SEALs, UDT, FROGMEN

Men Under Pressure

Also by Darryl Young
Published by Ivy Books:

THE ELEMENT OF SURPRISE: Navy SEALs in Vietnam

SEALs, UDT, FROGMEN

Men Under Pressure

Darryl Young

IVY BOOKS • NEW YORK

Ivy Books
Published by Ballantine Books

ISBN 0-8041-1064-6

Manufactured in the United States of America

It is often observable, that, in vessels of all kinds, the men who talk the most sailor lingo are the least sailor-like in reality. . . . On the other hand, when not actively engaged in his vocation, you would take the best specimen of a seaman for a landsman. When you see a fellow yawing about the docks like a homeward-bound Indiaman, a long Commodore's pennant of black ribbon flying from his mast-head, and fetching up a grog-shop with a slew of his hull, as if an Admiral were coming alongside a three-decker in his barge; you may put that man down for what man-of-war's-men call a *damn-my-eyes-tar*, that is, a humbug. And many damn-my-eyes humbugs there are in this man-of-war world of ours.

The Sea Witch
by Alexander Liang

Contents

Acknowledgments

I would like to thank the former members of Underwater Demolition and SEAL Team, and their families, who helped me secure documentation about a major part of our lives. Without their support, this project would not have become a reality. To them I am sincerely grateful.

To Hugh "Wild Bill" Mitchell and his wife Pat; Frank "The Marine" Lahr and his wife Charlotte; Mullie "Moe" Mulheren; Tim Reeves; Randy Kaiser; Pat Carter; Tom Shallcross; Dale Calabrese; Mike "The Chickenman" Ferrell; Frank "Fronk" Schroeder; Jerry Howard; Paul "PK" Barnes; "Iron Nick" Walsh; Rob Wogsland; Rick "Flex" Foster; Pierre "Remi" Remillard and his wife Shena; Tommy "Frogman" Marshall; Jack "Freddie the Frog" Tomlinson; Brian Curle; Dwight Daigle; Tim Oelker; Lloyd "Doc" Schrier; Dan Blocker; Dave Hostetter; Harlin "Funky" Funkhouser; Lance Green; John Passyka; Dave Perry; Clint "Bubba" Majors; Alan Vader; Rod Yonkers; Christopher John Caracci; Joseph Gannon; Robert "Petey" Nelms; B. Guilver; William Stubbs; Charles Greene; Manuel Solano; A. Brokes; C. Hoffman; John "Frenchy" Bisallion; Chris Christie; R. Micheels; Chester Tomassoni; Virgil "Stew" Stewart; J. Stauffer; Robert Marshall; G. Canizio; Harry Losey; and Russ Eoff. To all these men, their families (especially their wives), my wife Sandy, son Jamie, daughter Jennifer; Rose, my mother, and Billie and Willie, this book is dedicated.

Other People Who Have Contributed to the Success of This Book

Because of their support and contributing information, I can not forget to mention these friends—Owen Lock (my editor at Ivy Books); Jack "WordPerfect" Green; John "Frenchy"

French (Seabees); LDCR (Ret) John Keuter; Gary Linderer; Kenn Miller; Ralph "Stoner" Stafford; Daryl and Marge Buchanan; Bob "Machine Gun" Barry; Patrick Becroft; Terry and Ronnie Young; LCDR (Ret) Ben Blackburn; Dr. John Fuhrman; MCPO (Ret) Roger "Brown Water" Joy; Pete Schroeder (Recon); and Ned Kalbfleish. Thanks.

Prologue

After securing thirty-five to forty thousand words for this manuscript, I began to wonder why the hell I had even begun the project; I had already burned damn near a half a manuscript in the wood stove after abandoning it early-on because my editor was a little slow off the mark, then decided to begin all over again. And I had this attitude, "Why do today what I can do after I go fishin'?" When I reached fifty to sixty thousand words, I was nearly back to where I had been at the wood stove. By then I had become dedicated again but still had questions as to why I was spending my prime-time at the computer instead of fishin'. Then, when the computer word-count reached seventy thousand I fell back, regrouped, and tried to see just what I had collected here, it hit me like a slap in the face. But, the manuscript was still far from finished and still taking me away from my favorite pastime. But, like ascending from a deep dive, I was beginning to see the light as I neared the surface.

On a roll by then, except for an occasional fishin' trip, I couldn't stop. I even found ways to interview some Teammates while out on the lakes or floating the rivers of Western Montana. Because of the beautiful surroundings, this not only made my interviews more interesting and stress free but also kept up my fishin' habit that is required for my survival on this planet.

The events recorded on these pages, were experienced by my comrades then described or presented to me in personal interviews, phone conversations, or personal documents by the individuals themselves. All the men whose exploits are described within these pages were either members of the United States Navy's Underwater Demolition Teams or SEAL Team, in many cases both.

To fully, or even partially understand the functions that the Underwater Demolition Teams and SEAL teams (UDT/SEAL) have fulfilled throughout recent U.S. military history, one must attempt to put oneself in the mind of a Navy Frogman. The experiences recorded here will help you do exactly that.

Giving the reader a little knowledge of the flexibility and variety of operational duties that the Teams were—and are—involved in, straight from the men who experienced them, will also help give you an understanding of the way the Navy's Frogmen operated. It should also give the reader an idea of a few of the UDT/SEAL capabilities. These stories just touch a fraction of the overall operational picture of Frogman history. There were many stories I dared not, or could not—legally—print.

Some teammates keep their experiences to themselves. I respect their privacy. Other teammates welcomed my approach and appreciated the fact that someone else was interested in that important part of their lives. Asking my comrades to relate their experiences is one of the most difficult feats I've ever had to do, but I felt that it is very important for our families, friends, teammates, and the public in general to read about the Navy's Frogmen performing their duties and living their lives at that most important time of their sojourn on Earth. Whether it was liberty in Olongapo City, reconning the beaches of Guam, or a fire-fight in the Delta, what better way to relate the story than in the words of the men who have experienced the encounters.

Opening up a letter from a Teammate with whom I haven't been in contact for more than twenty years, a letter in which he related a personal experience for this manuscript was a very emotional occasion. Other interviews, letters and notes made me laugh till my sides ached. The sharing of experiences was good for all of us, as only a Frogman can relate to a Frogman—or a Frogman's nights in Olongapo City . . .

After reading accounts in this book, some people may think that UDT/SEAL training is cruel and inhumane and should be reorganized. They may ask, Why does this training have to be so difficult? Why do these men have to go through with this? The proper answer is simple to the men who "Have Been There!"

Number One—because of that difficult training, we had an outstanding survival record in combat. It helped us in times of need, in life-and-death situations; and improved our chances of returning home alive.

Number Two—we never *had* to go through the training; it was purely our choice. We were *all* volunteers.

Number Three—there seems to be a growing problem with "Wish-They-Were, Want-to-Be's," individuals claiming not only to have been members of the UDT/SEAL Teams, but other Special Operations Forces as well. The stories within the pages of this manuscript are not the contrived experiences of "Want-to-Be's" who for some reason have to fabricate their pasts.

These individuals go through life with poor "Visibility," with their swim fins on the wrong feet. They're always having to clear their face mask of the fog that's placed behind it while they spread a false representation of the way it really was. By spreading false suppositions to anyone who will listen, such people give those of us who have "Been There" bad names. The sad part is, the people who listen have no idea if a "Want-to-Be" is fabricating a story or not.

The pain we endured in UDT/SEAL training to qualify for the "Teams," the blood we shed in combat on foreign soil, and, most of all, the sacrifices made by our fallen comrades, force us to permit no one the right to claim he has "Been There" when in fact he has not.

Once he is identified, the situation can be very embarrassing to the phony. Sooner or later, especially when confronted by *real* Special Operations Forces personnel, who know exactly how their units operated, these individuals stick out like tadpoles in a drying pond. Very few of the phonies have the names, dates, places, and documents to substantiate their claims. Some do go as far as to fabricate paperwork such as Form DD-214. Others just lie, saying things like, "All my military records were destroyed," or "My military records are classified and not available to the public." And we see it in the fabricated motion pictures also—are there any teammates out there from Training Class 1121 out of Great Lakes? I know some of you are reading this . . . This subject, as I have observed from the time that I was discharged from active duty, actually gave me the motivation and incentive to go forward with the pages of this manuscript.

There's a special camaraderie and a common bond among Frogmen. We generally keep in touch. We still have reunions and parties. And most former Frogmen can still swim six miles underwater without tanks or fins. That's true! I know because some guy who graduated from UDT/SEAL Training Class Squadron 12 told me so the other day.

This special camaraderie among teammates was programmed into our hearts and minds through the good and bad times that we experienced as Frogmen in training, peacetime, and war, and will be riveted to us the rest of our lives. Because of our training, and our past experiences as Frogmen, we have the gift of self confidence, self-knowledge, and camaraderie that will help us throughout our lives.

Any time violent activities take place, whether manmade or natural, in peacetime or war, a man will naturally experience fear. Fearful or not, the men in these pages were highly trained and capable of performing their dangerous duties by concentrating on the task at hand and not letting their anxieties get the best of them. That's one reason only one UDT man was killed while reconning the beaches of Guam in 1944, and that nobody was ever left behind, dead or alive, on a mission in Nam, and that SEALs were the most highly decorated unit to serve in Vietnam.

For most of us, after years of civilian life, in our daily routines, at work or at play, we still make decisions the way we were trained back then—without even thinking about it. Standard Operating Procedures I guess you could call it. Whenever a difficult task or decision arises, the obstacles in our way can be overcome without too much hassle because "We have Been There before. No big deal."

For those teammates, our comrades and friends who have fallen in combat or for any other reason while in or out of the Teams, we think of you often because you were and still are a major segment in our lives. You will never be forgotten. The reason most of us stand today and our country is free is because of the sacrifices made by you and those others who were called. Most of the Protected, who haven't "Been There," or fought for the price of Freedom seem to forget—or will never know . . .

SEALs, UDT, FROGMEN

Men Under Pressure

The Definition of a Frogman
Dwight Daigle
SEAL Team 1 1967–1970

Gen-u-wine, shockproof, waterproof, chrome plated, antimagnetic, barrel-chested, rootin', tootin', parachutin', fightin', fuckin', frogman that never eats and never sleeps and takes forty men forty days and forty nights to track down, can see in the dark, breathe underwater, and fly.

Chapter One

The Early UDTs (The Underwater Demolition Team Handbook—First Edition, 1965)

During the earliest stages of preparation for an amphibious landing, a number of special organizations are expected to obtain intelligence information on possible beach landing sites.

It is during the final days and hours preceding the actual landing that two specially trained units are called upon to perform an amphibious reconnaissance. These two special units were the navy's underwater demolition teams and the Marine Corps' amphibious reconnaissance teams.

Marine Corps amphib recon teams, during World War II were clandestinely inserted into the expected landing area prior to the actual landing to provide intelligence to the landing force commander. Their assigned areas of operation were usually from the high-water line (high tide) inland.

The navy's underwater demolition teams (UDT) were responsible for collecting intelligence from the three-and-one-half fathom curve offshore to the high-water line on the beach of the anticipated amphibious landing site. They were also responsible for the clearance and destruction of any man-made or natural obstacles by demolition located within the assigned UDT area before the actual landing took place.

In addition, they would also collect information into the hinterland area (area past the first signs of vegetation from the beach). This includes intelligence about the enemy, their positions, firepower, movement, minefields, and types of vegetation and terrain the landing forces will encounter once they hit the beach. Also, samples of the beach itself are collected (sand, dirt, rock, etc.) and sent back to the ship for the analyst to determine if heavy vehicles can maneuver onto the shore.

The types of obstacles the UDT men might encounter could be natural or man-made. This may include coral, boulders, logs, enemy mines, steel, concrete, or mined natural or man-made obstacles.

Additional tasks would include channel location, marking and improving them, initial assault-wave guidance, along with the beach intelligence for the task force commander. There are even more responsibilities for the UDT men, which include clandestinely landing supplies, infiltrating and exfiltrating agents and guerrillas, harbor and river penetration and clearance, and surface or underwater attacks against ships or harbor installations.

Being combat-demolition experts, combat swimmers, and rubber-boat handlers in the early years, the UDT men later became qualified scuba divers and parachutists to expand their operational environment.

The UDT's were also capable of penetrating into and beyond the hinterland for intelligence gathering and demolition raids against enemy targets. Both the UDT and recon units operated in very small groups, helping to eliminate the possible detection by the enemy.

In early 1943, the navy formed the Navy Combat Demolition Unit (NCDU) from members of the navy construction battalions and the Navy/Marine Scout and Raider Volunteers. The rugged, strenuous training began at Fort Pierce, Florida. The purpose, to provide better preassault hydrographic information and to demolish any natural or man-made obstacles, giving the regular landing assault forces a better chance of survival.

Demolition work was emphasized and nonrestricted. New methods and explosives were developed for demolishing different types of obstacles the UDT men might encounter. The

UDT men had the opportunity to standardize and develop their own explosives according to their operational requirements.

The training given to the early UDTs at Fort Pierce, Florida, included endless hours of exhausting day and nighttime evaluations conducted in the insect-, snake-, and alligator-infested swamps. This intensive psychological and demanding physical training was based on the theory that a man is capable of ten times as much physical output as was usually thought.

The mud, insects, snakes, and alligators along with the demanding teamwork involved made the UDT men feel at home in this environment so future operations could be conducted successfully if they encountered that type of terrain.

Pause for a minute and place yourself in this harsh training situation, in your own mind if you can, and maybe you will comprehend why so few men graduate from a UDT/SEAL training. You are continuously exposed to immeasurable mandatory imsomnia, reeking mud and water, one evolution after another, fatigued from the constant on-the-go, along with the instructors constantly harassing you verbally and physically, making conditions miserable, trying to make you quit. To top this off, there are explosions going off all around you.

It takes a very determined motivated individual to hang in there just to complete the training course. Well over half the UDT trainees drop out of the all-volunteer training program. Those members who complete UDT/SEAL training are proud of their accomplishments and join the elite group of the UDTs then, or the present day SEAL teams.

The men of the early-day NCDUs did not anticipate any swimming, and their normal assignments were conducted only at low tide. Their uniforms at that time (Utah and Omaha Beaches at Normandy) consisted of impregnated, hooded, canvas fire-fighting suits, with field shoes and long stockings, also impregnated. A protective mask covered the bare part of the face and was used in the anticipation of the Germans using mustard gas.

The NCDUs lost thirty percent of their men at Utah Beach and 60 to 70 percent at Omaha Beach. Even under overwhelming odds, the NCDU men completed their mission, saving many American and Allied forces lives by opening up passageways through the obstacles for the landing craft coming ashore.

After the war in Europe, the navy Frogmen became known as the underwater demolition teams or UDT. They pulled combat operations and made hydrographic reconnaissance at Borneo, Peleliu, Saipan, Tinian, Guam, Lingayen, Leyte Gulf, Iwo Jima, and Okinawa.

Chapter Two

Hugh "Wild Bill" Mitchell UDT-3 1944

"What's a former navy frogman like you doing living way up here in Montana?" I asked eighty-year-old Wild Bill as he invited me into his home for an interview.

"It's as far away from the ocean as I could get," he replied.

Wild Bill, Mitch, or the Sheep Herder are some of his nicknames that his former teammates call Bill since way back in the early forties. One of his teammates even told me that Wild Bill was hung like a stud horse and liked to drink Wild Turkey. That's okay, Bill, we know that our teammates will say anything about us behind our backs when we're not around.

Wild Bill is a tall, lean, slender man who stared me straight in the eyes when he talked and said, "One thing about it, I'm not going to tell you any stories that aren't true. It makes me mad when I read some of this stuff that I know about, especially when it's about my old unit during that time. I got so mad at one book that I threw the SOB down and wouldn't pick it up again. You'll have a drink of whiskey, won't you?"

Bill was eager to tell me the stories about his days as a navy Frogman during World War II. He appreciated someone he could relate his story to, even though I was a younger generation Frogman. I was eager to listen to Wild Bill about the "way it was," back in the early days of UDT training and being a member of the Frogman family during World War II from someone who has been there and really understands. September 25, 1993, Wild Bill and Pat celebrated their fiftieth wedding anniversary.

The Reconnaissance of Guam

Well you see, I first came to this part of the country in 1932, from Lenoir, North Carolina. I broke horses; there was a lot of horses in this part of the country back then. I used to round up the wild mustangs down on the Jennings Range down there; that country was straight up and down. And then I got married, then was divorced later on. Then I went to the coast, out on the peninsula, and worked in the timber. I was high riggin' and toppin' trees. Well, when I was done with that, I signed up with the navy yard, and I got on.

I started out working as a blacksmith helper at the Puget Sound Naval Yard. I went in there as a helper and took the blacksmith training and got to be a first-class blacksmith. We were making parts for the *Saratoga* and the *Lexington*; they got shot up down in the South Pacific. They were ordering parts, and we were shipping them to them, of course they had the blueprints there in the navy yard for those ships. The ships weren't even back to the States yet; they just called their orders in.

I joined the navy while I was at the naval yard. I didn't really know what was going on, I just wanted to get in . . . see? I wanted to find out what the hell was going on. So I joined the naval reserves on 8 July 1943, began active service on 14 July 1943, and went in as a Seabee.

I volunteered for the navy out of the shipyard where I was

working, but they didn't want me to. They told me it takes three years to make a blacksmith out of ya; it only takes about six weeks to make a swabbie out of ya. But I still wanted to get in, so I went.

I was sent to Camp Perry, Virginia, to attend Seabee boot camp, the naval construction battalion at Williamsburg. I went through there, and when we got through, they put me into water purification. Well, that didn't sound too goddamn exciting to me, but a guy came along and was asking for volunteers for UDT. It was an all new outfit at that time. In my earlier life . . . I always did live on the edge . . . as far as I could . . . so I volunteered into it . . . see?

Well, they had big stories, of course; you know how the big stories goes. I think they said, "Go into this outfit, you'll see plenty of action!" In fact, they really didn't know anything about UDT because it was all new then. They said that in combat your life expectancy will be about eighty-six seconds. Well, I figured, goddamn, that ought to be exciting . . . as long as it lasts! So, I was a little bit crazy, and I went into it.

They didn't want us skinny guys like me; they didn't want to take us.

"We want those big guys, so when we get them in shape, they will be leaned down and ready to go," they said. But, needing men to fill the ranks, they took me anyway.

We went through this place, I think that they took us there intentionally, where these guys were all crippled up from the training and were waiting to get shipped out. They put us through there so we could talk to them before we decided to start the training. Then, we started our Frogman training right there in Camp Perry.

From Camp Perry, those of us that were left, were sent to Fort Pierce, Florida, for our formal UDT training. We went through all that training down there of course. We had such an elimination of men at Camp Perry that hardly any of them guys washed out at Fort Pierce. Oh yeah, you're damn right we had it; we had Hell Week right there in Fort Pierce, Florida. In my opinion, we was a lot luckier than you guys over there on the West Coast because we had that warm water down there in Florida. That Gulf Stream you know; that water wasn't cold to me.

We had no training class number that I can remember. We didn't do any of that parachuting like they do today. They started that later, after I got out. We mainly were trained to do beach recons and demolish obstacles on enemy-occupied beaches.

The funny thing about this was they called us Frogmen, but you know, when we went in the water we didn't even have fins or do any scuba diving or anything like that yet. All the operations that we went on, we never even had fins, just a little hard-rubber face mask that we had to take sandpaper to and custom fit them to our faces.

From Fort Pierce, after UDT Training, we were sent to Maui, Territory of Hawaii, and formed Underwater Demolition Team 3. UDT-3 was the first Underwater Demolition Team to be commissioned in the Pacific Fleet, and pretty nearly all of us were from the naval reserves. I was the oldest man on Team 3, and I'll tell you what, we didn't sit still much after we got started.

After more training at Maui, we were sent to Saipan, Tinian, and Guam. It took us a long time to get there, riding on an APD. After arriving at Saipan, our ship sailed to Guam, and then we were sent back to Tinian and Saipan and were on standby there. While we were there, we were attacked by Japanese aircraft several times, but they never hit our ship. They never needed us there, so we returned to Guam.

We were also on standby for Iwo Jima, but of course they never told us that at the time. They didn't need us for that one anyway. We found that out later. They had a couple of other teams there for that one.

I was a member of Section 1 in our outfit. I think that we had the worst beach on Guam to recon. While we were there, one of the warrant officers of UDT-3 was killed on a diversionary reconnaissance. Our team demolished 504 obstacles on Asan Beach with ninety-six hundred pounds of tetrytol in three days, and 90 obstacles on Adolup Point using one thousand pounds of tetrytol on another day, all under enemy fire. We were kept pretty busy while we were there. The concrete was reduced to rubble, and the steel beams would just be lying there after the explosion.

We took all the explosives to the beach in a rubber boat. We dragged the rubber boat right up onto the reefs and had to carry the powder on our backs and run to the obstacles while our fire support shot over our heads, and the Japs fired at us and back out to sea. Our fire support kept the Japs occupied while we did our job on the reef. They were firing both ways over our heads while we were in there workin'. Ocean swells would rock the UDT gunboats that were giving us fire support from the edge of the reef, and their rounds would even hit around us sometimes while we were conducting the recon. They were armed with .50-caliber machine guns and other weapons. Without this fire support, it would have been a very tough job for us, and more men would have gotten hurt or killed.

Some men got wounded, but we survived these difficult tasks because of the training that went before this. This is what saved us really. All that daylight stuff we did over there was done under enemy fire. We could tell the difference between our support fire and the enemy fire as it went over our heads because it sounded different.

We guided the first assault wave of Marines into the beach on D day through safe channels that we had clearly marked, and helped bring out the wounded later. I was the instigator of making that famous sign, the one that was left on the beach for the invading Marines, that read, WELCOME U.S. MARINES—NAVY SEABEES—UDT3. Who says that the Marines are the first ones ashore? After that first sign, there were several more made. Their CO had found one and destroyed it, thinking that it was the only one.

We didn't get to see much of the island, only the beach areas and not too far inland, we were kept too busy for that. After the invasion, we continued to work on Guam. They didn't let us sit still very long. We would gather unexploded shells, rockets, and ammunition and swim them out to deeper water and drop them off. We had to inflate one side of our life belts to help us float as we swam this unexploded ordnance out there. Our life belts were made of canvas-covered rubber, which had two floatation bladders in them. To inflate them, we had to mash this inflator system to activate the air inside them so they would blow up.

UDT's job was finished on Guam, and we set sail on September 28, 1944, to Eniwetok. We eventually ended up in the Leyte Gulf, Philippines, and did some beach recons there. We never found any obstacles on the beach, but we received a lot of enemy fire directed at us and our boats.

We had one man that got scared and swam back out to sea. He filed a false report as to what he did and saw while he supposedly swam to the beach. His swim buddy, Holmes, was ordered to swim back out with him. Later, Holmes came to me, and the first thing he did was tell me about it.

He said, "I don't want you to say anything about it." Later, one of our officers came to me and mentioned, "Something sure looks wrong with Holmes; he sure looks down."

I told him, "I would rather you go talk to Holmes; I think he'll tell you."

And so he did; Holmes told the officer that they didn't swim all the way into the beach. His swim buddy, being of a higher rank than Holmes, got scared with all the mortar shells landing around them and made him swim back out with him. There's some times in your life when a man is just scared. We couldn't have that shit out there, so I guess you know what happened next; he was kicked out of UDT and sent down the road. Many other men's lives counted on what we were doing there. They were depending on the results of our recons to get them safely into the beach.

We were getting ready to go in on a recon, and one of the boys was saying his prayers.

I said, "What the hell's the matter?"

He replied, "I feel a little nervous going in there, I thought that I would say a little prayer."

I said, "Ah hell, there's nothin' to it. If you go in there and get killed, you will be a hero. If you live through 'er, you'll probably go home and be a goddamn drunkard. Don't worry about it."

Anyway, there was nothing else for us to do there after the invasion, so we returned to Maui. We were put on the UDT training staff there for a while, because of our combat experience, until we were sent back to Fort Pierce, Florida.

After several months of even more training, developing different methods of demolishing various types of obstacles, we were sent to Oceanside, California. We were sittin' outside of Oceanside, aboard ship, when VJ day (Japan surrendered) came along, but we still had to go to Japan anyway. We had to go over and clear a beach at Wakayama for the occupational troops, and there wasn't a damn obstacle on it. But we had to go anyway.

After that, we returned to the States, and I was discharged from the naval reserves on 11 November 1945 as a chief shipfitter. There are very few service men that have a complete record of what they did in the war like I have. I still keep in touch with many of my teammates, and some of them even come all the way up here to Montana to see me. That really means a lot to me.

Wild Bill received the Bronze Star, American Campaign Medal, Asiatic-Pacific Campaign Medal, World War II Victory Medal, Navy Occupation Service Medal with "Asia" Clasp, Philippine Liberation Ribbon, and the Philippine Republic Presidential Unit Citation Badge awarded to Underwater Demolition Team 3.

Chapter Three

Mike C. Ferrell
UDT-12 1967–1970

Vietnam: A Personal Delirium

I was born in 1945, in Houston, Texas, and raised in Port Neches, Texas, down on the coast, next to Louisiana. After graduating from high school in 1964, I attended college at Stephen F. Austin, in Nacogdoches, Texas, until joining the navy. I was twenty-one years old when I joined, a little older than the typical profile of Vietnam vets.

The way I had it figured, the Vietnam War was escalating to such an extent that the armed forces were going to get me one way or another. It only mattered to me if I was going to be an enlisted man or an officer. So, I decided to join the navy as an enlisted man.

Why did I decide to join the UDT/SEAL teams? Well, this will probably make no sense to you, but here goes. Growing up on the Texas coast, I was a "surfer," lifeguard, and enjoyed all types of water sports. I remember putting on a set of diving tanks (with no training. Stupid, Stupid.) and cleaning the algae on the bottom of a swimming pool one day. I thought it was a pretty cool experience while floating around, and it was quiet and everything.

Anyway, a chief petty officer at the navy recruiter's office listened to what I was interested in and pulled a brochure out of his drawer. It was an underwater demolition team "Frogman" brochure, and it caught me hook, line, and sinker!

Here were these guys paddling an IBS (inflatable boat, small) through some "righteous" six-foot surf in California. They jumped out of planes, dove deep in the ocean, blew stuff up, and sometimes, they even shot people. But mostly, they liked to sneak around and find out things. The real bonus was, I got to stay in Coronado, California, and surf if I wasn't "touring" over in Nam!

Wowie, zowie, man, was I stoked! So I asked the guy, "How can I get into this UDT stuff after joining the navy?"

"Son, when you get to boot camp, they are going to be asking you a lot of questions as to what you want to do. What you tell them is, you are a good swimmer, love the ocean, and like to dive and stuff. And they will cut you orders for one of the underwater demolition teams. It's as simple as that!"

He forgot to mention that before I got assigned to the "teams," first, I had to pass the most difficult training the armed forces had to offer!

But that's okay; after boot camp, I passed the training and was assigned to one of the teams. And, before I shipped to Nam, I took a short leave and went back home to Texas for a visit. The first thing I did, was to bust into that chief's office and give him a good going over! By the time I was through with him, he had noticed my jump wings (parachute wings), and his mouth dropped open.

The chief said, "Congratulations, I knew you would make it!"

I replied laughingly, "That's right, you blackshoe (regular navy fleet sailor) puke! Come on, I'll buy you a beer!" That's how I got started in the teams!

Underwater Demolition/SEAL Team Training
Training Class 42

Well, I guess no matter what training class we went through, each class had to be a unique experience. But one difference was, my class was an extremely large one. We started with 183 trainees and graduated with only 69. Ah yes, Training Class 42 was so big that the instructors had to split us into two groups, Alpha and Bravo. I was assigned to Bravo. Our instructors were primarily Dick Allen and Vince Olivera, but there were others, too. Rascheck, Messenger, and Mr. Slight were also our UDT/SEAL instructors.

Dick Allen was a thick, muscular man, which was kind of unique for us frog-types; most thick, muscular men were not good swimmers. He was also a black man. However, as Frogman trainees, we were all very sensitive to the fact that we should never bring that subject to his attention, at least when he was "in our face." Know what I mean? He was capable of making our day a very, *very*, painful experience.

Vince Olivera was an Indian. He was in his late thirties or, maybe, forty years old, but the guy could definitely strike fear in your heart, and he knew exactly where all your tension strings were. His nickname was God, and that name was neatly printed on his uniform.

Olivera could run like the wind, smoking a cigar and chewing tobacco at the same time. One of his favorite tricks was to run side by side with you and blow cigar smoke in your face until you puked. He was my favorite! Somehow, he always knew how to wind my clock. He was always asking me what time it was.

"I believe it's time to hit the bay, Olivera," I would answer.

"That's right, Ferrell. Hit the bay!" "Hit the bay" meant jumping into San Diego Bay when you screwed up. The water temperature was in the low fifties.

All the trainees hated hitting the bay, but I especially hated it. It would really pump me up when only a few of us had to hit it. Olivera would always come to our morning inspection and find something wrong with me; UDT/SEAL instructors always knew what screws to turn.

For other trainees, maybe it was the running till they puked, the "O" course (obstacle course), or log PT. They always paid attention to the trainee's personal "screw," and what was so amazing, was only you, God, or Allen knew it.

All of the UDT/SEAL instructors were excellent. They had

tuned up the whole training program and knew exactly when to turn up the heat, and when to turn it down. They were fabulous in teaching respect—for them, each other, yourself, and the VC/NVA. But not necessarily for the regular navy. We all developed an attitude about the blackshoe navy. We were clearly different. The navy was something we tolerated, but consistently played with.

In UDT/SEAL training, we started out fully dressed and wearing boots, running four miles in the soft sand. By the end of the first month, we were running twelve to sixteen miles. I remember the first day of training. We had some yahoo who was the O-in-C (officer in charge) of the tadpoles (trainees). He was the real rah-rah type—"Do this, move over there, drop, pick that up," that sort of a guy. Anyway, I think it was in the first week of training that I ran past him on one of our beach runs. He was down on all fours, puking and crying like a baby. I didn't say anything to him as I ran by, but I sure wanted to. So much for Roman candles. I was glad when he quit.

Then Came Hell Week

During Hell Week, the instructors gave us only about two and a half hours of sleep during the whole week. Over half of the total class dropped out, except for us hardheads. Due to physical stress and sleep deprivation some of us were having hallucinations. Once you start losing sleep, under stressful conditions it only takes a day or two before your mind starts to get away from you. The hallucinations were so real and kind of "interactive" that you could pop in and pop out of 'em easily. Scary shit.

I saw a giant alligator. We were paddling our IBSs out in the ocean, down to Tijuana one night. I was the bow-line man and had the lead paddle on the starboard side of the IBS when a huge gator suddenly appeared and was getting closer and closer. Finally, I had had enough and smacked it with my paddle, splashing water all over the rest of the men in my boat crew. I hadn't told them anything about seeing the gator, and they probably thought that I was crazy enough as it was. The boat crew was pissed off from getting splashed and decided to give me a thirty-minute sleep break in the bottom of the IBS, which of course, was full of cold seawater. Hey, no problem, I was out like a light and didn't even realize that I was wet.

When I woke up, I was run over by an aircraft carrier! I could clearly see the red and green running lights on its bow. It was probably an airplane, but nobody could have convinced me of that. I remember throwing my arms up in front of my face and screaming as it was running over me, and then . . . poof . . . there was nothing there. I don't think that I was the only one "juicing" off of my own hallucinations. However, Hell Week taught me that it is possible to function and accomplish certain tasks while being what I would call, "over the wall" of sanity. Hell Week built internal confidence in myself and the people I worked with. By making it through this window, we trusted each other even more.

The experience of Hell Week would literally come to save my life on a future operation while in Vietnam. The instructors were watching us all pretty close during that week, and constantly tested our thinking capability as well. We only lost a couple of tadpoles during the training after Hell Week. Everyone else graduated.

Obviously, I wasn't doing too well . . . and then there was God . . . "Where? . . . Over there . . . Oh shit . . . run and hide!"

"Ferrell . . . Ferrell . . . What time is it?"

"Whoya, Olivera." Here I go again!

San Clemente Island

After Hell Week, our class began to do a lot of serious learning: compass courses, how to orient a grid map (thousand-meter squares), longitudes and latitudes, hours and minutes, true north versus magnetic north differentials, dive training, and sneak-and-peek tactics. Our class went to San Clemente Island to learn the Frogman's demolition and land-warfare tactics.

Alpha group had just returned from San Clemente, having lost two men out there, Greco and McCall. They drowned while loading underwater obstacles with explosives. One of the men became tangled in some lines and panicked, causing him to hold his swim buddy underwater. They both had sharp K-bar knives and could have cut themselves free, but didn't. I don't know which group it bothered most, Alpha or Bravo. I mean, after all, Bravo had not yet been out to San Clemente for that part of its training, and the class had already lost two men. What are they going to do to us out there on that island? we wondered. That's what I wanted to know. It was quite a loss for all of us.

Well, it wasn't long before I found out. Do you know what the linear detonation rate of C-4 (plastic explosive) is? I do; 28,500 feet per *second.* That's fast, buddy, and it does a good job of destroying things, too.

I liked playing with explosives. It was like—when you were a kid and played with fire works to see how far you could make a tin can jump up into the air. But with C-4, you can take a whole bridge out of the water! On the technical side, there is a lot of mathematics involved; in practice, just load it up on the high side, and Fire in the hole!

Throughout UDT/SEAL training, teammates developed really close friendships. I guess it boiled down to helping your friends out when they really needed it most. Nobody was so strong that he didn't need some help from another trainee at one time or another, nobody! So, I guess you reach down and help somebody out, even though it may be painful for you to do so at the time. Sooner or later, somebody is helping you out! That's when you realize that you have made yourself a lifelong "potnah," a buddy you will always remember. Somebody who's in the Teams!

Training really built a sense of teamwork and a heavy dose of esprit de corps. After a while, you quit keeping score of who's helping who, and you just help each other. It became a way of life and instinct, and it was beautiful. Espi, Remi, Bimini, Moth, Troxell, Ambrose—heck, all you guys, you know already. You guys know who you are. No offense to everyone I didn't mention. If you know—you know.

When we were out at San Clemente Island conducting night operations, for instance, our target objective was a small building out in the boonies, and we were making an amphibious assault from the ocean. The IBSs (inflatable boat, small) were loaded with C-4, and the surf was really cranking—a big left-break into the shore about eight feet high. We were supposed to have our guns (I always called my weapon a gun because I knew it pissed off the instructors) strapped to our chests while in the rubber boats so we wouldn't lose them in the surf zone. And everybody did—but me. No, I stuffed mine under the cross-tube of the IBS. As we were in line to make our approach to the shore, I was so taken by how neat the surf was, I forgot to sling my gun back across my chest. Then, there goes my gun into the ocean. Our IBS broached in the high surf, and when we finally got control, I couldn't find my gun. So, there I was, creeping around on the operation with a stick in my hand, playing war games. At least it was night, and the instructors didn't notice that I was packin' a stick instead of an M-16.

Well, about 0200, we were all mustered up and informed that we had to do the "op" all over again because we loaded the wrong target. I finally worked up enough courage and approached the instructor, Rascheck, and informed him that I had lost my gun in the surf zone. It was dark, and we all were wearing camouflage on our faces; he couldn't tell who I was.

He said, "Who's that?"

I said, "It's Ferrell, Rascheck."

I fully braced myself for death and destruction. But I was surprised at his response. "That's all right, Ferrell, continue the operation and load the proper objective this time."

After loading the proper target, we went back to the beach, and all the boat crews began humping their IBSs back to the shore for extraction out through the surf. Then, from up on a berm above the beach, a set of jeep headlights flashed on. There, standing out in front of the headlights, was God, or Rascheck, I don't remember which.

"Ferrell, you and your boat crew get up here," he yelled.

He continued after we mustered in front of him, "So, you lost your weapon, Ferrell. You and your boat crew go out in the surf and find it, right now."

We were wet, tired, freezing cold; it was night, and the rest of my boat crew was not very happy with the Chickenman (the name I was given by the other trainees. I had this bird thing that I use to do. I would get all perched up on one leg, get my head moving, spread those wings way out there, and start steppin' out, struttin' my stuff. Yes sir . . . I be lookin' for one of those gooney birds . . . Seen any?). My classmates were definitely taking some pain because of me, but you know what, Steve (Moth) Miller found it! It took about an hour, but he found it in eight feet of water in the heavy surf. (Hey Steve, I still owe you one buddy, you and the whole boat crew!) If any one of these guys needed anything, anytime, I would bust my ass to get it for them.

The Teams

Before we knew it, our Frogman training was over, and those of us who graduated were divided among the West Coast UDT/SEAL teams. But ironically, the instructors assigned me to SEAL Team 1. It was quite an accomplishment to make it through the rigorous UDT/SEAL training, but to get picked as a SEAL was a real ego buster for me! At that time, the instructors were cherry pickin' certain guys to build up the ranks of SEAL Team. Once in the SEALs, you were assigned to a fire team, and then went through SEAL cadre out in the desert at Niland, California. At the SEAL camp there we used live ammunition when we practiced operating and patrolling as a fire team.

However, I wasn't sure the SEAL Team was the right thing for me to do at the time, and I respectfully declined and requested to be assigned to one of the UDT teams. The instructors went berserk!

"Hey, no big deal, guys, I just want to go over for a tour with UDT first to get a feel for what I'm getting myself into," I said. God and I had a real private "come to Jesus" in his office on this one.

God said, "Ferrell, you afraid of being a SEAL?"

"You bet I am, Olivera, I'm afraid of being a Frog, too."

"That's not good enough Ferrell, this is strictly a volunteer outfit, and when you volunteer, you take all of it," Olivera replied. "I'm shippin' you out on one of those gray monsters (naval ship, i.e., blackshoe navy)."

That really pissed me off. "Now wait just a minute, Olivera, I joined this outfit to be a 'fightin', fuckin' Frogman,' and didn't even know anything about this SEAL stuff. You guys wrote a damn good specification to get into the teams, and the government spent a lot of money on me in training. I passed your course in the top 10 percent, and you are still going to ship me out?"

"That's right, Ferrell."

Now I am livid with anger (there he goes, winding my clock again) and very disappointed. "You do whatever you need to do."

I was definitely putting my absolute best fuck-you look on the network. But he didn't even blink. Then he dismissed me. Boy, I was pissed.

Olivera left me in the dark for a couple of days, but finally, with Machado, I was assigned to Underwater Demolition Team 12. Shortly thereafter, I deployed to Vietnam. My first assignment was with a UDT platoon on aboard the USS *Tunny*, a submarine designed especially for UDT/SEAL operations. Whew! Made it.

Chapter Four

Frank Lahr
1944

First Lieutenant Frank F. Lahr (The Marine), USMC, was the only Marine to stay with the navy Frogmen during World War II after UDT dropped army and Marine Corps personnel from its ranks. Mr. Lahr, with the help of his teammates, was responsible for an accurate account of Team 3's history. In order to keep the story straight, and as accurate as possible, Mr. Lahr had several teammates write down stories and information about Team 3 while these stories were still fresh on their minds, just before UDT-3 was decommissioned on 8 December 1945. I had the honor of meeting Mr. Frank Lahr and his wife Charlotte on September 8, 1993, on their visit to western Montana.

Introduction to UDT-3

UDT-3 was one of five original demolition teams formed in late March and April of 1944 at Maui, Territory of Hawaii. Lt. T. C. Crist, a former operations officer with UDT-2 and one of the original men in demolition, was designated commanding officer. With him, from UDT-1 and UDT-2, were three officers and eighteen enlisted men who had just returned from the Marshall Islands' campaign. To this nucleus of experienced combat demolition men were added twelve officers and sixty-three enlisted men, most of whom had recently completed six weeks of basic demolition training at Fort Pierce, Florida, after having been transferred from Camp Perry, Virginia. The enlisted men were all Seabees. Of the officers, eleven were combat engineers, four were of the line and one officer was from the Marine Corps. Although team organization, training and maneuvers took place at Waimanila, Oahu, and Maui, Territory of Hawaii, we must, in order to give a complete history, go way back to the beginning at Camp Perry, Virginia, where as early as June 1943 there were men known as "demos," and the "demo" song was sung.

Chapter Five

Joseph Gannon
1944

UDT Training—Camp Perry

More than half of UDT-3 personnel first heard of Demolition at Camp Perry, Williamsburg, Virginia, in invariably the same way. Lt. George Marion, known as "Little Jesus," was the recruiting officer, and he made his rounds of the boot camps, robbing the Seabees of nice, healthy, potential pick-

and-shovel men. His argument was very convincing, and he always managed to recruit an abundance of volunteers.

Once a man volunteered, he began two weeks of what was known as plain, ordinary hell. The purpose of this two-week training period was to determine the men who were unfit for demo, or who just couldn't take it. The average drafts lost as high as 60 percent of the volunteers in one week. At the termination of the weeding-out process, the training program was begun in earnest. There were four classes, each lasting two weeks. These classes included diving, small-boat handling, explosives, and Marine training.

The average day of a demo during the two weeks spent in Marine training went something like this. At 0500, reveille was sounded, and we fell out for PT. It was very easy to dope off then. Because of the darkness at that early hour, it was difficult for the officers to take an accurate muster. After approximately a half hour of limbering up, we marched to the chow hall and partook of pig in some form or another (Captain Ware's hog farm).

Muster for the day's routine was at 0630. The uniform of the day was white hats, a pair of dungaree shorts, and GI shoes and socks. We also had to carry an Enfield rifle and bayonet. Each man's rifle was inspected every morning. If anyone had a dirty rifle, his day would, indeed, be a hard one. At 0700, the long trek from the barracks to the dock began. We double-timed, with rifles at port, for two and a half miles. If you couldn't keep up, there was a yeoman or ensign following you in a jeep, taking down names and threatening to send you back to the Seabees. When we arrived for drill at the dock area, our day really began. Three hard and tough Marines took over. I'm sure most of the men remember corporals Sully Manson, Connolly, and Johnson. Their sole aim was to make life miserable for us. We usually started off with a half hour of close-order drill. Next, we took a few trips over the obstacle course. The rest of the morning was spent in tumbling and a form of torture known as the U.S. Marines Rifle PT. Just before chow, we took a run up to the swimming pool, and swam to cool off and clean up.

With chow over, we went back to some more tumbling and

another trip over the obstacle course. Midway in the afternoon, twelve sets of boxing gloves were brought out, and a novel little game was introduced to us by our ever-loving Sully. Twelve men put on the gloves and formed a circle—each man with his arms over the shoulders of the man on either side of him. When the whistle sounded, we were on our own. The idea was to keep from getting hit and yet spill a little blood yourself. This lasted for three minutes, and then twelve more men took over. Usually the boxing was alternated each day with judo. After everyone had had a crack at this crude sport, those who were able, fell out for a little bayonet drill and extended order (parade-ground practice at tactical formations).

After the extended order was completed, with the sun sinking low in the west, we started our long trek back to the barracks. After chow, most of the men went to the beer hall and tried to forget that they had to go through the same ordeal the next day.

The other classes we attended at Camp Perry were not quite so rugged, but they were interesting. Small boats were something new to most of us. We all learned how to handle LCVPs and LCMs. Also, we learned the rules of the road, signaling, and small-boat navigation.

Diving class was one of the most interesting of all the subjects at Camp Perry. We all started out in the indoor tank. There we learned the various shallow-water and deep-sea diving rigs. We then were sent down to twenty and thirty feet in the copper shallow-water helmet to get the feel of being alone in the cold, dark water. We learned to do work of all kinds underwater—lifesaving, hammering, welding, etc. After a week in the tank, we went out to a float in the middle of the York River. Here we used the deep-sea rig, and believe me, it was quite a thrill. At this point in the training, it was discovered that some of the men were not suitable for underwater work, so they were eliminated.

Those of us who remained will never forget the night (we dived at night, too) when the whole crew of fifty men acquired diarrhea; the meat in the sandwiches we had eaten was rotten, and it wasn't long before everyone had a case of the screaming screamies. We couldn't get a boat to come out for over an hour, and we took turns holding each other over the side of the barge. Finally, the boat did come and took the whole bunch of us to the hospital.

It was on this diving barge that we first saw and met the man who was to guide our destiny, Commander Kauffman. He came down to Camp Perry to look over the gang of Seabees who were to make up his first demolition team. He wasted no time in getting out to the barge, where he took his first dive in the deep-sea rig. I was on the phone during this dive and was more than pleased to learn that the commander could cuss like a Seabee. It seems that when he had gotten a few feet below the surface of the water, his ears began to ache; we had forgotten to tell him what to do under those conditions. He inquired in no uncertain terms as how to relieve the terrific pressure. Upon instructions from topside, we heard a loud gulp, and from then on, the dive proceeded normally.

It was there that the demos first began to acquire the characteristics for which they have since become famous. The soil around Camp Perry was very moist (some people referred to the whole camp as a bog), and explosive concussions were transmitted for long distances. Our night exercises shocked many a weary Seabee from his slumber, and it was said that Captain Ware himself was once thrown from his bunk. We do know that a limit was finally put on the maximum size of our charges, and of course, this was strictly observed. It was in this class that Mr. Flynn got a flying start on his flaming career as a booby-trap artist supreme. Why no one was killed still remains a mystery. His thirty-six hour problem, complete with sand flies and mosquitoes in the demo epic, was the beginning of various incidents which built up the demo spirit. After an extremely cold winter at Camp Perry, everyone looked forward to a real summer vacation at Fort Pierce, Florida.

Chapter Six

Dale Calabrese
UDT-11 1970–1975

Liberty in Olongapo

When I got out of UDT-11, I made a promise to myself. I promised I would never allow myself to become freezing cold from the water again. Well, that's a promise that I can't keep when it comes to an opportunity to bag some meat for my family.

It's opening day of archery season for white-tail deer here in Ohio. I'm sitting about twelve feet off the ground in the crotch of a wild cherry tree, waiting for the right doe to walk in front of my broadhead arrow. It's pouring with rain, and fifty degrees!

Here I am, cold and wet, and when I'm alone like this, sometimes I think about incidents in my life when I was a member of UDT-11.

I was in the Philippines in 1971, at the Subic Bay Naval Base, when I developed a taste for *ponsit* (spaghetti). I left the UDT barracks and headed out the main gate from the base into Olongapo City. As I'm walking across the bridge, just outside the main gate that crosses "Shit River," a river that borders the base and town that looks and smells the same, I heard someone call my name. I turned around and noticed a Filipino man; he was calling my name again. I didn't recognize the man at all, but he mentions that his sister does the laundry at our barracks. Boy, was I naive; I stood there and listened to him.

He continued on, telling me about his life story and how his mother was sick in bed. He said his mother needed someone to mail a letter for her from within the base (quicker delivery) and wanted to know if I would help him out since he could not go onto the base. I didn't think at the time to tell him to have his sister mail the letter when she goes to work the next day.

Then he wanted me to accompany him to his house so we could pick up the letter. Anyway, being the "nice guy" that I am—I was only going into town to get something to eat anyway . . . What the hell—I went with him.

We climbed into a jeepney (Filipino taxi) and rode into town, away from the main gate. A half hour later and farther into an unfamiliar section of Olongapo City, the jeepney stopped, and we got off. We walked down some alleys and ended up at a run-down shack. Things were really starting to look suspicious.

I wore a Rolex diving watch with a sterling silver handcrafted watch band. I had the watch band made while I was visiting the town of Bagio, Philippines. I also had a little cash in my pocket. Those were the only two items of value that I had.

I knew I should have stayed outside, but we both walked into the house anyway. As soon as I entered, I saw four Filipino's playing cards at a table in the largest room in the shack. The Filipino I had accompanied told me to sit down and play cards with these guys while he went into another room to get the letter. So, being the nice guy I am and not really thinkin' anything was wrong, I did.

Only a short time later, the four guys at the table wanted to play cards for my Rolex. That's when I fully realized that I was being set up. About that same time, the other Filipino I had come to the shack with came out of the room carrying a very large letter opener, about the size of a two-foot machete!

This is where all the fun started and where my UDT/SEAL training instinct took over. I instantly smacked the guy to the right of me in the jaw with my elbow. Then, as I stood up, the guy on my left stood up also. His mistake was exposing his groin, so I kicked his nuts up to his Adam's apple. He fell back into one of the other two. I couldn't believe the guy sitting across from me; he just sat there watching everything happening. I thought that he might be packin' a weapon and try to blow me away. Things were happening fast, too fast. I pushed the table, cards and all, into the dude with the machete as I made a quick exit out the front door. After I entered the street, I was lucky enough to find a three-wheeled taxi not too far away. I jumped into the back, told the driver to take me downtown, back to some territory that looked familiar to me.

Once I arrived downtown, my pulse became normal again, and my appetite returned. I soon learned that this type of incident was a common occurrence for unsuspecting sailors while on liberty in downtown Olongapo. Unfortunately, I had to learn that the hard way. I finally ended up getting my *ponsit*, and a lot less naive, I walked back to the base.

Chapter Seven

Jerry Howard
UDT-12 1967–1970

Operation Deep Channel

Call it Kinh Gay, Tuyen Nhon, the Blow Job, or by its code name, DEEP CHANNEL (some called it worse things than these)—it was neither deep nor a channel, but a canal, almost six miles long. On 6 January 1970, twenty-two frogmen from Underwater Demolition Team 12 began blasting a narrow, five-and-a-half mile canal across the remote Plain of Reeds in South Vietnam.

Before it was finished, nearly half the team had had a hand in it. When completed, the Kinh Gay (Gay Canal) was the first canal to be constructed with demolitions in Vietnam—and the largest combat demolition job in U.S. Naval history. It was also probably the most celebrated—two movies were made of it, and military dignitaries, totaling seventeen stars, appeared for the final blast.

This was the ultimate UDT job: it involved a third of a million pounds of high explosives (60 percent of the world supply of Mark-8 hose); miles of mud and water to wallow and swim in; brutal work and long hours, with no liberty and bad food, for over a month; and assorted dangers. The canal was blasted in plain view of the Cambodian border and across one of the largest enemy infiltration routes in South Vietnam—the Kinh Bo Bo. The time frame included Tet, to boot.

Operation DEEP CHANNEL was being undertaken to cut the enemy's busiest infiltration route into Saigon and the upper Mekong Delta near its origin at the Cambodian border. When completed, it would connect two major rivers, the Vam Co Tay and the Vam Co Dong, providing a vital interdiction route for naval patrol boats and a timesaving commercial route for the civilian population.

Time was not on the Frogmen's side. The expected Tet offensive early in February was rapidly approaching. Local intelligence sources warned that the area where the crew would be working would be heavily trafficked at night by the enemy. The headquarters for Viet Cong and North Vietnamese Army (NVA) battalions and a VC mobile force totaling 550 men was reported to be within twenty kilometers of the canal site, and intelligence warned that terrorist raids, mortar attacks, and booby-trapping should be expected during the operation.

The blasting would occur within sight of the Cambodian border on the Plain of Reeds, approximately thirty-five miles west of Saigon. The two rivers parallel the borders of the Parrot's Beak section of Cambodia, and join southwest of Saigon to form the handle of the giant slingshot, which feeds the Mekong Delta river system.

The Kinh Bo Bo, an overgrown, neglected canal, which runs southeast from the Parrot's Beak toward the confluence of the two rivers, was known to be the most important of numerous infiltration routes into Saigon from that part of Cambodia. The entire Parrot's Beak region was a major staging and rehabilitation area for the Viet Cong and NVA troops. Estimates of the number of enemy in the region ranged, at times, up to sixty thousand. Using the Kinh Bo Bo and related streams, the enemy could move virtually without interference to within ten miles of Saigon. A year earlier, in December 1968, ComNavForV (Commander Naval Forces Vietnam) had established Operation GIANT SLINGSHOT, in which a combined force of U.S. and Vietnamese Navy patrol craft had been ordered to interdict these rivers, canals, and their tributaries.

No navigable waterway offered access to the Kinh Bo Bo, and it had become clear to NavForV that the route would have to be heavily patrolled if the operation was to have a chance of success. The logical solution was to extend the Kinh Gay southwest to meet the Kinh Lagrange (two canals started in the past but never completed), thus opening a direct waterway between the villages of Tuyen Nhon and Tra Cu on the two rivers. This route would be thirty kilometers long, and would allow a twenty-minute reaction time to any point along the canal from either of the navy's advance tactical support bases (ATSBs) at Tuyen Nhon or Tra Cu.

Greetings from the Bank

ComNavForV had requested studies to determine the feasibility of dredging the distance between the existing canals, which had been dredged by the French in the 1940s and 1950s (the Kinh Gay had never been completed). Work on the Kinh Lagrange had been terminated in 1953 after Viet Minh had sabotaged the original dredge and its two replacements. The distance that remained to be made navigable was 8.6 kilometers, or 5.45 miles. A portion, 5.3 kilometers of this—from the end of the Lagrange to the intersection with the Kinh Bo Bo—was a large drainage ditch, long overgrown with weeds. Once, perhaps, it had been wide enough for a sampan, but now it was only a habitat for reptiles and birds, and a hiding place for enemy munitions. The remaining 3.3 kilometers had once been a navigable section of the Kinh Gay, but now could not bear even small motorized traffic without weed clearance and deepening.

In July 1969, the Force civil engineers had reported that dredging bids had ranged from $2.6 to $5 million, with completion estimates ranging from seven to eighteen months. Even the lowest cost was prohibitive, and the time inconceivable. A construction company operating in such remote, hazardous terrain would be exceptionally vulnerable and would require three permanently assigned U.S. Army platoons for security. Furthermore, because of its size, the dredge would create a canal much bigger than necessary for the PBRs (patrol boat, river) and indigenous craft to pass.

It had been suggested that the job might be done with demolitions, and seven specialists from UDT-12 were deployed to the area, with an assortment of demolitions, to determine if that was feasible. Lieutenant O'Keefe and Detachment Delta conducted test-blasting on the site in October, and proved that demolitions would be incomparably faster and cheaper than dredging. It was estimated that, provided the necessary explosives were on hand, a canal five feet deep, thirty feet wide, with turnaround areas every one thousand feet, could be completed in forty-five days for under $500,000. The great advantage was that the task could be accomplished exclusively with military assets. The job was assigned, and all were thrilled, except the people who would have to do it.

ComNavForV decided to proceed with the plans for the operation. Since UDTs deployed in the Western Pacific (WesPac) are assets of the commander, Seventh Fleet, permission had to be obtained to "borrow" enough additional men to do the task. Two officers and twenty enlisted men were deemed adequate for the job. UDT-12, Detachment Delta, originally comprising one officer and four enlisted men, was reinforced with six men who were on loan to NavForV (serving with other UDT units in country) and eleven others approved by ComSeventhFlt. The detachment was assigned to Task Group 194.9, GIANT SLINGSHOT.

Lt. (jg) Walter R. Harvey, U.S. Navy, was designated officer in charge of the job, and in mid-November, he was assigned to write the operation order and to oversee all preparations. With assistance from NavForV and the newly formed Naval Special Warfare Group, Vietnam Detachment—created to supervise UDTs sea, air, land (SEAL) teams, and mobile support teams in country—the lieutenant ordered the demolition material and made arrangements for ground security forces, artillery, and air support, equipment, berthing, and other logistical needs.

Tentative plans were made to begin the operation on 4 January 1970, the earliest possible date. All plans were contingent upon the arrival of the demolitions—6,200 lengths of Mark 8, Mod 2, explosive hose—230 tons representing 60 percent of the free world's supply. Only four hundred lengths were on hand in WesPac; the rest had to be shipped from the States, and the projected date of arrival in Vung Tau, RVN, was 8 January. It was decided to move the detachment up the river from the Naval Support Activity, Nha Be, on 4 January, and to begin work two days later with the four hundred lengths on hand—at least two days' supply. The remainder was expected to arrive by 9 or 10 January.

To allow for the uncertainties of in-country transportation, members of the new detachment had been released from their prior units before New Year's Day, and filtered into Nha Be over the holiday. On the morning of 4 January, the twenty-two men piled their gear into the well deck of an LCM-8 (landing craft, medium), amid forklifts, air mattresses, demolition equipment, and motion picture gear, the latter being the property of navy and DoD cinematographers who were aboard to document the event. Two Vietnamese Navy LDNNs, (Frogmen), were also aboard to assist with the rigging and hauling of the demolitions.

Many of the UDT men had not seen each other since before the team deployment in August, and were enjoying the reunion. The group included three chief petty officers and four first-class petty officers, the bulk of the team's senior enlisted men, and the best of the younger operators. About half of this group would be spelled by other team members by the time the job was finished.

Although they made jokes about the hazards of the job during the two-day trip to Ben Luc and Tuyen Nhon, most of the men were not without private apprehensions, especially those with the burden of responsibility—Lieutenant Harvey and Chief Gunner's Mate George B. McNair, who, for eighteen years, was a member of UDT and was the team's most experienced demolitions man. Auspicious, if silent, greetings were offered by seven NVA soldiers, who lay rotting on the banks of the Kinh Lagrange the day the group arrived.

And the Circus Began

Among the numerous problems confronting the planners was the transportation of 230 tons of explosives from the continental United States (CONUS) to Vietnam on time, and then moving them safely to the blasting site. For safety reasons, no more than three days' supply could be stockpiled at ATSB Tuyen Nhon.

Chief McNair had an immediate solution for the laying of explosives, which he believed would eliminate the transportation problem, increase the safety factor, and cut the operation time in half. The charges would be rigged by section at Vung Tau, flown by CH-46 Chinook helicopter to the canal site, connected, and blasted. This would eliminate the need for forklifts, boats, and a stopover in Tuyen Nhon. Lieutenant Harvey, however, was unable to obtain this crucial transportation service until the canal was almost half-finished, after many alternate methods had been tried and discarded.

The first weeks were a mishmash of experimentation, improvisation, and frustration, as we tried to find the best way to lay the hose with the gear available. C-130 aircraft, LCM-6s and 8s, ASPBs, PBRs, army airboats, skimmers, IBSs, and air mattresses were all used to get the explosive hose from Vung Tau to the canal. Alfa boats with one engine, Mike boats that didn't work at all, skimmers that sank, punctured air mattresses . . . but the canal progressed, nevertheless. The brute force of the UDT men, if slower, was ultimately dependable.

Lieutenant Harvey had to plan a second method. Demolitions would be flown to Tuyen Nhon and moved by forklift onto LCMs. Boats would carry the demolitions to near the blasting site, where it would be implanted by hand, with the assistance of flotation devices, then detonated. The obvious problem was moving the charges up the narrow canal as it progressed. It was questionable that even an LCM-6 could navigate the canal. Other, smaller, craft were to be available if that failed; and as a last resort, demolitions could be moved a long way by hand.

Another consideration was the spirit of the men, who were not comfortable about the open location of the job, its length, or the security measures provided for it. Lieutenant Harvey had to settle for army air-cushion vehicles (ACVs) and Civilian Irregular Defense Group soldiers (CIDG) in lieu of Regular-Army troops. The ACVs would circle the UDT men as they worked, providing a mobile perimeter, and four CIDG would ride each ACV. However, there were qualms about the CIDG, Vietnamese mercenaries whose reputation for reliability was unpredictable at best.

Ostensibly, Operation DEEP CHANNEL was just a bigger demolition job, but its situation was significantly different from any of the riverine reconnaissance, demolition, or patrolling work that the UDT had been doing in Vietnam since 1968. The Frogman would work unarmed, with both feet in deep mud, literally miles from any cover or concealment, amid poisonous krait snakes. Every afternoon at about the same hour, the UDT men would announce to the enemy their precise location and the day's progress with a multiton explosion, visible for twenty miles. They would then go home via exactly the same dangerous route they had used to come to work, with no alternate or escape routes, and they would rely entirely on unfamiliar men and machines for their defense.

Those were the very same conditions the UDT men had spent twenty arduous weeks in UDT/SEAL training learning to avoid, for obvious reasons. The crew was only slightly reassured by the fact that artillery from three locations, helicopter gunships, and fixed-wing planes would be available on an on-call basis.

The advanced tactical support base (ATSB) at Tuyen Nhon comprised a long row of hootches strung out along one side of the Kinh Lagrange. It was protected against the open grassy spaces by armed watchtowers, a complex network of barbed and concertina wire, and a field of claymore mines and trip flares. On one side of the base was a Special Forces camp; on the other, a short clay airstrip that could barely accommodate the C-130 aircraft, which would bring the demolitions.

The base was headquarters for U.S. and Vietnamese patrol craft, which were tied along the canal in front of the hootches—many PBRs, ASPBs (armored support patrol boats), monitors, ATCs (armored troop carriers), and LCMs. Although the base was primitive, mosquito-ridden, and muggy hot, certain human comforts were evident: electric fans, armchairs made by the local villagers, unopened tins of Christmas treats, and innumerable friendly dogs.

Just after dawn on the morning of 6 January, the UDT team boarded two ASPBs and two LCM-8s, one of which carried four hundred crated charges of explosives. The small convoy headed northwest on the Kinh Lagrange, toward Firebase Gettysburg where the blasting would begin. Along the banks of the Tuyen Nhon village, bleary-eyed children in undershorts watched the boats, still too sleepy to chase them along the river bank and yell for tins of C rations that the sailors often threw to them.

Across the Vam Co Tay River was the Plain of Reeds, an endless flat ocean of grass, with a few clumps of trees barely visible to the west in Cambodia. Boat crews manned their guns. From long habit, the UDTs carried M-16s. The desolate twelve-kilometer stretch between the river and the firebase was the likeliest place for an ambush.

Less than a mile from the firebase, the men passed by the seven brown bodies of enemy soldiers who had been gunned down by helicopters three days before.

The Kinh Lagrange ended abruptly at the firebase, where the French had stopped dredging. The security forces were already waiting: common radio frequencies and call signs were established, and the procedures were reviewed.

The LCM-8 had dropped its ramp in the mud at the end of the Lagrange. At 0840, work began without confusion. Under the supervision of Chief McNair, the crew commenced to rip apart the wooden crates that housed the demolitions. The well deck and ramp of the LCM provided a handy working platform for rigging.

During the October tests, the Mark-8 hose had been found to be more effective and faster than any combination of M-3 shaped charges, forty-pound cratering charges, or C-4 demolition packs. The hose consists of reinforced rubber fabric casing filled with composition-A and aluminum powder, with a TNT booster at either end. Each charge weighed 150 pounds, was 25 feet long, and was 2.5 inches in diameter. At one end it had a male brass coupling—at the other, a female—with a recession for an electric blasting cap. The charge looked so similar to a length of conventional fire hose that it was frequently mistaken for it.

For use on most of the canal, five lengths were lashed together into a pyramid to form a twenty-five-foot section of charge. Each charge was moved into its position along the canal bed and coupled with the ones before and after it. One end of the entire length was then fitted with a blasting cap and connected to a reel of electrical firing wire. The shot was detonated from four hundred or more feet away. In theory, there was no limit to the size or length of the charge. If 8.6 kilometers of explosives could be planted in one day, a twist of the wrist could detonate the whole business.

The first day's operation was surprisingly smooth. The goal was to complete the four-hundred-foot connecting link from the Lagrange to the Kinh Gay extension, and make the ninety-degree turn to the northeast toward the navigable portion of the Kinh Gay. One group uncrated and rigged the hose while two groups staggered through the water and mud and coupled the charges together. About half of this connecting link to the Kinh Gay extension was now a pond, which had been created during the October test. It was decided to blow the area again to assure continuity of the canal. Parts were so deep that men had to swim the charges into position on air mattresses.

Beyond this experimental section was muck and tangled growth, with a fast trickle of water just wide enough to permit the mattresses to be pulled upstream between the weeds. After a few minutes on the job, the crew members were so wet and filthy that they changed from whatever uniforms they had worn to swim trunks and boots. The motion picture teams, equally dirty, were recording this for posterity on a variety of cameras and recording machines.

By noon, the shot had been prepared almost as far as the turn. It had been decided to limit the length of this explosion because of the proximity of Firebase Gettysburg. This base, located 6.5 kilometers from the tip of the Parrot's Beak, was a cleared dirt area occupied by three army artillery platoons. Their full-time job was to provide gunfire support for any targets within range. Because of the demolition activity, artillery operations had been suspended for two days, and the weapons and projectiles had been sandbagged and covered to prevent possible damage from shock or falling debris. The base captain had moved his troops well to the rear in anticipation of the blast. They collected in a large crowd, where a carnival spirit prevailed; the occasion that had given them two day's rest was providing entertainment, too, a rare occurrence on the Plain of Reeds.

A Spectacular Black Explosion

The devise used for detonating an electrical explosion is called a "hell box," and for obvious reasons, its handle is never attached until all parties are ready for the explosion. It is the responsibility of the man supervising the shot to keep it on his person until that time. At 1210, Chief McNair twisted the handle, instantaneously detonating the first explosion of DEEP CHANNEL.

Before a blast there is a quiet, expectant calm. Suddenly, before there is any noise at all, a black wall five hundred feet long bursts upward from the flat land like a phalanx of geysers. The huge explosion and staggering shock wave follow, and the walls keep rising, hundreds of feet in the air and perfectly intact. At its peak, well over three hundred feet high, the wall begins to disintegrate. Millions of particles of soil and water are atomized and suspended for seconds, apparently motionless, looming like a ponderous thundercloud above the plain. Then, huge chunks of earth splatter noisily along the banks of the new canal behind the veil of black mist, which slowly begins to fall. The smaller chunks hit the ground first, and then everything streams back to earth in a heavy, hissing mud rain.

Like oil erupting from a new well, the mud from the blast coated everything with a sludgelike gray film. The mud, heaped in giant gooey gray gobs along the infant canal, yielded strange gems, fish, and krait snakes—somewhat dazed from their first airborne experience but not beyond one last fatal bite. Chief McNair and Lieutenant Harvey, black from the muck, emerged, grinning, and led the crew through mounds of sucking mud to survey the new stretch of canal.

The CIDG troops had left the ACVs and forged in the mud for the stunned fish, which, along with the krait snakes and other fauna, were scattered along the banks. The new canal was rapidly filling with water from the Kinh Lagrange; several UDT members plunged into it to test the depth. One fifty-foot section just before the turn was too shallow and would have to be blown again.

Two more shots were blown the first day: the second smoothed and widened the turn from the Kinh Lagrange onto the connecting segment, and the third eliminated most of the shallow spot and turned the corner, pointing the new water way toward the Kinh Gay and Tra Cu.

The labor involved in preparing this final shot indicated more serious problems to come. The LCM-8 which carried the demolitions could not navigate the new canal. The ASPBs could enter the canal, but with their four-foot draft, mud was sucked into the sea strainers and pumps, so they could not be used. For the third shot, the demolitions could not be brought by boat to the spot where the charges could be laid. Before the UDT men could begin to lay them, they would have to be moved by hand or floated the five-hundred-foot distance the first two shots had covered. If one thousand were to be implanted, the last charge would have to be moved fifteen hundred feet. Implications of this were obvious. If some mechanical means of moving the charges from Firebase Gettysburg up the new canal to the work site was not found, the men might end up moving the final charge of the operation 8.6 kilometers by hand. Lieutenant Harvey had envisioned this problem when his request for helicopters was turned down in December. He had been assured that an LCM-6 could traverse the canal, and would be available for the job. To date, however, no LCM-6 had arrived for work, and there was no indication that one was on its way.

The Sweetness of Mud

In spite of this dim prospect, the UDT crew was elated, if weary, on the return trip to the ATSB late that first afternoon. Their apprehensions had eased as they caught the spirit of teamwork in the mud, and the blast had been eminently satisfying. Oppressive as the mud was, it offered comic relief. People slipped and fell in it, wallowed in it, became stuck in it, and even flung wads of it at each other. Mud became an obsession, a way of life in itself. It worked its way into every possible crevice and pore of the body. We worked in it, played in it, even fought with it—sometimes on the PBRs—which displeased their drivers almost as much as the canal they would have to patrol at night. We were not their favorite people.

That evening, a crew meeting was called at the ATSB to discuss the problem of moving the demolitions up the canal, and to hear suggestions for improving the procedures. It was immediately decided to radio to CTG-194.9 (GIANT SLINGSHOT) to request an LCM-6 or an LCVP; even though we realized that those, too, might fail, they were worth a try. There were three other possibilities: hauling the demolitions up the canal by PBR, towing them with motorboats on flotation devices, or moving everything by hand.

In his planning, Lieutenant Harvey had relied heavily on the PBRs as the sure alternative if all else failed. But because of her size, each PBR could carry only small amounts of hose at a time, and on a given day, each boat would take quite a beating going up and down the new canal. Finally, the PBR commander at Tuyen Nhon stated flatly that he had other commitments for his boats and did not feel that he could subject them to such a beating on a regular basis.

Both of Detachment Delta's outboard engines were still awaiting repair in Nha Be, where they had been for two months, and no others were readily available to power the Boston whalers.

At this meeting, the crew also decided to uncrate and pyramid the hose on the LCM-8 in the mornings while en route to the first firebase. (The LCM-8 would continue to be used until replaced by a smaller craft.) The trip up the Kinh Lagrange took over an hour, which allowed time for rigging—and that freed everyone to haul the hose up the canal bed. The prospect of being on board a craft loaded with eight tons of explosives was not enticing, but the risk had to be taken.

The next morning, the crew had made an important discovery: the Vietnamese villagers craved the wood from the demolition crates, an unexpected dividend. They would use all they could get. Reaching the village of Tuyen Nhon, the crew stopped to buy ice, and found they could trade wood crates for it. Subsequently, the crates were traded for more ice, for food, for sundries made by the local Vietnamese, and for labor. Old women traded Afro combs, shower shoes, watermelons, and cheap sunglasses for the wood, and their children threw the crates in the canal and swam or paddled them a mile to the village. There was a desperation in the way the Vietnamese scavenged for what we casually threw away—the wood, the C rats, even the garbage from the evening meal.

When the crew reached the firebase, all charges were rigged. The next two days passed without unexpected problems. Charges were floated along the finished canal, and then pushed on air mattresses through the choked weeks and mire of the ditch. A trickle of water less than three feet wide ran swiftly southwest, allowing space for the air mattresses. Thus, the remainder of the four hundred lengths of Mark-8 hose on hand was expended, and the crew ceased operations for two days while waiting for the new supply of demolitions, which had arrived as scheduled at Vung Tau on 8 January.

During this stand-down, an LCM-6 arrived from somewhere down river. Ironically, no one, not even her crew, knew who was responsible for sending her to Tuyen Nhon. The boat was in disgraceful condition; one engine was dead, the other one dying. The steering was in disrepair, and the ramp didn't function at all. Shipfitters and enginemen in the UDT crew repaired one engine, the steering, and the ramp, making the craft marginally functional.

By this time, Lieutenant Harvey had made an agreement with the captain of the local CIDG forces to exchange labor for wooden crates. The CIDG began work on 10 January, and continued to uncrate and rig charges regularly under the supervision of one UDT man. This arrangement might have worked well had it not occurred to the CIDG captain that he should get an extra crate for himself for each man he provided. His greed irked Lieutenant Harvey, who promptly fired him and hired the local villagers. The villagers ended up rigging the hose in exchange for the crates.

Work began again on 11 January, using the renovated LCM-6. It performed, but not smoothly. Since the tide was in its neap phase, there was insignificant change in water level, and the LCM-6 could traverse the new canal and provide a working platform as the LCM-8 had done. Getting the boat up the canal was one thing, but coming back out was something else again. Indentations had been blasted every one thousand feet to provide space for the PBRs to turn around, but these were not big enough to accommodate an LCM. It was a difficult stunt indeed to back this craft down a twenty-five-foot-wide canal on one engine, but even that was infinitely preferable to moving the explosives by hand.

On the fourth day of this procedure, 14 January, the UDT crew encountered its second shallow spot one thousand meters from the first turn. This was the second of three such areas which would slow the operation. Three unsuccessful attempts were made to deepen that section with extra loads of explosives. The spot was deep enough to allow the passage of a PBR, but the LCM-6 could not cross it. It was decided to continue with the canal, returning to deepen the troublesome section later, time permitting, when an effective method for doing the job had been worked out.

The reason for the difficulty lay principally in the composition of the ground. Explosives must encounter resistance. The more resistance, the more effective the explosion. These shallow spots were narrow corridors of the plain that were less compact, and which contained more moisture and more absorbent organic materials than other areas. Because of their porosity, the abundant waters of the plain moved easily through these corridors. The canal happened to transect three of them. They absorbed the shock, and more sophisticated techniques would be needed to bring them to the required depth.

The LCM-6 limped along for several days after the shallow spot was reached, and then it was grounded there, and the demolitions were moved beyond by "other means." Initially, they were dragged and floated by hand, and then someone suggested that the air-cushion vehicles might be able to tow the charges. Motorized boats could not be used because of the density of the weeds. The O-in-C requested the service of ACVs from CTG 194.9, and was provided with a smaller variety of airboat, a craft similar to the type used in the Florida Everglades, which served the purpose well. Slowly, two thousand more meters were blasted. The hose had to be towed gently and carefully through the weeds, but the procedure saved considerable labor.

Anything that saved labor helped. Since the beginning of the operation, the forklift had been an invaluable tool for moving the crates of demolitions from the aircraft and for moving rigged charges into the well deck of the LCMs. About the time the second shallow spot was encountered, the forklift broke down, and for several days, the UDTs and CIDG troops had to do everything entirely by hand. Crates were broken open on the plane, and charges were carried off individually. They were then rigged as usual and carried by shoulder onto the well deck of the LCM. Such labor took its toll psychologically as well as physically.

During this week, the commander of Naval Forces, Vietnam, Vice Adm. Elmo Zumwalt, made the first of several visits to the canal site, where he was briefed on the progress and technical problems, and stayed to watch the day's explosion.

On the morning of 19 January, the daily load of demolitions came from Vung Tau, not by C-130 or Caribou aircraft as usual, but by CH-46 Chinook helicopter—exactly what Lieutenant Harvey had originally asked for, and which subsequent events had proven were badly needed. He reasoned now that if they could fly the 180-mile round-trip, they could probably hop the extra 10 to 15 miles to the canal site on the return route. He notified CTG 194.9 of this proposal, and suggested that the helos bring a cargo net of crated hose to ATSB Tuyen Nhon, exchange it there for a cargo net of rigged charges, drop these at the blasting site, and return to Vung Tau. Lieutenant

Harvey's conversation with Vice Admiral Zumwalt several days before had possibly had something to do with the prompt response to the request. The first day of helo operations would confirm that the idea was indeed worthwhile.

On 22 January, after about three kilometers had been completed, two helos delivered nets of twenty rigged charges down at a smoke signal along the canal site. The UDT crew assembled the charges along the bank, rolled them onto air mattresses or rubber boats, and floated them to the left and then to the right of where they had been dropped. A third cargo net appeared, and fifteen hundred feet were implanted and successfully detonated that day. The previous maximum distance achieved had been one thousand feet. The average had been about 750.

For each of the next three days, helos were promised, and each day the UDT crew traveled to the site by PBR and waited. The helicopters never came. Shortly after noon each day, Lieutenant Harvey secured the ACVs and CIDG troops and returned with his men to the ATSB. Previously, there had rarely been any time on the work site to relax or loiter, and now there were three long mornings. The crew was now a long distance from the relative security of the firebase, and with nothing to fill their time, the men began to grow impatient and anxious. At about 1600 on the third day, long after the UDT crew had returned, word came that two helicopters with demolitions would arrive at Tuyen Nhon at 1800. Because of the hour and absence of security, Lieutenant Harvey decided not to take his men to the canal site that evening, but his decision was overruled by the UDT-12 executive officer, who felt that an alert unit of twenty Frogmen, if necessary, could handle any of the smaller enemy units that would be moving through the area. FAC (forward air control) observer pilots regularly reported numerous sampans and small groups of enemy soldiers gathering along the Cambodian border before sunset, but rarely saw units of more than ten men.

The UDT crew departed from Tuyen Nhon about 1700 in PBRs, armed with M-16s, grenades, and a heavy load of ammunition. Much of their work would be done at twilight, possibly dusk—prime hours for the enemy to be crossing the approximate area of the canal. The regular daytime security forces had been secured; and the air-cushion vehicle platoon, which was normally assigned to set night ambushes along these infiltration routes, would not be present that night because of mechanical difficulties in Ben Luc, some distance away. Nor would helo gunships be available for overhead surveillance and protection. This meant that the UDT crew would have to provide its own security while working that evening. The likelihood of obtaining helicopters for emergency evacuation, if necessary, would be slim. A fourth consideration was that the tide was in its full-moon phase, and would be approaching low. There was some question as to whether the PBRs would be able to passage the canal at all, much less cross the shallow spot twenty-five hundred meters from the blasting site.

The UDT crew went—not encouraged by the situation, but eager to work, nevertheless. A perimeter guard was posted fifty meters from each side of the canal site: one man each beyond the limits of the workers and one man in the middle. The men worked with weapons, H-harnesses, and ammunition on their backs. The hose-carrying helos arrived on schedule; one thousand feet of explosives were rigged by 1945, and were detonated by 2000.

But now the tide had fallen too low. The PBRs had not been able to cross the shallow spot, and were awaiting instructions at the firebase. No helicopters were available in the area to extract the men. The UDT crew lost radio contact with Gettysburg, and then with the PBRs. Then they lost radio contact altogether.

There was no choice but to walk out. Darkness had fallen, and the moon had not yet risen. The UDT crew assumed a loose patrol formation in the chest-high grass along the canal, and began to sweep southwest in the same manner that they had searched the river banks for bunkers in other parts of Vietnam. They hand carried the demolition chest, air pumps, and most of the mattresses, a few of which were used to float the two 150-pound cargo nets, which they towed along the canal.

After they had covered almost half the distance back to the firebase, a helo approached, landed on a signal, and took the men to the PBRs. Caked with mud, they returned to the ATSB after 2200, to find that the chow hall and the showers had been secured.

The following day, the helicopters came in the morning and the UDT crew blasted a record twenty-five hundred feet in less than four-hours' time. When the helicopters became part of the routine, the UDT crew consumed the canal at a rate of nearly fifteen hundred feet per day. The most important psychological victory was reaching the Kinh Bo Bo, the focal point of the operation. The first 5.3 kilometers were by far the hardest: beyond the Bo Bo, the Kinh Gay was a recognizable canal. The remaining 3.3 kilometers were impenetrably choked with weeds and partly filled with sediment, but the pyramid charges could now be reduced from five to three sections each and still clear the canal effectively.

All records for progress were broken the day the crew blasted thirty-eight hundred feet of canal, using twenty-eight thousand pounds of explosives—probably the largest single blast in UDT history. This was more than one-eighth of the total distance of the canal.

By 8 February, the dedication day for the canal, only eight hundred feet remained to be blasted to connect the waters of the Song Vam Co Tay with the Song Vam Co Dong. Several areas still needed attention, notably two shallow spots and one corner, which had to be widened.

The solution for deepening the resistant corridors was the use of a multiple-delay explosion. Instead of the usual single-pyramided length, four were used. Two were implanted in midcanal eighteen inches apart, and two others were placed along the banks. All were connected to the firing reel and detonated as a single shot, but the center charges were rigged with a fifty-millisecond delay blasting cap. The outside charges went instantaneously, creating a partial vacuum that substantially reduced the resistance for the delayed charges. This method was used successfully to deepen both spots.

The dedication of the canal was originally planned for 10 February, but the date was changed to 8 February. We learned that senior officers also have a distaste for mud, particularly when it comes from the sky and there is no way to circumvent it. COMUSMACV, Gen. Creighton Abrams, U.S. Army, was the honored guest. With him were Vice Admiral Zumwalt, the Vietnamese chief of naval operations, and four army general officers. They had come to witness the final explosion. The UDT crew planted the last eight hundred feet of hose that morning. When the dignitaries arrived, Lieutenant Harvey briefed General Abrams on the progress and problems of the operation to date. Chief McNair explained the operation of the blasting machine, and the general took custody of the hell-box handle and detonated the final explosion. And there our distinguished visitors stood, transfixed by the spectacle and heedless of our warning to take adequate cover. To our undisguised amusement, they were drenched from starched hat to spit-shined boot. The general, who was not amused, was heard to quip to Vice Admiral Zumwalt: "We'll see if we can do the same for you some time."

Operation DEEP CHANNEL ended five days later on 13 February, after the last touches had been put onto the canal. The job had been completed in twenty-nine working days—only two-thirds of the anticipated time—at two-thirds of the anticipated cost.

The Tet offensive never materialized, and there was not a peep out of Charles. For his cooperation, we are most grateful. No one on the demolition crew was injured by the enemy or bitten by a krait snake, something of a miracle itself. Before the operation, Chief McNair had reasoned wryly, that, "The only reason the enemy might *not* get us is if they figure they can use the canal themselves." His theory—and the military success of the canal itself—remain to be proved. We left a million footprints, and a curse or two.

A graduate of Yale University in 1965 and Columbia University Graduate School of Journalism in 1966, Jerry Howard worked for several newspapers as reporter and copy editor prior to entering Officers Candidate School in January 1967. In December 1968, he completed Basic Underwater Demolition/SEAL Training (BUDS) in Class 42 at Coronado, California. Jerry served as platoon officer, intelligence officer, and public information officer with UDT-12 until May 1970. He served two tours in Vietnam and participated in Operation DEEP CHANNEL.

Since his release from active duty, Jerry has worked alternately as a free-lance magazine writer and photographer and a staff editor on various publications. He is now an associate editor at *New Age Journal* in Boston, and gets his testosterone off building stone walls in his backyard, where there is a lifetime supply of rocks.

Chapter Eight

Ensign B. Guilver & Ensign William Stubbs 1944

UDT Training—Fort Pierce, Florida

The inevitable physical examination was our introduction to NCDU (Naval Combat Demolition Unit), Fort Pierce, Florida. Forming usually after a brief visit to Palm Beach, this experience caught many of us with the Monday morning hangover complex. Unlike so many physicals, this one consisted of a good deal more than the cough-and-spread-your-cheeks inspection. It was a thorough examination, designed especially to weed out those with weak hearts and lungs. This was followed by a personal interview and a series of psychiatric tests. Mental ability and a stable temperament were of no less importance than physical fitness in the work of the demolitoneer. Incidentally, we are still at a loss to know how some of us got by. As a result of these tests, 20 percent of the applicants were dropped before actually beginning the training program. However, the 80 percent that qualified were new "demos" and ready to begin the six-to-ten week training program which the navy classified as extrahazardous duty.

The quarters that housed the men and officers were almost identical. Everyone ate the same chow, sweated under the same hot, humid Florida sun, and were bitten, but plenty, by the same mosquitoes and sand flies.

The actual training began with what we referred to as "Hell Week." When one speaks of hell, the conception is usually of a place where things too terrifying to imagine take place. Fort Pierce was definitely the place, and if the things that happened weren't too terrifying to imagine, it was because we had been ribbed about Hell Week ever since the morning we were first inducted at Fort Pierce. Hell Week was actually a well-planned program, during which the various instructors were given the opportunity to determine whether or not a man was suited for demolition. Actually, the men were under the impression that it was merely an attempt to prove how much a man could endure without proper sleep.

Early in the morning of the first day, we started off with a little exercise which consisted, merely, of running out to the North Island Quonset area, a short jaunt of two and a half miles. Later in the morning, we were indoctrinated in the use of rubber boats. This was accomplished by demonstration and oral lectures under a sun of such intensity that it was actually almost unbearable. The afternoon was spent putting into practice what we were supposed to have learned during the morning. In the evening, we had a night problem—paddling two miles out to sea and back. We got in early enough to get five hours' sleep.

The second day was the heralded "round the world." Looking back, it seems funny because it started out like all other days. The sun was shining brightly. We had our morning run and swim, our lecture, and then, about sundown, we entered our "P" (practical) work. We were to start out by crossing two jetties, both of which were studded with rocks. A mile beyond that we began a one-thousand-yard portage. "Up boat" was the horrible command that started the trip. After all of that we began the long pull up the channel between the two jetties. At first it was easy, nothing to do but paddle, but then it started—the mud flats, and I do mean mud! It was necessary for us to disembark and continue on foot, dragging our rubber boats behind us. To some it may have seemed easy, but we heavyweights suffered because our weight caused us to sink into the mud to our hips and beyond. Why did we do all of this? That question is still in the back of our minds, but we did it, and finished the course on time. Oh yes, we got four hours' sleep that night.

The third day was devoted to instructions on the subject of "sneak and peek," which is nothing but stealth and concealment. Of course we had our inevitable practical work, which was highlighted by mosquitoes and more mosquitoes, also snakes and sand flies. After crawling on our bellies for several hours, we finally secured and were able to get three hours' sleep.

The fourth day was easy. That is to say it was nothing but a day in which the less wise of us wore ourselves out for the next day, which was the climax to Hell Week. This day was filled with athletic contests—swimming, basketball, volleyball, and horseback riding, but with men as horses. With the end of the day, we thought it was the end for us as there was a forced march back to our boat landing—a distance of two and a half miles. A few men passed out, but everyone was on tap for the next day, "so solly day." It's funny, but everyone went out that night instead of going to bed, and with a 0300 reveille, most of us got two hours' sleep.

Friday was our fifth and last day of Hell Week. At 0300, we jumped out of the LCPR about fifty yards offshore, with full packs. We swam to the beach for a nice breakfast of damp K rations, during which we were instructed as to the procedure we would use during the next twenty hours. After a half hour, we were ready to begin a systematic infiltration of a booby-trapped jungle area. Just in case we missed the booby traps, instructors on both sides harassed us with all kinds of explosives, some of which exploded not more than ten feet away. Those of us who finally made it to the noon rendezvous for another meal of K rations made it there only in time to have a rubber hose, which is usually used for channel blasting, blow up in our faces, thus tossing mud and everything else in our food and faces. The afternoon was a continuation of the morning—infiltration and harassment. After successfully plunging, lunging, walking, or running through a stretch of jungle, which even Frank Buck would have thought twice before tackling, we arrived at the final phase of the problem, that of the foxhole ordeal. Actually it wasn't bad, once you managed to dig your foxhole. However, trying to dig a foxhole out of that dry, hard sand was plenty rough after a whole day of mental and physical strain.

The best way to end the description of Hell Week is to recall the celebration of the last night. At Fort Pierce, it was established custom to close all stores, board all windows, and in general, prepare for an invasion at the termination of Hell Week. All this was done as usual, but to no advantage when our demos hit town and raised more hell than was ever thought of on North Island. But that is another story, one that can only be told after the fourth drink, so I'd better be getting over to the club where I can get a good start on the rest of the boys.

The first mile-swim test was held the Saturday following Hell Week. All trainees were taken in LCPRs (landing craft personnel, ramp) a mile off shore. From each boat, the men hit the water to begin the long swim back to the beach. All along the way, athletics specialists were stationed in rubber boats to keep a sharp lookout for the weak and tired swimmers. Approximately two-thirds of the trainees passed this test. The other third was given extra swimming instructions and another opportunity to pass the test.

Actual demolition training began two days after the first mile swim. It was divided into three phases: (1) physical conditioning, which included calisthenics, long distance swimming, and small-boat handling; (2) theory of explosives; (3) practical work in the use of explosives.

Each morning, Monday through Friday, all hands mustered at 0815. After a few brief announcements, we proceeded in small boats to North Island. It was on this island that all demolition training was conducted. Much of the work was classified Secret, and we were cautioned not to mention, to anyone, what we did or saw. Trucks met us, we hoped, at the North Island boat landing and took us to the demo camp that was located two and a half miles inland.

The first part of the morning, 0930 to 1000, was devoted to calisthenics; 1000 to 1100 was devoted to swimming. During this period, the weak swimmers were given instructions while all the others swam a carefully marked half-mile course. At 1130, everyone assembled in the amphitheater for lectures on explosives. These lectures included everything from tying in trunk lines to capping bangalore torpedoes. In the afternoon, the essence of the morning lectures was put to practice. If the subject was knot tying, the men learned to tie the essential knots from all different positions—underwater, behind their backs, while swimming toward the obstacles, etc. If the subject was devoted to blowing iron rails, each man took his turn at placing charges until he could demolish a rail in the quickest possible time. Day in and day out, this routine was strictly adhered to. Many men that were found to be careless had to be dropped because, obviously, there could be no room in demolition for such men. One careless mistake could cost the lives of many teammates.

Finally, however, our training came to an end. Everyone who passed the program felt a pride in demolition and an eagerness to get into a team. Our weekends at the "G.W." and Pennsylvania, in Palm Beach, were at an end and our dates with the Spars were over. We were leaving for the West Coast and then overseas. We were going into the war as members of an underwater demolition team!

We were all a little proud of ourselves, and stopped off at our homes on the way out to the West Coast, at least those of us who were fortunate enough not to have to travel on a troop train.

We spent a very pleasant week in San Francisco before boarding a transport ship for Maui. This trip was by far the most enjoyable we spent aboard any ship because we were passengers on the famous luxury liner *Matsonia.*

While most of the future Team 3 members were undergoing

Hell Week and hearing the familiar cry of "Fire in the Hole," several other future UDT-3 members were obtaining their experience, firsthand, as members of the hastily formed teams, UDT-1 and -2, which had just recently taken part in the Marshall Island operation. Because many of the original UDT-3 members were formerly of Team 1 and -2, it is fitting that a history of these earliest of demolition teams be included. The account in Chapter Ten of the history of UDT-2 was written by one of the ten original members who joined Team 3 and stayed with it from March 1944 until the team was decommissioned in December 1945.

Chapter Nine

Tim Reeves

SEAL Team 1 1969–1972

Dwight Fisher

It appeared to be just another day when I went to check my mail. I received a letter and shoved it into my jeans pocket. When I got home, I noticed the shaky handwriting on the business envelope as I struggled to tear it open. I suppose Dwight's father doesn't write many letters. He probably finds it impersonal, but why didn't he just call? It must have been too important for him to say on the phone. These thoughts raced through my mind as I finally got the letter open. Apparently he had scribbled the message quickly and mailed it. I only had to read it once . . .

Dwight and I experienced many things together. When I first met him, we were fresh young recruits just out of navy boot camp. We became instant friends, not only because of our desire to complete the UDT/SEAL training we were about to begin but because of our innocence.

Dwight arrived at the naval amphibious base, Coronado, California, only minutes after I arrived. Sporting shaved heads and curious eyes, we must have looked like newly hatched humans. He walked over, and before putting down his seabag, asked politely, "Is this bunk taken?"

"Not as far as I know," I replied.

As he sat down, he said, "Are you going to be in Training Class 53?"

"Yeah," I answered, "I guess our class starts training on Monday."

"I can't believe I finally made it! I've heard so much about this place," looking around as if trying to find something to convince himself that he was really there.

About twenty men had already arrived to form Class 53, and more were expected before Monday.

"Did you go into the bathroom yet?" I asked.

"You mean the head don't you, sailor?" He corrected me jokingly.

"Whatever the case, there's a shark on the floor. Go check it out," I said.

When Dwight returned, he looked excited. I told him the trainees that started before us had left it there.

"Are you kidding me?" he said as he fell back on his bunk, looking up at the ceiling.

After talking with him for a while, I learned that Dwight was raised in a middle-class family in Wilmington, North Carolina. He had become a top cross-country runner while in high school.

I had plenty of opportunity to watch him run that next Monday as Class 53 started its eighteen-week training course with seventy-eight men. He ran like a deer, his resilient legs and strong jaw jutting forward. Only a few of us were expected to complete the training and become members of one of the underwater demolition teams, or Seal Team 1. Since UDT/SEAL training is an all-volunteer program, anyone can quit at any time. As the training progressed and got more difficult, trainees dropped out. This would strengthen Dwight's and my bonds of trust and friendship.

UDT/SEAL training was designed to weed out the weak and incompetent, and put together an elite functioning team of men to conduct clandestine warfare.

Dwight and I were assigned as swim buddies (mandatory for safety during training while on ocean swims). As a pair, we swam many miles together in perfect rhythm. Swimming sidestroke, with Dwight on his right side and I on my left, our eyes communicating through face masks, our fins propelled us swiftly through the open sea. We swam miles every day for nearly six months. Toward the end of training, we became the fastest swim pair in our class, keeping each other going many times.

One day, on an ocean swim, the swim pair directly behind us was catching up. Suddenly, my right leg cramped. Dwight could see the anguish in my eyes and the perspiration on my face through my face mask. He furrowed his forehead, puzzled, wondering what was the matter. I straightened up in the water, ripped off my face mask, and cried, "My fucking muscles cramped."

He ignored me, saying, "Come on, we've got to keep going!"

"Wait a minute," I yelled, "let me massage it."

"We don't have time," he answered, "they're catching up." The next thing I knew, as I doubled up in the water still in great pain, Dwight was grabbing the straps of my UDT life jacket and pulling me through the water. None of the instructors on the beach knew what was happening.

We were trained to work together, as a team. We lifted telephone poles, carried rubber rafts, performed night evolutions or maneuvers without sleep, and crawled through waist-deep mud. Teamwork was constantly stressed throughout the entire UDT/SEAL training program. After all, the efficient team would be the one with the greatest chance of coming back from Vietnam alive. This was also stressed by the instructors many times throughout training.

Twenty men graduated from UDT/SEAL Training Class 53. Fifteen of the original men who started, and five men who had been rolled back from Class 52. Five of us, myself included, received orders to SEAL Team 1, and the remainder went to the West Coast UDT teams. Dwight received orders to UDT-13.

Assignment to the teams involved additional intense training as a platoon before deploying to Vietnam. After arriving in Vietnam and operating with SEAL Team, it became clear to us why teamwork was stressed so much in training.

On September 28, 1970, my SEAL platoon engaged the Viet Cong in a particularly brutal firefight, which wounded all involved except our officer in charge and myself. Those of us not seriously wounded received some time off. I knew Dwight's UDT platoon was stationed at a very small camp named Sea Float near the southern tip of Vietnam. This seemed like a chance for me to visit him.

I managed to catch a helicopter going that way and soon was circling his camp. I was anxious to see him. From high above on the helo, I could see the defoliated perimeter of his camp and the triple-canopy jungle, which appeared to be crawling around it. Squeezed inside the perimeter of barbed wire were several plywood buildings with corrugated metal roofs. Several barges with plywood buildings were secured together in the center of the river. That had been the original base before the camp was moved to shore.

After landing on the helo pad, I jumped out of the chopper and wove my way past sandbag bunkers and through the mud, looking for the UDT hootch. Finding the hootch, I noticed the letters UDT and the green gun-toting frog painted on the main door. As I entered, I noticed a busy scene. Clothes, pictures, and memorabilia hung amidst a row of bunk beds. On the opposite wall was a gun rack, twenty feet long, filled with exotic weapons.

Dwight was standing by his bunk, talking with teammates, when he looked up and noticed me. He looked taller and leaner; in fact, he looked downright rugged, with long hair and a goatee. I remarked about his hairy face, he shrugged as if to say it was easier than shaving. Dwight asked, "Hey, what happened to your platoon yesterday? It sounded bad."

"We got shot up pretty bad, but everyone will be okay," I replied. "What have you been doing?"

His excitement grew as he sat on his bunk, telling me of one of his UDT experiences. "I got to go out with Red to blow up a Viet Cong weapons factory yesterday." Red was a member of Dwight's platoon who enjoyed working with demolitions and would do anything for an explosion.

Dwight went on, "Well, really, we first went by boat the night before, but we got lost. Red and I were in a sampan, and he kept wanting to go up these narrow canals. It was still dark, and I was scared shitless, but I didn't let Red know that. Anyway, after the sun finally came up, we decided to go back, get a helicopter, and rappel through the jungle canopy with our explosives."

My eyes widened. "Did you do that?"

"Yeah," he replied, "I got down that rope real fast. Sparky and Ross went first to set up security, so it wasn't too bad."

We continued talking about our combat experiences for a while, then I asked him about his girlfriend, Nancy. We always shared the latest about our romantic lives. I was happy to hear they were planning to get married.

Dwight opened a C-ration can of cheese and crackers, and we continued our conversation.

"Did you hear Palma and Banfield are up in Da Nang now?" he asked.

"I didn't know that. I know Staudenmeir is in Rach Soi," I replied.

I returned to my platoon the next day. I didn't see Dwight again until our platoons were transferred back to Coronado, three months later. With two years left in the navy, I found out where Dwight lived and went by to visit him and his new wife. His beard was gone, and his house was neat and clean.

The first thing he said was, "Did you hear what happened in Da Nang?"

I sat down on the front porch and told him I had heard the bad news, but he continued anyway.

"A booby trap killed Palma, and Banfield was hurt so bad he is being discharged from the navy. That helo crash killed five other friends stationed at Sea Float."

We talked about death and how it happens so quickly. A moment of silence was broken as Dwight jumped up and ran into the house to show me something. He returned a few seconds later with all kinds of literature on Amway. In Dwight's naturally excited way, he told me how it would make him rich some day. He went on, "It's a real good deal, and it's biodegradable. You'd be great at selling it, Tim, why don't you try? Here's everything you need."

I changed the subject. "Isn't that training you're doing in minisubmarines keeping you busy?"

"Yeah," he replied, "but this is a way to make some real money." A few months later, Dwight was trying to sell land in Apple Valley.

Dwight had a way about getting excited. He would become completely involved and motivated in anything he set his mind to, and would think of nothing else. Take the obstacle course, for example. He was good, in fact, he was one of the fastest men on his team and hoped to compete in the International Military Olympics before being discharged from the navy. The obstacle course contained eighteen obstacles and took six to seven minutes to complete. Precious seconds could be cut from a few obstacles by becoming adept at new methods of overcoming them. For example, Dwight had found he could hang at the top of the fifty-foot cargo net and fall several feet at a time. During each fall, he would catch himself and then drop again, repeating this method until he reached the ground.

"It's important," he said, "to keep your legs bent back behind you to keep them from getting tangled in the net." The new technique was a matter of saving only twenty seconds, but he practiced it and other timesaving methods on other obstacles for hours, making himself more proficient at completing the course.

The months passed quickly. I ended up in the hospital to get my tonsils taken out. Two days after my tonsillectomy, Dwight's wife came into my hospital room. Her eyes were red, and she put her head on my shoulder and cried for a moment before saying, "Dwight had a bad fall on the obstacle course and is in serious condition."

"Where is he?" I asked.

"Fourth floor, intensive care," she answered.

I waited until later that evening, then put on my bathrobe to see what was going on. Until then, I had never seen anyone in traction. He was droopy-eyed as I leaned over him and asked, "Do you hurt, Dwight?"

"They've got me drugged up. I fell from the cargo net. They think I broke my back," he continued with anguish. "My legs got hung up and flipped me upside down; it doesn't look good." He went on to assure me that he would find a way to overcome his problem and for me not to worry. I told him I would be there any time he needed me and I would see him tomorrow.

I visited Dwight several times during the next two weeks. Then, without a word, he was sent to a hospital in Long Beach, California for rehabilitation. While he was there, they would teach him to cope with a body that was paralyzed from the waist down. The last thing Dwight said to me before he left for Long Beach was, "I'm going to be the best damn paraplegic there is."

While Dwight was in Long Beach, I was discharged from the navy. We kept in contact through the mail. He spent two years in the Long Beach hospital. He got out, ready to take on the world.

After returning to his hometown, he learned to play the guitar, bought a special van to accommodate his wheelchair, and started college to earn a degree. Even though his wife had since divorced him, he never let his problems get in his way.

I admired Dwight so much, thinking all the time it could very well have been me. I wondered if I would have had the guts to go on with life in such a functional way if I were in Dwight's condition.

I had been traveling around Europe since my discharge from the navy three years earlier. Upon my return to the States, Dwight grabbed the first opportunity to come and visit me. His van and wheelchair were his mobility. He seemed proud when he drove up to see me in Saint Louis, but I noticed his legs had started melting away into bony limbs.

I took him around to meet my friends and noticed how he inspired people. His smile and enthusiasm were contagious, and he still had his love of life. He told me of his plans to build a house with wide doors and a long ramp instead of the stairs. That was to be his next accomplishment.

Two years later, in Wilmington, North Carolina, Dwight's house was finished. I went to visit him. As I pulled up in front of Dwight's huge wooden house, the front door swung open, and he came roaring down the ramp on the back wheels of his chair.

"Tim, ol' pal, it's good to see you again. Come on, let me show you my house." He sped around excitedly, showing me what still had to be done. We finally settled down on the front porch after returning from the garden. He told me that though his wife wanted to be set free, they were still in contact.

"I've met some women up at the university, and they treat me real good. Actually, I think they feel sorry for me, but I don't care. I'm just happy for the attention and companionship."

He took me up to the campus recreation hall, and we played pool. I wondered if the other students really knew what Dwight had been through. He told me they thought he was some kind of war hero.

I asked, "Dwight, do you have any bitterness from all this?"

"I lay on that sand below the cargo net for almost an hour, waiting for the ambulance. I knew I was hurt bad, and I was scared. Then I heard them coming, but it was just an old jeep. They put me in the back like a piece of meat, and I remember bouncing around on the floor. I screamed and pleaded with them to hold me still, but everything seemed like an illusion. If I have any bitterness, it's for that jeep ride to the hospital. I might not have become paralyzed if it wasn't for that."

I was shocked. I had not heard anything about that. Dwight must have kept that inside himself the whole time.

He continued to say he wasn't bitter, but I knew he was. Dwight was happy the navy had taken care of him by helping finance his van and house. He also admitted the accident was his own fault.

We decided to go out for dinner. On the way, he told me about all the problems he had getting into restaurants. The restaurant we went to used to have a series of four steps leading up to the entrance. He told me he had asked the manager to build a ramp, but got no response.

"One day," he said, "I wheeled up to the steps of that restaurant, crawled out of my wheelchair, and dragged myself and my chair up the steps in front of everyone. I must have made such a scene that the manager promised to build that ramp over there." He pointed to the ramp.

Dwight spun the seat around in his van, pushed his chair out the side door, and wheeled up the new ramp and into the restaurant. We ordered our dinners and sat back to catch up on each other's lives. I told him of my plans to travel to South America, and his eyes widened. He wanted to go but had too many loose ends to tie up first. We decided to keep in contact. I told him I'd look for a good place for him to come down and meet me.

The next six months were very difficult for me. I kept my eyes open for a place where Dwight could get around as I backpacked over the Andes and through the Amazon. I finally settled in Mendoza, Argentina, and wrote Dwight. He replied, saying he was ready, so I called him on the phone and told him to fly to Santiago, Chile. We set the time and date.

I arrived in Santiago the morning of our meeting and found a good room. Then, I went to the airport to meet him. As I stood on the observation deck watching the planes come in, I met a pretty girl named Sonia. I told her about my friend arriving and asked her if she would run up and give Dwight a big kiss to welcome him.

Dwight's flight arrived on time. He was a little bewildered from jet lag, culture shock, and the kiss on the cheek from Sonia. Sonia helped with the bags and said she would come back to town with us.

We arrived at the hotel and piled Dwight's two large two-hundred-pound suitcases on the sidewalk in front of the hotel. His gaze drifted up the long flight of stairs.

I said, "I'm sorry, Dwight, but it's a good room at a good price, and it's all I could find."

He answered, "It doesn't matter; grab my legs." He dove out of the chair and put his powerful hands on the first step. Up we went, wheelbarrow style, till we reached the top. Sonia and I carried everything up to the room as Dwight collapsed on the bed, totally exhausted.

Sonia began to massage him. I thought it might be a good time to go get dinner from the market place. When I returned, Dwight was happy to see me. After Sonia left, I said, "How was it?"

He was perturbed, saying, "Tim, I was freaked out for a while; man, that girl could have ripped us off for everything, and I couldn't have done anything about it. What's more, you have to realize I have to be very careful about diseases."

"I guess I have a lot to learn about paraplegics," I said.

"Oh, that's okay," he said, "I can't rely on you all the time. I'm going to have to keep working so I'm not that defenseless."

Before taking the train back to Argentina, Dwight and I decided to attend the international song festival in nearby Vina del Mar. After finding a ground floor room in a pension, we went to buy tickets for the night's performance. All the tickets had been sold out, but one of the promoters offered us free tickets in a position where Dwight could park his wheelchair.

With a couple of hours of spare time before the performance, we went out to dinner at a fancy restaurant with glass tables. Dwight wore his braces, which enabled him to stand upright and swing his lower body with the support of crutches. After a good dinner of *cebiche* (raw fish and lemon juice), we prepared to leave. Dwight, using the table for support while getting up, shattered the glass tabletop and legs into a pile of rubble. He sat back down, reached into his pocket, and pulled out his travelers' checks.

"How much?" he said, ready to take responsibility for his actions. The owner was trying to figure out the price of the table when a nicely dressed man from another table interrupted. "I will pay for everything," he said. Dwight would not hear of it. The man insisted, saying he was a local neurosurgeon and would feel honored to support Dwight's trip in this way. We returned to the pension to prepare for the performance that night. I had noticed earlier that Dwight would go into the bathroom for an hour at a time. I had not figured out what took him so long. This time I heard a terrible crash and ran to the bathroom and found Dwight sitting naked on the floor. He was sitting in a puddle of water, and the sink was barely attached to the wall. He had been using the sink for support while getting on and off the toilet, and it had collapsed under Dwight's weight. We managed to get the sink back into position.

After that night's performance, we heard about a private party for all the stars in the plushest hotel in town. We rushed back to our pension to get Dwight's braces and leave his wheelchair. We took a taxi to the hotel. Outside, a huge crowd of people had gathered, hoping to get a glimpse of some of the stars.

We were shocked as the taxi stopped right in front of the hotel and the crowd closed in. Dwight said, "Tim, those guards have machine guns!" I looked up and saw a long flight of marble steps leading up to the door. All along the steps were soldiers without smiles, and sure enough, they carried machine guns.

We acted like we knew what we were doing. Dwight hobbled to the first step as people watched and wondered. I stooped down on one knee in front of him and he fell on my back and wrapped his powerful arms around my shoulders. We had practiced this earlier as a quick way of getting up stairs. I carried Dwight and his crutches up the stairs and past the soldiers and then put him down. We walked into a grand ballroom where we saw celebrities such as Ray Coniff, Gina Lollobrigida, the musical group Chicago, and the Hues Corporation. We mingled and visited through the night.

A few days later, we arrived in Mendoza, Argentina, and in the confusion of getting a taxi, I left one of Dwight's suitcases on the sidewalk. The taxi waiting behind the taxi we caught picked it up and took it to the local police station. After making a few calls, we discovered what had happened to it, and went to the police station to recover it.

The police were ready to give us a hard time until they saw

Dwight come wheeling in. His condition explained some of the strange equipment that they found in the suitcase, but they didn't know what the Frisbee was. I laughed, and they became stern. Although they had no legal right to search the suitcase, you do not question the police in Argentina.

Dwight and I looked at each other, wondering how we were going to handle this situation. We both smiled at each other and turned back toward the captain to explain that it was just a toy. They grabbed at their guns when I picked it up and tossed it to Dwight. Dwight spun the Frisbee on his finger a few seconds then offered it to the captain. The captain stood up and laughed, which made the other policeman laugh too. The captain then returned Dwight's suitcase with everything in it, including seven heavy Spanish books. This made Dwight very happy.

For the next six months, Dwight and I lived in Mendoza. It is a beautiful city at the foot of the Andes Mountains, hidden by natural barriers. The people are educated, clean, and in love with life. It is a great place to learn Spanish because they are compassionate and curious. Dwight, in his condition, was made most welcome. For days, he would sit back and visit with friends who would stop by. Sometimes we would take the city bus to town, find a sidewalk cafe, and sip on a *cafe con leche*. People got used to seeing Dwight jump curbs and maneuver along crowded streets in his wheelchair. Going downhill, he would tuck up in a ball in his chair and run free on his back wheels.

Often we sat around with friends and reflected on our past experiences. Dwight would tell everyone how we had been swim buddies during UDT/SEAL training and how he had pulled me through the ocean. I would remind him of the night dive when he put his hand on a sleeping ray and screamed with fright all the way to the surface. Sometimes our friends would ask about Vietnam. We talked freely about our experiences, telling them we had lost some close buddies, but life goes on.

One day, we decided to have an *asado*. An *asado* is simply a picnic where there always seem to be plenty of guitars on hand. We cooked half a cow in a creek bed full of *damajuanas* of wine. No matter how good (or bad) they were each person took a turn playing a song on a guitar. Dwight played very well and was always a hit. More often though, he would lie on a big blanket with pillows and talk to the pretty women. Sometimes I could get him to wheel around and throw the Frisbee.

At one point, we set off on a trek for a month around Argentina. In Buenos Aires, Dwight rolled into tango bars and sat by the piano to enjoy the music and the dancers. In the southern Andes, he fished for trout. One day, he talked a ski resort owner into stopping the chair lift so he could get on and off. At the top was a view that took our breath away.

Everyday, he would accomplish something that he thought he would never do again. I told him how Jacques Costeau had said the coast around Puerto Madryn was one of the marine wonders of the world. He wanted to go the next day.

We went by bus and saw killer whales feeding along a beach. At another beach, we saw millions of penguins. The journey was intensely interesting. We talked at night for hours about what we had seen and what we would do the next day.

One evening while in a cafe, over a game of backgammon, I said, "I think we can rent scuba gear in this town."

"I've been wondering if I can still dive," he replied.

"Do you still swim like a fish?" I asked.

"It's really different with no leg power to propel me, and those tanks would make it even harder." He hesitated. "You'd have to be beside me all the time."

"Dwight, if you don't go diving one more time with me, then you may never want to go diving ever again," I said.

"Well, just remember that day you had that cramp and I had to pull you."

The next day we went into the local dive shop and rented some diving gear and a boat. Not knowing anything about our background, they thought we were crazy, but figured we knew what we were doing. That afternoon, we took the boat right off a point, dropped the anchor, and pulled on our wet suits. It was like going back in time for both of us. Dwight rolled overboard and hung onto the anchor line. I then buckled the tanks on his back. It didn't take long to discover his paralyzed legs floated uncontrollably. Dwight didn't hesitate, he reached back into the boat and grabbed two five-pound weights and shoved them into his booties. That seemed to work well, and he started down the anchor line.

It was good to see his eyes behind a face mask again. We passed through an endless amount of shrimp, and came to rest on the bottom at about sixty feet. Just as we had planned earlier, up on the surface, Dwight held on to my tanks, and I pulled him along the sandy bottom. We were both excited about diving again. We made a big circle and came to rest back at the anchor again. We gave each other the thumbs-up sign and just sat there until I could feel my tanks running low on air. Dwight pulled himself back up the anchor line to the surface. Back in the boat, we peeled off our wet suits and let the sun dry us.

I looked at Dwight and knew he was thinking of something. I broke the silence. "I must have used a lot of air pulling you around."

"I know," he said, "but if I had one of those torpedolike things that pulls divers, I'd have no trouble." Dwight seemed surprised that he could still dive as a sport. We returned to Mendoza to rest up for the trip home. The last week before we left, our friends had one last *asado* for us, and everyone was there. It was sad to be leaving our friends, but we were thinking of our next stop, Cuzco, Peru.

By now, I had become proficient at finding the perfect room for my friend and his wheelchair. It had to be on the ground floor, have wide doorjambs, strong towel racks and sinks for Dwight to use as supports.

After getting ourselves settled into our new room in Cuzco, we went out to see the town. The local people were shocked to see Dwight. He began to realize he was not in Argentina. Most of the people were Indians, and although they were friendly, they seemed dirty and uneducated. Many thought Dwight's wheelchair was some kind of toy. The kids would run up to the shiny object just to touch it. They looked at Dwight as if he were another rich North American with some crazy toy. There were many beggars along the streets with all sorts of handicaps. Dwight began to look at his problems through different eyes. Sitting in one alley was a man with deformed legs. He sat on a flat board with four small wheels attached to it that enabled him to push himself around. Dwight wheeled up in front of the crippled man and dropped some money in his can. Dwight told the man that he could not walk either, as he rolled up his pants and showed the beggar his twisted skinny legs. The beggar replied, "I thought in North America there was a cure for everything."

Everywhere we went, we met people who wanted to help. The Cuzco train station is known for pickpockets because of the crowds of tourists going up to see Machu Picchu. We met two young boys at the station who helped us board the train. After getting Dwight settled in his seat, I discovered the only place to put his wheelchair was in an open space between the two cars. The two boys said they would keep an eye on it, but every now and then I checked on it myself.

Suddenly, one of the boys came running into our car and said, "Señor, the chair is gone!" Dwight and I both panicked, and I ran to check on it. Sure enough, it was missing. Then I noticed the two boys were laughing and realized that they had moved the chair, playing a joke on us. When I finally returned to Dwight, he had a serious look on his face and said, "Tim, what if I lost my chair and you weren't here?"

"You'd just have to make some fast friends," I answered.

Machu Picchu is located on a steeply terraced mountaintop and built with huge rocks that are fitted closely together. A wheelchair is not practical there, especially on the oversized steps leading up the mountain. We went as far as we could into the ruins, where we met two hefty German ladies. After talking with them for awhile, I suggested that if they could carry Dwight's wheelchair, I could carry him on my back a little higher. With the help of our new lady friends, Dwight may very well have been the first paraplegic to see the great Incan hideaway from all angles.

Back in Cuzco, Dwight and I were relaxing in an outdoor restaurant. He said, to my surprise, "I want to try traveling by myself."

"What do you have in mind?" I asked.

"I figure I can fly to La Paz, Bolivia, and travel by bus back down to Argentina."

"Do you think you can get on buses and find a room by yourself?" I said.

"I just need a little help now and then, and the people are all so nice," he said.

Dwight was right, his Spanish was good, and he knew what to look for. So, one day I carried Dwight up one more flight of stairs, and we said good-bye as he boarded the airplane.

Two years later, I saw Dwight for the last time. I was on the East Coast of the United States, with two other friends from my navy days. We called Dwight from a little country town along the Intracoastal Waterway. We were all anxious to see Dwight. Dwight said he would come up and meet us.

That night there was a dance at the local VFW hall. We decided to attend the dance. We ended up dancing and flirting with some of the local women, which seemed to bother some of the local men. After the dance, several of these guys were waiting outside for us. They wanted to jump us, but were hesitant. Dwight loved the excitement, and sat straight up in his wheelchair as he led us to his van. There were only four of us and at least fifteen of them. They began to yell obscenities at us as we passed. Dwight just kept on smiling and continued toward the van. I asked Dwight if he wanted me to drive, but he just ignored me and crawled from the side door up to the driver's seat. He turned the van around and drove right through the mob. They pounded on the side of Dwight's van and scratched the paint.

After dropping off our other friends, we went for a ride. Dwight seemed anxious, and I asked him if anything was wrong. He answered with a curt, "No!"

I went on, "You've sure got guts, Dwight."

He grew angry, then said, "Hell, I was scared, but what was I supposed to do?"

"You could have gone to the van first and let us handle those assholes," I said.

He looked distant and then said, "I can't let people take on any added burden because of me. I have to continue to do everything I can myself. As long as I can be strong, I have to be."

"There's a difference between being strong and being silly," I said.

"I know, I know," he said. "Did you get that girl's phone number?" He changed the subject, so I let it lie.

What was happening with Dwight after this, is not clear to me. I know Dwight began to see a psychiatrist for posttraumatic stress syndrome. Silent anxieties seemed to be surfacing with him. His parents wrote me a letter, which said Dwight had driven his van to Panama and had it shipped back. After that, I heard he was in California. He would not let anyone know where he was going. I had the feeling he might have stopped at the rehabilitation center in Long Beach. I wrote him a letter, telling him that I was upset because he never came to visit me. I received no reply. His mother wrote me a letter a few months later telling me Dwight was doing "crazy things."

That was it, I had to try to contact him to find out what the problem was. I got in touch with his parents late one night after dinner. His mother and father both got on extensions and filled me in. His mother said, "Dwight won't have anything to do with his family, from his grandparents on down to his six-year-old niece. He gave his dogs away, left his house, and even bought a gun."

I thought about the night when I left him alone with Sonia and how he felt so defenseless. His father convinced me something was definitely wrong. He said it was almost as if Dwight was trying to find something that could defeat him. Dwight's mother was crying by then and told me she thought maybe he wanted someone to take care of him, that in effect, he was looking for an escape for having to be so strong. I told Dwight's parents that I wished he would come and spend some time with me. They said there was very little chance of that. I was stunned.

"Why not?" I asked with disappointment.

"Because he won't accept help from anyone. He insists on getting through life by himself," they answered. Dwight's parents were devastated. His mother was sobbing uncontrollably by this time, and his father could hardly speak.

On the road again, Dwight drove aimlessly. His life was full of problems. He struggled to overcome barriers constantly put in his way. On March 11, 1981, in Minnesota, outside a restaurant that probably had icy steps leading up to the door, Dwight killed himself with a gun.

Dear Tim,

Dwight killed himself March 11, 1981. Please call collect.

I will always remember you as his very dear friend.

E.W. Fisher

After I read Dwight's father's words, my thoughts drifted away. I could hear all the sounds of life going on outside, but it did not matter right then; my friend was dead. How did this happen? Perhaps if I had put all of our experiences together and all the times Dwight and I really talked, I would have realized then what I only now understand.

I stood gazing out the window, with Dwight's father's letter still in my hand. My friend had died without fanfare in some obscure town in a remote section of the country. To me, it seemed as if he could physically succeed in anything he wanted to, but he was only human. He did not want to be strong all the time. That, in itself, had taken an emotional toll on Dwight. His personal strength finally deteriorated, and little creeping self-doubts about his ability to cope on his own became more like wishes. He just could not continue to fight all the handicaps of his condition and still be the "superman" he was, and wanted to be. His lifelong quest to take care of himself was over.

Chapter Ten

Virgil Stewart
UDT-3 1943

Underwater Demolition Team 2

Underwater Demolition Team 2 was organized at Waimanilo, Oahu in December 1943. Lieutenant Crist, CEC, USNR was designated commanding officer. Three Marine officers, two naval officers, four army officers, thirty-five enlisted Marines, four enlisted army men, and twenty enlisted naval men formed the team.

The naval personnel had trained at Fort Pierce, and at the time the team was formed, they were training the army and Marines in the different phases of demolition. This consisted mostly of coral blasting and removal of obstacles. When the call came for a demolition team, the army and Marine personnel were combined with the navy to form UDT-1 and -2.

On December 23, 1943, UDT-2 went aboard the USS *Schley* (APD 14), and proceeded to San Diego, where they were to pick up four drone boats and demolition gear. At San Diego, Lieutenant Commander Koehler replaced Lieutenant Crist as commanding officer, and Lieutenant Crist became the operations officer.

Picking up our gear, we headed back out into the Pacific.

Our destination was the Marshall Islands, although, of course, we didn't know this at the time. We arrived at Roi and Namur, Kwajalein Atoll at 0300 on February 1, 1944 (D-2). All boats were put in the water immediately, with each one carrying one and a half tons of powder. Lieutenant Crist took two amphibious tractors and five men to recon the channels leading into the bay. The remainder of the men were loaded into the drone boats and, after laying off the island all day, landed on one of the smaller islands off Namur to set up camp. That night, two drone boats each took two rubber boats and their crews and went to Roi and Namur. The four rubber boat crews of six men each reconnoitered both beaches. Nothing was found, so no preassault work was necessary. The next morning we were to send the four drone boats, loaded with tetrytol, into Roi and Namur and blow them up. However, the radio and drone equipment became defective due to a rough sea, and the whole operation had to be called off. The next six days, after landing, we lived ashore on a small island which we called "Ivan." There, we demolished coral, trees, small boats, and anything else that would prevent landing craft from disembarking troops and supplies.

On February 9, 1944, UDT-2 boarded the USS *Bolivar* (PA 34) and headed to Pearl Harbor. From Pearl, the team returned to its old base at Waimanilo, Oahu. It was decided that underwater demolition teams would in the future be made up exclusively of naval personnel, so all Marines and army personnel were sent back to their old outfits, and Team 2 was dissolved. Most of the navy men formed the nucleus of UDT-3; the remainder became a harbor clearance unit.

Chapter Eleven

Mike Ferrell
UDT-12 1967–1970

First Tour In-Country

Assignment: Our platoon was attached to the USS *Tunny*, one of the two World War II era submarines that was brought out of mothballs (retirement), reconditioned, and fitted with a special "bubble" (chamber) on its deck that was capable of accommodating one platoon of combat-ready UDT/SEALs. The submarine was designed specifically for UDT/SEAL operations.

Objective: Conduct clandestine intelligence gathering, beach reconnaissance of suspected enemy supply camps located on the coast in both North and South Vietnam. Avoid contact with the enemy at all costs. Provide both cartography and intelligence reports to the appropriate higher-ups for potential amphibious beach assaults.

Number of Recons: Between twenty-five and twenty-eight. All operations and recons were to be conducted at night, under cover of darkness, combat ready, the beach party fully armed and all involved with full-body makeup (camouflage).

Let's Go Kill Those Communist Bastards

Our platoon trained aboard the USS *Tunny* for about two months, out of Subic Bay, Philippines. All types of extractions and insertions were evaluated, which meant do we "lock out" of the large bubble on the *Tunny*'s deck or do we lock out of a small internal chamber with four or five Frogmen at a time? How do we locate the sub and extract from the shore at night? Every member of our platoon became familiar with the sub, and we determined that the best clandestine methodology for our insertion was to use the internal chamber while the sub was submerged at night.

The lock-out chamber is inside the submarine and above the main deck. To reach it we climbed a ladder and passed through a watertight hatch. After entering the chamber, we closed and locked the hatch behind us. The chamber was a little taller than and about the size of three home water heaters put together. Depending on the type of equipment the swimmers required for the particular operation, the chamber was capable of holding as many as three to four men in the standing position.

Once all swimmers are inside the chamber and the watertight hatch is secured, a seawater valve is opened. The chamber is flooded to about neck height, and then the valve is shut off. Another watertight hatch on the side of the chamber opens directly into the open ocean. The top of this hatch is four feet or so beneath the waterline inside the chamber. Once the SEALs are ready to lock out, an air valve pressurizes the inside of the chamber until the pressure inside is equal to the pressure outside the submarine. At this time the submarine is approximately sixty feet below the surface, which is equal to two atmospheres (roughly thirty pounds of pressure per square inch). Once the chamber is equalized, the watertight side hatch can be kicked open, giving the swimmers access to the ocean.

Typically, a safety diver waited outside the door for it to be opened. His job was to assist the swimmers as they exited the submarine, making sure that they didn't bang themselves on any of the overhead equipment on the deck. One thing you should remember is that these lock outs were conducted at night, and the visibility was very poor.

A buoy line was secured to the submarine, leading to the surface where two IBSs were tied to it. Before the swimmers attempted to exit the sub through the side door, they hyperventilated to get plenty of oxygen saturation before "blowing and going" to the surface on their own breath. This is a very dangerous maneuver because a swimmer can very easily embolize himself if he rises to the surface too quickly without exhaling the entire way. The safety diver also assisted the swimmers coming out of the chamber by grabbing their hands and placing them on the buoy line. That way, the swimmers could free-ascend to the surface on their own.

Once the surface was reached, one of the IBSs was inflated, and we would wait in it until everyone involved in the mission was accounted for before beginning our long paddle toward shore.

During a clandestine extraction, this procedure was reversed. A swimmer free dived from the surface, pulling himself hand over hand down the buoy line until he reached the lock-out chamber. Entering through the side hatch, the swimmer breathed in the residual air pocket inside the chamber until it was full of swimmers. Then, the side door was closed, secured, and an exit valve pumped the seawater outside until the chamber was empty. The air pressure was then lowered until it equaled that of the inside of the submarine. The lower hatch could then be opened, and the swimmers would then climb down the ladder into the submarine.

Play Time Was Over

It was nighttime, and I was fully briefed on our mission. My eyes were adjusted to the outside dark environment as I climbed the ladder and entered the lock-out chamber on the submarine. I was wired, man, I'm talking really pumped up—all that training, the discipline, my *potnah's* around me, and of course the confidence. We could feel the power within us. It was magnificent! This was "in your face," scared to death, let's go to war! I'm not talking defense here; I'm talking offense. And when I got in that frame of mind, that's what I called *being focused*!

Anyway, I was grabbing air in the chamber; it was my time to "blow" to the surface. The safety diver was in position outside the chamber, the hatch was opened, and I was on my way up. Wow . . . the water outside the chamber became a bright green as I moved my hands through it. I guess it was caused from all the phosphorescent plankton that was in the water. It was beautiful.

Remember to breathe out the air as I rise to the surface . . . Don't embolize . . . Come on now . . . Quit playing with the funny green water and get to the surface, I kept thinking to myself as I tried to settle down.

I finally made it to the surface, located the IBSs, and swam to the one I was to ride in. A few teammates were already in the IBS. We waited in the IBS until all involved were present and accounted for, then we started the motors and headed toward shore. Everyone in the rubber boats kept a low silhouette.

Wow . . . what a trip! There was all kinds of stuff happening on the shore, a flare over that way, a helo firing a minigun over there, I guess that Charlie was in the area. He was there, and he was close.

As we motored closer to the beach, the realization was coming to me . . . Training was over . . . This is a real war, and people really die . . . This is the life that I have chosen . . . No one else put me here or made me come to this place. This is my responsibility. Now assume that responsibility for my *potnahs*, and myself, and *stay focused*!

As we got within several hundred yards of the beach, we killed the motors and began to use the paddles. After reaching about three hundred yards from the beach, we checked the depth and dropped an anchor. It was extremely hard to judge distance during the night.

The first swimmers into the water were the security party. They were responsible for guarding the beach party and to collect intelligence on any nearby villages, enemy forces, weapons, etc. Should they make contact with the enemy and have to engage, they were responsible for drawing the enemy fire away from the beach party to allow them time enough to swim to sea. Only then could the security party disengage and swim to sea themselves.

The next swimmers over the side were the beach party. This usually consisted of three men, the officer in charge, and two other swimmers. One of the swimmers attached the flutterboard line to himself and pulled it with him as he swam to the beach. The beach party was responsible for setting up the beach, holding the bitter end of the flutterboard line securely as the other end was in the IBS, keeping the swimmers in line, and signaling them the correct time to take their soundings. They had two flashlights with a long cone-shaped attachment over the bulbs. At the end of the cone was a small aperture about the size of a pencil with a dark red lens in it. The red-lens flashlights were used to point to sea, one several feet above the other, to give the swimmers something to line up on, which in turn allowed them to keep the flutterboard line straight and perpendicular to the beach. When the men with the lights turned them off, that was the signal for the swimmers to take their soundings and check out the bottom area. It was very important that the man with the flashlight didn't point it down or behind the beach area so the enemy could see it when it was on. The beach party also wrote down descriptions of the beach such as surf conditions, obstacles, etc.

The flutterboard line was just a line several hundred meters in length with a swimmer hanging on to it every twenty-five yards. The line had a knot tied in it every twenty-five yards, and at every hundred-foot interval, there were two knots tied. The line was stored on a wooden reel called a flutterboard. We usually had swimmers on the line every twenty-five yards, from the beach out to two hundred yards.

As the flutterboard line was reeled out toward the shore, the next swimmer who was to enter the water felt the line for the knot that was his signal to enter the water and swim on the line in that position toward shore. All the swimmers then lined up on the flashlight, and when the light went out, they took soundings and dived to look and feel for obstacles at their assigned positions on the flutterboard line. The beach party would then move down the beach twenty-five yards, and the process would be repeated until the entire beach had been reconned. A beach recon could easily go four thousand to six thousand yards down a beach.

When the reconnaissance was completed, the beach party and all the swimmers would then swim to sea and rejoin the IBSs. The men who'd manned the IBSs would then reel in the flutterboard line. The security party would then swim back to the IBSs. When all involved were present and accounted for at the two IBSs, the entire platoon would paddle farther out to sea and then motor away to locate the submarine. The submarine would stay submerged, with its periscope extended five or six feet above the water. The periscope had an infrared beacon attached to it, and we carried an infrared scope to search for the beacon.

Once the submarine was located, we would signal it that we were in range, and the sub would then surface underneath the IBS. We would then haul all of our equipment and IBSs into one of the large exterior bubbles on the *Tunny*'s deck, close and secure the door, and submerge again. This would only take about five minutes. However, if we encountered a heavy rain and large rolling seas, things could quickly get plenty complicated.

Once aboard, we would debrief, clean and stow our gear, eat, and begin drawing up underwater charts of the beach we had just reconned. The submarine would be on its way to the next beach to be reconned the next night.

These missions provided the amphibious force commander the villages' military strength, the hinterland information, and an underwater hydrographic map of the beach areas. The charts clearly showed obstacles that would hinder an amphibious landing. Once all the sounding points were laid out on a map, it would be clearly evident whether or not an amphibious landing was feasible at that particular beach.

What a rush, we all did it. We all motored, paddled, and then swam in. We got the job done, and got back out to sea undetected. We were all recovered by the sub, submerged, cleaned up our gear, and completed the charts as the submarine headed for the next beach to be reconned. I will never forget those first few precious moments of *self-realization*!

The sub moved offshore from the next beach area that we were to recon, stayed submerged, and observed any daytime activity on the beach by using its periscope. I think that in the month or so that we were operating off the coast of Vietnam, I only saw the sun twice. When I did get to see it, daylight hurt my eyes. By then our eyes were fully adjusted to nighttime operations. Even so, UDT men involved on our operations had to stay in low-light conditions for a few hours before we went out of the sub to insure that our eyes were adjusted to the dark environment as soon as we broke the surface.

On the lighter side, we had a man in our platoon whose name was Neal. On one night recon, there were heavy seas with at least fifteen-foot swells, and it was raining very hard. We were trying to extract and couldn't find the sub to signal it with our infrared light. The sub could only stick its periscope up above the surface about two feet. We were paddling around like whining lost puppies. Where is the fuckin' sub? Where is the fuckin' sub? Bam—Neal found it! It was sixty or seventy yards away from us, so we paddled toward it, but then it disappeared. Neal saw it again, it was over *there* this time, about fifty yards, so we paddled in that direction. Then, no sub again! We went through five or six of these exercises before someone else finally found the sub. Well, from that time forward, Neal earned the nickname Nighteyes Neal. Where's the sub, Nighteyes? Hey . . . heh . . . heh . . . Neal was a good UDT operator, a strong man, but every once in a while you had to reach out there and bring him in close to you. That's okay, Nighteyes, someone had to reach out there and bring me in close too.

The best that I could tell, most of the operations we conducted and the camps we located were in North Vietnam. You see, in South Vietnam something was always happening on shore near our operation. During night recons there, we could see flares and helos' miniguns cookin' over the land from our positions in the water.

Those miniguns were something else to watch. Their rate of fire was so fast that they didn't go *rat . . . rat . . . rat*, they went *whoooooooooooooop . . . whoooooooooooooop!* There was a tracer placed in the belt of ammo every fifth round, and at night, it looked like a dark red laser beam waving down to the ground from up above. Awesome! It seemed like something was always jammin', but, maybe on the next operation, things changed. There was total darkness, quiet, and nothing happening on shore. We were up there all right, we were operating north of the DMZ.

In all, we completed close to thirty missions while operating with the USS *Tunny*. We were only detected by the enemy twice. None of us was seriously injured or got wasted. I considered the overall operation a huge success. We kicked ass; now let's get this sub back to Subic Bay, slip over the bridge to Olongapo, and pah-tee! Which we did. With the same level of intensity. Just to keep our energy level up!

Chapter Twelve

Charles Greene
1944

UDT-3 at Maui

From San Francisco, we left for Pearl Harbor, arriving the latter part of March 1944. After making one liberty in Pearl, we left for Maui aboard an LCI.

The existing base at Maui was not one which would readily recall the comforts of home. Rows of dusty, dirty tents were set on a level plateau made up of volcanic rock. Everything was dry because rain never fell on our side of the island. The base was just being established, and it was not until we were ready to leave for Guam that showers were finally installed.

The bright spots of Maui, however, were beautiful sandy beaches, moderate surf, and invigorating ocean temperatures. The climate was ideal—warm in the daytime and cool in the evenings. Other compensating features were the liberty towns of Puunene and Wailuku, located eight and fifteen miles respectively from the base. Also, the naval air station at Puunene was used to advantage, especially the officers club and the walk located just outside of the Waves barracks. However, our stay at Maui was a brief one; scarcely enough for a good drunk on a lethal product known as Five Islands Whiskey.

Within two weeks of our arrival, Lieutenant Crist had managed to form us into a unit bearing the proud title of UDT-3. Actually, we had had only two weeks of training as a coordinated unit, and yet we carried out, successfully, the longest, most difficult preassault operation ever assigned an underwater demolition team. Most of the credit was due to Lieutenant Crist and the officers and men from the Teams 1 and 2, because it was they who organized and supervised the brief training period. However, each man must share the credit given, for only men above the average could have adjusted themselves, in such a short time, to a new organization such as demo, and so capably and courageously carry out the work required of them at Guam. The training was aimed at developing teamwork within the platoons and acquainting each officer with the men rather than stressing techniques, although we did get our first look at coral and had a little practice at blowing coral heads.

Together with UDT-4, our sister team throughout the war, we boarded the SS *Typhoon* on 17 April 1944. We didn't get underway until the following day and of course, our destination was unknown to everyone except the captain.

I'm sure that the men will always remember the *Typhoon* for its noon meals. On the cooks' better days, two crackers were served with an orange instead of the usual one. The chow tickets were carefully punched to make sure no demo men could gather excess weight before the coming invasion.

Several of the team personnel assisted with the maintenance and operation of the ship throughout the voyage. The famous battle cry over the PA system was, "Conklin, J. W., report to the forward troops' head on the double!"

The twenty-second of April, the day we crossed the Equator, was, indeed, a day of historical importance for all of us pollywogs. The traditional initiation started at breakfast and continued throughout the day. Till this day, I occasionally find grease which was rubbed upon us freely by the shellbacks. I guess the salt water showers weren't much help.

On 2 May, we left the SS *Typhoon* at Florida Island in the Solomon Islands for a taste of life on a beautiful South Sea island. The following morning, we were all ready to go back aboard the *Typhoon*.

Chapter Thirteen

Brian Curle

UDT-12 UDT-13 SEAL Team 1

1966–1970

The worst day as a frogman . . . was better than any great day in the regular navy . . . *B.C.*

My First Real Operation

UDT-12 had just added its second hash mark to its efficiency *E* (the *E* is not retroactive, so an *E* with two hash marks means top operational team three years in a row) when I came aboard, after graduating from UDT/SEAL Training Class 40 on May 5, 1967, at Coronado, California. It was cold in Coronado just then and it felt great to report for duty somewhere dry and warm for a change. Most of my rowdy friends from training were assigned to UDT-11, which was deployed on its WESPAC (West Pacific) cruise a few weeks before we graduated.

The staff and operators of UDT-12 expected us new guys to have our act together when we came across the street from the naval amphibious base and reported to our new unit. We started out as clean-up crews and were pulled out of the "new" pool, two or three at a time, to operate with different platoons. We had four-section duty, so we were cleaning and operating all the time.

Everyone in the teams went to school. There was jump school (parachuting), dive school, pathfinder school, SDVs (swimmer delivery vehicle), outboard motor school, photography, weapons, SERE school (survival, escape, resistance, and evasion), and demolition schools; man was I stoked. I went to assault boat coxswain school, right there on the Silver Strand at the amphibious base.

My platoon officer was the strictest and most demanding platoon officer of the four platoons in UDT-12, and I set out to fit in as a good operator. I became the 1st Platoon boat coxswain. One of my classmates from 40 was the boat engineman. I felt that I had died and gone to heaven.

First Platoon operated all the time—drop and pick up, dive ops, compass swims, night problems (operations), sub ops, mine searches, and recons, not to mention running all the daily platoon errands somewhere on the other side of San Diego Bay. It was fun to fill in the spots left over by platoon members finishing their active-duty time.

The day after a few of us UDT men returned from jump school, my platoon officer called me into his office and asked me if I would like to recover a space capsule. Apollo IV would be launched, orbit the earth twice, and be recovered in the Pacific Ocean near the Hawaiian Islands. Apollo IV would be the last unmanned space capsule; after that recovery, they would be carrying astronauts. It would involve long hours of training, distance swims in the ocean, and we would spend most of the time in and out of helicopters, cold and wet. I flashed back to the winter class I had graduated from in UDT/SEAL training a few months earlier. My answer was easy. All the billets on this operation were filled by veteran Frogmen, and the outcome was extremely important. As I left his office, he said, "This will be your first real operation, so don't screw it up." I flashed to my friends on Team-11 who had been operating for real for months now. I thanked him for having confidence in me and saluted him.

We had fulfilled all the tasks that my platoon officer said we would do, and more, over the last month. But now, this was Hawaii. The waters off the Hawaiian Islands were crisp, clear, and went from a royal blue to dark purple to charcoal. This was my first time in really deep water where the visibility was great. I shuddered as I peered through my face mask down into the great depth below my swim fins. My grip tightened on the flotation collar we had just attached to the practice capsule. The nasty taste of shark repellent mixed with the green marker dye made me take my face out of the water for a breath of fresh air. My next thought was . . . shark repellent . . . no land . . . no carrier . . . no chopper, and thousands of huge things swimming in the darkness under me. I gave a quick kick with my fins and climbed up onto the flotation collar. The risk of seasickness on a three-hour capsule ride in five-to-seven-foot seas seemed a better deal than my first deep-water weird-out.

Our pay records hadn't arrived from Coronado yet, and we had been in Hawaii a month. The "shot" had been delayed four times, and there were still some problems with the launch. We had spent the first five days living on the air force base and flying out of there to practice our recovery. But, after a bout with the shore patrol in a barefoot bar downtown, we were assigned to stay aboard the carrier *Bennington*, the one we were to use for the operation.

This was supposed to be a quick operation, and the *Bennington* had no quarters for us, so we took over an abandoned office space to live in, turning some lockers face down and using the back sides as our bunks. Then, we made hammocks out of some laundry bags. The whole month had been nothing but practice, and hot/cold status, not knowing if there would be any more delays.

The operation task force consisted of the carrier and three helicopters, Alpha flight, Bravo flight, and Charlie flight. Alpha flight was the senior, with the top-ranking pilot and recovery team. Bravo flight was next in seniority, with a lieutenant junior grade pilot and a first-class petty officer and two seamen for the recovery team. I was assigned to Charlie flight. The three flights of Frogmen riding in the helos would fan out over a large area of the ocean, and the flight closest to the landing of the returning space capsule would swoop in and attach the flotation collar to the unit to keep it from sinking. The *Bennington* would then pull up alongside the floating capsule, and the Frogmen would hook it up to the carrier's crane. The Apollo capsule would then be picked up and placed on a grated elevator and brought inside the ship through the side of the carrier. Most of the practices had been performed pretty much to perfection.

I stared out the door, hypnotized by the sparkling blue water. Our chopper skimmed the surface as we raced into the sunrise. I had my ear plugs in, so I was alone with my own thoughts—my first real op, and we were in the spotlight. A bump on my shoulder snapped me back to reality. "It's in the atmosphere, and we are dead on it," yelled my swim buddy.

Charlie was the first flight up and the farthest out on the recovery area. Hopefully, the capsule would land close to the carrier, and Alpha or Bravo flight would make short work of the recovery. Charlie flight was the backup, on the outer rim of the "recovery basket."

"There it is!" My swim buddy was pointing to it. We all moved closer to the door. What a rush! I followed my swim buddy's wet-suit sleeve, past his Rolex diver's watch, to a small bright object in the distance. It was high above us, and we were going full out, straight toward it. We flew up over its three huge orange-and-white parachutes. They were lit up by the morning sun. Even though it was charred, the Apollo capsule had a grayish gold tint to it. We were so close to it that I felt I could reach out and touch it. The capsule had charred streaks on its sides, and the top edges were really burned. It struck an extreme contrast to the orange parachutes, the shiny blue water below, and the bright sunlight. It was just hanging there after returning from space, and our eyes were the first to greet it. It had secrets of its own that no one knew yet. It had its own story and looked alone and tired. Wow—the recovery was on!

We circled above the capsule as it descended until splashdown and the chutes were in the water. As we prepared to kick the collar out of the chopper and jump in to secure it to the capsule, the chopper started to lift off. We hovered over it and thought it looked like a piece of nose cone. We kicked out our flotation collar and an IBS (inflatable boat, small), and all three of us jumped out behind it. The rubber boat was then inflated, and the collar was secured to the nose cone. Then we climbed in the IBS and floated the piece of the capsule beside us as we waited for the carrier.

The seas were running about two to three feet, and a light breeze was blowing. As the Apollo capsule bobbed with the swells, about twenty minutes went by before Bravo flight finally arrived. They hovered over the capsule for about three minutes then lifted off high and away, leaving plenty of room for Alpha flight. Two minutes later, Alpha arrived. By then, the parachutes were starting to sink into the deep blue water, and the ocean current had opened them up below the surface.

Alpha flight kicked out the collar, jumped in behind it, and started to secure it to the capsule. We had a ringside seat as we floated about two hundred yards away in our IBS. The seas had begun to pick up, to about five to seven feet, and the light breeze was turning into a wind. Clouds began to cover the morning sun, and when the *Bennington* finally arrived, the water looked dark against its hull.

We had been riding in our IBS for over an hour, and the parachutes were now hanging straight down below the capsule. They were affecting how the space capsule was floating in the growing seas. The *Bennington* tried to slip up next to the capsule just when it made a heavy roll, and the huge carrier ran smack into it. The Frogmen who were riding on the capsule saw what was happening in time and dove off and swam clear.

The capsule and the flotation collar banged along the side of the carrier as it scraped by. The Frogs swam back to the capsule after the carrier passed, and cut the parachutes free. Alpha flight then swam away from the capsule again and were recovered from the water by chopper, and Bravo flight took over in the water.

The wind had steadily increased, and the seas were now fifteen to eighteen feet high. The huge carrier took over an hour and a half to turn around and get into position to come alongside the capsule again. By this time, all the Frogmen had traded off riding on the capsule. We had already transported the nose cone, which was also the parachute cover, to the carrier by chopper. The nose cone cover had never before been recovered.

We had all been in the ocean for over seven hours by then. Most of us had some form of motion sickness. We were on our third recovery pass now, and the easiest task, hooking the cable loop that we attached to the top of the capsule over the crane hook on the carrier, had become the most difficult and crucial in the recovery operation. The huge, heavy carrier, crane, and weighted ball-hook, seemed to stay in one place but the capsule resembled a cork as it repeatedly banged off the side of the ship. Sometimes the capsule would ride up on a wave and crash into the underside of the grated elevator on to which it was supposed to be placed by the crane. The trick was to ride the capsule up one of the eighteen-foot waves and try to loop the cable over the crane's ball-hook. The carrier was almost still in the water, even in the rough seas, and extra lines were finally secured to the capsule to help stabilize it for more control.

We were all taking a beating and being very careful not to get hit by the ball-hook or get caught between the capsule and the ship. Alpha flight had entered the water again, and Charlie flight was finally relieved for a break. It felt good to put on my dry, warm sweats and pull the hood over my head. It also felt good that the deck didn't seem to be moving, even though I found it hard to stand in one spot.

After a few moments, my swim buddy and I walked over to the edge of the grated elevator. We could see Alpha battling the crane's ball-hook and the waves through the grating. The UDT officer in charge of the recovery was a full lieutenant, (03, the equivalent of an army captain) a big, strong, superman type. I really looked up to him and respected him, but he had his hands full.

The next wave crashed them into the underside of the grate, then dropped them down about forty feet. The following wave wasn't lined up right and the capsule banged into the crane ball-hook, knocking two of the Frogs off of the capsule and into the water. Both Frogmen were hanging onto the flotation collar when the next wave started up.

The lieutenant was riding on top of the capsule, with one hand on the cable and the other hand free. The next wave took him up past the ball-hook, and when the wave started down again, he grabbed the hook with his free hand and slung the cable over it. When the bottom fell out as the wave continued down, the lieutenant fell to the collar, and one of the other Frogs fell into the water. The third Frog was hanging on to the bottom of the flotation collar as the wave continued down. The ship's crew cheered from the deck of the carrier as the lieutenant scrambled back up to the top of the capsule to secure the cable from falling off the ball-hook. Then, he signaled for the crane to pull the capsule up onto the grated elevator. Seeing that the lieutenant had control of the situation, the other Frog joined his swim buddy in the water. He did this by waiting until the next wave washed back from the side of the ship, then riding it out to his swim buddy. Both of them were recovered by a chopper and brought back to the carrier. The Apollo space capsule was brought aboard and was safe now, forever.

That night, as the *Bennington* steamed back toward Pearl, I went down to look at my lonely buddy from outer space. The Apollo capsule was roped off at a good distance, and a lot of men were looking at it. The cameras and flashes proved that it was a star now. I knew then that I had participated in a great adventure. I went up to the flight deck to look at the stars and feel the wind.

Chapter Fourteen

Alford Brokes

UDT-3 May 1944

Life Ashore at Florida Island

To write a humorous story concerning our unpleasant stay at dear ol' Turner City, would require a vivid imagination, not to mention slander and prevarication. If ever God made a mistake, or if ever He intended to place a bit of hell on earth, then the Solomon Islands should be a tribute to Him. Surely, no man in Team 3 will walk any road but the straight and narrow after being there. The slim possibility that hell is worse, converted our best heathens. Our (physical) casualties were surprisingly low, but our continuous struggle and battles against the hells of nature proved too great a trial for even our strongest minds. Believe me, Mother Nature is strictly playing a dummy hand in the Solomons! And yet, through all our trials and tribulations, our broadened minds gave way to some consolation.

Fresh water? Hell yes, gallons of it. The continual rains held the dust down, kept us clean, and kept the mud bottomless. We realized that our underwater demolition team would soon take part in a tough operation, but if we were considering this life as part of our maneuvers, then that was carrying it a little too far.

The never-changing menu (except from Vienna sausage to la Spam) made us all appreciate K rations, which we also shared with the flies. The perforated canvas on stilts, which served as our quarters, we supposed was to let in the sunshine, which never came—except "California style." The sand crabs, who fell in love with us at first sight, kept the insects out of our shoes every night—while they slept in them. The squirming lizards made such wonderful bed companions—in spite of the fact that they weren't "night-lovers" (bless their little hearts). Lockers, privacy, and security, of which there were none, encouraged thievery and "tent-Peeping Toms" and thus eliminated monotony. Our broken-down cots, with their modernistic swayback appearance, served ideally as a trough to catch the water, which our tent roofs refused to stop, and in return kept us from being too-hot-to-sleep at night. What cooperation!

The chow lines leading to the "Ritz Garbage Cafeteria" were the right length in miles, and seemed to move at a definite lack of speed to bring its waiting victims to the point of starvation and so, through self-preservation, forced them to stomach the bilge water and dehydrated rations that were thrown at them. The green beer ration of two short ones per week for those who could find the end of the line (the beer came in cans because even its looks would hinder its sale), made us appreciate the contraband bootleg of "torpedo juice"—denatured alcohol and fermented fruit juices—which flowed none too freely from our local stills in the hills to our slums.

A pet snake, a slimy little devil, adopted us the day we arrived and insisted on sharing our limited comforts. He proved to be an excellent guard and very hospitable companion and would have been loved by all except for his one fault. He insisted on using our sacks as a head.

Mouldy clothes, sultry heat, moisture that would seal envelopes at the flaps and make them fall apart at the seams, outdoor movies at the "Cloudburst Theater," where the visibility was zero, beautiful (?) native women who could double for both Dracula and Tony Galento, landscapes that would shift a few feet downhill with every few inches of daily rainfall, and other, similar, discomforts inspired us all with thoughts of home. Ah yes! My friends, when we recall those trying days of our lives on Florida Island, we are all ready to fight the war over again just to give them back to the Japs! Though we may not have taught the lizards how to "cuddle" or sleep on their own side of the bed, nor convince the sand crabs that they should crawl out of our shoes in the morning and give thanks for the night's lodging, you can bet your life that we sure as hell tried.

And so in closing, I say to those of you, who either by mistake of choice or lack of choice will be the victims of such unfortunate fate as duty in the Solomon Islands, may God lend a helping hand and preserve your minds.

There were no tears shed as we carried our soaking seabags aboard the USS *Dent*, our first of species APD, on 16 May 1944. We engaged in maneuvers with the V Amphibious Corps, blasting obstacles and reconnoitering beaches along the coast of Guadalcanal. We also blew shots in coral and demolished a midget sub (with torpedos intact) that had been rusting away on the beach. On 4 June, we left the Solomon Islands and headed for the Marshall Islands. Now we had a nice (?) opportunity to give our wholehearted attention to our so-called home—the APD.

Chapter Fifteen

Darryl Young
SEAL Team 1 UDT-11
1969–1972

Bottom: the surface on which a body of water lies, the lowest part or place, the remotest or inmost point.

Sample: a representative part or a single item from a larger whole or group presented for inspection or shown as evidence.

Bottom Samples

I was eighteen years old during second phase of basic underwater demolition/SEAL training (BUDS) and attending weapons and explosives familiarization out on San Clemente Island, approximately forty-nine miles south of Los Angeles, California. San Clemente Island is about four miles wide at its widest point and eighteen miles long. It has a maximum altitude of 1,965 feet above the Pacific Ocean.

A naval reservation, the island is closed to the public except for extreme emergencies. All vessels that enter the area are warned that the vicinity of the island is dangerous because of gunfire, rockets, bombing, and other military activity. At the northern end of the island is a military airport that was built up and leveled off from the existing soil in the area. San Clemente has few roads or buildings, and its largest naval facility is at Wilson Cove on the northeast side of the island, approximately two miles south of the east end of the airport's runway.

The little vegetation that grows on San Clemente consists of cactus, grass, sagebrush, and the few eucalyptus trees left of the twenty-seven hundred that were planted in 1938. Because of the dry climate in the area, San Clemente has that barren look, but wild boar, deer, goats, mice, lizards, and thousands of birds inhabit the island. Its terrain consists of rocky, steep cliffs, rolling hills, and a few sandy beaches. Miles of kelp beds surround the island.

On a clear day, one can see Catalina Island, nineteen miles to the northwest, across the Outer Santa Barbara Passage. The navy has used San Clemente for years for ship bombardment and carrier air strikes at targets located offshore and on the island itself. The northern tip of San Clemente, north of the airport, is designated as the UDT/SEAL weapons and explosives training area. UDT/SEAL trainees spend three weeks on the island, practicing land warfare using live explosives and ammunition. Some of the best chow I ever ate while in the navy was at San Clemente's UDT/SEAL training camp.

Our original class of seventy-eight men had thinned out considerably since the first day of training. Only twenty of us remained, making it easy for the instructors to handle and keep track of. Quitters and those who wanted to continue training but just didn't have the stamina were no longer with us. But UDT/SEAL training hadn't become any easier during second phase, in fact, at times it seemed to be much tougher. More responsibilities were placed on the individual and the entire class as the training days advanced. Taking each day's evolutions one at a time seemed to be getting me by. Working with, and learning about, different types of high explosives on the surface and underwater, along with firing and cleaning exotic weapons of all types, kept my undivided attention. Practicing day and night hydrographic beach reconnaissance and obstacle demolition kept each man involved alert and on his toes. I paid close attention to what the instructors were teaching us, not wanting to fuck up or have any of my teammates do the same. There was absolutely no room for error with a fragmentation grenade or a twenty-pound haversack of C-4 explosives in our hands.

On one particular day, the instructors had our class out in Northwest Harbor, which was located at the north end of San Clemente Island, just offshore from the UDT/SEAL training camp. The water was clear, cold, and over twenty-five feet deep beneath us. We each had a K-bar knife and wore UDT swim trunks, inflatable life jackets, and fins and mask. We were to free dive to the ocean floor and bring up a bottom sample. While the instructors stayed on board an LCPL (landing craft, personnel launch), overseeing the evolution and acting as lifeguards, we trainees got to tread water on the swells of the deep blue cold waters of the Pacific Ocean, waiting our turns to dive to the bottom.

Without actually speaking, the instructors had a way of telling us that it was our turn to dive. But there was something about that shit-eatin' grin on their faces that bothered me; I wasn't about to tell them that. Up until then, I hadn't ever free dived to that depth before. Shit, I had no reason to. But since UDT/SEALs are responsible for charting and demolishing any obstacles from that depth into the beach during a hydrographic beach reconnaissance, it was mandatory for all hands involved in our training class to bring to the instructors something from the bottom, proving we had, indeed, been there.

As I bobbed around like a waterlogged cork in the water, waiting for the instructor's shit-eatin'-grin signal that would tell me it was my turn to dive, I remembered recovering a fishing pole from the bottom of the Eel River in northern California when I was a kid. It wasn't near the depth of that day's dive, but at my age at the time, it was deep. A friend of mine had dropped his fishing pole from a logjam on a big bend in the river and offered me two dollars if I would recover it for him. He wasn't as good a swimmer as I, and two bucks was a lot of money for a fool kid back then. Looking back on it, it was a real stupid thing to do because of the dangerous location we were in.

During the long rainy winter's high water, the river current had piled huge redwood logs and debris up against the bank and eroded a deep hole underneath. It was a great fishin' spot because of the deep hole, but a very dangerous place for kids our age to be without an adult present. It was the kind of place you never told your parents about, or they would have kicked your behind for being anywhere around that area.

From out on the logjam, looking down into the dark green, almost clear water, I couldn't see the silt-covered bottom. I was wishing I had a mask and fins. It was summertime, so there wasn't much of a current in the deep hole because the water had dropped considerably. Nevertheless, I wasn't too excited about diving under the logjam to recover the pole. My friend showed me about where he had dropped it, so equipped with just cutoff Levi's, I dove into the water and started down. I didn't get very far when I noticed his pole lying on the bottom, back under the logs and way beyond my reach. Not being able to hold my breath any longer, I returned to the surface and took a deep breath before starting down again. I remember the water getting colder and darker the deeper I dove back under the logs and debris. I reached the pole, grabbed it, and returned to the surface, being careful not to hit my head on the logs. I was pretty proud of myself for diving to that depth, I really didn't think I could do it.

This incident from my past kept going through my mind as I hovered on the surface of the Pacific with my face mask submerged. From time to time I watched the other trainees as they attempted to recover their bottom samples. That kept my mind off the cold water, which had felt good when I entered it, but was starting to make my body numb. I could see the sandy bottom very clearly. Looking up from my position in the water, I could also see the instructors shouting orders to one of the trainees.

Some of the trainees had no problem recovering a piece of the bottom. Others achieved their goal but were glad to return to the surface. Anyone not completing the mission had to keep trying till he made it, or be ejected from the training class. After all, this was part of a Frogman's duties.

Then, the grin was directed at me. Making damn sure my legs didn't splash the surface, I jackknifed into a dive. The instructors had also stressed that we not give our positions away by lifting any part of our bodies out of the water. Thank God

I've got fins to help propel me down and back, I thought to myself as I entered the silent world below the surface. Having fins and a mask gave me a bit of confidence. Thirty plus feet may not seem deep, but when you're down there, out of a human's natural environment and needing a breath of fresh air, it's plenty deep.

The deeper I dove, the more the pressure increased in my ears. My mask began to squeeze tighter against my face. *I've got to make it. All the other trainees have made it so far. I don't want to be the only one to fail,* I kept thinking. My thoughts turned to how cold the water was down here compared to the surface and how nice it would have been if the instructors had let us wear the brand new custom-made wet suits the navy had bought each man before we left Coronado. They were hanging in the barracks back at camp. That's the price our class had to pay for fuckin' up the other night on our night recon.

Equalizing the pressure on my ears and face mask as I reached the bottom, I grabbed a left hand full of sand. The bottom was perfectly flat, with no structures of any kind anywhere in sight. I took a 360-degree survey of the bottom area then placed my fins on the bottom and gave a big push toward the sky.

As I ascended toward the surface, needing air, I noticed the sand was sifting through my fingers and out of my hand. I took a tighter grip on my bottom samples in my left hand, wishing the "proof I was there" was a rock, small sea shell, or anything more solid than sand. Thrusting my body upward with every kick of my fins, I prayed that there would still be something to show the instructors when I reached the surface. I did not want to go back down a second time . . . if I didn't have to.

As I neared the surface, the sky grew lighter, and I could see the other trainees treading water and watching me through their face masks as if I were some strange creature from the deep.. Then, I broke free of the silent world and gasped a breath of salty sea air. As I held my left hand high into the air and opened it, as I, too, treaded water on the surface, the instructors inspected my proof-I-was-there sample. I tried to hide the evidence of breathing hard . . . like, no problem . . . easy day! Their shit-eatin' grins turned to a serious look staring at my hand and what little sand was left after sifting through my fingers, then they hollered, "Recover," meaning, "tread some more water, sailor."

The rest of that day was spent at the UDT/SEAL training camp on San Clemente Island, eating steak and drinkin' beer, which happen to be two of a Frogman's favorite pastimes. The camaraderie among our swim buddies, our teammates, and the teams was definitely being installed in our minds without our realizing it.

As our training progressed, we all became proficient at free diving to even greater depths and staying down longer. Nobody else screwed up on our next night reconnaissance either!

Chapter Sixteen

Charles Hoffman
UDT-3 1944

Life Aboard an APD

Today you will find hundreds of American boys trying to outlive the experiences of horror forced upon them by being passengers on APDs. In order for you to become acquainted with this unusual method of transportation, I will reveal some of the experiences of UDT-3 on two of these vile conveyances.

First, the USS *Dent*, once a ship of distinction (1918), but by 1944 a broken and "dehorned" (she lost two stacks in conversion) child of destiny. Thanks to an efficient and conscientious Chief Belly Robber, our chow was very good and the galley very clean. The crew was a good one, and the men tried to help us whenever possible. Old Lady *Dent*, however, had one very bad feature. In order to sleep in our bunk, we were forced to go below into an oven and fight for possession with many large roaches who, being there first, had the mistaken idea that they had prior and final claim to your rack. Despite her good points, the *Dent* was not to be for us, however. Several knowing old men came aboard one day while we lay at anchor and wisely shook their heads and doomed the *Dent*. We transferred from the *Dent* June 9, 1944, after a ride from Guadalcanal to the Marshall Islands, and went aboard the USS *Dickerson* (the Dirty Dick). The next day we left Eniwetok Atoll and started our journey to the Mariana Islands, then occupied by short, dirty animals resembling apes. Said animals wore hats and could write, so we were able to distinguish them from apes.

Except for a bad engine and a boiler coming apart en route, our trip on the *Dickerson* was uneventful. The food aboard this enigma left nothing to be desired. In fact, after one meal, you desired nothing more to eat until days later when pangs of hunger forced you to hold your nose and once more tempt fate. The galley was a place of beauty and sundry odors. The overhead had been decorated in the dim past with long greasy cobwebs, which conveniently fell into the food. The cook was short, and the cobwebs did not hit him in the head when he walked by, so he left them where they were.

Most of the men existed in some Spartan way below decks at night. I, for one, took several life jackets and ponchos and rigged a private sleeping quarters topside, atop our bangalore torpedo boxes. This proved to be clean, comfortable, and airy. After being awakened several mornings by Number 3 three-inch gun, thirty feet from my apartment, I became used to this slight inconvenience and really enjoyed my ringside seat for our daily air raids at Saipan.

The captain of the Dirty D was quite a character, being

found in various states of undress most of the time. His favorite attire while underway was skivvy shirt, baggy trousers, and run-over shoes. When being fired upon at Guam, he commanded the gunners to "shoot at what's a-shootin' at you." Said command brought desired results.

While at Saipan, and in our usual state of mechanical collapse, we were tied up to the *Cambria* to make boiler repairs. Being at anchor, both ships sought the protective cover of smoke pots during the air raids. One night, not content to sit idly by, some ambitious eager beavers climbed up into the LCPRs and took potshots at the Japs who were dropping flares into the smoke. This action elicited foul language from *Cambria*'s bridge; her skipper had the audacity to question our intelligence. We finally left the Marianas and plowed our merry way back to Maui; true to form, our floating kamikaze bait fell apart on the way and was towed for several hours by one of the ships we were escorting.

The *Dickerson* was later sunk at Okinawa, and many of her brave crew were lost there. Dirty Dick she was, but she answered all our prayers at Guam. Her fire support and cooperation with us in our work were wonderful.

Chapter Seventeen

Mike Ferrell
UDT-12 1967–1970

Location: Cu Chi, South Vietnam
Objective: Clear and secure seven bridges for the army.

Let's Go In-Country

Our platoon from the USS *Tunny* was broken up in Subic Bay, and we were reassigned with other UDT units in Vietnam. It's difficult for me to remember after all these years, but I think we were in the Nha Be area, about ten miles from Saigon. That's about the time I ran into Andy and Jack, two other UDT teammates. They had graduated from UDT/SEAL training a few classes before mine. They were excellent UDT operators, and we became *potnahs*.

Jack was a short guy, but built like a stump; a crazy coonass he was. Andy was a big strong man, and had a heavy deep southern accent. He could really wind your clock. He also had a special gift, if you would call it that. Apparently, he had some kind of stomach problem, and he could literally puke at will, anytime he wanted to.

Both of these guys loved—I mean *loved*—to maintain a high energy level. Neither of them would pick on you, but if you got in their face, you were going to lose. I didn't know too much about fightin' and wasn't too good at it; for sure, I lost more fights than I won. I was the type of guy who, if you really got me focused, I'd just as soon pull out my pistol and blow your kneecap off.

Anyhow, Andy, Jack, Joe, Swabby, Nighteyes, and others, including myself, were called up to Cu Chi, which was north of Saigon. We were to consult with the army boys about how to secure their bridges and prevent Charlie from blowing them up. Intelligence sources said that the army boys were completely surrounded by NVA, and the only exits were seven bridges in the area. When we got there, we could feel the tension in the air; this place was hot!

It was all "black-water diving"—below six feet you were completely blind and in total darkness. We checked all the bridge abutments for enemy explosives, and except for one, all were clean. One of the bridges had a large abutment that had a chain link fence that totally surrounded it underwater. A lot of scrap steel had been placed between the fence and the abutment to prevent explosive charges from being positioned directly on that part of the bridge.

Upon entering the water with my diving tanks to begin our investigation, I found that a length of detonation cord had been secured to the fence, near the surface. The cord ran down through the scrap steel into the dark water below the bridge. I couldn't see the detcord line, but I followed it by keeping it in my hands. The fact that there was absolutely no visibility was probably for the better, because if I could have seen the "magic maze" of steel I was getting into, I probably would have aborted the attempt. I wasn't worried as much about how much air I had as I would have been about diving into the scrap metal. I was getting a little nervous about what I might find down there.

It took me a while to reach the depth of twenty or twenty-five feet. I had to move slowly, upside down, right side up, twisting this way and that, but I kept following the detcord, finally sensing that I was getting close to the bridge abutment.

I started thinking, Okay, Mike, *stay focused*, think about what you're doing . . . concentrate. Whew, then my sweet Lord

Jesus sent me this little thought, "What do you gain if you find the charge, some free explosives? Do you really need any free explosives?"

No, I thought, what would I do with free explosives other than take them to the surface and detonate them? Then what would I have? . . . Nothing . . .

Bear in mind now, that me and Jesus are still having this little talk down there. "Mike, what do you gain if you come across a charge down here and it's booby-trapped?" "Just dead." "Mike, take out your ka-bar and cut the detcord." "Yes, Jesus, thank you for helping me to stay . . . focused!"

After I returned to the surface, I told everyone that someone had cut the detcord, it had just ended and didn't lead anywhere. Nobody had any questions. Andy was checking me out pretty good and had that *grin* on his face. Even though Andy and I were not talking, I was receiving the message over the UDT network—Good move, Chickenman, I would have done the same damn thing.

We made recommendations as how to prevent Charlie from floating a satchel charge down onto the bridges, and then we put on quite a show for the army officers at the party they gave us. Heck, I was in full bloom, doing the "Chickenman strut," and Andy was puking for show. We turned it upside down! Joe, Swabby, Nighteyes, and the rest of us were just singing our Frog songs and having a great time.

The Double Shuffle and the Buffalo Trick

Perhaps I should do a little explaining here. When we were in country, we were under orders authorizing us to wear civilian clothes, carry firearms and demolitions, and go just about anywhere we wanted to, at anytime. The special orders worked out well for us, especially when we were dealing with other branches of the armed forces. If officers from other branches did not have the proper authorization, they couldn't even look at our orders. With these priority orders, we could go to Tan Son Nhut airport in Saigon, or anyplace else, and log ourselves onto a flight manifest. Other military personnel were then bumped off the flight so we could get to where we needed to go—or really didn't need to go—in a hurry.

One of our teammates we knew from "somewhere" was a car thief, and a damn good one, too—new paint job, serial numbers, paperwork, and the whole works. One day, Daryl X and I wanted to go to the PX in Saigon from Nha Be to buy a bunch of electronic stuff (radios and TVs, etc.). We were going to trade this stuff to the Vietnamese back in Nha Be.

Anyway, this guy from "somewhere" loaned Daryl and me a jeep to drive to Saigon for a PX run. But, as we were coming out of the PX, we noticed some MPs had the hood of the jeep open, and it looked like they were checking serial numbers. We didn't know if the guy from "somewhere" had fixed the numbers on this jeep yet or not. Once again, it was time to *stay focused*!

I said to Daryl, "Hey, I have an idea, the EOD (explosive ordinance disposal) compound is not far from here. Let's catch a cab and go over there and spend the night and forget about the jeep." EOD was a sister outfit to UDT/SEALs; they had a beautiful compound in Saigon, their own bar, clean beds, good food, and we all got along very well. They were also a little crazy, like us.

Daryl thought about it for a minute and then said, "No, Ferrell, I am going to try and bullshit those guys and get the jeep."

Daryl was an aggressive, intimidating guy and, frankly, I thought he had at least a fifty-fifty chance of pulling it off. But, we needed a contingency plan quickly in case something went wrong.

I said, "Daryl, if I remember right, EOD has a lieutenant over there at their unit; here's what we'll do. If the MPs rip you off, tell them that you are temporally attached to EOD and your officer in charge is Lieutenant Ferrell, got it?"

The next thing I knew, Daryl was being driven away in handcuffs by the MPs. I took all the merchandise we'd bought over to the EOD compound and spent the night there.

Well, the next morning, this army MP officer calls the EOD compound and wants to speak to a Lieutenant Ferrell. "Hello, Lieutenant Ferrell here," I said when I got on the line.

"Mr. Ferrell, I am with the MPs, and we have one of your men over here."

"Who's that," I answered.

"A GMG2 Daryl X," said the MP officer.

"You found Daryl X? He's been AWOL for over a month. What has he done now?"

"We wrote him up for possession of a stolen vehicle," answered the MP.

"How can I get my hands on him?" I said. "I am personally going to fly this idiot to headquarters in Subic Bay and have him in captain's mast, court-martialed, and put in prison. I am deeply in your debt, sir, and would gladly write a letter of commendation to your superiors."

"Oh no, sir, that's not necessary; just come on down here and pick him up," the MP replied.

"Well, that's a problem, I don't have any transportation, and I'm in the process of requisitioning a vehicle. Would it be too much of an inconvenience for you to drop him off here at the EOD compound within the hour?"

"No problem, we'll be right over, sir," the MP said. Now, I had to find some lieutenant bars and real quick. Lady Luck was with me that day; the EOD lieutenant wasn't in, so I went to his sleeping quarters to get his bars for my collar. They looked kind of nice on me. I then returned to the lieutenant's office and waited.

A short time later, here came the MPs with their officer and Daryl in tow. I acted really pissed, but I didn't say anything at first, I just started signing the release papers. Once I had all my copies in my hand, I walked around the desk and got right in Daryl's face and gave him a great "what for" in front of the MPs. I asked the officer to unhandcuff Daryl, then I stiffened up, congratulated them on a job well done, and gave them a military salute. They all bristled with pride. Daryl and I laughed till we cried, tore up "my" copies of the MPs' papers, and returned the lieutenant's bars before he got back.

Now I could have been "given" some bars all right, the kind of bars that I couldn't have gotten out of. But, you've got to remember, my *potnah* was hanging way out there. Would we have done it again if given the chance? No way, we would have blown off the jeep and *didi maue*d (run away)! But it sure was a rush lookin' at those MPs' faces.

Chapter Eighteen

Frank Lahr
UDT-3 1944

Introduction:
Operational Report: Guam

W day at Guam was 21 July 1944. For a full week previous to the landing of the 3d Marine Division on Asan Beach, Underwater Demolition Team 3 had accomplished the most extensive preinvasion work ever assigned a demolition team in the full course of the Pacific War. Beginning on 14 July and continuing through the seven days until the landings, UDT-3 undertook, successfully, thirteen individual missions of reconnaissance or demolition and removed 620 obstacles (coral filled cribs) using 10,600 pounds of tetrytol.

Many of the reconnaissance missions were carried with the same operational technique and, therefore, are not written up separately in this account. Following the action report are accounts of: a typical night reconnaissance, a diversionary reconnaissance, and postassault work, all written by the men who participated in the particular work described.

Chapter Nineteen

F. Lahr
UDT-3 1944

Guam Operation

On 10 June 1944, UDT-3, aboard the USS *Dickerson* (APD 21), sortied from the Marshall Islands for the FORAGER Operation. The capture of Saipan and the recapture of Guam were the immediate program.

From 16 June to 1 July, the *Dickerson,* with UDT-3 aboard, performed patrol duty and screening work between Saipan and Guam. Air alerts were frequent, and we could always count on being awakened by the familiar sound—gong-gong-gong-gong. "Man your battle stations. Man your battle stations." Again, shortly after dark, a few bogies usually came down from the Volcano Islands. To vary the program, at night, the Japs often tried to sneak small boats around from the other side of the island and to land troops behind our beachhead. However, the LCIs that were closer inshore than we were usually had the fun with these boys.

On 1 July, we returned to Eniwetok, loaded up with 3-inch, 40mm, and 20mm shells, picked up our LCI(G)s, and sortied again for Guam. Captain Cane, skipper of the Dirty Dick, gave this famous command to the LCIs, "I'm leaving for Guam; you can follow."

We were in good company. With the DDs *Dewey* and *McDonold* and the four LCI(G)s, we made up our own Task Force Unit 53.1.14. The bombardment group, with the big guns of the *Pennsylvania* and the *Louisville,* among others, was on hand when we arrived off the west coast of Guam on 14 July. We immediately began reconnaissance operations upon orders from CTF 53.

Four officers were put aboard LCIs 471, 472, 473, and 469 to coordinate and direct fire support. These craft had never heard of a demolition team, and knew nothing of our technique or our need for close-in fire support.

The primary aim of those officers was to see that the gunboats got as close to the edge of the reef as possible, and from such a position did as much firing as possible. Many a time the LCI skipper protested, "Goddamn it, I'm almost aground now!" in reply to our request that he move in closer. Even so, these craft did a wonderful job, coming in so close to the edge of the reef that they had to back down to retire, as they were too near to swing around. Some of the crew augmented the automatic fire of the 40mm with potshots from carbines and tommy guns at anything and everything they saw that could possibly be considered a target.

Each morning would find the tiny LCIs nestled against one of the battleships or cruisers, looking like a midget courting a giant while case after case of 40mm and 20mm shells was lowered from the larger ship until even the decks of the LCIs were packed solidly with the shiny containers. Rockets were another item used very extensively and effectively by the LCIs. Just before the demolition teams went into the beach, a barrage of rockets would be fired at the shoreline to discourage the Japs from hanging around the area. That worked pretty well.

LCI 469 especially deserved credit. Though hit three times and suffering nineteen casualties, she was never absent from her station off Blue Beach when the team was going in to work. She would withdraw only long enough to transfer the wounded, then come back in, firing as much as ever.

Those same LCIs were later all sunk at Iwo Jima while supporting demolition operations. Their work at Iwo Jima was so outstanding that the unit was honored by a Presidential Citation, and many of their men were honored with individual awards.

Chapter Twenty

Frank Schroeder

UDT-11 1969–1972

Apollo 15

Frank Sherman Schroeder is a solidly built, blond giant with green eyes. Some people call him Brisket because of his "locomotive type" chest. One warm September day, we sat side by side in the back of my boat, keeping a close eye on our fishin' poles. It wasn't the first time we had spent hours together in quality time, doing one of the finer things in life—trout fishin' in Montana. Even if the fish didn't always bite. We reminisced a lot that day—UDT/SEAL training, Vietnam, the USS *Denver*, Tinian Island, fellow teammates, the Filipino women. We had the entire lake to ourselves.

Along with more than over two hundred other trainees, including several Vietnamese, Frank began UDT/SEAL training with Class 54 in September 1969. On February 13, 1970, approximately one-fourth of those anticipated potential Frogmen (the life of a Frogman looks transcendent to some, until after the training begins) graduated. The Vietnamese washed out three days into the training program. The newly graduated Frogmen were divided among the three West Coast underwater demolition teams (UDT), 11, 12, and 13, and SEAL Team 1, stationed at the naval amphibious base, Coronado, California. Frank received orders to UDT-11.

After more and intensive Frogman training, Frank deployed to Vietnam as a member of Foxtrot Platoon, UDT-11. They conducted beach recons, diving operations, and destroyed numerous Viet Cong bunker complexes with large amounts of advanced explosives. The men of UDT-11 were in constant danger of being captured or killed by the enemy as they performed their Frogman duties, sometimes armed with nothing more than a K-bar knife. After their tour in Nam, Frank's platoon was sent to the naval base in Subic Bay, Philippines. UDT had a West Pacific (WESPAC) detachment headquarters at Subic for UDT personnel to rotate through and operate from. Frank was only there for a short time before he received new orders to Okinawa, to an army Special Forces camp for parachute training. After successfully completing jump school, he returned to Coronado, California.

Lieutenant Nelson, the executive officer (XO) of UDT-11, approached Frank one day and asked if he would like to start training with the Astronaut Recovery Program. The recovery program consisted of two months of special training prior to the actual recovery of Apollo 15, a manned command module carrying David R. Scott, 39, the expedition's commander; James Erwin, 41, and Alfred M. Warden, 39.

The main objective of Apollo 15 was to recover moon samples. For the first time since Apollo 11 had landed two years earlier, an Apollo crew would not have to go through quarantine; scientists had decided before the Apollo 15 launch that the moon was germ free and posed no risk to life on earth. Nine UDT men from Team 11 were designated to train with the Astronaut Recovery Program from the thirty-five officers and one hundred enlisted men attached to UDT-11. Lieutenant (jg) Fred Schmidt, who had won a gold medal swimming with a relay team in the 1964 Olympics, was assigned the officer in charge of the "15" recovery program. Lieutenant (jg) Jon

Smart received the responsibility of second-in-command. WO1 Jerry Todd, QM1 Jake Jakubowski, SH2 Bill Ramos-Flores, GMG3 Rudy Davis, BT3 Rod "Yonk" Yonkers, RNSN Al Buehler, and SF3 Frank Schroeder.

The nine UDT swimmers, three officers and six enlisted men chosen for the recovery program formed three groups of three swimmers each. Only six of them would be airborne in two helo's during the actual recovery, the other three would be on standby aboard the *Okinawa* in case extra UDT swimmers were needed. All nine UDT Frogmen had to complete the same special training to prepare for the recovery.

Jumping from a Sikorsky SH-3 Delta twin-turbine engine helicopter, into San Diego Bay or the Pacific Ocean from ten to fifteen feet with special equipment seemed to be the daily routine. On one occasion, during a practice jump, Frank accidentally jumped from sixty feet.

"I didn't realize how high the helo was until I was on my way down. Instant enema," he told me just as a rainbow hit his hook. After playing the trout and landing it in the boat, he continued.

"My left swim fin repositioned itself up past my knee and painfully began to cut off my blood circulation. The impact didn't do much for the rest of my body either. I had a very difficult time repositioning the fin back down onto my foot before I could continue to work."

Frank's platoon trained hard for weeks in San Diego Bay and the Pacific Ocean. They finely tuned themselves so there would be no problems when it became time to perform the actual recovery. For their training, the recovery team used a practice command module the same size, shape, and weight as the real one. Some days, the command module would be transported from the UDT compound over to the naval amphibious base. A Mike boat, with a crane aboard, would hoist the practice module onto its deck and then transport it out into the bay, or out to sea, where the recovery team would begin its practice. Most days, however, the practice module would stay anchored in San Diego Bay, out of the way of shipping traffic. Frank said he had never been so seasick in his life as he was one day while riding on the module as it was being towed back to the base.

"Except for that incident, it's hard to believe the navy was paying us Frogmen for this much fun," Frank said.

"As the Sikorsky SH-3 hovered near the practice module, two UDT swimmers would throw out a large 150-pound rubber bag containing a flotation collar and a sea anchor, and then jump into the water, open the bag, and secure the flotation collar to the module. A rubber raft for the astronauts was then thrown out and inflated so that they could climb out after the capsule's hatch was opened."

Still tending his fishing pole, Frank continued, "Then, another swimmer would exit the aircraft and attach the sea anchor, which was thrown out to keep the module straight. After that the parachutes that slowed down the module's descent were recovered. As the flotation collar bag was opened, one UDT swimmer would swim around the module one way while the other swimmer swam the other way, towing the collar in each direction, completely surrounding the entire unit."

He stopped talking for a few seconds, thinking he had just got another bite, then continued. "The flotation collar was then secured to the module. A strap was then extended underneath the module and secured to the opposite side of the flotation collar to stabilize the capsule and prevent the entire unit from sinking. The flotation collar and raft were then inflated by CO_2 cartridges." The rubber raft was used for the UDT swimmers to stand in while they opened the module door, besides a stable place for the astronauts to ride until they could be recovered by a helo. After weeks of training and working as three-man teams, the entire training exercise took only three to five minutes.

After weeks of practice, the men of the recovery team found themselves on an aircraft en route to Hawaii. There they boarded the USS *Okinawa*, a converted World War II aircraft carrier, which had been refitted to support several different types of helicopters, making it an ideal ship for the Apollo 15 recovery. To practice and to be on line and ready for the recovery, the team then proceeded north of Hawaii a few days prior to splashdown. Doctor Stokin, the man from NASA in charge of the Astronaut Recovery Program, was also aboard the *Okinawa*, supervising the project. Several TV and news crews were also aboard.

A man from NASA gave Frank a Nikon underwater camera to take photographs of one of his team's practices while they were out at sea. Frank jumped from an SH-3 helo, and when he made contact with the water, the camera's strap broke. The last time he saw the camera, it was sinking out of sight into the deep blue Pacific, way beyond his free diving capabilities. No more cameras for Frank, he thought to himself as he watched it disappear into the deep blue sea.

A couple of days before the command module was expected, the *Okinawa* moved to within three miles of the expected landing site, approximately three hundred miles north of Oahu. All UDT swimmers were ready. Frank was put in charge of all the UDT diving gear.

The navy had made new one-eighth-inch-thick wet suits just for the UDT swimmers involved in the recovery program. They had red, white, and blue stripes across the chest and an American flag on the hood. They looked great, but the team really didn't need them in the warm waters north of Hawaii. Because the chances of exposure to radiation existed, it was mandatory the recovery team wear the wet suits. But that was the last recovery for which wet suits were worn.

The day before splashdown, the *Okinawa* moved to a predetermined location, closer to the recovery area. The UDT recovery team was to use two Sikorsky SH-3 Delta helicopters and divide two swim teams of three men each amongst them. Not all the UDT swimmers were going to be utilized, but two SH-3 helos would be airborne in the splashdown area, just in case.

Finally, the day had arrived. Frank's parents, two sisters, and his brother were glued to the TV back home in Malvern, Pennsylvania, in hopes of catching a glimpse of Frank. At 8:04 A.M. EST, the astronauts were awakened to the fast rhythm of the "Hawaiian War Chant." Excellent weather and calm seas awaited the conclusion of man's fourth and most scientifically rewarding moon flight. Aboard the command module were 170 pounds of moon rock and soil samples plus an eight-foot-long sample of the core below the lunar crust that was to be sent to

Houston, Texas, for scientists to study. Scientists estimated this moon expedition alone would be more rewarding than any of the first three lunar landings. Knowledge about the moon's age and other information would be derived from the materials brought back by Apollo 15.

Scott and Erwin sat their lunar module *Falcon* down on the plains of Hadley Base at 6:16 P.M. Friday, July 30. They had walked and driven seventeen miles over the lunar Apennine Mountain Valley that was formed billions of years ago. All the while, Warden peered down from the command module, circling the moon, at the rugged lunar terrain.

The afternoon of the splashdown, both SH-3s were airborne, loaded with the UDT swimmers and their equipment. The primary team of Frogmen, Schmidt, Jakubowski, and Davis rode in one helo while Jerry Todd, Al Beuler, and Frank rode together in the other helo as part of the standby team. Smart, Yonkers, and Ramos stayed aboard the *Okinawa*. The descending command module had been located on the *Okinawa*'s radar system. That information was being relayed to the helos, guiding the Frogmen toward their objective. They were very close. The command module was descending with "bull's-eye" accuracy, so accurate, in fact, that Apollo's course back from the moon disregarded two scheduled course corrections that were not needed. Their twelve-day $445 million mission would soon be over.

Then, there it was, but something looked wrong. One of the three parachutes used to slow down the command module on its descent had collapsed. At 4:46 EST, the command module hit the ocean surface harder than it was supposed to. The parachutes were immediately released to prevent the wind's dragging the module through the water. Schmidt, Jakubowski, and Davis pushed their equipment out of the helo and jumped out after it. The secondary SH-3 hovered close by, with the rest of the team aboard. The three UDT swimmers in the water immediately secured the flotation device to the module, inflating it and the rubber raft, then opened the door and freed the three astronauts. History was being made, right before the eyes of Frank and his teammates.

Everything was going according to schedule when a message from Dr. Stokin aboard the *Okinawa* came through to the secondary helo. They needed to recover the parachutes, especially the one that had collapsed, so that NASA could determine what had gone wrong with it.

From the secondary helo, we could see that the parachutes had drifted approximately 100 yards from the command module and started sinking. Frank's SH-3 moved into position over the chutes; he looked at Mr. Todd, Mr. Todd gave the signal, and that's all it took. Al Beuler and Frank were out the door, airborne toward the Pacific Ocean to help make U.S. history. A "Frogman's fantasy" was being created. Mr. Todd could very well have done the job himself, but was kind enough to let his men do the historical duties. To him, Frank is sincerely grateful.

The two Frogmen swam toward the parachutes. The chute that had collapsed was starting to sink fast. Al was collecting the other two as Frank dove for the collapsed one. It looked normal and was fully deployed underwater. He dove once but couldn't reach it because a metal ring on the suspension lines was pulling it down, and the chute had to be cut free from that ring. Frank and Al dove together, but it was still out of their reach.

With the parachute slowly sinking lower, even deeper, the two Frogmen knew they had time for, maybe, one more try. Taking deep breaths, they dove straight down, concentrating only on bringing the parachute back to the surface. This time, utilizing the entire potential of their bodies and the Frogman's need to succeed, they reached the chute. Frank quickly unsheathed his K-bar and cut the suspension lines from the metal ring. Pulling the parachute behind them, they kicked desperately for the surface. They were never so glad to return to the sunlight in their lives. There would have been no fourth chance.

Their SH-3 hovered overhead and dropped a line to recover the parachute. After all three parachutes were aboard the helo, they dropped the line to recover Al and Frank, then returned to the *Okinawa* with the parachutes. The *Okinawa* was already underway, moving closer toward the command module to recover it.

The astronauts were recovered by the SH-3 in which Schmidt and his swimmers were riding and flown to the *Okinawa*, but Schmidt and his team stayed with the command module until it could be recovered. When the *Okinawa* maneuvered in close to the module, the three UDT swimmers who'd been in reserve aboard the *Okinawa* entered the water to help recover the module. A line was shot from the carrier over the module to the UDT swimmers, and Yonkers secured it to the module, which was then slowly hoisted aboard, along with the UDT swimmers.

Although Frank never personally got to meet the astronauts, he did get to see them up close. Schmidt, however, got to talk to them on the module while it was in the water and afterward aboard the *Okinawa*. He was also interviewed by the TV and news crews.

Later that night, aboard the *Okinawa*, Frank went below decks to where the command module was being guarded by a sailor he knew. Brisket pulled a piece of yellow Mylar off the module for a souvenir. He has it to this day.

After the *Okinawa* returned to Hawaii, the Frogman recovery team flew back to Coronado, California, where they were given thirty-days' leave. So Frank climbed onto his Harley Davidson and rode from California to his hometown in Pennsylvania. While he was home on leave, Dr. Stokin from NASA called and wanted to know the exact condition at the time of recovery of the parachute that had malfunctioned. Frank told him that the canopies and lines looked normal to him and that the currents and weight of the metal ring tugging on it had opened it up.

After Frank's leave expired, he returned to the naval amphibious base and was assigned a new UDT platoon awaiting orders for another WESPAC cruise. I had just returned from Vietnam with Juliett Platoon, SEAL Team 1, and received my transfer request to UDT-11 so we both deployed for our second WesPac tour of duty, with Det Bravo, UDT-11.

Frank and I stay in close contact, and our phone bills will verify that fact. Good friends are hard to come by, and after the military and civilian experiences we have shared together over the last twenty-four years, I can look back on them all, good or bad, and truly feel the camaraderie.

Well, we might be trout fishin' in Montana, where some people only dream about fishin', but that doesn't mean the fish always bite. Frank landed two nice rainbows that day, using my pole, and losing most of my favorite lures.

Chapter Twenty-one

Mullie "Moe" Mulheren
UDT-3 1944

Section One—Guam

Our section's first job was a daylight reconnaissance of Asan Beach the afternoon of 14 July 1944, D-7. Two swimmers were used to explore the edge of the flat, level reef, which ran seaward two hundred yards. The fire support could not have been better; it kept the Japs in their holes throughout the reconnaissance. Only light small-arms fire and a few mortars opposed us. The two swimmers proceeded into the edge of the reef and out again with little trouble. Later the same afternoon, a diversionary reconnaissance was made at Agana Beach with little opposition, the LCPRs pulling to the edge of the reef as though they were dropping swimmers, then circling out to sea and back in to pick up the imaginary swimmers.

There was a flat, level reef that extended seaward anywhere

from seventy-five to three hundred yards. At low tide, this reef had little or no water covering it. At high tide, there was hardly enough water to cover a man crawling on it. So, to carry out a successful close-in reconnaissance, it was necessary for us to work under cover of darkness. Our first reconnaissance took place on the night of July 14, 1944, (D-7). With our afternoon work completed, we looked forward to the reconnaissance that night.

There were two thousand yards of beach to be covered. These two thousand yards were divided into four five-hundred-yard beaches. This gave each section five hundred yards of beach to cover. To accomplish this, each section used two rubber boats. The crew of each boat consisted of five enlisted men and one officer. This made a crew of six men; five swimmers and one man to remain with the boat at the edge of the reef. The man at the boat had a 536 radio.

At 2030 this same day, LCPR 1 with Section 1 aboard rendezvoused with LCI 471 located one thousand yards off Red Beach, our section's assigned five-hundred-yard beach. The night and weather conditions were perfect. Never was there a darker night; darkness being our sole protector, we welcomed it. Each LCPR—numbered 1, 2, 3, 4—was to rendezvous with the LCI and proceed into the beach on a compass course. In that way, each section was sure of hitting its assigned beach. Also, the LCI was standing by to give fire support if needed. As the LCPRs pulled slowly past the LCI, the crew and skipper shouted words of encouragement, which made us feel a little better, certain of ourselves for this first night job.

We proceeded in the LCPRs toward the beach and dropped the rubber boats and their crews at three hundred yards off the reef. With the rubber boats away, the LCPR withdrew to five hundred yards. It was very hard to judge distance at night.

The rubber boats proceeded toward their objective. Each boat paddled to a flank of the section's respective beach. The water was calm and very little surf broke on the reef, which was to our advantage. The boats were landed with no trouble at all. Two swimmers waded to the left of the rubber boat, two to the right, and one man down the center on the seaward side.

Apparently, the Japs never knew we were there! They could

be heard talking and seen lighting cigarettes on the beach. Also, a concrete mixer could be heard, and trucks running along the beach. We believe that the Japs were building obstacles. We should have just told them to cut it out, that way there'd have been less work for both us and the Japs!

With the exception of a few potholes, the reef was as level as a tabletop. It had a gradual slope at the seaward edge. No mines were found by any of the sections, but a number of obstacles were discovered.

With everyone safely back to the rubber boat, we proceeded to sea. Just as we were launching one rubber boat from the reef, a burst of machine-gun fire rang through the night. Whether the Japs saw or heard someone is still not known. No one was hit, but a lot of boys on that reef were scared out of a few years' growth.

Each rubber boat was equipped with a red light to be used to signal the LCPRs. As dark as it was, a black rubber boat was very hard to see. We paddled seaward for three hundred yards then flashed the red light seaward, and our LCPRs came in to pick us up. A successful reconnaissance was carried out by Section 1. We returned to the LCPR at approximately 2230. After some time, all the rubber boats had returned and been recovered, and all the PRs returned to the APD. Fire support was never called for while the team was on the reef at night.

At Guam, on our night reconnaissance, security was stressed very very much. While on the reef, one man remained with each of the eight rubber boats at all times. Also, the swimmers always worked in pairs, one man in the pair carrying a carbine. Generally however, the carbine was more of a hindrance than a help.

For identification while on the reef, a sign and countersign were used. If someone approached you in the dark, you asked him to identify himself. He was to answer with a girl's name, and you would answer back with a boy's name. If you asked again for his sign, he would answer with a different girl's name. You did likewise with a different boy's name. If you asked twice and received no answer, you were to shoot him. This system was used when the swimmers returned to the rubber boats.

The APD, LCPRs, LCIs and all rubber boats had call signs. When a red flare was sent up from the APD, it was a signal for everyone to withdraw from the reef immediately.

The intense darkness of the nights when we were working at Guam was something that had to be experienced to understand. The total blackness really put a strain on a person. Because we were working so close to shore, we could reasonably expect a Jap to show up at any minute, but it was impossible to visually identify anyone until they were close enough to stick a knife in you—had they been Japs.

The man left with the rubber boat had to be a man with wonderful nerves. He would be sitting all alone for a couple of hours at a stretch, and it was easy to imagine the shape of a Jap crawling out of the reef. A nervous man could have given away all security with a few careless shots at these imaginary targets. Fortunately, the Japs apparently never knew that we were carrying out night reconnaissances.

Night reconnaissance does have one bad feature. When something is located—obstacles, mines, etc.—it is very difficult to position it correctly on a chart. Every man should be familiar with the use of a lensatic compass as one way to locate position in the darkness by taking cross bearings on terrain features. Even so, only continued practice in extreme darkness will give a man a sense of direction and confidence in his own judgment and ability at night.

The afternoon of 15 July, our section carried out a successful diversionary reconnaissance of Dadi Beach. Heavy enemy fire was drawn, and we were caught in a cross fire until the USS *Pennsylvania* moved to within one thousand yards offshore and silenced a Jap battery on Orote Peninsula. There were no casualties in our section.

That same afternoon, a diversionary reconnaissance was conducted at Agat Beach which drew considerable enemy machine-gun and rifle fire. Still later in the same afternoon, we conducted a third diversionary reconnaissance between Facpi and Bangi Points. Section 1 lost one off its officers when its LCPR got caught on a coral head. Mr. Blowers was killed instantly by small-arms fire while trying to free the PR. After some time, the PR was freed, and it returned to the APD. The

APD withdrew, and Chief Carpenter R. A. Blowers was buried at sea that night.

But there was to be no rest for the weary. A night reconnaissance was scheduled for the same night, but due to heavy rain and *extreme* darkness, the operation was canceled. The cancellation was welcomed by all.

The afternoon of 16 July, Section 1 conducted a diversionary reconnaissance of Tumon Bay, where the enemy small-arms fire was so intense, we were unable to get within three hundred yards of the beach. The fire came from a solid-rock cliff, approximately five hundred feet high, located just to the left flank of the beach, and was the heaviest encountered throughout the entire operation. No UDT operations were conducted that night, and everyone had a good night's sleep.

On 17 July, all operations were to be conducted at night. We were to demolish the obstacles on Asan Beach. LCI 348 ran aground, delaying operations for several hours, and its crew had to be removed by our LCPRs. Eventually the rubber boats were launched, each carrying ten to twenty packs of tetrytol. But heavy rain began to fall early in the morning and continued for several hours. Because of the extreme dark, Section 1 was unable to locate its assigned obstacles and was extracted from the reef at dawn. We returned to the APD, ready for some sack duty, only to discover that our bunks were being occupied by the crew of LCI 348.

July 18 was a holiday for us. A night removal of obstacles on Red Beach was canceled just at dark.

The morning of 19 July, we carried out the operation that had been canceled the previous night. From a spectator's point of view, it looked like a suicide mission. The obstacles were some distance inshore from the high-water line, but our faithful LCI(G) made it just another easy job. Only small-arms fire here and there was encountered. The operation was conducted at low tide, leaving only bare inches of water on the reef. This made it extremely hard to drag the rubber boats loaded with "powder" across the reef to get to the beach. Section 1's "do or die boys" accomplished the task, but I have to admit that several of our teammates were so exhausted that they had to be dragged into the LCPR after the operation.

We thought that we were finished until D day, but apparently, Marine general Gieger aboard the flagship spotted some more obstacles and bet the admiral that his demo boys couldn't remove them. Again, the demo boys showed the gyrenes. On 20 July, Section 1 demolished the obstacles on the extreme left flank of Asan Beach. Little opposition from the enemy was encountered. This operation was the last of the demolition preassault work.

On D day (or William day as it was officially called), Section 1 directed traffic on the reef and removed many boatloads of wounded Marines from the beach.

Section 1 worked every day of the six days of postassault. We marked channels, demolished several small craft blocking Piti Channel, and sneaked in a little souvenir hunting on the side.

One of our best deals was made with the USS *Wyoming*. We were cruising about in our LCPR, loaded with useless junk; school books; parts of Jap uniforms; and a dirty banner which probably advertised a fire sale in Agana. We told the "shore duty" boys on the *Wyoming* that the banner was a regimental flag. We gave them all the junk in return for twenty gallons of ice cream, the first we had seen since leaving Pearl Harbor over three months earlier.

Chapter Twenty-two

Mike Ferrell
UDT-12 1967–1970

Operation Sea Float

We were pulling nine empty barges down the Ca Mau River, way down south near the Ca Mau Peninsula, which was located near the southern tip of South Vietnam. The nine barges were secured together, and we were towing them down the river to be used to set up a base camp. The barges were to be anchored in the middle of the river, near the village of Nam Cam. They would serve as a home for the UDT/SEALs, Sea Wolf helos, Swift boats, and a few other military units.

This area was heavy Indian country, a very stressful and scary place to be around because the area was infested with NVA and VC. The terrain consisted of hip-deep mud and triple-canopy jungle, which made for slow going on land; to slow us down on the water, the enemy would drop cables across the river. They definitely didn't want us down there. We had to literally fight our way there to get the new base camp established. I know that the team people understand what I'm talking about, especially the ones who have actually been to Sea Float.

This was definitely a place to stay *focused*. I mean that you could stick your arm out, close your eyes, and feel the tension in the air. The surrounding jungle was very thick and had not yet been defoliated; once you entered it, you couldn't see ten feet in any direction.

The NVA were usually well trained, wore uniforms, were well supplied, and were tough when agitated. They wouldn't run anywhere, but rather dug in and did the nasty. They also came to "probe" you and basically get in your face. The VC, or Charlie, were, mostly, South Vietnamese who were fightin' for the North. They were mostly hit-and-run, booby-trappers, a nuisance. Some VC were just made to fight, while others were fightin' for the cause.

Special Orders

We were strenuously operating out of our barges, and gettin' pissed off at the enemy down at Sea Float when we were told to report to Saigon. There I received special orders for me to immediately report to Okinawa for a classified briefing.

In Okinawa, the briefing room was full of high-level brass. It turned out that the USS *Pueblo* had been captured by the North Koreans, with its entire crew of about 125 men. We listened carefully to the briefing officers as they described a mission to destroy the ship where it was tied up in North Korea in order to deny the Russians access to some very sensitive intelligence-gathering equipment on board. We were to use the USS *Tunny* for the insertion operation, positioning it close enough to launch an SDV (swimmer delivery vehicle) from the bubble on her deck. To avoid leaving a trail of telltale bubbles on the surface, we were to use Emerson oxygen-rebreathers instead of normal scuba gear. After the target was hit, the minisub (SDV) would extract to sea and link back up with the *Tunny* and be retrieved underwater.

The whole mission bothered our officer that was in charge of us UDT men. He asked for permission for us to be excused from the briefing for a while so we could discuss the operation privately. As we discussed the operation, some rather interesting issues surfaced:

1. If the mission was successful, we could probably count on the North Koreans executing the crew.

2. What type of underwater detection technology do the North Koreans have in place, if any, and was it sophisticated enough to detect a small SDV?

3. If we missed the submarine on our extraction, what are our alternative escape routes? (This is an important feature in the mission planning of UDT/SEAL teams.)

We accumulated back in the briefing room with the officers, and our officer addressed these issues to them one by one. They were fully aware that the ship's crew was at risk. They also didn't know if the crew had been taken off the ship or not! The briefing officers had no idea of what underwater detection capabilities the North Koreans had, and they had no alternative clandestine escape routes figured out. The question was also raised as to why don't we send some troops over there and raise hell with them? The response was that every available man in the military was committed to the Vietnam situation!

This mission would break just about every tactical rule in our book. It went against UDT/SEAL training and common sense. Finally, our officer stood up and addressed the briefing officers again.

He said, "Gentlemen, I think we need to stand down on this one. We are already fightin' a hell of a war in Vietnam right now, and I think that's what we are going to do!"

I was proud of that man for his decision, and all of my *potnahs*, too.

Chapter Twenty-three

Gordan Canizio

UDT-3 15 July 1944

Daylight Diversionary Reconnaissance

UDT reconnaissance work being carried out as early as D-7 was objected to by some who feared that any activity on the future assault beaches would alert the enemy to the exact locations of future landings.

For this reason, diversionary reconnaissances were carried out. We figured that if we simulated a reconnaissance of three or four beaches, the Japs would be none the wiser to our actual plans. Of course, when we finally did the blasting work, the enemy knew that we intended to land. This was usually only a day or so before D day, and the bombardment fire from our ships and planes kept the enemy from reinforcing the defense of the selected beaches.

LCPRs were loaded from the APD. One five-man crew, and two officers were the only personnel. ChCarp Ralph Blowers was in charge of the boat; Lieutenant Marion (XO) went along as an observer. We arrived at our beach four minutes after leaving the ship. Mortar and small-arms fire was very heavy as we turned parallel to the beach, zigzagging at all times. At intervals, a stall was made to make the enemy think we were dropping our swimmers. We did this twice, and the small-arms fire became heavier than usual.

We retired out of range behind our LCI (gunboat) for five minutes, then returned to simulate picking up our swimmers. Mr. Blowers thought our distance from the beach was too far and gave the order to the coxswain (Canizio) to go in closer to the beach. The coxswain maneuvered in toward the beach at top speed, and all of a sudden, the PR ran aground on top of the reef. Mr. Blowers ordered the engine to be killed, and Chief Moore and the crew were ordered to abandon the LCPR and get in a rubber boat. As this was being done, we received a considerable amount of small-arms and machine-gun fire from the shore. As he was standing upright in the LCPR, Mr. Blowers ordered the men to belay his last order. At that time, he was struck by a bullet right through the neck and was killed instantly.

The coxswain then tried to get the PR off the reef. Starting the engine, he listened for the sound of the screw grinding against the reef. When that was not heard, he gunned the engine in reverse and then shifted gears to neutral, which left the LCPR drifting backwards. Doing this on and off, we finally slipped off the reef. Mr. Marion got off the deck and asked if everything was okay. I gave him a "Roger." We then headed back for the APD *Dickerson*. That night, Tokyo Rose announced that the Japs on Guam had repelled an attack. Hearing this, we knew our job was well done.

Section 4 was then given the task of removing the *Tokyo Maru* from the small-boat channel where it had been run aground by the crew during a desperate attempt to save it. The *Tokyo Maru* was a transport vessel, 310 feet in length. The quartermasters wheel was located on the fantail, right on the deck underneath the gun mount.

Chapter Twenty-four

Rick Foster
UDT-11 1967–1969

Rick started UDT/SEAL training with Class 42, one of the largest classes ever to attend Frogman training. In fact, the UDT/SEAL instructors had to divide the class into two groups, Alpha and Bravo. Rick was assigned to 42 Alpha, and the training began as usual.

Why Training Had to Be So Difficult

"During the second phase of training," Rick began, "Class 42 Alpha was out on San Clemente Island, conducting explosive and weapons training, another phase of hell. Our Frogman training was already over halfway behind us. We'd already survived the famous UDT/SEAL Hell Week."

One morning, the surf was a little rough, and the tide was higher than normal in Northwest Harbor, at the northernmost part of San Clemente Island. Northwest Harbor was located just offshore from the UDT/SEAL training compound. The explosives were real, and the members of our class were securing the haversacks of C-3 to simulated enemy concrete underwater obstacles that were on the ocean floor near the beach area. This part of training was conducted to teach the Frogman trainees how to properly demolish all the underwater obstacles in order to make the enemy beach area safer for the landing craft that would bring the invading troops and their equipment ashore.

As always during the grueling Frogman training, we were wet, cold, and tired from the demanding tasks involved. It was just another day of training. I was not trying to think much about the day's schedule and what the instructors had in store for us; I was just trying to do my best and get through with the day's evolution.

Strenuously trying to secure the C-3 explosive haversack correctly to our assigned concrete obstacle, my swim buddy and I were having our share of problems because of the extra high tide and the surging water conditions. It took me more than a couple of times, diving to the bottom in the deeper than normal water, to try and tie the haversack to the obstacle with the securing lines that were attached to the explosive sack. In that cold water, we wanted to do it right the first time because the instructors would make us do it all over again if we didn't.

I remember coming to the surface with blood in the bottom of my dive mask, probably caused by a sinus squeeze because I couldn't equalize the pressure in my face mask properly. But that was all part of Frogman training. If you didn't like it, all you had to do was quit. We were all volunteers; if we couldn't handle it, the instructors didn't want us in the program. We could be packing our seabags and on our way to another duty station within minutes.

All hands involved had been up since the wee hours of the morning. We had already finished morning PT and had our breakfast. About midmorning, while swimming in the harbor during the middle of the training evolution, one of the instructors began yelling for everyone to swim to shore and muster up. After reaching the sandy beach, I noticed the instructors pulling Greco and McCall, two of our teammates, out of the water. They had drowned while trying to secure the haversacks of explosives to their assigned obstacles.

We started talking among ourselves and became very angry at the instructors, thinking they had pushed the class too hard for the unusual surf conditions during the evolution. None of us had been doing very well at all as we tried to load the obstacles with the demolitions in the deep water and rough surf. I saw the shock on the instructors' faces, and the other trainees as well. At that point, I came real close to quitting, as did many of the other members of my class.

The instructors tried to explain to everyone exactly what had happened. One of the swim pair had become tangled in the haversack securing lines after the demolitions had been secured to the obstacle. Why he didn't cut himself lose with his K-bar knife wasn't clear to any of us. In or out of the water, we all carried a K-bar as part of our mandatory equipment everywhere we went on all our training evolutions. The tangled man's swim buddy had dived down to help, and his panicking swim buddy grabbed onto him and held him under. When the two men were finally discovered by the instructors, it was too late. They were both just below the surface.

I had seen dead people before, but not friends or teammates. These deaths were hard for me and my teammates to deal with. The instructors secured the evolution for the day, and we returned to our barracks to put on dry clothes. Then the instructors explained once again what had happened and how to avoid an incident like that. We then continued on with our daily training as usual, performing a different evolution, and everyone involved being more cautious.

At a later day, I heard a rumor that there was going to be an investigation because one of the drowned men had already completed nuclear submarine school. The navy apparently wanted to know why the military was spending money to have a man attend UDT/SEAL training when he had already completed the very expensive nuclear submarine school.

The loss of these two men was unfortunate, and a real disappointment for our training class. But later, those of us who completed the program became fully aware of why UDT/SEAL training was so tough. The training was designed to produce men who were the best at whatever they did and who could be counted on to succeed on even the toughest missions. Being in the teams would not have been the same, or meant as much to us, if the training had been easier. And the teams would not have been as useful to the navy. All the instructors were performing their job, and doing it well, teaching us from the experiences they had during their combat tours of duty. This training would help keep us alive during the "ultimate tests" that we would experience as Frogmen at home or on foreign soil.

After I had completed training, I was assigned to UDT-11 and later deployed with a platoon from that team to Vietnam, where I had already been as a fleet sailor stationed on an LSD (landing ship, dock). On my second tour, our platoon spent a lot of time swimming in muddy rivers, performing demolition work, mostly opening up waterways by demolishing obstacles that had been placed by the Vietnamese and Viet Cong. We also performed a few beach recons along the coast of Vietnam. After our tour with UDT-11 was completed, I was exhausted, and tired of blowing up obstacles. We were all ready to return home.

After our platoon returned to the States, volunteers were needed to go to Midway Island for a two-month demolition job. My platoon had stopped at Midway on its return trip from Vietnam, but stayed on the island only long enough to refuel and take a break from the long flight. Having only a few months left in the navy, I was getting pretty short, so I decided that I would like to go along on the demo job. I was flown back to Midway with eight or nine other Frogmen.

"Gooney Bird Island," what a place! Midway Island was crowded with fierce gooney birds, which could cause terrible injuries with their bite.

One of the men on the demo job with us was a black named Perkins who I used to say I dived with because sharks like dark meat. Of course, it was Perkins's opinion that sharks liked sweet white meat.

Actually, none of us in UDT really knew why we were going to Midway for the demo job. We were to work there with two civilian divers who worked for Western Electric. They would be in charge of the overall operation.

After arriving at Midway under a warm, clear blue tropical sky, we were introduced to the two Western Electric divers. We unloaded all of our gear from the plane, and then were escorted to the barracks we were to use while conducting the demo job.

We were to blow a trench through the coral reefs so a cable could be laid from the island out to sea. We were not going to have anything to do with laying the cable itself, just make a trench for it. I assumed that the cable was to be connected to sensing devices that were to be placed on the ocean floor to detect submarine activity.

After we were settled in our new home, the two W.E. men immediately showed us where the cable would be laid and where they wanted us to "cut" the reef with Mark-8 explosive hose. The W.E. men were top-notch master divers themselves, and at least one of them would be in the water with us on all our dives.

As we got underway on the demo job, we found the diving on Midway Island to be gorgeous. The visibility was a good seventy to eighty feet and crystal clear. But there was a very strong current, which made diving and swimming very difficult out past the reef. The sea floor offshore of Midway was infested with beautiful coral and large boulders. Several different kinds of sharks, including reef sharks, white-tip sharks, and hammerheads inhabited the waters offshore. Every time we entered the water, we encountered sharks. We had to constantly be on the alert and watch them very carefully. There was also a lot of other marine life in the area, and the colors of the coral were unbelievable. We encountered manta rays, tuna, and even a fifteen-foot whale, which had been washed over the reef during a storm and was almost dead. We all got together and helped move it back into the deeper water, where it finally swam to sea.

Because of the sharp coral, we had to wear wet suits to protect against cuts. And we wore long johns on top of them to protect the wet suits. If we were not diving in the deeper water, we wore coral booties, tennis shoes, or boondockers (navy-issue boots) to protect our feet.

We spent the first couple of days setting fifty-five–gallon drums in the water on each side of the trench we were blowing. We used four drums, welded together in pairs to make them taller so they stuck out of the water on the reef, and we cemented a wooden post in each welded pair so it stuck out of the top. The drums were positioned apart from one another on each side of the trench where the cable was to lay, and a line was tied between the posts, with a pulley dangling from its center. That way, instead of the cable being dragged over the sharp coral floor, it rode the pulley secured to the line between each pair of posts, which also made it easier to pull the cable to sea.

We used underwater cement to anchor the drums on the coral reef floor. The drums had to be very solid to support the weight of the cable when it was to be reeled out to sea. The bags of cement were lowered over the side of a Boston whaler, to a diver, from a wide plank that was hanging over the side the boat. The diver would have to be directly below the bag of cement in order to grab it, and next to the drums or wherever else it was to go, as once it was dropped off the plank, it took the diver straight to the bottom. Re-bar was also placed into the cement to help strengthen it. The clear, warm water in the area soon became very cloudy with cement dust, and we began banging into things a lot.

Next, we started laying Mark-8 explosive hose across the reef and blowing a trench wide enough to lay the cable. Each morning, we entered the water and checked our demo job, and swam around with the sharks. The job couldn't be checked immediately after the explosion because of the sharks that were attracted by the detonation of the explosives and the dead fish in the water.

We had to make up broom-handle length sticks with nails in the end to poke the sharks with when they got too close to us. Of course, we drove the nail into the sticks so that the blunt end pointed out; we didn't want to cause the sharks to bleed or make them mad, just keep them away from us while we were in the water. We also had a device called a "bang stick" that had a 12-gauge shotgun shell in one end. It was capable of killing a shark, but we didn't want to use it as that would spread their blood in the water, attracting more sharks to the area and causing a feeding frenzy.

The current was so strong at times that several of us couldn't make it back to our boat after a dive; the boat had to come to us. Jay Posselt blew out both of his ear drums on a dive at the beginning of the operation and became part of the boat crew for the rest of the time we were on the island.

On one dive, I was submerged in the water, waiting for my swim buddy to get into the Boston whaler, and we were being harassed by a fifteen-foot shark. I was trying to keep it away from us so that we could get out of the water, but the shark kept coming up close to me, circling, and then swimming a little ways away. He kept this up for a while, and I had to keep poking him with the little stick with the nail in it until it was my turn to climb in the boat. Finally, it was my turn to climb into our small boat, so I let go of my stick, and keeping an eye on the shark, I swam to the surface. As I did, the stick slowly spiraled down toward the ocean floor beneath me, sinking from the weight of the nail. When the stick came close to the shark, he darted at it, biting it in half as if it was a toothpick.

Another time when we were being harassed by sharks, I was surfacing to our boat with a full set of ninety-cubic-inch diving tanks, weight belt, and the rest of my gear. My adrenalin was pumpin' so hard that I grabbed the side of the Boston whaler, pulled *myself* over the gunwale, landed on my back in the boat, and the momentum flipped me right back out the other side into the water with the sharks again. I swam back to the Boston whaler and was helped back into the boat. Because of the weight of the tanks and weight belt, it usually takes another person or two in the boat to help pull the diver up over the side. It's very surprising what a man can do when several hungry sharks are on your ass.

The ever-present sharks were beginning to make me wonder why I had volunteered for the demo job. Back in the States, my buddies who were "short" were getting "early outs" and leaving the navy, and here I had to volunteer for a demolition job that had already brought me closer to death than my two tours to Vietnam! The water and the weather were beautiful, but I was ready to get out of the navy, alive!

There wasn't much to do on Midway Island as far as recreation goes, but while I was there, I ran into a buddy of mine who I grew up with. I also got into photography to pass my spare time. We did get to fly to Hawaii once every two weeks or so for a little R & R.

One day, some type of secret jet landed on Midway for refueling. It was painted completely black. Guards were posted up and down the runway on both sides, and two men who were stationed on the island took pictures of it, but their cameras were confiscated. Not just their film, but their cameras! The men who flew the jet were dressed up like astronauts. When the plane finally took off, it climbed straight up into the sky, and was gone. I had never seen anything disappear so fast in my life.

The time slowly rolled by, then one day, we decided to do a little DuPont fishing for a change in our diet. We obtained quite a few fish and an eighty-five-pound sea turtle with some of our explosives. We cooked the turtle up on the beach, along with the fish, and had a feast. Of course, the underwater explosions from the Mark-8 hose also killed a lot of fish.

Late one night, two of us were rousted out of bed by our UDT officer, and the three of us quickly boarded a tugboat, which took us out to sea to the buoy marking the end of the cable. We didn't have any weapons with us, and a Russian trawler was approaching at full speed from some distance away. We didn't have any idea if the Russians were checking out the cable, but my partner and I had to get off the tug and hang onto the buoy in the water in the middle of the night. Our instructions were to cut the buoy loose from the end of the cable if the Russian trawler got too close to it. As our feet dangled below the dark surface in the middle of the night, I couldn't help but think about the many sharks that we had been seeing on our dives. Needless to say, it scared me. I was also thinking, "Here goes another *Pueblo* incident!"

We were stuck out there for a long time, with nothing to defend ourselves with except a K-bar knife each. American jets, ships, and submarines were being scrambled toward our position at the time, but we were still hanging on to that damned buoy. Finally, the Russian trawler was diverted away from Midway Island, and we were then recovered by the tug.

Another day, near the completion of our demo job, we detonated a few lengths of Mark-8 hose for the trench. One of the

Western Electric men, a funny and wild sort of guy, wanted to dive on the explosion site right away to inspect it, instead of waiting for the next day as we had been doing. I think that he might have had something to prove to us. Anyway, he chose me to go along on the dive with him to inspect the blast site. We were working off of a beach-landing-type craft and had a Boston whaler with us as a safety boat. After we entered the water, we dove to the bottom where the explosives had just been detonated. The W.E. man was checking out the trench, and I was following him around, looking at all the sea creatures that had collected in the area for a free meal on all the dead fish.

Everything was fine with the freshly created trench; the Mark-8 hose had done its job, so the W.E. man gave me the signal to surface. As we started up, I quickly grabbed his fin and pulled him back down and pointed to a white-tip and a reef shark that had just entered our area above us. At first, I saw only one, then two. Then there were three, then eight. By the time I stopped counting them, eighteen were hovering close by. They just kept coming from all directions and soon they were swarming around us like angry bees. There were even a couple of hammerheads in the bunch.

We returned to the bottom and began to look for cover and something to hide behind. The larger sharks were kind of hanging around in the background as if they were waiting for something to happen. The little guys, maybe four or five feet long, were darting in and out, trying to get us. We were pushing them away with our hands, our fins, punching them with our fists, and using our wooden poles to avoid getting bitten.

Since trying to reach the surface was now out of the question, we began to move back up the freshly blown trench toward the shallower waters of the coral reef. I followed the W.E. man, watching our rear, as we worked our way, back-to-back, toward shore. We had at least a quarter mile to go to reach the shallower water. On the way, we stopped occasionally to hide in and hang onto the cracks and crevasses that lined the sides of the trench. Because of the swells that passed overhead toward shore and the strong current running through the trench, we were often thrown twenty-five feet in and then twenty-five feet back out again like feathers in the wind. Swimming was very difficult as we continued to move slowly through the rough, surging water. We were barely making any headway, and hanging on to whatever we could.

All of a sudden, my face mask was ripped from my face. I didn't know what had caused it, the strong current, a piece of coral, or a shark! Now my visibility had suddenly became very poor; I couldn't see the sharks or the W.E. man very well. I could still see the silhouette of the W.E. man, and figured he still had his mask, so I stayed close to him, and we continued our way through the trench. I was wishing we had waited a day to check out the freshly blasted area. As far as sharks went, it was bad enough entering the water a day after the blast.

I don't know how we ever fit in some of the small holes we picked to hide in; I do know we had sea urchins stickin' out of our wet suits and long johns when we left them—and holes from the sharks. Our hands and other parts of our bodies were getting cut by the sharp coral. I had never sucked the air out of a diving tank in my life like I did that day.

Finally, we reached the shallower water of the coral reef. It was a good thing, as we were both about out of air. The larger sharks stayed in the deeper water outside the reef, but several persistent smaller sharks had followed us in. We climbed out of the trench and worked our way across the reef to one of the fifty-five gallon drums that we had anchored in place a few days earlier. When we reached it, Mr. W.E. jumped up onto it, tanks and all. He didn't seem to be the wild and crazy guy that he'd been earlier. We were both exhausted by then. There was no room for me up on the drum with him so I stayed in the water at the bottom. But I had to constantly run in circles around the drum, with all my diving gear still on, as one of the smaller sharks was still chasing me.

I hollered to the Boston whaler that sharks were chasing us and for them to hurry up and come in to pick us up. When the boat finally arrived, the driver was laughing and said, "I don't see any sharks." I pointed out the fin moving across the top of the water.

We were then recovered from the water, and the W.E. man

got down on his knees and prayed. He said that in all of his years of diving, he had never experienced anything like that in his life. I think the experience made a religious man out of him!

Throughout the entire operation, except for a few cuts from the coral, some bruises, and getting banged up a bit, nobody was seriously injured. Being in and out of the salt water all the time actually helped heal the minor cuts. That was probably the one good thing about the whole operation.

I wouldn't mind going back to Midway again sometime, but only as a civilian, and not if I had to enter the water every day. Because of my experiences on Midway with the sharks, I do very little diving to this day. I still live next to the ocean, as I have all my life, and do a lot of fishin'. We fish for mako sharks and a lot of other fish. But I don't like to catch any shark that weighs more than two hundred pounds because they become hard to handle when they get near our boat. The mako is the fastest shark alive, and every time I catch one, it reminds me of the Midway Island demo job. I guess fishing them is my way at getting back at the sharks for the way they harassed us on Midway. That demo job has definitely left memories in my mind that I will never forget!

I was, and am now, proud of what we accomplished while I was in the navy underwater demolition teams. We all owe a lot to the UDT/SEAL training staff for helping us survive the conditions and environments in which we operated. The instructors are one reason that most of us survived the types of duties—combat or "administrative"—in which the UDT/SEAL teams were involved. If the training hadn't been so damn difficult, we definitely would have lost more men than we did.

Chapter Twenty-five

Joseph Gannon
UDT-3 1944

Section Two—Guam

After three days of reconnaissance and diversionary reconnaissance, the first blasting operations came off on the night of 17 July. We left the APD at approximately 2300 and proceeded to the edge of the reef off of Red Beach 2. Just outside the breakers, we disembarked into two rubber boats.

There were ten of us UDT men in all, five in each boat. Each rubber boat carried thirty twenty-pound bags of tetrytol. After we experienced quite a little difficulty in finding the obstacles, they were finally located at about fifty to seventy-five yards offshore. The job was quickly and quietly executed without any further trouble. The only thing we didn't like was waiting for the green flare so that we could pull the fuse lighter. Sitting around in the dark with the Japs only a few hundred yards away was no fun. As soon as the green flare was released, we pulled the fuse and returned to the LCPR at the edge of the reef. We arrived back at the Dirty Dick about dawn.

The next afternoon's operation was much different in that there was no need for stealth. We proceeded to the beach with plenty of point-blank fire support, smoke screens, and air support. The only drawback was the reef was high and dry. Our only alternative was to pack the powder on our backs to the obstacles that were located 150 yards away from the rubber boats. I guess we looked like a bunch of monkeys as we scrambled back and forth across the reef. However, we finally loaded the coral cribs, pulled the fuses, and everyone returned to the LCPR safely.

Our final day of blasting went off like clockwork. It took us only twelve minutes to load and blow sixty obstacles, despite the fact that they were located three hundred yards from the edge of the reef and directly on the beach. The only reason that we were able to accomplish this was due to the magnificent fire support afforded us, particularly by the LCIs. Time and again the men of these ships risked their lives in order that they might come in a little closer to the reef with more accurate fire.

Chapter Twenty-six

Mike Ferrell
UDT-12 1967–1970

Return to the World

Finally, it was time to return to the States after a nine-month tour. Man did I want to do some surfing, chase some round-eyed hard bodies, and do some partying! You bet!

I was becoming a short-timer now, only having to pull one more tour of duty with the teams. I was a seasoned warrior, a man who kept a squared-away uniform and highly spit-shined boots. But, I liked to reach beyond the military edge in terms of hair length, mustache, and a really nice, colored, beaded necklace that I had made while I was in Vietnam. The lifers didn't like my necklace, and they probably didn't like me personally, but they always knew that they could depend on me to get the job done, and I would assume the responsibilities for my actions. I always leveraged this to the max, but they allowed me some space to "push the envelope," so to speak.

The teams decided to send fifteen or twenty frog-types (UDT men) through SEAL cadre training. SEAL cadre was conducted around the Chocolate Mountains near Niland, California. By this point in my navy hitch, my attitude had been changing. I had the, "Yeah sure . . . whatever," attitude. After the last half of the first tour I had just completed, I hadn't been doing a lot of beach recons anyway.

Chief Stone was one of the cadre instructors. He was about thirty-five years old or so, a short but strong man with a heavy South Carolina accent. He was a squared-away lifer (career man), and had that keep-your-shit-in-a-neat-pile attitude. He was a good SEAL operator and instructor; he knew what he was doing. He was the absolute mirror image opposite of what I represented, but I would have been proud to operate with him anytime.

We were all packed up at the UDT/SEAL compound at the naval amphibious base in Coronado and ready to go to Niland for our cadre adventure. We had a six-by truck for transportation, but no assigned driver! My friend Oggie had the appropriate driver's license and volunteered to drive the truck. That should have raised the yellow caution flag because we usually never volunteered for anything. So, Oggie, Roger, and I were to take the six-by and all the gear to Niland.

Roger was a funny guy, had a good sense of humor, a level head and a laid-back attitude. He was a big man, and I always had the feeling that if you ever really got him pissed off enough, he would probably beat you till you quit moving, then he would go get a stick. But, he really never seemed to get angry about anything.

Several other vehicles were going to Niland, too, but we had the heaviest truck. All the other vehicles were going to boogie on down the highway ahead of us because our top speed was forty miles per hour or so.

So, Chief Stone said to Oggie, "Now you stay on this freeway going east, and we'll be waiting for you at the exit. It should take you about four or five hours." He wrote the information down and gave it to me.

So, Huey, Duey, and Louey are now on our way to Niland, and it's a nice warm sunny day. We had four to five hours of driving ahead of us, so we thought we would make the best of it. We were barely out of San Diego heading east when we decided to pull off the road to buy a couple quarts of beer. Boy did it taste good. We got back on the freeway and kept on driving. It seemed like we had been driving for a long time when I started getting the feeling that we were lost. We all made one of those "executive decisions" and decided to pull off the highway and buy another quart of beer, and a map. We then decided to take a few back roads to get to our destination, and after a while, we ended up at Niland.

All the guys were glad to see us, but the bad news was that the chief was still back out on the freeway at exit XXX, waiting for us, exactly as he said he was going to do. I began to feel very bad about the whole thing; we screwed up (Chief, if you read this, I apologize to you again. I shouldn't ought of done that).

I may have been good about making my own decisions while I was in country, but I had completely lost my *focus*—but that's just a shitty excuse. Anyway, after the chief finally arrived at the SEAL camp in Niland, he was all over our ass, and we deserved every bit of it. I was the senior man among the three of us and took the responsibility for our actions.

One night during cadre training, the chief was teaching us how to cover our fields of fire with a .50-caliber machine gun. We were all up on this berm where the .50 was sitting on a tripod.

The chief said, "This is your area of responsibility," as he pointed out into the desert night. "Short burst of three rounds, pause and move the weapon, then short burst of three rounds again. This will keep the barrel cool." The chief didn't know that I was already familiar with the .50-caliber machine gun and already had a tour in Nam.

After he instructed a few of the men by going through the process with them, he went away for a few minutes, and we were left alone. So, I got up in front of the men and started mimicking the chief. I was a Southerner too, and could duplicate the chief's accent, "Now . . . see dat dark tree over dare . . . Dat is yo left field a fire . . ."

I was really jammin' and had the whole platoon falling on the ground laughing like a bunch of six-year-olds at Christmas. I had just turned around to look out into my dark field of fire while doing my "Chickenman strut" at the same time, and as I turned back toward the class, there was Chief Stone standing in front of me! The whole cadre class was all of a sudden dead silent. Even though it was dark, I could see the smoke steaming off the chief's head.

"Well Ferrell," the chief said, "looks like it's your turn next, come on over here to the tripod. I'm going to teach you the proper method to cover your field of fire."

"Who, me?" I said. "Oh, you bet, Chief."

(When I was in Nam, we used to go on river recons by boat and carry the army and Marines along so they could perform their clear-and-sweep or search-and-destroy operations. We were operating close to the Cambodian border in an area called the "Parrot's Beak." This place was a long gradual curve in the river that wrapped around this blunted point near the Plain of Reeds. There was a heavy concentration of NVA in the area who were fully supplied and "in force." The NVA were heavily entrenched on the curve near the river banks and kicked ass every time we went by. We would have a convoy of maybe twenty to twenty-five boats that were strung out, end-to-end, about seventy-five to one hundred yards between them.

Swooosh . . . swooosh . . . swooosh, B-40 rockets, small arms, and everything else they could throw at us would come off of the river bank. I could hear the shrapnel ricocheting off of the metal of our boat as we took hits from the NVA. We were all wearing flak jackets and metal helmets, and I would man a .50-caliber machine gun and return the fire. I was giving it hell, scared out of my wits, and hoping that I was killing every one of those motherfuckers! The best I could tell, they were all dug in, down in spider holes, sticking their heads up just long enough to fire a rocket and pop back down again and reload. This experience was heavy on my mind as I was sittin' at the tripod.)

The man who had fired the .50 before me had finished the box of cartridges, so I reloaded with a new one. *Pow . . . pow . . . pow*, pause and move . . . *pow . . . pow . . . pow*, pause and move. The chief was yelling in my ear for me to move faster. The .50 made a lot of noise, and it was hard to hear him.

"Faster, faster," he kept screaming in my ear.

It was making me angry, and I was beginning to get *focused*! Just about then, something snapped in my mind. I pulled that Vietnam experience into my "Chickenman" head and began to fire completely on full auto; tracers were flyin' everywhere, and I was definitely covering my field of fire. The chief was yelling for me to stop, but it was too late, I was jammin'. The barrel turned from a dark red to white, and by the time I had finished, there was complete silence all around me except for the ringing in my ears. I can't remember how long it took, but I emptied the whole box of ammo.

Now the chief was jumping up and down and screaming at me. He was really pissed off and telling me that I could ruin a weapon like that. I just kept staring out into my field of fire, looking into the dark, still "flashing." When he had finished, I didn't say a word. I stood up and dusted myself off, looked him straight in the eye, and then walked away. I figured that he had gotten the message and there was no need to further anger the man. There wasn't room for the *pow . . . pow . . . pow*, pause and move, *pow . . . pow . . . pow* stuff at the "Beak" in Nam! The way I looked at it was, I would much rather prefer to be throwing everything I had, including the kitchen sink, at the enemy to suppress his fire and stay alive instead of lying face down in the mud with a perfectly good gun in my hands. I understood exactly what the chief was saying and the lesson being taught. But . . . I've been wanting one of those Stoner things anyway.

As you can see, I was plainly starting to develop an "attitude." I seemed to be getting angry at everything. Maybe I was psychologically pumping myself up for my next tour to Nam, I didn't know.

I *was* getting close to my second tour, but before I left, first I wanted to go home and see my mom and dad.

By the late sixties, support in the country for the Vietnam war was seriously eroding, and I was having second thoughts about the whole thing; I knew that we were not going to win the war, and I was caught right in the middle of it! I was seriously thinking about going to Canada—for real, forever. This was a very private thought, and I didn't share it with anyone. I could not afford to let anyone see even a small crack in my armor. The problem wasn't, "Hey, I'm scared that I am going to die." It was much more serious than that—the erosion of support from the people was cracking the very foundation of my soul. I believed in the "dream," and I still do—democracy, the commitment of America to the ideals of liberty, apple pie, protection of our rights, freedom of religion, stopping communism, and the whole value system. My entire life seemed to be breaking down. It was a very confusing time.

I went home on leave, and it was a tough visit. God bless my parents! They brought a different perspective to my delirium and helped me reevaluate my thoughts. They probably saved my life! Had I decided to go to Canada, leaving my *potnahs* dangling in the wind and letting them spill their blood for me, I feel confident that my sense of guilt would have destroyed me. Thank you, Momma and Dad, thank you my sweet Jesus; your gift of wisdom saved my life.

Chapter Twenty-seven

Alford Brokes
UDT-3 1944

First Daylight Blasting Job: Guam

"Chittum, where in the hell's my little whistle?" was the desperate and famous command of Chief Carpenter Racine.

It marked the opening statement of our last-minute briefing on that exciting morning of July 18. This was to be our first daylight blasting job in action. Roger hour was but a matter of minutes away. Our jobs were assigned, and the gear was ready.

Nerves were pitched for unlimited excitement. And again, barked the biteless, "Who saw my whistle?" It was to play a very important part in this historical act.

If enemy fire became too intense, V. O. Racine was to give us a toot on his whistle, the signal to return fire as well as to return to the ship. It was understood, however, that if he was eliminated early in the game, the whistle would pass down the chain of command, Schommer being the next in line, etc. If too many of us were removed at once, it was also understood that the remaining men could use their own discretion. What an honor . . . What reserved authority . . .

However, the whistle was neither found nor needed, and Sections 1 and 3 successfully removed 150 obstacles with three thousand pounds of tetrytol. Thirteen minutes after our embarkation from the APD, the shot was laid and ready to fire. Everyone was too tired to be scared now, and Roger hour caught a few of the guys in careless positions. Timmy, for instance, was taking advantage of his first chance to get a good look at the beach. He was sitting behind one of the obstacles closest to the beach, taking in the show with an amused grin. What a position . . . What excitement . . . What a target! Especially since our smoke screen had drifted between us and our fire support. Skaggs, also too tired to move, just flopped down in the open, forgetting all about security and that we were going to set off the shot—or better yet, not giving a damn. Green was draped out halfway between the obstacles and the rubber boat, and Brokes was dragging himself from one obstacle to another, making final checks and tie-ins. Then, the time came for the shot, and Schommer gave the word and pulled the fuse. Everyone, well almost everyone, set a new one-hundred-yard-dash record returning to the rubber boat. A quick muster proved that the chief's lungs were no match for the LCI's 40mm's.

"Where in the hell's Timmy and D.E.?" Racine barked.

"Probably taking five for a short one," was Irish's bright remark. Just then, our sightseers came double-timing back to the rubber boats, D.E. in the lead.

"Ready to fire?" Tim shouted when he reached us.

"Had you stayed on that charge another three minutes you wouldn't have to ask," someone answered.

The explosion found us safely in the LCPR, well on our way to "Keyhole." The job was a success, and the strained faces and tense bodies of the men finally relaxed.

"That's a hell of a lot of work just for a shot of brandy," Irish remarked. But knowing him, we realized that he was the last to think so. To those of you who take our places in this outfit, I'd like to wish the best of luck. The demo teams have made history and an honorable name for themselves throughout World War II, and in the eyes of other service units, they are tops. It is up to you to "Carry on."

Chapter Twenty-eight

Paul "P. K." Barnes
SEAL Team 1 1969–1971

This incident occurred near Rach Soi, South Vietnam, while P. K. was attached with Kilo Platoon, SEAL Team 1. Among the members of Kilo Platoon were Tommy Dixon, Wade Puckett, Dave Perry, Tim Staudenmeir, Chuck Holler, Bobby Smith, Ron Garces, John Lynch, Billy Cheatham, Ron Quear, Harold "Happy" Baker, John Marsh, and Gary Stubblefield. P. K. replaced Baker after he became sick and was sent back to the States.

This operation is still fresh on P. K.'s mind, even after all the years that have passed. It's something that no man, after experiencing, can forget easily. For P. K., the word *hero* is an understatement. This is a prime example of the navy SEALs "All For One and One For All" attitude that P. K. inherited back in his early days of UDT/SEAL training as a member of Class 54.

This is a letter sent to me from P. K.

Kilo Platoon: Rach Soi, South Vietnam

Date: December 11, 1970.

Officers in charge: Lt. John Marsh and Lt. (jg) Gary Stubblefield.

Mission: Interdict any Viet Cong gunrunners encountered offshore in the Gulf of Thailand.

Transportation: Light SEAL support craft (LSSC) and Vietnamese sampan (small narrow wooden boat).

Intelligence sources: Word of mouth throughout local village, general statements from Kit Carson Scouts (ex-Viet Cong), and a hunch from our officer in charge, Mr. Marsh.

Personnel on mission and weapons carried:

Mr. Marsh—British 9mm Sten gun with silencer, 350 rounds of ammo.

Mr. Lac (South Vietnamese SEAL/LDNN)—M-16 with 350 rounds of ammo.

P. K. Barnes—Stoner 63-A light machine gun with 400 rounds of linked ammo and a 9mm Model 39 Smith and Wesson pistol.

Ut (Kit Carson Scout—ex-Viet Cong)—M-16 with 350 rounds of ammo.

Long (Kit Carson Scout—ex-Viet Cong)—Ak-47 with 350 rounds of ammo.

Concussion grenades, illumination pop-flares, and emergency signal flares were also taken along.

Uniforms—Vietnamese black pajamas and coral booties or sneakers.

Jack Tomlinson receiving his award for the design of the UDT emblem, “Freddy the Frog,” in 1953.

Ensign Chris Christie (foreground) and Chief Petty Officer (CPO) Jim Chittum securing explosive haversacks to beach obstacles on a beach at Fort Pierce, Florida, during a training exercise. [Photo: Chris Christie]

1st Platoon UDT-3, 1945. Hugh "Wild Bill" Mitchell (bottom row left), Mullie "Moe" Mulheren (third from right in top row). [Photo: Wild Bill Mitchell]

Tommy Marshall being decorated for the rescue of two young girls and their grandfather.

One year later, Tommy Marshall in Vietnam.

Swimmer delivery vehicle.

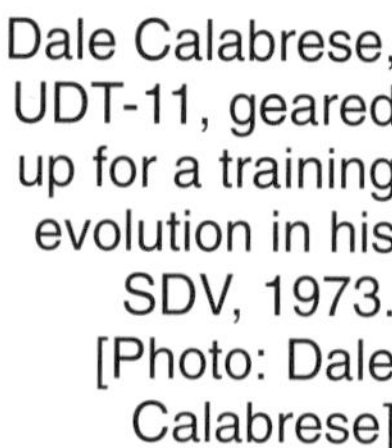

Dale Calabrese, UDT-11, geared up for a training evolution in his SDV, 1973. [Photo: Dale Calabrese]

Ambushed

At approximately 0045 hours, the LSSC took our five-man SEAL waterborne patrol, with a Vietnamese sampan in tow, into the Gulf of Thailand, under a crystal clear, warm night. The stars were shining brightly as we maneuvered several hundred yards from shore then headed northwest from the village of Rach Gia. We were operating on a hunch from Mr. Marsh, as we didn't really have any solid intelligence for our mission. Mr. Marsh had suspected that the Viet Cong were running weapons in our operating area. He wanted to interdict the gunrunners and put a damper on their activities. It wasn't unusual for SEAL teams to operate on a hunch and collect their own intel.

After traveling northwest for a while, we located a small concentration of various-size Vietnamese sampans, situated approximately one-half mile from our position. We knew from previous operations that the Vietnamese fished this area at night. They always used lanterns to mark their position and to see what they were doing while fishing.

The LSSC backed off on its throttles and came to a full stop. We loaded ourselves and our weapons and necessary equipment into the sampan. We did this very gingerly (Americans do not sit well in Vietnamese sampans), being careful not to capsize the sampan. To man the radio, Garces, a member of our platoon, stayed on the LSSC along with the MST (mobile support team) crew.

Mr. Marsh was kneeling in the bow, Mr. Lac directly behind him. I was in the middle, the radio in the bottom of the sampan in front of me. Ut was behind me, and Long was standing near the stern, steering our motorized sampan. It was normal for Vietnamese to stand while the sampan was underway.

We kept our weapons low in the boat, out of sight, until we got in close. Trying to look as normal as we could to the locals, so we could get in close and mingle without being compromised, we were disguised as Vietnamese fisherman, wearing black pajamas. The only exception was the camouflage paint on our faces. We proceeded quietly toward the concentration of Vietnamese fishing boats while the LSSC slipped away and headed back out to sea to wait for our extraction call.

We were soon in the middle of the fishing boats. We checked four different sampans and found nothing but old ladies and children, fishing or sleeping. The small lanterns on the sampans marked their location for other boat traffic in the area and made it easy for us to choose the next one to investigate. We continued quietly toward another small sampan that was to the far right of our position, maybe one hundred yards away.

As we proceeded in that direction, a large, fifteen-foot sampan, loaded with some type of cargo, came from out of nowhere and crossed our bow from left to right, no more than five yards away. None of us in our sampan had seen it coming because there was no light or lantern on board. Five Vietnamese occupants could be seen silhouetted on board the large sampan. After finding nothing in the other sampans, we had become too relaxed and almost ran right into them.

Mr. Marsh immediately came up to a crouch, raising his weapon, as Mr. Lac shouted, "*Laidai* (come here/stop)." The occupants on board the large sampan immediately opened fire on us with full-automatic weapons. Within five to seven seconds, Mr. Marsh fell back in the sampan, wounded severely in the hip; Mr. Lac was killed instantly with wounds to his head and neck; Ut was killed instantly with bullets to his head and lower abdomen, and Long was severely wounded in the upper thigh and shoulder. I immediately emptied the one hundred rounds from my Stoner, in one continuous burst, into the Viet Cong, spraying their sampan back and forth, from side to side, until it and the occupants disappeared beneath the water's surface.

Although I was in the center of our sampan with everyone else in front and behind me killed or seriously wounded, the only injury I sustained was a piece of shrapnel to my scalp from the front sight of my Stoner, which had been struck by the enemy fire. Except for the adrenalin that rushed through my body, the urine that filled my black pajamas, and the shrapnel in my head, I was fine—shaken up, but fine.

The sudden exchange of automatic-weapons fire had put

many holes in our sampan, and it was sinking fast. Mr. Marsh, in severe pain but still in command, grabbed Lac and inflated his UDT life jacket which, surprisingly, wasn't full of holes. He then inflated his own. I attempted to use our radio to contact the LSSC, but it was full of water from bullet holes, too. All it would do was gurgle and squawk, no call was made.

Long hung onto Ut's body while I put some wraps on his thigh with a bandage to try and stop the bleeding. We then both inflated our life jackets, and held Ut, along with the radio and our weapons. By this time, we all were floating in the dark, blood-filled water; our sampan was gone.

The shoreline was still a mile or two to the east. Sitting in the water about sixty to seventy yards away from us, as all this was taking place, was a larger Vietnamese fishing vessel. It began to slowly pull away from us. In my best Vietnamese, I screamed for them to come back, but they kept on going. We didn't know if they were Viet Cong or not. I pulled out my Smith and Wesson 9mm pistol and fired six rounds over their head, along with some stronger Vietnamese language. They decided to see things my way, and turned their boat around toward us.

As they pulled up next to us, we got into position to help each other on board. I kept my 9mm ready, just in case. Mr. Marsh and I loaded the dead and wounded Vietnamese onto the fishing boat, then I helped him get in. After I climbed in, I shot up two emergency signal flares to alert the LSSC and call it in. I then gave Mr. Marsh and Long a shot of morphine and checked over their wounds.

The LSSC finally arrived, recovered us from the fishing boat, and radioed for a helicopter to get the wounded to the hospital. We kept them as comfortable as possible until a lone navy Sea Wolf gunship showed up. It was the closest helo to our location, but we were in a small boat, and it couldn't land to pick up the wounded.

Mr. Marsh, being the athlete that he was, had us lift him up to where he could grab the skid of the helo as it hovered above us. While he held on tight, the helo pulled him up and away from the LSSC. If he'd fallen, he'd have been back in the water, but the crew on the helo finally pulled him inside. The rest of us, including Long, swiftly returned to Rach Soi, with the LSSC, to get to the hospital and for a debriefing.

The next morning, several SEALs, including myself, returned to the same location to search for the Viet Cong sampan and their weapons. We found none.

Follow Up

In early January 1971, I was transferred to Xray Platoon, which was located in Ben Tre. I was seriously wounded on February 28, 1971, during a Viet Cong B-40 rocket ambush while operating on board an LSSC. I lost my left leg, badly burning my right leg, and receiving an AK-47 round in my cheek.

I spent two months in the 3d Surgical Hospital in Binh Thuy, four months in the Philadelphia Naval Hospital, and was medically retired from the navy in July 1971.

I graduated from Syracuse University in 1976 and now reside in a small town in upstate New York with my wife of twenty-one years and my three children.

P. K. received the Silver Star and a Purple Heart for his heroic actions on 11 December 1970. He also received a Bronze Star and another Purple Heart on February 28, 1971.

Chapter Twenty-nine

John Bisallion
UDT-3 1944

Section Three—Guam

Section 3 was ordered in on the evening of 14 July to make the first reconnaissance with Section 1. At approximately 2100, the command was given to lower the boats. At the rail, all personnel boarded the boats, and the word was passed to lower away and prepare to shove off.

Two of Section 3's men who participated were MM1c Charley Greene, and SF1c W. O. Behne. The rest of us have often wondered what would have happened to Charlie if Behne hadn't been with him. It seems that his curiosity couldn't be satisfied as readily as the next man's. Greene kept crawling closer and closer to the beach until he was ordered not to go any farther. We all have our suspicions that he was intending to get close enough to do a little bartering.

Chief Chittum was also having himself a grand time. I guess he thought he was back in Peoria, because there he was, walking around with a white range marker that the Japs used to aim mortar fire. He was walking around, shouting how he had found it. It's a wonder that we didn't have the whole Jap army on our neck due to the racket he made.

One night, when the men were in their rubber boats signaling to the LCPRs to come in and pick them up, the signal light happened to be seen by the Japs on the beach. A heavy burst of machine-gun fire immediately followed. All hands at once put into practice the training they had received in underwater swimming. No one was hit.

On D minus four, the night the team conducted its first blasting job, things didn't turn out so well for Section 3. Sections 2 and 4 located their obstacles and disposed of them. Our rows of obstacles were supposed to be between theirs, but darned if we could find them.

On the second blasting job, we used two rubber boats loaded with powder. For some of us, it was the first time on the reef, which was, again, completely exposed. I'm certain that most of us will admit that we were pretty darned scared, but not too scared to do the job. Things were a lot tougher than anticipated. Between the emotional strain and the labor of running a hundred yards through a foot of water carrying forty pounds of tetrytol on our backs, it wasn't long before we were worn out. For the first time, we really appreciated the rugged physical training program given us prior to this operation. The obstacle course and grueling runs we had often griped about now were seen as blessings in disguise.

During his first day in, Bob Michaels had the unpleasant experience of swallowing some of the polluted water in the vicinity of the reef. It made him very sick, and it wasn't exactly safe to hang over the gunwale of the PR. We well remember the amount of wisecracks directed to old Doc Riegel about how he could no longer hide in the bilges of Number 3 PR.

Upon reaching the PR, a sea painter was secured to our rubber boat's gunwale, and the coxswain immediately proceeded at full speed to clear the range of the Jap's guns. ChCarp Charles Young had stood up in the rubber boat, and the sudden burst of speed caused him to lose his balance; he toppled into the drink. We went back and fished him out without much trouble.

It seems that all the excitement happened the first few days, and if I were to continue writing about the operation, I would merely be repeating myself. I would like to say though, that I have never met a finer group of fellows anywhere. And the men who take over our platoon after all of us seagoing civilians leave for home are going to have a heck of a job upholding the reputation established by the old men.

Chapter Thirty

Mike Ferrell
UDT-12 1967–1970

Location: Base Camp Tuyen Nhon, within sight of the Cambodian border, smack-dab in the middle of the Plain of Reeds.

Objective: Connect the Kinh Lagrange to the Kinh Gay by use of explosives, thereby connecting the Co Tay River to the Co Dong River (commonly known as "The Slingshot").

Purpose: Intelligence sources indicated that there are fifteen thousand NVA soldiers across the Cambodian border, who were infiltrating South Vietnam through the Plain of Reeds. The canal must be deep and wide enough such that a PBR (patrol boat, river) can navigate and patrol the waterway, thereby resisting and interdicting the infiltration of the enemy.

The Ditch

This job was magnificent. I was assigned to the evaluation team and stayed with the entire operation from start to the very end, when the last shot was blown. The evaluation team consisted of a few UDT men who were to examine and experiment with different types of explosives to determine which would work the best.

After experimenting, we determined that the most effective explosive was twenty-five-foot Mark-8 hose. Mark-8 hose (flexible linear demolition charge) has an explosive charge consisting of fifty pounds of 70/30 Composition A-3 and aluminum powder that is packed inside a two-inch rubberized hose. To insure detonation, there is a booster at each end of the twenty-five-foot lengths (seventy-six to seventy-nine grams of granulated TNT). Each length of Mark-8 hose weighs 150 pounds. Mark-8 hose can be coupled together to form longer lengths.

In order to create a channel large enough for a PBR to maneuver through, we would have to pyramid five lengths of hose together by laying three down and stacking the other two on top of them. Then the whole works was tied together and the whole 750-pound mass manually carried and dragged to the blasting site, where each hose was coupled together with one or two other pyramided lengths. The total weight of five lengths of Mark-8 hose tied together is 750 pounds, and it took a lot of men and work to get it into position. After one thousand feet was laid in position and coupled together, it was primed and wired to a hell box. Then, the most incredible "fire-in-the-hole" that I had ever seen, was created. All of this took place right in plain sight of Cambodia, where the NVA could witness it, too.

From start to finish, half of the men in UDT-12 were involved with the project at one time or another. When completed, the project had used 60 percent of the free world's Mark-8 hose, and we were literally sitting on it during the Tet of 1970. That could have been very interesting if it had been Tet of 1968 instead of Tet, 1970.

The local army firebases that were in the area wouldn't even let us into the security of their compounds. They were literally scared to death of us and all of our explosives. We had to move away from their bases and scratch around on the ground like a bunch of dogs and put up our own tents where we could play with our explosives.

This operation was the largest combat demolition job in naval history, and too many people were involved to give recognition to everyone, but it was a credit to all the UDT/SEAL team members who have ever walked the face of this earth. Men like Mr. Harvey, Chicken McNair, Andy Willingham, Oggie Osborne, Roger Charf, Kuntze, and Francis Ingalina, just to mention a few.

After the evaluation phase was completed, there was a tremendous amount of logistics to be worked out. So, having a little time off, a couple of teammates and myself went down to Binh Thuy to hang out with some SEAL friends for a while and "cruise."

Back at the Ditch

Back at the Kinh Gay, we began laying Mark-8 hose again. The usual procedure for us was to take a PBR, Boston whaler, or some other type of river craft to the blasting site from our camp. Everyday, we were able to take our boats through the new portion of the canal we were building. Even as far as we were inland from the South China Sea, the tides affected our area of operation. To avoid our boats' getting high centered in the mud, we had to work along with the high tides. Usually, I would drive a Boston whaler and lead or follow the PBR to our blast site. I preferred to follow the PBR because I could almost surf the wake of the larger boat with my whaler.

After arriving at the blast site, we would radio for a Chinook helo to pick up explosives at Tuyen Nhon and drop them off at the end of the last blast site. Most of the time, we were operating in hip-deep mud, with a foot or so of water flowing over the top. After trying several different techniques to "body" the explosive hose around, our preferred method was to secure the five lengths of explosive hose together, place them on air mattresses, move those into the mud, float them into position, couple the several lengths together, then drop the whole works in place into the canal. The canal that we were opening up with explosives was a little less than six miles long, which required approximately thirty one thousand-foot pyramided sections of Mark-8 hose. It was bustin' bone, weary, filthy work every day.

The operating area had many other hazards other than the NVA and Viet Cong. The "Reeds" were heavily infested with krait snakes and black cobras, not to mention the many different types of insects. Both snakes were very poisonous and if bitten, their poison would work on your nervous system. I didn't need that to happen to me, my nervous system was already being worked on just being in the area! The krait snakes were not very aggressive, and they had very small mouths, which was to our advantage. They had to nibble on you or bite you in an area where they could get a hold of your skin before they could get their fangs in.

The entire Plain of Reeds was saturated with listening devices that were monitored by three different firebases located at Tra Cu, Tuyen, and another one on the Bo Bo Canal. When disturbed, these listening devices would alert the firebase to enemy activity in that area. The particular firebase could then shift its artillery to the area covered by the specific device and pound it with high explosives. Sometimes they would pound different areas all night long. I never did get used to it and would be wakened up all the time by the loud noise.

At one place, the bodies of dead NVA soldiers were lying on the banks of the Lagrange Canal, but nobody gave a damn, and as far as I was concerned, they looked like great NVA to me.

One day, while we were at "The Ditch," loading the explosives, the tide suddenly started going out fast, and our PBR became stranded. Nobody wanted to be stranded out in the Reeds overnight. The executive officer in charge of UDT-12 had come to the blast site and just happened to be with us at the time. Francis Ingalina and I were told by the executive officer to take the Boston whaler out, and the rest of the men, including himself, would walk out with their weapons—just seven or eight M-16s and limited ammo. So, Francis and I jumped into our Boston whaler and hauled ass to the closest firebase, near the Bo Bo Canal. I went to their helo dispatcher and requested a couple of helos to extract our teammates from the Reeds.

The dispatcher agreed and rerouted two army slicks to the area.

After the choppers recovered the UDT men and brought them to the firebase, the executive officer approached me and asked whose idea it was for the helo extraction? I told him that it was mine.

He said, "Ferrell, we could have walked out of there with no problem; we had weapons."

I just said, "Yes, sir," and then he walked away. I guess I made him angry because I didn't ask for his permission; that didn't even occur to me at the time. Maybe he just wanted an adrenalin pump or he had been in the office too long. But I had an entire different movie going on in my head about the situation. It was getting dark, there were fifteen thousand NVA on the horizon, and the army's howitzers were being fired every night, which proved there was regular enemy movement in the area. I mean, after all, that's why we were building the channel. I wasn't worried about the PBR, it was heavily armed, and if we'd had to spend the night there, we could have set up a secure perimeter around it and dug in. But if they tried to walk out and ran into just one fully supplied platoon of NVA, the NVA would have gone through my *potnahs* like shit through a goose! Why take an unnecessary risk by walking out?

On this tour to Vietnam, most of the usual scare-you-to-death stuff didn't bother me as much. I was having too much fun blowing up the canal—especially when we took turns on the hell box, and I was in charge of detonating a one thousand-foot shot. When it came time to do that, we'd get a head count to make sure everyone was safe, look to the left, look to the right, make sure the area was clear, yell "Fire in the Hole," twist the handle of the hell box, and . . . *baawhoooooom*!

Damn what a rush! The sky would fill with mud and water, and it would all start to rain back down on us. Huge blobs of mud would start hitting the ground all around us, making loud *splats*. It seemed like it took forever for all the mud and water to return to the earth. Then, we would look at each other with a big grin and giggle like a bunch of six-year-olds at Christmas. We were all completely covered in mud from head to foot. Whoyaaa!

That was sure fun, but this is the best part. For the last shot on the canal, General Abrams and Admiral Zumwalt showed up with all their high-ranking officials and photographers and several high-ranking Vietnamese officers. The photographers were all over the place, taking pictures of everything. All of the visitors had freshly pressed uniforms, shined boots, and polished brass. They were all saying, "Yes, sir, yes, sir," and saluting each other. Then these two gooks get in the water, and we have to jump in with them. We had to uncouple the charge so the photographers can take pictures of the two gooks participating in the program. Boy were we pissed! Well, I forget who was in charge of the operation just then, but we had the muckety-mucks go downwind from the blast site sixty or seventy yards. We had detonated so many explosive charges throughout the operation that our electrical wire was constantly getting shorter with each blast. We were getting closer and closer to the charge each time we detonated one. As we were "fidgeting" with all the things that we needed to do before the blast, the photographers kept creeping closer and closer with General Abrams, Admiral Zumwalt, and all the others in tow. Then we were ready . . . all clear . . . (someone *had* mentioned earlier that they were gettin' awful close, but we'd told them once where to stand. Not *our* problem) . . . fire in the hole . . . *baawhoooooom*!

As the huge mud cloud started falling all around everyone, there was absolutely nowhere to run for cover. We knew exactly what was going to happen. All of us UDT men fell in the mud and started rolling around, laughing our asses off. I was really proud of the job we did there, and boy did we get a great send-off!

Chapter Thirty-one

Manuel Solano and Chester Tomassoni
Section Four UDT-3 1944

D Day at Guam

The first wave of Marines had already landed. A few of the more adventurous amtracks had been blown up by land mines. Consequently, it was necessary for several of us to go ashore and do a little mine disposal work. Section 4, working under Doc Barge, was given the dangerous assignment. So there we went, fifteen tired and proven men—but none too eager.

We were split into groups of five. Doc took charge of his crew, which consisted of Tommy, Mike, Whalen, the Mex, and N.G. Actually, this mine detail ended up as a souvenir hunt, but some work did get accomplished.

Whalen was the first to find an unexploded mortar shell. He nonchalantly put it into his pocket, figuring he could save his energy if he gathered a few at a time before swimming out to the edge of the reef and dropping them. Mike quickly talked him out of the idea. Whalen is that kind of guy.

Mike and the Mex discovered a jeep which had somehow or another fallen into sixteen feet of water. How it got there, we'll never know, but the Mex decided to go down and see if a mine had been the cause and also to check for other mines. There was one thing he had to be careful of though, the so-called "dumb Japs" had a peculiar habit of laying mines where they were least expected.

However, down went Mex, and up he came with a yell, "Hey, Mike, stick around, I think I've found something." Back down he went, and this time he came to the surface with a bottle of Four Roses! He passed it over to Mike, took a short breath, and went back down again, and came up with another bottle! This was the best salvage work accomplished by anyone in the entire Pacific.

We stayed ashore instead of going back out to the APD, and, the expression on the faces of those Marines when they saw our bottles . . . We finally opened one and offered a drink to the bulldozer operator. Before he finished, there was a line of at least twenty Marines.

This guy with the bulldozer was diggin' up the Jap pillboxes, and our chief pharmacist mate, Doc Riegel, was removing the valuables from the dead Japs as fast as they were uncovered. What a stench!

Upon returning to the ship, we found that our day's haul included twenty-five mortars, four tank mines, several unexploded bombs, and, oh yes, two quarts of Stateside whiskey. Not a bad day.

During our full week of postassault work, we did any job the beachmaster or Marine engineers could find for us. Here is a brief list:

1. Selected and marked seven beaching places for LSTs;
2. Located and removed five antiboat mines from Green and Red-2 beaches;
3. Surveyed and marked Tepungan and Piti channels;
4. Removed the stern of a four hundred-foot Japanese freighter blocking the harbor outlet to Piti Channel;
5. Removed, by blasting, a total of eight barges and sampans blocking Piti Channel;
6. Attempted to enlarge the turning basin at the causeway in Tepungan Channel;
7. Blasted a two hundred-foot-wide unloading slot in the

reef at Dadi Beach, using sixteen thousand pounds of tetrytol.

This eight-ton shot was an opportunity to use the last of our powder. On the afternoon of 28 July, we were released by CTF 53 and set out for Maui. We could all look back and feel well satisfied that we had earned our spurs as a team at Guam.

Chapter Thirty-two

Dale Calabrese

UDT-11 1970–1975

Triton Island

Triton Island is not your typical desert island. In fact, it was only a coral reef, three feet above sea level, one-half mile wide, and one mile long. It is located off the coast of Vietnam, and its ownership is claimed by North Vietnam, North Korea, South Korea, USSR, China, and maybe one or two other countries. The only inhabitants were birds and giant sea turtles.

My UDT platoon, under the leadership of Lieutenant junior grade Bean, was attached to the USS *Mount Vernon* (LSD-39). The *Mount Vernon* is designated as a landing ship, dock (LSD) and is capable of taking on helicopters on its stern helo pad. It has a stern gate, which can be lowered to partly fill the hull with water so that small boats and amphibious watercraft can enter or exit the ship. for storage, repairs, or transport.

While aboard the *Mount Vernon*, our platoon kept busy by keeping our PT boat in shape. The PT boat was used for UDT operations and finding remote beaches for our platoon to drink San Miguel beer.

Riding on a ship for months can become very boring if you don't stay busy. Not being part of the regular ship's crew, we had no duties or watches to stand. As UDT personnel, we could be activated at any time to perform any type of job from clearing a ship's screws of debris to reconning a hostile beach. For this reason, we were always on standby. We had to be very flexible and ready to go anywhere, anytime.

At times, it seemed like the toughest job we had to perform was morning PT (physical training). It was also mandatory for all UDT personnel to have suntans. While operating in a tropical environment, getting a sunburn could put you out of business, jeopardizing a mission. For that reason, while aboard ship, we played volley ball on the helo deck and laid around on lounge chairs in the "sun conditioning" position while the ship's crew went on with its normal duties. Proper sun conditioning had to be performed in UDT swim trunks.

At times, sun conditioning seemed to cause problems with the ship's crew. The men had the, why-should-they-be-allowed-to-lie-around-in-swim-trunks-all-day-while-I-have-to-work-in-these-hot-dungarees syndrome. The ship's crew complained so much that our officer had to report to the ship's captain and explain to him the necessity and requirement of UDT's sun conditioning.

Once, while cruising with a convoy around the West Pacific, we were caught in the middle of a typhoon. The swells in the ocean were over thirty feet high. The excitement sure broke the monotony of our regular daily routine aboard the ship. The USS *Denver* (LPD-9) was cruising behind us. When our ship dropped into the trough of a wave, the *Denver* disappeared from sight. At the time, the *Mount Vernon* was experiencing problems and listing to the starboard so badly that we could almost touch the water.

During the typhoon, a merchant ship transporting ammunition from Vietnam ran aground right in the middle of Triton Island; the *Mount Vernon* was called upon to move to that location to unload the munitions. We arrived on site to find the stranded ship high and dry on the island. By the looks of it, a thirty-foot wave must have picked it up and set it down on top of the island. Our platoon was going to get an opportunity to utilize our UDT/SEAL capabilities.

Because of the way the munitions ship was situated, there was no way to get a LCU (landing craft, utility) alongside for the off-loading to take place. Our platoon was going to blow a channel thirty feet wide by six feet deep through the coral reef, large enough to maneuver an LCU in alongside the munitions ship so that the off-loading of its cargo could take place.

Our job became very interesting, not only to us, but to the ship's crew, which soon understood why sun conditioning was so important. Our platoon was shuttled by helicopter from the *Mount Vernon* to the island. The entire first day was spent reconning the situation. This involved scavenging the ship for everything from hatch covers to brass. There was not a lot to see on the island, except for a lot of unusual sea shells.

Once the recon was completed, our platoon started blowing the channel through the coral. The water near the stern of the ship was only a couple of feet deep at high tide. The shallow water extended forty yards behind the stern of the ship, where the reef dropped straight off into the ocean. We could stand on the edge of the reef and drop a coin in front of us and watch it disappear into crystal clear water of the abyss.

Our operation involved two UDT men being shuttled by helo back and forth from the *Mount Vernon* to Triton Island with the necessary explosives, MK-8 Mod-2 hose, or flexible linear demolition charge. As the careful reader already knows, Mark-8 hose is a twenty-five-foot length of two-inch diameter rubber hose (resembling a fire hose), with a main charge of fifty pounds of 70/30 composition A-3 and aluminum powder. The charge contains an Mk-8 Mod-0 booster in the female end, and an Mk-12 Mod-0 booster in the male end. Each booster contains seventy-six to seventy-nine grams of granulated TNT. On the female end of the explosive charge, the Mk-8 Mod-0 booster contains an activator well for installation of a blasting cap.

The Mk-8 Mod-0 hose may be used for clearing channels through sandbars and coral reefs. It can also be coupled together by connecting the male and female ends to create one continuous explosive hose. It can be wrapped around irregularly shaped obstacles on the surface or underwater, and it can be woven together, forming a mat, which can be placed over an obstacle. Several hoses are tied side by side to create a larger explosive charge. Mk-8 Mod-0 hoses come packed in lengths of three, a total weight of 450 pounds.

Our platoon worked for several days, laying and snaking the Mk-8 hose on top of the coral, from the stern of the munitions ship out to the open sea. We wanted to detonate all the explosive at one time because after the explosion, the water would be too murky for several hours to assess our accomplishments or to lay more explosives to further open the new channel.

After securing the entire explosive operation, Mr. Bean decided we were ready to detonate. We packed up all the gear that was spread around the munitions ship and Triton Island, and the entire platoon was shuttled by helo back out to the waiting *Mount Vernon.*

For the last week, the ship's crew watched and wondered about our operation as the platoon was shuttled back and forth. They lined up along the ship's rails every time the helo came or left again. They could not see anything of our operation on the island because the *Mount Vernon* was anchored over a mile offshore. Only the silhouette of the munitions ship could be made out.

The detonation of explosives was scheduled to go about supper time. Looking around the *Mount Vernon*, you would think we were entering San Diego Bay after being out to sea for nine months. It looked like the entire ship's crew was on deck to witness our platoon's explosion.

Mr. Bean had the honor of detonating our week's work. Even though we were over a mile away, he yelled, "Fire in the hole," and we watched as water and coral shot straight up into the blue sky, followed, a couple of seconds later, by the sound of the explosion.

The next morning, our platoon took its last helo ride back to Triton Island to inspect the new canal. The Mk-8 hose had performed perfectly—the canal could not have been any better if a sculptor had carved it out. It was wide, deep, and long enough for an LCU to maneuver right up to the munitions ship to off-load its cargo. With another UDT job perfectly executed, the *Mount Vernon* sailed back to Subic Bay, Philippines.

Chapter Thirty-three

Manuel Solano
UDT-3 1944

Postassault Work on the *Tokyo Maru*

D day plus 2, Mr. Gordon, Cochrane, Pony Boy, Donohue, Mex, and Tommy went out to inspect the ship and to estimate the amount of tetrytol which would be needed. The inspection showed that the fantail was nearest shore and about twenty-five feet below the surface, while the rest of the ship was in deeper water. We figured that it would take about two tons of explosives, so when we returned later to do the blasting after the inspection, we brought back four tons to do the job.

First, we stripped the ship of all possible souvenirs, then we proceeded to lay the charges. We laid about half a ton of tetrytol around the deck beneath the gun turret on the fantail, then we systematically (?) threw or dropped a few packs down her hold. We then laid packs of explosives in a line from bow to stern on her deck, with one pack every two feet. We also systematically dropped, or laid, a half a ton right down her smoke stack.

After the powder had been laid, we proceeded up the channel a safe distance, about a hundred yards away. Then it was "Fire in the hole," and away she went. The gun mount went up out of sight, and it had been under twenty-five feet of water!

The next day, we inspected our job and found that we had split that ship right in two, lengthwise. The explosion had also flattened the ship like a discarded beer can. It was a perfect job so we went on to hunt for more souvenirs.

Chapter Thirty-four

Pierre Remillard
UDT-11 1967–1971

This is a true story, like all the stories in this book, about one of our teammates as seen through the eyes of Pierre Andre Remillard. Pierre and Tommy were members of Underwater Demolition Team 11 (UDT-11) and both men are two-tour veterans of the Vietnam War.

Tommy Marshall
A Frogman Through and Through

The Tommy Marshall story is a real story, about a real hero. There were a lot of heros in the teams, right? There were a lot of men who did great things, under the worst possible conditions, under a lot of stress. But the Tommy Marshall story is about an honest-to-goodness real situation that didn't have anything to do with the war—didn't have anything to do with Vietnam. It was one of the most heroic things that anybody I ever knew in the teams did in a real spontaneous heroic way, because nothing was planned or set up. It was something that happened in Tom's life, and mine, and definitely in all the peoples' lives who were there at the time. In fact, it was absolutely a pure miracle for everybody involved. Tommy Marshall was a Frogman through and through, but that day . . . he was an angel.

The first time I saw Tom was in 1967 at the UDT/SEAL compound at the naval amphibious base on the Silver Strand, just south of Coronado, California. He had just graduated from UDT/SEAL training, Class 43, and being assigned to UDT-11, had crossed the highway to the main part of the base.

Tommy looked like all the rest of the new guys, brand-new starched greens, new shiny boots, fresh short haircut, and no UDT/SEAL issue Rolex watch, but there were things that were different about Tom. For one thing, he was about six feet three, had a big North Carolina kid-style grin, freckleless face, and red hair. Tommy Marshall was a 20-year-old, 215-pound event waiting to happen.

Tom had grown up in North Carolina, where he had spent most of his childhood days in the water, hanging on to a surfboard and dreaming about the California waves. He was a natural athlete and an extremely strong swimmer and felt very much at ease in the water. He had a muscular build, with huge shoulders, big arms, and lats that looked like they were carved out of granite. Time and time again, I watched Tom and his surfboard power through the biggest waves that the Pacific Ocean could lay down on the Silver Strand. He would get that big ol' grin on his face after catching a wave, like the big kid that he was, and turn his surfboard back out toward sea, and do it again and again. It seemed like all Tommy ever wanted to do was be in the California sunshine and the surf.

Tom's responsibility with UDT-11 became centered around the SDV (swimmer delivery vehicle) program, operating the two-man submarines. One of my other best friends, Albert "The Owl" Arnold, was also in the SDV Program. Tommy and The Owl's friendship started during our first tour to Vietnam. After that tour, Tommy and The Owl spent most of their nights thoroughly enjoying themselves while maneuvering their SDV around San Diego Bay on training exercises.

Tom loved the camaraderie of the teams. We all became family in those few formative months that we all spent together, preparing ourselves for the inevitable task that lay before us, the next trip to the ever-lovin' fuckin' Nam.

Everybody had gone through the same training, and that right of passage—plus a combat tour to Vietnam—developed a common bond among us teammates. This is where a man had to "put up or shut up," and Tommy had "put up" time and time again. He went on every combat mission that was assigned to our team and always kept his cool under fire.

There were many other things which naturally happened between most of us that strengthened individual relationships. One of these things was surely the Tradewinds, the Frogman bar in Coronado. It was a Frogman bar and nothing else. The bartenders were in the teams or had been in the teams; all the patrons were in the teams or had been in the teams. Absolutely *no* blackshoe fleet-sailors were allowed, and no civilians came to the Tradewinds, except for women. There were always a few of them hanging around watching the show.

Tommy loved the Tradewinds and all his Frog Brothers who drank an endless supply of beer. It was a tradition at the Tradewinds that money was always set aside so that if a man was killed in combat, there would be a keg or two of beer for his teammates. Friday nights also saw a free keg of beer for the Frogs.

Tom was different; he never drank alcohol. He had told me a story one time about his father and alcohol. I can't remember it all, but it was a classic case, and Tom never needed to drink.

Basically, Tommy was always in great shape, ready for anything that could take place, and he had already proved that in Vietnam. He was definitely in control, physically and mentally, which is what this story is all about.

Now on occasion, Tom would be involved in the raucous horseplay, which was not uncommon in the Tradewinds because more beer was poured there over peoples' heads than in their mouths. I believe that Tom absorbed enough beer through his clothes and skin that I'm sure he had to feel some kick from the alcohol.

After our first tour in the Nam, Tommy Marshall had become a big part of the people that I hung around with. We were all seasoned Frogmen with a combat tour behind us. We were no longer separated by the length of our hair, our rank, or the number of our training class—the things that had separated us in the past. There was a group of about ten of us who became real close friends. We all lived together on the beach or next door to each other on the beach. Within our group we had total support. This group consisted of Steve Miller, Jay Posselt, The Owl, Mike "The Brose" Ambrose, Greg "Eggplant" Moore, Tommy Marshall, myself, and a few others.

Sometime during this period of Stateside duty, I received a phone call from my brother informing me that our mother had died. So I took off on emergency leave and went home to the funeral. Of course, all my teammates felt bad for me for what had happened.

While I was at home on leave, a float trip was organized for the Colorado River to perform some UDT training exercises. Knowing that I would like to go along and needed some time to occupy my mind after what I had just gone through, my teammates signed me up for the float trip.

When I returned from leave, my name was on the float list, along with Lt. (jg) Edward Brown, Lt. (jg) Michael Shannon McCreary, SN Robert Anderson, QM2 Danny Batchelor, GMG3 Gerald Boward, AN Tommy Bracken, AN Craig Danielson, BUR3 Lance "Call Me Lance" Green, HM1 Thomas Holmes, GMG3 Tommy Marshall, SN Michael McAtamney, FN Ronald McReynolds, AME3 Stephen "Moth"

Miller, SFP3 Dennis "Rud" Rutherford, ADJ3 Joseph "Pancho Mango" Via, and MM1 Gary Weller.

Our group mustered in the UDT compound at 0600 hours on 20 May 1969. We packed all our gear onto a bus that shuttled us to the North Island Naval Air Station. From there, we loaded our gear aboard a C-47, which flew us over the Colorado River, near the town of Needles, California. The first function of the trip was to insert by parachute into our starting point near the river. This meant jumping with full gear, three IBSs (inflatable boat, small), and enough equipment to sustain us for a nine-day float down the river. Our objective was to float down the river from the starting point, paddle through Lake Havasu, portage Parker Dam, and continue as far as we could downstream during that time period.

Steve Miller and I were designated as the two wind dummies, the first two jumpers out of the plane, to judge the wind conditions so the rest of our group could see where we landed before they jumped. That way, the plane, could make the necessary corrections before the rest of our team jumped, making sure all our gear would land close to the anticipated landing zone and not get blown off course.

The jump went fine, and except for a few hangovers from too much drinking the night before, nobody was the worse for the wear. Once everyone was on the ground, we were assigned boat crews. I was assigned to a boat crew with Steve "Moth" Miller, Jay "Bird" Posselt, The Owl, Tommy Bracken, Lance Green, Tommy Marshall, and our officer, Shannon McCreary.

We shoved off in the early afternoon, after inflating the IBSs and loading all our gear. We had plenty of wine and beer to get us to Lake Havasu, which we towed behind our IBSs in the cool water. We spent the first few nights on the river and floating through Lake Havasu. By the end of the seventh day, we were at the upper side of Parker Dam.

We portaged the IBSs and all our gear around the very large concrete obstacle in the river and spent the night drinking and playing pool at a riverside hot spot called Charlie's Bar. It was located not too far downstream from the dam. Charlie's Bar was a great party spot on the river. There were lots of V-8 ski boats, lots of girls, and three great pool tables, which allowed us to drink beer for free due to fact that I had a hot stick and more or less controlled the game from the minute we arrived.

The morning of the twenty-eighth, everyone was pretty hung over, except for Tommy Marshall. He wasn't allowed to pour beer on himself or anybody else the night before. About 1000 hours, we launched our boats back into the river and continued on our journey. By noon, we were about three miles south of Parker Dam. We were all as lazy as the river, which had widened considerably. Everyone was in the kicked-back-rest mode, enjoying the scenery, and telling a few lies about the night before.

As we floated, I looked up and noticed an older motor home parked on the river bank. Our position was approximately one hundred yards upstream a little and to the center of the river.

The water was smooth as glass, and we were all lazily floating with the current as we watched an older couple, their daughter, and two small girls, setting up a picnic near the river's edge. It was a real scene, almost like slow motion. The river current moved our rubber boats slowly along, and none of us had much energy because of the postalcoholic state we were in. Time seemed to stand still.

As we continued drifting, we watched the grandpa and two little girls walk over to the edge of the river. At this point, we were just about straight out from their position on the riverbank, still a good fifty to seventy yards from shore. As we continued watching them, we saw the two girls go down the bank, holding each other's hand. Then one of them fell into the water. All of a sudden, the girl in the water went under, pulling her sister with her. They both started thrashing about near the surface as the river current pulled them farther from shore. The grandmother and mother of the girls ran to the river bank and began screaming and going hysterical. The grandpa, standing right there, immediately jumped into the water after them and grabbed one of the thrashing girls. But the weight of his wet clothes along with that of the panicking girls, caused him to go under. He didn't return to the surface.

Now it took about thirty seconds for all this to happen right before our eyes as we floated downstream below them. Time seemed to be standing still as we waited for the elderly man to surface. But he didn't come up. We began to realize that some real trouble was brewing there, so a couple of men from our IBS dived into the water and started swimming back up stream.

Al "The Owl" Arnold was one of the first swimmers. While in Vietnam, The Owl had made a reputation as a very fast and strong swimmer. He was also known as "The Night Train" for the night mission that he and Tommy had swam on in Vietnam. But because of the strong river current, the men who dived out of the IBS were unable to get anywhere close to the little girls and their grandpa.

Then, Tommy Marshall does a flat-out speed dive out of the IBS and starts swimming toward shore instead of upstream. The current was pulling him downstream also, but he was swimming just as fast as his big surfer arms could pull him. It looked like he was swimming through twelve-foot surf on the Silver Strand as he took the Colorado River in giant chunks with every stroke of his mighty arms. Meanwhile, as Tommy swam toward the beach, the other swimmers returned to the IBS and pulled themselves back in. We all proceeded toward shore with the IBSs as fast as we could paddle. Tommy finally reached the riverbank, but he was about seventy yards below where the two little girls and their grandpa had entered the water.

Tommy ran up the rocky beach toward the area where the little girls are panicking, thrashing on the surface. The mother of the little girls and their grandmother were standing, hysterical, on the riverbank where the three had entered the water. They were really losing it! But Tommy was running flat-out over the rocks toward them as we yelled encouragement; he was the only chance of survival for the three of them. At a certain point on the beach, where I thought the submerged grandpa might have drifted to, I yelled, "Now Tommy!"

Tommy reentered the murky green water, with absolutely no regard for his own safety. He went under, and didn't come up, right? Now, we're lookin' and waiting for Tommy; he's disappeared, too. After what seems a *long* time, he finally came to the surface. He had the unconscious grandpa by the nape of his neck and one of the little girls under his arm. As he swam toward the beach pulling the two behind him, the other little girl frantically grabbed onto Tommy's shoulder for support. Tommy was unable to hold all three of them up and swim at the same time, so he submerged again and walked on the bottom through the river current toward shore, holding all three of them on the surface above him. The little girls held onto each other as Tommy worked his way toward shore.

Finally, the rest of us reached the shore with the IBS and ran as fast as we could back up the rocky beach to help Tommy. He had now worked his way to about waist deep and was close to shore. He was very tired, just the swim and the run up the beach had worn him out. The mother and grandmother were still absolutely hysterical as members of our boat crew gave artificial respiration to the grandpa and finally got him breathing again.

It was a miracle, and nothing else, that we were floating by at that particular moment with Tommy Marshall in our group. The mother and grandmother were still out of it. The two little girls were scared, but just fine. Their grandpa was very weak, but very much alive. Tommy Marshall was a friggin' hero to everyone who was there. He was the angel that they needed, but Tommy was "aw-shucksin'" it, like it was nothing. He didn't want all the attention.

Later on, the people involved wanted to invite Tom to their hometown for a parade to recognize him for what he had done, but Tom didn't want to go. He received the Navy and Marine Corps Medal, for heroism, from Adm. John J. Hyland, commander in chief U.S. Pacific Fleet, for the president of the United States.

Tommy Marshall is a very unique man, not only to his teammates, but to hundreds of other people whose lives he has touched in some way or another. As a lifeguard at La Jolla, California, he saved many people who had gotten into trouble in the water. But this particular incident that I witnessed on the Colorado River was an inspiration to me, one I'll never forget as long as I live. I love Tommy Marshall for that, not only because he was an honest-to-goodness, real navy Frogman, but because he is an honest-to-goodness hero! He still hangs out in the California sunshine, with the same ol' North Carolina grin on his face, waiting for the wave of the day.

Chapter Thirty-five

Frank Lahr
UDT-3 1944

Leyte Operation

We arrived at Maui 10 August and went on a ten-day inter-island leave (which was counted as annual leave!). We scarcely had time to tell our leave stories to one another when we again packed our seabags and climbed aboard another APD. Two officers and six men left the team at this time. As our complement was high,' the officers were not replaced, but we did add eight new men to the team. We expected to go to Yap, in the Carolines. En route to the Marshall Islands, however, orders were changed. Yap was to be passed, and the liberation of the Philippines was to commence at a much earlier date than heretofore hoped for.

Our floating target for this trip was the USS *Talbot*, another vulnerable four-stacker converted to a transport. One good point of this ship was the fact that it lacked the roaches of the *Dent* and *Dickerson.* We slept alone in our bunks for a change and didn't have to shake out our clothes before wearing them each morning.

The *Talbot* had her faults however, and one of the worst was running into battleships at night. Luckily, she gave this sport up after coming out second best with the *Pennsylvania* at Saipan. As on other APDs, there was fresh water to drink, but damn little left over. The ship headed for rain clouds whenever they were anywhere near our course, and we would stand out on the weather decks, washing ourselves down. Usually, there would be just enough rain to wet us down. We would soap up and then out would come the sun. Upon occasion, this was just a wee bit aggravating.

On this trip, we crossed the equator again but this time, there were only a few pollywogs. We saw to it that they weren't slighted in any of the ceremonies of the "Ancient Order of the Deep."

We reached Manus in the Admiralty Islands 5 October and spent a week there. It was an excellent opportunity for us to get in shape and do a lot of swimming. There was a long, flat reef at Manus, with beautiful coral formations at its edge. The water was amazingly clear, and with our glasses on, we could see a hundred feet in any direction. We worked harder at collecting shells and cat-eyes than we ever did at PT. Each morning, we broke out the rubber boats and paddled (unless we could get one of the "never-fail" outboard motors to working) to the reef. We wore heavy shoes to avoid getting cut by the coral. Sand shoes did not hold up well enough.

The USS *Talbot*, UDT-3 aboard, sortied from Seeadler Harbor, Manus Island, Admiralty Islands on 12 October 1944, in company with bombardment, fire support, and associated groups (T.G. 77.2). When we left Manus, we stored our seashells in cans of sand at various locations about the ship. About two days out, the *Talbot* smelled like a garbage scow. Louis Gordon had hidden his collection, the largest of all (Louie never went at anything halfheartedly), somewhere near the section of bilges reserved for the troop officers. When the shells' occupants began to decompose, Louie made several enemies till, one night, someone played the hero by deep-sixin' them.

The voyage to Leyte was marked by a storm on 15 October, which abated sufficiently to permit fueling from the USS *Mis-*

sissippi on the sixteenth. During the night of 16–17 October, the wind increased to gale force and necessitated slowing from sixteen to twelve knots. The storm delayed sweeping operations in Leyte Gulf, and Group Able of the fire support unit and the APDs were delayed four hours in entering Leyte Gulf. We finally arrived off the southern beaches of Leyte at 1400, 18 October 1944 (D-2).

Without benefit of a thoroughly planned bombardment, operations began immediately. It was planned to have the village of Dulag burned by air bombing, and to bombard the beaches and adjacent areas for two hours preceding Roger hour (the time the LCPRs leave the APD with UDT aboard). But prior to the action, it was evident that the bad weather had prevented the air bombing of Dulag and that the scheduled period of preliminary bombardment would be reduced to one hour.

Close-in-support destroyers were to be in position thirty minutes prior to Roger hour to begin their close support and counterbattery fire as necessary. The whole reconnaissance was planned to last no longer that ninety minutes.

At 1512, all boats were in the water. The *Talbot* was approximately twenty-four hundred yards offshore. Sections 1 and 3 were to make a swimming reconnaissance of Yellow 1 and Yellow 2 beaches, respectively. Sections 2 and 4 were to stand by and assist as needed. The commanding officer was in LCPR number 4, and the executive officer was aboard the APD.

This is a description of the technique and procedure followed by the 1st Section. However, it applies equally as well to the method followed by the 3d Section, which had a similar mission on another five-hundred-yard beach.

The plan as designed and carried out called for evasive tactics on the part of the LCPR coxswain from one thousand yards to five hundred yards, at which distance the six swimmers were dropped off. At varying speeds, LCPRs followed zigzag courses with legs of fifty to one hundred yards at angles of 135 and 45 degrees to the beach. The zigzagging would make it less obvious when the boat ran parallel to the shoreline while dropping off the swimmers, and it was also intended to confuse enemy observers as to the course of the boat, lessening the chance of its being hit by direct shellfire.

All except the six swimmers wore full greens, helmets, swim shoes, and uninflated life belts. Kapok life jackets were recommended for the men remaining in the boat as they offered excellent protection against shrapnel. Since there was no reef edge to reconnoiter, six swimmers were considered sufficient, and with deep water known to exist close to shore, the only possible place the Japs could have planted mines or obstacles was right on the beach itself. The plan called for three pairs of swimmers to swim directly into the flanks and center of the beach, diving to find the two-fathom line on the way in.

The six swimmers wore swim trunks, swim shoes, uninflated life belts. Each carried a .38 revolver in a shoulder holster. Until they went over the side of the PR, the swimmers wore helmets. Swim fins were not available to our team at that time. Face masks were not worn as the water inside of seven hundred yards was very muddy due to the recent storm and the fact that the mouth of a river was on the flank of the beach. Wearing them would have been a risk with no compensating advantages.

The swimmers also carried several lengths of Primacord, each three feet long, with a balsa-wood float attached. The purpose of these was for tying about the horns of any mines encountered. This, of course, was before the development of chemical-pencil mine clips. The balsa-wood floats would mark the locations of mines and make it a quick and simple process to run a trunk line of Primacord to them.

On the way into the beach with the LCPR, only the boat officer, lookout man (a man who could judge the depth of the water visually), and the coxswain were visible above the gunwales. At five hundred yards off the northern or right flank of Yellow 1 Beach, the boat officer gave the word for the swimmers to stand by. The PR turned so as to run south, parallel to the beach. At the same time, the first pair of swimmers—myself and one enlisted man—rolled, not jumped, over the seaward side of the PR. We did this just forward of the engine-box housing, showing as low a silhouette as possible.

We had debated the danger of being caught in the screw while going close over the side of the boat, which was proceeding at full speed. As it turned out, we got tossed about a bit, but there was no danger. Two other swimmers, one a chief petty officer, were dropped opposite the approximate center of the beach and the third pair, the section leader and an enlisted man, were dropped opposite the left flank of the beach. The LCPR retired to one thousand yards offshore, after dropping all swimmers, and zigzagged back and forth, attempting to draw fire and keep the enemy from concentrating on the swimmers.

The reconnaissance was conducted like this. The officer in the first swim pair, and the designated man in the other two swim pairs, swam ahead about fifteen yards while his partner remained behind and off to one side. When the lead man touched bottom, which turned out to be less than twenty-five yards from the shoreline, he moved in a ways and started zigzagging parallel to the shore, feeling with his arms and legs for mines and other obstacles. The rear man had the mission of maintaining a strict lookout up and down the beach for any enemy personnel.

The first two swimmers were to go to their left along the shoreline, while the second and third pair were to move to their right, always maintaining at least a fifteen-yard interval between men to prevent offering a concentrated target to the enemy. They were to move in this manner until they all joined together. Then, after the reconnaissance, all the swimmers were to swim seaward four hundred yards, line up parallel to the beach, twenty-five yards apart from each other, and be picked up by the LCPR.

The chief petty officer in charge of the middle pair of swimmers became frightened by the heavy volume of small-arms fire from the enemy approximately one hundred yards offshore and ordered his swim partner to turn about and return to sea with him—the only instance in the history of UDT-3 where a man didn't carry out an assignment because of fear. Needless to say, this man was dropped from the team as soon as possible. The other four swimmers proceeded on into the flanks and, in fact, did not notice the center pair swim out.

Underwater, the muddy water limited visibility to less than a foot, and considerable debris, including many coconuts, was floating close to shore. This was an advantage as it made the heads of the swimmers less conspicuous. Otherwise, a Jap with a couple of stones and a poor throwing arm could have gotten us!

Our .38s were more of a morale booster than offensive weapons. We could not spot any of the enemy, although we could hear the *ping* of the bullets and see the splashes where they hit the water. A small sand dune on the shore may have prevented the enemy from bringing accurate fire to bear on us as we were close in to shore. We hoped that when the swimmers rolled into the water, they were unnoticed, but they were spotted when they were about halfway to the beach, and drew considerable enemy fire. The only living thing observed was a scrawny dog that ran up and down the beach, barking at us.

The left flank swim pair, though the last ones dropped from the PR, had covered 350 yards of the 500-yard beach when they reached the first pair, who had made little headway against a strong drift. After these four swimmers joined, they swam out to sea. They had figured that the other pair had already swam out.

After reaching a safe distance from shore, the swimmers compared results and agreed that nothing was found in the way of obstacles and mines. The boat officer brought the LCPR inside of four hundred yards to pick up the swimmers, drawing considerable enemy fire as he did so. While in the water swimming out to sea, the swimmers felt quite secure. It would have been much safer to hold off bringing the boat in and let the swimmers go out as far as one thousand yards.

The rubber-boat pickup technique had not yet been developed, so as the boat came alongside, the swimmers had to grab ahold of a ladder on the seaward side of the boat and climb aboard. This method is not satisfactory as it necessitates slowing down the LCPR. The men in the PR reported that quite a lot of enemy mortar and machine-gun fire was drawn due to the ineffectiveness of our bombardment.

No mines or man-made obstacles were discovered by any of the swimmers. The one-and two-fathom lines were determined, and the beach adjudged ideal for an amphibious assault and the beaching of LSTs. The surf was negligible. No casualties were suffered by UDT-3, though UDT-4, operating right next to us, was shot up and lost one of its LCPRs.

From the time of leaving the APD until returning to the ship, the entire operation consumed eighty-two minutes. Reports from each platoon leader were turned over to the commanding officer, who then made an oral report to the group commander. Two days later, MacArthur would say "I have returned."

Conclusion

This brief reconnaissance completed the work of UDT-3 at Leyte, and as it developed, it was the last work we would do under enemy fire. There was no call for any work on D-1 or on D day, 20 October 1944. On D+1, UDT-3 was called upon by the group beachmaster to survey the sandbar at the mouth of the Dulag River to determine the feasibility of blasting the bar. The project was considered impractical, and no demolition work was done. UDT-3 was then released, and the *Talbot* ordered to proceed to Manus.

During our five-day period at Leyte, no casualties were suffered, and no actual demolition was done. The *Talbot* was involved in four antiaircraft actions against single Jap Aircraft, which the gunners didn't get, and one of our TBFs which they did get, mistaking it for a Val because its wheels were down. Yes, someone got hell for this!

The night of 21–22 October 1944, the *Talbot* took screening station, and we sortied from Leyte Gulf. The *Talbot* reached Manus on 27 October, and on 1 November, UDT-3 was transferred to the USS *President Hayes.* On 11 November we departed for the Hawaiian Islands.

Crew Members of Section One
UDT-3 Leyte Operation
October 18, 1944

Swimmers

Lahr, Lieutenant Williamson	Right flank
Moore, Chief gunner's mate Holmes	Center
Jacobson, Ensign Hart	Left flank

Boat Crew

Frazier, Warrant officer	Boat officer
Brady, Warrant officer	Coxswain
Foster, Warrant officer	Deck and lead line
Purvis, Warrant officer	Machine gun
Maher, Warrant officer	Machine gun
Swain, Warrant officer	First aid
Murphy, Warrant officer	G10
Sims, Warrant officer	536 (hand-held radio)
Mitchell, Warrant officer	Carbine
Mulheren, Warrant officer	Standby machine gun

Chapter Thirty-six

Pat Carter

SEAL Team 1 1970–1972

The Dirty Thirty

I joined the navy from Seattle, Washington, right after high school, on August 19, 1969. I joined on the buddy system with a friend named Steve Nelson. I wanted to go into the submarines like my brother Mike, who was a year older than I and already in the navy.

During boot camp in San Diego, Steve and I met Randy Kaiser, another member of our boot camp company, and we all became close friends. One day, our company and another company from the same barracks complex had marched across the naval training center and were standing in front of a building. Our company commander (CO) and the CO of the other company came out of the building and yelled, "Attench-ut." After everyone snapped to, I moved just a little bit, and the CO noticed me, so he had me spend the rest of the day with the other CO's company. Both companies were about to enter the building to watch a film, but we didn't know what it was about.

It turned out that UDT/SEAL instructors had come over from the naval amphibious base and were showing a recruiting film. They were also giving a screening test the next day in Coronado to anyone who wished to volunteer for UDT/SEAL training. The test would consist of timed runs and swims and some demanding physical exercises. It looked like something fun to do, and besides, Randy and I wanted to get away from our regular boot camp routine for awhile. So, after the film, Randy and I decided to try out.

During the screening test, I came very close to not making the qualifying time for swimming but I was a fantastic runner and lapped just about everybody else taking the test. After the test was over, I was exhausted. Of the several dozen men who had taken the test, only four of us achieved the qualifying times and completed all the exercises. Randy and I and Steve Nelson all qualified, but Steve was later turned down due to poor eyesight.

After boot camp, I was sent to basic electronics school, an eight-week-long course, also in San Diego. Then I was sent to Treasure Island in San Francisco to attend electronic technician school (ET). I had always had trouble with algebra, I just never could grasp it. So after six weeks at ET school, I just wanted out of there.

So, from ET school, I was sent to UDT/SEAL training at the naval amphibious base in Coronado, California. I arrived in March 1969, right after my birthday. I was assigned to Training Class 57, which was to begin in three weeks. So new trainees who were arriving at the amphib base had time for pretraining to get in shape for what lay ahead.

The first day of pretraining was rough. The next day, I could hardly do any of the sit-ups, I was so sore. Randy Kaiser showed up a few days before our newly formed training class started. He had just finished his "A" school (Advanced Individual Training). Then came the day Class 57 started training.

By then, thanks to the three weeks of pretraining, I was in a lot better shape. I started first phase of training, which was then six weeks long, and made it all the way through Hell Week. But I injured my wrist a week later during second phase and was rolled back to Training Class 58, which was going through its pretraining. Randy stayed with Class 57 and graduated with it.

I started UDT/SEAL training all over again and had to go through Hell Week one more time. There are not too many people who have gone through Hell Week twice, but if a man wanted to be a Frogman as badly as I did, he had to go through with it. At least I was in a lot better shape and knew what to expect from the instructors and Hell Week.

The Friday before my second Hell Week, we were on Turner Field, with instructor Terry Moy, doing morning PT. Moy was leading the exercises. We did 250 four-count burpies, 250 six-count flutter kicks, and 1000 deep knee-bends, and Moy did every one of them with us. Then we ran sixteen miles to Tijuana. After the run, Moy took us to the Old Plank Inn, and our entire class got shit-faced. After that was over, we loaded up on a flatbed truck and returned to the naval amphibious base. The next day, Hell Week started all over again for me.

During the third phase of training, diving phase, our class was performing underwater compass swims in San Diego Bay. We were all on board an LCPL (landing craft, personnel launch), sitting in different positions in swim pairs, waiting for the diving officer to give us the command to enter the water. I was sitting on the port side of the bow with my swim buddy, Mike Sideler, fully geared up with twin-90 diving tanks, waiting for the signal. The LCPL was moving forward very slowly, and the signal was finally given for Mike and me to go over the side. Holding onto our marker buoy with both hands, a standard procedure, I entered the water backwards, and went underwater in the normal way. The boat continued to move slowly forward as the command was given for the dive pair on the port aft side to go overboard. Mike and I were just reaching the surface to adjust our compass on the attack board when I was hit in the head by the diving tanks of one of the other swim pairs. The force of the tanks split my head wide open, along with cutting my double-hose regulator in half. I was unable to dive with the class the rest of the day.

Another time during diving phase, I was on a dive using the Mark-6, a very sophisticated rebreathing diving device, which uses a mixture of 40/60 percent nitrogen and oxygen. My canister of beryline, which absorbs carbon dioxide from the breath, flooded with water, and I began to get a weird taste in my mouth, along with getting dizzy. I informed Mike, and we both surfaced immediately. This problem could have cost me my life if I hadn't surfaced right away and gotten some fresh air. But eventually, I finished training and graduated with Class 58 without any further problems.

After graduating from UDT/SEAL training, I was assigned to SEAL Team 1. Right away, several of us were sent to jump school at Fort Benning, Georgia, for three weeks of parachute training. It always amazed me how the army took three weeks to teach SEALs what they could have learned in an afternoon. While we were there, a couple of us put on our dress blues and went to downtown Columbus to do a little bar hopping. I was astonished at all the women we attracted with our navy uniforms.

After parachute training, I returned to the SEAL team compound and was assigned to the armory. Then, I was assigned to Juliett Platoon, which was just starting to accumulate fourteen men to train for Vietnam. Darryl Young was the highest ranking enlisted man in the newly forming platoon at that time. He had just returned from Vietnam himself and was also assigned to work in the armory. Until he transferred to UDT-11, Darryl was in charge of making up the platoon's weekly schedule, which included rapelling down the side of Otey Dam without breaking a gallon bottle of Red Mountain Wine, and other fun SEAL duties.

After Darryl's transfer, our platoon parachuted from thirty-five hundred feet near the navy's SERE (survival, escape, resistance, and evasion) school. We were training for the rescue of American prisoners who were being held in Viet Cong POW camps. I was the fourth man out of the UH-46 helicopter, and a deployment bag wrapped around my feet, wrist, and my neck, which left me hanging there for a matter of seconds. I was lucky it didn't break my neck or kill me. I hurt all night, but we completed the operation, sneaking up on the guards and rescuing the "prisoners."

Another time, we trucked two platoons to the Colorado River, with four IBSs and all our gear. Two of the IBSs had motors, which towed the other two through the slow moving waters of the Colorado. It was hotter than a son of a bitch, so we took along fourteen cases of beer, a lot of food, and spent an entire week there. During the trip, the temperature was over a hundred degrees, so I slipped over the side of the IBS to cool myself. I was hanging on to the side of the IBS, and my foot drifted under and hit the prop. The top of my left foot received a huge cut; it's lucky it wasn't cut off! I still enjoyed the trip.

Juliett Platoon was finally scheduled to deploy to Vietnam in February 1972 but never made it. We were to go to Sea Float (Solid Anchor) located in southern South Vietnam. Meanwhile, Mike Platoon (Randy Kaiser's) was pulled out of Vietnam. And that was the last SEAL platoon in Vietnam. My platoon just missed deploying to the Vietnam War!

Now, SEAL Team 1 had to cut back its size since SEALs were no longer needed in such numbers. Instead of stopping the training classes, which would bring more men into the teams, they sent more than thirty men from SEAL Team to the fleet. Pat Carter was one of them. The Dirty Thirty they were called. Why send qualified, well-trained SEALs to the fleet when the navy could have given early outs to the short-timers who wanted out anyway? After spending thousands of dollars to train these men in the schools they had attended, the teams betrayed them. Pat, like most of the men who were transferred, had never gotten in any trouble while he was in the teams. His quarterly marks were outstanding.

Pat ended up on board the USS White Sands, *which carried the navy's deep diving bathyscaphe* Trieste. *There he was as-*

signed all the prediving checks before it was deployed underwater. Since he had completed UDT/SEAL training and was a qualified SEAL, he was allowed to wear the SEAL Trident on his dress blues, but other men who were transferred threw theirs in the ocean. After Pat Carter gave so much of himself to train for our country to reach a goal that few men have accomplished, he was shit-canned to the fleet and given absolutely no excuse from the Department of the Navy. You can bet that if the Vietnam war was still going on, SEAL Team would have kept all those men and used them in that conflict.

To Pat, after what SEAL Team did to him, the navy never was the same; he hated it from then on. It was all he could do to stay in until his enlistment was completed. To this day, Pat and his comrades feel betrayed. They were highly trained and ready to kill or be killed in combat for our country.

Chapter Thirty-seven

Robert Micheels
UDT-3 1944

Section Two—Leyte

The water was a little choppy because of the typhoon that had just passed by, but it proved to be to our advantage while making swimmer reconnaissance. UDT-3's section of the beach was located opposite the town of Dulag. As we arrived off the beach a few hours late, we didn't get the full preliminary bombardment planned. However, as we lowered all boats to the rail, the bombardment group was lobbing shells, ranging from 20mm to 16-inch stuff, at our beach to keep the slant-eyes dug in. This also prevented them from getting too many ideas as to what was going on. The air corps was on the ball also, busy bombing the town of Dulag. The order finally came to lower away all boats and cast off from the APD at 1512.

Section 2 was a standby for Section 1. The section leader had drawn to see who got the opportunity to make the reconnaissance. We had lost, and hence drew the standby job. Up to the time the swimmers were dropped by Section 1, everything seemed rather quiet except, of course, for the comforting thunder from our own support fire.

It seems that the swimmers had no more than gotten into the water when the Japs began to throw their whole arsenal at us. The volume of fire from machine guns and mortars was intense. The first mortar round hit quite a distance from the boat, but that one shot was still too close for comfort. It seemed as though the boat was literally picked right out of the water. We were all sprayed by the water from the explosion, so believe me, we knew that it was close. That one was the closest we had, but one of the UDT-4 boats, up the line a few hundred yards, happened to be in the wrong place at the right time and received a direct hit. Luckily, no one was killed, but several men were injured, and their boat quickly sank.

On each of our LCPRs were mounted two .30-caliber machine guns. The port gunner in our boat had a close call. Actually, the only thing that he felt was a slight brushing past his knees. When we finally got a chance to look around, we found that a bullet had come through the port side of the boat, right by the gun mount, glanced off a helmet, then embedded itself in the starboard side of the boat.

At 1600, the swimmers were heading back to sea. The LCPRs proceeded in to recover them, and we all returned to the APD and sat about the fantail, downing brandy and batting the breeze.

Chapter Thirty-eight

Jack Tomlinson
UDT-2 UDT-21
1953

Freddy the Frog

When I was fresh out of high school, I was fortunate to land a position as a linoset designer with Armstrong World Industries. Armstrong is the world's leading flooring manufacturing and has its corporate offices and main plant in my hometown of Lancaster, Pennsylvania.

After graduating from high school, I joined the naval reserve in my hometown. My older brother, Sandy, was my hero. He was already in the navy, serving aboard an aircraft carrier. To me, he was nine feet tall. I wanted to be just like him and be in the navy, too.

One day, because of an error in my naval reserve records, I was notified that I was to be drafted into the army. After contacting my reserve unit, I was informed that I might not be able to clear up the mistake in time to miss being drafted. Not wanting to be a foot soldier, I decided that the best thing for me to do was to sign over into active duty with the regular navy.

I took my boot training at Great Lakes Training Center, near Chicago. There, because of my civilian training, I requested draftsman school. I was accepted, and after completing boot camp, was sent to Port Hueneme, California, a Seabee training base.

Most draftsman graduates get assigned to a Seabee outfit, but this was not to be for me. When my orders arrived, I couldn't believe my eyes. I was assigned to Underwater Demolition Team 2 (UDT-2) as a cartographer (mapmaker). I had heard of these men, but knew that I was not up to their standards. At least I would be in Little Creek, Virginia, which was close to my home in Pennsylvania.

I reported for duty at Little Creek and was put to work in the chart shop with UDT-2. It wasn't long before I was approached by a UDT member and was asked to try out for the next UDT training class. I was a lean, skinny kid and certainly didn't think I could measure up to the rigorous physical training I had read about that the UDT trainees had to go through. I declined and requested a transfer to another outfit. The Old Man, Lt. Comdr. Frank Kane, said I didn't have to go through UDT training, but there was no way I was getting a transfer. I was to stay with UDT-2 as a cartographer, and that was that!

I worked very hard at my rate, received my regular advancements, and was sent on several training exercises with the team. As time went by and I watched the men perform their duties, my admiration for them continued to grow. I thought many times of my situation and finally decided to attend the next training class.

It was winter in Virginia at the time, and very cold, when Training Class 8 began with about eighty-eight men. The training was much harder than I could ever have imagined, and every day I wanted to quit. To this day, I don't know what made me go on and finish, but I did. One day at a time, the training continued until Hell Week arrived. What an appropriate name for that portion of UDT training. I thought it would never end and none of us would ever make it through.

The UDT instructors would roust us out of bunks in the wee hours of the morning and herd us out of our barracks toward the cold, wet sands of the Atlantic beaches. We ran, walked, crawled, and then ran some more. Men who I thought were giants would throw up, pass out, or even run blind, as if in a trance. As skinny as I was, I didn't know how I was to keep up with the rest of the class. After a while, I came to realize that it was not the size of a man that would carry him through the training but the heart and mind of the individual himself. I found I could close my mind to the obvious and place myself in another world, tuning out the taunts of the instructors. In the strenuous running, the trick was to get my second wind, then I knew that I could make it back to our camp. At least I had made it through the training for that night.

Each day during Hell Week, after what seemed to be an eternity, we were allowed to eat and sleep. This, too, like all other areas of the training program, was to be short-lived. The instructors would come into our camp screaming and yelling for all of us to fall in. It seemed like we were only asleep for a few minutes, and of course, this is what the instructors wanted us to think.

During Hell Week, the UDT instructors did everything they could think of to make us quit. Physical and mental abuse were part of the Frogman program. The instructors continued, day and night, to harass us relentlessly. Many of the trainees gave up and quit. *Hell Week was really hell!*

Then, Hell Week was finally over. Those of us who remained were sent to Saint Thomas, Virgin Islands, for training in underwater work, endurance swimming, and the handling of various types of explosives. It was in this part of training that the buddy system was introduced. From that day on, we never went into the water without our swim buddy and K-bar knife. In those days, many times, when the UDTs were in a combat situation, the K-bar knife was the only weapon they carried.

We earned our swim fins by swimming a certain distance in a required time, and then learned to use them on longer and longer swims. We also learned to use our fins to elevate our upper bodies out of the water when the cast and recovery boat came by to snatch us out of the water. The boat never stopped to recover us. We would all line up in a straight line in the water by guiding off of each other. As the boat approached us at battle speed, we were to grab a snare ring that was placed into our hands by a pickup man riding in a rubber boat secured to the side of the main boat. It didn't take us long to realize that the fingers on our hands were the weakest part of our bodies. After having the snare pulled from your hands a few times, you developed a method of snaking your arm through the ring and grabbing your wrist with the opposite hand. I never missed a pickup after I learned that.

Finally, UDT training was completed. UDT Training Class 8 graduated on April 12, 1952, with thirty-three men out of the eighty-eight that began. Five officers were among the graduates of my class. I was assigned back to UDT-2 (later to be redesignated UDT-21) and continued to work at my rate as a cartographer.

I married a girl named Pat, from back home, and saved all the money I could to send to her. I did drawings, painted murals on the chart shop walls, lettered footlockers and other things to earn extra money. I had some experience in silk-screen printing, and designed T-shirts for our team.

One day, our team was to participate in a large amphibious exercise. I had designed a cover for the operations manual, showing Frogmen attacking two enemy ships. It was silk-screened in several colors, and it blew the Old Man's mind. He presented it to the fleet operations officer and was asked if we could continue to provide covers for future operations. The commanding officer of our unit gave me a blank check to purchase any equipment and supplies I needed. I thought I had landed in heaven. I was very proud of the many covers I had designed and often wish I had saved samples of each one.

I continued with my drawings and cartography work, and one day, my partner in the chart shop told me about a contest going on within the Atlantic Fleet. The contest was for someone to design a shoulder patch for the UDT. The contest was open to all members of the Atlantic Fleet. The Seabees, along with the amphibious forces, were the only ones that I knew of who already had shoulder patches. This is where my early design training came into play.

I began to sketch some preliminary designs. To me the term "Frogman" immediately conjured up the image of a frog. Of course, a frog alone was not going to cut it. He had to be tough, so the snarl on his face was created. UDT work involved explosives, thus came the stick of dynamite (even though the UDTs didn't use dynamite). I then added the white hat to represent the navy, but it still was not ready, and I wasn't satisfied.

I put my design away for a while, but it was never out of my mind. I often thought back to my UDT training and to one of our instructors named Mark O. Lewis. Lewis smoked cigars, and when we were berthed in the bow of the small DE (destroyer escort) that took us south for part of our training, he stood in the hatchway, puffing on that cigar, trying to make us all sick. That was it! That's what I needed to complete the frog design. Lewis's cigar was placed in the frog's mouth, showing the glowing ashes. That triggered the idea of lighting the fuse on the stick of dynamite, and my design was complete. In all, I submitted three different designs for the contest.

To my total surprise, I was announced the winner. I was speechless. Out of thirty-five entries that were submitted to a board of seven judges, I had won first, second, and third place. I knew that some of the competition had more formal experience than I, and that made the honor of winning much more appreciated.

Lieutenant Commander Kane came to me personally and congratulated me for winning the contest. It was decided that I would present the final design to the admiral myself. Lieutenant Commander Kane took me to Vice Adm. F. G. Farion's ship, and the presentation was made in his stateroom. To say the least, I was scared to death. Imagine me talking to an admiral, and I wasn't even in trouble! I received a wristwatch for my frog design.

Several additional awards came my way as a result of winning the contest. Articles were written in the Norfolk papers, and I was named "Sailor of the Week" and presented with the keys to the city (replicas). My brief day in the sun continued when I was invited to be interviewed on a Norfolk radio station. I knew it wouldn't last, but the attention was great for a while.

After I won the contest and the design was accepted, nothing else seemed to happen. I was told that the shoulder patches were not to be worn by the navy Frogmen until the design had been approved by the Navy Board. Time went on, and I soon forgot about my design of the frog patch.

I was discharged from the navy at the rate of DM2 (draftsman mate second class) in 1954 and returned to my work with Armstrong World Industries. I had no more thoughts about the patch that I had designed while in the navy.

After I retired from Armstrong World Industries in 1989, my wife and I purchased a second home in Leesburg, Florida. One day, while trying to find a place to park at an art show, I was following a van, which had a personalized license plate that read, UDT-11. On the van's bumper was a sticker about the Frogman museum in Fort Pierce, Florida. My wife and I got the address of the museum, and a few weeks later, we made the trip. There in the UDT/SEAL museum, hanging on the wall, was a copy of my frog design. For some forty years, I never even knew that the navy had finally, officially, adopted my design.

A burly veteran at the museum (later identified as the museum curator, CPO Jim Watson) approached me about the UDT/SEAL emblem I was wearing on my cap. I told him I was in a UDT team while in the navy. At that time, my wife blurted out, "Yes, and he designed that frog emblem," pointing to a copy of my frog design that was hanging overhead. She continued to bend Watson's ear about the design and my part in désigning it.

Watson grabbed me and took me back to his curator's office. "Do you know how long we've been looking for you?" he asked. He told me how the museum staff and the Vietnam vets had referred to my design as "Freddy the Frog." They had no idea who had created it. The museum had contacted several people, including the Disney studio, but were notified that none of them had created the design. Watson was elated that, after his years of searching, I just walked in off the street and introduced myself.

Today, over forty-one years later, my design hangs in the navy's Frogman museum at Fort Pierce, Florida, which has photos and documents about my winning the design contest. Several SEAL teams have made variations of the design for their use, and that's okay with me; my design lives on!

I was no hero, had no great adventures, nor did I perform any feats of courage. The only thing I had really accomplished in my military service was to endure the rigors of UDT training to become a navy Frogman. After I became a member of UDT-2, I designed the shoulder patch which became the standard patch for the UDTs. Many a navy Frogman would wear this patch with pride and honor for years to come.

It brings back many fond memories of my UDT service and my teammates. My design is still intact after forty-one years, and of that, I am very proud. The one thing I do miss, however, is the fact that I was never allowed the privilege of wearing my own design when I was on active duty with the UDTs.

Chapter Thirty-nine

Chester Tomassoni
UDT-3 1944

Section Four—Leyte

As with Section 2, we were to stand by; to assist Section 3 if it ran into trouble. We had swimmers ready to go in, and we kept an eye on the boat and the other swimmers of Section 3. Lieutenant Crist, our commanding officer, and Doc Barge were in our boat—Doc, with his helmet on backwards as always. When we were between five hundred and six hundred yards from the beach, there was quite a burst of machine-gun fire right across our bow. It seemed that we could almost reach out and touch those tracer shells, but none of us was going to try it! Lew, the coxswain, made a sharp turn and followed a zigzag course, roughly parallel to the beach, keeping to the seaward of the boats carrying the operating platoons.

Some mortar rounds hit close enough to get the boat good and wet, and the thing that made us so mad was the fact that we could actually see a Jap mortar team loading and firing at us. The Japs were on a level spot up the side of the hill a ways, protected on three sides from direct fire by the existing terrain features. They were well out of range of our light machine guns, so we radioed back to the *Talbot*, giving them the mortar's location.

Each boat had a "blown up" gunnery-grid chart of the area just in back of the beaches. We could call for fire on any two hundred-yard-square sector by merely giving the standard target square number and letter. With our enlarged charts, we could locate the target closer than this, and did so as best we could. When we pulled out, we could still see the monkeys dropping shells down the tube. We could also follow the flight of the shells in the air. They were so located that it would take a direct hit on them to get rid of them. Bob Stearns, our sharpshooter on the fantail, took some potshots at them as we pulled away. It made us feel good to shoot back, but it apparently didn't bother them a bit.

One thing we'll all remember, is the sight of six or eight men hugging the space behind the engine box. Our curiosity was quickly satisfied as to what was going on, and we were content to get just as low as we could in that boat—Doc Riegel, our junior medic, used to pass us the brandy from his vantage point in the bilges of the LCPR.

Conclusion
Frank Lahr, USMC

Our reconnaissance of D-2 indicated no obstacles or mines, so there was nothing to do from here on. On D day, while the famous "I have returned" speech was going around the world, we were all busy making ash trays out of three-inch shell cases and watching the waves of the LCVPs go past us into the beach. It was a smooth landing for the Marines at our particular beach. By the afternoon of D day, the LSTs were unloading on the same beaches that we had reconnoitered.

We were released the afternoon of 21 October, and that night sortied from Leyte Gulf. Our five-day stay at Leyte had not been marked by any particular exciting moments after we finished our reconnaissance. There were four air raids that didn't amount to much. The only time the *Talbot*'s gunners did some right smart shooting was when they brought down an American TBF that someone hollered was a Jap. What looked like "meat balls," were the burning wings. Some other eager gunners had nailed this poor plane first. Evidently, the fact that its wheels were down made it look like a Val to some.

On our way back to Manus, we read the reports of the great battle of Leyte Gulf. We were mighty thankful that the *Talbot* wasn't in on that fight! We reached Manus on 27 October, and on 1 November, UDT-3 was transferred to the USS *President Hayes.*

Chapter Forty

Pierre Remillard
UDT-11 1967–1971

So . . . you want to be a Frogman?

I moved to Richland, Washington, in 1963. It was summertime, and Richland was hotter than hell. Richland, Washington, was the last stop for a kid who had been bouncing between real achievement and serious trouble since the eighth grade or so. Richland was the "Home of Atomic Energy," and the Hanford Nuclear Reservation was a big deal along that stretch of the Columbia River. I didn't know much about atomic energy or Hanford, but President John F. Kennedy came there that year, and as an Explorer Scout, I actually got to shake his hand.

I met Brad Pugh that year. I was a junior, and he was a sophomore at Richland High. He was on the gymnastics team with me that winter. In the spring of 1964, we were both on the track team together, and because of these common interests, we became friends. Friends enough that I had dinner at his house a few times.

Brad's older brother was in the navy. He was a Frogman in Underwater Demolition Team 12, and Brad idolized him. I had never met him, but I saw pictures, and heard stories, and I dreamed. I dreamed about submarines, and mines, moonless beaches, enemy sentries, Aqualungs, and knives strapped to my legs. I didn't know what I was really getting into, but I knew I wanted to get into it. Brad and I spent a lot of time in those couple of years going to gymnastic meets, going to track meets, and talking about becoming Frogmen in the navy.

I graduated in 1965 and went to Columbian Basin Junior College. A year went by, college sort of happened. I lettered in cross-country, mostly running across the desert outside of town. After a while, I guess I didn't care one way or the other about CBJC. Instead of looking to transfer somewhere else, I decided to join the navy.

By October of 1966, I was at boot camp, San Diego, California. Boot camp, boot camp. Boot camp really wasn't so tough. We did some exercising, not much more than high school PE class, and I was in pretty good shape already. So I did a lot of push-ups on my own and tried to keep fit. Just before Christmas, I got a chance to take a UDT training test, and that got me to thinking about Brad Pugh. I had lost contact with him after high school, and I wondered if he was in the navy.

The UDT training test was my chance to get into UDT training! I couldn't believe it. The instructors from the UDT school were too much. Blue-and-gold T-shirts, stretched over tanned muscles, divers' watches, coral boots—shit, these guys were in great shape.

Because of my gymnastics and track background, the strength and exercising parts of the test were easy for me. Hell, the running was a breeze. Then came the swimming test. I forget exactly how far it was, but halfway through it, I was wishing that I had done more swimming and less diving-board posing at the old pool. To make a sad story short, I did not make the cut time for the swim that day. All of a sudden my dreams were in my back pocket, I was just another boot who had tried out for UDT and didn't make it. Damn, it had looked so close!

I finished boot camp with orders for gunner's mate "A" school, and after two short weeks at home, found myself at the Great Lakes Naval Station, Waukegan, Illinois, with a shaved head, a San Diego suntan, and a snow shovel in my hand. I was doing duty as an E-2 in what seemed like an eternal winter.

There's not much to say about "A" school. Oh, I learned about guns and the mechanics of naval weapons, hydraulics and electrical stuff, but mostly I played handball with Jimmy Tyrone, from New Orleans—played handball and dreamed about getting *anywhere* away from Waukegan. I mean thirty-two dollars every two weeks, a handball court, a letter from home, and a few Lucky Strikes was about it.

Jimmy and I played handball at the base gym, and we were getting pretty damn good, when we met these two guys who looked like great players. We started talking to them one day while waiting for a court, and right away they asked us to play a partner's game. We were young, and competitive as hell, and after a week or so of doubles, we beat their butts. Well, maybe we didn't beat their butts, but we did win one game, and they weren't actually killing us on the courts, so we became friends, sort of.

It turned out that these two guys were recruiters for the East-Coast UDT training detachment, and they told us that we should take the training test. They know that we're in good shape and all that, right? I mean, we beat their butts at least once, right? I asked one of them if I passed the test there in Great Lakes Naval Station, could I get orders to the West Coast to train in Coronado, California?

"Well," he said. "No way. If you qualify, you have to train on the East Coast."

Not me, I wanted that San Diego sunshine, I wanted to be closer to home. I wanted to be a Frogman, and I was sure I could be a Frogman in Coronado.

Now I was either the luckiest "dickhead" who ever walked the plank, or Frogman fate just works in strange ways, but I was the only one in my class of about forty-five gunner's mates to get orders to the West Coast. San Diego! Right where I wanted to be. The only trouble was that I had orders to catch up with an AKA, a troop transport ship that was coming into San Diego about thirty days after I got there.

After arriving on the West Coast, I fetched up "in transit" at the San Diego Naval Station. I still made my thirty-two dollars every two weeks, and my hair was still short, and I still had a good grip on the broom handle, but I was in San Diego, and I knew there were better things to come for this blue-eyed boy, this want-to-be Frogman.

Transit is transit, and after a few days in transients barracks, I'm sitting on my bunk, smokin' a Lucky and rereading a letter from home, when this guy came up to me and handed me orders to the Coronado naval amphibious base. It seemed that the troop transport is a "Gator Navy" ship, you know, shallow water, Marines, and all that stuff, and I've been hanging around polluting the cruiser and destroyer people. So off I went, with orders to Coronado. Another transient barracks and another broom, but this time I can look out the window and see these guys running down the street in swimming trunks. Everyone's in step, yelling "Hoo yah, hoo yah," and I just know that they have to be in UDT training. Damn! San Diego, Waukegan, San Diego, Coronado, UDT trainees right outside my window, and all I'm waiting for is troop transport!

I spend the next few days getting used to yet another bunk, another guy in charge, and more chores. I am the lowest man on the watch list, so naturally I get the 2000 to 0400 watch in the barracks. What fun. All these guys seem like they've been in the navy forever. They're going out on dates, telling stories about the girls on the beach.

So I'm walking around on duty watch, basically cleaning up and watching all the important military shit that goes on in the barracks at that time of the evening—you know, card games, guys bullshitting about one thing or another, guys reading, guys getting ready to hit the street, stuff like that. As I walk into a sleeping area, I actually bump right into this guy wearing civies. I look up at him, and he looks at me, and I'll be going to hell, it's Brad Pugh! Unbeknownst to me, Brad had joined the navy right after he graduated from high school. He was about six months ahead of me, and he had just that very week graduated from UDT Training Class 41. I'll be damned, Brad Pugh was standing right before my very eyes, an honest-to-goodness, no-shit Frogman!

Well, we sit down, in total nineteen-year-old shock, and he

tells me that there's a graduation party at the chief's club that very Friday. He tells me that I should come to the party with him. He says he'll introduce me to Olivera and that Olivera could help get me into training. "As a matter of fact," he says, "Class 42 just started Monday, and you could make it. I know you can!"

Needless to say, my wheels started spinning. It's one thing to tell a couple of strangers you're not quite ready to take the test, or write home that you flunked the swim, but it's something else to tell your buddy Brad, "Thanks, but no thanks." I never really worried about whether or not I could make it through training, but now, *I knew* that I was going to have to prove it. Now I really had to be committed to this thing, no backing out, no excuses. Now my enthusiasm was overriding any possible hidden fears of failure.

Up to this point in my life, I had always let my need for competition or recognition lead me into situations that compelled me to come through. I had been looking for this test of manhood all along, and now I had the opportunity in hand, or so I thought. I only hoped I could stay on track.

Friday night finally came. I got off watch and went lookin' for Brad. He had been busy at UDT/SEAL area, getting measured for his wet suit, collecting his weapons, knives, fins, and most important, his submariner Rolex. All living proof that he had made it through training. He was a Frogman! The UDT/SEAL compound (area) was right on the beach of the Pacific Ocean, across the Silver Strand highway from the main gate of the naval amphibious base.

Brad told me that he would meet me in the TV lounge at 1900 hours. Feeling the excitement build, I killed time over a sandwich at the bowling alley, and at 1900 hours sharp, Brad and I are walking into the chief's club, what a deal! As soon as we walked into the lounge, Brad starts "who-yahhing" everyone.

Frogmen for sure, young, enthusiastic, almost childlike with enthusiasm, but men somehow, men through some common bond that I just didn't share. And they're all lookin' at me like I was some sort of reject.

I was awed, no doubt, but hey, didn't anybody know that I

held the pole vault record at Richland High School—fourteen feet one inch? Didn't anybody know that I could really run a pool table? I mean, I can make it through training . . . I haven't . . . But I know I could . . . No shit . . . Just ask Brad . . . He knows! I got third in the state in the parallel bars . . . I was ranked nationally in the AAU . . . He knows . . . Just ask him . . .

Well, as I come out of my own little trance of insecurity, I look up and see this big Indian, in a pair of starched fatigue shorts, combat boots, drum-tight, blue-and-gold T-shirt, and black, black sunglasses. Now this guy is "bad" lookin'. He's got a perfect cigar-store Indian nose, and he's looking at Brad with an expression that shouts, "what kind of dumb new-guy trip are you on?" I hear Brad explaining that I'm his friend from high school.

Brad looks at me and said, "Pierre, I'd like you to meet Olivera. Olivera, this is—"

Well, Olivera takes one look at me and asks Brad, "Who in the hell told you you could bring a black-shoe to the party?"

Brad said, "I wanted to introduce him to you, and vice versa; I think he can make it through UDT training, and we always talked about UDT, and . . ."

Brad is stumbling through the "whys" while Olivera is walking away mumbling, not really to himself, about some "new-guy shit," and if a person wasn't in the team, he had better get his ass out of there soon, if not sooner! Finally Brad looks at me kinda' funny, and I decide I might as well leave. What the hell, I wasn't really there anyway . . .

On the slow walk back to the transients barracks, I realize that I had just left a place where everyone was part of something shared. Olivera and all the other Frogmen in that lounge were in the same energy, a camaraderie. They all felt that they were part of a team, a team that they had worked hard to make.

I hadn't realized just how big a deal it was. I guess I was hurt by what had happened in there, but I was also beginning to realize more about life and myself. My self-esteem had been banged pretty hard that night; no one likes to be told to get lost. Maybe I was a little pissed off, too. In any case, my enthusiasm to find out more was stronger than ever. I wanted to show Olivera and Brad, and mostly myself, that I was serious, that one setback wasn't going to stop me from realizing my dream. I was completely exhausted by the time I got back to the barracks; I went straight to my rack and fell asleep, wondering just how I was going to get into UDT training. Looking back on it now, I would like to think that Olivera saw a promising young recruit and that he started his mind games on me right away. Maybe that's just wishful thinking.

Saturday, I saw Brad, and we talked about the night before. He told me it wasn't a big deal, and that he would ask about getting me in to talk to someone in the UDT training area.

"Better yet," he said, "just go over to the training unit Monday morning and ask to see Commander Wilson, the skipper of UDT training." We talked about the old days in Richland for a few minutes, and then he split. I grabbed a candy bar and ended up watching TV the rest of the night. Ah, the joys of being in transit . . .

Monday morning muster at the transients barracks; all were present and accounted for. We got our national security sweeping assignments, and I told the third-class petty officer in charge that I was going over to see if I could get into UDT training. He said, "Fine, but don't take too long; muster again at noon."

Zero eight hundred hours in Coronado, the morning air is cool on the Strand as I turn the corner and see all sixty guys of Bravo Section of Class 42 standing tall, on the line, in the road between the training area and San Diego Bay. I kind of "suck it up," take a deep breath, and continue to walk toward them. Olivera is the man in charge, he is standing in front of the formation, and he turns to see what's coming.

As soon as he sees me he starts walking right at my face. "What is a 'black-shoe' squid doing on this road?" he asked.

I hold my ground and say, "I would like to talk to someone about getting into UDT training." I tell him that I'm the friend of Brad Pugh, the one who left the party the other night.

That was all that he needed to bring it all back. He puts his arm around my neck, and as we start walking toward the formation, he says, with a big grin, "Come right this way, my boy." He tells me right then and there, in front of all the trainees, in a loud voice so God and everyone else can hear, that they're going on a little run down the Silver Strand that very morning. He says that he can get me some boots and greens, and if I can make the run with them, then I could just go get my stuff and move right into the training barracks that very day.

"I can make the run," I said, "at least I would like to try it."

So he walks me back to the supply building, and I get a pair of combat boots, some large wool socks, green fatigue pants, a T-shirt, and a helmet liner. He tells me to get them on and join the ranks, "I mean today, puke . . . Immediately . . . Can you hear me? Now, now, now, now! Get movin'!"

Well, well, if this isn't something. I recognized the energy that I had felt at the party. It was weaker, not nearly as easy to put my finger on, but it was there. All at once, I felt different again. These guys had only been in training for six days, but their esprit was already starting to build. Needless to say, I wasn't part of it. I was just a runner in a pack of would-be Frogmen, everyone with shaved heads—all but me.

First, we ran across the base, out the main gate, across the highway, and over to the beach behind the UDT/SEAL compound. Once we got there, we all got to cool our feet off by standing knee-deep in fifty-five-degree water in the surf zone for about thirty seconds. Then we formed up again in the soft, hot, ankle-deep sand. We were facing south, toward Imperial Beach, and I started wondering just how far this little run was going to go.

This was the second week of training for Class 42. The first week they made the short runs. They ran one mile the first couple days, two miles for a couple of days, and three miles the fifth day of that first week. This being the first day of week number two, how about four miles! Four miles with wet feet? Oh don't worry, they'll dry out before we run back into the water . . . they'll dry out after they turn into twenty-pound balls of dry sand, sand caking up to your knees as you slog over the logs that Olivera is leading us through . . . they'll dry out after you roll down the sand hill that Olivera just ran you up! Olivera is now running backwards in front of the formation—and smoking a cigar, no shit—this guy wasn't kidding when he said, "If you can make it!"

I did make it! I'm sure that I was as surprised as Olivera that I did. True to his Frogman word, when we got back to the training area, Olivera told me, "Just go over and get your seabag and move on in."

That is exactly what I did. Then I hit the showers and collapsed on my bunk without saying a word to anyone.

It soon became obvious, even to me, that this was the "real thing." I was sleeping in the UDT training barracks. I was getting up every morning and running to the chow hall. I was running to the PT field. I was doing all the push-ups . . . and the flutter kicks! I was going on the famous runs down the Silver Strand, and I was experiencing all the physical and mental hardships that all Frogman trainees experience. But the camaraderie, the common shield that I thought held these would-be Frogmen together still eluded me. I still felt different, and it wasn't just the length of my hair.

The first four weeks of training didn't give a guy much time to make friends. There was always something more for us to do, something that took all of your energy, mental and physical. Just getting through to the next day took about all the energy I had. Still, during these first four weeks, I began to realize that I was becoming a part of something. It happened slowly, I'm sure it was nothing that I suddenly became aware of. It just seemed to establish itself in subtle ways.

Those early training schedules were set up to break any weak links. The instructors had it all their way. They not only put you up against the wall physically, but they also never let you forget that at the end of the four-week period, if you could make it, was Hell Week. Officers or enlisted, just knowing that Hell Week was the next thing up, could convince you to quit. All the little physical injuries—the scrapes and bruises, the rashes that went from the inside of one thigh over to the other, and the blisters on the back of your heels that you could stick your thumb into. The pulled leg muscles and the aching backs were in themselves enough to make you want to quit. And, the reward for all of those things was—Hell Week! Huh? Shit, oh dear! I realized that it was better not to have any close friends during this time because they might quit, and I might quit with them.

Every day, someone else packed it in, and they always seemed to take someone with them. Every night in the barracks, there was another empty bunk or two. My rack was at one end of the barracks, and I began to have some communication with two other guys, named Willy and Abe. We weren't friends, yet, but every night, we could see each other sitting on our bunks. So every night, we knew that at least we were still there.

There were fewer and fewer people in the barracks, and the weeks rolled on. Just being there . . . just experiencing every run . . . bracing every time somebody "hit the bay" . . . realizing that your eyes were meeting the same eyes in the course of the day . . . told me that finally I was becoming a part of it.

By the end of those first four weeks, every one who was left was part of "it." Each one of us knew common pain. We had seen each other at our weakest and strongest points. We had helped and been helped by each other, and we were stronger individuals because each one of us knew that he had support from within our group as well as strength within himself.

Hell Week was Hell Week! More of the same, but a lot worse, or maybe a lot more. We lost a few more guys, but the common bond that I could feel every time that I sat on my bunk and saw Willy and Abe, or any time my eyes connected with anyone else who felt what I was feeling, became stronger and stronger. Things happened every day to one or all of us that built that bond. We had made it.

A few days after Hell Week was over, I was standing in the pay line with all the other people who had survived. Pay was going to be nice for me because I was broke, worse than broke; I didn't even have any toothpaste. Everyone got paid, except me.

I told Olivera that I didn't get a check and asked him what I should do? Well, he gets his familiar, "no shit, puke," grin on his face and asks me how long it's been since I got paid. I tell him it's been about a month, or maybe six weeks. He tells me to drop and give him fifty push-ups, then tells me to run on down to disbursing to see where my checks are.

The disbursing officer of the amphib base was busy when I got there, lots of guys in khaki uniforms or dungarees. I stood there in my helmet liner, totally worn fatigues and combat boots for about half an hour before a yeoman asked me what I needed. I tell him my name, rank, and serial number and that I haven't been paid for at least a month. He goes over to his desk and shuffles some papers for a few minutes, finally reaches into this file next to the desk, and pulls out three checks—six weeks' worth of pay!

As he's walking toward me, I'm starting to feel relieved just knowing that he has my money in his hand. The problem was, as he laid them down in front of me, I could read "UA" (unauthorized absence) on them—written on each of them in red ink! He looks up at me and asks me where in the hell I've been for the last six weeks?

He doesn't know? I tell him that I haven't been anywhere. I know for a fact that I haven't been UA, hell, I've been in UDT training for the whole time! I've been running up and down the beach with Olivera! The yeoman gathers up the checks and says he'll be right back. He wants me to wait in the chair by his desk.

Now, I'm sitting in this chair, and I know where my checks are. That's good news. But, why would anybody think I was AWOL? I mean, I've been too busy even to go off base for five minutes. I haven't even been out of the barracks alone. AWOL? There has to be a mistake!

The yeoman comes back with this lieutenant junior grade and the jaygee tells me to come with him. We go into his office, and he asks me if I've ever heard of the chain-of-command. He says he called the UDT training area and that a Commander Wilson there did tell him that I had, in fact, been training with Class 42 for about six weeks and that I had just made it through Hell Week. However, the aforementioned Commander Wilson couldn't find any orders for me! This jaygee asks me if maybe I should have told the transit people that I was staying over at the UDT training area, sort of camping out with the Frogmen?

It seems that the day I went over to the training area and ran into Olivera and made the run and moved into the training barracks was the last day that anyone who was supposed to know where I was had any idea where I might actually be!

.The rest of that memorable day was spent spiraling from one office to another. I stood at attention in my smelly fatigues while another officer told me about the chain of command and how things work in the navy. The last office I remember walking into was in the administrative building of the amphib base command, and wouldn't you know it, there sat Commander Wilson in Class A khakis, and Olivera in combat boots, starched fatigue shorts, a blue-and-gold T-shirt, and sunglasses.

There was a lot said in that office, almost none of it by me. I stood and listened to Olivera and Commander Wilson explain why he should let me back, that they believed I would make it in the teams, and that he should try to get me orders. What I remember clearly was that the officer who owned the big desk wanted my head on a platter, while Olivera and Commander Wilson wanted the rest of me!

I had, in fact, been AWOL. I had, in fact, broken the rules, *all* of the rules. However, I had done what I needed to do. What I had to do to get where I wanted to be, which was in UDT training, on the West Coast.

I left that office that day with Olivera and Commander Wilson and sat in the bay for what seemed like forever. I continued to train with 42 Bravo. From then on, every day that Class 42 mustered on the road by the bay in the morning, Olivera would pull me out of ranks and ask me if I wanted to quit.

Olivera would say, "You know, Remillard, you don't have any orders to be here; are you sure you don't want to quit and return to the transients barracks and take it easy on yourself?"

"No, Olivera," I would answer, "I'll just keep on training."

My ship had come and gone, and I didn't even know it. Orders were cut for me for UDT/SEAL training. Finally, I started receiving my checks, and everything was eventually squared away, as far as my orders were concerned.

So, training continued as normal, if you want to call UDT/SEAL training normal. Finally Class 42 Bravo entered its diving phase. For 42 Bravo, diving was moved to second phase while Alpha was in its demolition-and-land-warfare phase.

One day, Bravo had a 110-foot bounce dive, which was to be conducted outside San Diego Bay, past Point Loma, to where the ocean reached that depth. On this particular day, we were to dive down to the depth of 110 feet on a long rope called a trunk line. The trunk line was nothing more than a long length of rope with a heavy chunk of lead secured to one end. We would dive, one trainee at a time, with Olivera and show him that we could clear our mask, turn our tanks off, and buddy breathe with him for a while.

For UDT training, a bounce dive was an easy day, as we trainees would call it. It would take several hours to get to the required depth outside the bay by riding on a slow-moving boat from the training area. The dive wouldn't take very long; then we would take the long ride back and secure our equipment for the day. It was a great time to get some rest.

Anyway, after we anchored at the correct depth, the ramp on the bow of the boat was lowered into the water. The trunk line was thrown overboard, with extra line to put the lead weight below the 110-foot mark so it wouldn't interfere with the divers. After he informed us that we couldn't wear our new wet suits, Olivera asked the class for a volunteer to go on the first dive with him. Needless to say, the whole class was real bummed out.

Shit, I thought to myself, it's September, and the water's cold. So, like a dummy, I volunteered to be the first trainee down the clump line. I didn't want to wait for everybody else to do it and sit around freezing my ass off, waiting to get colder and have my anxiety build up. Even though we would have less than ten minutes of bottom time, I just wanted to get the dive over with!

The ocean was surging, and the ramp would come out of the water and splash back down again. Olivera explained to me exactly what we were going to do, and then we carefully worked our way down the traction cleats on the ramp and jumped clear of it when it was safe. This was difficult due to the weight of the twin ninety-cubic-inch diving tanks and the lead-weight belt that were strapped to our bodies. We swam back close to the ramp, keeping our distance from the head-crushing steel contraption, then we submerged several feet below it and grabbed the clump line. We didn't hang on very tightly, as the line would have pulled us up and down with the surface swells. I followed Olivera down the line, letting it slide slowly through my hands as we equalized our eardrums according to the pressure from the depth. The deeper we dived, the darker and colder it became. I could see light and the bottom of our boat if I looked up. I was wishin' I had my wet suit.

It didn't take us very long to reach the 110-foot mark on the clump line. Olivera looked at me, and then he pulled my mask off to confuse me a little bit. I recovered my mask, cleared it. No problem. Then he reached around to the valve on my manifold and turned my air off, real tight; he had a habit, back in the swimming pool at the base when we were just learning how to dive, of turning our air off so tight that you had to take the tanks off and hold them between your legs to turn them back on. All this without swimming to the surface.

Then, he kept his mouthpiece in his mouth and waited until he knew I needed a breath of air real bad, till I was beggin' him for it. Finally, he hands me his mouthpiece, and I'm needin' air so bad that I slammed it into my mouth and sucked it as fast and hard as I could. I sucked up a giant plug of Indian chewin' tobacco that Olivera had been chewin' all along. So now, not knowing what the hell I have inhaled, I can't catch my breath. I was in kind of a panic situation at first, then I realize what has happened and try to get the chewin' tobacco out of my mouth and lungs. With burning watery eyes and a horrible taste in my mouth, I finally got control of myself and looked over at Olivera, who had a big grin on his face. We began to buddy breathe for a while, and I was more cautious every time I took his regulator from him.

My time was up at the 110-foot depth. The grin on Olivera's face and the tap on my shoulder signaling me to surface was proof to me that I had passed the test. I got my air turned back on and started breathing from my own regulator again. We then slowly began to work our way back up the clump line toward the surface, the boat, and my dry clothes.

Before surfacing, we swam away from the boat's ramp. The only way to get back on the boat was to swim close to the ramp, wait till it went underwater from the swell action, and swim up onto it as fast and far as you could while hanging onto one of the many traction cleats. Because of the heavy weight we were carrying, the swell action, and the slippery deck of the boat, another instructor and a couple of trainees would help pull us the rest of the way onto the boat.

Then it was someone else's turn, and I could get into my dry clothes. I made sure to tell as many classmates as possible to watch out for that first hit off Olivera's regulator.

Once I got in UDT training, I stuck it out until it was over, or so I thought. I had taken a path least traveled, and I hadn't quit. I remember graduation day . . . all my classmates . . . and how proud we all were . . . I remember the common shield and the camaraderie, and I feel it even to this day. I know that there are hundreds of reasons for me to feel a part of the teams . . . the things that we did together . . . the running and swimming . . . the ever-lovin', fuckin' Nam . . . all of it. But the strengths that we learned in training, the truths that bond us together as men, that we learned in UDT/SEAL training will forever give me strength. Thanks forever to Willy and Abe, to The Moth, The Owl, Mike "The V-Body" Ambrose, to Blues Butler, Jay The Birdman Posselt, to the Chickenman, to the officers and men of Class 42.

Chapter Forty-one

Charles Greene
UDT-3 1944

Aboard the USS *President Hayes*

Being aboard a large ship, a relatively new one, was like stepping into a new world after the long months we had existed aboard various APDs. While still at Manus, daily liberty parties were sent ashore for all hands not on the inevitable working details. From the looks of the returning liberty hounds, there was no shortage of beer.

Duffy's Tavern was the name of the fleet recreational beach here at Manus, and considering this unheard-of island had been secured from the Japs only eight months ago, wonders had been done building up the base to make it a springboard for the attack on the Philippine Islands. Four-lane roads were everywhere, hacked out of the jungle. The waterpower from the rivers back in the mountain jungle was harnessed to provide power plants that were big enough to light a fair-size city. On the recreation island, there were facilities for everything, from drinking beer to playing handball. As before when we were here, we spent a good deal of our time hunting cat-eyes on the edge of the reef.

We left Manus on 11 November and had a very pleasant trip

back to Maui. There were the inevitable long chow lines, but there were always a couple of good arguments going with the ever-famous UDT-6 while we stood in line. But our buddy team, UDT-4, was also along with us on this trip, and we didn't listen to many of the stories of Team 6.

Thanksgiving Day, November 23, found us with plenty to be thankful for. After a wonderful meal aboard ship, we disembarked at Maui. (That dissenting noise you hear is the officers' sounding off. They didn't get the good meal that we did. Too bad!)

Chapter Forty-two

Mike Ferrell
UDT-12 1967–1970

Back to Sea Float

Our platoon had only twenty-one days left in country when Oggie, McGee, and I were assigned to an operation down at Sea Float. The UDT/SEAL teams had been stationed at Sea Float since we had hauled the barges down there during my first tour. I was a little angry that I was sent there, especially when I was so short.

Baker, Atkinson (The Lizard), and Chief Kinnard were seasoned team warriors who were also stationed at Sea Float. Mr. Kirkland was the officer in charge of the overall operation. He had graduated from UDT/SEAL Training Class 42, also, and was a very good officer and operator. Maybe a little rah, rah, but okay.

Each UDT or SEAL man who was to participate in the operation was assigned twelve to fifteen Montagnards for a three-day, two-night extended mission. My team was assigned a Green Beret, a good operator.

The Yards were mercenaries, paid by the Vietnamese government for enemy bodies and weapons that they collected. What the white man had done to the American Indians, the Vietnamese did to the Montagnards. The Vietnamese took their land and pushed them up into the Central Highlands. Now the Yards were fightin' for the South Vietnamese. They despised the NVA and Viet Cong, and in my opinion, they were the best foreign outfit that I had ever had the privilege of operating with. We couldn't speak the same language, but we were patient enough with each other to play one hell of a game of charades out in the bush.

We were to be inserted into the jungle in predetermined areas around Sea Float and be extracted three days later in the late afternoon. Most of the canals had been heavily defoliated with Agent Orange since I had been here on my last tour. Based on the terrain, we were to patrol about three klicks. Our mission was to search for arms, food caches, and weapons, and to destroy all the bunkers and villages we could locate. Also, we were to take prisoners for interrogation, and extract by helo any innocent Vietnamese we could find.

I could orient a grid map very well by then, and navigate through the jungle. My camouflage makeup was outstanding. I had all the radio frequencies and passwords for our boat support, helo extraction, and air strikes. I carried a Swiss seat (seven-foot section of rope used to make a rappelling seat) on my H harness for emergency helo extraction, and all the ammo, grenades, and pop flares that I could carry. All that training, the confidence, and the power were there, but this one was different. I was going out with total strangers. Even so, I loaded all the data properly in my little Chickenman head and was ready to make some friends.

We left Sea Float and were inserted into the jungle in our

designated operating area. Ca Mau was less secure and had a higher concentration of NVA and Viet Cong than any other area in South Vietnam. I was gettin' scared and nervous. But there was also another part of me that wanted to get a little payback for the Beak and those river recons up at the Beak.

This was the only time that I had been on an operation where we were split up and I wasn't operating with my *potnahs*. And I had also never been out in the bush on an operation for more than twenty-four hours straight. This time, though, instead of the enemy seeing me coming, I was going to see him first, by taking it real slow and keeping real quiet, smelling the air, listening real hard, and paying special attention to noise discipline.

The Ca Mau jungle was still considered the NVA's hideout. You couldn't believe how hard it was to get around there. It could take twelve hours of some real humpin' in the deep mud to go the distance of three football fields. The terrain was incredible—hip-deep mud, and mosquitoes so thick that you could wave your arm through the air and feel them. The Ca Mau also had snakes, spiders, and just about every type of insect imaginable. Heck, I believe there are animals living down there that our scientists don't even know exist.

There were also these incredibly large half-inch, aggressive green ants that lived in the trees. If you bumped into a branch, they fell on you like rain and ate your ass. They would crawl up your nose, in your ears, and everywhere else. The ants were intelligent, too. One day during the operation, I was standing next to a tree when I looked at a leaf on one of its branches. There, staring back at me at eye level about four inches away from my left shoulder, was one of the green ants. I stood there staring back at it. He reared up on his hind legs for about ten seconds, and his little antennae started going around in circles. Then, without any warning, the little critter actually jumped on me, trying to bite me, pick me up, and carry me back up into the tree to feed all of his *potnahs*! Damn, what an animal. What we need to do for the next war is to train those little ants and supply them with guns and let them do the fightin'!

We had been inserted early in the morning and covered a lot of ground that day, stopping all the time to get used to the jungle sounds and listen for the enemy. Move for a while, stop, listen, move, stop, and listen some more. I liked the way the Yards patrolled. The Green Beret was okay, too. And they were probably checking me out. We were all paying close attention, looking around a lot and being very quiet.

Toward late afternoon, we came across this large rice paddy, approximately 150 yards across. Our course should have carried us straight across it. It was a real temptation to break cover and walk across it after patrolling through all the thick vegetation and crawling in the deep mud.

No way, Mike . . . stay out of the paddy . . . stealth and concealment . . . you know what to do, I thought to myself.

About fifty yards from the corner of the rice paddy, as we were patrolling around its perimeter, the Yards became excited and were looking over toward the other side. Everyone stopped and got down. I slowly turned and moved to a small hole in the vegetation where I could see out into the paddy. I saw an unarmed Viet Cong, wearing black pajamas and carrying a fishing net. He was walking down a dike and heading straight toward us, coming right down our nose. Good thing we hadn't broken cover and walked across the rice paddy.

As the VC walked out into the open a little more, maybe about twenty yards or so, another VC had popped out of the jungle behind him. Then, four more came out of the jungle right behind him. All six of them seemed to be fishing. My heart was really beginning to pound now, and I had to go down the line in our patrol and calm my little pit bulls down. They were getting excited, talking, and moving around too much. It was time for all of us to turn ourselves into trees. The thought occurred to me to let the first VC walk right up to us before we opened up so we could try to capture him for a field interrogation and collect some fresh intel, then we could quietly snuff his ass if we had to. But it was getting very close to dark . . .

I checked down our line both ways, and everyone looked ready. The first VC was no more than twenty yards from us now . . . I squeezed off the first round . . .

By the time I moved my weapon to our secondary targets, they had all dropped down. It was not clear to me how many of the VC we had hit and how many had dived behind the dikes for cover. We had all opened up on them at the same time. All of a sudden, the Yards broke cover and entered the rice paddy. I quickly yelled *lai dai* (come here) to pull them back into the bush.

I talked to the Green Beret, "If we move further around the corner of the rice paddy, we may move right into them, so let's move back one hundred yards the way we had come in and set up an ambush site with claymores to protect ourselves."

We both agreed, so we all hauled ass back in the direction that we had come in from and reestablished ourselves. I'm sure that the Yards were a little pissed off at me because I wouldn't let them get to the bodies, but I was pissed off at them for breaking cover. Thick triple-canopy jungle surrounded the rice paddy that concealed us, and if anybody had been on the other side, they would have known exactly where the shots had come from. It would have been a lot easier for the VC to look for us.

Something was still bothering me, so I got together with the Green Beret again. "If we were the VC, and there were only six of us, and we were hungry, would we talk the newest guy into going out and getting us some fish?" I said. "What if there were several NVA soldiers over on the other side of the paddy? Why don't we call in an air strike and have them soften up the other side of the paddy just in case?" So that's what we did.

About a half hour later, a Black Pony (OV-10 Bronco) showed up. We made radio communication with the plane and informed him that we would shoot up a flare to mark our position. We told him that his target was three hundred to five hundred meters due southeast from the flare. We also told him to work the area very well, but not to go beyond five hundred meters because of other friendlies in the area.

He replied, "Roger that," and proceeded to throw ordnance right on target.

That should have deterred the enemy from probing us from our front, and they would have had to cover a lot of ground to sneak up on us from the rear.

Everything stayed pretty quiet and normal till late that night. All the Yards were settling in and getting some sleep when suddenly I heard a sound like, *doink . . . doink.* It wasn't really too unusual, but it was keeping me wide-awake. I wondered if it could have been a bird or some other animal. A little while later I heard *doink, doink* again. Still nothing unusual, but it was keeping me alert. About an hour later, I heard *doink, doink* again. That one seemed to be behind me. *Doink, doink*—that one sounded like it was down the line. They're going to probe us, I thought. I was getting focused by then. My head and eyes were clear. My nostrils were flared, and my ears were three-feet around. In other words, I was getting scared and paying *close* attention.

There were no other abnormal sounds for a long time, then—*doink . . . doink . . . doink . . . doink . . . doink . . . doink.* It sounded like they had our entire perimeter marked. The sounds started to become a lot more regular, like they were marking our position, and theirs as well. The good news was the noises weren't getting any louder. One thing was for sure, the strange noise was surely keeping me from getting any sleep at all. Maybe some gook was warning the local river traffic to stay away, unfriendlies were present.

I was glad when the morning came. We patrolled out into the paddies to check for bodies but overnight, someone had dragged them off. Not all of them could have gotten up and walked out on their own; at least I know of one of them that didn't.

We continued on with our mission, patrolling until we came across a vacant village with warm food still inside some of the hootches. They must have heard us coming and split. We burned all the hootches, blew up the bunkers, and destroyed the boats. We took everything to the ground and made it of no use to the enemy.

Then, after patrolling farther, we met up with Chief Kinnard and his group of Yards. We both came onto another village that was located across a river from our position. We could see several VC milling around sampans, and since it was starting to get dark, we decided it was time to find an area where we could set up the night's ambush. We patrolled back into the jungle and found a smaller tributary that fronted another rice paddy.

Just before dark, Kinnard collected his Yards and returned to the area near the village to set up his own ambush site. I was exhausted, but still wrapped tight, maybe too tight. The Yards set out the claymores and points to keep watch, ate a little chow, and nestled in for the night. The Yards were good operators.

As tired as I was, I still couldn't sleep. There were no more *doink, doinks*, which made me think that it really had been Charlie the night before. There were lots of mosquitoes, too many to deal with, so I just sat there in the mud and let them suck my blood. It was the beginning of a very long, slow night.

Later, as I sat in the mud, looking through some cover that we had placed on the canal bank, I saw a sampan moving very slowly in our direction. It was moving perpendicular to our ambush line, on the far left side of the tributary. I looked deeper into the rice paddies across the canal to see if there were any more dark shadows moving out there. Nothing . . . Great!

The sampan came down the main tributary and then made a left turn right in front of our left point. After each stroke, the VC held their paddles low to the surface so that dripping water wouldn't make any noise. I thought that our left point should have been stirring people up long since, but he must have fallen asleep. Now, the sampan had come to a complete stop right in front of me. I slowly reached down, grabbed a clump of mud, and threw it on the man next to me to get his attention. I signaled him with a full open hand, spread fingers, right in front of my face. That meant that there was imminent danger and it's close, get ready to rock and roll. I turned back to the sampan, and I could make out the curved bow slowly, faintly bobbing in the water. Just as I started to squeeze the trigger, the bow of the sampan did something strange—it became a plant leaf. It was really a reflection from the leaf of a plant that was bobbing in the light breeze. That scared the hell out of me; the whole incident was just a hallucination. I was getting out of control, and that could be dangerous! Dangerous to me and my *potnahs*. I got up and looked both ways, up and down the canal—nothing. I was able to get a little catnap after that incident, and once again, I was glad to see the morning light.

The next day was typical. We located a large occupied village, marked all the VC suspects for interrogation, and extracted the whole works by helo. We then burned the hootches to the ground and destroyed all the bunkers. We made it on time to our extraction site at the river and were recovered by boat. Baker was on board with his group of Yards, and he, too, looked totally exhausted. I felt worse than he looked. I never told anyone about my favorite plant.

Collectively, the operation was a success, and letters of commendation were written up for it. But it was ironic, that after two tours to Vietnam and all the ops I went on, that the thing that scared me the most was myself. At least I was now aware of it.

I left Vietnam a couple of weeks later, taking a commercial jet home, round eyes in it and everything.

Chapter Forty-three

Robert Nelms
UDT-3 1944

Maui Training Staff

Ah, Maui, land of tropical beauty, lovely hula girls, cherubic, healthy, husky islanders and, last but not least, demolition. It was toward the end of November that the islanders received their greatest shock since Pearl Harbor. The cause of the commotion was a ragged horde that poured ashore with the rays of the setting sun. God knows, we looked like anything but American sailors, but there really was no cause for alarm; it was only Team 3 returning home from outlandish places such as Guam and Leyte. Upon returning, we were informed that we had been selected for the rather dubious honor of the training staff.

First, however, there were several pleasant days of leave. Most of us went to Hawaii and tried our worn-out charms on the local belles. As most of us failed in this, good old island liquor was resorted to, with the result that upon returning from leave, most of us had substituted a barroom pallor for the salty tans we'd picked up in the Pacific.

There was quite a luau thrown for the officers our first night back. A luau is a Hawaiian-native word which we chose to interpret as "get good and drunk." Perhaps you heard all about "The Doctor" trying to dance the hula with a five-foot Hawaiian gal and scaring her half to death. At that point, the Marine and Jake had to carry him home. Home, of course, is the colloquial expression meaning the "damn base."

Our leave was all too short, and soon we were all back at the Maui base. Lieutenant Crist, soon to be lieutenant commander, took over as the base training officer. He began a well-rounded, eight-week program, which each team coming in from Fort Pierce was to undergo before leaving for an operation. It was Team 3's job to teach different phases of this program.

Now this instructing is quite an art, especially if a student asks a question that the instructor can't answer. Using various noises and gestures, the instructor leaves the student with the idea that he knows the answer but doesn't wish to divulge the information at the present moment.

Team 3 got along fine on the training staff because, although none of them knew anything, all of them could yell like hell. There was one phase of the course affectionately called Marine training. This included such things as familiarization with hand grenades, gunnery, compass reading, reconnaissance, bivouacking, forced marches, judo, and of course, strengthening the morale of each and every student.

The instructors' special joy was the three-to-four-day bivouac in which the students were landed on a designated island and forced to march a distance of twelve miles through carefully placed minefields. There were also sniper traps and instructors whose job it was to capture the students' scouts and infiltrate their ranks. We tried to make this period as rough as possible because we wanted those men who couldn't take it to drop out.

Christmas at Maui, of course, lacked the snow at home, but we had most everything else, even to the Christmas tree procured by Petey Nelms. A big athletic program was A.J. Stone's idea of a Merry Christmas, among other items. There was a rubber boat race over a mile course for the officers. Our noble men, having celebrated Christmas Eve with sixteen quarts of champagne and three roast ducks, were not exactly in the pink of condition for the race. Wally Schied clinched the booby prize for our crew.

Team 3 was in charge of the training at Maüi from early December 1944 to March 1945. Looking back, it wasn't bad duty at all. Although the quarters and conditions at the base left much to be desired, there were many advantages—the beaches were among the most beautiful in the world, the climate was ideal, and the training work was diversified enough not to become boring. The island liquor, while not great, was potent. There were even a few women now and then—never enough of course, but better than nothing.

Chapter Forty-four

Jerry Howard

UDT-12 1968-1970

For countless Vietnamese children and a few bands of Viet Cong guerrillas, the tanned Frogmen who walked and swam along their pristine beaches became almost as familiar as the sunrise which brought them. In 1968 alone, UDT-12 surveyed more than 120 miles of coast line.

This year our friends waited in vain. We surveyed three beaches—two at night—and covered little more than a mile. Our calling was elsewhere, in our secondary mission. There were bunkers, bridges, miles of canals, and the chance to meditate on the irony that destroying things can sometimes be con-

structive. Each deployment defines itself; this is only part of the story of what happened.

Sea Float

Sea Float was a clump of nine barges anchored in the middle of a brackish river in Ca Mau province, at the very southern tip of the Mekong Delta in Vietnam. Ca Mau was less secure, and had a higher concentration of NVA and VC, than any other province in South Vietnam.

From the air, it seemed a vast wasteland of brown, green, and mud-gray mangroves and defoliated forest. Nor would the reality of the ground disappoint the aerial observer: prickly, gnarled mangroves ripping at clothing: hip-deep mud like tar, thousands of tiny streams, water vipers and carnivorous fire ants one can not see from above. Only the rivers offered freedom of movement, which was relative: enemy B-40 rockets, machine guns, or homemade fifty-five-gallon-drum antipersonnel mines sometimes interfered with progress.

The Approximate End of the World

On patrols and ground sweeps, UDT usually worked as a demolition element with Biet Hai Rangers or Montagnard mercenary troops. They would insert by Yabuda junk or Swift boat and search for pinpoint targets—base camps, arms caches, tunnel complexes, or supplies, usually along the waterways. Although an average sweep covered twenty-five hundred meters, a few went for seven thousand—slogging through muck and tangle and sudden streams, always listening, always watching for trip wires and strange movements, always uneasy, waiting . . . getting very tired.

There was a constant threat of ambush, and more times than not, the patrols received some kind of hostile fire. If this was one of the most dangerous areas in Vietnam, with the right luck, it was also one of the most lucrative: huge quantities of food, arms, supplies, and important enemy officials were just there for the finding.

On January 20, 1969, the UDT members of Det Golf—Mr.

Kirkland, Chief Kinnard, GMG1 Baker, and DM3 Atkinson—set out with a force of eighty Montagnard mercenaries and their Special Forces advisers for the Bo De River, where they would insert for a week's operation, searching for the enemy, his structures, and supplies. One UDT man was assigned to each of four platoons as its demolition capability. All carried automatic weapons, heavy loads of ammunition, grenades, plastic explosives and fuses, Vietnamese dried rations, and light fishing tackle.

The Longest Night

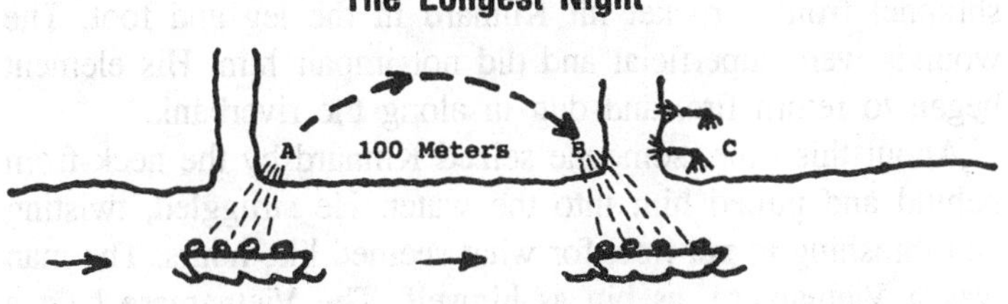

They were inserted about 4:00 P.M. and swept on foot up the Rach Cai, a canal fifty meters wide. Chief Kinnard's group surprised and killed three men in a sampan. One man was the executive officer of an NVA company; another, a supply officer who had just contracted to buy fifty thousand pounds of rice.

The next night, about nine o'clock, the same group spotted two sampans—one of them very large—moving down the canal (see sketch, point A). Chief Kinnard's group took them under fire, knocking out both motors and killing several men. Kinnard saw about nine more enemy trying to escape by paddling upstream in the two disabled boats. He grouped several Montagnards and moved them quickly through the dense undergrowth to an area they had searched earlier, the wide mouth of a small tributary one hundred meters farther up the Rach Cai (point B). There he set up another ambush for the slowly moving sampans.

When the enemy passed this point, Kinnard yelled *lai dai* (come here) and an Anglo-Saxon expletive. The men in the sampan stood up, as he had expected, and were immediately gunned to death. The smaller sampan sank. The larger, which was heavily laden with supplies, was near the bank, but drifting away. Kinnard swam to it, towed it back, and tied the bow line to a stump on shore. While he was in the water, automatic-weapons fire burst from across the Rach Cai (point D), clearly aimed at him. His element returned fire, enabling him to get back on the ambush site. Then more fire came from across the tributary (point C)—B-40 rockets, machine guns, and AK-47s. For a time, the enemy fire was so intense that his group was pinned to the ground, unable to return fire. During this barrage, shrapnel from a rocket hit Kinnard in the leg and foot. The wounds were superficial and did not impair him. His element began to return fire, and dug in along the riverbank.

About this time, someone seized Kinnard by the neck from behind and pulled him into the water. He struggled, twisting and thrashing to get free, for what seemed like hours. The man was a Vietnamese, as big as himself. The Vietnamese held a pistol in one hand and swore constantly in articulate English while he struggled. Kinnard found firm footing on the shallow bottom and eventually got a grip around the other man's neck and the arm with the pistol. Slowly he forced him under the water and tried to pry the gun from his hand. The man weakened from lack of oxygen and relinquished it. Then Kinnard pulled his head out of the water, held the man's pistol to his forehead, and shot him twice in the brain.

He pulled the dead Vietnamese out of the water and resumed shooting from his position. Kinnard did not know until later that the man was an NVA lieutenant colonel. The machine-gun fire across the tributary continued. Kinnard threw grenades for some period of time; about midnight the guns were silenced. The B-40 rockets also stopped, but small-arms fire continued in intermittent bursts until daybreak.

The men held in their position until daylight. The other elements were too far away to risk coming to help in the dark, and no air support could be obtained. At dawn, Kinnard discovered from the uniform and papers on the man he had killed that he was a ranking officer, apparently in the area to attend a major planning conference. Four of the men dead on the floor of the sampan were his staff officers. All totaled, eighteen enemy were dead. Inside the sampan were four AK-47 rifles, 4 pistols, 3800 rounds of ammunition, 1 B-40 rocket launcher, 3 rockets, 6 radios, 2 sampan motors with 150 pounds of spare parts, 100 pounds of American tools, 40 pounds of clothing and uniforms, and pounds of medicine and documents.

The documents were among the most important ever found in the region, crucial information on forthcoming operations, on locations of base camps and headquarters, weapons, capabilities, leaders and the names of Popular Force personnel and hamlet chiefs who were undercover Viet Cong.

There was nothing to explain why the NVA colonel had chosen to subdue Kinnard himself, or why he had not immediately used his pistol instead of his bare hands. Kinnard had been lucky on another count: most of the shrapnel that hit him was stopped by his boot. Two weeks later there was almost no evidence of the wounds. The Special Forces adviser with the platoon recommended Kinnard for the Silver Star.

The operation had lasted for only four days. Elsewhere with the other platoons, there was less action. The elements of Kirkland, Baker, and Atkinson accounted for only 7 kills, 20 sampans, 7 motors, 250 pounds each of rice and salt, 75 pounds each of tobacco, dried fish and clothing, and 30 pounds of medical supplies. One bunker, three cisterns, and seventeen hootches were destroyed.

Chapter Forty-five

Frank Lahr
UDT-3 1945

Home We Go!
Duty at Fort Pierce

Early in April, when we finally received the word that we were heading Stateside, there wasn't a happier bunch of guys. All of us had at least a year overseas, which isn't a record in itself, but it's long enough to do a little thinking.

UDT-3 left Maui on March 27, 1945, and arrived at Pearl Harbor April 1. We left Pearl Harbor and arrived in San Francisco April 7. We were given leave until May 1, at which time we were to report to the Naval Combat Demolition Unit, Amphibious Training Base, Fort Pierce, Florida. We were once again to be instructors, but actually the duty seemed just a good excuse for more time in the States.

Lt.(jg) Robert Parson Marshall, former executive officer of UDT-5, succeeded Lieutenant Commander Crist as commanding officer of Team 3 when Mr. Crist was assigned to Maui to resume duties as officer in charge of the training there. UDT-3's organization became very extensive. The CEC warrant officers, who had done so much to build up UDT-3, were released. Many enlisted men failed to pass the rigid physical examination and also had to be released. Consequently, it was Lieutenant Marshall's job to recruit and train ten new officers and forty-six enlisted men and work them in with the old team members to develop a coordinated unit. We had three weeks to accomplish this before shoving off for Oceanside, California.

Among the more pleasant jobs was a choice assignment that went to Bob Whalen, Fred Hart, Moe Mulheren, Tommy Maher, Earl Durden, and me. This was one month of temporary duty in marine testing of cold-water swimsuits. We "lucky boys" flew up to Boston, procured a station wagon, and drove up to Rockland, Maine, where we set up headquarters in the local motel. The bar of the hotel was known throughout the state as the "Passion Pit," and for good reason.

We worked hard up there (no laughing please). The water was at a temperature of fifty degrees most of the time. Although the two hours we spent inside a swimsuit every day took quite a bit out of us, we still found time to take in the beauties of the New England woods. We always managed to find several lobsters in the course of a day's work, and one has never lived until he can watch the setting sun while looking out over a quiet lake in the New England woods, a beer in one hand and a steaming lobster claw in the other. A woman and a fire were necessary as props, of course. This duty came to an end all too soon, and we flew back to Florida to rejoin the team, which was undergoing a good bit of reorganization.

UDT-3's maneuvers had to be extensive in order to form a smooth running outfit out of the combination of old hands and new men. Any doubt that the old salts had as to the worth of the new replacements quickly gave way to open admiration as the spirit and ability of the new men became evident. The more experienced petty officers quickly saw that instead of having to teach these men how to operate, these replacements knew many new techniques that the old salts had never been exposed to. Also, they were all very good swimmers, something new to those of us who had swum from that reef at Guam by hanging on to our inflated life belts.

The work at Fort Pierce consisted of blasting paths through bands of obstacles. A standard system was worked out in which Section 1 took the seaward row of obstacles, Section 2 took the ones just inshore, Section 3 took the beach obstacles, and Section 4 struggled mightily with the seawall.

Chapter Forty-six

Darryl Young

SEAL Team 1 UDT-11 1969–1972

Tinian Island 1971

John Collier, one of the strongest members of our sixteen-man platoon, grabbed the bitter end of the flutterboard line and secured it to his web belt. With his swim fins in hand, he began to walk, towing the line seaward across the level coral reef through the warm, knee-deep, crystal clear water. Another member of our platoon held the flutterboard securely in place, while the rest of us loitered around the white-sand beach, checking over our gear and watching the flutterboard slowly unravel.

Everyone else designated to enter the water, myself included, waited for a small piece of colored rag called a bunting marker that was secured to the flutterboard line at twenty-five-yard increments. The bunting marker marked the position where the next UDT swimmer would grab the line and proceed to sea. Six members of our platoon, the beach party, were to stay on the beach to work the beach equipment.

Scattered large, white cumulus clouds slowly moved across

the blue sky, constantly transforming themselves into odd looking configurations. I felt that I could almost reach out and feel their soft, cottony surface. A warm, tropical offshore breeze blew in from the sea. The larger island of Saipan, a long and low strip of green on the blue horizon, could be observed to the north. Knife-like gray coral and serrated lava figures, high and dry for thousands of years, protruded out of the hinterland sand and low vegetation behind the beach, where contact was made with a lush, green jungle wall. The scene reminded me of *Robinson Crusoe* and Pitcairn Island, where the *Bounty* ended up.

Tinian was a truly lush tropical island paradise, a feast for the eyes and mind after spending weeks at sea on board a large naval vessel. There were no Holiday Inns, fancy restaurants, paved highways, busy intersections, or crowded international airports to destroy the exquisite view and natural sounds of the surf crashing on the far edge of the coral reef. It was the kind of environment you only dream about or get to visit once in your life—if you're that fortunate.

It was great to get off our ship and finally function as a platoon, the way we'd been trained, instead of traveling around with limited leeway on what we UDT men called the "big gray monsters," i.e., the navy's vessels. This mission would give me an opportunity to accumulate more exotic tropical seashells for the collection I had started when our platoon was in Okinawa. Tinian was an ideal location for just that.

The majority of the time our platoon spent on board the big gray monsters was consumed by morning PT, followed by a couple hours of sun conditioning. We maintained our UDT equipment and kept ourselves in shape for any situation that might arise that would require UDT capabilities. In Vietnam, the war was still going on. That was not far to the west, and we were prepared to deploy there on a moment's notice, if needed.

Our not functioning as part of the ship's crew angered some of the fleet sailors, and a constant line of complaints seemed to always float down from above. That was nothing new for a UDT platoon to be deployed on board a naval vessel as an assault readiness group (ARG). If the officer in charge of the

UDTs went to bat and stuck up for his men, none of us would have to perform regular ship's duties or stand watches. Those tasks were not why we had dedicated ourselves to the months of extraordinarily rigorous training to become Frogmen. And besides, we may be required to perform our Frogman functions on a moment's notice, for just about any situation, anywhere the U.S. military may demand.

After transferring to UDT-11 from SEAL Team 1, I was trying to make the best of my second overseas tour. The reality, that I might never have the chance to return to an environment like Tinian's after I got out of the navy (a little over a year away), was starting to sink in. After all, a cruise on a civilian ship to a tropical island paradise would cost major bucks. So I thought I would take advantage of the situation.

Our platoon departed San Diego back in September, on board the USS *Denver*, with two F-4 phantoms lashed to its helo flight deck, en route to Vietnam. The ship cruised from San Diego to Hawaii, then to Japan and Okinawa, where we finally got to conduct several hydrographic beach recons and recovered all the pieces we could find of a lost fluorescent orange experimental missile that plunged into the sea after malfunctioning. On the way to Okinawa from Japan, we were caught in a typhoon with thirty- to forty-foot waves that crashed over the bow and superstructure of the *Denver*, making the bulkheads flex as the ship maneuvered through the storm.

After spending time in Okinawa, we transferred to the USS *Schenectady* while the USS *Denver* sailed to Da Nang to deliver the two F-4 Phantoms. Our new gray monster, the *Schenectady*, cruised southeast to Guam and then north to Tinian, where we arrived in early November. The *Schenectady* anchored in the bay off Tinian Town because there were no docking facilities for a large vessel anywhere on the island.

Tinian Island, part of the chain of Mariana Islands, is located about 150 miles north of Guam. It is largely surrounded by jagged coral reefs that extend several hundred yards out to sea, lava shores, and frequently cliffs. Very few ships travel to Tinian regularly as it isn't located near major shipping lanes, so tourists are rare there. When their mail and supplies arrive, it's a pretty big occasion for the locals.

Consisting of coastal plains and low, broad plateaus, with a wide variety of vegetation, Tinian is approximately twelve miles long and three miles wide. Tinian itself was a plateau, a tableland rising from the crystal clear, warm waters of the Pacific Ocean. The shoreline was composed of sheer and undercut walls of rusty brown and gray lava. Even though in long stretches it was only five or six feet above the water, it still effectively barred amphibious assault by American forces during World War II. The Japanese made good use of this natural barrier.

Each of the four days the *Schenectady* was anchored in the bay, our UDT platoon descended a long set of stairs from her side to a boat waiting to take us and our gear ashore. Then we traveled by military six-by truck to the beaches that were to be reconned. Each night, our platoon returned to the *Schenectady* to prepare for the next day's recon.

We were the first UDT platoon to recon beaches that were last reconned by the UDTs during World War II when the Japanese occupied the island. It had been more than twenty-seven years since the U.S. Navy's underwater demolition teams had reconned the beaches of Tinian.

1944

UDT was fairly new to the U.S. military back then. New techniques and equipment developed since the invasion of Normandy made the UDT men more maneuverable and increased their chances of completing their missions and surviving with fewer casualties in an ocean-swimming, combat environment. Not only did the UDT men have to cope with the possibilities of making contact with the enemy Japanese soldiers, their obstacles, mines, and weapons, but the creatures that lurked just off the reef could be just as deadly.

In 1944, the island was occupied by nine thousand Japanese who were placed there to defend an airstrip and the island itself. Tinian had great strategic value to the United States. A full-scale invasion by our forces was needed to secure the island and its runway. By securing Tinian, America would be within striking distance (fifteen hundred miles) of mainland Japan, using B-29 bombers. Maps, charts, and intelligence about the offshore waters were very limited, and there were no prewar inhabitants available for interrogation.

During this period, Tinian Town was considered to have the better airstrip for the B-29 bombers. At first only two beaches were considered for an amphibious landing, Asiga Bay on the east coast and the bay at Tinian Town on the southwestern coast. At Tinian Town, more than a mile of good sand beach stretched behind reefs and shoals, traversed by several navigable channels. A concrete pier offered essential facilities for unloading of heavy material and equipment. There and only there, was the beach area extensive enough to receive assault craft in the widely deployed waves, which, as the Japanese commanders had learned from their observations of Saipan, were the essence of our assault tactics. The main blow of the assault force was thought to have to fall at Tinian Town because of the wide beach.

The Japanese confidently prepared for the main assault from the Americans at Asiga Bay and Tinian Town. Behind the narrow sands of Asiga Bay, designated as Yellow Beach, the Japanese built a defense system from which a battalion might stand off the seaborne attack of a regiment and more. Then, as an added precaution, they formed a mobile reserve force of their finest troops to be stationed in the southeast, ready to reinforce the defenders at Asiga Bay or Tinian Town as the situation might demand.

But they concentrated their efforts at the Tinian Town beaches. They strengthened existing defenses to make the ground behind the sands a second Tarawa—they sowed the reefs, the channels, the shoals, and the beaches with mines. Safe from our aerial reconnaissance, in the thickets and woodlands of the high ground to the northwest and southeast of the town, they concealed machine guns and artillery to trap assault waves in a terrible cross fire. All the big guns of their hidden coastal batteries were trained toward the beaches. Many of them were British six-inchers, brought to Tinian from captured ships or from Singapore.

For thirty-nine days, the Japanese watched from Tinian as the Americans invaded Saipan to the north. They witnessed the violence of our first assault wave and the bloody, yet unrelenting, progress of our campaign. They heard the voices of our guns on Saipan multiply day after day, and they felt the silence when the guns ceased firing—the silence which meant that of their twenty-four thousand brothers-in-arms on Saipan, one thousand had been taken prisoner and twenty-three thousand had died.

For thirty-nine days they waited, knowing that their turn would come. By day, from sea and air, we blasted their fixed positions and emplacements, their roads and villages, and Tinian Town. By night, our star shells filled their broken sleep with fear. In the first days, their own artillery threw occasional shells toward our ships, our beachhead on Saipan, or our planes on Aslito Airfield, also on Saipan. When they discovered that every gun of theirs that opened fire on us invited immediate counterbattery fire, they ceased firing. The nine thousand Japanese occupying Tinian waited to face the conquerors of the twenty-four thousand comrades on Saipan.

For thirty-nine days the Japanese labored through the hours of darkness to construct and repair their defenses. Under our daylight bombardment, the houses on Tinian collapsed into dusty piles of rubble and splinters and torn corrugated-iron roofing.

Meanwhile, two other small beaches were accidently discovered that were not visible on the aerial photographs taken earlier. They were designated as beaches White 1 and 2 and were located directly across the channel from Saipan, on Tinian's north shore. Passing at sea along the straight line off Tinian's northeastern coast from Ushi Point on Saipan Channel to Faibus San Hilo Point, four and a half miles to the southwest, men might have looked shoreward a hundred times without noticing that at two places the white thread of foam against the sheer lava walls was different from elsewhere—less fluid and less brightly gleaming. At those two points, the whiteness was the sand of two little beaches, two scarcely visible indentations in the lava, where over the years, the waves had pushed back the walls a few yards and eroded them into banks of brown rubble. The northern beach, White 1, was only 65 yards wide and the other, White 2, was 130 yards wide. Their combined span was less than one half of a normal battalion front. Both beaches were flanked by large jagged lava rock and coral outcroppings.

If the two beaches were to be utilized, the lava barriers in the hinterland would have to be breached for an opening large enough to insert a vital steady flow of the men, equipment, heavy weapons, ammunition, and supplies needed to establish a position on the island.

Asiga Bay (Yellow Beach), one of the other possible landing sites, was approximately four hundred yards long but was considered too risky for a large-scale assault. Of the four possible assault beaches, White 1 and 2, and Yellow Beach were the main beaches to be reconned and charted by the UDT men. The beach at Tinian Town was out of the question, as that is where the Japanese were expecting the invasion.

On July 10, 1944, a combined force of UDT swimmers and Marines headed for Tinian to commence the recon. The Marines were responsible for a recon of the beach and hinterland area, and the UDT men were responsible for the recon of the waters off the beaches. The famous UDT fast insertion and extraction, cast and recovery, or drop and pickup, utilizing the rubber sling to the left arm, was first utilized by UDT-5 on June 14, 1944, on the island of Saipan, across a two-and-a-half-mile channel to the north. This successful system was also used during the recons of Tinian by the UDT men.

A strong current running offshore of beaches White 1 and 2 made the recon difficult, but few obstacles were located in the water by the UDT men, or on the beach and into the hinterland by the Marines. This wasn't the situation at Yellow Beach.

At Yellow Beach, the eight UDT men in the water and twenty Marines who went ashore found the Japanese forces on Tinian had placed barbed-wire entanglements in the water and on the beach, as well as mines and other obstacles. Assuming that beaches White 1 and 2 were too small for an American beach landing, the Japanese had concentrated on reinforcing Yellow Beach.

The information brought back from the recon indicated that the cliffs facing Yellow Beach had gun emplacements and fortified bunkers, as well as sentries patrolling the beach itself.

Underwater, the UDT men located large potholes, boulders, and floating mines anchored just below the surface.

Based on intelligence gathered by the UDT men and the Marines on these possible landing sites, an amphibious invasion was planned for July 24, 1944, utilizing beaches White 1 and 2. These beaches were very small, but it seemed that the Japanese were not expecting an invasion to take place there. Another detailed investigation of the waters off those two beaches was conducted by the UDT men prior to the invasion, and a demolition swim to destroy obstacles was not considered necessary.

During the actual amphibious landing, White 1 and 2 were discovered to be heavily mined when the troops made it to shore, and the preinvasion bombardment by the support ships had only destroyed about one-third of the mines on White 2. Being demolition experts, the UDT men assisted the engineers and bomb-disposal teams in clearing the mines and booby traps the Japanese had put there. White Beach 2 was considered safe by midafternoon the day of the invasion.

In winning the battle for Tinian from the nine thousand Japanese, who now lay dead, we had won an island less than fifteen hundred miles from Tokyo. Tinian's forty-eight square miles of flat and gently rolling fields made it the finest potential air base in the Central Pacific. The possibility of launching B-29 bombers to mainland Japan had become a reality, possibly shortening the war in the Pacific and saving millions of lives. The cost to the United States: 190 dead, 1,515 wounded, and 24 missing, a cost in startling contrast to its great strategic worth. If the beach landings had taken place on either of the other two beaches, our losses would have been far greater.

After Tinian Island had been secured, the UDTs moved on to the south to recon the island of Guam.

The first atomic bomb was launched on a B-29 bomber from Tinian Island, August 6, 1945, destination Hiroshima. Eighty thousand Japanese were killed, but the nation still wouldn't surrender. A second bomb was launched three days later, destination Nagasaki. This time forty thousand Japanese were killed. The Japanese finally surrendered a few days later.

1971

So there I was, standing on White Beach 1, looking inland toward the hinterland from the water's edge at the beach openings in the lava and coral through which American troops and their equipment had stormed more than twenty-seven years ago. Looking around, it was difficult for me to believe that not that many years ago this island was ripped apart from the shells of our ships' guns, and nine thousand Japanese were killed trying to defend their positions. Over the years, the island had partially restored itself, but looking around, the evidence of the battle's scars still remained.

The airstrip, used to launch the B-29 bomber attack on Japan, had been reclaimed by jungle. The ride in the back of the military six-by to this particular location on the island was, in itself, an experience I'll never forget. The road was so overgrown with vegetation that we and our equipment were buried alive beneath leaves and branches while riding in the bed of the truck. The truck bulldozed its way through the jungle, pushing back both outside mirrors,, streamlining itself as though it could adjust to the impenetrable jungle. Instead, the jungle adjusted to the powerful, military diesel truck.

Live ammunition, grenades, bombs, old anchors, jeeps, conex boxes (large metal storage containers), and other pieces of rusty war equipment still lay around on the beach and underwater like ancient fossils, exposing themselves after Mother Nature had revealed them from their interminable resting place. Near my feet, in the water close to shore, was a rusted pineapple grenade. With my SEAL training and explosives background, I was normally interested in all types of demolitions, but we all avoided prehistoric ordinance. It had had its chance twenty-seven years ago as far as I was concerned. Tim Oelker, one of the members of our platoon, photographed the grenade with his 35mm camera. That was good enough for me.

I could only look around and imagine what had taken place here back in the midforties and what it might have been like to be one of the soldiers, on either side, to have done battle here so *far* from anywhere else. I was experienced in combat so I could relate to the fighting that took place there, even though it was long ago.

Each swimmer in our platoon who was assigned to enter the water carried a lead line, a small chunk of lead with a twenty-foot line attached that is marked every foot so the swimmer can take a sounding and determine the water's depth. Each of us wore around our neck on a lanyard a Plexiglas slate with grease pencil for recording the depth and information regarding any obstacles on the sea floor. A UDT inflatable life jacket, web belt carrying a rusty-trusty K-bar knife, with a day-and-night emergency flare attached, face mask, and swim fins were also worn. Levi's and snorkels were optional equipment.

The beach to be reconned had already been set up with a baseline, using a lensatic compass from the determined right flank of the beach. The right flank was determined as a starting point because of the direction of the ocean current. Taking advantage of the current would make swimming during the recon much easier.

The straight baseline, shot with the compass from the right flank to the opposite flank of the beach, had to be established before the UDT administrative parallel hydrographic beach reconnaissance could begin. This was fulfilled by six members of our platoon designated as a beach party. They were to stay on the beach and were responsible for determining the current's direction, its speed, the type of waves and their heights, the high-water line, the baseline, the range pole positions, and any obstacles on the beach and into the hinterland.

The flutterboard is nothing more than a large wooden spool, holding several hundred feet of small diameter nylon line, similar in size to the suspension line found on a parachute. It incorporates two handles, one for carrying and holding it securely on the beach, and the other for reeling in the line when the beach recon has been terminated.

The flutterboard line, with the bunting markers placed every twenty-five yards, is mainly used to keep us in our assigned positions while in the water and help us line up on two range poles of different heights, with a different colored flag on each pole. The poles are positioned perpendicular (ninety degrees) from the baseline on the beach, close to the high-water line, using a compass, the shorter pole at the water's edge and the taller one several yards inland. The flutterboard can also be used to mark the twenty-five-foot increments for the range poles on the baseline before it is pulled to sea by the outboard swimmer.

Our flutterboard line continued seaward, accumulating a swimmer at each bunting marker. I was third man from the outboard swimmer, the man on the bitter end of the line. The line continued seaward until the outboard swimmer sent word back down the column of swimmers to the men on the beach that he had reached the twenty-one-foot depth with his lead line, the depth that UDT is responsible for while collecting hydrographic information to create a chart.

When the twenty-foot depth is determined, the line stops unraveling, and all the swimmers line up on the two range poles positioned on the beach. When all the swimmers are on line, the after range-pole man (furthest inland from the beach) waves his range-pole flag. The flag is waved only when all swimmers involved are in a straight line perpendicular to the beach baseline. As the flag is waved, we drop our lead lines and record the depth of the water in each swimmer's position on the flutterboard line. We then let go of the flutterboard line and free dive to the sea floor to inspect our area for obstacles, man-made or natural, and record all this information on our slate.

The majority of our swimmers were only standing in the knee-deep water on the wide, flat, shallow reef floor. Nevertheless, any UDT man on the flutterboard line is considered a swimmer and is responsible for collecting the same hydrographic information as the men treading water in the deeper areas. Swimmers located in shallow water (one to two feet deep) were not required to wear swim fins, but they had to watch out for old ordnance that might barely be visible in the sand. The UDT swimmer inboard on the line tends the flutterboard at the water's edge.

As the swimmers are investigating their assigned areas, the beach party moves the range poles down the beach, twenty-five yards toward the opposite beach flank and again positions them ninety degrees to the baseline with the compass. The beach party always stays ahead of the swimmers by marking the range-pole positions ahead of time. The swimmers, after investigating and recording their areas on their slates, tow the line through the water to the next position, and again line up on the two range poles for their next inspection of the bottom in that area. It is important that the swimmers stay on line, swim at the same speed, and do not hang on the line while performing the recon.

The hydrographic beach reconnaissance is conducted this way from one beach flank to the other, accumulating all the hydrographic information from the seafloor as the swimmers stay on their bunting markers. This information can be used to create an accurate underwater chart of all obstacles, depths, and beach gradients in the anticipated amphibious beach-landing area. This process, like all types of UDT hydrographic beach recons, takes many hours of practice. By the time a new Frogman graduates from UDT/SEAL training, he is very proficient at it.

Tennis shoes or coral booties (canvas shoes with rubber bottoms that swim fins will fit over) were mandatory for all hands involved, to protect our feet from the jagged coral that broke up the sandy bottom of the reef's floor. Some teammates wore Levi's to help protect their legs. Others, myself included, wore only UDT swim trunks.

This beach was a far cry from the stench of the Vietnamese mud and the waters of the Mekong Delta area where I had grown so accustomed to crawling and wading through less than a year ago. This was the kind of Frogman duty I had dreamed about, and joined the navy for in the first place. I would rather take my chances in the shark-infested water and put up with the sea snakes and dangerous jellyfish any day than fight Viet Cong and NVA soldiers.

I was amazed at how warm and clear the water was. In fact, being submerged, I could see for over a hundred meters in all directions. We could insure complete coverage of our surrounding positions in those existing visibility conditions. The water was so clear that no one on the flutterboard line really had to dive to the bottom to see what was there; it could be seen from the surface. But, diving to the bottom made me more aware of and familiar with my surroundings. Without a doubt, this was the clearest water I had ever swam in.

What a contrast from other beaches and rivers I've reconned in the past, where the visibility was so poor I couldn't see a hand if put to my face mask. We had to "feel" for obstacles in those circumstances, not knowing what the hell was lurking beneath the surface or what we might grab onto.

Now and then, adding to the beauty of this tropical paradise, a giant sea turtle would glide by, seemingly unconcerned at our intrusion. While in the water, it seemed that every time I turned around I saw another strange creature that before I had encountered only on TV or as photographs in a book. There were fragile little sea-horselike things with growths like angel wings on their back that would swim right up to my face mask. Giant coral heads of all sizes, shapes, and colors, bloomed toward the surface from the bottom, creating natural condominiums for a wide variety of fish. There were more exotic fish and sea shells of different sizes and shapes than I could remember seeing anywhere else.

A local who our platoon used as a guide, escorted us to all the beaches we were to recon. He knew the best, fastest, and easiest way to get anywhere on his island. The day before, back at the first beach we reconned on Tinian, the waters just off the reef were infested with sharks. Before we entered the water, our guide told us that we were crazy. He also told us that when the people of the village fish there, the sharks ate most of their fish before they could get them to the boat.

Our guide was right about the sharks and about our being crazy for entering the water. Immediately upon entering the water, we counted eight large white-tip sharks and several large barracuda at the edge of the reef. They never aggravated us as they curiously maneuvered close by during the recon. We kept a close eye on them anyway. The sharks gave me the feeling we were all as vulnerable as bottom feeders. They were just a sample of what we were to see our four days at Tinian.

Besides the sharp coral and the ever-present sharks, barracuda, sea snakes, and jellyfish, the only other thing to be concerned about was the pounding surf at the edge of the coral reef. Being slammed into the coral by the "wave of the day" could result in numerous stitches to head and body.

Our flutterboard line was stretched over one hundred yards across the flat reef from the shore. Those of us in deeper water at the reef's edge, were getting a fantastic view of the jagged coral as it dropped off into a dark blue, beautiful abyss, the color blue that would look proper painted on a custom '57 Chevy.

Collier, the outboard swimmer, was treading water at his designated position and making every effort to stay on line with the two range poles. Swimming with the current is much easier if the recon moves right along, but if it slows down for any reason, the outboard line man really has to work hard to hold his position. That was one of the disadvantages of being the outboard swimmer. It was a constant battle, treading water against the surf action and the current while trying to keep the line straight, taking soundings, and diving to inspect the bottom at the same time. Every time a wave crashed on the reef's edge, the line was pulled shoreward, along with the swimmers in the surf zone. It takes a very strong swimmer as the outboard line man, or the man positioned in the surf zone, to endure the entire length of the beach during any beach recon.

As the line of swimmers moved down the beach, staying on their bunting marker, the twenty-one-foot depth would fluctuate closer or farther from the baseline. Swimmers were added to, or subtracted from, the flutterboard line as needed, making it longer or shorter according to the seafloor's gradient changes. In my assigned area, just outside the plunging surf zone, past the edge of the reef where the large creatures lurked, crevices twenty feet deep with ridges eight feet across extended straight out and down into the sea, disappearing into the dark depths. The crevices were filled with a variety of exotic tropical fish, feeding on the sides of the coral or just swimming around. The bottom had scattered conglomerations of seashells, rocks, and an occasional unexploded bomb from a plane or a projectile from a ship's gun.

I collected a few shells as I moved along, stashing them in a small nylon-mesh bag I carried with me on most dives. The sharks lingered near the reef's steep drop-off's, occasionally entering to investigate one of the deep crevices.

At times during the recon, I would be in an area just inside the surf zone, where my feet would make contact with a coral ridge. This would let me stand for a few moments with my head out of the water, giving me some relief from having to tread water, at least until the next wave came in when I would have to deal with the plunging surf, watching the waves and maneuvering my body to avoid getting thrown against the sharp coral.

While standing on one coral ridge, I could look into the water, with my face mask, into deep crevices to either side of me. They resembled large steep-walled cracks in the earth. As the flutterboard line moved to its next position, twenty-five yards away, I was treading water over a crevice twenty feet deep.

Facing seaward, the ridges resembled lava fingers of consistent size, long seized by fungal, jagged coral, which extended steeply down and out from the level and secure reef, finally ending up at the deepest place on earth, the Mariana Trench, located just a few miles offshore! Looking down into that '57 Chevy dark blue, I wondered how deep it really was and what creatures lurked down there?

At one point during the recon, while I was treading water over one of the crevices, a six-foot white-tip shark came up from out of nowhere and cruised past me, so close that I had to lift my feet to avoid him making contact with my fins. The shark was swimming in the direction of Frank Schroeder, the next man on the line toward shore from me.

I hollered to Frank, "Shark coming your way." He stuck his face mask in the water, pulled his K-bar knife from its scabbard, and dived toward the shark to meet it head-on. The shark, noticing him coming, turned, and with one kick of its tail disappeared past me into the clear dark blue depths below the coral reef.

As we lined up on the last lane at the opposite flank of the beach, both range poles waved simultaneously, indicating the end of the recon. All UDT men in the water took their last sounding, and those of us treading water dove to the bottom to investigate the ocean floor's characteristics. The flutterboard line was then reeled back onto the flutterboard.

After each of us completed his last investigation of our area, it was time to return to shore. Those of us treading water swam to the edge of the coral reef, took off our fins, and carefully climbed up on it. We then walked back through the knee-deep water to the beach.

At the beach, the UDT cartographer (man in charge of creating the chart), debriefed each swimmer in swim order on the flutterboard line and collected all the hydrographic information. It was recorded on a rough chart, along with information regarding the hinterland area. The beach recon was now secured.

That night, back on board the *Schenectady*, an official chart was created of the entire beach area from the hinterland to the twenty-one-foot depth. This chart accurately exposed all obstacles, whether natural or man-made, on the surface and underwater within the beach-landing area. Coral would be considered a natural obstacle, while concrete, steel, etc., would be man-made. If needed, our platoon could go back to a beach we had reconned, along with the proper demolitions to neutralize the obstacles, making the bottom safe for amphibious landing craft.

This type of UDT operation just scratches the surface of the naval special warfare capabilities. There are many other types of hydrographic beach recons the UDTs perform to chart the bottom areas of possible beach-landing areas. They can be conducted administratively, in peacetime, or in a combat situation, day or night.

After transferring from SEAL Team 1, except for operating with my new platoon's inexperienced officer in charge, I looked forward to, and enjoyed, the duties our platoon performed with UDT-11. We had an excellent platoon of qualified enlisted men who were capable of performing any type of UDT function that may be required anywhere in the world.

So, we left Tinian Island late one evening to the sounds of the vibrating gray monster, as it got underway, and the colors of another tropical sunset. In only four days, our platoon had reconned every possible amphibious beach-landing site on

Tinian Island. Our destination was now Okinawa, where we were to meet up with the USS *Denver* once again. That long, thin, green island lying in the blue Pacific, so far from anywhere else, where giant sea shells lay around in great quantities, will always be on my mind.

Like many other things I had the opportunity of experiencing during my naval obligation, I'll never forget the island of Tinian as long as *I* live. The battle that took place there in World War II, the friendly natives, the clear, deep, dark blue '57 Chevy waters of its rugged shoreline, and the one hundred plus meter visibility. The beautiful, odd-shaped coral figures, the eighty-degree water temperature, the turtles and tropical fish, the barracudas, sea snakes, jellyfish, and last of all, the white-tip sharks with big, ugly, white teeth that lurked near the edge of the coral reef. Waiting to greet us each time we entered the water, they could be depended on.

But most of all, the entire seashell collection I accumulated from the many dives I swam on, during my second WesPac tour. They were stolen from me, later in the tour, by some Marines who were on board the *Denver* after we returned. Who knows, maybe I'll return to Tinian someday and start a new collection.

Chapter Forty-seven

Robert Marshall
UDT-3 1945

Oceanside, California to Wakayama, Japan

UDT-3 reported to Oceanside, California, on August 8, 1945. Everyone had their twenty-days' leave behind them and, of course, had accumulated a new and better bunch of leave stories. When we arrived, we were very much up in the air as to what the score was as far as our immediate future was concerned. Back at Fort Pierce, the scuttlebutt was that we would receive some cold-water training for the "big push." Everyone was pretty well certain that that indicated Japan. There were, of course, tens of guesses as to the date. But the consensus seemed to indicate sometime in the late fall. We had a suspicion that it would really be a rugged few weeks of cold-water training. We were greatly pleased upon arriving at the ATB to find that it was one of the better camps that UDT had been thrown into. The barracks were plainly livable. The chow was better than that of good old Fort Pierce, and of course, the sand flies and mosquitoes were entirely absent, this being California.

After a few days had passed, we quickly saw that this was to be a real demo conclave. UDT teams from everywhere started to arrive. People we hadn't seen for months started to show their faces. More and more brass turned up also. Everywhere we went, there was a captain. It was obvious that the demos were gathering for something big, and it was also obvious that Hirohito and his boys were fast getting enough of it.

Rumor pressed on the heel of rumor. First we heard that the war was to be over in a week. Then we heard that it was to be over in a few hours. Then the papers came out with a statement that the Japs had said that they would fight to the death, regardless of the cost. Then, came the big news—the atom bomb was dropped on Hiroshima!

It was unbelievable, fantastic, beyond the wildest imagination of the human brain. It really looked like the end to us, and bets were flying thick and fast that we would all be home in a week at the latest. All this time, Oceanside was still slowly gaining UDTs. Teams were showing up from leave, Maui, Borneo, Okinawa, and God knows where. A tentative training schedule was being set up to run some six weeks, complete with en masse APD problems and all the fixings. Gear was arriving by the trainloads to outfit the teams for what looked like the grandest of demo operations. Flak suits, swimsuits, and zoot suits. Tommy guns, grease guns, and son of a guns all piled up in glorious confusion. Then the last word was that the entire base was put on forty-eight–hour notice, and everyone was restricted to the base. The newspapers were still flowing with every supposition in the world.

The team COs were then called together and told that we would be expected to draw all our gear, get the personnel together, and be ready to load off on APDs within twenty-four hours. It was said that twenty APDs would be on hand the following morning—and they were!

The ship we drew was the USS *Ira Jeffery*, APD 44. The captain was Lt. Comdr. William Doheny, USNR, with Lt. Wayne T. Ash for the executive officer. Of course, the ship was the new type of APD, that is to say, one which had been converted from a destroyer escort and not from an old flush-decker. It was a real revelation to the old-timers in our team.

We loaded every bit of gear that we could beg, borrow, and steal. We must have signed our names for at least a thousand dollars worth of gear for every minute of the day. The troop space looked like a veritable Waldorf, and the troop officers' space reminded one of the bridal suite at the Royal Hawaiian. The CO's and XO's cabins were like something out of this world. Of course, with all these sumptuous appointments, there were some few who started to bitch before the cruise even began, but honestly, we simply loved it. There was only one big trouble though, *the war was over*! Yes, the very day that we boarded the *Ira J*, 15 August 1945, the big news was finally announced.

That night as we sat at the movies, we saw the mad celebration ashore, and it sure looked swell. Later, we read about it in the newspapers. As for us on board, we shot red flares into the air. Thank God that we weren't ashore with all the drunks, riff-raff, and wild women, especially the latter. My gosh . . . if we would have been in Hollywood that night . . . you can't tell what might have happened . . . Damn it!

Seriously though, we all did feel slightly let down at the whole proceedings. It seemed like kind of a dirty trick to be so close to the celebrations, yet so far away. But the war was over. The following evening, 16 August 1945, we set sail, twenty APDs with twenty demo outfits aboard.

The first few days were spent straightening the gear away. It was a terrible mess inasmuch as it was just thrown from the deck of an LCT (landing craft, tank) to the hold of the ship. Much of the gear had been stowed at Maui where the *Ira Jeffery* would have to pick it up on the way. We did not have the powder aboard at this time.

Things soon settled down into a fairly smooth routine. We set up a continuous watch over our gear, which was continued throughout the cruise. We set up our own MAA's (master-at-arms) in the quarters and designated mess cooks and a chow-hall MAA. Doc Quiggle performed the duties of CMAA (chief master-at-arms) and was assisted by Stew and Fred Hart. Rylands served as the boss in the chow hall throughout the stay on the *Ira J*. They all did an A-1 job and were in no little way responsible for the comparative comfort of all hands. They enforced a standard of cleanliness, which meant a lot.

At the same time, a tentative setup was made with the ship

concerning the LCPRs. In general, the UDT boat officer and the ship's boat officer worked together in regard to the boats. We were given complete freedom to make all alterations which were desired, and immediately proceeded with this work.

At this time, we were asked if we had any volunteers who would like to stand junior officer-of-the-deck (JOOD) watches. Several of the junior officers of the team desired to do this and were encouraged to do so by the CO. Although it does cut down on sack time, it was thought that, in general, it makes the time pass more pleasantly. There is no reason why this is not practical prior to the serious planning stage of the operation.

At the request of the ship's captain, the UDTs also stood some enlisted watches. Suffice to say, the team and the ship got along amicably despite being jammed together on an APD. It can be done without hurting the interests of either party with concessions, favors, and a little common sense on the parts of both organizations.

We arrived at Pearl Harbor on 22 August and were soon alongside an ammo dock in order to pick up our powder. We loaded approximately thirty tons of explosives, which we were able to stow in their original boxes. It is believed that this is the preferable stowage, that is to say, the safest. All the explosives were stowed in the ship's troop magazine space. That night, liberty was granted . . . with no casualties.

We got our first glimpse of a small stream that was soon to turn into a mighty torrent while we were at Pearl. That was the UDT article which the *Honolulu Advertiser* published. It felt good to see ourselves in print, and the paper boy sold out in a very short time. Of course, all the old-timers turned up their noses at some of the fancy tales that were told in this article, but you can be sure that, secretly, these clippings were put aside to bring forth ten and twenty years from now in order to impress the newer generations. After so much secrecy, it seemed almost sacrilege to see the innermost workings of UDT spread open to the public eye.

Also at Pearl Harbor, the first of another mighty torrent was started. Here the team lost its first members to demobilization. Jake, the team's XO, and also the team's photographer's mate, along with S. A. Featherston, departed us and started back to the States. Jake was one of the oldest old-timers of them all, while Featherston was one of the newer members of the team.

The newest pastime for all naval personnel became a game that we called count your points. This game had a great resemblance to the game of blackjack, with the slight difference that the number to get was forty-four instead of twenty-one. Forty-four points and home you went. I might mention that this was the first time that anyone really learned to appreciate the value of his Silver Star, which was the equivalent of the magic forty-four points. Jake was discharged on this angle. The Marine, Frank Lahr, replaced Jake as the executive officer of UDT-3. The Marine had also received the Silver Star, but the Marines played the game a slightly different way, and his didn't count.

While at Pearl we also procured as much of our missing gear as possible. However, due to the confusion, we were not able to get much besides some of our photo gear and a small amount of recreational equipment. We also saw Lieutenant Commander Crist and Burt Hawks who were both over from Maui, trying to get discharged because of their Silver Stars. Of course, with all the demos being in port together, a party developed, and the DESPAC (Destroyer Pacific) officers club was properly christened with no fatal consequences . . . noted.

We started out our speed run once more with a somewhat diminished squadron. The teams split up and only the *Jeffery*, the *Blessman*, and the *Hobby* were present, transporting UDT-3, UDT-7, and UDT-5 respectively. We were told at Pearl that this would be the group with which we would operate, although we were not told at this time where or when the operation would be.

During our passage to Eniwetok, we continued preparations for any eventuality and went forward with the work on the boats and guns, and prepared for string reconnaissances. The weather was at all times fair. We had some practice with the .50-calibers, the carbines, the .45s, and submachine guns under the direction of Bill Munro, the gunnery officer for our team. This exercise was carried out with only one small incident. Petey Nelms scared the CO out of a couple of days of his life in showing him how to operate one of the new "squirt guns" (submachine guns).

We steamed into Manila Bay on the morning of 5 September and got a great kick out of all the Japanese shipping sitting on the bottom of the bay. Each of us also felt a lump rise in our throats as we passed Corregidor. It is believed that Captain Williams set some kind of record in bringing this group of APDs out to the Philippine Islands in nineteen days total.

At Manila, we finally caught up with the group with which we were to operate, and for the first time we got some idea where we were to go. Captain Williams got the dope from commander Amphibious Group Eight, Admiral Noble, and passed it on to us. We were to take part in the occupation of Japan on the island of Honshu. To be exact, we would operate in the vicinity of Kobe.

This first plan anticipated that we would conduct a reconnaissance of beaches just to the west of the city of Kobe. However, just before we left Manila, this was changed to the town of Wakayama, which is about thirty miles to the south of the Kobe–Osaka area. This change was made because the bay that forms the entrance to the Kobe–Osaka landing beaches was strewn with U.S. pressure mines which cannot be successfully swept. The plans at this time were not very detailed nor was the date definitely set, but the tentative date for K day was to be 25 September. In the meantime, we were ordered up to Subic Bay to await more-detailed plans and to conduct rehearsals and training.

Before leaving Manila, all hands got the opportunity to go ashore, and I am sure no one will ever forget the sight of utter ruin which the town afforded. It made all hands thank God that the war never reached the States. Between the Japs and ourselves, there certainly was not much left. Except for the shore patrol, which was its usual, vigilant self, everything seemed in a state of complete disorganization. Our team's CO was awarded a type of citation for his ability to borrow a jeep under such difficult conditions. We shoved off for Subic Bay at noon on the seventh and arrived there around 1600.

While at Subic Bay, we were able to get in quite a bit of swimming, which everyone needed very badly. Personnel who had never before been in the Pacific got a kick out of swimming out over the coral reef, which lay to the seaward side of the recreation island. We also ran several experiments in conjunction with the ship to determine whether or not we would be able to use the ship's radar to track LCPRs during hydrographic reconnaissance. The results of this experiment were disappointing, and the technique was not used later.

On several days, different methods of reconnaissance were tried out. It was finally decided that the "string recon" from about four hundred yards into the beach, combined with a profile taken from a PR from four hundred yards out gave the best results. With this system, we decided that conditions in Japan warranted taking a chance, putting a small party ashore to assist with the inshore end of the string recon. This procedure was run through several times, and most of the wrinkles were ironed out.

The USS *Blessman* came up from Manila in a few days, and in company with her, we moved up the coast to Lingayen Gulf on the fourteenth. The next morning we anchored in San Fernando Harbor. We dropped the USS *Hobby*, with UDT-5 aboard, at this time. The original plans had been changed to the extent that UDT-5 was now to go to a different area for its operations. At San Fernando, we perfected our plans, in conjunction with UDT-7.

On the seventeenth, a complete rehearsal was held off Watenek Beach, just south of San Fernando. As usual, the runthrough was invaluable in locating errors and rough spots in our plans. This was particularly true where two or more teams were working together. The rehearsal was generally considered to be okay and became the order for the work to be done at Wakayama. While at San Fernando, we picked up three officers as passengers who all had some interest in the results of the demo work. They were Commander Graff, the group beachmaster, Lt. Cornell Larson, the army shore party commander, and Lieutenant Mitchell, the Seabee officer in charge of pontoon causeways.

On the eighteenth, we shoved off from Lingayen for Okinawa, which was to be the last stop before Japan itself. During this trip we caught the tail end of a typhoon; it was far from a pleasant trip. We arrived at Buckner Bay on the twentieth. After refueling the next morning, we left on the final stage of our journey to Japan.

Chapter Forty-eight

Tom Shallcross

SEAL Team 1 1970–1972

Dedicated, Motivated, and Loyal

I joined the navy in 1969 from a small town fifteen miles out of Great Lakes, Illinois. I had mentioned to the navy recruiter that I wouldn't mind trying out for the UDT/SEAL teams, but that wasn't my main reason for joining the navy. I was sent to San Diego, California, for boot camp and was assigned to Company 688. I had heard and read a little about the UDT/SEAL teams before I joined, but didn't think I had the "hair" to try out for it.

After graduating from boot camp, I was sent to ET (electronics technician) school at Treasure Island, in San Francisco Bay. I attended ET school for about sixteen weeks, and then I had had enough of that and got orders to BUDS (basic underwater demolition/SEAL training), the naval amphibious base in Coronado, California. About a week before UDT/SEAL Training Class 58 began, I arrived at the amphib base and started pretraining.

After Class 58 started its formal training, in the summer of 1970, I became injured during the second week and was rolled back to Class 59. While waiting for Class 59 to begin training, I was sent out to San Clemente Island to gofer around the UDT/SEAL camp, where Class 57 was performing its explosive work.

Class 59 began training in September 1970 with about one hundred men. We were the first training class to move into the new UDT/SEAL barracks that had been constructed near the UDT/SEAL compound, across the highway from the amphib base.

While we were in training, the instructors asked for volunteers to box in the smokers. I had always been told not to volunteer for anything, and I used to try to hide behind somebody in our ranks when the instructors asked our class.

The instructors would always say, "What, there are no volunteers? Shallcross, you're a volunteer . . . aren't you . . . you like to box, don't you? I'll just put your name down here!" Whenever they couldn't get boxers for the smokers, they would just come down to the UDT/SEAL training area and grab some guys. I got volunteered for two of them, and I lost them both. It was just something else in training that would aggravate us.

I was about the fifth fastest guy in our training class. Williams and Moy always used me as an example for the poor guys who couldn't run.

I was also a good swimmer. Usually, on our timed runs, I finished the swims within the third pair.

We graduated from UDT/SEAL training with about sixty men and weren't even in the teams a week when we were sent to jump school at Fort Benning, Georgia. That was in February 1971. Our whole training class attended. We arrived about a week before jump school began, so we got to help the army. While we were moving some lockers from one barracks to another, using a six-by, we hooked one end of a chain around the porch it had backed up to and the other to the bumper of the six-by, thinking that the army driver wouldn't be able to pull the truck away. But, the driver, not knowing about the chain, jumped in the truck and started to take off, pulling the porch off the front of the building. We had thought the truck would just come to a stop.

During morning muster one day, one of the officers approached us and said, "Could you guys keep it down, all these army guys want to be just like ya," meaning we were not disciplined very well. This was about the funniest three weeks that I ever had in the service. We were used to eatin' all we could eat back in the navy chow halls. We were only allowed one trip through the chow line at jump school. Most of us ate at the PX because the chow was better there.

Some British troops were going through jump school at the same time, and we became good friends. They hung around us because they couldn't get along with the army troops.

On my second jump, we were all lined up near the runway to board a C-119 aircraft. The group before us boarded its plane, and it took off down the runway. The plane left the ground and was barely flying over these pine trees, just like you see in the movies. Pretty soon, the plane started coughing and spitting and dipped down below the tree line. Finally, the engines revved up, and it circled around and came back and landed. All the jumpers got off and boarded another 119, then this guy came out with a screw driver and a crescent wrench and worked on the C-119 for a few minutes. Then they gave the signal for us to board that same plane! I was a nervous wreck. I expected the plane to blow up. Needless to say, we were all glad to bail out of that aircraft when it finally flew over the jump zone. I really did like jumpin'; it was a lot of fun.

Once, when I was on the ground after a jump, one of the black-hat instructors was yelling in his megaphone up into the air, "You with the Mae West, pull your reserve."

Everyone hanging in the air panicked, lookin' around to see if their parachute was open.

Once we were on the ground, we really had to watch out for jumpers' helmets falling from above. Once a helmet landed close to me, from a jumper that left a different aircraft after I had landed. Those stupid army helmets would fall off of you all the time, and if one would have hit you while you were on the ground . . .

After jump school, we returned to Coronado, formed Foxtrot Platoon, and went through SEAL cadre training out at Niland, California. Training as a platoon, getting ready to deploy to Vietnam, moved along pretty fast. We were scheduled to deploy in June 1971. That date was then moved to July 1971. Our platoon was all dressed, packed, and ready to deploy when the date was moved to November 1971.

Our platoon conducted a practice nighttime parachute jump on the SERE school (survival, escape, resistance, and evasion) in California, training for BRIGHT LIGHT operations, the rescue of American prisoners of war in Vietnam. As I jumped from the helo, I made a lousy exit. I was packin' the M-60 machine gun and had a malfunction in my parachute. I looked up and—the suspension lines were wrapped around my weapon. The chute was open and I *thought* that I was descending slowly enough, but it was dark and I couldn't tell just how fast I was falling. The chute above me was kind of fluffin' up and had a big rip in it. I looked around for my teammates to determine if I was falling any faster than them so I could pull my reserve. Then, all of a sudden, I hit the ground real hard, with a thud, and my knees hit me in the chest. I remember, after opening my eyes, saying to myself, wow, and looking up and seeing all the silhouettes of my teammates hanging in the sky way above me. Then, the next thing I remember, was footsteps coming around me and one of my teammates saying, "Damn, Shallcross, you were smokin'!"

Surprisingly, I didn't have a scratch on me, but the drop sure knocked the shit out of me. We continued the mission and liberated the POW camp.

On another parachute jump, we were to simulate blowing up an enemy radio station. Our officer in charge had a canister of real C-4 explosives strapped to one of his legs. After our officer was to jump from the helo, he was to unstrap the canister and let it hang twenty feet below him so it would hit the ground first.

The jumpmaster yelled, "Get Ready!"

As our officer stood up to get ready to exit the helo, he hit his head on the upper part of the door. When he fell back, he accidently pulled the release cord that secured the canister to his leg. The large canister bounced along the deck and out the back of the helo, but the line that would let the canister hang twenty feet below was still secured to him. The very next second, the canister of explosives jerked him right out of the helo with it. The man directly behind him tried to grab him, but it was too late. I'll never forget the look on the officer's face as he watched the canister bouncing along the deck and out the back of the helo. He knew what was going to happen next. Talk about wide-open mouth and big bulging eyes!

The officer was supposed to have been the first man in our platoon out of the helo in 1st Squad, and I was to be the first man out in 2nd Squad, after the helo circled over the drop zone again. But, now the officer had prematurely exited the helo all by himself. The rest of his squad was just standing there. We weren't even over the drop zone yet, and everybody was laughing so hard that they forgot that they were nervous and still had to make the jump. The jumpmaster looked at the rest of us and just shook his head, which meant, We'll look for him later.

We continued to the jump zone, and the rest of us exited the aircraft with no problems. We didn't have any explosives with us for the operation because our officer-in-charge was somewhere out there, five miles away from his platoon.

Another time, our platoon was practicing a nighttime hootch search-and-seizure. The instructor would wait in the hootch for us, one squad at a time, to sneak up on and take control of him and the hootch. I was in the first squad to hit the hootch, and we successfully took control of it and our prisoner, the instructor. We were now told to go sit down out of the way; it was time for the second squad to do the task.

Meanwhile, an illegal Mexican walked up, and the instructor offered him a cup of coffee. The Mexican border was not far away. They went inside the hootch and were drinking their coffee while the second squad was maneuvering into position. The second squad never knew anything about the Mexican who was inside the hootch with the instructor, and he never knew anything about the second squad's sneaking up on them.

Well, here came the second squad, shooting up the night sky with their blanks and showing no mercy to the two men inside the hootch. They had the instructor and the Mexican face down in the sand with a foot on the back of their heads and putting plastic handcuffs on them as they roughed them up a bit. I couldn't see the expression on the Mexican's face, but I knew he was just scared to death. The Mexican finally broke loose and ran off, screaming, into the dark night, with his hands still cuffed behind his back, and the second squad firing M-16 blanks at him while yelling, "Hey, that's not fair! We shot you. You're dead!" We never saw him again!

Anyway, SEAL Team kept about half of our class and I ended up with the "Dirty Thirty." SEAL Team was cutting back on their ranks and over thirty teammates were sent to other duty stations. I was sent to the fleet after all that I had gone through to get into the Teams. I was a dedicated, highly motivated, and loyal individual. To get into the Teams I had made it through all the rigorous training. I performed all my duties to the best of my ability and all my quarterly marks while I was in SEAL Team were outstanding. We were given no logical reason for their decision to drop us from the Teams. I always wanted a chance to prove to myself, my teammates, and my country what I learned and trained for. I ended up throwing my SEAL "Trident" into the Pacific Ocean because of this treatment. To this day, I am still aggravated for what SEAL Team did to me and the other members of the "Dirty Thirty!"

I would like to add that this aggravation is not as deep as it sounds. Although I was very disappointed, my SEAL training and sense of humor helped me adapt very well to many situations to this day. Whether it was a recreation dive for lobsters off of Point Loma with the Teams or untangling the mooring lines of an Oil Tanker in a sumpy, smelly bay with a bunch of "Black Shoe" fleet sailors, I always made sure to have the best time that I could. I met many great people during my days in the Navy. I'm proud to know every one of them. . . . God Bless the "Dirty Thirty!"

Chapter Forty-nine

Frank Lahr
UDT-3 1945

Introduction to Wakayama Operation

As for all demo teams, UDT-3 operations during the occupation of Japan were unique. We had never before been able to make our plans on the assumption that there would be no resistance. Because of the peculiar circumstances, the operations reported on below bear little resemblances to previous UDT procedures. Actually, however, we at all times kept in mind the possibility of either organized resistance or of scattered fire from fanatics.

Our boats were fully armed, and all men going ashore were protected. In regard to this shore party, it might be mentioned that the odds were weighed both ways, and it was decided that the advantages to be gained from the use of the shore party overruled the amount of risk involved. In any case of resistance, the orders were specific that total withdrawal would be executed, and then a normal UDT swimming reconnaissance would be started. Our assessment of the odds was borne out, and the operation was completed as planned.

Chapter Fifty

Rob Wogsland

SEAL Team 1 1968–1970

Wogsland . . . Put Your Mask On

I joined the navy from Fargo, North Dakota and was assigned to boot camp Company 204 at the naval training center (NTC), San Diego, California. During boot, I became acquainted with Hall Kuykendall, a man from another company, which shared the same barracks complex.

Hall was the kind of person who you didn't forget, even if you'd never met him. He had this strong southern drawl, and I hadn't heard anybody talk so funny in my life.

During boot camp, UDT/SEAL instructors would come to the NTC once or twice a week to give a mandatory screening test for those who wanted to see if they could qualify to go into that training. This test was just an average sample of what the first phase of Frogman training was all about—push-ups, pull-ups, timed runs, timed swims, and other calisthenics, along with a lot of "you're nothing but a little maggot puke" type language mixed in with a little shoving around. I showed up for the test, but failed because I didn't finish the timed run in the qualifying time. Only about a quarter of the men who showed up qualified.

After boot camp, I was sent to the radioman's school that was also located at the NTC. Hall was attending the same school.

We became real good friends. We had a great incentive on each other to try to become navy Frogmen.

While at radioman's school, the UDT/SEAL instructors came around regularly to give the screening test to anyone interested in volunteering for the training. Hall and I both took the screening test this time. Hall passed, but I failed, for the second time.

I felt that if I didn't pass the test, I was going down the road. I wanted to go with Hall real bad, and had to get my act together and pass the test.

Not wanting to give up, I took the test each time the instructors gave it, failing in the timed run each time. Hall was there each time, watching me take the test, giving me a lot of encouragement.

I just kept plugging away at it, I really wanted to pass.

Hall had already passed the screening test, and the fact that my new friend would be going in a different direction after radioman's school if I didn't pass the test had a psychological effect on me. Hall's having passed the test was a great incentive to me, making me try harder each time the instructors gave the test.

It wasn't until the UDT/SEAL instructors showed up to give the screening test the seventh time that I finally made the required run. Both instructors giving the test that day knew I wasn't going to give up trying to pass the test.

When it came to the run, they ran with me. They ran the whole run with me, the two instructors. They kept looking at their watch and helping me pace myself. They were really encouraging and a lot of help to me.

I was a terrible runner. I was always crowding the time. But, I wanted to see what it was all about. Now, with my eighth try, I had qualified. But that was just the beginning.

Hall and I finished radioman's school and reported to the naval amphibious base, Coronado, California, a week before our class started training. It was the first week of November 1968, and we started pretraining to get in shape for the beginning of the eighteen-week UDT/SEAL training course.

Some of the other trainees in my class were Hurrel, Bunkie, Burky, Hampton, and Lieutenant Dill. Dividing the class up into seven-man boat crews that were each assigned an inflatable boat, small (IBS), our winter training class began.

I was still plagued with the difficult runs that the training had to offer, always coming in near the last of the group. It was the hardest part of UDT/SEAL training for me. I had no problems with any other part of the training, but I seemed to always end up with Hurrel and a few other select trainees in the "goon squad," a term used by the instructors to indicate those who needed a little extracurricular activity in the surf zone for screwing up or not keeping up with the class. I was one of the three or four worst runners in our class. I just didn't know how to run.

A trainee had two choices if he couldn't keep up with the training program, and those choices were usually determined by the instructors: Drop back to the training class behind and try again, or drop out of training completely.

The first week in December 1968, my class experienced Hell Week, the week in UDT/SEAL training that weeds out most of the weak, the quitters, nonhackers, and the men who have changed their minds about being a Frogman. Our class was in the mud flats just north of Imperial Beach. We had been awake for four days without sleep. We had spent the entire day in the flats, after paddling our IBSs the twelve miles from the naval amphibious base earlier that morning.

Evolution after evolution against each seven-man boat crew kept the class awake and constantly moving. As it was December, even in San Diego it was pretty cold. The mud was deep, maybe two and a half or three feet. The boat crews lined up on the mudbank, and when the instructor gave the command, the trainees would do sommersaults head first across the mud flats and back, trying not to be the last boat crew back.

The mud was cold and full of tiny broken seashells that left small cuts on any part of the body that wasn't protected. As we stood in line in boat-crew order, waiting for the next "game," the mud would begin to dry, leaving a smelly gray crust all over our bodies.

We used our fingers to clean the mud from our eyes, nose, and mouth the best we could.

Going through the mud with our boat crew on the next evolution, the mud would thicken on the body and fall off in chunks as we waited for the instructors to assign us something else to do. Working together as a team was the only way to complete most of the evolutions the instructors assigned us, especially log PT, which consisted of each boat crew lifting telephone-pole size logs over their heads while lying on their backs in the mud or just carrying them around constantly, pushing them to the sky. If one man within a boat crew wouldn't or couldn't do his part, the entire crew would have to pay by doing push-ups in the mud or starting the evolution all over again.

Then came lunch, yes, in the mud. But first, we had to sing for our lunch. If the instructors were satisfied with our singing, we got to eat. Box lunches were passed around to the hungry potential Frogmen and we sat in the mud in boat-crew order and ate with muddy hands. There was nowhere to wipe or wash them off. Shaking the mud from our hands was the cleanest we could get them. Wiping the mud from our faces helped a little; it was the best we could do. It was so easy to just say, "Fuck it, I quit," and the instructors would have us to a warm shower in no time.

As the long day in the mud came to an end, we lined up next to our IBSs for the long paddle back up San Diego Bay to the naval amphibious base. If we were lucky, the instructors wouldn't let any air out of our IBSs (making it harder to paddle on the long journey back to the base).

The instructors gave one last instruction to us as we put our IBSs in the bay. "Every man had better have the same mud on him when he reaches the Amphib Base. Nobody had better wash it off."

The long paddle began, bucking a strong head wind, as the instructors drove back to the base.

We were having a heck of a time paddling into this wind, just trying to get anywhere. It seemed like we weren't making any headway at times, and our boat crew decided that what we should do is beach the IBS and get up on the Silver Strand highway and hitchhike instead of paddle. So we did. We were the only boat crew to do this, and somebody pulled over with a pickup, and we loaded up the IBS and took off down the road. The man in the truck had some association with the teams, but I can't remember what. He knew who we were and what we were doing and everything, and he pulled over anyway, but it just so happened that one of the vehicles in the traffic on the highway that day heading north was a little silver-gray Sunbeam with one of the meanest, toughest, legendary, dedicated instructors named Olivera. We never knew he was behind us, watching us the entire time. I remember we were pretty tired after spending the last four days awake.

Still caked with the stench of the Imperial Beach mud, our boat crew rode in the back of the truck, underneath and on top of the IBS. On the way, we had to decide whether to stop before we got to the Amphib Base and get back in the bay or just carry our IBS through the main gate and back to the training area. No big deal, the trainees carried their IBSs over their heads through the main gate all the time anyway.

We knew the instructors would be waiting for us, and we had to show up like everybody else, but we didn't want to be the first boat crew to return to the base. I remember, there were one or two people that wanted to just go through the main gate. All the rest of the trainees in our class were still in the bay, paddling their asses off against the wind.

We decided to get off about a mile from the base and wait on the beach until we could see the other trainees out in the bay before getting back in the main group. That would give us time to rest up before the instructors assigned new evolutions to us. And that's what we did.

Once the other trainees finally showed up, our boat crew paddled out and met the entire group and continued back to the base in the middle of the pack, still unaware that Olivera knew about what we had done. All the boat crews climbed out of the bay and lined up in boat-crew order in front of the training area, singing training songs and shivering, still caked with I.B. mud.

The class proctor, Moy, came out of the instructors shack and addressed the officer in charge of our training class, Lieutenant Dill. He then got a garden hose and began to spray down all the trainees.

The water was very cold, and I knew that by the way Moy was acting toward our boat crew that we had been found out. We were receiving most of the cold water. I felt like returning to the mud flats and paddling the entire length to make up for our mistake, but it was too late. I was really afraid. In fact, I was cringing. I remember standing in formation, and people on either side of me were breaking ranks and quitting. You know, I think just about everybody was having a real hard time at that point. This was the part of Hell Week that most made me want to quit. It just looked so easy. I wanted to step out of ranks and walk away with those other guys who were heading for a warm shower and dry clothes.

The warm shower was less than fifty yards away. I stood there with chattering teeth, shivering, as the instructors kept paying particular attention to our boat crew with the garden hose.

I just knew they had found out somehow about our ride in the pickup. I remember standing there and wanting, really wanting, to quit real bad.

I was just about to hang it up when I heard Hall's voice. Hall was standing next to me, in another boat crew.

Hall said, "We're not going to quit, are we, Rob?" I just stood there, looking back at him and not saying anything, shivering as I collected more of the cold water that was washing off the insulating coating of mud.

Hall's voice came back again, louder this time, "We're not going to quit, are we, Rob?" He seemed to know exactly what I was thinking.

Finally, I replied, "No, we're not going to quit."

If it hadn't have been for Hall standing there, I would have been in that warm shower. I would have quit, I know I would have.

Hall was always an encouragement, not only for me, but to other members of our training class too.

Hall and I both completed Hell Week and started UDT/

SEAL training's second phase, which consisted of demolitions and land warfare. The timed swims and demanding runs were still a major part of training, and they always had to be completed in a faster time. Then, during the twelfth week of training, the "Little Olympics," a demanding test of physical endurance, was introduced to our class. It consisted of timed runs, ocean swims, and the obstacle course.

Then, along with five other men from his training class, I couldn't make one of the timed runs again. All six of us, Hurrel included, were dropped back to Class 50, which had just started their second phase of training. We had to start second phase all over with our new class.

I was assigned swim buddies with Chaldecas, a member of Class 50. Hurrel was assigned to swim with Hampton, another man who'd started with Class 50. Hurrel was a short man, and one of the biggest morale boosters in the training class. He seemed to keep the class's spirits up even during the worst of times.

UDT/SEAL training had a strict rule for the trainees to comply with during their timed ocean swims. Each swim pair was not to be farther than six feet apart during any swim. While on an ocean swim one day, Hurrel and Hampton were noticed by the instructors, swimming twelve to fifteen feet apart. After the swim was over and all of us trainees were on the beach, Moy brought out a thick, heavy piece of ship's mooring hawser (Manila rope used to secure ships to a dock) approximately six feet long. A loop was braided on each end. One loop went around Hurrel's neck and arm and the other around Hampton. They had to wear the rope, attached to the both of them, everywhere they went for a week, the head and the chow hall included. You can imagine what the other people stationed on the Naval Amphibious Base thought as Class 50 ran by with these two trainees tied together.

This not only taught Hurrel and Hampton a lesson, but made the other trainees aware that they had better stay within the six-foot limit of their swim buddy or they would receive the same treatment.

Another time, I left my dive mask on the beach after a

three-mile ocean swim. I had left it on the sand for just a moment. When I turned around to grab it, there was Moy.

Moy said, "Wogsland, that's going to cost you."

Our class then ran from the beach to the chow hall for lunch. It was very hard to try and pull something and get away with it with the UDT/SEAL instructors. They seemed to always be one step ahead of the trainees and very seldom forgot anything.

When our class reached the chow hall Moy said, "Wogsland, put your mask on." I did. Then he looked at his watch and said, "Take it off next week at this time!" I wore that damn mask on my face, breathing through my mouth, for the entire week, while running the obstacle course, to the head, and even eating in the chow hall. I never set my mask down again after any swim throughout the rest of the training program. It was very embarrassing running around everywhere we went with everyone lookin' at me, and I couldn't wait till the week's training was secured so I could take off my mask!

The day we graduated from UDT/SEAL training was a proud one for me and my teammates. My class was divided between the UDT and SEAL teams on the West Coast. I was assigned to SEAL Team 1. The world's toughest military training was now behind us.

The new Frogmen were issued their team operating gear, then a few teammates and I were sent to parachute training at Fort Benning, Georgia.

Once jump school was completed, we returned to Coronado and attended SEAL cadre training and other schools before forming a new fourteen-man platoon. I was now a member of Echo Platoon, SEAL Team 1. We deployed to Vietnam in late February 1970.

Chapter Fifty-one

James Stauffer
UDT-3 1945

String Reconnaissance

On the morning of 23 September 1945, the APD *Ira Jeffery*, with UDT-3 aboard, steamed into Wakanoura Wan. Our mission was to make a reconnaissance of the one-thousand-yard beach near Wakayama in preparation for the landing of occupational forces on 25 September. UDT-17 had a similar mission on an adjacent one-thousand-yard beach.

At 0730, our APD was in position, four thousand yards off Blue Beach. Two destroyers stood by at two thousand yards for fire support if called upon. Platoons 1 and 2 were to make a series of reconnaissances from the beach out to three hundred yards. Platoon 3 was to continue the profile from three hundred yards out to one thousand yards from the high-water line.

At 0730, the LCPRs were loaded and shoved off to the beach in column. At one thousand yards, all boats rendezvoused. Upon signal from Lieutenant Marshall in the control boat, Platoon 1 proceeded into three hundred yards from the beach. As previously rehearsed, Lieutenant Lahr and the five-man beach party were dropped off with their rubber boat. This LCPR then cruised parallel to the beach and dropped off six swimmers at two-hundred-yard intervals. Three of these swimmers were from the 1st Platoon and three were from the 2d Platoon, one of the latter being an officer. These swimmers then proceeded into the beach, looking for mines and obstacles.

After the swimmers were dropped off, the LCPR retired to one thousand yards and waited for the 3d Platoon, designated as the hydrographic platoon, to drop buoys locating the starting points for the string recon.

After the beach extremities had been marked and the buoys dropped, Platoons 1 and 2 proceeded in to three hundred yards. Platoon 1 sent in one rubber boat with five men at buoy number 1, on the extreme right flank of the beach, to begin their string reconnaissance. This crew was to make their string recon at buoys 1 and 2.

A second rubber boat was dropped at buoy number 3. This crew was to make one profile. The 2d Platoon did likewise at buoys 4, 5, and 6 with two five-man crews. The platoon leader stayed in the LCPR to better direct operations.

In casting off one of its rubber boats, the 1st Platoon caught the line in a cleat and the pull of the LCPR on the line caused the rubber boat to overturn. The boat was righted quickly, and only some carbines were lost.

The string-line reconnaissance was planned so that when the LCPR was just outside the surf, a man would take in a reel and lead line, and one of the swimmers already ashore would secure it at the high-water line. When this was accomplished, as the line unwound soundings would be taken every twenty-five yards from the high-water mark out. Four men paddled, one man recorded data, and one man took soundings. All pertinent data was recorded on a Plexiglas slate, with location and mean time noted.

The first morning our reconnaissance slowed up because each rubber-boat crew only had one reel. It was suggested that reels be made expendable and plenty provided. They should be made sturdily and practical, with a convenient handle to hold onto for winding and unwinding. Markings on the line should be outstanding and accurate. A reel should be devised that can be towed by a swimmer, leaving one hand free.

LCPR number 1 lay off the beach until the string reconnaissance parties in the rubber boats had completed their work. The time from leaving the APD until each rubber-boat crew had completed two three-hundred-yard-long string recons was sixty minutes. When the beach party returned, all personnel were accounted for, and we returned to the ship.

After all the information was gathered, it had to be put to useable form. The slates with the data were used by the platoon leaders to make rough charts. These were then used by the team cartographer to turn out a finished sketch, which was included in his report. The information that the beach party had obtained was also included on the sketch.

Chapter Fifty-two

Randy Kaiser

SEAL Team 1 1970–1973

There's nothing like the stress-free environment of fishing on your favorite lake, kicked back, enjoying the scenery, the warm weather, and the camaraderie of teammates . . . that is unless you fish for bass the way Randy Kaiser does. To Randy, bass fishin' is a "second job"; it would be his first if he had things his way.

Randy has won three bass tournaments in Washington State in the last couple of years, and he takes his fishin' very seriously. I had the honor of interviewing Randy aboard his boat on my favorite lake here in western Montana and not only learned a little about his experiences as a member of SEAL Team 1, but also learned a lot about Randy's special techniques in bass fishin'.

The Tiger Men

I joined the navy from Freeport, Illinois, which is located about one hundred miles west of Chicago. I had dropped out of high school, and in those days that was a guaranteed ticket to Vietnam. I didn't even know if I really wanted to be there, in the navy that is, but I figured that I had better do something. So, I joined the navy rather than get drafted into the army.

I enlisted in the first part of May 1969 on the 120-day delay program and began active duty with Boot Camp Company 581 at the naval training center in San Diego, California. That was August 17, 1969. After a few days of navy life, there I was, folding my underwear and all my other new clothes so perfectly and wondering, "Why did I do this? This sucks."

I met a guy named Pat Carter the first day of boot camp, and we became good friends. Pat was a stalky guy with dark hair, brown eyes, five feet eleven. He had joined the navy on the buddy system with his friend Steve Nelson. One day, our company marched over to a building and watched a movie called *Men With Green Faces*. I had never even heard of UDT or SEAL team before that. I saw that movie and thought, God, that looks cool. Seeing those guys rappelling, swimming, and parachuting made me realize right then and there that that's what I wanted to do. That's when Pat, Steve, and I decided that we wanted to go into the UDT/SEAL teams.

So, I think it was the very next day, they picked up Pat, Steve, and myself, along with everybody else from boot camp who wanted to try to pass the UDT/SEAL screening test, and bussed us all over to Coronado, where the test was to be conducted. I figured that, if nothing else, at least I would have the chance of getting away from boot camp for awhile.

Once we reached Coronado, the instructors ran us from the UDT/SEAL compound, north up the beach to the rock jetty near the Hotel del Coronado, then back down the beach a couple of miles to the obstacle course. They had us do a few things there, like dips on the parallel bars, push-ups, sit-ups—so many of each in a certain amount of time. But nothing seemed to be too strenuous. Pat and I passed the first part of the test, but Steve didn't. Then, the instructors found out that I had a little bit of a problem with my eyesight. I didn't have 20/20 vision, which was a requirement to get into UDT/SEAL training. I had to get a waiver before I was accepted for UDT/SEAL training.

After boot camp, I was sent to SF school (ship fitter) and Pat was sent to ET (basic electronics) school. I didn't see Pat for quite a while, until one day in late February or early March, after I had finished my "A" school. I showed up at the naval amphibious base in Coronado with my seabag and all my gear, and as I was walking in through the main gate, I ran into Pat and somebody else as they were walking out. Pat had already been there for about three weeks and had started pretraining, which was getting him in shape for what lay ahead.

UDT/SEAL training had a pretraining course at that time, and I didn't get in on it because I had had to complete my "A" school and was late arriving at the amphib base. If I remember right, I showed up on a Friday and our training class, Class 57, started the following Monday, with over ninety trainees. Pat and I both began training with Class 57 that following Monday.

All the normal UDT/SEAL stuff went on in our training class, if you want to call that training normal. We had an instructor whose name was Williams, a black man, about seven feet two, who was a first class petty officer. We didn't have Hatchet or Olivera for instructors at that time. Moy *was* one of our instructors, and I think that Olivera showed up for a couple of our runs during the first week or two of training. After that it was turned over to Moy and Williams.

Moy was designated our class proctor. He resembled something that evolution had forgotten. He stood about five feet nine or maybe even five feet ten and had a body of two hundred pounds of bulging muscle. His face closely resembled a rabid pit bull, with a gold front tooth. When he stood in front of our class, screaming orders at us, wearing his UDT/SEAL blue-and-gold T-shirt and UDT swim trunks, he gave all trainees the impression that he was the meanest son of a bitch on earth. From a trainee's point of view, his looks were definitely intimidating.

That first day of training, the instructors called everybody into their office one at a time for an interview. After I had finished answering Williams's questions, Williams got up and said, "I'll tell you one thing, boy. You ain't ever going to make it, boy, I'm going to see to it that you don't!" I was standing there at attention, lookin' up at him. All I could see was his two giant black nostrils, like eyeballs, staring down at me. I stood at attention in front of his desk the whole time and absorbed everything that he was saying to me.

He just scared the hell out of me, you know, because I was trying to be as serious as I could with the guy! I thought that the whole time I was impressing him with my answers to his questions.

I remember especially that during training Moy got our whole class all lined up, standing out in San Diego Bay, one morning. It was the third or fourth week of training, and someone had screwed up on an inspection or something. I don't remember who it was, but Moy was yelling at everybody in our class because it was the fifth or sixth time that the same guy screwed up the inspection, and everyone in our training class had let him get away with it.

We were all standing in San Diego Bay, and Moy was on the concrete causeway above us yelling over a bullhorn. "Okay, this is going to be the simplest evolution you'll ever have to do in training. When I do this"—he held his thumb down—"I want everyone to go down. When I do this," holding his thumb up, "I want everyone to come up at the same exact time. We will do this evolution until everyone comes to the surface at the same time and you all get it right. Until all of you come up together, you will all stay in the bay."

Well, when we were down there, underwater, we couldn't see his signal! Everyone was chokin' to death and swallowing water, wondering how in the hell we were going to do it right and come to the surface at the same time.

We were in the bay for three or four hours, going under at the same time and trying to figure out just how we could see his signal to come up together. That was about the closest I had ever come to quitting. It wasn't that the evolution was hard or anything, it was the fact that he was just pissing everyone off. There was no way that we could do it correctly, or do anything about it, but quit.

This game went on until we finally got it right, somehow, or he was just tired of playing with us. Eight or nine men quit UDT/SEAL training during Moy's "easy evolution." They had decided that they really didn't want to stay in training any longer.

One Sunday morning, about the seventh or eighth week of training, after Hell Week, Moy came into our barracks carrying a case of beer under one arm and a radio in his other hand. There were a lot of trainees in our barracks that morning, getting dressed in their civilian clothes and ready to go into town.

Moy said, "Hey, who wants to listen to the ball game with me this morning?"

Figuring that Moy might just have a human side, everyone came running out of the barracks, in their civilian clothes and street shoes and followed Moy over to the base armory. There were some stairs that went up to the second floor of the armory, around the back side of the building, and Moy climbed up a few steps and sat down, with his radio tuned in to the ball game, and opened his first can of cold beer. He then told everybody who had followed him, and expected to get one of his beers, to "Get down there, dummies," in the "leaning-rest" position (push-up). That was the moment when we realized that we had screwed up.

I can't remember which teams were playing, but every time the team scored that Moy didn't want to win, we had to give him twenty-five push-ups. Every time his team scored, we had to sing him a Frogman song, all the while staying in the leaning-rest position. This was really pissing everyone off because we were all dressed in our civilian clothes and ready to go to town that Sunday morning. We couldn't figure out why he was screwing with us, after all, our class had already gone through Hell Week. We stayed in the leaning-rest position throughout the entire ball game while Moy drank that entire case of cold beer himself.

Pat Carter was injured near the end of the second phase of training and was rolled back to Class 58. He was very disappointed, but had no intention of quitting UDT training. He had to go through Hell Week all over again with Class 58, which few men had ever had to do.

Three days before Class 57 graduated from training, we had three officers quit. I think they found out that they were going to be assigned to SEAL Team, and they didn't like that. They wanted to be assigned to a UDT team, and I think the reality of them being assigned to SEAL Team made them decide to quit. I never did get the whole story, but it was kind of disappointing, and the morale of the entire training class suffered when we saw the officers quit so close to the end of training.

Class 57 graduated from UDT/SEAL training with only thirty-nine men. Some men were assigned to SEAL Team 1, and the rest were divided among the three West Coast UDT teams. I was assigned to SEAL Team 1. I attended SBI (Seal basic indoctrination, or cadre training), at the SEAL camp in the desert out in Niland, California. From there, I was sent to the army jump school at Fort Benning, Georgia. When I returned from parachute training, I was assigned to Mike Platoon, and after even more training as a platoon, we deployed to Vietnam about the middle of August. I don't remember the exact date.

Once we arrived in country, and before we were allowed to proceed to our operating area, our platoon was taken to the MACV compound in Saigon. We were all sat down and given a course and written test on the "rules of engagement"—don't shoot any gooks unless they shoot at you first! We all thought that this was nonsense, but we had to go through with it anyway. After we had all passed the test, we were allowed to proceed to our base camp at the village of Ben Luc, in the Mekong Delta near the Vam Co Dong and the Vam Co Tay rivers, about thirty-five miles south of Saigon.

On our very first operation, we went by boat on a twenty-foot-wide canal and inserted into the jungle. I was the grenadier, carrying a Car-15 with an XM-203 grenade launcher attached beneath it, and was the fourth or fifth man in the patrol. The boat had left the area and gone back down the canal and we were about fifteen minutes into the patrol when I heard, back behind me, "Shoot the motherfucker . . . just let me . . . just shoot the fucker and leave him here . . . we can't get out of here now . . . they can't bring that boat back in here!"

I thought to myself, Wow, we're only fifteen minutes into our patrol and we have already captured a prisoner . . . This is great . . . My first mission, and we are really doing great!

The noise kept going on back behind me for some time, and I began to wonder what was really going on. I could hear the bushes rustling and someone being pushed around. I held my position, training my weapon into the surrounding jungle and concentrating on signs of the enemy. Finally, word was passed up to me, and I found out what exactly was going on.

Our problem was a corpsman who had just been assigned to the platoon but had never been through UDT/SEAL training. Our corpsmen were volunteers who had been assigned to the teams and wanted to operate with us. Most of them, at least, had to go through SEAL cadre training. But I don't think this guy knew what he was getting himself into. He was a quiet guy and came from a well-educated, wealthy family background. He didn't have to be doing what he was doing, or be in the navy for that matter. He hadn't been through SEAL cadre training or anything else to prepare him for what SEALs do. It was really rare for the teams to put someone in that position. Our platoon needed a corpsman, and I guess that this guy had just volunteered and was assigned to us.

But our new corpsman had had enough of being a SEAL and froze up, broke down, then started crying, right in the middle of the patrol. All our team members were really pissed off. Why he hadn't decided that he didn't really want to be a SEAL at some point before he was twenty minutes into his first operation, I'll never know. He could have gotten all of us killed. One of the members of our platoon was so mad, in fact, that he kept telling our officer that he wanted to shoot the corpsman and continue on with the mission. The corpsman was so scared that he kept trying to crawl off into the jungle.

One of the members of our platoon kept having to grab him by his belt and pull him back.

I felt a little sorry for the guy, but at the same time, our lives were being placed in jeopardy because of one man who couldn't handle a SEAL patrol. Hell, we hadn't even seen or made contact with the enemy yet! We finally had to get on the radio and call the boat back to extract him.

The little canal that we had inserted off of was choked with overhanging trees and vegetation, a perfect place to get hit by the enemy. We set up security on the canal bank until the boat arrived to extract the corpsman. Our officer decided that we would stay behind and go on with the operation anyway.

After returning to camp the next morning, the corpsman got up and gave everyone in our platoon a great big apology. It probably took a lot of balls on his behalf, but he didn't have much choice. I guess that he'd thought he was going to be giving little children shots, lookin' in their ears for infections, and passing out Hershey bars, or something. Anyway, down the road he went, and we were without a corpsman for a while. Our next corpsman was an older man and an experienced SEAL operator.

The operation that sticks out in my mind the most after all these years is when we set up an ambush in the Plain of Reeds along the Kinh Bo Bo, sometime in September of 1971. We had intelligence that there was a lot of NVA movement through a certain area during the night, but we didn't know how good it was. The source had no idea of what type or how many NVA moved through the area. On the operation, we were somewhere out in the Plain of Reeds on that Kinh Bo Bo.

The Plain of Reeds is just what its name says, a large expanse of reeds, dotted with clumps of very dense vegetation. The Plain of Reeds is located north of the Mekong River and west of Saigon. It extends west into Cambodia and covers an area of several hundred square miles.

The Kinh Bo Bo wasn't a very big canal, not more than fifteen or twenty feet wide. We were to stay out there on ambush until dawn the next morning or until we made contact with the enemy. There was nothing but reeds and thick vegetation in the area where we were to set up the ambush, no trees. The vegetation grew very thick throughout the Plain of Reeds and choked some of the canals to where a sampan couldn't pass through.

We had to insert by helicopter because there was no other way to get into the area except by sampan. Other than the few very small canals that ran through the area, there were no other routes into that place. This was the third or fourth operation that I had been on in country. We really didn't know what we would run into in that area, but all the intelligence sources had indicated that there were fairly large groups of NVA movement through there.

We inserted by helo fairly late one afternoon, with eight or nine SEALS and one Kit Carson scout, about two miles from our anticipated ambush site on the Kinh Bo Bo. We went in with three men sitting in each doorway, on each side of the chopper, and made sure that we were seen as we went over two small hamlets close to the area we were operating in. Other teammates were riding inside the helo, down out of sight, to take the place of the men in the doors after we had inserted. They would be seen on the return flight.

When we were about two miles out from our insertion point, I felt a tap on my right shoulder. I turned around to see my platoon officer nod his head at me. It was time to lock and load our weapons. I heard four bolts slam shut and everyone gave the "thumbs-up." Just then, the helo made a sharp bank to the right and in what seemed like seconds, we went from three thousand five hundred feet to fifteen feet off the reeds. What a rush!

We went in real quick, I mean the helo just went in and everybody jumped from the skids very quickly. The other men in the helo moved into the doors and sat there so it would look like the helo hadn't even stopped. This only took a second, and then the helo left again, cruising back past the hamlets to make sure that it was noticed all the men were still sitting in the doors.

After inserting, we formed a perimeter and stayed low in the reeds. This only took a matter of seconds. Everyone involved knew the exact spot to be in and the field of fire to cover. We lay there, watching and listening for the enemy, about an hour, which was longer than normal. On most insertions, we waited quietly for fifteen or twenty minutes. But, because we had inserted during the daylight hours under limited cover, we took the extra time to make certain that we hadn't been detected.

We began patrolling very slowly for about two miles through the reeds to get to the banks of the Kinh Bo Bo. The reeds were very thick, and we couldn't see very far in any direction. Our point man had to use his compass to guide us to the canal. We arrived at our ambush site about nine o'clock that evening and set up in our predetermined positions in the reeds on the canal bank. Then, I put out one of our claymore mines out on the right flank while someone else did the same on our left flank and out behind us.

It wasn't at all like, or didn't remind me of, training back in the States. I climbed up on that canal bank, and the vegetation was much thicker than in other places of the plain that we had patrolled through. It was so thick, in fact, that I could barely make my way through it.

We had a variety of weapons among us, including a couple of Stoner machine guns, two M-60s, M-16s, and I carried a Car-15 with an XM-203 grenade launcher attached to it. My first round in the grenade launcher was double-0 buckshot, which would leave a pattern about the size of a barn door at close range. After that was fired, I would load it with HE (high explosive).

I was wearing a standard H harness with five canteen pouches on a web belt, which were filled with 40mm HE, 00 buckshot, flechette, and illumination rounds. Under that, I wore a magazine vest that held six thirty-round magazines for my Car-15. Also secured to my H harness were two frag grenades and, of course, my rusty-trusty K-bar knife. I was packin' about fifty-five pounds total.

It took me a long time to set up my claymore. All my gear kept getting tangled up in the thick vegetation, which I had to push my way through while trying to be as quiet as possible. I figured that everyone in the world must have heard me out there. I remember how pushing through the reeds was draining me of all my energy, especially after patrolling through it for several hours already.

Anyway, I got my claymore set out and returned to my position, which was the fourth or fifth man, in the middle of our ambush from the upstream man. I felt real comfortable there, in that position on the canal bank. It was only my third or forth operation, and all the firepower of the rest of our squad was on either side of me. On the canal bank now, we settled in for what might be a long—or short—night, whatever the case might be.

I was sitting between two teammates who I had gone through training with. On my left was Hoover, Coon Ass we called him as he was a Louisiana bayou boy. He was packin' one of the M-60s, which he had lightened from twenty-three pounds to about sixteen. On my right was Challis, a Stoner man.

As my thoughts turned to the task at hand, I doubted very seriously that the claymore I had set out there would be effective unless someone happened to be right on top of it when it was detonated. I tried to position it where it would be most effective to the enemy if he happened to come along from that direction. I knew that I had set it up correctly, but those reeds were so damn thick.

After I returned to my position, we each tied a length of five- or ten-pound-test fishing line to our hands, down the entire length of the ambush line. We had a Starlight Scope at each end of the ambush line, and if anyone with the Starlight Scope saw someone coming, he was to give a couple of small jerks on the fishin' line, which would alert the next man down the line that the enemy was coming. He in turn, would do the same, and so on until every member of the ambush was alerted. It was a very dark night, and we were spread out far enough apart from each other that it was difficult to see the man on either side.

We sat there on ambush for what seemed like forever. We were all down in the muddy water near the edge of the canal bank. In fact, I was about waist-deep in the reeds, and my legs extended in the water out into the canal. I could feel the lung fish, mud skippers, or whatever they were called crawling around my legs and crotch area, making little squawking noises, but I couldn't see them. The lung fish could crawl up on land. They had a head like a frog, with bulging eyes and a body with fins and a fish's tail. They were crawling behind my magazine vest, in my clothes, and everywhere else, but I had to maintain noise discipline and could not swat them away because that might compromise our position. The thousands—millions—of mosquitoes showed no mercy on the bare parts of my hands and face either. Who knows what else was crawling around out there, also?

Between the insects and the bloodsuckin' leeches, I wasn't really worried. The leeches couldn't attach themselves to me because I was wearing panty hose! Many SEALs wore them to prevent the leeches from attaching themselves to our legs. They couldn't suck our blood through them, and since we had to be in this environment for hours, any relief from the bloodsuckers was welcome. The only problem with using them was they would only last about two operations before falling apart, and they were difficult to find in country. I often wondered what might have happened had I been captured by the VC and they had found out that "the men with green faces" wore panty hose!

A long time had passed, and in fact, I think it was a little after midnight or maybe one o'clock. It was a real calm night and extremely dark. All of a sudden, I could feel little waves hitting me on my lap. There was no wind, and the water was glassed off, so I began wondering what was making these waves. I didn't know what the hell was going on but figured that something was happening out in front of me. I couldn't see a thing in any direction. Then I felt a couple of small jerks on the fishin' line. Someone was coming down the canal.

My heart began pounding as soon as that fishin' line was tugged. I put the Car-15 to my shoulder and pointed it out into the canal. I figured that anybody "out there" would be able to hear my heart beat, too; I mean it was going *boom*, *boom*, *boom*, *boom*! I'm sittin' there in the water with my weapon and just ready to go . . . and then . . . after a long time . . . nothing happened . . . I mean nobody initiated the ambush by firing a weapon. The waves stopped after a few minutes, and everything was back to normal for a while.

There was a long pause, and then the waves began lapping

up against me again. I couldn't see a thing out in front of me. Only my two teammates with the Starlight Scopes knew what was going on. The waves kept coming and slapping up against me, and pretty soon I could hear gooks talking out in the canal in front of me. Then, some more tugs on the fishin' line, but again, nobody initiated the ambush. I figured that we were letting an NVA point element pass by in trade for a larger and more important target that was to follow.

More tugs came my way, and I passed the signal on. I sat there in the ready-to-blow-the-gooks-away-position for at least two hours. I would start to put my weapon down, and then some more tugs would come my way. The waves kept lapping up against my waist in the calm, dark, warm night, and I could hear lots of gooks talking, bullshitting, and even laughing quietly now. They had absolutely no idea that they were being watched by the men with green faces. This went on all night long.

It continued like that for a long time, and then we heard sampan motors going by out in front of us, more voices, and gooks talking and moving back behind us in the reeds. The whole damn night, I didn't know what the fuck was going on except that I knew there was a lot of gooks out there. One burp, fart, or click of the safety on anyone's weapon could have spelled disaster for us all. If just one of us had forgotten what we had been taught in UDT/SEAL training, it would have been all over for us.

At the briefing before the operation, our officer wanted to put a rope across the canal, downstream from our ambush position, to stop any sampan after we ambushed it. That way we could stop the sampan and search it for weapons and documents. I was to be the man to swim the rope across the canal and secure it to the opposite side. Getting ready for the operation, I even practiced swimming across a canal with a rope near our camp. At the last minute, another member of our platoon talked the officer out of the idea because if some gooks happened to come along, I might be stranded on the opposite canal bank during a firefight. Also, it would only take a minute for a swimmer to swim out and recover the sampan. I, and I'm sure every member of our ambush team, was glad that we did not have a rope stretched across the canal as originally planned.

We sat there all night and didn't dare move from our positions. Then as quickly as it had started, the noise stopped, and we heard no more movement. We extracted by helo just after light the next morning and flew back to camp for a debriefing. I finally found out at the debriefing just what exactly was going on out there only a few feet from my position hidden in the reeds.

An estimated six to seven hundred NVA moved past our position during the night. They had moved in front of us in the canal, on the opposite bank, and behind us. While I was sitting in the muddy water dark, trying to figure out just what the hell was going on out in front of me a few feet, my two teammates with the Starlight Scopes had watched the NVA as they passed out in front of us, carrying weapons, boxes, mortars, and other gear. We didn't dare initiate any fire as we were heavily outnumbered. I remember when the first sampan came through; I felt those first little waves lapping up against me. That was one or two small sampans, with only a couple of gooks, acting as a point element for what was to follow. There was a pause before the next bunch of larger sampans came through, and then there was a constant movement of the enemy all night long.

The NVA couldn't have been very far away from us when we extracted. If only one of us had not had the self-discipline and acted as we were taught in training . . . or . . . if only one gook had run into us in the dark as they pushed their way through the reeds . . .

After returning to our camp for the debriefing, I noticed that our officer looked a little odd. I think that he was shocked by what he had seen through the Starlight Scope. The intelligence that we brought back about the NVA's movement into that area was very important. Saigon wasn't very far away to the southeast. For the next few days, B-52 strikes were called in, and they leveled the Plain of Reeds in that area.

On Thanksgiving Day, a helo was shot down, and our platoon was called out at about four o'clock in the morning. Our officer came running into the hootch and said, "Get your shit together and muster up at the helo pad; we're being scrambled!" Everybody ran around, grabbing their gear and pulling on their pants, then heading down to the helo pad.

At the helo pad, our officer gave us a quick briefing and told us that a UH-46 had been shot down. We were going to fly to the crash site and set up security. To this day, I believe that the site was in Cambodia because we flew over the Plain of Reeds and continued on for about another forty-five minutes. I could tell by the direction we left our base that we had to be heading west. The sun was coming up to our backs. They flew us out on navy Sea Wolf gunships, which was unusual, but they were the only helos that were available at the time. It was hard enough for a Sea Wolf to get itself off the ground with all its ammo and crew, and we used two of them, carrying a squad in each. We were definitely loaded for bear.

They were just getting the last of the people off the UH-46 and out of there as we arrived. It had been carrying Marines, and there had been some casualties. On our way in, we had spotted a small patrol of Viet Cong that was moving in from about three hundred yards to the south. Our chief petty officer took four or five men and went out to block them after we landed. The UH-46 had been shot up pretty bad, I mean it was riddled with holes. The whole back end was blown off of it. A rocket had to have taken the tail section off that thing. We spent our whole damn Thanksgiving Day out there at the crash site, keeping everybody and everything away from the helo until it was removed.

While we were in country, we also had a joint POW operation, with army Special Forces and two other agencies involved in the thing. We had prepared for it for two days, but at the last minute, for whatever reason, they called it off.

Another time, we were returning early one morning from an operation on which we used one of our boats. We had killed a fairly high-level Viet Cong. I assumed that he was high-level because of the nice pistol he was packin'. Not all Viet Cong got to pack nice pistols. Anyhow, it was early in the morning, and all the Vietnamese were getting on their boats and hanging around the dock. At the end of the dock, a small group of Vietnamese men and women was huddled around a small fire, cooking something on a stick. As we secured our boat to the dock and got off, we carried this dead VC past these Vietnamese people. I will never forget the horrified look on their faces and in their eyes as we passed them.

They were mumbling something that sounded like, "*Nuy-Nai Nuy-Nai.*"

I asked our Vietnamese scout, Tan, what they were saying. Tan replied, "The village people call you the tiger men. The tiger man is said to be the most feared of all natural predators in the Southeast Asian jungles."

In October or November 1969, Nixon said that he was going to start bringing home the troops. Mike Platoon was the last direct-action platoon to operate in Vietnam. There was one other direct-action SEAL platoon in country while we were there, but they returned to the States about a month before we did. Another SEAL platoon was on standby, stationed off the Vietnam coast aboard a carrier. But whether they operated in Vietnam or not, I don't know.

Our platoon pulled out of Vietnam about the end of December. Our tour was cut short about a month and a half because all of the American troops were pulling out about that time. We were pretty damn happy about getting to go home a little early. In fact, we made it home for Christmas; nobody back home had expected us before sometime in February.

I am proud of what we did in Vietnam. I don't know how many patriots were there. I wasn't really a patriot, and I'm not really a whole lot today, but I enjoyed what I did and being a member of SEAL Team 1. Before an operation I would feel that little bit of anxiety and that adrenalin rush. But once I was on the boat or aboard the helicopter it was fine—I was ready to go.

Chapter Fifty-three

Frank Lahr
UDT-3 1945

Critique of a String Reconnaissance—Wakayama, Japan

In order to make an effective and accurate string reconnaissance, conditions must be very favorable. Practicality limits the size of the line used to one-eighth-inch white line. Actually we used chalk line, which is much thinner and much less satisfactory. It could take very little strain, and could not be pulled tight enough to make the overall result accurate; estimates had to be made to allow for the bow in the line when plotting the data on the final chart. Strain on the line is caused by either or both of two factors—surf and drift (current).

The likelihood of enemy opposition is another factor that must be considered when planning a string reconnaissance. One man must expose himself on the beach to secure the end of the string. Also, rubber boats are used to carry the party with the string and the sounding lines, and a rubber boat is a considerably better target than an individual swimmer. We had experimented conducting string reconnaissance using swimmers without rubber boats, working in fairly heavy surf at Fort

Pierce, and the results were not satisfactory. Much better control and more accurate results are obtained using rubber boats.

However, there are advantages to a string recon, which, incidently, was devised and used with good results by UDT-5 at Saipan under heavy enemy fire. At Wakayama, the conditions were ideal. We experienced no surf, and negligible current. There was no enemy opposition. Our information was accurate to the extent that LSTs, LCMs, and DUKWs beached along the areas we marked as suitable with no damage to any of the amphibious craft. Conceivably this could have been done without benefit of our string reconnaissance, but the argument against this can be stated simply.

On an adjacent stretch of beach, another UDT team had made its recon using swimmers only and no string recon. The beachmaster requested us to make a string recon of this same beach. Our results were checked against theirs, and there was considerable disagreement. However, our results indicating where craft could and could not be beached safely were used successfully by the beachmaster. Of course, this particular form of string recon could, normally, only be used for postassault work, and is offered as such.

Chapter Fifty-four

Mike Ferrell
UDT-12 1967–1970

So . . . What Did I Learn?

I was back Stateside for another seven or eight months before I was discharged from the navy. Just before I got out, Mr. Harvey and our CO, Jack Couture (Smiling Jack), called me into the office. The captain made me a proposal. He felt that I had officer potential and was pleased with my past military duties and performance. I had received several medals and had never been written up for anything (if they only knew). He was willing to pay my way to San Diego State, and I would be able to collect my military pay and still be attached to the teams. After graduating, I would have been returned to the teams as an officer. I felt a great sense of pride and was complimented.

However, I was against the Vietnam War and thought it was a waste of human life and endeavor. I had returned to Nam only because of my commitment to the teams. No one made me volunteer for the teams. I had consciously chosen that path in my life. When I was a young man, commitment to the teams was the first real commitment that I had made to anything, and damn it, I was going to make it a good one whatever it took.

I regretfully turned down the CO's offer. I didn't tell him or anyone else in the teams, my feelings about the war. The only ones who knew about my feelings were my parents. I could no longer commit myself to that war. In retrospect, it was probably one of the biggest mistakes that I have made in my life; by the time I'd graduated from college, the Vietnam War would have been over.

I loved the teams, the people, my brothers, and the camaraderie; I guess we were all adrenalin-junky renegades. I have never experienced working with a more professional outfit. Our performance throughout the war was outstanding. We had zero MIAs, and throughout the UDT/SEAL involvement in the Vietnam War, from 1962 to 1972 we lost only forty-nine men. Given the types of duties and missions that we were involved in, that's incredible! The psychologists should probably put all of us under a clear glass bubble and study us very carefully!

This has been a painful story for me to tell. It took a lot of reaching back into "black holes" that were tough for me to deal with. There are veteran friends of mine who don't even live in this country anymore. Others are still on drugs. They were fine men in their youth, with discipline and focus, but it hurts me to see them now.

As teammates, we have our winners too. Bob Kerry, who ran for president of the United States of America on the Democratic ticket, was a graduate of UDT/SEAL Training Class 42. A lot of us hold good jobs, have careers, families, and are regular people. But, I have to admit, it took a lot of work to get me there. But then again, life's kind of tough sometimes, isn't it?

In closing, I would like to offer a special thanks to all the air, ground, and boat-support units that stood in there with us and gave 'em hell. There is no question that you guys saved our butts a lot more than once. The craziest army warrant officers that piloted the Hueys, the Cobras; the navy's Black Ponies and Sea Wolves; the River Rats; the PBR crews, and the crew of the USS *Tunny*. You all have my deepest appreciation! I love you, no shit—you buy me Honda? Whooooo Yaaaaa!!!

Chapter Fifty-five

Chris Christie
UDT-3 1945

Hydrographic Platoon—Wakayama, Japan

A profile is a cross section of the bottom of the ocean, showing the depth and composition of the bottom. These characteristics must be known from the high-water line out to the three-fathom line, for the beachmaster to judge where and when to bring in amphibious craft, especially the large LSTs. The string reconnaissance is satisfactory for getting this information about a steeply sloping beach, but where the slope is very gradual, this method becomes less satisfactory. The strain in the line becomes greater as more line is paid out. This results in a greater bow in the final results. Also, the time required to conduct a string reconnaissance one thousand yards long could be objectionable.

At Wakayama, the three-fathom line extended out to one thousand yards. As previously described, a string recon was conducted from the high-water line out to three hundred yards. From three hundred to one thousand yards we used a system developed by our commanding officer, Lieutenant R. P. Marshall. Section 3 was designated as the hydrographic platoon, and they made ten such profiles, each seven hundred yards long. The average time was four and a half minutes!

This is a description of their technique.

Previously, markers had been set up every two hundred yards on the beach to definitely locate the profile on a chart. The hydrographic platoon then dropped alternate red and black buoys approximately three hundred yards from the beach on predetermined compass bearings so that the line "marker buoy" was perpendicular to the shoreline. The LCPR then moved out from each buoy on this marker buoy. Two men took soundings with lead lines, standing on the gunwales forward of the gun tubs. The platoon leader would visually judge distance and call out when the lead men were to cast their lines. The boat was run at a steady speed, approximately two-thirds full speed, and the time of each sounding was recorded.

This served as a partial check on the visual estimation of the platoon leader. Actually, the process was very simple, and obviously the success of this method demands an expert at judging distance. With a good man judging the distance and calling when to throw the line, with a good coxswain maintaining a steady course and speed, and with experienced men casting the lead lines (two men would always cast their lines together and the average of their readings was recorded as one), this would be an altogether satisfactory method. Section 3 had all of these, and their results were very satisfactory.

This system proved its worth when a sandbar, which would otherwise have stopped an LST, was located six hundred yards offshore. The beachmaster directed the craft around the sandbar, thus preventing any hitch in the unloading of supplies.

Chapter Fifty-six

Christopher John Caracci
SEAL Team 1 SEAL Team 6
1979–1985

The Making of a Rat-SEAL

The year was 1981. And the war machine had apparently decided that the navy should be properly prepared in the event that SEAL Team could be used in the Middle East. Our assignment probably had something to do with Khadaffi. With the hard part completed, that is to say, someone's at least remembering to get us into the game, all that was left was to decide what we needed to know and how we were going to learn it!

As SEAL Team world responsibilities are divided, the assignment went to SEAL Team 1, my first love because of Mr. Grey Rather (my first SEAL mentor) and the support of former UDT/SEAL member Brian Curle. My platoon was being formed, and unknown to most of us, we were about to be transformed from marine mammals to guinea pigs. Our SEAL platoon would be the first of its kind; our main theater of operation would be in the desert and there would be a good chance that we would have some of the first "real" assignments in some time. With this in mind, the officer in charge (OIC) would have to be someone special.

As it turned out, our whole platoon fell into that category

because the OIC handpicked the majority of the men from his own people. The officer in charge would be the key to a successful mission because there were not enough combat veterans left in the teams to handle every situation that might turn up.

The OIC selected was Lieutenant R. J. Thomas, a former enlisted man who had been highly decorated as a SEAL in Vietnam. Mr. Thomas had been awarded the Navy Cross, second only to the Congressional Medal of Honor. The word was that he had saved a lot of lives after the helicopter he was riding in was shot down. Injured, with a broken back from one of the rounds that brought down the helo, he was still able to drag other people free from the flaming wreckage and also to eliminate a large number of pursuing enemy.

Mr. Thomas was also one of the finest shots in the American military. I had been taught how to shoot by Mr. Thomas, and it would be a long time before anyone would be able to improve on my shooting skills. He was the kind of man who was either liked or hated; he was *very* confident in his ways. That alone causes insecurity in many, and his fantastic and comical arrogance didn't help soothe anyone's fears.

Our assistant OIC (AOIC), Ensign Christopher R. Lindsay, was a graduate of Duke University and a superior athlete. His combination of intellect and physical ability would bring him instant success in the Teams. Having gone through BUD/S training together, he and I developed a lifelong bond. Lindsay was appreciated as an officer who could perform as well as anyone, yet he could motivate his men like a Chief. We were glad to work with and for him, although the times we worked "for" him were mainly when the brass was around and we all knew that.

Then there was the Chief, the backbone and funny-bone of our platoon, Jim "Ka-Bar" Kauber. Ka-Bar was a free-fall specialist, and served for several years as a member of the navy jump team known as the "Leap Frogs." He was a good leader and acted as a buffer between Mr. Thomas and the rest of us, which was not an easy job. I will always remember Chief most for teaching us that humor was as much a part of the Teams as swimming.

Our platoon also included two first-class petty officers. Because he had the greater time in service, our leading petty officer (LPO) was Dave LaConte. Dave was a PT (physical training) machine, a biker—Harley, of course—and another great guy. After I was discharged from the navy, I heard the sad news that Dave had been shot nine times in an accident in Thailand. As I understood it, Dave survived but was a little slower after that, which probably meant that he was even with the rest of us.

Our other first-class petty officer was Andy Nelson, one of the kindest Frogmen that I have ever had the pleasure of working with. Andy was a walking SEAL Team encyclopedia, there for any of us making sure we knew our stuff at any time, twenty-four hours a day.

Tony Pascoe was our platoon's corpsman. He was a little fireplug of a guy who was either bodybuilding or practicing his martial arts, that is, if he wasn't caring for us. I once asked Tony to help me with an injured seagull that I had found on the beach with its wing half severed. Tony compassionately helped me nurse the bird, whose wing could not be saved. Eventually, the seagull recovered and was adopted by a bird shelter.

The rest of us who made up the platoon were fairly new. Tom Vawter was the communications man. Tom carried the big radio on his back and sometimes walked point. Roger Meek and Randy Paulus were our first-lieutenant reps, which meant they were responsible for all the mechanical stuff like vehicles, engines, boats, etc. Bill Sandborn was an M-60 machine gunner, my counterpart in the other squad, but he was excused from the platoon during this period because his house and property were being threatened by California brushfires. Bob Schmidt was the only other man in our platoon who was as young as me. His responsibility included packing parachutes because we were still jumping "old rounds" (T-10s) at that time. He also did quite a bit of sewing on our ammo vests and assorted operating gear.

Like most SEAL platoons, this group was full of heart, and we would be ready for anything when the time came. However, the most important thing about the group was the senior

Frogs, from the LPO on up. We had some of the best experience going for us, not only as SEALs, but as people. Our officers knew the secret of leadership which was that of respect, not performance ordered or demanded. Their respect was well earned.

A good leader does not have his men work for him, but with him! We did not respect our seniors because their rank made them somebody special, we respected them because their rank was earned, something that differentiated us from most of the civilian world and a good portion of the rest of the military.

Our new platoon was to be ready for any real-world scenario in the Middle East. The Teams' next step was to find a source for the field expertise we needed. Due to our unique assignment and the expertise it required, the navy chose an outside source, as was often the case when the know-how required could not be found within the SEAL community. In this case we chose Mr. Dave Ganci of the Arizona Outdoor Institute, now located in Prescott, Arizona.

Mr. Ganci's academic qualifications included degrees in physical geography and desert survival. The essential characteristic that Mr. Ganci demonstrated was his willingness to go all out, pushing us and himself to the maximum and often beyond what we perceived to be our limits. With the need for his specific skills approved and security cleared, Dave was brought into the fold and developed our program, which started with a five-day survival course tailored just for us.

The first day and a half were spent in the classroom, where we were exposed to the general theory of the mental and physical challenges associated with the task we were expected to perform. The course taught us to recognize possible pitfalls so as to avoid them, and coping skills for those problems that could not be avoided.

In the navy's attempt to learn the maximum human potential for their SEAL Team and to create a worst-case scenario, we guinea pigs were placed in every unavoidable adverse condition. The data gathered during our survival course was to be used as a gauge for the maximum sustainable and survival capabilities of any individual or platoon under similar conditions. Mental, physical, and intellectual preparation is essential for the successful completion of any SEAL mission, but we would have to push ourselves beyond our perceived limits and to maximize our potential for the safe and successful completion of our required tasks, not just for ourselves, but for documentation and the education of future "Frogs."

After our classroom session was completed we conducted practical exercises outside, which included the use of solar stills, a technique of drawing water out of plant life, and the identification of plants that we would be exposed to in our actual operating environment. The next four days our platoon spent in the desert to acquire invaluable field experience.

It was July, and the temperature in the sun was 120 degrees or so. We began our field survival training with the worst case—no food or water. For gear we had only our knives, emergency medical supplies, and some water collection devices such as plastic bags for solar stills and surgical tubing for hard to reach areas. Our survival course took place near the southeastern border of California in the Chocolate Mountains.

In the next four days we moved approximately 40 miles, during the day usually taking cover in whatever shade that could be found, then moving by night in temperatures that still ranged between ninety and one hundred degrees. Our main objective was to find life-sustaining water. After the second day without food, we quickly learned that it was easy to live without, but that water was paramount to our survival. It seemed that the sensation of hunger for food was not triggered until the body fluid level was replenished to some minimum level. We traveled to abandoned ranches and mine shafts and took cues from the natural geography such as rock formations and gullies in search of water.

In an effort to locate water, we took note of the vegetation which was a sure sign of water and we followed wildlife whether insects or coyotes. Several times we traveled all night to a site that on the map looked like it might be an abandoned mine shaft or potential water hole only to find the possible source to be dry or barely trickling. Sometimes we had to dig, and other times we found the water in the middle of the night at a time of great desperation, which meant drinking it but not necessarily seeing it.

Once we traveled all night to a prospective location, and upon arrival, we were all in bad shape. Luckily, we found water there and we drank as much as possible—"tanked up." When daylight finally came to the desert the next morning, we saw that the water from which we drank the night before contained insect bodies and larvae. And a dead, decaying bat floated on its surface. But to us, at that stage, any water was good water in this, the purest of battles between man and nature.

On our last day in the field, we moved approximately nine miles during the hottest part of the day—as if we had to escape and evade the enemy during an actual mission. Several brothers had consumed enough and wanted no more warm water; they refused to drink, figuring that the course was nearly completed. Needless to say, *they* did not finish the last trek of the course; we had to call in an emergency vehicle to extract them.

Many more lessons were learned and a great deal of experience gained. As always in the Teams, there are a select few who always try to muscle everything instead of using their most valuable weapon—the mind. This course demonstrated the power of mind over muscle. One thing is for sure, for the mission to be successful and every Frogman to be mission oriented, the Frogman would have to survive, that was his personal commitment to his brothers and the Teams. After all, that is what a team is! I like to think this lesson is learned during training. That is why we always live as we train and train as we live!

After the survival course, we contracted Mr. Ganci to stay on with us as we were going to use what was learned on an actual week-long mission with a live target and live ammunition. The training mission would be based on a standard SEAL target, in this case a small, remote, simulated airbase located in the same area of operation as the survival course and manned by a company of U.S. Marines assigned to us just for the training mission.

The base was constructed by the SEAL Team 1 cadre and would contain six actual U.S. jet fuselages, reconstructed wings and tails, and all other support equipment. There was lodging for the company of Marines, fuel sites, and vehicle support. There were security patrols, foot and vehicular. The completed base was a work of art from the concertina wire to the planes.

The scenario was simple. We would insert from the air by parachute, then patrol on foot ten to fifteen miles to our objective. We were to penetrate security, destroy the target, and then extract to our rendezvous point.

The Marines would man the site for three days, during which we would strike. That may seem like a large window of time, but after all, the enemy already knew that we were coming. Once our platoon had penetrated to within striking distance, we would identify ourselves over the radio, then mark our location with a flare or fragmentation grenade. The airbase site would then "go administrative," all the Marines would be evacuated, and then we would blow it up from our position. After that, the Marine reaction force had thirty minutes to respond and pursue at will.

Other support for this historical event was supplied by our very good friends from the Australian Special Air Service (SAS), Captain Dean Pie and Sergeant Len Smith. SEAL Team shared a special relationship with the Aussie SAS. I'm not sure how this came about, but I'm glad it was so. One of the great things about SEAL Team was that we had the opportunity to work with every other special operations unit in the free world and wanted to work with the others, if you know what I mean. If I had a choice of selecting only one special unit out of all the foreign ones that we have had the pleasure of working with, I would choose the Australians.

With everything in place, the airbase mission kicked off three days after the desert survival course, obviously not leaving us with a whole lot of time for recovery. But that's the way we liked it! Mr. Ganci would be waiting at the drop zone with our Aussie friends. Mr. Ganci then planned to follow us through the entire operation in order to monitor our progress and newfound skills.

Warning and patrol-leader's orders were given as in any other mission. Our equipment would be different, though. Our target was large and its complete destruction would have to be done from a distance so we had to change from our platoon's

Standard Operating Procedure (SOP). First the M-60 machine gun was eliminated: too much weight for the distance we would be required to cover. We still needed firepower for the destruction of the planes, so we chose the 60mm mortar to augment our normal load out. In addition, we doubled our Light Anti-tank Weapon (LAW) load for backup. Mr. Thomas had had the rest of the platoon carrying M-14s already as our platoon SOP weapons along with match-grade .45-caliber handguns, since he did not believe that there were any other caliber weapons worthwhile. He detested the .223 and the 9mm. As far as I was concerned, Mr. Thomas's opinions were based on real-life experiences so that was no problem to me.

All geared up and ready, we were notified that the Air Force C-130 we would be jumping out of had an onboard computer which they wanted to use to calculate our drop point. This was usually done by our own people, but we decided to be good sailors. That proved to be our first mistake!

Our platoon was all geared up on board the aircraft and, according to the computer, over the drop zone. The Australians were in communications with the bird from the drop zone. Periodically, the ground winds were twenty knots steady and gusting up to thirty to thirty-five. SOP on a training jump is to abort if the wind speed is greater than fifteen knots. Well, the story I got was that there was a miscommunication between our aircraft and the ground, and instead of aborting the mission, we proceeded.

We all exited the aircraft using round T-10 canopies (parachutes) that were not very maneuverable in strong winds. Therefore we drifted with the wind. Bad enough that we were in for one hell of a ride, we also found out that the computer had dropped us off course about three miles, directly over the only high-tension wires in the entire desert. As fate would have it, the aircraft had proceeded off course directly in line with this very deadly obstacle.

We are trained for this possibility, as things don't always go as they are planned. The correct procedure in this situation is to put your arms up along the back riser straps of the parachute while keeping your feet and legs together, and begin an oscillating motion to reduce the possibility of getting snagged in the wires. Of course, you have to see the wires in order to initiate the escape-drill technique. It is also important to bear in mind that in a jump such as this, which is performed in full combat gear, each jumper is carrying a minimum of an eighty-pound pack tied between his legs. The accepted technique is to drop the pack just prior to landing so it dangles at the end of a ten foot drop line. In this manner you will not be carrying the additional weight when you land.

The first jumper to approach the lines was Rick Benjamin. Mr. Lindsay was next in line and then myself. I watched in disbelief as Rick headed directly for the high-power lines. Just prior to making contact, he looked back at us as if to say, "Do you believe this?" As he turned back around, he drifted right into the lines at chest level.

The sudden stop caused his arms to fall down on top of the wires. I began my own emergency evasive maneuver, a massive riser slip. Instead of using the parachute toggle lines, which would affect the direction of the chute too gradually and slightly, I pulled down on the risers trying to direct the parachute away from the lines in a more aggressive manner. To no avail, I was still being blown directly toward the hot wires.

Mr. Lindsay seemed well aware of the impending doom; I could see the determination in his actions as he vigorously began the fish-flopping oscillation technique just before his collision. It worked; he weaved his body right through the lines almost without a hitch. If his chute hadn't tangled, he would have made it safely through the lines perfectly. I watched Mr. Lindsay dangling through the wires as I got closer, and was still concerned for his safety because the voltage in these wires is so immense that even the nylon suspension lines of the chute might act as a conductor. To make matters worse, he was dangling nearly twenty-five feet above the ground. Now it was my turn. . . .

I knew I had a chance to clear the wires but that meant not dropping my pack; I would have to land with it. That was not going to be fun because I was carrying the 60mm mortar, three mortar rounds, one LAW rocket, my M-14 with two hundred rounds of ammunition, all my rations for the week, and almost six gallons of water. Except for the mortar, it was pretty much the average weight of gear.

With some fairly frantic rocking, I was able to clear the wires. As I drifted directly over both of my Teammates, I could hear the low-bass buzz of the extremely heavy current jolt and arc through Rick's body. I could also see the flash of Rick's body jerked from the shock. By the way he looked, I was sure he was dead. I wasn't sure about Mr. Lindsay's condition, as he was motionless as he dangled from his suspension lines. I now had to prepare for what I hoped would be a once-in-a-lifetime landing, and for all I knew, I might be cashing in my life's allotment right at that very moment!

Because of the high winds the descent was like riding in a car with a rusted-out floor, watching the road pass underneath. The majority of Frogmen go through army Airborne training, or navy appreciation as we call it, at Fort Benning, Georgia. In that school, they refer to your parachute landing as a PLF (parachute landing fall), a technique where one learns to fall to the ground while under a parachute at about eight miles per hour. So at thirty miles per hour, all I could muster up was the "L" part of it, and that was into the side of a dried-out wash. My whole right side struck the ground when I was on the downswing of my pendulum motion. I hit so hard that I was knocked out.

When I came to, slowly I began injury analysis to see if all my circuits were working. After feeling nothing wrong, I slowly got up to my feet. I looked over toward the wires and to my surprise no one was hung up! I had been knocked out for at least twenty minutes.

I mounted all my gear, got my weapons online, and approached the activity under the wires. I could see that Rick was burned from his right side all the way to his left. The worst damage had been done to his right arm; it was unrecognizable. The rest of his upper torso had at least third-degree burns and his chest and back had some second-degree burns, mostly toward his left side. Andy Nelson was holding the IV bottle, which he was administering to Rick. I saw a medevac helicopter already inbound. The Australians had called for it as soon as Rick's situation had developed.

Mr. Lindsay's shirt was on the ground next to him, burned as well. Later he told me that he had wiggled free of the power lines and had fallen to the ground. He knew that Rick was going to drop through the lines at any moment; it was only a matter of time before his harness would melt through. The electricity was heating the metal in Rick's harness.

When Mr. Lindsay finally got to the ground, he ran beneath Rick and waited. Sure enough, Rick began to fall through the lines and as he did, Mr. Lindsay attempted to catch him. That was about a thirty-foot fall for Rick, and needless to say, a lot of weight and momentum to try and catch. As Rick fell, Mr. Lindsay did a great job of breaking the fall with his body, and they both hit the ground together. Mr. Lindsay had successfully saved Rick from further injury and, remarkably, without hurting himself. Rick was still on fire when he hit the ground, his skin was burning before Mr. Lindsay's eyes. Mr. Lindsay removed his shirt and with it and his own hands smothered the fire.

Andy Nelson arrived soon after Mr. Lindsay began treating Rick for shock. Andy had been forced to land with his pack as well, and was suffering from a severe back sprain. Andy could see that Rick was in shock and in dire need of fluids. He took his IV from his pack and administered it to Rick. All SEAL Team members were cross-trained for medical emergencies, and Andy Nelson's actions were testament to his years of experience.

Tony Pascoe, our Corpsman, was surely earning his pay that day. He had survived the drop and was busy analyzing and tending to all of the injured, of which there were many. Tony had been at Rick's side right after Andy had arrived, and was checking over Mr. Lindsay's and Andy's work. He stabilized Rick as much as possible, then went back and forth checking on everyone else until he was satisfied about each man's condition. Although Rick was the only man to be medevaced, he was not the only injury. After he was on his way to a medical facility, it was time to salvage the mission.

Those of us still on our feet began to scour the drop zone for our missing Teammates. Of the original thirteen, only ten of us were able to continue the operation. The other two men who had been injured were Chief Ka-Bar, whom I spent a good while picking cactus out of, and Bob Schmidt. Their injuries ranged from concussion and badly sprained joints to massive Cholla cactus poisoning, from which we all suffered a little.

The equipment from our three injured comrades was divided among the remaining ten of us. At that point, we even enlisted Mr. Ganci. He wanted to get a true taste of the action so we gave him a pack in which he carried some mortar rounds and his own gear. We also gave him an M-14, unloaded of course. He was with us for the long haul. . . .

We left the drop zone with heavier packs and had less than half of our water, as many of our containers did not survive the high-impact landing. Initially we lost some motivation, but that was only for a short time. We traveled approximately nine miles that night before laying up the next day in as much cover as we could find.

On the second night we moved another nine miles, which put us about two miles from the target. The next step would be to put out recon teams to check out the target for security patrols, etc. Mr. Thomas and Dave LaConte would be on one team because the OIC liked making his decisions based on firsthand observation. Others would not agree with his tactic, but sometimes the man making the decisions has to see the site firsthand in order to make the right assessment. The other recon team would be made up of Andy Nelson and Tom Vawter.

Both teams went out after a brief rest so that they could recon the site during the night and return to our position before dawn. Each team would maneuver to the site from a different angle so the whole area would be covered. Mr. Lindsay and the rest of us would stay behind. We would provide support if there was a problem.

All went pretty smoothly for a while, then we heard shooting. Problem. Andy and Tom had been observed during their recon and were under fire from a small Marine mobile security patrol. Later we learned that the recon team didn't think the Marines had night vision gear with them so they took some liberties in their movement. Needless to say, that was the wrong answer!

Mr. Thomas's team arrived back at our position with Mr.

Thomas spitting and sputtering some fine expletives about the other team's carelessness. Mr. Thomas did not like it when things went wrong, and in the game of war it's easy to see why. Apparently, the other team had decided to escape and evade (E&E) from the Marines instead of returning to us, and that decision brought upon them the full Thomas wrath, which is great to witness as long as it's not directed at you. To compound the situation, Andy Nelson's back injury from the jump had by then crippled him to the point that he was removed from the operation. Tom would join up with us later at a rendezvous point for our extraction.

The next day proved to be no break in the action. We holed up in some foothills and dried washes while observing the target area. The terrain was well suited to our needs because it afforded us a good vantage point to the target, provided us with an escape route, and gave us an opportunity for water. We positioned ourselves in the foothills at the base of some mountains where water runoff would collect. One very important thing to remember about water in the desert is that it is the most important element of life for every living creature in that environment, from the smallest insect to the largest mountain lion, all of which become ferocious in their quests for survival. This is where the next big battle took place!

Due to our .308 rifle, we didn't anticipate any problems with the big creatures, but we overlooked the insects, the bees to be exact. After all, we were big hairy-chested Frogmen and no measly insect could bother us. Wrong!

The battle with the bees was incredible. We were attacked constantly. Anywhere there was fluid the bees swarmed. Our canteens had to be covered because the bees would be all over the neck of the containers if they could find a drop of water. When we drank, we had to cover our heads or they would dart into our mouths or land on our lips. We even took a great risk in urinating because the bees followed the stream right back to us! So we developed a new technique called "peeing on the run"!

While the battle of the bees waged on, we began to formulate our plan for striking the airbase. We were down two more men and their equipment was again divided among us. Our penetration would now be more difficult because we had lost the element of surprise, and we now had to carry the remaining team and gear.

Meanwhile, the bee problem grew worse; we had all been stung several times each and some of us were very ill from the venom. Mike Miller, Randy Paulus, and Mr. Lindsay were worst off. They were so bad, in fact, that antiserum had to be flown out to us as an administrative project. Along with the serum would come more water.

As the grind of the mission worsened, so did our consumption of water; the formula developed in the survival course no longer worked. Later in the day, a frustrated Mr. Lindsay had had enough and he waged his own blitzkrieg on the bees. He came running down the wash swinging and kicking wildly at the swarm like he was fighting the Invisible Man, all the while maintaining an excellent war cry. His attack was one that would have made Warner Brothers' Tasmanian Devil proud. Although I think the casualty rate Mr. Lindsay claimed for the bees was a little inflated, our morale was certainly lifted.

Paulus and Miller were dangerously ill by then and would also have to be removed from the operation. Thus, we were down to six men, six of us carrying the gear of thirteen and faced with hitting a target the size of a small airfield!

The third night we were to attack. Our plan was completed and we had come too far to abort the mission. It was decided that we would be on the site at 0300, that would give us time to make the foothills on the other side of the desert floor under the cloak of nightfall.

We proceeded to a point approximately 300 meters past the target towards our first rendezvous point along our E&E route. At that point we would download and take only what was necessary to hit the target then break contact to escape—this included all weapons and ammunition and our backup gear, which consisted of five LAW rockets apiece, as well as the mortar and five of the mortar rounds apiece. The rest of the gear we would pick up on the run after hitting the target.

We doubled back to the target and penetrated along the route Mr. Thomas and LaConte had planned, completely undetected, even though the Marines knew we were coming. After we identified our location, the operation turned administrative and all the Marines were evacuated. The success of the hit was built around the firepower of the 60mm mortar, whose responsibility was borne by Nelson and myself. As everyone positioned themselves in attack formation with security and backup positions in place, we fired the first mortar round. . . .

The mortar rounds didn't fire after being dropped down the tube; the firing mechanism had been damaged on the jump, and unless we had dismantled it at the time, we would never have known. We carried that damn thing and all the rounds the whole time for nothing!

We immediately went to our backup and began firing on the target with all the LAW rockets and rifle fire, trying to at least knock out the nose cones and down the planes. The planes were damaged sufficiently, but damage to the base was minimal. The race was on! Like a bat out of hell we moved through the dark desert, picked up our gear, and headed for the foothills while we still had the night on our side.

Upon reaching the foothills undetected, we felt safe to hole up for the day. Sentry assignments were made and everyone else would try to rest up for the final leg. The SEAL Team 1 training cadre were assisting the Marines in their endeavor to locate us.

Bill Allman was within the cadre group. He was a personal friend and an excellent tracker, among other things. Bill had trailed us to the foothills and the Marines were in hot pursuit. It was now mid-afternoon and I was on sentry duty. I learned a valuable lesson here: although it is positive to pick a high spot to observe from, if at all possible, try to make it a place you can move from while under observation from the enemy.

I was on a very high rock in some brush with a great vantage point, and noticed a distant Marine patrol rise on one of the hills. They appeared to be off a good distance but I felt Mr. Thomas should know about it. I called down to the sleeping crew in the wash and received no response. Then I yelled because I could hear the sound of vehicles approaching, but no one awoke. I went for broke and moved from my position into the open, whereby the Marines came barreling down the wash right on top of us.

The unit I had seen was the main body but the scouts were obviously a good distance ahead of them. At one point, we were all at point-blank range from each other, exchanging fire and concussion grenades. All the while, Mr. Thomas was barking orders, giving us a blow-by-blow of the Marines he was killing and chewing me out for not telling him they were coming. Mr. Thomas wanted to stay and fight the Marines hand-to-hand but he thought better about it as, by then, the larger element was flying to our position as well.

We were now in the hills, but we had very little gear and almost no water. After the Marine attack, most of our equipment was left behind, and we had left a large cache of water for Nelson and Vawter in case they returned to our other site. It was clear now that we should have gone a little farther to the sanctuary of the mountains instead of settling at the foothills, thinking we were safe . . . Oh well!

It was now the fourth night and we had still another concept that we had to try—to locate a cache hidden in enemy territory. The coordinates would be given to us by an "underground operative" via radio and we would have to find the needle in a haystack. The assignment was given to Mr. Lindsay, and he was to take one man with him—me.

Mr. Lindsay and I headed out from the mountains to the desert floor about a mile and a half and, believe it or not, we found the buried cache. We were actually thrilled that we had found it because there were no landmarks. We had just dug around and wished for the best while avoiding the enemy, who had us surrounded. After finding the cache, we tied all the water and ammo on each other and headed back to deliver the goods.

At daybreak, we patrolled to our extraction point and ended the operation. As always, a very lengthy debriefing was conducted as soon as everyone was recovered. The lessons learned on that mission were invaluable, because shortly after it, we were deployed to North Africa and conducted assignments in several countries. Our missions were varied and we were locked and loaded the entire time. Everything went the way it was supposed to—in and out, and no one knew that we were there.

There was no question in my mind that the key to our success was the extreme level of realism that we focused on in our training and the fact that we knew when to enlist the expertise of people like Mr. Ganci. One of the main concepts being reinforced by that training was the development of our most important weapon—our minds.

Although our bodies are just the vessels which carry our minds, great lengths are taken for physical development, as it is of equal importance in overcoming the elements of a physical hell. Probably the most important thing I learned was the fundamental SEAL Team concept—persevere and complete the mission. This concept was generally not spoken of specifically, but like most mental aspects of the Teams, it was learned by necessity. Sometimes mental fortitude is the only way to survive. And, in the most pure sense, sometimes just to survive is to complete the most important mission. However, each warrior must be prepared to sacrifice himself for the success of the whole. . . .

Chapter Fifty-seven

Frank Lahr
UDT-3 1945

The Beach and Inshore Reconnaissance Party—Wakayama, Japan

The plan to set ashore a party to mark the beach to assist in the profile marking and then make an island reconnaissance assumed no organized enemy resistance. Without considerable modification, this plan could not be used if the enemy had offered resistance. It is a definite advantage, we found, to first find out as much about the beach conditions as possible before carrying out any operation as detailed as a string reconnaissance.

The beach group consisted of myself in charge, a corpsman, and two two-man reconnaissance teams, the petty officer in charge of which had field training and mapping experience while on the staff at Maui.

Each of the two-man teams carried a tiny 536 FM transceiver, as did the officer in charge. All wore helmets, full greens, life belts, swim shoes, and carried carbines and .45s. Flares were also taken along to use as signals should the radios fail to operate. Beach marking flags were carried in to mark the location for the profiles, which the operational sections were to make. These markers were blue bunting secured to the end of a five-foot-long steel rod; one-fourth inch welding rods were used for this. Because our markers were too small to be easily seen from the LCPRs, it was recommended that for marking beaches we use either yellow or blue bunting, depending on whether the background was dark or light, five-feet square, and held upright by a set of steel rods. This combination could easily be spotted by the naked eye from one thousand yards out to sea.

All the gear was lashed to the inflated life belts. In case the rubber boat overturned, or had it been necessary to ditch the boat on the way into the beach, no gear would have been lost. We could all swim right into the beach, towing our gear, if that happened. We also carried a plywood board with a sketch of the area, made from aerial photographs, penciled upon it.

We were towed in our rubber boat from one thousand yards into three hundred yards by LCPR number 1. We were cut loose then and paddled the rest of the way into the beach. As we approached the beach, several Japanese were standing about, apparently harmless but curious. We left them strictly alone, at first, and went about our work.

Immediately upon hitting the beach, a large blue marker was placed upon the flank of our beach, dividing our beach from that which UDT-17 was to reconnoiter. They had agreed to wait for us to do this, and thus any confusion as to who was to cover what area was avoided. One of the pair of men then proceeded to place a yellow marker every two hundred yards along the one-thousand-yard beach. Two factors were important in doing this; first of all, the men had to know their stride, running and walking, in wet sand so that the distance would be accurate. Secondly, these marking flags were to furnish the baseline for measuring distances seaward, as well as marking the proper interval between profiles. The string recon parties were to secure the end of their line near the base of each marker. With a four-foot tide and a beach with a slope of one in twenty, considerable error could result unless the same datum point, namely the high-water line, was used in all cases so that the men as they paced off the distances also had to make certain they placed the markers at the high-water line. This was no easy task when the tide was going out.

Meanwhile, the other two-man team was measuring the width and slope of the beach and noting its stability for military traffic. When the first pair had finished placing their markers along the beach, one man returned along the dune line, noting the immediate beach exits, while the other man came back along the beach, checking the locations of four small boat hulks.

From the time of hitting the beach until the second pair returned took less than fifteen minutes. During this time, however, the six reconnaissance swimmers who had been dropped off the LCPR just after we were cut loose, had made their way into the beach and found no mines or obstacles except for the four hulks previously mentioned. These six swimmers reported to the officer with the beach party, giving him their information and their estimates as to the location of the one- and two-fathom lines.

All this information was reported via 536 radios to the commanding officer in LCPR number 4, which had been designated as the control boat. The go-ahead signal was then given to the hydrographic platoon by the CO, who then proceeded as described in the previous pages.

Our shore party now left the beach and began an inland reconnaissance, with the purpose of locating beach exits and noting the terrain inshore. All information as to possible exits, extent and nature of wooded areas, rice paddies, streams, and so on, as well as the location of permanent buildings, was recorded on the sketch board. Roads and railroads were marked in, with comments as to their state of repair, width, and usability.

This five-man party (the corpsman had been left behind), covered the area inland for one mile all along the one-thousand-yard beach, returned to their rubber boat, and were aboard the LCPR seventy-five minutes after first landing.

No outright hostility on the part of the Japs was encountered. General reaction to our appearance was a combination of fear and curiosity, with curiosity soon gaining the upper hand. We, UDT, were the first Americans that these Japanese people had ever seen.

Chapter Fifty-eight

Clint "Bubba" Majors
Seal Team 1 1969–1976

X-Ray Platoon

I was sleeping, and I had planned to sleep in all morning. In my dreams I could still hear old songs from the late fifties, echoes of the "real world" back home. All we could do was dream about it. On a day like this, the "boss" had to wake me up early!

Sunday, February 28, 1971. I wasn't wild about working on Sunday. Sunday you went to church with the family—but how long ago had that been now: months, weeks, years? I was not sure. The past . . . what was I thinking? It was Vietnam and Sunday did not exist in a war zone!

Boredom and frustration, men in black pajamas toting AK-47s, leeches and rampant humidity: this was the real world now, the essence of a new lifestyle. Constant monsoon rains created a fragrance of wet, moldy earth that kindled thoughts of my childhood. But life here was oddly different, full of darkness and emptiness. The emptiness carried a fragrance of death, and that scent was never to leave my mind.

The delta was very pleasant and peaceful in many respects, but there was a void, a quietness, and fear. Even the birds and animals were gone. In the heart of the delta you could almost smell and feel terror.

This was Vietnam, the final testing grounds, the furnace, the forge where the SEAL trident was to be wrought into shape. Death was no stranger here. God. I was barely old enough for this, but to be able to play the game, the sacrifice was almost worth it. Life, death, frustration and the building of cold emptiness: it was all part of the game. Today would be my last operation in Southeast Asia, though I didn't know it yet.

There was a job to do and we, America, had signed on to do it. B-52 bombing strikes had been called in on the downtown area of Ben Tre during the Tet Offensive of '68. An army major wrote in his reports that day, "We had to destroy the city to save the people." If we had to fight a war, the delta was the place to be, one of Charlie's strongholds. A place which we had to destroy to save the people.

SEALs came to play Charlie's game in Charlie's backyard, and we played to win. We would obtain peace only through fire superiority, the way we were taught. SEAL Team 1: When you care enough to send the very, very best—that was us! We lived by many mottos and one of them was: "For the Lord Giveth and the SEAL Taketh Away."

It had been almost an hour and a half since the "boss," Mr.

Collins, had woken me. I'd called six other team members to the operation briefing; CWO2 Jones, EN1 Doyle, PT2 Mike Walsh, SN Paul "PK" Barnes, FN Don Barns, and SN Jim McCarthy. I was to be the patrol leader on this operation. It was to be a simple weapons cache recovery, based on decent intel from a *cheiu hoi* by the name of Tran Van Pham.

At 1000 hours we got on step in the LSSC (light SEAL support craft) from Ben Tre and headed several clicks downriver with seven SEALs and two boat-support personnel. The "light's" standard weaponry consisted of two M-60 machine guns and one M2HB 50-caliber machine gun. The boat was also equipped with two radios, a PRC-77 and a VRC-46. Between us SEALs, we carried three CAR-15s, one M-16-XM-203 combo, and three Stoner 63A light machine guns. We also carried a PRC-77 radio.

We passed the 10th ARVN Regiment fire-support base and continued downstream. After insertion, the recovery of the cache went easily, too easily. Tran Van Pham knew exactly where we were going and there were no problems. The cache consisted of several British Lee Enfield rifles, two 30-caliber carbines, three well-used SKS rifles, several hundred rounds of ammo, and approximately 60 pounds of ground sulfur. We returned to the light, loaded the cache, and headed for home.

On step, traveling at a speed of approximately fifty-three miles per hour, we made a smooth S curve and headed back upriver toward the 10th ARVN fire-support base. I was relaxed, sitting on the dashboard next to the coxswain on the starboard side of the boat. I was daydreaming, my back toward the bow and my feet hanging inside. My left boot was resting on the *chieu hoi*'s right shoulder as he squatted Vietnamese-style against the ceramic armor plating of the forward starboard boat-crew cockpit.

About a half-mile downstream from the ARVN fire-support base, I was staring over my left shoulder toward the river bank to my left. I was suddenly brought back to reality as two Viet Cong wearing black pajamas rose up from hiding places at the river's edge. God, this couldn't be happening!

It was just like a speeded-up silent movie from the thirties.

First they were there, then they weren't, then they were there again, each holding a B-41 rocket launcher on his shoulder. I was trying to bring my CAR-15 to a firing position on my shoulder as puffs of gray smoke erupted on the river bank. The impact and explosion of the first rocket as it slammed into the starboard side of the light, crumbled my CAR-15 in my hands. I couldn't hear anything but the *whoosh* of the first B-41 rocket as it ripped through the boat and passed out the other side.

Then, a second eruption and a *whoosh* as the other projectile grazed the boat with a glancing blow. My sixty-five-pound PRC-77 radio and my backpack took the brunt of the second explosion, and I was slammed facedown inside the boat. In shock and only half conscious, I tried to get up. Tran Van Pham, the *cheiu hoi*, had been blown in half right below my left boot. The first rocket had struck the boat exactly where he had been squatting.

Jim McCarthy, who had been standing to the *cheiu hoi*'s left, was laying facedown in a spreading pool of blood. As I tried to get up, I realized that my face had been resting in what remained of his right buttock. There was no movement or sound on Jim's part, and his right arm looked like it had just come out of a meat grinder. Since I believed he was dead, I disregarded him.

I reached for the handset of my radio, but it was gone. The whole radio and aluminum frame was gone; only the nylon webbing was left. I found the handset for one of the boat's radios and immediately began radioing for support. Giving the grid coordinate to the 10th ARVN Regiment fire-support base, I requested an emergency medevac and any additional air support we could receive.

As the boat sat in the water, we continued to receive enemy small-arms fire. My only function seemed to be a constant radioing for help. P. K. Barnes propped himself up against the ceramic armor plating of the bulkhead; his left leg was gone and his right leg was seriously burned. He reached up, took off a bandanna from his head, and made a tourniquet around his leg. He then calmly fieldstripped his CAR-15, placed the barrel inside the tourniquet, and slowly tightened it down, stopping the flow of blood to a trickle. Removing his belt, P. K. then secured the gun barrel to his thigh. With the immediate emergency medical treatment taken care of, P. K. reached into his tiger-stripe cammo pocket for a cigarette, placed it in his lips, and stared at me before his eyes rolled back as he passed out.

Only two or three minutes had passed since the explosions had rocked the LSSC. Chief Warrant Officer Jones, acting as assistant patrol leader, manned the 50-caliber machine gun and was passing out orders. I was trying to survey the damage while other SEAL squad members helped to suppress the incoming enemy fire. McClaren, one of the boat-crew members, also was missing his left leg.

From out of nowhere, second squad from our platoon arrived to assist in fighting back the enemy and help with the medevac of the wounded. I continued to call for support, and soon noticed an army slick flying high above us. The helo was carrying South Vietnamese ARVNs. I made contact with the helo, informing them that we had severely wounded Americans and were badly in need of assistance. They rerouted and came to help us.

The helo carrying the ARVNs landed nearby in a clearing on the river bank. EM1 Lou DiCroce helped me load P. K. and McClaren on the ARVN helo. As we gently placed P. K. inside the helo, his eyes opened. He grabbed me by my arm and said, "Maj, don't let them cut off my other leg, buddy."

A second helo, this time a medevac, arrived and touched down on the riverbank. Don Barns, PT2 Walsh, QM1 Cronk (the LSSC coxswain), and myself boarded the second helo, and it took off toward the Third Surgical Hospital in Binh Thuy. All of us had suffered shattered ear drums. Don Barns also had shrapnel wounds to his face, and I had shrapnel wounds to my right leg. After arriving at Binh Thuy and being treated for our wounds, we were billeted for the night.

To our dismay, those of us that were not seriously wounded were held for follow-up treatment until the second of March. I located the hospital beds of McClaren and my teammate P. K. Barnes. As I approached their beds, both men held up an extra hospital-issue shoe and asked if I've seen anyone in need of two right shoes. While P. K. and McClaren seemed in good humor, they were also in need of more support than I could give.

The afternoon quickly passed and turned into another frustrating night. Early Wednesday morning, McClaren was flown out to a naval hospital in Japan. After a short visit and a few tears, I bid P. K. farewell and headed for the Army airport to catch a helo back to our base camp.

With my SEAL Team 1 priority orders, it was no problem securing a seat on the next bird toward Ben Tre. Twenty-five minutes before departure time I was on the helo and waiting. As I sat there, I caught sight of a figure moving around the other helos. As the man got closer I realized that it was Doc Brown, a corpsman from another SEAL platoon. Doc was going from helo to helo looking inside; I wondered what he was searching for.

As Doc got closer, still searching each bird, I noticed he had a fifth of liquor in his hand. As he approached the front of the helo that I was sitting in, he noticed me.

Doc said, "Majors, come on, let's go get drunk!"

"No," I replied, "I've got to get back to work."

"Not right now," he said, "You've got time; let's spend the morning getting drunk!"

As SEALs, we worked hard and we played hard, too, but not today; I had to get back to what was left of my platoon.

"No thanks, Doc, I've got to get back to Ben Tre," I said. Doc knew that I meant it.

Doc raised his head and looked straight at me. I could see the tears in his eyes as he said, "Majors, they're all either dead or here at the hospital. No one is left in your platoon at Ben Tre. They got caught in a river ambush last night. There's no one left at Ben Tre!"

I was in shock. I can't remember if I cried, but I did scream. Part of myself died that day. Doc Brown just wanted to get me drunk to ease me into that bitter, empty pain. Sunday, February 28, 1971, five United States Navy SEALs were wounded in action along with two boat crew members. One Vietnamese *cheiu hoi* was killed.

X-Ray Platoon was the hardest-hit platoon to serve in Vietnam. According to CIA intelligence sources whom we worked closely with, a South Vietnamese LDNN (SEAL) named Thang who was attached to our platoon was giving the Viet Cong information about our missions. Three days after our platoon returned to the States, the SEAL platoon that relieved us took care of Thang.

It has been said that not many people who served in Vietnam were there to serve their country, most were just there. I don't know about that. I do know that some of us got to do what we were trained to do and even play out some of our fantasies. We had a special job to do: Our mission was to disrupt the existing Viet Cong infrastructure, to halt the continuance and growth of the Viet Cong community—we were good at our jobs.

Chapter Fifty-nine

William Stubbs
UDT-3 1945

The Demolition of the YMS 478
Wakayama, Japan

The western Pacific is an area frequented by heavy tropical typhoons. One of these storms was raging in the vicinity of Wakayama, Japan, around 15 September 1945. The seas were shipped into a tempest, filled with death and destruction, which had to be ridden out by any unfortunate ships in the vicinity. One of these ships was the ill-fated U.S. Navy Minesweeper YMS 478, which slipped anchor in the middle of the worst of this storm.

The captain and all its crew worked valiantly for hours to best the fury of pent-up seas, and only when the lives of the crew were in imminent peril was the word passed to abandon ship. Many men chose to ride it out, others jumped. After a hectic three hours of the ship's pounding upon the rocks, the storm abated, leaving the ship high and dry upon the beach at a seventy-five-degree list. Two men were found dead, and many more were injured. All personal gear was lost.

Naturally a ship of her size and mission carried quite a bit of sensitive gear, which the U.S. Navy felt reluctant to pass on to the so-recent enemies, Japan. It was therefore necessary to do away with all the gear, and UDT-3, Section 2 was selected for the job.

Section 2 was taken over to the YMS on a bright and sunny morning to look over its newly appointed task. We were met by the captain of the ill-fated ship, who gave full and complete instructions as to which parts of the ship contained the most important gear—radar gear, sound gear, charts, navigation instruments, along with the wheelhouse became the main objectives.

After receiving this dope from the captain, the men were instructed as to their particular tasks, which included breaking the keel of the ship in order to prevent its ever becoming seaworthy again under the flag of the Rising Sun.

The explosive charges were positioned to the satisfaction of all. The plan called for breaking the keel systematically in three places by situating the charges in the water at concentrated positions. The confidential gear was disposed of mainly by the use of Primacord wrappings. The ship was now ready for the explosion, and the area was cleared, although fire hoses were held in readiness.

Section 2 took up its new positions at the summit of a hill, where the hell box was placed. After once more ascertaining that the immediate area was clear, that old demolition cry of

"Fire in the hole" rang out through the crisp, cool Japanese air.

After the air had cleared and the shrapnel had settled down, Section 2 rushed headlong down the hillside to view its work. It was successful, i.e., all the destruction that was expected had been accomplished. After seeing the results, the captain of the YMS was at first crestfallen because he realized that he no longer had a command. He then recognized the good job that had been done and immediately requested us to finish the job with a complete demolition of the ship. But, it was chow time, so we all returned to the APD for chow-down.

That afternoon after chow, Section 2 returned, and once more loaded the ship with bags of tetrytol to finish the job. We found that our morning explosion had proven the advantageous use of compartmentation. Our next task was to place the charges as to take fullest advantage of this. We did this by hanging charges from the overhead, and then closing all the hatches and doors. We planned to cut the ship into three different sections, along with cutting it longitudinally, which we set about doing. After placing the charges thusly, we again retired to our vantage point on the hilltop. Again, "Fire in the hole," and again, an ear-rending explosion occurred, and shrapnel fell, but this time wires many feet above our heads went up in flame as the houses overlooking the ship slipped from their foundations. The houses in Japan are constructed flimsily, like mere shacks in the States.

The job was completely finished, and only a pile of kindling remained to show what had once been a minesweeper. That night, we mentioned that it was an excellent thing that we had the "handy-billies" in attendance because the wreckage caught fire. Handy-billies were the portable pumps we used for fire-fighting or dewaterizing.

Aside from the feelings of a lieutenant commander, who as senior short patrol officer had to listen to the cries of those Japs whose homes we had shaken up, our job was quite a success.

Chapter Sixty

Frank Lahr
UDT-3 1945

Conclusion—UDT-3 Decommissioning

On 19 November, the *Ira Jeffery* pulled into San Diego Bay, and UDT-3 moved ashore to the amphibious training base at Coronado. We were the last demolition team in the Pacific. Our standby job at Nagoya, Japan, was the last appearance of a UDT Team in World War II.

Decommissioning took up our first two weeks back in the States. Twenty-six men were discharged from the service, ten regular navy men of the team remained in post-war demolition, and four men signed over from the reserves to the regular navy to remain in demolition. The remainder of the men were given leave and reported into their home naval districts to sweat out their few months left in the service.

UDT-3 ceased to exist on paper on 8 December 1945, but it will forever be uppermost in the memories of the enlisted men and officers who served with the team, when the sea stories of the war are told. At over twenty months, it had the longest life, and we believe was the most exciting of all the UDTs.

Chapter Sixty-one

Dale Calabrese
UDT-11 1970–1975

Meanwhile, back up in the crotch of the cherry tree ...

SDV

Until today, my driver and I had been performing training runs in San Diego Bay. I was the navigator on a swimmer delivery vehicle (SDV), attached to an SDV platoon with UDT-11.

The SDV is a four-man minisubmarine with a fiberglass hull. It is powered by sixteen silver-nitrate batteries. It is also built of nondetectable materials. With compressed air tanks attached to the vehicle for controlling ballast and for the diver to breathe, along with his separate diving tanks, two divers can stay submerged for up to six hours.

The minisub has a top speed approaching six knots and has a dive capability of well over one hundred feet deep. The SDV is mainly used for clandestine operations, delivering divers, their weapons, and explosives to within swimming distance of their objective. According to the type of mission, the divers then stay submerged or swim on the surface to their objective.

In your wildest imagination, do not discard the possibilities of delivering a hand-carried nuclear weapon.

We deployed to San Clemente Island for our first SDV training operation in the open sea. My partner and I would be making our very first ocean run outside of San Diego Bay, where the water will be much clearer, colder, and deeper.

I charted our compass course on a plastic swimmer slate, and we ran through our checklist, double-checking everything, before we started our run. Everything looked fine, so we began our descent. After reaching a depth of twenty feet, we leveled off. The visibility was great, nothing else around us but kelp beds. The ocean bottom at our location was not beyond our limitations.

Everything was going according to correct procedure, water temperature sixty-eight degrees, 360-degree compass heading, and maintaining the twenty-foot depth. Even though we had a predetermined course to follow, we were not restricted the way we were in the confines of San Diego Bay.

Suddenly, from out of the clear blue sea, on our starboard side, we came across a huge dark shadow, a large dark wall that blocked the light and visibility in that direction. I strained my eyes through my face mask trying to figure out what the dark wall was. The driver and I were wearing communication face masks and began talking back and forth, wondering what this dark wall was and where it had suddenly come from. It seemed to be getting closer and darker, and my driver slowed down and began maneuvering to our port a little. I was straining my eyes harder, trying to make out some kind of detail in the object, when all of a sudden, I saw a huge eyeball blink, just a few feet from my face mask.

I didn't have to tell my driver we had encountered a whale and for him to turn hard to port; he was already doing it! Not wanting to make contact with the huge sea creature, we kept turning away until our SDV was forced into a kelp bed, and a frond of kelp caught the SDV's canopy and slid it all the way open. I was pinned to the back of the SDV, and my face mask was ripped off. My swim buddy and I were both wearing small emergency reserve tanks with regulators, which we immediately started using. The SDV then became dead in the water, hanging in the kelp at twenty feet. The whale continued on its course as if nothing at all had happened.

After getting control of my surroundings and getting oriented again, I exited the SDV to assess the damage. The propeller and rudder were tangled in the kelp, and the SDV continued to hang helplessly in the lush green, underwater jungle. My partner and I cut the kelp away with our K-bar knives, climbed back inside, and got the SDV back on its correct course without either of us having to swim to the surface.

What seemed like hours must have only been a few minutes. When we completed our training exercise and surfaced, the safety boat that had been following us never even knew what had happened while we were down below.

It is an experience like this during training that gives you the confidence to handle any predicament you are involved in, whether it is an administrative or combat situation. Whether you are operating with two men or a platoon, teamwork will always help to insure the success of a mission.

Now that I'm cold and soaked to the bone, I'm going to keep that promise I made to myself years ago. Before I freeze, I'm climbing down out of the crotch of this wild cherry tree and going home. No doe today.

A Chronological Account of UDT-3's Movement

1944

March UDT-3 organized at Maui, Territory of Hawaii. T. C. Crist is the CO.
April 18 Left Pearl Harbor aboard the SS *Typhoon*.
April 27 Arrived at New Hebrides.
May 1 Left New Hebrides to Guadalcanal.
May 3 Arrived at Guadalcanal.
May 5 Left Guadalcanal to Florida Island aboard the SS *Azalea City*.
May 6 Arrived at Florida Island.
May 6–16 Living ashore, Turner City.
May 12 Maneuvers to Guadalcanal aboard LCI 467.
May 14 Arrived back at Florida Island.
May 18 Left Pervis Bay to Guadalcanal aboard USS *Dent*, APD 9.
May 21 Arrived back at Pervis Bay.
June 4 Left Pervis Bay to Roi and Namur.
June 8 Arrived at Roi and Namur and transferred to the USS *Dickerson*, APB 21.
June 10 Left Roi and Namur to Saipan.
June 14 Arrived at Saipan.
June 15 D day on Saipan.
June 16 Arrived at Guam.
June 16–July 2 Underwent daily air attacks off Guam and Saipan.
July 2 Left Saipan to the Marshalls.

July 6 Arrived at Eniwetok.

July 14 Arrived at Guam.

(1) Daylight reconnaissance of two thousand yards of Asan Beach.

(2) Daylight diversionary reconnaissance of Agana Beach.

(3) Night reconnaissance to the high-water line of all four landing beaches at Asan.

July 15

(4) Daylight diversionary reconnaissance of Dadi Beach.

(5) Reconnaissance of Agat Beach, two thousand yards.

(6) Diversionary reconnaissance of beach between Facpi and Bangi Points. CWO R. A. Blowers was killed.

(7) Night reconnaissance of Agat Beaches.

July 16

(8) Diversionary reconnaissance of Tumon Bay.

July 17

(9) Night removal of 120 obstacles on Asan Beaches using two thousand four hundred pounds of tetrytol.

July 18

(10) Daylight removal of 150 obstacles on Asan Beaches using three thousand pounds of tetrytol.

July 19

(11) Daylight removal of 110 obstacles on Asan Beaches using two thousand two hundred pounds of tetrytol.

(12) Daylight removal of 124 obstacles on Asan Beaches using two thousand pounds of tetrytol.

July 20

(13) Daylight removal of ninety obstacles near Adolup Point using one thousand pounds of tetrytol.

July 21 W day on Guam.

July 28 Left Guam to Eniwetok.

August 1 Arrived at Eniwetok.
August 1 Left Eniwetok to Maui.
August 10 Arrived at Maui.
September 13 Left Maui to Pearl Harbor aboard the USS *Talbot*, APD 7.
September 15 Left Pearl Harbor to Eniwetok.
September 25 Arrived at Eniwetok.
September 28 Left Eniwetok to Admiralty Islands.
October 12 Left Admiralty Islands to the Philippines.
October 18 Arrived at Leyte, Philippines, and conducted preinvasion recon.
October 20 A day on Leyte.
October 22 Left Philippines to Admiralty Islands.
October 27 Arrived at Admiralty Islands.
November 11 Left Admiralty Islands to Marshalls aboard the USS *President Hayes*, PA 20.
November 16 Arrived at Marshalls.
November 16 Left Marshalls to Maui.
November 23 Arrived at Maui.

1945

March 27 Left Maui to Pearl Harbor.
April 1 Left Pearl Harbor to San Francisco aboard the USS *Hyde*.
April 6 Arrived at San Francisco.
April 9 Left San Francisco to Fort Pierce, Florida (Home).
May 1 Arrived at Fort Pierce.
June 9 Lt.(jg) R. P. Marshall succeeded Lt. Comdr. T. C. Crist as CO.
July 19 Left Fort Pierce to Oceanside, California.
August 8 Arrived at Oceanside, California.
August 14 V-J Day (victory in Japan), embarked aboard the USS *Ira Jeffery*, APD 44.
August 16 Left Oceanside to Pearl Harbor.
August 22 Arrived at Pearl Harbor.
August 24 Left Pearl Harbor to Eniwetok.
August 30 Arrived at Eniwetok.
September 2 Arrived in Ulithi.

September 6 Arrived in Manila, Philippines.
September 10 Arrived in Subic Bay, Philippines.
September 15 Arrived in Lingayen Gulf, Philippines.
September 18 Left Lingayen Gulf to Okinawa.
September 23 Arrived in Wakayama, Honshu, Japan.
September 25 D day on Wakayama.
October 25 Left Wakayama to Nagoya, Japan.
October 26 Arrived in Nagoya, Japan.
October 27 Left Nagoya for Guam.
November 2 Arrived in Guam.
November 3 Left Guam to Eniwetok.
November 6 Arrived at Eniwetok.
November 11 Arrived at Pearl Harbor.
November 14 Left Pearl Harbor.
November 19 Arrived at San Diego, California. Disembarked to amphibious training base, Coronado, California.
December 8 Last of UDT-3 men left today. UDT-3 decommissioned this date.

Invasions Performed by UDT-3

July 21—Guam
October 20—Leyte, Philippines.
September 25—Wakayama, Japan.

Original Personnel of UDT-3 and Casualties April 1944

Name/Rank	Sources of Personnel
*Lt. T. C. Crist	Seabee Battalion, Johnson Island—UDT-2
*Lt.(jg) G. C. Marion	Camp Perry
*Lt.(jg) W. T. Hawks	Bomb Disposal
*Ens. C. Emery	Bomb Disposal
*Ens. L. P. Luehrs	Bomb Disposal—UDT-1
*Ens. W. W. Schied	Bomb Disposal
*Ens. M. Jacobson	Seabees
*Ens. J. J. Breen	Seabees
*Ens. W. J. Dezell	Seabees
*2d Lt. F. F. Lahr	Marine Engineers
*ChCarp R. A. Blowers	Camp Perry—KIA Guam Operation
*ChCarp V. O. Racine	Seabees
*ChCarp R. Barge	Camp Perry
*ChCarp C. L. Young	Seabees
*ChCarp W. L. Gordon	Seabees
*ChCarp E. E. Frazier	Seabees
^RM3c J. L. Allen	Camp Perry
^GM3c J. E. Bagnell	Camp Perry
^CMM O. C. Baker	Camp Perry
^SK2c J. H. Barfield	Camp Perry

^SK2c F. L. Barnett	Camp Perry
^S2c E. J. Barta	Camp Perry—UDT-1
^SF1c W. O. Behne	Camp Perry
^S1c J. M. Bisallion	Camp Perry—UDT-1
^S1c J. M. Brady	Small Boat Pool—UDT-2
^CM3c A. L. Brokes	Camp Perry
^S1c W. K. Brown	Camp Perry
^S1c E. L. Carlson	Small Boat Pool—UDT-2
^F1c G. J. Canizio	Small Boat Pool—UDT-1
^MM2c W. R. Cardoza	Camp Perry
^F1c M. Chapman	Camp Perry
^S1c M. B. Chase	Camp Perry
^CM1c H. Chilton	Camp Perry
^CMM J. R. Chittum	Camp Perry
^COX B. M. Christinson	Small Boat Pool
^SF3c W. D. Cochran	Small Boat Pool
^SF2c J. Conklin	Camp Perry—UDT-1
^S1c E. Davis	Camp Perry
^SF1c J. W. Donahue	Camp Perry—UDT-2
^GM3c E. W. Durden	Camp Perry—UDT-1
^MM3c L. G. Foote	Camp Perry
^GM3c D. B. Gable	Camp Perry
^S1c J. E. Gannon	Camp Perry
^GM3c V. D. Gilkey	Camp Perry—UDT-2
^MM1c C. E. Greene	Camp Perry—UDT-1
^GM2c F. C. Hart	Camp Perry
^GM3c L. L. Harrison	Camp Perry
^EM2c L. L. Houk	Small Boat Pool
^AOM1c C. W. Hoffman	Camp Perry—UDT-2
^MM2c E. Holmes	Camp Perry
^CM2c W. W. Irish	Camp Perry
^CBM R. E. Hustead	Camp Perry
^COX D. C. Iverson	Small Boat Pool—UDT-2
^S1c J. Jenkins	Camp Perry
^S1c I. S. Johnson	Camp Perry—UDT-2
^COX L. E. Kirkbride	Camp Perry
^S1c J. L. Lepore	Camp Perry
^MoMM3c G. S. Lewis	Small Boat Pool
^CEM H. E. Little	Camp Perry

^GM3c T. C. Maher	Camp Perry
^GM3c H. A. Mathews	Camp Perry
^MM2c C. M. Massey	Camp Perry
^S1c R. L. Micheels	Camp Perry—UDT-1
^SF1c H. G. Mitchell	Camp Perry
^GM1c F. C. Moore	Camp Perry
^S1c Mulheren	Camp Perry
^S1c R. R. Nelms	Camp Perry
^COX E. P. Parker	Camp Perry
^CM2c N. G. Parker	Camp Perry
^MM1c E. Pollock	Camp Perry
^SF1c J. F. Quiggle	Camp Perry
^GM2c A. H. Rahn	Camp Perry
^S1c R. E. Reid	Camp Perry
^CPhM C. V. Reigle	Small Boat Pool
^SK1c J. H. Reinhardt	Camp Perry—UDT-2
^MM1c R. J. Robinson	Camp Perry
^GM3c K. J. Rylands	Camp Perry—UDT-2
^MoMM2c R. M. Schantz	Camp Perry
^CCM J. Schommer	Camp Perry
^GM1c M. Semanchick	Camp Perry
^S1c L. A. Shaw	Camp Perry
^RM3c E. L. Shepherd	Camp Perry
^COX H. K. Sims	Camp Perry
^CM2c D. E. Skaggs	Camp Perry
^F1c R. W. Smith	Camp Perry—UDT-2
^CM3c M. C. Solano	Camp Perry
^CM3c E. J. Spellman	Camp Perry
^SF2c V. R. Stewart	Camp Perry
^F1c A. J. Stone	Camp Perry—UDT-2
^RM3c H. W. Stump	Small Boat Pool
^MoMM3c W. E. Swain	Camp Perry
^COX W. A. Timmerman	Camp Perry
^MM2c C. A. Tomassoni	Camp Perry
^S1c S. R. Wagner	Small Boat Pool
^MM3c R. J. Whalen	Camp Perry
^RM2c R. M. Wood	Small Boat Pool

*Received the Silver Star for the Guam operation.
^Received the Bronze Star for the Guam operation.

Lt. T. C. Crist—Bronze Star for the Marshalls operation with UDT-2.

Lt.(jg) W. L. Hawks—Bronze Star for the Marshalls operation with UDT-2.

Ens. L. P. Luhers—Silver Star for Marshalls operation with UDT-1.

Lt.(jg) R. P. Marshall—Silver Star for the Marianas operation with UDT-5.

Casualties

ChCarp R. A. Blowers	Killed in action July 15, 1944, at Guam.
CM2c W. W. Irish	Killed in maneuvers July 1945, at Fort Pierce, Florida.

There were other changes in the ranks of UDT-3 for the Guam Operation, Leyte Gulf, and Wakayama, Japan. Some men were added, and some men were discharged or changed duty stations.

The Yonahlossee Riding Camp for Girls

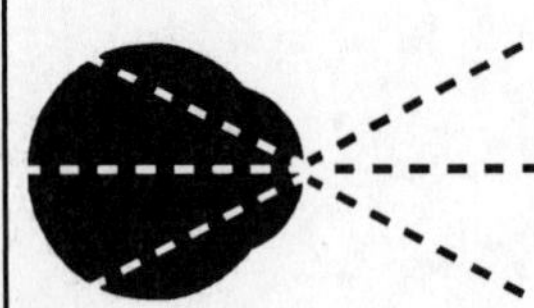

This Large Print Book carries the Seal of Approval of N.A.V.H.

The Yonahlossee Riding Camp for Girls

Anton DiSclafani

THORNDIKE PRESS
A part of Gale, Cengage Learning

GALE
CENGAGE Learning

Detroit • New York • San Francisco • New Haven, Conn • Waterville, Maine • London

This is a work of fiction. Names, characters, places, and incidents either are the product of the author's imagination or are used fictitiously, and any resemblance to actual persons, living or dead, businesses, companies, events, or locales is entirely coincidental.

Thorndike Press® Large Print Basic.
The text of this Large Print edition is unabridged.
Other aspects of the book may vary from the original edition.
Set in 16 pt. Plantin.

LIBRARY OF CONGRESS CATALOGING-IN-PUBLICATION DATA

DiSclafani, Anton.
The Yonahlossee Riding Camp for girls / by Anton DiSclafani. — Large print edition.
pages ; cm. — (Thorndike Press large print basic)
ISBN 978-1-4104-6025-7 (hardcover) — ISBN 1-4104-6025-8 (hardcover) 1. Riding club—Fiction. 2. Children of the rich—Fiction. 3. Large type books. I. Title.
PS3604.I84Y66 2013b
813'.6—dc23 2013015943

Published in 2013 by arrangement with Riverhead Books, a member of Penguin Group (USA) Inc.

Printed in the United States of America
1 2 3 4 5 6 7 17 16 15 14 13

For Mat

1

I was fifteen years old when my parents sent me away to the Yonahlossee Riding Camp for Girls. The camp was located in Blowing Rock, North Carolina, concealed in the Blue Ridge Mountains. You could drive by the entrance and never see it, not unless you were looking, and carefully; my father missed it four times before I finally signaled that we had arrived.

My father drove me from Florida to North Carolina: my parents did not trust me enough to let me ride the train alone.

The last day, we ascended into the upper reaches of the mountains, at which point our journey slowed considerably. The road looked half made, narrow and overgrown; it twisted and turned at sharp angles.

My father spoke little when he drove; he believed one should always concentrate on the road ahead. He'd bought his first car, a Chrysler Roadster, five years earlier, in

1925, so an automobile was not a habit for him but an innovation. We stopped in Atlanta on the first night, and after we checked into our hotel, my father told me to dress nicely. I wore my lavender silk dress with the dropped waist and rosette detailing. I carried my mother's mink stole, which I had taken despite Mother's instruction not to do so. When I was a child I was allowed to wear the stole on special occasions — Christmas dinner, Easter brunch — and I had come to think of the fur as mine. But now that I wore it on my own, it felt like a burden, an accessory too elegant for me. I felt young for the dress, though it was not the dress but my body that made me feel this way. My breasts were tender and new, I still carried myself in the furtive way of an immature girl. My father, in his gray pinstripe suit, didn't look much different than usual, except that he had tucked a lime-green handkerchief in his coat pocket. Not the lime green of today, fluorescent and harsh. We didn't have colors like that then. No, I mean the true color of a lime, palely bright.

At the entrance to the restaurant, I took my father's arm like my mother usually did, and he looked at me, startled. I smiled and tried not to cry. I still clung to the hope that perhaps my father would not leave me in North Carolina, that he had another plan for us. My eyes were swollen from two weeks of weeping, and I knew it pained my father to see anyone cry.

The country was in the midst of the Great Depression, but my family had not suffered. My father was a physician, and people would always pay for their health. And there was family money besides, which my parents would come to depend on. But only after my father's patients were so poor they couldn't even offer him a token from the garden in exchange for his services. I saw all this after I came back from Yonahlossee. The Depression had meant something different to me when I left.

I rarely ventured outside my home. We lived in a tiny town in central Florida, named after a dead Indian chief. It was unbearably hot in the summers — this in the days before air-conditioning — and crisp and lovely in the winters. The winters were perfect, they made up for the summers. We rarely saw our neighbors, but I had all I needed right there: we had a thousand acres to ourselves, and sometimes I would leave with a packed lunch in the morning on Sasi, my pony, and return only as the sun was setting, in time for dinner, without having seen a single person while riding.

And then I thought of my twin, Sam. I had him most of all.

My father and I ate filet mignon and roasted beets at the hotel's restaurant. Plate-glass windows almost as tall as the restaurant were the central decoration. When I tried to look outside to the quiet street, I saw a blurred reflection of myself, lavender and awkward. We were the only people there, and my father complimented my dress twice.

"You look lovely, Thea."

My full name was Theodora, a family name. The story goes, Sam shortened it to Thea when we were two. The beets tasted flat and dirty against my tongue; I tried not to think about what my brother was doing while I ate.

My father told me again that at the camp I would ride every day except Sunday. I thanked him. I was leaving Sasi behind in Florida, but it was just as well because I had outgrown him. I kicked his elbows when I posted. The thought of my pretty paint pony pained me terribly now. His coat, Mother always said, was distinctively beautiful, divided evenly between black and white patches. I thought of his eyes, one blue, one brown, which wasn't so unusual in horses: if white hair surrounded the eye, it was blue; black hair, brown.

Our meal, our last meal together for a year, was mostly silent. I had never before eaten alone with my father. My mother, yes, several times, and with Sam, of course. I didn't know what to say to my father. With all the trouble at home, I was afraid to say anything.

"You'll come home soon," my father said, over coffee and crème brûlée, "after all this mess is settled," and it was my turn to be startled by my father's behavior. I sipped my coffee quickly and singed my lips. I was only allowed a taste of Mother's at home. My father rarely spoke of unpleasantness, any kind, personal or remote. Perhaps that's why I knew as little about the Depression as I did.

He smiled at me, his small, kind smile, and I felt my eyes warm. When my mother smiled you saw all her teeth; her face revealed itself. But my father's smile was something you had to look closely for. In this moment, his smile meant he still loved me, after all I had done. I wanted him to tell me that things would be fine. But my father was not a liar. Things would not be fine; they couldn't ever be that way again.

I have never loved a place again like I loved my first home, where I was born, where I lived until the mess commenced. One could dismiss my love of place by explaining that I was attached to the people who lived there, my mother, father, and brother. That is true, I did love these people, but I cannot remember my family without remembering the gardens where they walked, the sun porches where they read, the bedrooms where they retired. I loved the house separately from my family. I knew the house, it knew me, we found solace in each other. Absurd, but there was magic in that place.

I confess that I was as sad to leave my home as to leave my family. I had never been away from it for more than a few nights, and I knew in my bones that it would be changed when I returned.

I would be changed as well. When my parents met me again at the train station in Orlando, all that time later, they might as well have been meeting an entirely new person.

I left my home, my lovely home, and was taken to the Yonahlossee Riding Camp for Girls, an enclave for wealthy young women, staffed by graduates of the camp awaiting marriage.

I came of age, as they say, at the Yonahlossee Riding Camp for Girls.

But then, I knew nothing about the place except that it was where my parents were sending me so they wouldn't have to see me. It was dusk when we arrived, a melancholy hour I've always hated. Under the cover of enormous oak trees we drove up the long gravel road that seemed to go on forever; it occurred to me that it might be weeks before I traveled this road again.

My father clutched the wheel and squinted, completing very carefully the task at hand, which was how he had always done things. We pulled up to a square — it was indeed called the Square, I would later learn — of birch-shingled cabins and my father began to turn the automobile off; I looked around for another girl, but there was no one. I opened my own door — "Thea," my father called, but I ignored him. I set my feet on the loamy soil, so different from the ground in Florida now, which was parched from the summer. The air smelled wet here, but not like the ocean. The ocean was always close to you in Florida, even when you lived hours away, like we did; here you were boxed in, on all sides, by mountains.

I peered up at the building in front of me

while my father fiddled with the car — he would not leave it until he was sure everything was turned off properly. Even now. And this building was something like I had never seen before, half built into the mountain. The stilts that supported it reminded me of horses' legs, tall and wobbly, not meant to sustain such weight. I always had the feeling that the building should fall, would fall. Later, so much later, our headmaster told me that this was, in fact, the safest way to build in the mountains. I never believed him.

Since it was a Sunday, the camp had already eaten dinner, but I didn't know that then and I was overcome by a terrible sensation of dread and longing. This was not my home, my family was elsewhere.

A man approached, appearing as if out of thin air, and held out his hand when he was still much too far away, ten, twelve feet, for my father to possibly accept it. I thought for an instant that he resembled my brother.

"I'm Henry Holmes," he called out, "the headmaster."

The first thing I thought about Henry Holmes was that his title was odd: I didn't know summer camps had headmasters. Then he reached us and first my father shook his hand; next Mr. Holmes held the tips of my fingers and bowed slightly. I inclined my head.

"Thea," my father said. "Theodora, but call her Thea."

I nodded and blushed. I was not used to strangers, and Mr. Holmes was handsome, with dark, glossy brown hair that looked in need of a trim. His shirtsleeves were neatly rolled up, and now that he was close I could see that he did not, in fact, resemble Sam. Sam had a happy, open face, with round hazel eyes — Mother's eyes; Sam always looked kind, calm. Mr. Holmes's face was a tiny bit tense, his lips drawn together in consideration. And he was a man, with a shadow of a beard. My brother was a boy.

At that moment I would have seen Sam's face in anyone's. I had taken one of his monogrammed handkerchiefs, which was what the adults I read about in books did, gave their loved ones a memento. But of course Sam had not given me anything; I had taken it. The handkerchief lay flat against my torso, beneath my dress; no one in the world knew it was there but me. I pressed my hand to my stomach and looked Mr. Holmes in the eye, as my mother had taught me to do with strangers. I couldn't ever remember meeting a man whom I was not related to, though surely I must have.

"We're pleased you've decided to join us," he said, and his voice seemed softer when he spoke to me, as if he were trying to show sympathy not with his words but with the way they sounded when they reached my ears. I told him that I was pleased to be here as well. He must have guessed that some unpleasantness had sent me to the camp so late in the season. I was enrolling in the middle of the summer; I wondered what excuse my father had made.

Mr. Holmes led us up the tall staircase to the Castle, and though I would only learn later that this was what everyone called this edifice, I thought even then that it looked like a fortress, imposing and elegant. The staircase was uncovered and it must have just rained, because the wood was slick. I stepped carefully. Two gas lamps flanked the door at the top of the stairs. The twin flames burned steadily, orange and red within their glass houses. Mr. Holmes opened a thick oak door, painted navy blue with yellow trim, the camp's colors, and led us through the front room, which served as the dining hall and worship site.

Mr. Holmes paused by the front bay window.

"So unlike Florida," my father said. He smiled at me, and I could see that he was pained. He had started to gray around the temples in the past year, and I saw, suddenly, that my father would become old.

Mr. Holmes waved us into his office, where I sat on a brown velvet settee while my father and Mr. Holmes took care of the necessary matters. I could feel Mr. Holmes watching me, but I did not look up.

I coughed, and my father turned his head. "Wait outside, Thea?" I left and wandered down the hall outside the office. From where I stood I could see the tables that were already set for the next meal, tables that tomorrow morning would surely be filled with girls. Hundreds of them. I wanted so badly to be elsewhere.

I turned back to Mr. Holmes's office, and was confronted by a wall of photographs, which I had somehow missed before. Horses, and astride them, their girls. I went closer and read the tiny script engraved beneath each photo, touched the brass and felt the words. On each plaque there was the name of a horse, and beneath that the name of a girl, and then, finally, *First Place, Spring Show,* and the year. There were photos from the 1800s. The horses hadn't changed much, but the earliest girls rode sidesaddle, their legs hobbled together, hanging uselessly. You could see the march of time, both through the quality of the photographs and the girls' names and clothes and hairstyles; the last two had grown shorter as time progressed. So many people had passed through this place. The most recent photograph featured a tall girl with white-blond hair and patrician features, astride a giant horse; they dwarfed the man who stood next to them, presenting the award. *Leona Keller,* it read, *King's Dominion, First Place, Spring Show, 1930.*

I noticed a small, marble-topped table by Mr. Holmes's office door, two neat stacks of brochures on top of it. *Yonahlossee Riding Camp for Girls,* the first one said, *A Summer Equestrian Respite for Young Ladies Since 1876.* Beneath the cursive script was a row of smiling girls, in white blouses and white skirts, each holding a horse. The horses' ears were all flipped forward, their attention earned by something behind the camera.

At first I thought the brochures in the next stack were simply older versions. Their covers featured a photograph of what must have been the entire student body, a mass of girls straightened into rows for a picture, each one of them staring solemnly into the camera. *Yonahlossee Riding School for Girls,* the same cursive script read, *Educating*

Young Ladies Since 1902.

I heard a voice behind Mr. Holmes's door, and slipped away and went to the window. I held a hand to the glass, my thumb blocked half of a mountain range. The view was stunning, I had never seen anything like it. Florida was flat and hot, for as far as I could see from this window there were mountain peaks, slate-gray, snaked with trees, puncturing the clouds that hung so low they must not have been ordinary clouds. The clouds I was used to floated high in the sky.

I was not so angry with my situation that I could not discern beauty.

I was assigned to Augusta House. All of the cabins were named after the founders' relatives — we had Mary House, Spivey House, Minerva House. Mr. Holmes led me and my father through the Square, but I trailed a foot or two behind so I didn't have to speak. Mr. Holmes's stride was enormous; he was tall and lanky and towered over my father, who had always been on the small side. Sam, who had shot up like a weed over the past few months, was taller than him now. Sam might be eating at the moment, or maybe dinner was done. Perhaps he was still wearing his day clothes: shorts and a button-down linen shirt, an outfit chosen to make the sun bearable. We never wore sleeves in the summer, but in Atlanta every man I'd seen had worn a full suit, despite the heat. Mr. Holmes wore a suit now, had emerged with Father from his office wearing a jacket.

My father walked quickly to keep up and wanted to leave his hands in his pockets, but kept removing them, instinctively, for balance.

I wondered if I would recognize the back of Father's head in a crowd. Surely I would recognize Sam's, his coarse, thick hair that Mother coaxed to lie flat every time she passed by, drawing a hand over his head by habit.

Mr. Holmes opened the door to Augusta House and walked through first, but before he did he turned and gave me a little smile; I could hear him tell the girls they had a visitor, and when my father and I walked in a moment later, five girls stood by their bunk beds, hands behind their backs, motionless. It was almost dark now, and the light from a wall sconce was the only source of illumination in the room. I thought it odd that Mr. Holmes, a grown man, had entered a cabin full of girls without knocking. But they had known he was coming. I wondered what else they knew.

"This is Theodora Atwell, she has come to us from Florida."

The girls nodded in tandem, and a panic seized me. Did they do everything in tandem? How would I know?

"And this," Mr. Holmes said, starting with the girl on the left, "is Elisabeth Gilliam, Gates Weeks, Mary Abbott McClellan, Victoria Harpen, and Eva Louise Crayton."

"Pleased to meet you," I said, and all of the girls inclined their heads slightly. Elisabeth, the first girl, broke her stance and broke the order, and I was so grateful. These were just girls, like me. She tucked a piece of ash-brown hair behind her ear and smiled; her smile was crooked. She seemed kindhearted. I liked her blue eyes; they were wide set, like a horse's. She would be my Sissy.

I wondered, in that dimly lit cabin that smelled so strongly of wood, what had brought each girl there. Or who had brought them. We each had half of a bunk bed, a tiny closet, a washstand, a desk, a vanity. Our house mistresses roomed with each other in another cabin; we girls were to be left completely alone. I took my father's hand, which hung by his side, and hoped the other girls would not think me childish. His grip surprised me, and then I knew it was true, he meant to leave me here. I tugged my hand free of his and stepped forward.

"I'm pleased to be here."

My father kissed my cheek and pressed me to him in a sort of clumsy half hug; now I was embarrassed instead of sad, all these girls watching. Mr. Holmes turned his head politely. Then they left, and I stood there alone in this room full of girls and felt terrified. I was accustomed to the feeling of fear — it threaded itself through my brain each time I tried a higher jump — but that fear was accompanied by a certain exhilaration.

Now I watched the unreadable faces of all these girls and they watched me and I felt frightened in a way I had never felt frightened before. There was no place to go but here, no one to take comfort in except myself. I started to cross my arms in front of my chest but then an instinct told me to stop: I didn't want any of these girls to know I was scared.

"Theodora?" the pretty girl with the full figure asked, and I remembered her name. Eva.

"Thea," I mumbled. But I wasn't from a family that mumbled. I cleared my throat. "Thea. A nickname."

"Well, that's better," Eva said, and

grinned. "Theodora's a mouthful."

I hesitated — was she making fun of my name? But then she patted the bunk beside her. "This is you. You're my bottom."

Sissy laughed. The sound startled, then comforted me. "Have you ever slept on a bunk bed?" she asked. "I have the bottom, too. It's the worst, but you're here so late."

I pointed at my trunk, which rested at the foot of my bottom bunk; pointing was bad manners, now the girls would think I had none, but poor manners were better than explaining why I had come so late.

"My trunk's already here," I said.

"One of the men brought it," Mary Abbott chimed in. Her voice was fragile-sounding.

"But not the handsome one!" Eva said, and Sissy laughed.

Gates turned from her desk, where she had been writing something — a letter? I wondered to whom — and I could see she did not approve.

"Oh, Gates," Eva said. "Don't be so serious. It's just chatter." Eva turned to me, languidly; she moved about like she didn't have a care in the world. "There are two men here who do chores. One is very handsome. And the other . . . you'll see." I felt my face go hot, and quickly walked to my bunk so the other girls wouldn't see. I blushed at the drop of a hat. I busied myself with my trunk, and after a moment I noticed that everyone was changing into their nightclothes. I changed out of my clothes quickly — no other girl had ever seen me naked. Only Mother, and she was not a girl. I was careful to hide the handkerchief as I disrobed — the other girls would think me childish if they saw I'd hidden a piece of fabric from my brother beneath my clothes. Or worse than childish: odd.

Our nightgowns were all the same — mine had been laid upon the bed — soft cotton shifts with V-necklines, a mid-calf hemline, *YRC* embroidered over our left breasts. Over our hearts. The nightgown I had brought with me was high collared, ankle length, ruffled at the wrists. It would have given me away immediately. Mother had told me that I'd be wearing a uniform, so I didn't need to pack much; the idea had made me furious back home. I was going to be treated like everyone else! But now I was glad. I had not known my nightgown was all wrong.

The girls left in pairs — Eva and Sissy, Gates and Victoria — until only Mary Abbott and I remained. I had no choice but to follow. I didn't want to ask where we were going, but I did.

"The privies. I know what you're thinking, how can we not have a toilet in our cabins?" she asked. She dropped her voice conspiratorially: "They think it's good for us." Her accent was very Southern. Mr. Holmes had an accent, but I couldn't place it — he spoke in clipped tones, the opposite of how everyone in Augusta House spoke. I didn't have an accent, not compared to these girls. "But at least there's indoor plumbing. And running water for our baths."

I nodded at Mary Abbott, unsure of how to respond. I'd always had indoor plumbing, and running water.

Eva and Sissy passed us on their way back to the cabin, along with pairs of other girls from other cabins. We looked like ghosts in our nightgowns, and I hated this place, hated these girls, my first clear, unconfused sentiment since I'd arrived. I wrapped my shawl tighter around my shoulders and hated my mother.

The privies were spotless — I was grateful for that. I didn't wait for Mary Abbott, rushed back to the cabin without once meeting anyone's eye. When we'd passed Eva and Sissy, I knew by how they smiled that Mary Abbott was not someone I wanted to align myself with. I was already in bed when Mary Abbott came in; she looked at me for a long second, wistfully, I thought, but that was unreasonable, she'd known me for an hour — and then someone entered the cabin, too young to be a woman, too old to be a girl. She barely looked at any of us. When she saw me, she nodded — "Theodora Atwell. Glad to see you've settled in." And then she turned off our lights.

"Good night, girls," she called as she left the room.

"Good night, Henny," everyone called back, in unison.

The girls said good night to each other then, in sleepy whispers; I thought they were done when Eva spoke.

"Good night, Thea," she whispered, and all the other girls followed suit, my name whispered five times, and it seemed astonishing that I knew which voice belonged to whom; it seemed astonishing that already these girls laid claim to me.

The last girl I had known was Milly, a neighbor, and she had moved away years ago. She carried a doll with her, always. I thought she was boring, which in my family was least what you wanted to be. Other people were boring; the Atwells were interesting.

Sam liked Milly, though. She would watch him tend to his terrariums, help him carve branches of trees into a more manageable size, listen with interest as Sam explained how his huge cane toad transmitted poison from the glands behind its eyes. Only Sam was able to pick the toad up; when I tried, it puffed to twice its normal size. Sam had a carefulness about him that animals trusted. People, too.

I did not like Milly there with Sam when I returned from a ride. And so I stole Milly's doll and buried it behind the barn. She never came back.

Sam knew what I had done. I had been cruel, and Sam hated cruelty. I think he did not understand it, the impulse to harm another living creature. It's why he couldn't ride. The thought of pressing a spur into a horse's tender side, or lifting a whip against a dumb animal — well, Sam could not imagine it.

He was ashamed of me, and I was almost ashamed of myself, but Milly was quickly forgotten, ground into the dust of a child's memory.

A girl muttered something nonsensical, talking in her sleep.

"Shh," Gates said, "shh," and the muttering stopped.

In Atlanta, my father and I had slept in separate rooms. We'd never traveled alone before, so I didn't know how to interpret this, but in my great big room I'd cried, and then slapped myself for being so silly and desperate: this was nothing, I told myself, take hold of yourself. I'd fallen asleep to the noise of cars underneath my window, wondering if my father heard the same in the room across the hall, wondering if he was even awake to hear it or dead to the world.

The cars outside my window had made me feel less lonely, though that was silly — the men and women in those cars were no friends of mine.

I wondered if Sam was still awake now, listening to the Emathla crickets. I wondered what else he had heard, today, what else he had done. Mother would still be awake, reading, listening to the radio; Father would still be driving if I had to guess, twisting carefully through the mountains.

I thought of my cousin, Georgie, and wanted to weep, but I would not let myself. I had wept enough for a lifetime. Two lifetimes. Three.

The next morning a bell woke me. I sat up quickly and banged my head on Eva's bunk. Her face appeared next to mine, from her top bunk.

"You look like a bat," I said, and she looked at me dreamily, and I admired her pretty skin, her plump cheeks.

I massaged my scalp and waited for the other girls to rise. But no one moved for a few minutes; instead they lay in their beds and yawned and stretched. I had never been alone with so many girls for so long. Mother had sent me and Sam to the Emathla school for two weeks before deciding it wasn't good enough for us; but the differences between me and those children, the sons and daughters of country people, had been so clear. Here I did not know where I stood.

All the girls looked dazed, lying in their beds. Eva was the tallest among us; Mary Abbott the shortest. Victoria was the thinnest girl, but she was too thin, with a collarbone so sharp she looked starved. My hair was neither dark nor light; I was neither short nor tall. At home I almost never saw other children. Father taught us our lessons, and when Sam and I did see another boy or girl, in town, we were always looked at closely, because we were twins and resembled each other uncannily: we both had Father's strong nose, and high, broad cheekbones. Our faces were sculpted, Mother said. And we both had Mother's hair, a rich auburn color and coarsely wavy. It felt the same, when you touched it. Our resemblance made people notice us. Here, without Sam, I was just like everyone else except a little darker, because of the Florida sun.

Another person entered, clearly a maid — I could tell by her uniform.

"Good morning, Docey," Eva called, and Docey smiled quickly in her direction, then poured water into each of our washstands. Then everyone rose and went to them — they were plain, simple walnut, but their bowls were painted prettily with delicate flowers. The rim of mine was chipped. Docey was smaller than any of us. If I had to guess, I'd say she was no more than five feet, but stronger, with mousy-brown hair pinned into a tight bun and a lazy eye. She spoke with an accent that was rough and quick, Southern, messier than everyone else's. Later I would learn her accent signaled she was from the poorest part of Appalachia.

After we washed and dressed, we walked through the Square to the same building I'd come to last night, with Father. I'd slept with Sam's handkerchief under my pillow. I'd wanted to put it underneath my clothes again, but the risk that Eva or Sissy — I wanted to impress them most — would see was too great.

When I stepped outside, I was shocked by the sheer mass of the girls. There were so many of them, all dressed in white skirts and blouses with Peter Pan collars, *YRC* again embroidered over our hearts. My father had told me that there would be almost two hundred girls, I suppose to prepare me, but I wasn't prepared, not for this army. The only thing that immediately distinguished them from one another was their hair — a girl with tight curls glanced at me and whispered something to her friend, and I realized I was gawking. I stepped into the crowd and tried to keep up, tried to pace my gait with theirs. I looked at all the girls' legs and realized no one wore stockings; from the waist down, we looked like a crowd of children.

Sissy caught up with me. Her brown hair was cut in a fashionable bob. I touched my own hair, which fell well over my shoulders. I'd wanted a bob, but Mother hadn't wanted me to cut it.

"You're a quick walker," she said.

I slowed my pace. "Yes."

"It's hot in Florida." Her voice was husky; it contrasted sharply with her delicate features.

"Where are you from?" I asked.

"Monroeville."

She acted as if I must know where that was. I pretended that I did.

"What does your father do?" she asked.

"He's a doctor. And he owns orange groves." The last part wasn't technically true — the citrus was in my mother's family — but I assumed owning land gave you currency here.

"I love oranges!" she said, smiling her crooked smile, and I smiled back at her enthusiasm. Oranges weren't a treat to me. They were a given.

"What does your father do?" I asked.

"He manages my grandfather's affairs. And rides horses. That's why he sent me here, to learn how to ride. But I'm afraid I haven't taken to it."

"No?"

"It's too dirty," she said. Then added quickly, "But don't think I'm like that," and glanced at me sideways. "I just like other things better."

I was surprised by the sound of my laughter. I hadn't laughed in weeks.

The other girls swarmed around us as we entered the dining hall. Clustered at tables draped with toile cloths, they spoke among themselves, and I could see they liked it here, felt at home.

Sissy pointed out my table, where Mary Abbott, Victoria, and Henny sat amid others. Mary Abbott grinned excitedly when she saw me, and I gave a small smile in return, then chose the seat farthest from her.

"Hello, Theodora," Henny said. I started to tell her about my name, but Mary Abbott piped in.

"She goes by Thea." Henny didn't acknowledge that Mary Abbott had spoken, went on and introduced the others at the table, a mix of younger and older girls and a teacher, Miss Metcalfe, who had very smooth skin and small, pearly teeth.

There were steaming platters of food — eggs, bacon *and* ham, raspberry muffins, grits — but I had no appetite. Mostly, everyone ignored me, and I was grateful. I thought that Sam would have loved all this food; he had started to eat like a horse the past few months. I knew exactly where he was right now: out back, tending to one of his injured animals, or feeding the insects in one of his terrariums, rearranging a branch so a lizard had a better place to sun himself. He didn't always have an injured animal to tend to, but he'd been raising a nest of baby squirrels for a few weeks. Their mother had vanished.

"Can I ask you a question?" Molly said, halfway through the meal. She had buckteeth, which made her seem younger than she was. Her thin brown hair hung loose, an inch past her waist. It needed to be cut.

"May I . . ." Henny corrected. She was chubby, with a double chin and an unfortunately placed mole on her left temple. She wasn't homely, exactly, but there was the mole. I did not like Henny but I was relieved by her presence, that there was a near-adult here along with Miss Metcalfe to keep order.

Molly continued. "Why are you here so late?"

"Pardon?"

"Why didn't you come at the beginning like the rest of us?"

I waited for Henny to intervene, but she sat quietly, like the others at the table, watching me. Alice Hunt Morgan, from Memphis, Tennessee, traced the rim of her glass. I'd called her Alice and she'd corrected me: Alice Hunt, she'd said, that's my full name. Now everyone waited for my answer. They were all curious, and I couldn't blame them: I was an interloper.

"It was a late birthday present," I said, "we were in Europe on holiday because it gets so hot in Florida during the summer."

I paused. The girls waited, heads tilted. Molly rolled a piece of her ratty hair between her fingers. "We go every year and I didn't want to miss it, but my father wanted me to come to camp, too. So he arranged it." I shrugged my shoulders, as if to say it was all in the hands of generous and capable adults.

"Where in Europe?" Molly asked, but by then the other girls were tired of me, had returned to one another.

"Paris," I said. "I love Paris in the summer."

Molly nodded and looked away, satisfied. I felt the back of my head for a tender spot from this morning, but there was nothing. I looked across the room and found Sissy, who smiled at me. I smiled back.

"Thea," Henny said. So she had heard Mary Abbott; Mary Abbott was a girl one didn't have to acknowledge. "Drink up." She nodded at my milk. I contemplated the glass, which I had barely touched. At home we drank orange or grapefruit juice, depending on the season. Never milk. Mother had an aversion to it. We stirred milk into our tea sometimes, or Sam and I had it with dessert. For lunch at Yonahlossee, I'd soon learn, a glass pitcher of sweet iced tea, a chunk of ice floating in the amber, would rest next to Henny's plate, and she would dole it out among us carefully. This iced tea was thick and syrupy, and, I had to admit, delicious. Years later I'd crave this iced tea, its cool weight on my tongue, the bitterness of the strong tea offset by the copious amounts of sugar; I'd learn that to miss the Yonahlossee sweet tea was something of a tradition among us.

But that would be later. For now I stared at my glass of pale milk and tried not to cry.

"Thea," Henny said again, her voice low, but I knew I would cry if I looked up. Then I could feel her gaze lift; everyone turned their seats around in the same direction and I thought this was some strange way of leaving until I heard his voice.

"Good morning, girls," Mr. Holmes said.

"Good morning, Mr. Holmes," everyone chorused but me, and Mr. Holmes seemed quietly delighted at this response, even though he must hear it every morning.

After he had delivered morning announcements and led us in worship, a woman approached me, too old to be a house mistress. She was plump and short, with a pretty face.

"I'm Mrs. Holmes, the headmistress. Follow me," she said, and gestured toward the stairwell at the edge of the room. I tried to keep the surprise from my face, but she saw anyway, looked at me for a second too long so I would know I had erred. But I also knew I could not be the first person who had been surprised that she was married to Mr. Holmes. When I'd seen her this morning, I'd thought she was head housekeeper, or some other staff person; even from across the room she had a matronly, interfering way about her. She struck me as impatient. I followed her obediently, slowed down so that I would not overtake her. Her waist seemed unnaturally small, as if she were cinched in, and I realized she must be wearing a corset. Even Mother didn't wear those. But Mother was so slim she didn't need one.

Mrs. Holmes's office was on the third floor, and by the time we reached it she was out of breath. As she opened the door, I stood close enough so that I could see how tightly her brown hair was bound into a bun; her hair was graying, which you could not see from a distance.

Her office was elegantly appointed, the settee upon which she gestured for me to sit upholstered in a modern plaid.

"Theodora Atwell," she began. "You're at Henny's table?" Before I could answer, she continued. "I've known Henny for a very long time. She's exceptionally capable." This seemed like a warning. She looked down at the papers in front of her. "From Emathla, Florida. I've always thought that to live in Florida as a gardener would be sublime. You could grow anything."

Mother said that very same thing. But I didn't want to think about Mother. "Everyone calls me Thea."

"Oh, I know," Mrs. Holmes said, and smiled at me. I wondered if Mr. Holmes had already told her what to call me, if they spoke often about the girls here. They must.

"Tell me, Thea," she said, as she lowered herself into her shiny wooden chair and gazed at me from across her desk, hewn from the same wood, also polished to a sheen, "how are you liking it so far?"

"Very much," I said, because there was nothing else I could say.

"The founders of Yonahlossee were very progressive individuals. They started this camp in 1876, eleven years after the War Between the States. Why, Thea, was this such an important time in our nation's history?"

I knew this, at least. My own great-grandfather had fled the War Between the States. "Because the South was poor almost beyond belief. Because it was a terrible time for this part of the country. Everything was changing, rapidly, and no one was sure what would happen to the South."

I had impressed her. "Yes." She nodded. Then she told me about Louisa and Hanes Bell, who had never had children of their own but who had made it their mission to provide a summer respite for females in this rapidly changing — she used my words — world. Places like this already existed in the North, for girls and boys, and in the South, for boys, but the Bells had seen a lack and filled it.

"And then the camp became a school, as demand for the place grew." Before, she had sounded like she was rattling off a speech, one she had given before many times. Now she looked at me intently, but I didn't know why. "So now Yonahlossee is a camp for certain girls and a school for others. But in both cases it is a place for young women to learn how to become ladies. Because, Thea, becoming a lady is not simply a thing which happens, like magic." She snapped her fingers, then shook her head. "No, quite the opposite: becoming a lady is a lesson you must learn.

"In this world of uncertainty," she finished, "a lady is more important than she ever was."

She was referring to the financial crisis, of

course. It seemed sad that the Bells had never had children, especially since they'd devoted their lives to the young. Something must have been wrong with Louisa's organs. I had very little idea of what Mrs. Holmes meant: she might as well have been speaking Greek. A lady was now more important than she ever was?

"And the name?" I asked, because Mrs. Holmes was looking at me expectantly. "Yonahlossee?"

"Oh," Mrs. Holmes said, and made a small, flinging gesture. "An old Indian name. It has nothing to do with the camp, really. The name of Mrs. Bell's horse."

I waited for her to continue, to say something about equestrienne pursuits. I smiled to myself; Sasi was an old Indian name, too. Mother had named him after I couldn't think of anything. Sasi was an old Muskogee word, meaning "is there." As in, the flower is there. Mother had said that, exactly. I remembered her voice so clearly.

"I hope you'll like it here," she said, and put her elbows on the table, and stared at me frankly, her small hands folded in front of her.

"I feel sure I will." And I had liked it, a moment ago, liked hearing about Louisa Bell; Yonahlossee seemed like a kinder place now that I knew it was named after a horse. But remembering Mother, and Sasi, had turned me gray again.

"Your mother was sure you would."

I was so confused for a second — had she read my mind?

"Your mother is a friend of mine. An old friend."

This was impossible. My mother didn't have any old friends; we were all she needed. How many times had I heard her say that she and Father had stumbled into their private utopia out here in the Florida wilderness?

"You have her hair," Mrs. Holmes said, and then I knew it was true, she had known Mother.

"We went to finishing school together," she continued, "in Raleigh. Miss Petit's."

My eyes blurred, and I thought for an instant that I was having an allergic reaction, like one of Father's patients; to a bee sting, a berry.

I bit my lip, and it was hard to breathe; then I started to cry.

"Oh, Thea, I didn't mean to upset you. Did your mother not tell you that we knew each other?"

I shook my head.

"Yes, I know all about you. She entrusted

you to me, in a way. Another place might not have been suitable for you.

"Do we understand each other, Thea?" Mrs. Holmes asked, after a moment.

I nodded.

"Please look at me."

I did as she asked. Her eyes were almond-shaped. That I was looking into the same eyes my mother had once looked into seemed impossible.

"And there's another thing: if you notice anything unusual, anything . . . bodily, please come and see me at once."

"Bodily?" I repeated.

"Bodily. I'll expect you know what I mean if it happens."

I told her I understood, even though I didn't.

As I walked alone to the stables for my evaluation, I thought she must mean my monthly cycle. But I already had that, and knew what to do myself.

I was glad no girl could see my red eyes; I was grateful that I had the walk to compose myself. My understanding had been that Yonahlossee was a place arrived at by accident, by circumstance.

The path past the privies narrowed into a lane wide enough for two people; trees rose on either side, blocking out most of the sunlight. I shivered, and was relieved when I emerged suddenly into a large circle of flat space, bordered by mountains.

I gasped, in spite of myself; I had told myself I would try not to be surprised by everything new at Yonahlossee. But I had never seen anything like this; I hadn't even known something like this existed. There were three stone barns, all in a row, and they were massive compared to my barn at home, as if they housed an army of horses. My barn at home was barely a barn at all, I realized, compared to this. Horses hung their heads out of their stall windows, and I saw an Appaloosa with a spotted head, a breed I'd only read about, never seen.

Grooms milled about the grounds, pushing wheelbarrows or leading horses. One man caught me staring, and I turned away, blushing; he looked like Docey's male counterpart, skinny and wiry, capable.

There were five riding rings, two with jumps. Everything looked perfect and new, the rings freshly raked, the fences newly painted. I wondered where Yonahlossee got all its money. The few towns we had driven through on the way here had looked very poor — the buildings falling down, the people dirty — but I knew we were entering

Appalachia, which was poor anyway, aside from the financial crisis. Father mentioned a terrible drought. Another reference to unpleasantness, uncharacteristic, but I was quickly learning that my life was turning into a series of surprises.

"It's unexpected, isn't it?" a voice asked, and I spun around to find a tall man standing at my left. A horse, already saddled and bridled, stood at his side.

"You startled me," I said, my hand clapped over my heart, as was my habit when surprised. I hoped my red eyes didn't give me away.

The man laughed. He had a German accent; I'd met a German man before, Mr. Buch, who used to come visit my father every year or so for business about the oranges.

"You're German?"

"Yes. I'm Mr. Albrecht."

"I'm Thea Atwell, pleased to meet you." I curtsied slightly, to compensate for my rudeness. I recognized Mr. Albrecht from the photographs hanging on the wall. He was the man who presented the awards. He was extremely thin, with a flat chin, which surprised me. I thought Germans came with square jaws. But his skin was smooth, for a man, and his teeth straight. He was, if not handsome, passable. He seemed as old as my father.

"And this," he said, "is Luther." He stroked the ridge of Luther's neck, and Luther lowered his head and watched me. Luther was a homely horse, dull brown with a too-large head and small ears. But he had kind eyes.

"He's the first horse everyone here rides. Your father said you were an experienced rider?"

"Yes."

"You shouldn't have any trouble with Luther. Tap him on over the jumps, keep him steady through the doubles. He'll jump anything, but sometimes he balks if you're shy."

Mr. Albrecht gave me a leg up, and I settled into the saddle while he adjusted my stirrups. My heart raced, from some mixture of the shock I'd just experienced at the hand of Mrs. Holmes and the anticipation of riding in front of a stranger. Luther was huge, over sixteen hands, maybe even seventeen, the largest horse I'd been on. That doesn't matter, I told myself. Control is control. Mr. Albrecht mapped out the course, and I followed him to the farthest ring. He gave me ten minutes to warm up, and I trotted around the ring, testing

Luther. I tugged on my left rein and he tugged back; I gave him a sharp jerk. Mr. Albrecht stood by the gate and watched. He had a simultaneously formal and relaxed air about him; he stood with his hands in his pockets, his head cocked, his white shirt spotless, his breeches neatly ironed and creased.

I tried to ignore the figure of Mr. Albrecht watching me ride. When he told me it was time, I halted Luther from a trot and then asked him to canter from a walk; I wanted his reflexes sharp. Another man had joined Mr. Albrecht by the gate; I squinted — Mr. Holmes. He waved, and I bowed my head in response. I wasn't wearing a helmet, no one in those days did, and though other people wore gloves, they dulled the feeling in my hands. The jumps I was to clear were over three feet tall; we weren't afraid of anything, in those days. We didn't know there was anything to be afraid of.

I completed the course in a blur. I could never remember my courses after I'd finished them, someone would have to tell me if I'd knocked down a rail, or made a wrong turn. After I jumped the last combination, I cantered Luther around the perimeter of the ring until the tension in both our bodies eased. I walked over to where Mr. Albrecht stood; Mr. Holmes was gone.

Mr. Albrecht nodded, and slapped Luther's neck.

"Cool him out. You did well."

I could still see Mr. Holmes; he hadn't reached the trail yet, where the woods would swallow him. I wondered how long it would be until Sam was as tall as Mr. Holmes. Right now he was still a child, or half child, half adult, like me.

I held on to the reins by the buckle at their end and let Luther hang his head. We walked leisurely around the ring. That Yonahlossee was not a place picked at random disturbed me, but also confirmed that my parents' plan was beyond my understanding. Mother had chosen a place a little like paradise, as far as horses were concerned; at least there was that. That my mother could have been friends with a person like Mrs. Holmes was almost unbelievable; yet I had to believe it. My mother had been cruel to me in the past few weeks in a way that I knew I deserved but was nonetheless hard to bear. My parents had not sent me into the arms of strangers; instead they had sent me into the arms of a woman who knew at least part of my terrible secret. But what part had my mother told her? Surely not everything.

Mr. Albrecht had disappeared into the barn. I stopped Luther and dismounted; then I did a childish thing. I wept into his hot shoulder, salty with sweat, and for the first time in weeks I felt comfort.

2

The tunnel of woods from the stables to the Square was dark, and though I'd never been scared of being by myself, I hurried. All the other girls were in class. What kind of animals lurked in the North Carolina woods, what kind of poisonous plants? I knew all of that in Florida. Here I was an innocent.

There wouldn't be as much to be wary of here, at least concerning the natural world. Winter came every year and weeded the animals, the plants. In Florida nothing died, nothing retreated.

When it was cool enough, Sam and I liked to roam out back, past the orange grove, miles away from the house. One day, when we were eleven, I brought Sasi with us, because it was one of the last tolerable days before summer. Sasi was young then, too, could be ridden for hours and hours and still have something left. Sam was walking ahead of me, looking for blackberries; I was on horseback, following him. It was April, a few weeks too early for blackberries, but Sam thought we might get lucky.

"Is Sasi tired?" Sam called out.

"No," I said. "He likes it out here."

"Do you like it out here, Sasi?" Sam asked, in an English accent, and I giggled.

We walked some more. Sam disappeared into a throng of bushes.

"Even if you find any, they'll be tart," I said.

Sam reappeared, empty-handed.

"Because it's too early," I explained.

Sam grinned. "I knew what you meant the first time."

I turned around and reached into my saddlebag for a canteen; there was a sudden dip, a feeling of weightlessness, and then buzzing. At first I didn't understand the noise, but when I felt a sting on my cheek I knew that Sasi had stepped into an underground nest of yellow jackets.

"Sam!" I screamed. I slipped off Sasi, who was stomping his hooves into the dirt, clouds of dust rising around his legs. "Sam!"

"Thea," he said, and his voice infuriated me: it was so calm, so slow.

"Help," I cried, slapping at my cheeks. "Hurry!"

"Thea," he said, "listen to me. Listen," he said, as he walked toward me.

I shook my head furiously; I could feel my cheeks swell, my throat tighten. I could see red welts rise on my arm, I felt them on my neck. I tasted bile.

"Thea," Sam said, and when he reached me he touched my forearm. "Look at me."

But I couldn't. I looked at Sasi, who was furiously biting his leg where he had been stung; I looked beyond Sam, at the miles and miles of scrub oak and oak trees; I looked at the sky, which was blue, not a cloud in sight. I could hear my heart beat. I could smell my sweat.

"It's not a full nest," Sam said, but he sounded like he was speaking from a great distance. "There aren't enough of them. But if you aren't calm you'll make it worse. All right, Thea? See," he continued, "they're gone."

I looked at him. "Sasi?" I asked.

"Sasi will be fine. He's so big," he said, and I understood that I was not so big, that my labored breathing, my hot, scratchy face were evidence of my smallness.

"How many stings?" I asked, my voice high.

"Not that many." But I knew he was lying. Sam had never been able to lie to me.

"Ahh," I gasped, my throat feeling tighter and tighter, "ahh." We were miles from the house. I knew what happened if you were stung too many times by yellow jackets; your throat swelled, you stopped breathing, and it all happened very quickly.

I started to cry, and claw at my neck, and I could feel the welts my fingernails made, and I knew I was going to die.

"Thea!" Sam said, almost shouted. "You'll make it worse. Look at me." He put his hand on my cheek and it felt so cool against my inflamed skin. He held my face and made me look into his eyes, he would not let me look away, and gradually my breathing became easier. Like a snake charmer, I whispered under my breath.

"Just listen to me," Sam said, and helped me into the saddle, and walked beside me and held my hand while Sasi trudged on, all the while keeping up a steady stream of conversation — about early blackberries, about a new jump Sasi and I should try, about Mother and Father, about Georgie, about nothing. It was the sound of his voice that was important.

When we arrived back home, late because of how slowly we had walked, Mother saw me and cried out; my face was swollen, my lips and eyelids puffy. Sam raised a hand to his forehead to sweep away his hair and I noticed that it shook, terribly, proof that he had also been scared; his fear proof that I had been in danger, that Sam had saved me with his calmness. He had always been like that, still where I was frantic.

But here I would never be miles away from camp. I would be watched, in a way I never had been.

I knocked before I opened the cabin door, a habit I'd soon forget. Our cabin was never locked, none of the buildings here were. Perhaps the headmaster's cabin, perched beyond the Square. Or maybe there was a safe somewhere in the Castle, with camp valuables. I didn't care, Docey or anyone could have anything she wanted of my things, I hadn't brought much that was good.

"Hello," I called, as I started to take off my boots by the door. A flurry of dust motes slanted through the morning light. All was in perfect order, left that way by Docey. I didn't even have to make my bed here.

I pulled my boots off. The thin socks I wore while riding were damp with sweat, and the air felt cool on my feet and calves. I needed to dust the insides of my boots with talcum powder. I knew that the barn would keep a supply, but I hadn't looked. Of all the time spent with a horse, riding was such a small part of it.

I went to Sissy's closet first, found only clothes. Half her closet was occupied by party dresses, the silk soft beneath my fingertips. I thought I had a lot of clothes, but Sissy's wardrobe was triple the size of mine. And for the last year Mother hadn't bought any new clothes for herself or me. She said it would be in bad taste, with how poor everyone was becoming.

In Sissy's desk I found a few pens, a letter from her mother, *received* spelled wrong, the *i* and the *e* reversed. The letter was short, recounted a week she and Sissy's father had spent "doing much of nothing." A novel that looked brand-new, called *The Art of Friendship.* I traced the embossed lily on its red cover. Silly, Mother would have said. There was a hairbrush on her vanity, matted with her brown hair. Three bottles of French perfume in her drawer, full. I hadn't noticed any scent on her. In the back of the drawer I found a rolled-up velvet pouch, with little compartments for jewelry. I held a pair of ruby studs to the light, each stone identical to the other, flawless and deep pink. An oval locket, engraved with initials — not Sissy's — and a braided lock of hair behind the glass. I wondered who had died. I didn't have any jewelry this nice. Mother had said I would have her jewelry one day, but I wondered if this was still true. It was all kept in a safe. As if anyone would bother it, or us, where we lived.

The ruby earrings hurt to put in. I met resistance in both ears, especially the left, which was pierced slightly crooked. Mother and Idella had pierced them, with a hot needle and a piece of thread. I put them in less to see what they looked like and more to open the holes in my ears, but they didn't suit me anyway, were too large and surprising. Mother might have said they brought out the auburn in my hair. Despite living so far out of town, she knew what was in vogue. There was a stack of magazines in our downstairs sunroom, but Mother also read books, the same ones Father did. Still, I didn't have dresses like this, and I had never been given a piece of jewelry nearly this fine.

What had Sissy's mother said when she had given her the earrings? Maybe she had presented them to her before a party, dropped them into Sissy's hand and closed her own around her daughter's. The posts would have stung her palm, but the feeling would have been pleasurable. I'd never been to a party, only to restaurants. I could see

Sissy at a dance, in the navy blue silk from her closet, the rubies offsetting her brown hair, her smooth skin, colored by the summer sun. Passed from boy to boy, flirting in her husky voice. I was suddenly angry at my parents for sending me to Yonahlossee unprepared. They'd kept me sheltered all my life, and then sent me here, ignorant of so many things.

Eva's desk was next to Sissy's, under the window. The Square was still empty. There was a thick stack of pictures in her drawer. Her father was very heavy, had gotten heavier as the photographs progressed. Her mother was plump. Eva would have to be careful, which I'm sure she knew. She might lose her figure entirely after children, like I assumed Mrs. Holmes had. It happened to some women — Mother had told me this. The pictures were tied with a ribbon, but the rest was a mess — a tangle of paper and jewelry and pots of rouge and cream. There were sentences in French. The tins of makeup were hollowed out at the center. I wondered if she was a fast girl in a world where boys were involved. I knew about fast girls from books.

Mary Abbott's drawer was very spare. I almost didn't bother with her. Her closet was nearly empty except for a few homely dresses and Yonahlossee uniforms. Her thick letters were from her father. The postmark was Raleigh, which wasn't far from here. Mary Abbott dressed the same as the rest of us, so there was no way to know without looking in her closet that her things weren't as nice as ours. Her family must have had enough money to send her here, so perhaps the bareness of her wardrobe was due to some religious fervor. I scanned a letter; indeed, God was mentioned a few times. I liked putting the pieces together like this. I returned the letters and opened a small compact; inside, taped to the mirror, was a picture of a baby. I recognized Mary Abbott's features — her thin lips, her shocked-looking eyes. I touched the photograph, softly, and smiled. She had been pretty.

I was terrified before I knew by what; I must have seen a shadow out of the corner of my eye; then I turned and saw Mr. Holmes through the window. Mr. Holmes also turned, and glanced inside, straight at me. He was more handsome than any movie star I had seen: his angular jaw, his dark eyes, framed by dark eyelashes and darker eyebrows. I stared at Mr. Holmes for another ten, fifteen seconds as he passed by, and he looked so nice that I almost thought, Let him find me. He'll understand. But he didn't stop, and I was instantly relieved the sun was too bright for him to see inside. Of course he would not have understood. I would have looked like a thief. Or worse, a lurker.

I closed Mary Abbott's drawer in a fit of relief, and as I did I heard the tap of a hard sole against the floor.

"Hello?"

It was Docey, with a stack of towels. She said nothing. I didn't know where to look because of her wandering eye.

"I was looking for powder," I said. I walked to my bed and picked up my boots. "To sprinkle inside." My face was hot. I held my boots to my chest, the leather still warm. She watched me for what felt like a long moment and I saw how this would go: she would tell, I would be an outsider.

"That's fine," Docey said, and it took me a second to catch what she said, because of her accent. She turned her back to me and went to each girl's closet, removing the dirty towel and replacing it with a clean one, accumulating a mass of dirty linen in her arms. When she was done, I thought maybe she'd leave without saying anything. She looked about my age, but she had a pale, ageless face. There wasn't a trace of any sort of figure beneath her uniform. She was lean and small. I'd been stupid. I'd let myself be caught.

At my closet, she paused, as if to ask permission. I nodded, and as she got my towel, she spoke: "I'll let you get back." At the door she turned briefly, and in a gesture so minute I might have imagined it, she brought her hand to her ear. I felt my own ear, the earrings I had forgotten. She wouldn't tell.

Eva and I waited outside the cabin in our robes for Sissy.

"She's always late," Eva murmured, "her only fault." The comment struck me as odd, because Eva didn't seem like the critical type, but then she grinned. When Sissy emerged, we left. The sun had gone down an hour ago and it was chilly, but my robe was thick and plush.

"Are you settling in?" Sissy asked.

I laughed. "Mr. Holmes asked the same question yesterday."

"What did you tell him?"

"I told him I was. What else could I say?"

"Well, Mr. Holmes could make you say anything." She whispered into my ear, "Henry."

I giggled.

"Those eyes," she said, and swooned. "But

just so you know, he doesn't flirt. He thinks he's our father."

"Mrs. Holmes would slap your hand with a ruler if she heard you," Eva said. "Did she already give you the founder's speech? About how grateful we should all be for women's education?"

"She said Yonahlossee was named after a horse." I liked this, walking in a group. Other girls glanced at us curiously, admiringly.

"Oh. She doesn't like horses," Sissy said. "She doesn't like anything."

She had apparently liked my mother, but never in a million years would I have said so.

"Yonahlossee is hard at first," Eva said. "I couldn't get out of bed. I couldn't manage to get up at the morning bell. I would miss breakfast, even my first class. At home I slept until noon every day."

I couldn't imagine sleeping until noon. Sam woke me every morning before the sun rose. A tap on my shoulder was all it took; I was ready, eager to get started on the day. Sam was amused by my impatience. I had to ride early at home, to avoid the heat; Sasi was tacked by sunrise. "Didn't you have things to do?"

"No. That's why they sent me here. Because there was nothing to do at home. But I was fine, actually. I liked having nothing to do." Eva was taller than both of us, and she moved languidly. Her skin always looked slightly moist, in a pretty way, as if she'd just taken a bath. She did seem lazy.

"Didn't you get in trouble?"

She lifted her shoulders and let them drop again, lazily. "You don't really get in trouble here, Thea. Mrs. Holmes talked to me. And I got used to getting up."

"You can get in trouble here," Sissy said. "I wouldn't cross Mrs. Holmes."

"Who gets in trouble?" I asked.

"Last month Gates's sister and another girl were caught smoking. Last year a girl was meeting a boy from Asheville in the woods. The smokers got a warning. The other girl got sent away the next day. No one knew what happened to her until Mrs. Holmes announced it after morning prayer. It was like she disappeared."

We were at the bathhouse now, which was nothing more than a large room full of tubs, set about five feet apart from one another, in rows. Docey wove her way through naked girls, handing out towels.

"Nobody looks," Sissy whispered as we walked in, fiddling with a delicate diamond horseshoe that hung from her neck. Which wasn't true — I looked. Everybody looked. Bath hour was an exercise in avoiding being caught looking. Mary Abbott was the scrawniest of us, looked like you could blow her over, light as a feather. I was thin, but my limbs were defined from riding. The hot water felt good and I closed my eyes and submerged my head. I scrubbed my scalp, the greasy spot at my crown. The room was steamy with all the hot water, perfumed by the various soaps and lotions.

We were silent while we bathed, as if pretending we were alone.

Then Docey stood over me with a towel and it was over.

"Thank you." But she had already moved on to another girl. I noted that no one else thanked her. I tried to modestly slide into my nightclothes, which proved impossible. I spotted a girl with white-blond hair in a tub near the corner, and the way her face was perched just above the water sent a chill down my spine.

Docey was attending to Mary Abbott. Gates and Victoria were shielding each other with their towels while they dressed, but you could see perfectly the shapes of their bodies. This was bizarre, I felt very keenly. The strangest thing so far in the strangest week of my life. I knew we were safe, but it seemed foolish to put us all together like this, all in one place, naked.

Victoria hurried past us on the way back to our cabins, and Sissy studied her retreating figure. Victoria had very close-set eyes, and a long, narrow face; improbably, she was pretty.

"Victoria," Sissy said.

"She looks like a very pretty, very thin monkey."

Sissy burst out laughing, had to stop and lean against a tree because she was laughing so hard. The only other person I could make laugh this hard was Sam. I stood nervously; what would I say when she was done laughing? We still had several minutes to fill.

"She does!" Sissy exclaimed, finally.

"You can't ever take a bath when you feel like it, can you?" I asked Sissy, after a moment had passed.

She shook her head as we walked. "I guess you could sneak in. Like a bath bandit." She grinned, her blue eyes crinkling, and I couldn't help but grin back. She was so lighthearted.

"Hold still," she said, and darted behind me. I felt my hair lifted from my neck.

"What —" I started, surprised, but Sissy only wrung the water out of it, for the second time that night.

"There," she murmured, still behind me, her hands in my hair. "Why did you come so late, Thea?"

She dabbed water from my neck with her towel. My mother had barely hugged me when I left. It had pained Sam to look at me. This was the first time in weeks someone had touched me and not been angry, and I was surprised at how vulnerable and loved it made me feel. I wanted to offer Sissy something.

"I was sent away." As soon as I spoke I regretted it. What had I been thinking? That this girl would offer solace, this girl who knew nothing about me?

Sissy dropped my hair, which she had twisted into a rope, onto my neck. I thought I could feel her deciding.

"Oh," she said finally. "Well, I was, too, in a way. Sent away to learn how to be a lady." She deepened her voice, turned everything into a joke. And I was so grateful. Sissy's cheeks were red from the steam, and her hair hung damply. She did not seem like the girl from her desk, with all that jewelry and perfume. Sissy was friends with nearly everyone here, there was always a girl waving to her, sidling up next to her to impart some bit of news. I wondered why she had chosen me, and hoped it was something besides my novelty. It seemed like it was.

"I left a girl, but returned a lady," Sissy intoned, in the same voice, and on and on back to the cabin, where I begged her to stop, I was laughing so hard. I felt a little bit like I was walking on air — to think that I had been nervous about filling the time as we walked back to the cabin. There was nothing to be nervous about around Sissy.

We entered Augusta House a pair. Our beds were already turned back by Docey, like we were at a hotel. Eva smiled at us, unconcerned, but Mary Abbott didn't like the look of us together, I could tell. We prepared for bed: Sissy patted cream onto her cheeks, Victoria brushed her hair. Eva's leg dangled over her bunk, next to my face. Her toenails were painted. She was reading the book from Sissy's desk.

Gates was hard at work at her desk, practicing her handwriting, which was terrible, loopy and vague. Miss Lee, our matronly elocution and etiquette teacher, had shaken her head in dismay over Gates's work today. Gates paused, and shook her hand dramatically. "It aches!" she cried. Her dirty-blond hair was cut into a bob, and two barrettes, adorned with tiny pearls, were clipped above each ear. She seemed like a girl who would not want hair in her face.

"Wait until classes begin," Sissy said. "Then it'll really hurt."

Gates grimaced, and everyone laughed, even Mary Abbott.

"What other classes will they have?" I asked. "The schoolgirls," I added, when Sissy looked at me blankly. Our mornings were devoted to classes: elocution, then etiquette, then French, then instrument (piano for me). Then lunch, then rest hour, then riding, then "leisure" pursuits: bird-watching, botany, painting. Then free time until dinner, which we usually spent in the Hall in the Castle, short for Study Hall, though no one seemed to study there. I was bad at bird-watching: all I ever spotted were hawks and hummingbirds, which were a dime a dozen.

"The schoolgirls?" Sissy asked.

Gates put her book down, carefully, making sure to mark her place with a silver bookmark. I knew from my snooping that it was monogrammed. "Some of the girls leave," she began, slowly, "but most of us stay." Her voice was high, excited. She watched me solemnly. I felt my neck warm, the telltale sign of a blush.

"I know," I said.

"It's just," Sissy said, "we're all schoolgirls. This is a year-round cabin." She looked at me carefully for a moment, and I smiled. She didn't understand that I was not a schoolgirl, that I was only in a year-round cabin because there had been no place else to put me.

Gates returned to her handwriting, pressing so deeply into the paper as she wrote that it tore; she cried out again in exasperation. Sissy lay back onto her pillows and picked up her needlework, a pretty embroidery of a mountain stream. I watched her patiently color in the stream, stitch by blue stitch. This place was so odd. Yesterday a dozen of us had sat outside behind easels, facing the mountains, and been directed to paint them. Henny walked behind us, murmuring approvingly at some paintings, clucking sadly at others. I had received a cluck, of course; I wasn't good at spotting birds, or stitching straight lines, or painting a leaf that looked like a leaf, pursuits I couldn't ever imagine pursuing once I left this place.

It was called the Yonahlossee Riding Camp for Girls, but it was neither a camp nor a place for girls. We were supposed to be made ladies here. I thought about where that left me. I still thought of myself as a girl, but I was not like my cabinmates. I would never be a girl like that again.

And had I ever been like them? At home I had been a girl among boys and men. There had been no one prettier, or richer, or in any way better than I was. I did wonder, of course, if such a person existed, and knew that she must, but then the thought had dropped from my head. My place in my family was so well defined I'd had no need to wonder about what could be for too long.

My mother was our standard of beauty. I knew nothing about curling my hair because Mother still wore hers up. And she had never painted her nails; the thought made me smile. I had always thought of her as timeless, like women I saw in the prints of paintings Father showed us during our lessons. But now I could see she was old-fashioned, of a different world. No less beautiful, but perhaps less becoming.

Henny bustled in and switched off all the lights, told us good night.

Gates lit a candle, to read. I touched the handkerchief beneath my pillow.

3

A letter from Father arrived on my seventh day at Yonahlossee. The postmark was from Atlanta. I pressed his letter to my lips. His script was slanted and flowery, like a woman's. I had never in my life received a letter. A postcard once or twice from Georgie, when he was in Missouri visiting his mother's family. But anyone could see a postcard — it was read first by Mother before she handed it to me. No one in the world knew what was inside the letter except for my father, and now me.

Dear Thea,

I was so very sorry to drive away from the camp. Although I must say that it is a beautiful place to spend some time. Before your mother knew me, she loved to be around other people; her coming out lasted nearly a year. I see so much of her in you.

We all love you very much. Take care of yourself at the camp. Think of it as an opportunity to learn more, from different (perhaps better) teachers. It bears repeating that your family is your tribe; this is but an interruption in our lives. We kept you too secluded at home. We should have sent you away sooner. You will learn how to behave around other children there, Thea. I hope that is not too much to ask. We know what's best for you, though at this moment you may believe, very fervently, otherwise. That is the way of parents and their children.

Love,
Father

He had called it a camp, not a school — I was here until the end of summer, no longer. I placed the letter back into its envelope and slid it under my pillow, next to Sam's handkerchief. I was not a child. And it *was* a punishment, to be sent here, even though he and Mother had said it was not; he had as good as admitted it in his letter. Anyway, he was just parroting what Mother had said. She was the one who had always decided what to do with us.

But mostly, I missed Father. I could hear his voice, softly reading the words. Miss Lee would have told him to speak up.

My cabinmates were whispering about an announcement Mr. Holmes had made at lunch; Sissy told me I was lucky, here one week and already a dance to attend. Most of the girls waited months and months for a dance, the bright spot of a boy turning the winter months bearable.

I closed my eyes, even though no girl used rest hour to nap. But I was exhausted: I'd stayed up last night memorizing a Robert Frost poem, "The Cow in Apple Time," for elocution. I'd read Frost before, at home, but Miss Lee was only interested in how we pronounced each word, how we measured our voices, not in what the poem might have meant.

Though Yonahlossee was an odd place to me, it was quickly turning familiar. Not missing home had at first seemed inconceivable, but I understood how the human heart operated, that it was fickle, capricious.

I was born in the house my parents sent me away from, built by my father as a gift for his new bride. My mother's family was New Florida, as those families were called, those that went there after the War Between the States when Georgia was no longer a tenable place to live. My great-grandfather,

Theodore Fisk — for whom I'm named — decided on Florida because it was close, and he had heard the land there, worthless, was for the taking.

He and his wife were crackers first; wealthy landowners later. When the railroad was built — Henry Flagler was said to have been entertained and wooed in the Fisk family home — my mother's family's fortune multiplied exponentially. Mrs. Fisk served Mr. Flagler a piece of key lime pie, a delicacy the Northern man had never tasted. Citrus was from then on shipped by railroad, and an industry was born.

My father's family was Old Florida, of Spanish descent. They weren't as wealthy as my mother's side: they'd herded cattle on land that no one owned until Florida began to sell this land, and then it became impossible to drive the cattle south, through newly erected fences and homesteads, toward the coast, where they would be shipped to Cuba.

Florida was a different place then. My father and his older brother, George, would require a new way of life. My father, Felix, went to Atlanta Medical School on scholarship; George, to law school in Illinois, but they both came back — each with a new wife. My mother, Elizabeth, was in her second year at Agnes Scott College and was expected to find a husband in Georgia when she met my father at a semiformal dance. She was twenty years old; he five years older. It was a perfect match.

George and his new wife, Carrie, settled in Gainesville, a stone's throw from Emathla. My father could have practiced medicine anywhere, but he wanted to help people, so he went to a place where he was the only doctor for miles and miles. This was how it was always explained to me and Sam, anyway: we could have lived anywhere, but lived here because of my father's goodness. And at first Mother, accustomed to the bustle of Miami, thought she would be lonely in such a rural place. But the magic of our home was that it destroyed loneliness. You could see other people — and Mother did, once every few weeks, tea with a neighbor, a Camellia Society meeting — but other people and places only made you love your home, your people, more.

These were my people: Sam, my mother and father; Uncle George and Aunt Carrie and their son, my cousin, Georgie.

That was our first story, how we had come to be situated in this little piece of heaven carved from the Florida wilderness. Luck, partly, but also love: Mother and Father had become engaged two weeks after meeting. George and Carrie and Georgie were part of this story, of course, not central to it but it is easy now to see how the story would have collapsed without them. We needed them in Gainesville to illuminate our own lives.

The bell rang, signaling the end of rest hour, and I woke with a start.

"Finally!" Gates said. She liked to ride as much as I did. Everyone else was already pulling on their breeches and boots. This was the first time I was going to ride with everyone else, and I was both nervous and excited, a combination I loved. I tugged my boots on with boot hooks, and saw Sissy out of the corner of my eye, watching. She smiled, I smiled back. I was eager to please her.

I tucked my shirt into my breeches. We wore white breeches here; even the suede at the knees was white. Our clothes were laundered by the maids so it didn't matter to us how dirty we got, but it seemed silly to dress us exclusively in white.

When I walked outside the cabin into the smell of pine trees and sunshine, I saw Sissy had waited for me.

"A letter?"

"From my mother." I remembered from my snooping that Eva and Sissy's fathers had not written to them, only their mothers.

"My mother writes me," Sissy said, "three times a week. But her letters are so boring. My sister, hardly ever, only when she's made to."

Other girls flocked around us, all identically dressed. They waved at Sissy, and because I was with her, at me. I smiled back. I'd never smiled at so many people in my life.

"I hate writing letters," I said, "it takes so long to write what you could say in half the time." There were butterflies in my stomach; I was glad Sissy provided a distraction.

Another girl walked by, so close she grazed my arm. I started to say something, then stopped. She was the girl with the white hair I'd seen bathing in the bathhouse. And, I realized with the small, pleasurable shock of recognition, the girl from the horse photograph, from the Castle. I knew even before Sissy said her name.

"That's Leona."

We both watched Leona disappear around a bend. We had passed the privies, now we were almost at the stables. Leona was a giant, her strides covered twice the ground of my own. Her white-blond hair was pinned into a tidy bun. Her boots were navy blue, the only girl among us who didn't have black boots.

"She's from Fort Worth," Sissy said. She said *Fort Worth* as if she were saying some other, more improbable place — Constantinople, Port-au-Prince. She was whispering now, even though Leona had disappeared. "Her father is an oil speculator who made it big, her mother is royalty. She has her own horse, shipped by train. She's trained by masters. The shipping costs were more than her room and board." Leona had not said hello to Sissy. I wondered if Sissy meant that Leona's mother was truly royalty, and decided she must not. I didn't know very much about the world, but I didn't think there were any princesses in Texas. "She ignores everyone, mostly."

Leona from Fort Worth, Thea from Emathla. Out of all the places in this world, I was at the Yonahlossee Riding Camp for Girls. It was half past one in the afternoon. I was one among dozens of girls on our way to our daily riding lesson. Sissy had threaded her arm through mine; her skin was soft, she smelled faintly of rosewater. At home, Mother would be out in the garden, a towel around her neck to soak up the sweat, a worn, floppy hat on her head to protect her fair skin. My father would be working. Thursday was one of his traveling days, so he would be at someone's house, giving an injection, listening to an account of pain. And Sam.

He would be feeding his squirrels. They had to be fed often, more often than a human baby — which was what Mother always said, that Sam tended to his animals more faithfully than most human parents did their children. And he was faithful, my brother, faithful and good. It was not the first time Sam had raised a litter of squirrels — raccoons got their mothers all the time. Their nests were always hidden in nooks that only Sam was patient enough to find.

When I had said good-bye, after everything had happened, he was out back on the porch, holding one of them.

"It has hair now," I said, because I did not know what else to say. It was early in the morning, but still hot. The squirrel was less ugly than it had been a week ago. It looked so vulnerable; I could see why Sam loved it.

He wore his clothes from yesterday. His hair was wild, stuck out in all directions from his head. It scared me a bit. I wanted to smooth it down, but knew not to touch him. The rims of his eyes were pink. In that moment, his hazel eyes were so dark they almost looked brown. I knew in full sunlight they would look light again, translucent. Our eyes were different. Mine were plain brown, like Father's.

"Did you sleep?" I asked, though I knew the answer. I had not slept, either; in fact, I had gone into Sam's room, hoping to find him. Instead, in the dim room, I could faintly see the outlines of his made bed, which looked so perfect and untouched I started to cry, though I could not say why. The sight of his perfect bed, made first by Sam, then straightened later by Mother, disturbed me. His electric fan was trained at the space where he would have slept, and it droned on and on, cooling nothing.

I switched it off and went to his window, which provided a view of our backyard. But to call it a backyard was false; it was the beginning of our thousand acres. There was no fence, no border. Mother's gardens ran into the orange grove. These oranges weren't for sale, but for my mother, who loved them, said she could not live without them.

Sam sat in the grass, next to Mother's rose garden, which was blooming. I could not smell it from here, but he could. I watched him for a long time; he didn't move, sat still as a statue. He had always been able to sit still for longer than I; I was fidgety, restless.

I could not see his face. Only his narrow back, his skinny arms. His voice was beginning to change. I knew what happened to boys' voices; Georgie was two years older and his had changed a few years ago. I could hear Sam's voice right now, a child's voice, so pretty and light. I wished I could make a recording of it before it was gone.

If Sam had turned to face me, I would have seen his bruised eye, the small cut above it. Minor injuries, healing quickly. Father called them superficial. This was the first time I could remember seeing Sam hurt. I tried very hard to remember another time but could not. I had broken my arm, twice, and bruised myself more times than I could count. That was what happened when you rode horses. But Sam did not court danger. It was not his way.

He turned his head as if he had heard something, and he probably had: the rustle of an animal in the bushes. I saw his profile in the moonlight. We both had Father's nose, which was strong but handsome. I thought for a second that he could feel me watching him. I put my hand to the window.

"Sam," I murmured.

He peered down at something, and I knew he held one of the infant squirrels; how unmoored he was, how badly I must have hurt him, was confirmed. Because how many times had he told me not to touch a baby wild animal, that if I did, it would become accustomed to human scent and, once released into the wild, be unafraid of humans. And wild animals needed to be afraid of us, to survive.

"Thea?" Sissy asked. "Have I lost you?"

I looked sideways at her. She did not know the dark recesses of my heart. I knew Sam thought of me as often as I thought of him; that when he was not asleep I was on his mind. On it, threatening to displace everything else like a weight dropped in water. But he could not imagine my life here, which might be a curse or a blessing. I did not know.

Soon we arrived at the barn and parted ways. I took a deep breath: the smell in a barn was always the same, hay tinged with manure. It was a smell you either liked or did not. A groom — the handsome one Eva had mentioned my first night here — showed me to my horse: Naari, a flea-bitten gray mare with a pink muzzle.

"Thank you," I said to the groom, "I'll tack her up."

I clicked my tongue and Naari looked up from her hay. There were hundreds of brown dots scattered across her white coat, hence the term, which I'd always thought was an ugly way to describe such a beautiful pattern. I was excited, though I tried not to be. I did not want to get too attached to Naari, because I would have to leave her here when I left.

After I had tacked her up, I stood in a single-file line with the other girls in my group, the horses so close Naari's muzzle almost touched the reddish tail of the chestnut in front of her. Leona stood at the front of the line, the de facto leader of my group. Her gelding was huge, like his owner. He was beautiful, a big bay with white stockings and a white blaze down his face. I also recognized him from the picture.

Sissy was in the intermediate class; I could see her in the next ring on a skinny Appaloosa, her brown bob flying in her face as she posted. I was in the advanced class, with twenty or so other girls, among them Gates, Leona, and a girl named Jettie, who sat at my dining table. The advanced class was the smallest class, and the privilege of being in it was enormous: you did not have to share your horse. All the other horses were shared except for ours.

Sissy was the weakest rider of her group. I realized it would be easier to be friends with her because I was better, much better, on a horse.

I watched Mr. Albrecht shout out instructions in his quiet, firm way. I liked him. Mother had taught me less and less about riding as the years passed, and though she occasionally offered advice now, I mainly schooled myself. Mr. Albrecht was a jumping master trained in Germany, he had won an individual bronze medal in the 1920 Belgium Olympics, and a team silver. He had already helped me with my seat, taught me a new way of sinking into the saddle that I found most effective. The Yonahlossee horses were all purebred; our courses designed by a jumping consultant, a friend of Mr. Albrecht's from Germany; the barns were almost nicer, at least as nice, as our cabins, their corridors lined with bricks, the stalls with two windows each for ventilation and thick, sturdy shutters for the winter. Despite Mrs. Holmes's best intentions, the rest of our education was secondary to horses, as I'd learned my first day when I'd skipped morning classes for my riding evaluation.

At home, Father tutored us from seven in the morning until ten, when he left to see his patients. Idella, our maid, served us breakfast while he explained ideas from books to us. The girls in my cabin thought it odd that I had never been to a real school before, but they didn't know: we were lucky to be tutored by Father, who was brilliant, who was certainly smarter than the Emathla schoolteacher. I rode all afternoon, and Sam played tennis against the garage wall, and tended to his terrariums, his rescued animals.

"Advanced!" Mr. Albrecht called. "Come!" He clapped his hands.

Leona mounted, and for an instant she and her horse looked like a centaur: part horse, part girl. Then the rest of us swung up into our saddles. Gates cut a pretty figure on a horse, slim and elegant and ramrod-straight. Jettie, short and stocky, looked powerful in the saddle.

We stood on our horses for a moment while the first group filed past us, their horses' chests flecked with white spit. It was summer, in the early afternoon. In Emathla you stayed inside during this part of the day, when the sun was high. It would have been dangerous to ride right now; you might kill your horse. During the summer I rose before anyone else and rode at dawn, before our lessons, and even then I had to carry an old handkerchief to wipe Sasi's sweat from the reins. Sam and I would go out anyway, sometimes in the afternoon, and then we were giddy from the heat and danger of it — Mother would be furious if she knew — our brains boiled in our heads, the sun was so powerful it felt like we were lit from the inside. We would climb oak trees, me coaxing Sam higher and higher, and then lie in the embrace of a branch for hours, watching for some sign of life below — only the reptiles, impervious to the heat, presented themselves: thick black snakes, harmless, and bright green, darting lizards.

I bet it never got that hot here. These girls — they wouldn't know how to survive in such heat. Then Leona's enormous horse — he must have been over eighteen hands — began to walk, and Naari moved beneath me. We circled the ring in a single file, and then, one by one, as if orchestrated, the horses broke off and carved out their own space; I headed toward the far end of the ring, closest to the mountains. I was a Florida girl, used to hazy skies and flatness; the mountains were like clouds to me, so large and expressive they seemed like something you could reach for.

Naari was twitchy and quick; I knew immediately I would like her. She was too smart, I could already tell that by the way she tested me, twisting her barrel so she could carry her weight unevenly, tugging on the left side to see if I would notice. I did notice, I corrected her sharply, tugged back on the left rein, squeezed my calves against her sides so she'd speed up and straighten out. She was intelligent but fearful, two traits that always seemed to accompany each other in horses. A squirrel climbed up onto a post and Naari skittered sideways.

I thought about the future weeks, when we would know and understand each other, and I was nearly lifted out of the saddle in anticipation. Sometimes anticipation affected me in this way, as if I could feel it coursing through my veins. I suppose it was a girlish habit.

I watched Leona lead King in a figure eight. He kept dropping his shoulder on the diagonal, and she corrected him. She stared straight ahead, which was where, Mother was always reminding me, you were supposed to look — Look where you want to go, and Sasi will follow you there. Looking at my hands was a habit I couldn't quite break; neither could I pretend a broom was hooked through my arms, to keep my back arched and my arms positioned in just the right way. Leona passed through the diagonal again, and this time King trotted through smoothly. Leona turned him, abruptly, and met my gaze briefly and I squeezed Naari into a trot, embarrassed that I had been caught watching.

We filed out of the ring when our riding time was over, Leona still led, but that was fine. She was more technically expert than I, had been schooled by masters, but she wasn't better. I wasn't as physically strong a rider as Jettie, or as pretty as Gates, but I had a way with horses; I could get them to do anything I wanted. I felt strangely powerful: I was a girl of fifteen, locked away in the mountains, surrounded by strangers. But I would be all right; I would emerge from this place.

I fiddled with my books as Mr. Holmes led morning prayer. I could feel Henny watching me from the corner of my eye. Sometimes I looked up and studied the ceiling when we were supposed to be praying. I had never seen anything like it before, tin stamped with an intricate pattern of flowers. Rhododendron, Sissy had told me, and later pointed out a cluster of bushes with a pretty pink flower that lined the path to the barn. I wondered, as I often did, who had done it, and if the work had taken hours or days, days or months, and let Mr. Holmes's voice recede into the background. As far as

I could tell, he asked for the same things every morning: health, happiness, and prosperity. I couldn't get used to all this sitting still; first at breakfast, then here, then all through classes. By the time lunch hour came, I felt like a caged animal.

And though I still missed my home, terribly, I was getting used to this new order of things. I was learning. I knew, for example, that though Yonahlossee had first seemed enormous, it was not even as large as our farm, only three hundred acres, and most of it was mountain land, uninhabitable.

Mr. Holmes shuffled a stack of papers on his lectern. We all paid attention, for the most part. Mrs. Holmes had caught my eye a few times when she noticed my attention wandering. She sat beside her husband, along with their three girls. When I wasn't watching the ceiling I was watching the Holmes girls, who fascinated me. Just now Sarabeth put her hand over Decca's, to stop her fidgeting. Sarabeth was the oldest, at eleven, and reminded me of her mother. Rachel was next, ten, and she was moody, a storm always passing over her face, or threatening to pass over, while her father spoke. I was jealous of them. The distinction between the Holmes girls and everyone else was very clear: they were not alone.

Decca was tall and dark like her father, and even at seven you could tell that she would continue to be tall and dark, would grow, it seemed almost certain, to be beautiful. It was unfair that nature had been so precise: each child born prettier, Sarabeth the first attempt, Decca perfect.

Decca caught my eye, and I looked away, but not before I saw her smile. I wondered what she thought of me. Did she think I was pretty? Did the other girls? I wasn't sure where I landed on this list. My mother was beautiful, this I knew, both because I could see for myself and also because it was a fact in our family. She had even modeled for a milliner, briefly, before she met Father. I looked like her, but I had always known I was not beautiful. I had my mother's hair, which was auburn and wavy, wild. I'd once seen a picture of Amelia Earhart in a magazine; the caption had called her handsome. I thought that's what I was. Handsome.

"And there's something more," he said, and paused. He looked up, out into our midst. He stood in front of the window, which afforded the most perfect view of the mountains in the whole camp. When he looked out at us like this, it was as if the room disappeared, as if we were all on top of a mountain. Alice Hunt straightened beside me. We all felt it. "Something very serious." Heads snapped up. "You all know Herbert Hoover?" A titter spread through the room. "Oh, of course not personally." He smiled, and I found myself smiling back. "Though I dare say some of you *might* have met him." Out of the corner of my eye I studied Leona, who sat next to Sissy. Maybe Leona was one of the girls who might have met the president? "Our president has lately spoken of his belief that our country will recover from this financial crisis." He held up a newspaper, though we were all too far away to see it. A girl in front of me yawned. "This is a little old, of course." He paused, as if anticipating our laughter, which of course followed. All of the magazines and newspapers were, at the very least, "a little old." More often they were months and months old, sent to us by our mothers and sisters.

"Here our president declares the Depression over." He tapped the paper, lightly, with his fingertip. "He asks for our continued effort in supporting the economy."

Gates, who sat a row ahead, raised her hand.

"Yes, Gates?" Mr. Holmes said. He folded the paper neatly while Gates spoke.

"How can we help?" she asked. I thought

that she was perhaps being impertinent, but Mr. Holmes didn't seem to think so.

"A good question," he said, "and one best answered by your fathers. To put it bluntly, money begets money." Even Mrs. Holmes smiled a little bit, behind her husband. "Encourage your fathers to invest, to spend, to trust the banks."

At first I didn't understand what had triggered the merry laughter that followed Mr. Holmes's answer. Sissy was giggling next to me, and as I watched her pretty fingers cover her mouth I understood completely: there was nothing we could do to help. We were but daughters. The idea that we would offer our fathers financial counsel was, indeed, laughable. I smiled, too, but not because I was amused; I smiled so that I was indistinguishable from the other girls.

"Let us pray that by the time you leave Yonahlossee, you will reenter a world that will be happier," Mr. Holmes said, and stepped back so that his wife could step forward.

I hadn't heard the name Hoover since I'd left home. I thought of Uncle George, who had returned from Miami the last time and said he would not go back, that it was useless, that the bank could take it all. How President Hoover was handling the crisis was a point of contention between my father and his brother: my father thought he was handling things fine. Uncle George thought more needed to be done, and soon.

Everyone here seemed so rich and Southern, impervious to the slings and arrows of the world. And there was me, who had learned to ride from Mother, on a pony without papers. My middle name was not an important family name, my family did not have five homes stateside, or spend Christmas in Venice. We were fine, because of the citrus money, but my father was a physician, not a cotton magnate or an oil king.

Yonahlossee was where important Southern men sent their daughters. I would later learn more: an Astor, via marriage to the Langhornes of Virginia, had graduated the year before I arrived. One of the girls counted Robert E. Lee as a relative. Her family owned rubber plants in Malaysia. There were other girls' schools, but Yonahlossee was the oldest, and it must have provided a certain comfort to these men, locked away as it was in the mountains; nobody could reach their daughters here. Nobody could touch them. After World War II, these same men would begin to send their daughters to Northern schools, where they would become worldly. But in this moment, worldly wasn't what anyone was after. The South was still a land unto itself, in some ways it was a land that time had forgotten. There were girls here who refused to believe, or at least admit, that the North had claimed victory in the War Between the States.

"Thank you, Mr. Holmes," Mrs. Holmes began. There was still tittering, somewhere from the back, and Mrs. Holmes abruptly stopped speaking. "Girls!" The tittering disappeared.

"On that same note, but perhaps more specifically" — here she smiled, almost imperceptibly — "allow me to bring your attention to a way you might do more than simply keep those less fortunate than you in your prayers." Her elocution was perfect. Miss Lee would have approved. "In the spirit of Christian charity, please consider making a pledge for a contribution to a Fund for the Mill Girls, who live a few hours' drive from us and enjoy none of our benefits."

Jettie and Henny stood and walked to the front of the room, carrying a papered box with FUND FOR MILL GIRLS carefully lettered on it in red. Jettie placed a stack of small papers next to it, along with a cup of pencils, and girls started to rise and scribble figures on the papers, then fold them and drop them into the box. It resembled the kind of box Mother had brought home from the Red Cross, for which she had volunteered when we were very small.

"Thank you in advance for your generosity," Mrs. Holmes said. I didn't have any money, not a single cent. I'd never had any money, or at least any that I could touch. "All right, girls," Mrs. Holmes said. This is what she always said when she finished. It was a place maintained by routine. Mrs. Holmes was nice enough, I supposed. But not too nice, which was how you had to act if anyone was going to listen to you. That's how I was when I rode.

Henny stood. We were going to class — I had elocution, then etiquette, one right after the other. They were so boring I could have cried. My parents had never seemed interested in a daughter who had perfect handwriting, or could spot the difference between an olive fork and a lemon fork (an olive fork had two tines; a lemon fork, three), but I wondered if Mother knew or any longer cared exactly what kind of education I was getting. Someone pinched my arm.

"Ow," I cried. It was Eva.

"Sorry." But she was giggling. "You just always look so lost in your own world. I ate so much! I love hash-brown day." She smoothed her hands over her waist.

I smiled. "I stuff myself like a roasted pig at every meal." And it was true. I did. My appetite had reappeared after the first few days.

"Eva," I said, as we climbed the stairs to our classroom, "I didn't bring any money with me."

It felt like a dirty word, *money,* but Eva didn't seem bothered. I'd never met someone so unconcerned.

"Oh, that," she said. "You just ask your father."

I nodded, and knew I would never request money from my father. It would mean that I cared about this place.

"My father," Eva continued, "says he gives enough with tuition. And Mrs. Holmes comes knocking every winter, in person, for donations to the school. My father says she's very persuasive." She smiled, and I noticed she had dusted her face with powder, her cheeks with rouge, but very subtly. "She'll probably visit your parents, too. But maybe not, since you're from Florida." She paused, and bit her lip. "I didn't mean —"

"No," I said, "it's fine." We had reached

our classroom; I could see Miss Lee's broad back from behind, writing in cursive on the board. "I know Florida's . . ." I trailed off, and Eva looked at me expectantly. "A strange place," I finished. "Not for everyone."

4

The day of the dance another letter arrived, this one from Mother. It was long, over two pages of my mother's rose-scented stationery, her initials engraved at the top of the thick, cream-colored paper. *EAC,* the *E* and *C* flanking the ornately drawn *A.* Elizabeth Collins Atwell.

My mother had surprising handwriting, inconsistent and loopy. *Dear Thea,* the letter began, and went on about the vegetable and herb garden and the swarms of bees and butterflies it attracted, before concluding:

> Sam is fine, as fine as can be expected. No one knows quite what to expect, though. It's all undecided, will stay that way for a while I predict. Sometimes I'm so angry with you. Other times I'm so sorry for you. Such a terrible thing. May God grant them and us peace.

Everyone here misses you. Do the mountains make you feel small, Thea?

I glanced around the room and saw that Mary Abbott was staring at me. I stared back. Her eyes unnerved me, pale, almost colorless. Mary Abbott relented, shrugged her small shoulders, and mouthed *Sorry* across the room, though of course she wasn't.

I lay back on my thin pillow (my pillows at home were plump and perfect, I wished I'd brought one with me) and ran my fingertips along the smooth wooden planks of our floor, marked by an infinite number of scratches. Girls wearing riding boots inside, Docey pulling the beds out to make them, dropped books. At home, no one was allowed to wear shoes in the house, only visitors, and if anything fell and my mother heard there would be a price to pay.

Sissy spun around the room, humming a waltz. When she was next to our bunk, Eva climbed down and bowed, held out her hand. Sissy accepted it, and they began to dance, Eva playing the boy's part. They both wore white skirts. Eva was taller, and more solid; her hair alone seemed to outweigh Sissy. They looked like mother and daughter dancing. Even I knew that waltzing was old news, but there was no jazz at Yonahlossee. Because it was hypnotizing, Mary Abbott had explained.

Both Sissy and Eva came from families that entertained regularly. Eva from a North Carolina cotton empire and Sissy from Monroeville, which she referred to as the center of the earth, where her father did something vague in her father's family business, and was also the mayor. All her jewelry was from her mother's side; I assumed most of the money was from her, too.

Only Mary Abbott and I were unexcited about this evening, when boys from a boarding school in Asheville would arrive at eight o'clock, and we would all be expected to dance the evening away. I pretended to be excited, at least; Mary Abbott didn't know how to pretend.

"Another one," Mary Abbott said when Eva had bowed and Sissy had curtsied, the waltz over. We were all startled by Mary Abbott's voice. We respected rules at Yonahlossee, and though it was likely no house mistress would pass by during rest hour, we knew they could.

Mary Abbott rose and clapped her hands like a child who wanted her way. Her squinty eyes were bright. Eva told me Mary Abbott's father was a Methodist preacher, that her mother had died when she was an infant.

"Shh," Victoria whispered, a finger on her lips.

Eva put a hand on her hip and studied Mary Abbott, amused.

"You'll see plenty of dancing tonight," Sissy whispered. "I wouldn't worry."

Mary Abbott lay back on her bed and folded her arms. I wondered what she thought she was missing now that Eva and Sissy had stopped dancing. When I saw my friends twirling around the room, I saw two innocents.

Mother's favorite story — more beloved than the story of how she and Father met — was the story of our births, transformed into a kind of fairy tale by her, the mother who carried twins and did not know it. My brother and I were born during an early winter storm: it snowed, birds dropped from the sky, dead from the unexpected freeze, all the plants in my mother's garden shriveled and turned from green to deep russet. My parents were expecting a large boy, because my mother carried so low. So I was the surprise, not Sam. I was the child no one expected.

There was no history of twins in our family. When we were born, our family was cautious, especially of me. I had either sapped Sam's strength and was the stronger twin, or Sam had enfeebled me. I was either a selfish or useless girl. My father tried to dispel these notions, said there was no evidence. But even he was worried, a boy and a girl born together, contrary to the order of things.

We were cranky babies, both colicky. My mother lay in bed for weeks, my father tended to her and then to his other patients, who were always my father's responsibility, always, the only doctor in Emathla. A woman from town took care of the new babies, Theodora and Samuel, us. My mother had only just begun painting scenes from Grimms' fairy tales when we arrived: a swath of Rapunzel's hair circled the wall of our nursery, only partly painted gold. The mural had been painted over years ago, but I still remembered it so clearly. I had loved it.

I spoke first, at nine months; Sam waited another five, though he spoke to me earlier, in the dark, in the soft light of morning, when the rest of the house was asleep. My first word was *orange,* which I mangled, but my parents knew what I meant. My mother liked to attribute it to my inherited knowledge of citrus. Sam and I cut teeth late, we were both bald until age two, we hated nap time, we loved bread and orange marmalade.

But there was still the gloom of our early days: the surprise of us, then my mother's convalescence. There was always the possibility of death with childbirth, an unavoidable risk, so even before my mother went into labor there was concern she might not handle it well. The winter storm, snow on the ground for the first time in a decade, my mother in bed from the contractions. It must *mean* something, their babies born on *this* day, not any of the other, snowless days.

First me — A girl! my father said, so my mother would know. Everyone would have preferred a boy for the first child, that went without saying, a person to inherit it all; then, as my father toweled me off and clipped my umbilical cord even closer, so it would not be agitated by clothes, another head crowned and was born quickly, much more quickly than I was, and — A boy. My father did not shout this time, ashamed, confused: he'd wanted a boy and gotten a girl, but now a boy? Something was wrong; the gods didn't grant wishes like that, without expecting something given in return, in gratitude.

My mother was in too much pain to hold us properly, so the woman from town cleaned us, smoothed our patchy hair, twisted bits of cotton and coaxed the mucus from our noses and mouths, the afterbirth from our ears. We were tiny. My father held each of us, one after another, to my mother's breast. We ate indifferently while my mother writhed. My mother had decided during her confinement that she would nurse her child. It was the style then to bring in a wet nurse, but who from Emathla would be suitable? Who could nourish her child as well as she could?

Dead birds littered the lawn outside. Later, by moonlight and a lantern, my father would collect them in a wheelbarrow and burn them in the rubbish heap, watch feathers float from the plume of smoke, blue feathers, scarlet, brown, white that did not hide dirt. He would watch and consider. He would feel vaguely hopeful, by the moonlight, his breath its own plume in the air, his babies small and pale but healthy, as far as the human eye could tell.

Mother would tell us that we were loved even before we were born. But that wasn't quite true: one of us was loved, the other unknown.

We would not ever leave. I had known

about Miss Petit's, the school where Mother had gone, but I would never be sent there. There was no need. Soon I would go away to a finishing school in Orlando, but only for a few weeks, only long enough to interact with girls my own age, see how they behaved. Mother assured me that I wouldn't have any trouble learning the ropes. This was to prepare me for my coming out, which would happen before I graduated from college. I would go to Agnes Scott, like Mother, and Sam would go to Emory. We were to be educated. Our minds were fine, important — Atwell minds.

Sam would become either a doctor or a lawyer. It didn't matter. Something to do on the side, while he managed our farm. We made our real money in citrus farther south — crops and land now attended to by Mother's brother on our behalf — and Sam and I would inherit that, too, but right now Mother's brother tended to it.

I would live where my husband did, but somewhere nearby. Gainesville, perhaps. Not everyone was lucky enough to live in such a secluded place; not everyone was lucky enough to make a living in the way Father did, on his own terms. And he was lucky like this because of Mother's money. He was a philanthropist — that's what

Mother said. He helped people, and many of those people could not pay.

This was the story of our futures. And it was always a joint future, a combined venture.

But Mother might as well have been speaking Greek when she mentioned these things — that Sam and I would marry, and live apart. We had never been farther south than Orlando, farther north than Gainesville. I had never even seen a college. When I pictured it, I saw my own house, peppered with people. That's how I conceived of Yonahlossee, too, before I entered its world: my own beloved home, threaded with strings of girls. Of course I knew this would not be true. Of course. But I knew in my brain, not in my heart.

And Georgie? He would live somewhere nearby, it was assumed. But his future was not as well mapped as ours. He was not Mother's child. I would say that Georgie was like a brother except that he was not; I could see him more clearly, because he was separate from me.

People can lie about their childhoods, they can make up any sort of story and you must believe them, unless you were there with them, unless you saw for yourself. It is a burden to know a person so well. Sometimes a gift, but always a burden.

It was a relief that my lavender dress, the same one I'd worn to the dinner with my father in the hotel, seemed stylish enough.

I shivered. It was almost eight o'clock in the evening but the sun still shone, a different kind of light from daylight, less severe, bluer. It had rained earlier, and the air tasted damp, the packed-dirt path springy beneath our feet. Swarms of fireflies darted through the throngs of girls. I was still enchanted by them. It was too hot for them in Florida, there we only had mosquitoes and enormous, noisy dragonflies.

I had hesitated to wear my mother's mink stole, afraid it might be too good for the occasion, but furs abounded. Alice Hunt brushed by me, a dead fox wrapped around her neck.

I raised my hand in a wave, but she wouldn't meet my eye. She wasn't the kind of girl who gave anyone the time of day. My cheeks burned. It was so hard to remember whom to be friendly to, whom to coolly ignore.

"Alice Hunt," Sissy called, and Alice Hunt stopped, turned around slowly. Everyone gave Sissy the time of day.

"Sissy," she said, her gray eyes briefly darting in my direction. "Thea."

Then she was on her way again, off to join the rest of the Memphis girls, who all had a soft manner about them, spoke barely above a whisper, and almost never looked directly at you. They had a way of looking through you. They were widely recognized as the camp's most snobbish clique.

"The sun never sets on Memphis," Sissy murmured under her breath, and I giggled, though the first time she'd said this I'd had to puzzle out what she'd meant. She was full of sayings like this: Mrs. Holmes was wound tighter than Dick's hatband; Leona's family was in high cotton. More like she's in high oil, I'd said, and then Sissy had laughed.

Girls swarmed around Sissy and me as we walked, dressed in their colorful silks, fur capelets and shimmering shawls upon their shoulders, diamond barrettes in their hair. I saw Katherine Hayes, from Atlanta, who was the biggest gossip at camp. Her throng of Atlanta girls surrounded her, all laughing dramatically. It seemed to me that they were all named Katherine, but only Katherine Hayes was allowed to use her full name. The rest were called Kate. Katherine had wildly curly brown hair; she wore a navy-blue sleeveless dress, which was the closest anyone came to black. I knew from the magazines that it was in vogue for the stars to wear black. But that was in Hollywood. People in the South didn't wear black unless someone had died.

Katherine's fingernails were painted red. The Atlanta girls were big-city, walked around camp with their bobbed hair and painted fingernails (Mrs. Holmes would order their nails scrubbed whenever she saw them); they were always gesturing and laughing as if everyone was watching. And generally, everyone was watching, like now. They *would* scrub their nails, and then give Mrs. Holmes a few days to forget before they all appeared with freshly coated fingernails, all the same hue, like a band of exotically clawed birds.

We all wore stockings, and so our legs gleamed. Most girls' hemlines, including my own, were modest, but if Eva sat a certain way you caught a glimpse of her knees.

There was so much of the world to see, and most of us had never held a boy's hand. We wanted to do more than that, anyway, we wanted boys to hold not just our hands but all of us, gather us into their sturdy arms and ring our slippery curls around their thick but tender fingers.

But none of that could happen, not to the good and correct daughters of wealthy and powerful men, with family names and family connections and family duties. We would be debs first, wives second. We would all be married one day, hopefully after we turned eighteen but before we turned twenty-one, though I doubt any of us tied marriage to passion. We'd seen our parents, our aunts and uncles, our sisters and their husbands. We weren't stupid. We understood that desire was a dangerous thing that needed to be carefully handled, like a mother's antique perfume bottle, passed down to the eldest daughter when she turned sixteen.

Yet I did not have as much to put at risk as other Yonahlossee girls. I saw this now. My family was never in society pages; my mistake could not have ruined any of my father's business deals. I had only risked my family's connections to each other.

"I can see the boys," Sissy whispered.

I whispered, too. "They won't bite." We were almost at the Castle, and the boys stood in a line, their backs facing the windows. They were dressed in light-colored summer suits and bow ties, like they were playing dress-up with their fathers' clothes. I couldn't remember the last time I'd seen Sam or Georgie in a suit, even though my parents had given one to Georgie for his last birthday. They'd said he'd be applying to college soon; this was when that still seemed possible.

Sissy giggled. She was giddy tonight, and I was glad for the distraction, glad not to think of Georgie and the suit he had not yet worn, at least not in my presence.

The staircase to the Castle was narrow, only three girls could fit on it at a time. Mary Abbott, her hair pinned back in a high, old-fashioned bun, joined us on the bottom step. Sissy and I linked arms. I offered my left to Mary Abbott, who clasped my hand instead.

"Your hand is cold," Mary Abbott said. Her voice was higher than it normally was, her eyes wide.

"Yours is damp." It felt like a dead, wet thing in mine.

"Will you find a beau tonight, Mary Abbott?" Sissy asked, teasing. Sissy's dress was pale green. Its square neckline was embroidered in iridescent silver, which seemed to illuminate Sissy's long, slender neck. Her hair had been curled that afternoon, like mine, but unlike mine her hair wouldn't hold curls. Eva had powdered all our faces, save Mary Abbott's, and Sissy's light freckles had disappeared. She had painted our lips with gloss, too, but very subtly, so Mrs. Holmes wouldn't notice. Paint was forbidden, but this was apparently one of Yonahlossee's more bendable rules, since most of the girls I saw tonight looked a little brighter than they usually did, their features lit. Surely Mrs. Holmes noticed. She wasn't stupid. You had to pick your battles, I supposed.

Sissy wore a strand of pearls clasped by a bright ruby, and a turquoise ring, the stone as big as a nickel, flanked by two round diamonds. She wore her ruby earrings, too; they matched the necklace. I'd never seen anyone, not even my mother, wear such grand jewelry. She was so thin that the ornate jewels seemed to wear her — her everyday necklace, the diamond-studded horseshoe, suited her better — but still, Sissy, if not beautiful, was nearly incandescent tonight. Her wide-set eyes — any wider, and she would have looked odd — emphasized her otherworldly quality. She looked like one of the fairies from *A Midsummer Night's Dream.*

Sissy had startled Mary Abbott. "None of us will. We're not old enough."

"How old do we have to be?" I asked.

"Old enough to want one," Mary Abbott said, and dropped my hand, giving it a final squeeze that was hard enough to make me wince. Then she sped ahead, hiked her too-long dress up to her calves and took the stairs two at a time until she was stuck behind another threesome of girls. I looked at Sissy.

"She's odd."

"Don't be unkind," she said, "it doesn't suit you."

I was surprised, wanted to ask Sissy what she meant, but we had almost reached the top of the stairs, and we were nervous. The gas lights at the door burned, like they always did, morning and night, though during the day you could hardly see them. Then the door was opened by Mr. Holmes, who smiled at us. He was opening the door for each set of girls, then letting it close again, then swinging it open — when really, he should have just propped the door open, like it was when we filed in for our meals and classes.

Though that would have ruined the effect, we would have been able to see in advance.

Our dining hall had been transformed. The Yonahlossee garden must have been robbed of all its flowers. They were everywhere, as far as a girl or boy could see. In vases, arranged by color: clusters of blood-red, burnt orange, pale yellow, electric pink, pure white, flecked cream. The smaller, heirloom roses, which bloomed in dense clumps, had been woven into a thick rope that dangled from the ceiling, high enough that we could not reach it, not even our tallest girl. I'd never seen so many flowers out of a garden. My mother always thought it a shame to cut them, and when she did she never arranged her flowers according to a single color, like this. The harsh electric lighting had been switched off, for tonight; instead, huge silver candelabras held candles as thick as my forearm. The candelabras themselves were taller than I was, beautiful in the way that a weapon was beautiful: I would stay away from them, lest one of their otherworldly flames, as big as a fist, catch my dress on fire.

A group of gray-haired men was seated at the opposite end of the dining hall, partially obscured by an Oriental folding screen. Perhaps they weren't supposed to look at us. They sat at attention on their stools, each with an instrument: the band.

The boys stood in their perfect line, stretched from one end of the dining hall to the other, distinguished only by the random sparkle from a wayward gem when it caught the light, while the girls messily clumped opposite them. I wondered if the boys had flasks hidden in their pockets, like Eva said they would. I knew from morning announcements that Mrs. Holmes was a vocal prohibitionist: drink was evil and immoral. Miss Brooks stood near them, as if to stop an errant boy before he made it to the other side. Miss Brooks led us on our bird-watching and botany walks in the afternoons and taught history during the school year, and though she seemed dull she was nice. I liked her, at least compared to Miss Lee, who watched everyone like a hawk.

Docey and another maid served us punch out of a giant crystal bowl. I inclined my head to Docey, who didn't acknowledge me. A formal serving outfit, like the kind that the maids in hotels wore, had replaced her normal uniform: a starched black pinafore, a crisp white blouse underneath.

"Docey's dressed up," I whispered to Sissy when we both had our punch.

"Look," Sissy said, "no, don't look, they'll see."

This was the first time I had seen Sissy nervous. And it was the closest I had ever been to a group of boys. I knew what they expected of us. I also knew what we were supposed to expect from them, which was very different — to be led in handfuls of dances, twirled around the room underneath the watchful eyes of adults. We wanted a certain handsome boy to take a fancy to us, to become half of a pair for a night. And then, maybe most of all, we wanted them to leave, so that we could pine away.

I didn't answer Sissy. I was nervous, too, but for a different reason. Silly as this sounds, I had never been around a boy I wasn't related to. Surely Mother and Father hadn't known that there would be a dance, with a busload of boys in attendance.

Henny and Jettie and another senior, Martha Ladue, entered the dining hall, and something about Henny looked strange, and it was a second before I realized that her mole had been powdered over. Martha was the most beautiful girl at camp. She looked like Louise Brooks, except prettier, calmer.

Sissy nudged me. Leona was at the door, dressed in a dull gray silk, a diamond-and-pearl choker around her throat. Everyone watched her, it was impossible not to, for Leona was the type of girl who commanded a room's attention; she was tall, almost six feet, and her white hair hung down to her waist, which was a style for younger girls. I wondered if it had ever been cut.

Mr. Holmes called us to attention at that moment. He stood at the head of the room then, Mrs. Holmes stood next to him, a corsage of a striped cream-and-red rose on her wrist. Mr. Holmes towered over his wife, as slender as she was plump. She wore the same pearl earrings, the old-fashioned skirt that fell to the floor, that she did every day.

"Let the dance commence," Mr. Holmes said, gesturing to the band, which struck up a song. We fanned out so that a boy could approach us definitively, without our having to wonder if he was really after our cabin-mate, our best friend. The boys rushed toward us; I took a step back, impulsively, bumping Leona.

"Pardon me."

"Pardon accepted," she said; I forgot to worry about the boys and instead peered up at Leona, who stared ahead, probably hoping that a tall boy would ask her to dance. She was even taller when you were close to her. I looked down and saw that her shoes were flat, and dyed silver to match her dress. The rest of us wore heels when we dressed up. I supposed she was rich enough to have any type of shoe made, in any color she wanted.

"Thea." I looked up, surprised by the sound of my name. I hadn't thought Leona knew who I was. "Someone wants you," Leona said impatiently, and I turned to face a skinny, pale boy.

"May I have the pleasure of this dance?" he asked, and I accepted his arm, realizing as we walked that a slow song was playing, which meant I would have to get close to this boy. His voice was unsteady. I looked back to Leona as I was escorted to the dance floor. She was watching, which satisfied me for some reason.

"Thea, pleased to meet you," I said, nodding my head since I couldn't curtsy, not while we were walking. I hoped I was remembering all my manners.

"Harry, pleased to meet you," he said.

Before I knew it we were dancing, caught up in the flock. I recognized the song — "Carolina Moon" — even absent the words. It was one of Mother's favorite songs, and it seemed foolish, now, that I had just thought the melody was pretty, had never connected it to a place. Here I was, in Carolina, dancing to its slow, sad anthem.

"Where's your home?" I asked.

"Mainly here," he answered, after a pause. He did not dance particularly well. He led, but barely. And yet he smelled like Sam, and Georgie; I had forgotten the smell of boys, which was so different — sharper, more pungent — from the smell of girls.

"And when you're not here?"

"Louisiana. My family's in the lumber

business." He was eager to please, Harry. His answers were questions — Mainly here? Louisiana? The lumber business?

There were boys I would have swooned over here — there was a tall, black-haired boy, in a pale blue jacket, and Sissy had snagged a handsome redhead — but Harry was not one of them. Molly, the first-year from my table, twirled by, her knotty hair combed. Even the youngest of us danced. Sissy had told me these dances were progressive; before the Holmeses, each girl was assigned a boy whom she danced with the entire night. He would escort her to the Castle, her white satin dancing shoes carefully tucked under his arm. There had been members of the board — Sissy's grandfather, for one — who had fought hard against the change, who thought that Yonahlossee dances should model themselves on the old, prewar debutante balls.

When the waltz ended, I curtsied, Harry bowed, and I excused myself to the refreshment table. I accepted another cup of punch from Docey, who met my eyes briefly.

I felt a hand cup my elbow; for an instant I thought it was a boy, and I blushed, but then I turned and saw Sissy.

"Done already?" she asked.

"A little parched." I lifted my half-empty

punch cup. "You're not dancing?"

"Did you see the boy I was dancing with?" I nodded. "Boone. I like him." She lowered her voice. "I *really* like him."

I felt a strange pang of jealousy. We stood for a second, lulled into a trance by the music. I studied my punch, which was blue, strangely — almost black. Swollen blackberries bobbed on the surface, which the younger girls had picked yesterday with Mrs. Holmes during elocution class. My mother's citrus sherbet punch, an old family recipe, was light pink, tasted cold and sweet and creamy, only slightly tangy.

Sissy broke the silence. "I saw you talking to Leona."

"Not really. For a second. She knew my name."

"I'm surprised. I thought she only knew her horse's name."

"You don't like her?" I asked.

Sissy shrugged impatiently. "It doesn't matter, with Leona. Like her or hate her, she doesn't give a whit about anybody but her horse. She's so rich, Thea." She looked at me. "She can do anything she wants. She doesn't have to care about anybody."

In fact, though Sissy claimed Leona and Martha Ladue were the richest girls here, I knew Sissy was wealthy, too. Everyone did.

And her family's fortune wasn't new, like Leona's; it had lost that ugly sheen. Eva told me the funds to build the new riding rings had been donated by Sissy's grandfather; Sissy's mother and aunt were alumnae, and Sissy's father and grandfather sat on the camp's governing board.

Yet pretending your family wasn't wealthy, as Sissy did — this seemed to be part of the game. Sissy played this game so beautifully, moved so easily and naturally through Yonahlossee, was able to effortlessly wind her way through its hierarchies. She knew who was on scholarship (ten girls every year, including our own Mary Abbott), who was smart (she said I'd earned the reputation as a smart girl, which both flattered and unnerved me), and who was related (so many of the girls were cousins). She knew who might be sent away soon, because of her father's financial problems, despite Mr. Holmes's assurances that the country's situation was improving (Victoria's position at the camp was growing shakier by the moment). She knew who mattered, who didn't, though she was kind to both the former and the latter. The Kentucky girls, for instance, didn't matter, were hillbillies, though I didn't see why. Molly looked like all the other first-years; take away the Atlanta girls' stylish hair, remove the Memphis girls' gold lockets, emblazoned with their initials, and we all looked the same.

Sissy's blue eyes were earnest and perfectly round. A child's eyes. She had chosen me, out of all these girls. I was so grateful. When I left here, I would remember her always. Perhaps we would even visit.

I understood, suddenly, how lonely Mother must have been in Emathla, with only our aunt to call a friend. And I was angry that she had not ever allowed me my own, that she had not ever let anyone else in.

The waltzes continued. I danced with three more boys; one complimented my copper hair — he called it that, copper — and another's hands were so wet and slimy they felt like snakes. After we were finished, I excused myself and resolved not to dance again for the rest of the evening. I retired to the chairs set up for this purpose — I had seen earlier that boys could not, or would not, approach a sitting girl — and chatted with Henny, who cheerfully criticized girls' dresses. I let myself daydream, imagined my father would walk through at any moment — after this dance, before this one — no, now, in the middle of this interminable waltz, he wouldn't care about interrupting us: he would want to get to me too badly. Maybe my brother would come — then all the girls could see how handsome he was — or maybe all three of them, Father, Mother, Sam, and I would forgive them right away, be done with Yonahlossee forever.

Mary Abbott was standing alone by the door, nervously tapping her scuffed black shoe on the floor, as if she couldn't wait to make her escape. I felt sorry for her. It would cost me something, I knew, to cross the room and stand with her. Another test, to see what kind of girl I was. It didn't matter if I crossed the room or not; I had already failed, at home, in a way that could not be forgiven.

I had been feeling hopeful, imagining my family coming to retrieve me, and now I felt miserable, the sight of Mary Abbott, my indecision over whether or not to help her — my daydreams of Father interrupting this dance were just that. A fantasy, concocted in my wrong brain.

I looked at the ground, at my nice shoes, worn only once before, at Easter dinner, when I had sat between Georgie and Sam. When I looked up again I had decided I would cross the room, skirt the dancers, and be a friend to Mary Abbott.

But I didn't have to. Mr. Holmes was standing next to her, gesturing at the dance floor, smiling. Mary Abbott spoke, and Mr. Holmes listened attentively. He was so handsome, with his shock of dark hair, his thick eyebrows. His nose was crooked, veered a tiny bit to the left, and I wondered if he'd broken it playing sports.

Mary Abbott smiled now, and Mr. Holmes pointed to a set of chairs, and offered his arm to Mary Abbott; she took it, and followed him, and I watched Mr. Holmes wait for Mary Abbott to sit, then take a seat himself, and I realized he was kind, that he had also noted Mary Abbott's unease, but that he had, unlike me, responded to it. Offered solace. I wondered what he would have done in Father's position, if Mr. Holmes's niceness would have shredded beneath the weight of a bad daughter.

His kindness made me homesick. It reminded me that I had once only known kindness. I watched Mr. Holmes murmur something to Mary Abbott, and I wondered what they were talking about — I knew firsthand that Mary Abbott was not good at small talk — and *I* wanted to be Mary Abbott, I wanted to be murmured to by Mr. Holmes.

"Don't you think, Thea?"

I turned to Henny reluctantly. “Hmm?”

“Don’t you think the dress is too much for Sissy? She always does that, parades around in things too fine. She looks foolish.” Her voice had hardened.

We all look foolish, I thought. Less like girls at a camp dance and more like ladies at a ball. I think she looks beautiful, I began to say, but the words caught in my throat. Henny looked at me closely, like she was deciding about me, too. I had thought everyone liked Sissy; no, loved her. What could Henny possibly have against her? Just then Sissy twirled by, still with the redhead, as if summoned, and caught my eye and smiled enormously, as if she were the happiest girl in the world.

“Like a fool,” Henny muttered, and then the handsome black-haired boy appeared in front of me, and I remembered where I was. She was jealous of Sissy. And who wouldn’t be?

“Thea?” he asked, and offered his arm. He led me onto the dance floor, and my resolve not to dance vanished. He was very direct in how he held me and guided my body; I felt lucky that he had chosen me, but also surprised — he had broken the unspoken chair rule — was I the kind of girl that boys liked?

"I'm David."

"And you already know who I am."

He smiled. His shoulders were so broad they strained his jacket. His thick black hair was pomaded back from his broad forehead in the modern style, and his teeth were very big and white and straight. He was almost too handsome.

"How old are you?" I asked. It took him a second to answer, and blood rushed to my face — I had made a mistake, already. But then he spoke.

"Seventeen."

"And an athlete?"

"Football. Track. I'm stronger than I am fast. Feel," he said jokingly, and I touched the muscle that he offered.

The music turned slow, and David gathered me closer. He smelled faintly of cologne. In another world, this would have made me so happy, that David had chosen me out of all the other girls. I could feel the admiring, jealous glances of my campmates. And why had he chosen me? Because I'd looked like I hadn't wanted to be chosen. The customs with boys were all wrong. And besides, I didn't want David. I was done with that. I didn't want to be gathered, ever again.

A tap on my shoulder. I opened my eyes

and saw Mrs. Holmes, then the couples beyond her, who had stopped dancing and watched us.

"Too close, Thea." But surely we were no closer than any of the other girls? Or maybe we had been closer than I thought, and I hadn't noticed? That I hadn't known how close was too close horrified me.

"I'm sorry," I said softly. I didn't know what to do, what the etiquette was in these situations. Should I leave, or was I meant to stay and bear everyone's disapproval? The music still played, but very few people were dancing. David turned his face to the floor and suddenly I thought of my father, how he had not defended me. He had wanted me to stay, I know he had. But he had let Mother win that battle. Yet the world had not ended, even though it had seemed like it might.

Mrs. Holmes watched me. Not very much had changed since the days of white satin shoes that were not allowed to meet the earth. She did not tell me to go, or stay, so I nodded to David and left on my own, made my way through all the warm, glittering bodies. When I reached the edge of the floor, I saw that not everyone was watching. Couples had resumed dancing. Henny chatted with a group of girls. Perhaps about me, but perhaps not. I can save this, I thought. I have to; there was nowhere else to go, at least not right now.

My character was not what it should have been. Nobody had told me that, but I knew. And perhaps I had danced inappropriately; perhaps I was no longer the best judge of what was and was not appropriate. *What is wrong with you?* Mother had asked. And what was? I felt my forehead, flushed and hot. And then I turned to face whoever was watching me — I could feel eyes upon me like a touch.

Mr. Holmes. He offered a small smile, and I knew that he was trying to be kind, as he had been earlier to Mary Abbott. And at first I felt a sick feeling rise in my throat, because I did not want to be pitied; but then this feeling was replaced by a hopeful feeling: Mr. Holmes did not think I was bad. He watched me for a second more before politely averting his eyes. He did not see me the way all the other adults now saw me: my parents, Mrs. Holmes. But he was not a boy, either, like David. He was not drawn to me simply because I was pretty enough, available: a girl at a dance. He liked me, I realized. And I liked him.

I was still more child than adult. I was not a monster but a confused, wronged girl. It would be years, though, before I would understand. In those two weeks at home, Mother had been angry, Father mainly mute, as if there was nothing to be said. They blamed me. And so I came to Yonahlossee a person worthy of blame.

5

Most of the time, my home was very quiet, and my life was constant in the way of happy childhoods. Mother took Sam and me to Orlando once in the winter and once in the summer, where we shopped and dined in a restaurant, perhaps saw a picture, spent the night in a hotel. These excursions were exciting, though I hated to miss a ride, but they, too, were part of our custom.

Sam and I accompanied Mother to town once a month and trailed her from store to store while she ran errands. People knew us; she was the doctor's wife, and we were the doctor's children. Mother was charming in the stores as she told little stories, said funny things while she fingered plain fabrics we would never buy — we bought our clothes in Orlando or from catalogues — and placed orders.

Mother thought gossip was vile. So she did not ever say that the other people in

Emathla were beneath us. But we knew anyway. Now I understand that my mother's status was complicated; my father was a country doctor, there was no other woman who occupied the same position as she did. In Gainesville, where there were other physicians, and lawyers, like my uncle, perhaps Mother would have had friends. But what Mother wanted, truly wanted, was, and always would be, a mystery to me. It does not seem possible that a woman so charming and beautiful could find her life's happiness with three people: me, Sam, my father. And once every few weeks, my aunt and uncle and cousin.

But back then I did not ponder my mother's happiness. I was a child. I just wanted the drive to end, so I could get to Sasi.

I rode him once a day, sometimes twice. I never skipped a day. If I was sick, I rode; if it rained, I rode. I spent hours and hours in the barn each day, but only sat in the saddle for a small fraction of that time. The rest of the time was devoted to chores, but they weren't chores to me, couldn't possibly be placed in the same category as weeding Mother's garden with Sam, or helping Idella polish our infinite collection of silver. I cleaned my bridle daily, my saddle weekly; curried Sasi's coat until it shone. Carved the packed dirt from his hooves and squirted iodine onto his tender frog to prevent thrush. I picked manure and spread fresh hay in his stall, changed his water and fed him a mix of sweet feed and oats at eight in the morning, a lighter meal of grain at four in the afternoon. I did these things every day; I took pleasure in them. No one had to remind me.

Mother rode, in her youth. Sidesaddle, which she said she didn't mind, which I'd tried once or twice and hated. Sasi would not take a single step without my asking first. And sidesaddle, one leg hooked over the saddle, rendered me powerless.

Sam could often be found with me at the barn, especially in the afternoons. He didn't ride, but he liked Sasi, and he would arrange courses for us that included elaborate combinations, exact distances between jumps. The trick was turning Sam on to a task; after that he was fully engrossed, a dog with a bone. He would time us and record in his notebook our numbers and how many jumps we had knocked over. And beside that he would write a number, one through ten — his own ranking of how well we had done.

And sometimes, though we weren't supposed to do this, because Mother didn't think it was safe, I would bring Sasi out back and take his saddle off, and convince Sam to sit behind me. I loved riding bareback, though it was painful, less the padding of the saddle: but that was the beauty of it, too — nothing between me and Sasi, like the Indians rode. I could feel every twitch of his muscles, every slight hesitation or surge of interest. Sasi did not think — he simply acted. And in order to ride well, you had to stop yourself from thinking, had to act on instinct alone, and this was something I'd always done well.

Sam would have to cling to me, fiercely, in order to stay on; Sasi, excited by the new weight upon his back, would sidestep and arch his neck, trot elaborately. He knew what was coming, how I would let him go, give him his head and let him gallop until he tired; could he hear Sam as he whispered, frightened, into my hair, begging me to stop? Could he feel me shake my head and turn a deaf ear to my brother? And finally, could he feel Sam relax against me, and, as we swerved to the right to avoid a branch, feel him gasp with fear but also with pleasure?

Fear makes a horse go faster, so I liked having Sam's fear up there with me, goading Sasi on. And this was good for Sam, I thought, I knew — he needed to let himself be scared sometimes, in order to experience the pleasure that risk brought.

Father was usually gone until nighttime, and Mother gardened and tended to the house for most of the day.

Sam and I eagerly anticipated our cousin's family's visits, when Mother and Father would act lighthearted, when Sam and I would spend countless hours with Georgie. But I liked it when they left, too, at the end of the weekend; I liked having my family back to myself again, I liked spending uninterrupted hours in the barn, where I went less when Georgie was here, because he was afraid of horses.

Father saw his patients every day, but even so, he never seemed to particularly care about people. Besides, of course, keeping them in good health, which he cared about deeply. The Atwells on their thousand acres were *almost an island,* my joke with Sam. But it wasn't entirely a joke, for an ocean might as well have surrounded us.

"Thea?"

I opened my eyes, slowly. Georgie stood over me. He had arrived yesterday with his parents.

"Wake up, Thea," he whispered.

Sam was snoring softly. My stomach ached, fiercely, and I wanted to sleep. We slept in my room, Georgie in my other twin bed and Sam on the floor, though I noticed how Mother had hesitated over the sleeping arrangements this time.

"Thea," he said again, "it's almost morning."

"Yes," I agreed, "now go back to sleep."

"If I'm not tired?"

I closed my eyes against Georgie's voice.

"Come downstairs with me," he whispered, tugging my hand. "Please."

"I'm tired."

"Come anyway." His features were softer in the dim light. He looked at me hopefully, and put his hand on my cheek. It felt strangely tender, but good; I could feel my heart quicken. I threw off the covers. I wanted to wake Sam, but Georgie shook his head. Sam and I did what Georgie wanted, mainly. He was older and stronger than either of us.

"Follow me," he said, and we made our way through the sleeping house that felt dead it was so quiet.

"I should have put on more clothes," I said, once we were outside in the chilly air. It was fall, almost Thanksgiving, though the leaves didn't change here, instead died suddenly and quickly. Fall was a mixed blessing: I could ride during the day, because of the cool temperature, but I couldn't stay out as late because dark came earlier.

"Aren't you tired?"

Georgie shook his head. "I can't sleep. Here," he said, and patted the damp ground. "Sit."

I lingered. "I might go say hi to Sasi."

"Don't. He's probably sleeping."

I laughed and sat down next to him, folded my nightgown over my legs. "Horses only sleep an hour a day."

"Maybe I'm like a horse."

"They sleep standing up," I continued. "So that they're ready to run, at a moment's notice."

"Do horses say things like that? A moment's notice?"

"To me. Sasi says all sorts of things to me."

Georgie nodded, but he didn't smile. I could tell his mind was elsewhere. He seemed pensive, which I took note of because it was so unusual. Usually he moved through the world so easily, was himself such easy company, always in good humor.

"Do you think you'll live here forever?" he asked. We were sitting at the back of my house, the view that was most familiar to me; the porch where we would all sit later, while the adults sipped their drinks. The glass French doors that opened to the less formal sitting room, where we sat in the evenings when we didn't have company.

"I hadn't thought about it." I lay back in the grass, still sleepy. "I suppose I'll live wherever my husband does." The words were strange in my mouth. But it was true; I knew I would live where he did.

"What if he takes you to the moon?" He winked at me, and I thought, there he is.

I laughed. "Then I'll bring you and Sam along so you can see it, too. But first I'm going to sleep awhile."

"Then so am I." He lay down next to me. "Sweet dreams," he said, which was what Aunt Carrie always said. He took my hand, and though I expected him to let it go after a second, like he usually did, he did not.

"Thank you," I murmured. I closed my eyes. I was nearly asleep when I felt Georgie's fingers on my arm, so lightly, running down the length of it. I looked up and he was watching me, smiling; I closed my eyes and tried not to fall asleep, tried to remain in this trancelike state between sleep and waking. The pleasure of my cousin's touch was almost too much, but I did not want it to stop.

Then the sun was bright overhead, and my thighs were sticky with sweat. Even when the air was crisp, like now, the sun was always overhead, following.

"Georgie," I said, and shook his inert shoulder. "We fell asleep."

My uncle and father sat on the porch, a sheaf of papers in front of them; usually my father was making his rounds right now, visiting his patients. We saw them before they saw us; my slender father, his delicate doctor's hands, and my rotund uncle. They'd both had sons who resembled them.

Uncle George looked at me blankly as I approached; I kissed him on the cheek anyway.

"What are you doing out here?" my father asked. He took out his father's pocket watch, which he always kept with him. Uncle George teased him about it, called him nostalgic. And it was true that almost every other man I had seen — not that I had seen many — wore wristwatches. "It's too early."

"We fell asleep," Georgie said.

I was going to elaborate but I could see my father didn't care. When I'd asked my father what Uncle George got from their father that was like the pocket watch, he'd only smiled.

"Why don't you go on inside," he said. "It's still early. Don't wake Mother."

My father, forty years old this June, had started to gray, his dark brown hair turned peppery. Uncle George was balding. They'd both aged, Father more handsomely.

When we were upstairs, I found the blood on my underclothes. I sat down on the edge of the tub and felt; my fingers were covered with a sheen of red-brown, but this blood was different; it clumped, formed clots.

I heard the floor creak outside the door. Sam, getting up. There was only a door between my cousin, who had fallen back into bed, my brother, and me. And there was no lock, either, and I wanted one so badly right now. Sam would knock first, but still — the thin fact of a door was inadequate. I pressed an old towel to my underclothes. I would burn it, later. I would tell Mother, later. My family was progressive in certain ways, and I'd known to expect this. But still, the thought of either Georgie or Sam finding out made me want to die.

Later that day, Georgie, Sam, and I went hunting for a snake for one of Sam's terrariums. I'd fitted one of Mother's belts to myself. Ordinarily I'd be riding, but I'd announced at breakfast that Sasi was lame.

Mother had looked at me curiously — Sasi was a sound pony — and I had turned my head. The thought of pulling on breeches over the contraption between my legs seemed impossible. Aunt Carrie was back at the house, with Mother, and they'd told us to be careful, which was advice they gave regardless of activity, and so meant nothing.

"What were you doing last night?" Sam asked, and I knew immediately he was a little hurt we hadn't asked him.

"What do you mean?" Georgie's tone was playful.

"I woke up and you weren't there. Neither was Thea."

"Georgie couldn't sleep," I said, "and so he woke me up! I wouldn't let him wake you up."

"What are we looking for, exactly?" Georgie asked, oblivious to Sam's hurt feelings. But Sam seemed to accept my explanation.

"Snakes," Sam said.

"I bet I'll find one," Georgie said, and grinned. "I know where they hide."

"Remember," Sam said, "don't kill it."

Georgie crossed his heart. "Promise!"

Sam laughed. Georgie had accidentally squashed one of Sam's tree frogs last month, and he was always picking up lizards the wrong way and severing their bodies from their tails. Sam was gentler: he knew how to entice a lizard into his cupped hands, how to pinch a snake by its neck and wind its body around his wrist.

"Poor snake," I murmured. "Do you think it really wants to come live with you?"

Sam grinned. "Better than getting eaten by a bigger snake, or a bird."

Georgie stopped and unscrewed the cap of his canteen, then tilted it to his mouth. We each had one strapped across our backs. I took a sip from mine, too; I liked how the water tasted cool, slightly metallic. Aunt Carrie let Georgie grow his hair longer than my mother let Sam grow his, so my cousin had a wild look about him now, his brown hair unkempt, bleached in streaks by the sun. My brother knelt and examined a palmful of dirt. Georgie was changing, next to Sam; there was hair when he lifted his arms, and his sweat smelled ripe and musky. From this vantage point, Georgie looked almost like a man, muscle-bound and thick. Sam was still impossibly skinny, in the way of boys, his spine stretched taut against his skin.

"If we're lucky," Sam said, standing, "we'll see a coral snake. They're so beautiful. I see some snake tracks, but I don't know which kind. But we're near water."

Coral snakes lived near water; I knew that from Sam. Or maybe I had always known it.

"Hopefully we won't be lucky," Georgie said, "since they're deadly."

Sam and I gazed at him. Coral snakes *were* deadly, but they were shy. And they had to chew on you for a long time before any venom was transmitted. We knew what to be afraid of in the Florida wilderness, but we were taught to be unafraid of the natural world. The smaller the animal, the more afraid it was of us. And when I was on my pony, my father told me, I was a terrifying creature — snakes could feel our footsteps from miles away, and bears and panthers could smell us before they saw us.

Sam was a very cautious naturalist. His terrariums were full of reptiles that were not poisonous. He only wanted to see a coral snake, not capture it.

"You're such a city boy," I said. "You'd have a better chance of choking on your water than being bitten by a coral snake."

"I'll take my chances with the canteen," Georgie said, and grinned. He took another sip of water.

Sam started to delve into the specifics of the coral snake's bite, and then he moved on to the pygmy rattlesnake, in order to provide context, and I started to walk again, hoping to move things along. I didn't want to be out here too long. I didn't know how long the belt would last.

"Quiet," I whispered, when I saw the grass shiver slightly. I pointed.

"Could be a lizard," Sam said softly. He dropped to his knees, then crawled to the edge of the grass, which came up to our waists.

Georgie and I watched him, trying to stand as still as possible. Sam could move as quietly as an Indian. We could not. I held my breath and Sam reached into the grass and pulled out a long black snake, an orange band encircling its neck. I felt a flash of pride; Sam was quick.

"Good eye, Thea," he said, and showed us the snake's belly, which was beautifully vermillion. "He's at least twelve inches."

We watched the snake writhe around in Sam's net.

"Diadophis p. punctatus," he said.

"Diadophis," Georgie said, "this was not your lucky day."

"But it was mine," Sam said, happy.

I watched the snake, motionless in the net, as if it had accepted its fate. It was fully grown, an adult, and unblemished. A lucky snake. Sam would not keep him forever in a glass house, but the snake would not know that.

Mother was in my bedroom when I came in from out back, sitting on the edge of my unmade bed.

"There's blood on your sheets," she said, and I looked to where she pointed.

"I was going to tell you today."

She stood, and I thought she was going to leave, but then she came very close to me and untucked my blouse before I could stop her.

"Where did you get this?" Her hand lingered on the belt. I looked out the window, at the great oak that hovered over our house like a parent. Father said it kept us cool in the summers, warm in the winters.

"I'm sorry," I said quickly. "I'm sorry."

She nodded, and took my hand between hers, as if entreating me. But I was her daughter, I didn't need entreating. "Do you know what this means?"

"That I can't ride."

She laughed. "No. It means you can have a child now."

I was horrified. My mother smiled at me very, very kindly and I wanted her to be angry at me, anything but this tenderness.

Usually I eagerly received my mother's affection, but I did not want any more attention drawn to this thing that had happened to me, to my body. I had not wanted it to happen. I had not asked for it.

"Of course not now," she continued, "but someday. Doesn't that please you, Thea?"

I shook my head. My mother drew me close and pressed my head to her chest.

"Oh, don't cry. I didn't mean to alarm you. I only don't want you to think that this is anything to be ashamed of."

I sprung back. "You won't tell anyone?"

"Of course not. This is between us. A woman's matter." She smiled faintly. "It's nothing to be ashamed of, Thea. Nothing."

I nodded. I didn't know what to say, so I thanked my mother, and she responded in kind, out of habit, as she left the room.

"You're welcome."

I was very good at focusing my mind. That's what Father called it. Mother called it ignoring the consequences. I had bled twice before this, the first time more than a year ago. And I had kept it a secret because I was confused by the thing that was happening to me. I didn't understand how something I had expected could make me feel so ashamed. And I knew telling made a thing real. I flung myself on my now-made bed, which wasn't something we were allowed to do, and pressed my face into my pillow and wished that I would hear a voice, Georgie's or Sam's or even Aunt Carrie's — just a sign that life went on without me, that my bleeding was not really a great or particularly exciting fact. I was a girl, the only girl in our world. How different I was from Georgie and Sam had been articulated by Mother. I felt, for the first time in my life, apart, adrift. A floating girl.

Now I understand that the relief I could see, faintly, on Mother's face was relief that I was normal. She must have been worried, her daughter fourteen, almost fifteen, and still not menstruating. She's simply a late bloomer — I'm sure Father would have told her this, uttered these exact words or something so close, and Mother would have agreed with him or not, but still she would have gone away and worried.

My father came home later than he had promised, and Mother was waiting for him by the front door. I was afraid she was going to tell him I'd started menstruating, so I waited in the sun porch where I could hear them.

"They're waiting outside," my mother said, and my father nodded.

"How are they?" He put down his black doctor's bag, which was always with him. "How do they seem?"

"Fine," she said, and helped him out of his white coat.

"Fine?"

"Fine, Felix." Her voice was soft but firm. The conversation of adults was often coded, impenetrable. And though I usually cared very little about the adult matters my mother and father discussed, this was something else, something that involved my aunt and uncle, and, by extension, Georgie. And I cared about Georgie, deeply.

I waited a second and then followed them to the back deck, where the adults went to have cocktails before dinner. I was surprised by my disappointment that Mother hadn't mentioned me to Father. Everyone sat in our low deck chairs, green-painted metal, around a table set with canapés and a bottle of champagne for the ladies, a decanter of whiskey for the men. Though liquor was technically illegal, getting it was like a game everyone played, and won. Uncle George knew someone in Gainesville who kept him, and us, supplied. This was usually my favorite part of the visits, the time when the adults were happiest.

I walked up behind Father, kissed the top

of his head. He smiled up at me, and Uncle George winked at me. Georgie and Sam sat on the ground, a little bit behind everyone, watching the snake. Sam had filled a terrarium with dirt and moss and rocks; a miniature of the snake's former home. I sat down next to them.

Aunt Carrie caught my eye and smiled. "Is your pony better, Thea?"

I looked at my aunt blankly before I remembered. "Oh, yes," I said. "He just needs to rest for a few days."

"Good." She smiled and smoothed her skirt over her plump stomach.

My father watched my mother as she tipped the champagne bottle to her glass, lifted it away just as the bubbles threatened to flood the rim. We were all watching her, now, and I thought of what she had said earlier, about being a woman. It seemed very womanly, to have everyone watching you.

"Well," Uncle George said, and paused. He held a pipe in his hand, a thin stream of smoke curling to the heavens. I loved the smell. Idella stepped onto the porch then, carrying a platter of tiny chive biscuits. Sam stood and grabbed a handful before she set it down on the table.

"Sam," Mother chided softly. She seemed

distracted. All of the adults did.

"It's eating. That's soon. The last one didn't eat for days," Sam said, ignoring Mother, kneeling down and pointing at the snake, which was indeed eating an earthworm. I shuddered.

"Are you going to catch all its food?" Georgie asked. "Seems like a lot of work."

Sam swallowed the last of his biscuit. I tapped my cheek, to show him there was a crumb, but he was lost in the world of the snake. He could do this, devote himself completely to an animal; I could, too, with Sasi, but it seemed entirely different. Sasi was warm-blooded, like me.

Sam gently lifted the snake from the terrarium and stroked its head. The snake seemed calm, mollified. Mother said it was Sam's gift, calming animals that frightened most people. He lowered the snake to the wooden ground and it started to slither away, slowly. "It needs its exercise," Sam murmured, as he crawled on his hands and knees to follow it.

Georgie looked at me and rolled his eyes, and I smiled. I could not imagine loving a snake as much as my brother did.

"He's a snake charmer," I said, and Georgie began to say something else, but then we both turned, drawn by the odd, unmistakable sound of someone weeping. My aunt. I felt chilled. I couldn't ever remember seeing her cry. In fact, I'd only seen my mother cry once before, when her horse had to be put down; my father, never.

I turned to Georgie, but he was watching his mother.

"It's worthless now?" my mother asked quietly. "All of it?"

My aunt closed her eyes, and pressed her fingers to her lips. My uncle watched his pipe, which he held carefully, pinched between his thumb and finger. He would not meet Mother's eye. Neither of them spoke. I turned to my cousin again, and there were bright red splotches on his cheeks and forehead, the redness colonizing his fair skin. He knew.

"Miami," Aunt Carrie said dolefully, and shook her head. "Miami."

Miami was where Uncle George had been going for years, since I could remember. He drove down there once a month, to look after his property, property he would eventually sell.

My father said nothing, sat very still, his hands on his knees, his face blank. But I understood that this blankness meant something: my father was angry.

"Tell her, George," Aunt Carrie said, "tell her."

Uncle George looked at his wife, and she nodded. "Go on."

"To put it plainly, as I told my brother this morning, I owe the bank more than it's worth. It was a foolish investment from the beginning," he said finally. "But it seemed a sure thing. Bryan himself called the light 'God's Sunshine.' Everyone wanted a piece, Elizabeth. There were so many people who wanted to live there . . ." He trailed off. "It seemed a sure thing."

When my father spoke, his voice was soft but clear. "Nothing in this life is sure, George." A bright red cardinal landed on the railing, and gave a little chirp. My father turned his head in the direction of the sound, gazed at the bird for a moment, and then turned back to his brother. "Nothing."

"Especially land speculation," my uncle said, and laughed nervously.

I felt sick to my stomach. The air was thick, the adults were so distracted they hadn't noticed me and Georgie. Sam was still following his snake.

Georgie stood, and walked off the porch into the backyard without asking to be excused. I waited for an adult to call him back, but they just watched him go, their foreheads creased, and I was suddenly so angry at everyone — my stupid brother, my stupid parents, my stupid aunt and uncle.

I ran after Georgie. My mother called after me — "Thea!" — but I ignored her.

When I caught up to him, I touched his shoulder.

He spun around. "What do you want?"

I couldn't say anything. I didn't know what I would say. His meanness surprised me; Georgie was never mean to me.

"Let's go to the barn," I said quietly. I knew he would follow me. When Sasi heard me, he nickered and swung his pretty head over the stall door. It was nearly time for him to eat. I patted his broad forehead, and waited. I sensed that Georgie would speak when he was ready.

I murmured to Sasi, told him what a good boy he was. I hoped the bleeding would not last too long this time. I hated not riding, hated spending a day or two reestablishing things with Sasi before we could begin again where we had left off.

"My father thought we were going to be rich," Georgie said, from behind me, "like you."

Sasi nipped my hand, lightly, mouthy because he was hungry.

"We're not rich," I said.

Georgie gave a short, hard laugh. "You have the oranges."

It was true. We did have the oranges.

"Do you know what it means to mortgage your house, Thea?" he asked. He stepped closer to me. He touched the tail of my braid, and I shivered. "It means my father borrowed money from the bank against our house."

"Why?" I could barely breathe. Georgie's finger lingered on my back, toying with my hair.

"To buy more land, in Miami," Georgie said. "He was happy to sell soon." He was almost whispering. "And now the country is doing very badly, and he can't pay the bank back, and he asked for money. From your father."

I could feel Georgie's breath on my neck. I could smell him: strong, oily, like he had been out in the woods.

Very badly. Those were our parents' words. Father had said the same thing about the country last week. But our parents' world was separate from ours, another place entirely. Georgie need not worry about the matters of adults. I spun around and faced my cousin, who looked mournful, the opposite of how God had made him to look. I took his hand.

"They'll take care of it. You'll see."

I could see Georgie wanted to believe me.

"Trust me," I said.

I would show Georgie I was not afraid. Money meant nothing to me, then. If Uncle George borrowed money from my family, that was fine, because everything was shared in a family, and besides, there was always more money. There was always another set of silk drapes from Orlando, another pony, another ivory-handled knife.

"All right," he said. The old Georgie had returned to me. "All right. I'll trust you, Thea."

He kissed me on the cheek. I blushed, but I was pleased because I had pleased my cousin, because I had cheered him up, because I had shown him that the money did not matter.

I believed all those things I told my cousin that day. I had everything I loved in the world within one hundred feet: my parents, my aunt and uncle, my brother. My cousin and pony within arm's reach. My understanding of our world, I thought, was complete.

6

The rain fell in sheets. Naari and I were halted at the head of the ring, next to Mr. Albrecht, watching Leona complete her course. She rode badly today, perhaps distracted by the rain. She and King had nicked several jumps, knocked two over entirely.

"Hold his head!" Mr. Albrecht shouted, his voice dulled by the wind. He held an umbrella, which Naari eyed warily. We were to be assessed individually, today, my first time, but I wasn't nervous.

When Leona was finished I nudged Naari into a trot from our standstill: she was distracted by the storm, and her ears flicked back and forth. I murmured to her, kicked her twice, and she gave me her attention for a moment. We passed Leona, who was muttering furiously to King.

"Knees, Thea," Mr. Albrecht yelled. My knees had a tendency to slide upward during jumps.

"One minute." Mr. Albrecht timed our courses, as we would be timed in a competition. I slid my right heel back and asked Naari to canter.

"Time," Mr. Albrecht called, and we were nearly aligned with the first jump, but not quite. I had learned early on, before Mr. Albrecht, to forget my mistakes. Remembering could easily ruin a course.

"Now," I hissed to Naari as we cleared the first jump, but barely. The rain seemed to quicken, or maybe I was just going faster. The wind whipped. There was no thunder or lightning — camp rules would force us to take cover, then — but I could hear the weak branches of the oak trees snapping.

A pelt of Spanish moss flew into our path, and Naari skittered. I tapped her shoulder with my crop and tightened the reins.

"Balance," I heard Mr. Albrecht yell, but he was barely there.

I directed Naari toward a triple, the most difficult combination of the course.

"Two, two, two," I repeated to myself — there was room for two strides between each jump, no more, no less.

"Yes," screamed Mr. Albrecht. *"Gut!"* I could barely hear him. "Now," I heard him yell, and I cleared the first jump. One, two

— Naari soared over the second jump, I could barely feel her beneath me, she was a coil between my legs.

And then the last jump. We were nearly done. The wind picked up, then, between the second and third jumps, and Mr. Albrecht's umbrella flew toward us. Naari swerved to the right, and I lost my right stirrup, and then I heard the unmistakable crack of leather, and my saddle slid to the left. My girth has broken, I thought, incredulously. I looked toward Mr. Albrecht, as if to say — Do you see this?

But then the saddle lurched even farther to the left, and I couldn't believe my bad luck — how could I straighten myself out, move the saddle to the right, when I had lost my right stirrup? It was impossible. I felt horribly dizzy all of a sudden, perched at an angle nearly parallel to the ground.

"Circle her." Mr. Albrecht yelled. "Circle."

But I was so disoriented I didn't even know which rein was right and which was left. I pressed my right leg to Naari's flank as hard as I could, the only pressure that was keeping me from hurtling to the ground. And I would not fall cleanly. I could see from my vantage point that the girth had not broken completely, so if I fell I would likely be trapped beneath Naari, tied to her by the stirrup I had not lost.

"Do something," Mr. Albrecht called desperately. "Something!"

Naari galloped by them, and Leona flashed through my tilted field of vision; she was looking at her hand, held in front of her in its navy glove, fingers splayed, palm upturned. Dye streaked her forearm.

In a burst of strength, I somehow threw my arm around Naari's neck, and hitched myself upright again. And then the world was back to its normal order, and I was able to turn Naari in a circle until she slowed.

Mr. Albrecht approached us, holding out his hand to Naari, who looked at him warily. "It is all right," he murmured, and then to me: "Are you all right, Thea?"

I nodded. I felt fine, strangely fine. I knew I should have felt relieved, or still scared, but instead I felt blank; relaxed, even. I had been so close to an accident; but wasn't I always that close, whenever I was on top of a horse?

Leona stood in the same place as before, watching us, and I understood that I had witnessed a weakness: Leona hadn't wanted to watch. She had been afraid.

"She's spooky," Leona said later, at the barn, as we sponged warm water over our horses' backs. Steam rose. "King's not. He's dull. That's how a horse should be, dull and obedient."

"I like my horses smart," I said lightly.

"Too smart for their own good, is that how you like them? You lost your stirrup, you almost fell. She would have dragged you around the ring if you had."

"But I didn't." Naari was exhausted, stood perfectly still in the cross ties.

"But you could have," Leona said. I was about to argue, but Leona continued: "The duller a horse is, the better." She slapped King on the neck. "People are killed in horseback riding accidents, Thea." She unhooked King's cross ties; Naari started at the sound of the metal snaps against the concrete floor of the wash rack. "You should request a different horse.

"But," she said, as she led King past us, "you won't, because you're proud. A horse is a weapon."

I stopped and looked at her, and I realized that I had something Leona did not. I was fearless. And that counted for something.

"Smart horses will work for you," I said. "Once you win them over. Dumb horses" — and here I looked at King — "they don't care enough." Leona stared at me, then turned her face away quickly, her long blond braid snapping like a whip; we both knew I was right.

I was currying the saddle marks from Naari's back when Leona appeared again.

"I want to tell you something," she said. Her tone was neutral. "I come from a riding family."

I banged my curry comb against the wall. A curry comb–shaped clump of hair fell to the floor.

"I know." We all knew.

"Yes," she continued, "a family where everyone rides." She paused. "My sister walked behind a horse, too close, and she was kicked in the head. She died."

I didn't say anything.

"It was a long time ago. I was born later. She died in three days." She held up three fingers. "It was not the horse's fault. It was her fault, she walked where she should not have. It is never the horse, Thea."

She turned, then, and began to stride away in precisely measured steps.

"Leona," I called.

She turned. "Yes?"

"I'm sorry for your sister." I took a step forward, and though I must have been more than twenty feet away from this girl, this exquisite giant, she took a step back.

Leona shook her head. "It was before me."

As I watched Leona walk away, I could

"She rode in the rain for hours las
Mrs. Holmes said, "she chilled hei
the bone. And," she added, and lowere
voice, "she's been very homesick."

"An equestrienne?"

"Yes," I said. Mrs. Holmes went to ti
closet and pulled out a stack of whit
towels; I saw a reflection of myself in a mirror that was nailed to the door as it swung shut. I looked very pale. "All the girls ride," Mrs. Holmes said, as if it were an unavoidable, slightly disappointing activity.

I wondered if she was angry at Mr. Albrecht — whom she seemed to like, who sat at the head table with the Holmes family — for letting me ride in the rain.

"I didn't make myself sick," I said. I wasn't the kind of girl who would do that.

Mrs. Holmes said nothing. Mr. Holmes had become easy to read, for me; his face was always moving in response to the things girls said, always expressing pleasure or dismay or confusion, but Mrs. Holmes was entirely self-composed, a trait I admired in spite of myself. I would like to learn to be that composed. Her clothes were so old-fashioned, of another era: her skirt that fell to the floor, her cameo that closed her blouse at the neck to prevent even the tiniest glimpse of skin. The Holmeses were

see that her disclosure did not mean a door into her soul had opened slightly and forever, as it would have with Sissy. But I liked Leona, in spite of her imperiousness. In spite of what Sissy said. I felt linked to her: we were the best riders here.

Mary Abbott knelt beside my bunk.

"Thea," she whispered. "Thea."

I opened my eyes. There was no moon, and the cabin was dark as coal. I saw Mary Abbott by the flash of her pale skin. My chest felt tight.

Yes, I wanted to say, but my voice would not come.

"Your breathing," Mary Abbott said, "it woke me."

I sat up too quickly and banged my head on the bottom of Eva's bunk, which I hadn't done since my first morning here. My hair caught, my scalp burned. I tried to speak again and my voice came out as a bark.

"You don't sound well."

I shook my head and began to cry. I couldn't speak, I could barely breathe. When I'd gone to sleep I'd only had a cold. I'd felt a bit achy, but otherwise fine.

Sissy came to me then, and pushed Mary Abbott aside. She took my hand and felt my forehead.

“Fetch Henny.” Mary Abbott disappeared.

Sissy freed my hair from the metal netting. “Lie back,” she whispered.

“Thea?” Eva’s head hung over the bed.

I tried to speak — Nothing, I wanted to say — but Sissy shook her head.

“Quiet.”

Sissy wasn’t allowed to accompany me to the Castle, where I spent the night in the windowless infirmary. Mrs. Holmes checked on me every hour while I slept fitfully, alone for the first time in months, nothing to lull me to sleep but the sound of the wind disturbing the trees. I had become used to the sounds girls made: Gates snored lightly when she first fell asleep, and occasionally Sissy spoke to herself, in nonsense, until Victoria reached down and tapped her. And there was always the heavy sound of breathing to soothe when I woke and believed, for the briefest instant, that I was at home in my own bed, where I used to belong.

I fell into a delirium. Mrs. Holmes was careful not to touch me when she slid the thermometer in my mouth, held it there with the tip of her finger against my tongue’s thrusts.

“Leave it, Thea.” But I would not, my quiet resistance.

“Mother,” I said.

“She’s not here, Thea,” she said quietly.

My breathing became more labored as t
night wore on; my fever rose. Each time
woke I thought I was home.

Another figure followed Mrs. Holmes in
the room — by this time, perhaps, I tru
was delirious — I saw the sharp, sli
outline of a tall man.

“Sam,” I called.

“Hush,” Mrs. Holmes said.

Mother would come to me, once s
learned that I was ill. She would have to.

When I opened my eyes again, Mrs. Holn
and a man — the doctor, I knew — sto
over me.

“May I examine you, Thea?” he asked.

I covered my heart with my hand, emb
rassed. I wondered if he’d lifted my gown
hear. Even through my stuffed nose,
doctor smelled musty. He didn’t wea
white doctor’s coat, like my father did wh
he saw patients. He wore instead a regu
suit. It was Sunday, he had made a spe
trip to see me. He was short and fat,
matched Mrs. Holmes better than M
Holmes did. His wife was probably tall a
slender; that was how the world worked.

He took my wrist in his hand and pres
his fingers to it, to feel my pulse.

considered progressive: they'd done away with sidesaddle when they'd taken over, for which I, at least, was grateful. And under the Holmeses' direction, many girls applied to ladies' colleges as seniors, and though some married before they could go, many actually went. And yet here Mrs. Holmes sat like a relic of an earlier time.

The doctor felt my neck. "An illness is a mysterious and often inexplicable event, Mrs. Holmes. To know its cause would mean that you knew more than God, Mrs. Holmes. Knew more than science."

Mrs. Holmes murmured, but the murmur gave away neither assent nor dissent, and the doctor chuckled and winked at me, asked me to sit up so that he could place the cold stethoscope, warmed by his breath, on my back. I wore only my nightgown, no underclothes.

I was nearly naked in front of this man. My chest ached, and it pained me to breathe deeply, but still I was ashamed.

I closed my eyes and took deep breaths when the doctor asked me to. I was relieved I was not at home, because then Father would have examined me and seen me unclothed. But if I were at home, I would have been well.

"A bad cold," the doctor announced when

he was done. I liked him. He had taken my side.

There was a knock on the door and I put down my book.

"Come in," I called.

It was Mr. Holmes. He was wearing a suit; it was Wednesday, camp life continued without me. Everyone here dressed formally; Mr. Albrecht wore a black show coat with his breeches, and the female teachers wore nice, if plain, dresses. I smoothed the covers over my lap.

He folded himself into the chair by my bed, which seemed too small for him.

"Hello," he said, and smiled. He was too tall to ride horses, it would be hard for him to keep his balance. Maybe if he had learned when he was a child, but it was almost impossible to teach a tall adult how to ride. It should feel strange, I knew, to be alone in a room with a man who was not family for the first time in my life. And yet it did not.

"Hello. How are you today?"

"I'm just fine. I should be asking that of you. Do you feel better?"

I nodded.

"What are you reading?" He gestured to my book.

"Howards End."

"Do you like to read?"

"I love books."

He picked up the book and examined its cover. "I love them, too. There's such cruelty and such goodness in Forster's world. But I don't want to ruin it for you. I see you're only halfway through."

"That could be said of any book, couldn't it?" I asked shyly. But I knew I was correct. "If the people in them are real."

"I suppose it could."

I could tell I had surprised and pleased Mr. Holmes. We were quiet for a moment.

"I'm concerned, Thea. Mrs. Holmes thinks you are homesick —" I started to protest, but he held up his hand. "It's nothing to be ashamed of, Thea. Many of the girls are homesick. It always goes away. But you've been here for two months."

I fiddled with a piece of my hair. It hadn't been washed in almost a week. I must look wild to Mr. Holmes, pale and unkempt.

"But I'm not homesick," I said. "I'm going home soon."

He tilted his head, and I could tell he was trying not to look surprised.

"When summer session ends," I continued. "Next week."

Mr. Holmes did not speak for a moment. "Thea," he said finally, "you won't be leaving Yonahlossee next week."

"But I will," I said. "There must be some sort of misunderstanding." This was what Mother had said last year, when an Emathla shopkeeper had ordered the wrong hair tonic for Father. But even as I protested, I knew that Mr. Holmes would not lie to me. I traced the cover of my book. "How long, then?" I asked. I could not look at him. Surely they would bring me home for Thanksgiving. We'd never spent a holiday apart.

"Your father reserved a space for a year."

"A year," I repeated. "A year." The cover of the book blurred. I could not fathom it. Father had not told me himself. He had let a stranger do his bidding. My father was weak. I saw that so clearly now.

Mr. Holmes spoke again. His voice was kind. "You are liked here. This is not a place of punishment, regardless of your parents' intention. It is a privilege, to be here." He paused, and the pleasure his voice had brought disappeared. I looked at him, and offered a small smile, so that he would go on. "You'll make of it what you will, but please don't hate it. I imagine you might grow to love it."

I said nothing. I did not trust my voice. He stood, as if to go. He must have thought

I wanted to be alone. I wanted nothing less.

"Do they know I'm sick?" I asked.

He didn't want to answer, I could see he didn't want to, but he nodded, and pursed his lips together, and I could tell he thought my parents were terrible. He was thinking of his own girls, how quickly he would go to them if they fell ill, and I wanted to tell him that he was correct, my parents were awful, but I also wanted him to know that they loved me, that he did not know what I had done. That he should not judge them. And that none of us knew how we would act, under certain circumstances. None of us, including him.

"They are concerned," he said hesitantly.

The sound of my laugh surprised him; he looked at me curiously.

"You must think I'm a fool," I said, before he could go on. "A rube." A word I would never have been allowed to say at home. Slang, common.

"Thea," he said, shaking his head. He was so close I could see the stubble where his beard fought to grow. "I have never for an instant thought you were a fool. I do not pretend to understand the intricacies of other families." He paused, and shook his head. "I'm sorry. I should speak plainly. I do not know your parents, Thea. I do not understand the way in which your family operates. But I know that things have a way of working themselves out, if not immediately, then eventually."

Before he left, he said one last thing: "It has always been a great comfort to me that I could bring a book anywhere, to any place. To any part of my life. I'm glad to see you're taking the same comfort."

When he closed the door and the room was empty again, I sobbed into my pillow. I had not cried like this since home. I must mean so little to them that they had not told me themselves. My chest was on fire, I could hardly breathe. I made it to the wastebasket in time and retched into it. The taste was bitter in my mouth. I'd eaten nothing, but still my body produced enough to expel.

I opened the closet where the supplies were kept and stared at my reflection. I was ugly already, pale and dirty and sharply thin. Now my eyes were swollen and red. My lips were cracked. I looked like some kind of monster; it seemed impossible that my family would ever recognize me. I'd never spent more than a night away from my home, and that was only in Gainesville with Georgie.

When Sam and I were ten, young enough

not to be told directly what had happened but old enough to put the pieces together, a woman in Emathla killed herself. She put her infant to bed on a cold night with a quilt; she came back in the morning to find him dead, his face in the quilt. She'd smothered him by trying to protect him, and after she found him, after my father had come and examined the body, after the funeral, the condolences, the stream of calls from neighbors and well-wishers, she'd drunk a bottle of ammonia. My father was called to the house again, though she was already dead when he arrived, and Sam heard him tell my mother that her throat was badly burned, that she'd found a way to punish herself even as she died.

Sam had found me in the tack room, excited by the news, not quite sure what it all meant. I had understood. Not much scared me, but this had: that a person could be so brutal to herself.

There were other stories of people who sought their own death, some successful, some not. I had a closet of infirmary supplies at my disposal. Sharp scissors, a selection of pills, bottles of alcohol and disinfectants. It seemed uncharacteristically careless of Mrs. Holmes that she had not locked the closet.

The woman had been young, newly married, probably no more than twenty; not so much older than me. I watched myself smooth my hair, the way my hand so easily clasped and released, over and over again until I stopped. I *would* stop, I would close the closet doors and return to my bed, perhaps start my book again where I had left off.

I wanted to be alive. I wanted to live. I was not weak. And in order to do that, I would make a home here. I would make a home without my family.

A slice of light fell upon my bedspread, and I could feel someone looming near the bed. Sam, I thought, half asleep; here to pull me out of bed like he did nearly every morning.

"Thea?"

"Sissy," I said, and sat up straight.

"You look like you've seen a ghost!"

"I was surprised," I said, drawing my covers around me more tightly. Sissy did look like a ghost, pale in the near darkness.

"Mrs. Holmes let me come. I'm her favorite," she said, and framed her face with her hands. She waited for me to laugh, but I couldn't.

I was silent for a moment, and so was she; then I switched on the lamp, illuminating us both.

"She probably thinks you're a good influence," I said finally, avoiding her pressing gaze.

"What's wrong, Thea?"

I looked at her briefly. She looked so concerned, so upset for my sake.

"My parents aren't coming to get me." She looked unsurprised. "You knew," I said.

"I figured," she said. "I hoped."

"I want to go home." I was embarrassed by the sound of my voice, thick and overwrought. I covered my face.

"But why?" she interrupted, and gently pulled my hands from my face. "What's so good about there?"

I looked at her incredulously. "I miss it," I said. "I miss my brother."

"Your brother, who hasn't written you a single letter?"

"But," I sputtered, "it's not his fault. You don't know what I did, Sissy." Sissy could not understand. I felt sorry for her, that she hadn't ever loved her sister like I loved Sam.

"Try me." She gazed at me levelly; I'd never seen her so firm.

"But I don't want to try you." I was feeling desperate. I put my hand to my throat. "I want to go home."

She paused. "The rumor was that you

were sent away because of a boy."

"The rumor?" I repeated.

She gave a short laugh. "There's always a rumor. Some girl knows someone who knows someone who knows your parents. Something like that." She tilted her head. "Is it true?"

"Yes," I said, and the words that were both true and a lie tumbled from my throat so easily. "I was sent away because of a boy."

"Believe me, you're not the only one." She felt for my hand, through the covers. Her touch was surprisingly strong. "I'm sorry that you can't go home. But look what you have here — me!" I smiled — I couldn't help it. "And people who send you chocolates." She picked up a box from my nightstand. "What's so good about home? They'd send you away anyway, in a few years, with a husband." She fiddled with the bow on the box and seemed hesitant suddenly.

"Sissy?"

She looked up. "I need your help."

Some people were so easy to read. What would that be like, to wear your heart on your sleeve as Sissy did? My life might be better now, if my heart weren't so carefully tucked away.

"With Boone?" I asked. The cabin had known he was writing her letters, and that she was writing back. She'd shown me parts of them. I could picture his blocky, masculine handwriting.

"I'm in love," she said very seriously. I wanted to laugh.

"How can you be in love with him?" I asked. "You've only spent an evening in his company." Then it occurred to me that this wasn't necessarily the case. "Isn't that right?"

Sissy turned her cheek, and I noticed a small scar near her ear. From chicken pox, perhaps. I thought of my own letter, from David, which had been brief. It was a perfectly reasonable letter, one I should have been glad to have received. But boys were trouble. Boys didn't know how to behave. I'd taken it to the Castle and thrown it into the fire when no one was looking. I knew from the other girls that unless I wrote back, David wouldn't send me another letter. It would be the height of bad manners, to write a lady again when she hadn't responded the first time.

I tapped Sissy's wrist. "Sissy?"

"Only once," she said finally.

"Sissy." The disappointment in my voice surprised me.

"Don't scold me." She took my hand. "I can't help it."

"But if you're caught, you'll be sent home."

"Oh, that would be the least of my worries. My grandfather would murder me. He'd marry me off to some boring Monroeville boy in an instant." She snapped her fingers, then paused. When she spoke again, her voice was softer. "He wouldn't think twice about it." She shuddered. "If I play my cards right, *I'll* decide who I marry. And I won't get caught. Not if you help me." She squeezed my hand, as if entreating me, as if it were up to me whether or not Sissy and Boone could be together. And I saw that Sissy was good, that she had learned to move through this world and love people, and let them love her back; that she did not love too intensely, as I did, or not at all, as I imagined Leona did.

"Of course," I said, "of course I'll help you."

She needed me to help her meet him in the woods at night, after the rest of camp was asleep. My bed was near the window, on which Boone could easily signal his arrival with a tap. And I would sleep in Sissy's bed once she was gone, because Mary Abbott, who was the lightest sleeper in the cabin, faced Sissy's bed. This had been my idea — Sissy had told me how good I was at this. That she didn't seem to appreciate the risk she was taking made me want to help her more. One false step and Sissy would be gone, removed from Yonahlossee as quickly as if she had never existed.

Was there something about me that spoke of a receptiveness to this sort of thing? An explicitness in my nature, some quality I was unaware of that made me bad? This was all fun for Sissy. And I wanted it to be that way for her, because she was not like I was.

I thought about the woman in Emathla who had smothered her child with love. I thought about Mother, how isolated she had kept us, how now she had turned me out completely, had thrown me to the wolves. She had known I was sick, and not even telephoned. Father — he had let Mother have her way with us. But knowing all this, how completely I had been cast out, and how Father could not even bring himself to tell me, made being in this place easier. How could I go home, now? What kind of home would it be? I wondered. Would it be any home at all? Yesterday Mrs. Holmes had told me I could use the telephone. She felt sorry for me. I had considered her offer for a moment, considered the sound of my family's voices, which I had never heard before except in person. And then I shook my head no.

They had kept Sam, because he had not done anything bad. But my poor twin — there was this world here, among other people, and he knew nothing of it.

7

When I left the windowless infirmary after three weeks, the first thing I noticed were the trees, covered now in a brilliant palette of reds and oranges, bright and rich, indescribable, really. The colors, I thought; in Florida the leaves never changed colors, or even died, instead appeared everlasting. I'd read about fall in other places, and Eva had mentioned the colors, but it had happened so quickly; while I had been away, the world turned into a painting; it almost hurt my eyes to look.

I closed my eyes against the electric color. Why should it be surprising that this beauty signaled death? Eva had told me the Indian myth: four hunters tracked a bear into the sky and killed him; he bled scarlet from the heavens, onto the leaves of all the trees as he died.

I had gotten sicker before I'd gotten better, and Mrs. Holmes had kept me confined because she had not wanted to note the health of all the other girls. Thank God for health and happiness, everyone said, or murmured, or shouted, depending on the girl. A chorus as I reentered my camp routine, made my way from Augusta House to the dining hall, clinging to Sissy's arm, out of weakness, but out of shyness, too: the girls had become strangers in my absence. Henny was engaged to a boy from home. Katherine Hayes's uncle had murdered his wife and shot himself in the head upon learning that his railroad fortune had evaporated. A teacher had almost been bitten by a rabid raccoon; Mr. Holmes had heard her screams and shot the animal just in time. Jettie had been caught drinking, for the second time, by Mrs. Holmes; the real story there was that she had been drinking alone. Like a man. She was not allowed to ride for a week, which even seemed a worse punishment than embroidering handkerchiefs. Gossip abounded. And Augusta House was one girl smaller: Victoria had left, gone back to Jackson, Mississippi. The clothing stores her family owned had collapsed all at once, like a house of cards. The bunk above Sissy was empty now, but she stayed put. She said she was afraid of falling.

Camp was smaller now, too, by a third:

the summer girls had gone home.

Mrs. Holmes left every winter for three weeks to visit the vast troupe of Yonahlossee alumnae, scattered about the South. Mr. Holmes could not go, apparently, because he was not Southern, and, as Sissy put it, Southerners liked to exchange money with other Southerners. Sissy had learned from her grandfather, who sat on Yonahlossee's board, that Mrs. Holmes would double the length of her fund-raising trip this year. But no one was supposed to know, lest they think Yonahlossee's fortunes were falling.

"But won't everyone notice when she's gone?" I asked.

"You'd be surprised at how little girls around here notice," Sissy said. "And everyone will be glad to have Mrs. Holmes gone. Mr. Holmes's punishments are half as bad as hers."

I would be glad to have her gone. She knew everything about me.

I was not allowed to ride. The muscles in my calves had grown small during my convalescence, my arms had turned flabby, my shoulders bony. I could hook my hands around my waist if I sucked in all my breath, hard; I had turned weak, for the first time in my life that I could remember. For the first time since infancy.

I slipped away to the barn one afternoon, when all the other girls were studying at the Hall. Now instead of bird-watching, botany, and painting we had history, literature, and home economics; math and science didn't seem to exist in this mountain enclave. We didn't have much homework, either, or nothing that took very much time. I liked literature, unsurprisingly, taught by bland Miss Brooks. She became impassioned, though, when referring to books she loved, and watching her I sometimes thought, isn't that always the way? A dull girl charmed by a book?

Mainly girls gossiped in the Hall, or read magazines. Naari did not seem pleased to see me, as Sasi would have; she didn't know me as well. But it was a comfort to see her, anyway, it was a comfort to smell the smell of horses, to smooth her forelock against her broad face, to pet her impossibly soft muzzle. Like silk, I thought, but no, it was softer than that.

I heard footsteps behind me and turned, expecting a groom. But it was little Decca Holmes, holding a short crop. Holding it out to me, it seemed.

"I found this," she said. There was a smudge of dirt on her cheek. She was very pretty, with her mother's almond-shaped eyes and her father's dark features. Her hair was always braided tightly, in pigtails, but they were loose right now, strands of dark brown hair, almost black, falling in her face.

I accepted the crop. "Thank you," I said. And after that I did not know what to say.

"What's it called?" Decca asked.

"A crop." She seemed to want more of an answer, so I spelled it. But she only looked at me quizzically.

"Crop," she repeated. "Crop!" She held out her hand, and I gave it back to her. "What is it used for?" she asked.

"To nudge the horse along, when he's being lazy," I said. The quizzical look, again. "To hit him. To make him go faster."

"Like a spanking?" Decca asked.

"Exactly."

The handsome groom entered the barn, and Naari swung her head over the stall door at the sound of his footsteps. It was feeding time. Decca jumped back, and eyed Naari nervously.

"Don't be scared," I said. "She's just hungry. She's excited, like you are, for dessert." I thought it was strange that a girl who had been raised around horses was afraid of them. They were the gentlest creatures in the world. But I couldn't remember ever seeing a Holmes girl ride.

"Do you want to give her a sugar cube?" I asked. Decca pushed her hair out of her eyes and nodded.

I showed her how to hold her hand flat, so that Naari would not accidentally catch one of her fingers. Naari lifted the sugar cube from Decca's hand delicately, and then crunched it between her back teeth.

Decca giggled. "It tickled!"

We walked back to the Castle together, Decca's small, sticky hand in mine. I was her friend now, it seemed. Being around her had not made me miss my family more, as I had assumed it would; Decca made me miss my family less. She reminded me of Sam, his curiosity, his quiet intensity. She was so observant, and this was how Sam had been, still was: he watched everyone, everything.

Mrs. Holmes was surprised to see us enter the dining room together, but then she smiled at her youngest daughter, who ran to greet her. Mrs. Holmes tucked Decca's errant hair back into place as Decca spoke. That was what mothers did: they never simply listened. They straightened, and fixed; they ordered their children's worlds while they listened. And if they were good at it, like Mrs. Holmes was, like my mother had been, their children never noticed. Decca sat down for dinner, her hair neatened, none the wiser.

I asked Mr. Holmes if I could speak to him the next day, then followed him into his office, where I'd last been with my father. We passed Jettie, who caught my eye and smiled. I liked Jettie. There was something unaffected about her.

Mr. Holmes's office was full of leather, brass-studded furniture, the brown velvet settee I had sat on when I first came — surely where all the ladies and children sat, behind their husbands and fathers. I wondered if my father had noticed it, or if he had been so focused on the task at hand — transferring the responsibility of my safekeeping to a man he had never met — that the room around him had slipped away.

"Thea, you're feeling much better?"

"Yes, thank you."

He folded his hand underneath his chin. He seemed a little too sensitive to heroically kill a raccoon.

"I have an idea," I began, but that seemed too childish. "I have a proposition."

"Please," Mr. Holmes said, and nodded. "Continue." He seemed amused.

"Your daughters. I'd like to teach them."

"Teach them how, Thea?" There was no gray in Mr. Holmes's hair, as there was in

Father's, and his skin was unlined. He was thirty or thirty-one, nobody knew for sure, and Sarabeth was eleven, which meant he had been very young indeed when he had become a father. A few years older than I was now. While it was rumored that Mrs. Holmes was older than her husband, I alone knew her age, approximately the same as my mother's: thirty-six. It was unusual in those days that the husband be younger than the wife — my own father was five years older than my mother — and I liked Mr. Holmes more for it. His marriage made him seem generous. It made perfect sense that he and Mrs. Holmes had had children as soon as they'd married; age was not kind to women.

"To ride," I said, feeling bolder; something about the way he watched me so closely, almost eagerly, made me want to continue. I gestured at the framed photograph on his desk, the three Holmes girls all in white. "Decca said that she and her sisters don't ride, but that they want to."

"Did she say that?" Mr. Holmes asked.

I nodded. "And Mr. Albrecht would help me. I wouldn't be alone with them."

"I'm not concerned about you being alone with them, Thea." He looked at the photograph. "They do need to know how to ride, their mother and I agree. Especially Sarabeth and Rachel. But Decca seems so young."

I shook my head and inched to the edge of my chair. "Oh, no," I said, "the younger, the better. It will be second nature to her, if she learns early enough."

He looked at some papers on his desk, smiled, as if at some private joke. I waited; I wanted this, I wanted this very badly. And was taking advantage of, or at least depending on, Mr. Holmes's kindness. If anyone would let me have my way in this, it would be him.

"Please," I said, "I need to be around horses. And I'm not allowed to ride until I'm stronger." I hoped my voice didn't sound too desperate, but knew it probably did, because I could feel the desperation surging through my brain. And what I did not say was that I wanted to be around his girls, that they were a family and I had none here. That his presence brought comfort; that being near his daughters meant being nearer to him. I could never say that.

"All right, Thea," he said, after a moment. "You've convinced me. And I will convince Mrs. Holmes."

Did he guess my reasons, which were twofold? Horses and girls, girls and horses.

I wanted to be around children around horses; I wanted to see the Holmes girls learn to love a beast. I wanted their father to watch me.

I was distracted during history class, could not remember the site of Grant's great War Between the States defeat.

"Shiloh," Leona answered when I could not. Sam would have been ashamed — he had all the dates of those battles memorized.

History, then French, then the day was half over; finally, lunch.

"I'll see you," I said to Sissy, who was chatting with Eva. I ran to catch Leona, who walked alone.

"No running," a house mistress called, the voice sounded like Henny's, but I didn't look. I slowed and weaved in and out of the girls making their way to the dining hall, masses of them, so many girls! I'd forgotten the sheer size of us when we moved from one place to another. I brushed a little too close to Alice Hunt and she glared at me; I mouthed an apology.

Leona didn't turn around, gave no signal she had heard me. I was out of breath, my feet were heavy, and I could feel a sheen of sweat forming on my upper lip. I felt desperate, suddenly, unwell and crude.

"Thea," Leona said calmly, when I

reached her side.

"Hello," I said, and settled into her pace. "I wanted to thank you for the chocolates," I said, "they were delicious." Scrumptious, I had almost said, Mother's highest praise, delivered on rare occasions.

"It was nothing. I told my mother and she arranged it."

"She sent them from Texas?"

Leona laughed. "Yes, across the country." I was so close to her I could see a little crop of white-blond hair on her upper lip, blighting her otherwise faultless face. Leona turned her head to look at me, and I felt as if she'd caught me staring.

I blushed.

"No, they were not shipped all the way from Texas." She sounded amused. "They would melt. But they were Swiss chocolates. Could you tell the difference?"

"Yes, of course."

We were approaching the entrance to the dining hall and Leona paused for a beat, took the open door from another girl, and waved me through as if she were the man.

I found my table and slid into my seat. I looked at the meal: fried chicken, a camp favorite; green beans, roasted potatoes. I had no appetite, but the iced tea was still appealing. Henny, a ruby-and-diamond engagement ring now upon her plump finger, had clearly been told to watch my eating habits, and all her sideways glances made me nervous. I took the smallest piece of fried chicken I could find, a wing, and an extra spoonful of roasted potatoes to compensate. The thought of consuming flesh made me sick. In the infirmary, I had begun to picture my lungs, huge slabs of red meat, throbbing, as if they each contained their own heart, turning black at the edges. On days I felt worse, I imagined the black creeping steadily toward the lung's center, approaching. On days I felt better, the black receded.

I listened to Molly pester Henny with questions about the raccoon. Across the dining room, I saw Sissy nodding sympathetically, murmuring to slender Katherine Hayes, whom I recognized across the room by her curls. I wondered if her uncle had the same curls. I felt sorry for her, but wondered if she'd loved her uncle as much as I'd loved mine. I was jealous, too, because she was blameless.

I turned back to my plate. Henny caught my eye, and I tried to smile reassuringly. In another week I would be just another Yonahlossee girl. I'd been sick, I'd become well, I was here again.

8

Dear Thea,

We're told you're well. The mountain air is better for you than the air here, I'm sure. And all those girls for you, all those horses. Are your teachers teaching well?

You haven't sent a letter in almost a month. I hope that your silence is a sign of how busy you are, at the camp.

Nothing seems to have changed — Sam and I continue with his lessons, your mother is out in the garden all day, preparing all her precious flora for winter.

Take pity on your parents and send us a letter. Be merciful, Thea, it is a capacity that God has granted only us.

And nary a week until your birthday. Happy You Day. (I will shout the other half to Sam!) Did you think I would forget? That day was the happiest day of my life, of all our lives.

Love,
Father

It was true, I had not written a letter since I'd been in the infirmary, since I'd learned that I would not be returning home at the end of the summer. I was angry — they'd known I was ill, and had not come to get me — but as my anger dissipated, I saw that I needed to not think of them in order to survive here. I would train myself not to want my family. I needed to live my Yonahlossee life without thinking of how to frame it in a letter for my parents and brother.

I put the letter in my vanity drawer, along with Sam's handkerchief, which I had not been able to bring with me to the infirmary. I had missed it, at first, but then the want had disappeared.

If I had been stronger I would not have opened their letters, which came once a week. Mother and Father alternated the task. They were brief, briefer now that I gave them no reply. I was glum after their letters; Sissy noticed. But I was not strong enough to leave them unopened. There might be some news of Sam inside, or even Georgie.

■ ■ ■ ■

Thanksgiving at Yonahlossee was a small affair, a more elaborate version of Sunday dinner. Sissy was gone for the week, pining away in Monroeville; that she would miss her weekly tryst with Boone, who came every Thursday, would hang over her week like a cloud. Mary Abbott was the only girl from Augusta House who hadn't gone home, and the atmosphere in the dining hall was solemn, almost.

"Thea!" Decca called out when I entered the dining hall with Mary Abbott. I scanned the room and saw that girls sat out of place. I felt sorry for Mary Abbott, who I knew would have jumped at the chance to follow me, but you did not sit at the head table without an invitation, and Decca wound her hand through mine while thoroughly ignoring Mary Abbott, as only a child could.

Decca led me to the head table, where a few teachers sat along with Alice Hunt, who must have also been granted a head-table invitation. Miss Brooks smiled at me, and I smiled back. Mr. and Mrs. Holmes were at either end of the table, as if they were hosting the dinner. Which they were, I suppose. Mr. Albrecht sat next to Mrs. Holmes; he smiled when he saw me. Sissy told me Mr. Albrecht and Mrs. Holmes were friends. Nobody cared, though, because Mr. Albrecht wasn't handsome and Mrs. Holmes wasn't beautiful.

"Here," Decca said, and pointed to the chair next to her, only sitting down herself after she made sure I was settled, even lifting my napkin from my plate and tossing it into my lap. Mr. Holmes watched her with his amused expression.

"Thea," he said, "I'm glad that you could join us. You're quite famous in the Holmes household. Decca especially is your biggest fan." Decca nodded seriously. Sarabeth grinned at me, but Rachel looked as if she had been crying, her cheeks mottled and pink.

"I'm flattered," I said, and I was.

True to form, Alice Hunt barely looked at me. I watched the girls file in and saw Leona, her hair pulled back into a tight bun. She looked straight at me, as if she had caught me thinking about her, but her expression revealed nothing. There had been whispers that her family was suffering financially. That was how Sissy had put it — suffering, as if lack of money was a wound. Which it was, the worst kind. But Sissy didn't believe the rumors, and I hadn't, either — Leona's very bearing, the way she carried herself around the room — seemed wealthy, but I wondered why she hadn't gone home for Thanksgiving.

Mrs. Holmes wore an old-fashioned mourning cameo pinned at her throat, the hair of the dead intricately plaited behind glass. You had to look closely to see that it was hair at all; it almost looked like a piece of textured fabric. I knew from my lessons that the Victorians had been wild about mourning jewelry, just another way, along with séances, they had tried and failed to reach the dead. Or perhaps they had not failed — Father did not believe in spirits, but how could he know, for sure?

Mother had a mourning locket, passed down to her from her great-grandmother. It was pure gold, designating the loss of her five-year-old son. My parents might as well be dead: the thought sprang into my head, unbidden, and I was ashamed. I was a nasty girl, with nasty thoughts.

Mrs. Holmes noticed me looking and her hand went to her throat. It was easy to see how Mrs. Holmes could have been pretty before she'd lost her figure.

I wondered who she had lost, or if she wore the piece for fashion's sake. I wondered how she and Mr. Holmes had met. It was camp lore that Mr. Holmes had defected from the North to the South, and though nobody could say for sure why, the wilder speculations involved gambling debts, a lost love (not Mrs. Holmes).

I had thought that we would be allowed to dress in our own clothes for Thanksgiving, but even the Holmes girls wore starched white shirts. Sarabeth was almost old enough to be part of the first-year class, but I doubted she would ever live in a cabin.

I had begun to love the Holmes girls, especially Decca, who loved me back. Sarabeth, who so resembled her mother, had turned pretty to me, her inherited stoutness transformed into a charming plumpness. Rachel, quiet and afraid of the world, I hoped I would teach to be unafraid, at least as far as horses were concerned. And finally, Decca; her path seemed already lit by a charmed light. She was the natural rider of the three girls, which was perhaps why I loved her most.

I was needed suddenly, and I liked the feeling, being needed instead of needing. Decca held out her arm, and I noticed a diamond-and-emerald bracelet clasped around her thin wrist.

"That's beautiful," I said, and traced the rectangular emerald baguettes that alternated with sparkling round diamonds. It was much too fine a thing for Decca to be wearing; even Alice Hunt studied the bracelet attentively.

"The girls got into my jewelry this morning," Mrs. Holmes said. "Decca chose to ornament herself most exquisitely." She sighed, but not unkindly; the holiday must have put her in good cheer. It occurred to me that Mrs. Holmes had fared better than my mother, at least in terms of jewelry. Mother kept all of her finest jewels in a safe.

Decca beamed. "I'm exquisite!" she shouted, and Sarabeth put her finger to her lips.

The room fell silent, as it always did, but I had never observed so closely how it all worked. Before Mr. Holmes's knees had straightened, the room was silent.

"Hand," Decca whispered, when I kept my hands folded at my skirt, oblivious. Apparently the head table held hands.

Mr. Holmes bowed his head, but still his voice projected, deep and melodious. I watched him as best I could with my neck bent. He thanked God for all the normal things: us, health, happiness, and, because of Thanksgiving, the spirit of generosity.

"And please remember those who are not as fortunate as us, in this time of great instability. May God grant them and us mercy." He stopped, and seemed to want to say something else, but nothing came. A few girls fidgeted. It was hard to hold our attention for very long. "We are not untouched by the tragedies of late. The girls who have had to return home — hold them in your prayers." He had our attention, now. It had never been said, by him or Mrs. Holmes, that the girls who had left had done so because their fathers could no longer afford tuition. We knew, of course, but not officially. Mrs. Holmes frowned, but the source of her displeasure — her husband's revelation or the sadness of the lost girls — wasn't clear, at least not to me.

"Amen," we chorused. Decca held on to my hand, and smiled up at me. Her two front teeth had a gap between them, only a small space, and though I knew it probably would disappear when she lost her baby teeth, I half hoped it wouldn't. She tugged on my hand and laughed, inexplicably, before she dropped it. She was always involved in a game, most often played by herself. Children *were* careless and unpredictable, as I had feared, but that was the fun of them.

"What kind of dressing does your mother make?" Sarabeth asked suddenly, as the food was still being served. The subtext was clear: Why are you here, and not there? Sarabeth seemed to have inherited her mother's shrewdness.

"She doesn't," I said.

"Our mother makes corn bread dressing," Decca said, "for our own Thanksgiving."

"Take your elbow off the table, Decca," Mrs. Holmes said.

"Your own Thanksgiving?" I asked.

"Tomorrow," Mrs. Holmes replied. "The girls have to learn how to cook, how to set a table. They won't be served all their lives. One would imagine." She was ladling gravy as she spoke, her eyes darting back and forth from her plate to her girls. Where would all the other girls learn these things, I wondered. I knew how to roll out a passable piecrust, how to clean a chicken; this year, Idella was supposed to teach me how to put up preserves. But I didn't much care for cooking, or any of the domestic arts.

"Do you eat snakes down in Florida?" Rachel asked. "Alligators?"

I blushed. Eva had told me my blushing was the curse of a redhead, though my hair wasn't truly red. Close enough, Eva had said.

Mrs. Holmes glared at Rachel. "Rachel," she said, "that is not an appropriate question for the table." Rachel nodded. She hadn't meant to be inappropriate; it was so hard to know, sometimes, what was and what wasn't.

"That's fine," I said, and smiled. "No snakes, but I've eaten plenty of crabs. And crawfish."

"Crayfish," Mr. Holmes corrected, and winked at the girls. "We have a Southerner on our hands."

Alice Hunt perked up at this reference, eager, I assumed, to lay claim to the South.

I laughed. "Hardly." But his daughters were little Southern girls, with their smocked dresses and Southern accents and big bows clipped to their hair.

"You're from the southernmost state. What else would you be if not a Southerner?"

"I'm a Floridian. And we're a different breed."

"Unbound by the rules of society and civilization, a breed apart?"

We were the only people at the table speaking, and I felt, suddenly, as if onstage. I was drawing too much attention to myself. Alice Hunt patted the corners of her mouth with a white linen napkin, so gently.

"I can't speak for everyone from the state," I said lightly, but even as I spoke, my voice sounded cold, serious. "But Florida's a different place. And besides, I don't think we're Southern enough for the rest of the South."

Alice Hunt nodded, and I had a feeling it was the first and last time she would ever agree with me. Mr. Holmes looked at me for a long second. Then Rachel, who hadn't touched her food, began to cry. Her arms were crossed, and she looked fiercely at her plate. We all gazed at her, stupidly, before Mr. Holmes broke the silence.

"Oh, Rachel," he murmured.

Then Mrs. Holmes rose. "Come with me, dear."

After they were gone, the table was quiet. "Rachel's had a difficult week," Mr. Holmes said to the table at large, but no one responded. I nodded, and he looked grateful. "She's quite sensitive."

Leona found me at the end of the meal, as I slowly made my way out of the dining hall.

"Thea," she said, and threaded her arm through mine. I looked at her, surprised. "Full moon tonight." We were descending the stairs now, and I looked up and saw the moon was, indeed, full.

I waited for her to say something else — Isn't it beautiful, makes me miss home —

something to account for her arm through mine, for the anticipation that made her voice almost quiver, which was something Leona's voice never did. Leona was steely in her stoicism. Her behavior was rare at Yonahlossee, where there was always a girl crying, a girl giggling, a girl flinging her head from side to side in delight or hysteria or some combination.

"The perfect time for a night ride," she said, and looked at me; her expression was hopeful, and I realized that she hoped I would go with her.

The barn was empty, but we were silent just in case. Mr. Holmes would be disappointed in me if he knew I'd disobeyed the doctor's orders, but there was little chance he'd come down here tonight. Besides, it was more exciting this way, to pretend we might be caught, to pretend that we risked something tonight; there was so little we ever risked at Yonahlossee. We could fail our classes, smoke in the woods, be insolent to our teachers, and all we would get was a warning. It was only boys that were a true risk to one's place at Yonahlossee, one's reputation. For all of Mrs. Holmes's talk of education, of carving a place for women in this world, the worst thing we could do here was give ourselves away too easily.

Leona and I tiptoed, did not let the hard soles of our boots meet the ground, though there was no one to hear except the horses — who all watched us curiously, eyes wide, ears tipped forward, their necks pressed against their stall doors. I slipped Naari's bit into her mouth and led her to the front of the barn; she whuffed into my shoulder, nervously, and I murmured soothingly. She was a ball of energy, and after I mounted she danced beneath me like some sort of overgrown sprite, clumsily, her hooves knocking against each other. She was out of practice, too.

Leona led on a trail wide enough for only one horse. Though Naari didn't like it, kept trying to pull ahead of King, I held her back, slid the bit over her tongue, shifted my weight to keep her attention.

We rode on the trail briefly before we came to a large clearing, where we both let our horses go without speaking, stood up in our stirrups and let them fly beneath us. I was so close to Leona our boots brushed; this was how horses raced, neck and neck. The moon was an orb above us, lighting our way; for a while, there wasn't an ending to this, just the blank space of the field for as far as I could see. I gave Naari her head and felt the stinging cold in my ears, the warmth of my calves where they touched Naari's barrel. My hair, which I had not had a chance to braid, whipped my cheeks. I could do this forever, was how I felt; and what else is there to say about galloping? A feeling so close to fear. One misstep and Naari might break a leg, and I would certainly fall, hurtled to the ground with astounding velocity.

You don't want it to ever end. I knew Leona felt the same way. Naari moved so fast beneath me I could hardly feel her move at all. Father had told us that history was a lesson, a way to never forget what had happened before us. And now I knew from my own experience that you could never leave the past behind. But galloping that Thanksgiving night, the first Thanksgiving I had ever spent away from my family, I *was* leaving the past behind. And however illusory this feeling was, the faster we went, the more of it was lost.

Naari and I pulled ahead — she was small and compact, built to be faster than King — but then I sensed Leona at her flank, and without looking I knew Leona was racing us. Before, I had simply let Naari run, but now I pressed my legs around her throbbing sides and touched her lightly with my spurs, which was all it took. She shot in front of King, whom I could hear breathing furiously behind us.

Afterward, Leona and I walked the length of the field, our mounts spent. I had never raced before, only galloped solo on my pony.

"She's fast," Leona said, which I knew was half a compliment, half a signal that I had nothing to do with Naari's speed. But horses weren't raced without jockeys.

She spoke again. "Other girls don't like me." She paused. "They think I'm cold." And I knew now she was speaking of Sissy, who had used that exact word. "I don't care what they think. All I care about is horses." I watched her profile as she spoke, her square jaw offset prettily by her sloped nose. I looked down at my hands, red and chapped from gripping the reins so tightly in the cold.

"I know . . ." I meant to go on, but I couldn't find the words, let my voice slip into the night. I knew what it was like, to love horses. But I also knew what it was like to love humans. I knew what it was like to want, to desire so intensely you were willing to throw everything else into its fire. There was a reason that I was not at home for Thanksgiving this year. And Leona? Were the whispers true? It did not seem so — she acted the same as ever. Quiet, impenetrable, strong.

I lay in bed that night and thought of Mother. I first sat on a horse when I was still a baby, tucked in the saddle in front of Mother, on her old horse, Chikee. He died when I was seven, and that was when Mother stopped riding for good. I used to pity her, quietly, for not riding. Surely she must have missed it, I thought. Surely it was a loss.

I can't remember being told exactly why Mother stopped riding, but I had a vague notion that it related to the pain that sometimes beset her, the pain that was a result of our births. But Mother did not complain.

Mother brought Chikee to the marriage. He was almost twenty-one when he died, ancient for a horse. He was buried where he fell, in the pasture; Father had to hire several men to dig a hole large enough for him. In pictures he is handsome and dark, with gentle eyes. Mother loved him. It is a simple thing, to love a horse.

Mother said that I rode with my head, not with my heart. And that riding with my head would serve me well in many instances, but it would not earn Sasi's enduring loyalty. I always thought that was a romantic view of it.

I rolled over and faced the window. It was like looking into nothing, the night was so black. I had wanted her there, tonight. I had wanted her to see how I floated above the earth. Would she have loved me, then? Watched me and known in her heart that I was her daughter, her daughter who could ride so beautifully, sit atop and not interfere with a horse going as fast as time and space would allow. Mother, it was as if we were floating. Mother, if you cannot love me with your heart, then at least with your head.

And then a face appeared, and at first I thought I had conjured Mother from my thoughts. But no, a boy. I sat up, my heart racing, though by now I had realized it was Boone. I hurried outside, relieved by Mary Abbott's snoring.

Boone looked at me expectantly, and I realized he must not have gotten Sissy's letter. "She's not here," I said. "She's in Monroeville."

I'd never been this close to him. Usually I saw him briefly, recognizable by his shock of red hair, before I woke Sissy.

But now I was so close I could see his face fall, faintly, as I delivered the news. I knew that he had to borrow a car, drive over an hour, to get here. We stood at the edge of the woods. He took out a slender case and offered me a cigarette with the assurance that I would take it, which made me do exactly that. He cupped his hand around the tip as he lit it, with a silver lighter, and I could see why Sissy liked him. He was quiet and completely at ease with himself.

He leaned against the tree and studied me in his calm way. Meanwhile, I noticed the tip of the cigarette was receding quickly and I tried to take a drag like the stars in the movies did. No one in my family smoked.

Boone smiled. "You've never done this before?" he asked gently.

I shook my head, embarrassed.

"Just think of it like breathing," he said, and demonstrated.

"But with a cigarette," I replied, and he laughed. He wore his clothes casually: a shirt that was pressed, but not crisply; a belt that was cinched around his narrow waist, but not tightly.

I felt suddenly as if we were going behind Sissy's back. She would not like this: me here, with him.

"I should go," I said, and let my cigarette fall to the ground. Boone moved forward and I thought for a second that he was going to kiss me; he crushed the cigarette into the leaves with his shoe and then retreated, and I was such a foolish girl, seeing signs where none existed; believing, always, that I was an object of desire.

"Thea," Boone said, and it was a bit of a shock that he knew my name. "Does Sissy . . ." Two girls passed by Augusta House. I recognized one of the voices as Jettie's.

I turned back to Boone. "Does Sissy?"

"Does she say anything?"

"Many things," I said, and Boone smiled. He seemed earnest.

"She likes you," I said. "And you?"

He nodded slowly. "I want to make sure I'm doing everything right."

I smiled. That was impossible. "I wouldn't worry . . . But you should leave, now. Someone might see us."

I turned, and he said my name again. I looked back.

"David?" he asked. "He's my friend."

I had not imagined they talked about us like we talked about them. But of course they did. I shrugged. "We'll see."

Boone was not the type of boy to press an issue. He seemed very kind. Whatever Boone and Sissy had gotten themselves into — and who knew, really — at least he was kind. Perhaps he would not make her regret him.

■ ■ ■ ■

Dear Sam,

I'm writing in the dark (there's the moon, like a sun, brighter than it ever is in Florida). All the rest of the girls are asleep.

Did you have orange cake? Were there candles?

I would describe how it is here, how different from home, but I don't know where to begin. It is exactly the opposite of home. There are so many girls.

I went for a night ride last week. It was pure fun, Sam. Sometimes I forget why I'm here, sometimes all of that just slips away.

I've never written you a letter before. Or received one from you. Not ever. Do I sound like myself, Sam? How would you sound, I wonder. I suppose you might not be reading this at all. You might like to pretend I don't exist, that I won't ever return home, and I can't say I blame you, Sam, I can't say that at all.

I think of you at home and wonder if you do the same things you did when I was there. I wonder if you and Mother and Father have any new jokes, or if Idella has made any new foods. You won't know this until you go away, too, but it is impossible to think that life continues on without me. Does that sound proud? I don't mean it to be. I think you know what I mean.

When you go away you will see that there are other people in the world besides me. And Mother and Father. There are so many girls here. Hundreds of them. They have names I've never heard before: Harper, Roberta, Mary Abbott, Leona. I like them. Not all of them, but many of them. I think once you have seen how many other people there are in the world you won't hate me as much. Although I know you don't hate me — you were very clear on that point. You hate what I did. But is there a difference, Sam?

I'm teaching three little girls how to ride. Well, one isn't that little — she's just turned twelve. But my favorite, Decca, is seven years old. She reminds me of you — she's good with animals, horses all like her immediately. She's so young. She doesn't know about anything. She asks the strangest questions. Yesterday she asked why I was a girl and not a boy, as if I had any choice in the matter. I don't remember much from when we were six. I remember you.

You can't know how lonely I am sometimes.

I'll stop before I'm too sad. But before I do, I have to ask — does our cousin continue to heal?

Your Sister,
Thea

I knew there was a very good chance that Mother would read any letter I wrote. She might not even give it to Sam. I thought she would, but I wasn't certain; she had always given us our privacy, had called it our autonomy, as if we had any real idea of what that meant. Mother read books on child rearing, and marked passages for Father to read. She considered herself progressive. That Sam and I were allowed to roam freely most of the day was evidence of her progressiveness, of her desire to raise children who thought and acted independently.

Mother had sent me a birthday present, from everyone, though I doubted Sam had any part in it, and a signal from him was all I'd wanted. A pair of drop pearl earrings, with diamond filigree. They were small but beautiful. I tucked them into my vanity drawer without showing anyone. They were her earrings, she wore them on special occasions. It was a mystery, why she had sent them to me. Did she think I'd have a chance to wear them, here? I would, probably, at a dance, but she couldn't have known that. The gift seemed like a gesture, an extravagant one, but I saw it as what it truly was: a way not to see me. They were just earrings, earrings she never wore anyway.

"Happy You Day," Mother would have exclaimed when she first saw us, at the breakfast table, kissing Sam's temple and then mine. "Happy Birthday to You and You."

Last year, for our birthday, Idella had baked a spice cake with orange frosting. She made her own orange extract every year, my great-grandmother's recipe. Last year, my present had been a new dress and two books from Father. I'd wanted perfume from Paris, something I'd seen in a magazine, and I was disappointed I hadn't gotten it. But who would you wear it for, Mother had asked, amused. Sasi?

Last year, things were just beginning in earnest. Sam had received a hunting rifle, and Georgie had been given a matching one even though it wasn't his birthday. Sam had wanted a chemistry set he'd seen in a magazine, not a rifle, and he'd been so disappointed when he'd been handed the long box, clearly a gun.

My parents were always doing that, giving Georgie a present to match Sam's. And my cousin and aunt and uncle were always there, had celebrated all our birthdays with us. As we had celebrated all Georgie's with him. Even his birthday celebrations took place at our house, with a cake baked by Idella, though Aunt Carrie was a marvelous cook. It had never seemed strange. Our house was, of course, where everyone wanted to be. Just the presence of Uncle George and Aunt Carrie's neighbors felt like an intrusion. And we had all the land out back to play on.

I told no one about my birthday this year, not even Sissy, who was pleased that Boone had revealed to me how much he liked her. "See?" she'd said. "He loves me." And I'd had to agree; it did seem that way.

I wondered what Sam had received for his birthday. I should have sent him a book along with my letter; a book where someone makes a mistake and pays the consequences. But that could be any of the books I loved: *The Portrait of a Lady, The House of Mirth, The Age of Innocence.* And Sam would not read a book I'd sent him.

At Yonahlossee we celebrated after dinner, each girl took a slice of an enormous sheet cake; but, mercifully, my birthday had gone unnoticed. Perhaps, in the Thanksgiving preparations, it had fallen by the wayside. Or perhaps Mrs. Holmes had not wanted me to have a birthday celebration. Either way, I was grateful.

9

Last Thanksgiving, I spent the morning in Uncle George and Aunt Carrie's guest room, sleeping and running to the toilet to vomit. I could hear my aunt and mother in the kitchen, cooking; Sam and Georgie up and down the stairs. I loved this chaotic preparation, cursed the illness and my father, who could not fix it though he was a doctor.

I was dozing, half awake; I opened my eyes and saw Georgie, sitting next to me on the edge of the bed.

"You came to visit me."

"Yeah." He grinned. "Yeah, I did."

Perhaps because I had just been asleep, had woken, and my brain had not yet reset itself; perhaps because I had been sick, and now was feeling a little better — I can't say why, but my cousin sitting next to me filled me with an intense pleasure. I felt almost buoyant; my hands tingled. His grin seemed like some kind of path to another world.

"I'm glad," I said, and my voice sounded strange. I touched his hand, above the covers. "Thank you."

"Sam came, too," he said, and I realized my brother was there, sitting in the corner of the room. They had both come to see me, to wake me from my nap. Then Uncle George tapped on the door and told us to come downstairs, and though I'm sure we all went, I'm also sure that I walked around in a kind of dream, still woozy, not completely understanding the pleasure I'd felt with Georgie but greedy for it, not wanting it to disappear.

Aunt Carrie was a marvelous cook, the compliment my father routinely gave her. My mother was not; she didn't care enough about eating her food — picked at her meals, ate half of her plate — to care about preparing it. Her thinness was part of her beauty; her sharp angles carved a space for her wherever she went — my mother was a woman you were required to look at. Mother's beauty was delicate, fragile: a swan's neck, abrupt cheekbones, eyes that could never decide between hazel and green.

Aunt Carrie was plain. In her youth, I imagined, she looked sturdy in that Midwestern way: straw-blond hair, dark blue eyes, a capable figure. When I knew her, Aunt Carrie was what Mother referred to as stocky, in a constant battle with her figure, and I wondered what happened to her figure after the trouble, whether or not she abstained from food in grief or turned to it for comfort. So when I thought of her at Yonahlossee, I saw her in two ways: as slender and pinched, her full cheeks replaced by dull hollows; or obese and slovenly, her ncck folded, her arms ringed with fat. That she would look the same as when I last saw her was impossible.

I woke early the day after Thanksgiving, my sense of time disrupted as it is in illness. I felt completely well. I slept in the bed, Georgie and Sam on the floor; I sat up and saw Georgie was gone. My brother was a lump beneath an old blue quilt.

Aunt Carrie had little flair when it came to decorating. The guest room would have been better plain, in simple solids instead of competing florals. I fingered the duvet cover; burgundy cotton embroidered with gold medallions. Stiff and ugly, the whole room was a study in burgundy — the curtains, the chairs, the Oriental rug. The brooding, mahogany bedroom set. Mother had been acquiring more and more art deco furniture, which was all clean lines and simple geometry. Aunt Carrie's house looked like it was out of the last century.

Still, the house held a certain charm, my family lived there.

The door opened, and a chink of light shone through the curtains and cast a shadow over my cousin's face. I had wished him here and he had come; I felt nervous, suddenly, as I watched him enter the room, watched him shut the door a little too firmly, a thick thud and surely Mother would come see how I was. But no one came.

Georgie was losing his baby fat, developing an athletic posture, suddenly broad instead of awkward. I was still skin and bones.

"Are you up?" he asked.

"Almost."

I lifted the covers and he got into bed beside me.

"I ate some pie for breakfast."

"You couldn't wait for brunch?"

"I'll eat again," Georgie said, "don't worry."

He shifted onto his side, and I could feel him staring. I closed my eyes. The cover rustled, and Georgie put his finger on the bridge of my nose, and traced it to its tip.

"Such a pretty nose," he said, half seriously.

I giggled, and pulled the top sheet up over my face. Georgie's hand was trapped, he moved it to my throat and my breath quickened, but it was not unusual for Georgie and me to find ourselves in intimate postures. We had always had an easy affection with each other, the consequence of being children together. But this felt, I knew even then, in that moment, different. I couldn't see Georgie, his hand rested warmly on my throat. His fingers moved, slightly, and I shivered. I rolled onto my side and faced him, pulled the sheet over both of us. His hand was beneath my cheek, now, his eyes were closed. We were so near I could feel his breath on my face, moist and peppery. I could hear perfectly each intake of breath. I put my hand on Georgie's shoulder; he didn't move. I shifted and felt that my nipples had hardened beneath my nightgown. I arched my back, to be closer to him, and in that instant there was a knock at the door, and Mother entered.

"Rise and shine," she said, and I sat up, flushed, revealing Georgie as well, who had curled into a ball and was feigning sleep.

Mother paused at the foot of the bed, her eyes traveled over me, then Georgie, and I crossed my arms over my chest, though I knew she could see nothing.

"Feeling better, Thea?" Her face was calm and unreadable.

Georgie and I had slept in the same bed just last month. We had done nothing wrong.

"Yes, thank you. Ready for brunch."

"All right," she said. "Georgie, why don't you wake up and come downstairs with me? I think your mother wants you."

My mother had always been a bad liar. Her voice became thin, turned up at the ends of her words.

I sat in bed after they had gone, a little stunned.

"Morning, sunshine," Sam said, and I jumped. I had forgotten he was here. He lay on his pallet, his head propped up by his bent elbow.

"You're up?"

"Evidently." His voice was strange, and he would not meet my eyes, stared at some spot near the door. He had a perfect view of the bed. I wondered how long he'd been awake. The tone of his voice — sullen, brooding — made me feel as if I'd been caught a second time.

We ate brunch, and I watched, relieved, as Sam's sour mood lifted, as he and Georgie competed over who could eat the most crepes. "Sam," Aunt Carrie said, "it's time for *you* to grow."

Mother had cast her glance sideways at Aunt Carrie at that comment, but that had been the only note of tension I'd noticed. Nobody had uttered the word *Miami,* for which I was grateful. It had been a place I only knew about, because of our orange groves there, but never visited; now it was where Uncle George had been imprudent.

Father made me take a sip of his champagne to settle my stomach. I waved goodbye to Georgie from the back window of the car, stopping only when Sam tugged at my sleeve, pulling me down next to him. I sat down willingly. I felt guilty, though I didn't know why; like I had done something wrong, though I couldn't have said what.

The day after Thanksgiving, Mother and Idella disappeared into the basement and emerged with our Christmas decorations: glass ornaments so fragile we weren't allowed to touch them; four hand-carved wooden reindeer purchased from a catalogue; a long, slender Santa whittled from a single piece of wood. A silver nativity set passed down for generations through my father's family, Spanish names engraved on the underside of each figurine: José, María, Jesús.

The next week, as we sat in the sunroom with Father for our lessons, we heard thumping and pounding as my mother and Idella put everything in its proper position.

"Do you think they need help?" Sam asked, his finger planted somewhere on his book so he would not lose his place.

Father ignored him, and I kept reading: we were in the middle of mythology, which I loved. So expansive and lovely, those gods and their heavens. We were supposed to keep quiet while we read. Father was strict about this rule, at least as strict as he ever was.

I raised my eyes and met Sam's gaze; he watched me impassively. I lowered my eyes and returned to the tale of Narcissus.

I wore an old dress of Mother's, a cotton shift with a square neckline. The dress hung on my frame. I was of average height for a girl my age, but almost too thin. Because I only rarely saw other girls my own age, only had Mother to truly compare myself to, I didn't realize that girls were not immediately women once they reached a certain age, that there was an awkward dividing period. I was too comfortable in my own skin, perhaps. I wore Mother's old casual dresses because they made me feel more adult.

Father closed his book, signaling our lesson was over.

"All right," he said, "you may go attend to your other, more pressing matters, like helping your mother." He smiled. Sam and I stood; I went to my father and kissed him on the forehead before I left the room, flattening my dress against my chest with my palm as I leaned over him. Half girl, half woman.

Later I helped Mother wind Christmas greenery through the banister on the front porch's staircase, then above the windows. The sun shone directly overhead, mean today; I was hot, my skin felt thin, my underarms and forehead were beaded with sweat. Mother worked hard, and fast. Father said she was more efficient than any man. More and more, Mother liked me to help her with house chores. When I complained, she told me that I had to learn, that keeping house was an art. And, of course, my complaint was oblique: we never challenged Mother or Father, especially Mother.

When we were done, we stood in front of the house and admired it. Mother always liked this part — after she set her table for a holiday she would gaze at it for a few minutes, taken by its beauty, admiring her delicate china and starched linens.

"They look like eyebrows," I said of the greenery above the windows. "Thick eyebrows. Like the house is watching you."

I wasn't happy, out here doing this tedious work while Sam was doing whatever he pleased.

I waited for my mother to finish gazing. She started to say something, but seemed to hesitate, which was unusual: my mother never hesitated.

"Georgie is coming to stay with us for a bit," she said, finally.

I said nothing. Georgie often stayed with us. Yet I could feel her unease. I thought she was going to bring up the money. I didn't care about the money. "Damned foolish," my father had said to Mother, when they thought we weren't listening. But we had been, me and Sam. It was easy to eavesdrop — they'd never seemed to notice that the door to their bedroom blocked no sound — but usually there was no need, their nighttime conversations were of no interest to us.

"Aunt Carrie's mother is ill. She's going there to be with her."

"There" meant somewhere in Missouri, the tiny Midwestern town that had always sounded awful: small, flat, plain.

"Georgie's going to be here for a few weeks, then," Mother continued, "and he'll sleep in Sam's room this time. With Sam."

"Why can't he stay at his own home? With Uncle George?" Though I did, in fact, want to see Georgie, I was angry — what did she mean, that Georgie and Sam would sleep separately from me? We had always slept in the same room. Don't cut off your nose to spite your face, I told myself.

Mother didn't scold me for my tone, which was cross; she looked pensive instead.

But then her face resolved itself into seriousness, and I looked down at my shoes.

"Uncle George has to be in Miami."

That was enough. I understood — she could stop. But she would not.

"To meet with his bank. So Georgie will be coming here, because a sixteen-year-old boy cannot stay alone for a week. He'll bring his schoolwork with him."

I raised my head and was met by Mother's firm gaze, her stern face. This was how she looked at you when she wanted acquiescence; if Sam were here, he would have kicked a puff of dirt, or shrugged, disguised as putting his hands in his pockets. But I only ever knew how to meet Mother's gaze.

I shifted my eyes and looked beyond her: such a view my home provided. Stands of giant oaks, broken occasionally by orderly groves of orange trees. Miles of thick green growth. Nothing seemed far away, there was so little opportunity for perspective in all the flatness. This lack of distance had always been comforting to me, since I was a child, everything so close even when it wasn't.

"Why can't I sleep in the same room?" I asked. I felt near tears.

She pulled me close before I had a chance to react. "Don't cry," she said. She smoothed my hair, which she knew I loved. I relented.

"Thea," she murmured, "you're getting older."

"I'm not."

"It's natural. It's the way things happen. Do you understand?" She cupped my chin in her hand and tilted my face up.

"I feel the same."

"But you're not the same. You'll still be close, you and your brother and Georgie. But there are certain things you can't do anymore. Do you understand?"

I nodded.

"Say it, please." Her voice was kind but firm.

"Yes."

"Oh, Thea." She patted my cheek. "Everything will be fine. It's just sleeping."

I slipped from her grasp and trotted away.

"Be good," she called from behind me, a phrase uttered so often it meant nothing.

I was mean to Sasi that day. He was sluggish over the cross rails, warming up, and I pointed my toes out and jabbed his flank with my spurs. This was a problem we'd been having for the past few weeks, this clumsiness over the cross rails; there was always a problem, a difficulty, when one rode: that was the whole point of the endeavor, the constant striving. And this reaching depended both on me and my mount, and, more generally, on our natures. I was obsessed, as Father said; at the very least I was a perfectionist. And a horse was a dumb animal, clearly he could not want the same things that I wanted, but he could want to please me, and today I felt no eagerness from him.

And then it was over, quickly, as my fights with him usually were: we fought deeply and briefly.

As I was turned in the saddle, examining the welts my whip had made on Sasi's flanks, I saw Sam perched on the fence, one leg hiked up, his chin resting on it. I wondered how long he'd been there; I wondered if he'd seen me turn the whip over in my hand so that I could wield it more powerfully. Would he have even known that was wrong? Mother would have. She would have made me stop, immediately, no, no, no, her voice an incline.

I nudged Sasi forward. His head hung low. I had exhausted him. He would forget; he might have already forgotten. But he wouldn't forget the fear, and the memory of pain would be replaced by an instinct of mistrust. That was the problem with horses; they were too dumb to remember properly, but there was still a memory to contend with, a memory that could not be reasoned away.

"Georgie's coming tomorrow."

"I know," I said. I tried to smile, but the effort felt too great. I watched Sam sitting there with his leg hiked up. I could never hike my leg up like that; even in breeches, the posture would be terrible manners, unladylike. I knew that other twins, the twins I read about in books, were identical; I wondered how it would be if Sam had been a girl, like me. It was the first time I had ever wondered that. We would both have to sleep separately from Georgie, then. We would both have started menstruating.

Sam tilted his head, trying to read my thoughts, and I smiled. Sam as a girl was impossible. I was our only girl.

"I have to sleep separately from you and Georgie," I said, pulling Sasi to a halt. He stopped willingly.

Sam nodded. "I know. Mother told me." He paused. "All we're doing is sleeping, Thea."

I nudged Sasi into a walk again so Sam would not see my red face. I was furious Mother had told Sam. We were not the same person, after all.

"Thea?" Sam called, but I ignored him.

Sasi stood still and tired in the cross ties as I sponged warm water over his tense muscles. I traced the cross-stitch of raised lines the whip had left on his haunches. I felt ashamed. I put my arms around Sasi's damp neck and he hung his head low. He loved me. I could feel his enormous heart, pumping in his plump pony's chest. Drawings of his pretty face were in all my notebooks. Sorry, I wanted to say, so sorry, but knew it was useless.

I felt sorry over Sam, too.

Usually I was calm and fair while riding, even when I was frustrated. I promised myself that I would not allow it to happen again. That I would not be so easily undone. I told myself I would be different next time, but what good were those promises, made as they were in the calm of the aftermath.

"Go," Georgie said, and folded laced fingers over his eyes. Sam and I ran in opposite directions, quietly, the air crisp and cool, the sun bright, one of Florida's perfect winter days.

I tiptoed into the barn, so that my heels would not clap against the cement floor. We'd been playing for hours, and I was tired, ready for dinner, but I would not be the one to suggest finishing.

"Hello," I whispered to Sasi, who stood at his hay, munching impassively. This was a lazy hiding spot, one I'd used before; I was hoping Georgie had forgotten. Or would come into the barn last, like he usually did. I was losing this game. Our rank was figured according to a complicated system. The more dangerous the spot, the more valuable. The rules never changed, but we were always adding new ones, so that the point of the game had unofficially become, over the years, that you were never safe.

We were too old to be doing this, Georgie nearly seventeen, Sam and I newly fifteen. But Georgie had suggested playing, and Sam's eyes had lighted up.

I crouched in the front corner of the stall, underneath the feed trough. This was not a hiding spot worth much, Sam was probably at the top of our oak tree. I watched Sasi's slender, knobby legs; each time he swallowed, his entire throat leapt like a wave.

Georgie appeared in the stall window. He'd crept around the side of the barn so quietly I hadn't suspected. I pressed my spine into the cold corner and prayed Sasi wouldn't move.

"Hey there," Georgie said, and made an uncertain kissing noise with his mouth. Sasi swung his head around.

Georgie waited for an instant more and then he was off. I slunk out of the stall, tiptoed out the same way I had come. When I reached the end of the barn, I peered around the edge instead of making a run for it straightaway, and this was my tactical error.

Georgie, creeping along the barn's outside wall, saw me and smiled.

"I knew you'd be in here," he said.

I took a step backward, out of his sight.

"Don't even try," he called. "I don't want to run."

I ran anyway, toward the other end of the barn, but even though we were matched in speed (I was fast, for a girl), Georgie had the advantage, had me trapped, as long as I was inside and he was not.

"I told you I didn't want to run," he said, as he met me at the other end; I turned the other way, but it was too late. He grabbed my dress and I tripped to a stop. I expected him to let me go immediately and continue for Sam, but he held my dress and tugged me to the wall.

"What did I tell you?"

I looked at him. This was not the way we played.

"Go get Sam," I said.

"I told you not to try," he said.

He put both hands on my shoulders, suddenly, and pressed me to the wall. I could hear Sasi rhythmically chomping hay.

I relaxed under Georgie's grip; his face was so close to mine I could see the faint, scattered stubble of his shaved moustache. I hadn't known he'd started shaving.

"Very bad, Thea," he said, and smiled, and I smiled, too, and then he was gone, to get Sam.

I was restless, restless. I went to bed at the same time as Sam and Georgie and listened to them talk through our closed doors and then there was silence, and I was still awake. I felt the curve of my breast beneath my nightgown, the swollen tip, the smooth, smooth skin.

Usually I stayed in bed until sleep came, but tonight I wanted out. I stood outside the boys' door and listened for snoring, signs of sleep.

The French doors that closed the living room from the lower landing were fragile, all glass panes and brass fittings, but I knew how to open them quietly. The Christmas tree rose to the ceiling and we'd had to trim the top in order to fit the angel: faceless, hairless, dressed in a luminescent gold gown. Idella's cousin delivered our tree every year. I wrapped my blanket tighter around my shoulders, shivered.

Whenever I see a Christmas tree now, adorned with a mismatched collection of ornaments, I'm embarrassed for it. Mother's tree was beautiful: purple and red glass orbs, handblown, because of this slightly irregular — you could see the place on each where the blower had folded over the hot glass, closing the globe. The ornaments were so thin they seemed almost liquid when the tree was lit.

Mother used candles to light the tree, dozens of them, held by special glass holders. It was dangerous but beautiful. The rage then was to use electric, colored lights, red and blue and orange and green — but

Mother hated all that color, thought it vulgar.

Someone was on the landing, then walking down the stairs, then the seventh step groaned and I knew it was Georgie; we all knew to skip that step.

"Shh," I said, as he came through, but he caught the sharp tongue of the lock with his hip. I drew in a quick breath: the door rattled, a hollow, familiar sound that was likely to wake Mother. If she found us, I knew she would think I had not been good. And my explanation — that I had done nothing, that Georgie had followed me downstairs — well, she would not believe me. I saw all this clearly as I watched Georgie walk past me, toward the front door, and I was chilled, then furious at my cousin.

"Stop," I hissed, but Georgie was already half outside; he looked back at me and beckoned. I ran to the door, needing to reach it before Georgie closed it roughly.

"What are you doing?" I whispered, as I pulled the door almost closed behind me.

"I'm watching the moon," he answered, in his normal tone.

"Watch it from inside."

He shrugged, and turned to me: "No." His voice was sluggish, sleepy. When he looked at me, his eyes were off center, distracted.

So I watched the moon, too, full and fat.

"How long are you going to stand here?" I asked.

"Why?"

"I'm cold."

"You woke me," he said. He seemed moody, this visit, spent more time in Sam's room, alone. He said he was reading, but Georgie never read.

"How did I wake you?" I had been so quiet.

"I always know where you are, Thea," he said.

"Only God always knows where I am," I replied softly.

"Is He watching now?" Georgie asked, also softly. He took a step closer. Another one. And then he was an inch or two from my face, his breath milky and thick.

"Of course," I said, but I had lost track of what we were talking about.

He touched my hair, and then let his hand fall to my neck.

We examined each other: my blanket had fallen from my shoulders, I was naked and cold underneath my white nightdress. My eyes were large from exhaustion. Georgie's face was swollen with sleep, his features babyish. Sweet — he looked sweet. His hair had gotten even longer in Aunt Carrie's absence, fallen forward over his eyes and lent him an air that was equal parts raffish and shy.

He put his face closer to mine and kissed me on the lips. Then he touched my cheek, and kissed me again, and parted my lips with his.

I knew that we were kissing, but I had never seen anyone kiss like this. Father kissed Mother on her cheek in our presence. People in my books kissed, but *this* had never been described, how warm Georgie's tongue was in my mouth, how strange and lovely it felt, in equal measures, as if the strangeness made it lovely.

I was not raised in a house where pleasure meant guilt. And this — Georgie's tongue in my mouth, like a live thing, the face that I had known since birth so close now, closer than ever before: this was bliss.

10

The Holmes girls waited at my cabin door. "Hello," they said, almost in chorus, and claimed my hands. They had stopped curtsying after the first week. Mr. Holmes stood with them, watching with an amused expression. His hands were in his pockets, and he inclined his head when I smiled at him. I hadn't spoken to him since Thanksgiving, a few weeks before.

I noticed the other girls' glances. Thea Atwell and the Holmes girls, plus Mr. Holmes.

Girls waved to him as we passed, girls I'd never spoken to: Roberta, Laura Bonnell, Hattie. Mr. Holmes acknowledged them with a dip of his head, but he didn't take his hands from his pockets.

At the barn, I cross-tied Luther and Bright, and the girls curried in a frenzy, stopping only to knock their combs against the wall. Bright was an old, black pony, who had wise eyes: many, many children had sat on his back. I watched and pointed out missed spots. Mr. Holmes kept his distance from the horses, especially Luther, which was funny: ponies were notoriously mean, horses gentle. Everyone was eager today; Decca lifted Bright's hoof and pointed to his tender frog, then showed her father how to dislodge the dirt with a pick. Bright's forelock was tangled, and Rachel unknotted it gently.

After we'd tacked the horses, we led them to the ring where we rode; Mr. Holmes stood outside the ring and watched, in a pose all men seemed to adopt — his arms rested on the top rung of the fence; one leg hiked up to the middle board, his knee bent.

Mr. Holmes watched Decca work through her routine — the same routine I'd worked through when I was a young girl, which Mother had taught me — leaning into the ring like he owned it, like he wasn't afraid of horses.

"Your legs are so strong, Decca," he called out, and Decca nodded, pleased.

My father's German friend, Mr. Buch, once told me I looked Turkish in profile. The comment had delighted me; I liked thinking I looked like someone from another place. I was careful not to let on, lest Sam think me vain. You were supposed to be pretty, you were supposed to be beautiful, but you were not supposed to care.

I wondered what Mr. Holmes thought of my profile, if he had ever seen a Turkish girl. Probably not.

"Change beats," I called to Decca, who was mastering posting. "Good," I called again.

We'd developed our own language; or, rather, the girls had become fluent in my tongue. No one had fallen yet, or even come close. I fell all the time, in my youth, and luckily never sustained more than a sprained ankle. But I fell because I was a daredevil, and no one watched me. The Holmes girls were always watched.

Later, after they had dismounted, Mr. Holmes praised them. "Good, girls," he said, and though Decca and Sarabeth beamed up at him, Rachel wedged herself between Decca and her father and took his hand.

Decca looked outraged, but then Mr. Holmes held up his other hand.

"I have two," Mr. Holmes said, and Decca accepted his hand, and I thought how different Sam and I had been from the Holmes girls, who competed with each other, who always, at least in my presence, tried to court their father's attention, tried to walk a little bit ahead of the other sisters.

Later the girls stood in the barn's wide corridor, Bright and Luther in cross ties, and curried away saddle marks. I stood in the tack room, where I could keep an eye on them, and cleaned, wiped the sweat off the bridles, the grass off the bits.

"Do the girls do that?" Mr. Holmes asked.

I jumped. "Pardon?"

"I apologize. I sneaked in." He moved closer, examining my handiwork. "Do the girls do this usually?"

"They know how and Sarabeth does a good job, but Rachel and Decca are too small."

"Too small to clean?"

"Too uncoordinated."

Mr. Holmes nodded, and examined my handiwork. He smelled thick, like oil. I was an expert tack cleaner, the buckles on my bridles shone, the brow bands gleamed. He made a sound — a sigh? — and lowered himself carefully on top of a trunk. I massaged balm into the reins and waited for him to say something else. But neither of us spoke. I could see him out of the corner of my eye, and it seemed that he watched me, intently, and I began to enjoy our silence, which felt companionable but not completely neutral: we were both aware of each other.

Mother had taught me how to clean tack, how to make stiff leather supple, how to extend the life of all the equipment you needed for riding. I had always taken good care of my tack, taken pride in this task, which pleased Mother. I was her daughter, in so many ways. We both appreciated order.

Girls came in and out with their saddles. Leona came in, a saddle blanket damp with King's sweat over her arm, and dipped her head in my direction. She had been warmer to me since our night ride, but almost imperceptibly: she caught my eye more often, tilted her head in a nod when we passed each other at the Castle; at the bath-house she had even murmured something about how the night ride had done King good. After we had finished with the horses, Mr. Holmes escorted us back to the Square.

"I'll be seeing you soon, I'm sure," he said, and the girls also thanked me, a chorus behind him. It started to rain, lightly.

I waved.

"Such an opportunity," he said, as I turned away, "for the girls to learn about horses."

"The pleasure's all mine." I remembered my first day here, months ago, Father by my side, Mr. Holmes a stranger.

I wasn't as good a teacher to the girls as Mother had been to me. She had always been able to anticipate what I would try next — how I would shift my weight in the saddle, how I would tug the right rein instead of the left — what Sasi would try next, and this prescience had made her an eerily good teacher. I saw that now. I wasn't as good at predicting what these girls would do, but of course Mother had known me better than I knew the Holmes girls. Her prescience had extended beyond the ring: she knew when Sam had rushed through his arithmetic, when I had used a nice towel to clean up a mess. Mother knew everything. But she had not known about Georgie. It had all happened right under her pretty nose.

I turned from Masters — a charming cottage, really, covered with birch shingles — and joined the mass of girls also returning from the ring. Perhaps Mother had sent me here partly because she was angry at herself, for not realizing what was happening in her very own house. For not knowing me as well as she thought she had; for not stopping it.

Sissy ran up beside me, eager to hear about the headmaster watching me teach. I smiled at her, the crowd of girls milling around us. I was one of them. We would stop at our cabins first and change quickly, but we would not be given long enough to wash away the smell of horses.

On Christmas Eve I was the only girl left in Augusta House. Even Mary Abbott's family had scraped together the money to bring her home. Mainly, the girls who stayed were scholarship girls. And then girls who made various excuses: their family was traveling this year; it was too long a trip for too short a time. I had made that excuse, exactly, and for me it seemed at least a little bit conceivable: Emathla, Florida, was very far away from the Yonahlossee Riding Camp for Girls.

The night bell had rung hours ago, but I couldn't fall asleep. It hadn't even been a question in my mind, whether or not I would return home for the holidays; of course I wouldn't. We had sung carols at the Castle tonight, trimmed a giant tree. I had been spared an inquisition by the Holmes girls, because everyone who had not gone home sat together, at a large table; the Holmeses sat at the opposite end from me. Decca had found her way onto my lap by the end of the dinner, but she was too young to care why I had not left.

I heard something outside and thought it might be Boone again, not knowing Sissy had gone home. But of course it wouldn't be him — he was surely home with his perfect family, exchanging perfect gifts.

Someone laughed, but the sound was eerie. It seemed to be coming from right outside my window.

I heard it again, the same laugh, high-pitched. It chilled me to the bone, one of Mother's expressions. I peeked outside my window, very carefully. I saw the back of a girl, dressed in her white nightgown, without a coat, her hair wild. She turned and I recognized her squat profile: Jettie.

I bundled myself up and hurried outside, one of Sissy's extra coats in my hand.

"Jettie," I whispered, "why are you out here?" I handed her the coat but she shook her head. Her eyes were glassy, and she held up an amber-colored bottle.

"I'm very warm already," she said. "I don't need a coat."

I put my finger on my lips.

"Why?" she asked, even more loudly. "What could happen?"

I placed Sissy's coat around her shoulders and took the bottle away. She was moving too slowly to stop me.

"If Mrs. Holmes saw you," I said, "she'd

have a fit."

Jettie smiled. "I'd just get Henny to save me. She's Mrs. Holmes's favorite. They're cut from the same cloth. May I have my bottle back, please?"

I sat down next to her. "As long as you keep your coat on," I said.

"It's a deal." She took a swig from the bottle, like a man. "Thea Atwell. You were big news when you came. Katherine Hayes told everyone there was some trouble with a boy." Jettie looked me up and down, frankly. I pulled my coat more tightly around me. "But nobody cares about you anymore. That's the way of the world."

"You're drunk," I said.

"You're right." She laughed her odd laugh. "I know why you're not home, but do you know why I'm not home? I'll tell you," she continued. "If you can keep a secret."

"I can," I said cautiously. I wasn't sure I wanted to know Jettie's secrets.

"My father lost his job. So now I have to marry. And I don't want to." Her voice had turned fierce. "That's the last thing in the world I want. But Mother says I have to. And Henny says I'm selfish. What do you think?" She brought her face very close to mine — I noticed a faint scar on her temple.

"The boy you're going to marry, is he nice?"

"He's not a boy," she said. "He's a man. He's old. Rich. Tobacco rich. And he's nice enough, but I don't like them. Men. There's something wrong with me. I'd prefer being alone."

She looked like she might cry. I took the bottle from her and tilted it to my lips. I almost spit, the taste was so strong.

"I'll tell you something else." She began to cry then, in earnest. "I don't want to leave," she said. "I don't want to go away from her. From here. I don't understand. It's not as if we're starving. We aren't Appalachians." Her gaze drifted off to the distance.

Yonahlossee, an island of rich girls in the middle of the poorest. I thought of Docey, her family. We had put together a box of Christmas food for the Mill Girls: ham, pie, potatoes. Mrs. Holmes had said it would be delivered in time for Christmas dinner.

"Thea," Jettie murmured, "life is so hard once you grow up."

"Maybe it's better," I said, finally.

"What?"

"Not to like boys. Men. They're nothing but trouble."

She looked at me for a long second.

"Don't be a fool, Thea."

I smiled, then poured the rest of the bottle onto the ground while Jettie watched. More liquor would only make her sadder. She rose then, and walked unsteadily away. She looked like a pony: short and sturdy.

"Remember," she called. "It's a secret."

I traced my lips with my finger, mimed throwing away a key.

I woke the next morning and the world was white.

I slipped on my boots and stepped outside without my coat into a foot of snow.

"Hello," someone called, and I saw Mr. Holmes, walking across the Square, carrying a wrench.

I waved and crossed my arms. I should have dressed before coming out here. My hands were chapped. I needed gloves, but did not want to write and ask Mother.

"Merry Christmas," he said. "One of the pipes burst." He brandished his wrench. "There's no water in the Castle, and our handyman is home for the holiday." He stopped when he reached me, a single line of footprints behind him.

"I've never seen snow before," I said — "not like this."

"No?" He looked around, at the expanse

of white, white everywhere, on the roofs, on the trees, on the mountains. "I love the cold," he said.

He was wearing an old coat, the top button missing. "I suppose it makes you miss home," I said.

"You remembered." He looked pleased. "Yes, it reminds me of Boston."

"I've only ever known heat. But this," I said, "this is beautiful." And Sam was not here to see it.

"My mother used to say God was angry when it snowed, but I've never seen it that way."

"What is He then, if not angry?"

Mr. Holmes laughed; a white puff. "Contemplative." He paused. "It seems as if you're liking Yonahlossee, Thea."

I nodded. I was turning colder and colder, but I didn't want to leave. I started to speak, but stopped.

"What were you going to say?" he asked.

There was a little red nick above Mr. Holmes's lip, where he had cut it shaving. He and his family would celebrate their own Christmas, before we gathered for dinner in the Castle. I wanted to be there, with him. I wanted him to invite me. I suddenly wanted it very badly. Ask me, I thought, as he watched me expectantly. Ask me.

But of course he would not. I was not a Holmes. I wondered if this would be my last Christmas without my family, and understood in that instant it would not: I could see so many of them in my future, unfurled before me, empty. I did not know where I would be, but I knew my family would be absent.

Mr. Holmes was still watching me, curiously.

"I like it here," I said. I paused. I didn't trust my voice. "But I miss my home, too."

He seemed unsurprised. "Of course you do, Thea. Of course you do."

My Christmas present from home: a cashmere coat, deep burgundy, with silver-plated buttons. *Merry, merry, happy, happy,* the card read, the writing someone else's, the saying Mother's. The tag was scripted with the name of an Asheville clothing store. Held to my face, in the mirror, the coat made my hair shine against the red. I unfastened my braid and took a handful: it was getting long, growing quickly, thick. A strange portrait I made in the silvered mirror, my eyes swollen with sleep, my lips dry from the cold, the coat bold and opulent. I touched the mirror. Mother had never even seen the coat, the color. It was an extravagant gift — unlike her, and unlike me. She must have felt guilty, not bringing me home even for Christmas. She didn't know that I wouldn't have gone if they'd offered.

I stuffed the coat into one of my empty drawers.

Last Christmas we hadn't exchanged presents. Mother had told me and Sam about it beforehand, and though I had grumbled at first, Mother had reminded me that Georgie's family was troubled — she'd used that exact word, *troubled* — and we didn't want to trouble them further. And besides, she'd added, we don't need Christmas presents; we have all we need already, don't we? And what was there to say but yes, though I would have liked a new bridle, a smarter pair of breeches.

A few days before Christmas we'd built a bonfire. Aunt Carrie was back from Missouri, her mother better. We stood in front of the fire for what felt like a long time. Father put his arm gently around my shoulders. Mother and Idella came out with mugs of cocoa.

"Oh, no," Aunt Carrie said, smoothing her hand over her plump stomach.

I watched my cousin while I ate and tried very hard to pretend I wasn't, wasn't watching or interested in anything at all, particularly. He stayed close to Sam, deferred to him, it seemed. We never drank cocoa. It was too rich, I felt heavy as I drank and so I tipped my mug into the fire. I felt Mother watching me, so I focused on the fire, the smoke and the sizzle.

We were all quiet, that night. It's tempting to assume we all knew we were on the cusp of something.

Georgie stayed away from me until the fire started to fizzle and the men decided not to add wood. I was over-warm, and seated a foot or two farther away from the fire than everyone else. Georgie left his mother's side and knelt next to me, but he was silent and I was glad. I uncrossed my arms — the air had a bite to it — and rested my palms on the cool grass, and Georgie leaned back and rested his dry hand on top of mine. We were blocked from sight, it was not a brave gesture. We sat like this for ten, fifteen minutes, and what I felt in that short time, the anticipation, the pleasure, the eerie feeling of bliss — well, this was all still new to me. A week since my cousin had kissed me, and I was another person. Or perhaps not another person, but I suddenly cared about completely different things, and that seemed the same thing.

We had not kissed again, or even spoken of it. But Georgie touched me, now, all the time, held my hand in the barn like it was nothing. We had moved so easily into this; and now I wanted more.

The next day I sat alone on the front porch steps, watching our quiet yard. Georgie had replaced Sasi in my daydreams. I thought about him more than I had imagined it was possible to think about something, which was to say, always.

The front door whined. I turned, and Georgie stood in the door frame. This all seemed like magic. I had been hoping he would find me, and he had; there was something so delicious about the way he courted me in my home, the way he seemed to always find me. When I saw him now, when I was close to him, my groin throbbed and then there was a slickness between my legs, which seemed to come almost immediately. He smiled back, but his head was inclined and I couldn't tell if he was shy or smug.

He sat down next to me and put his hand over mine.

"We shouldn't," I whispered.

"Everyone's out back." He kissed my forehead, and I drew back, stunned, and I couldn't sort out why: that he would be so bold, kissing me where anyone could see, but also the pleasure of his lips on my forehead.

"Georgie."

"Can't I kiss my cousin on the forehead?" he asked. He challenged. He seemed so large next to me; if I had seen him as a stranger in town I would have thought he was a young man.

I touched his cheek. I liked how small my hand was next to his face.

"Did you shave this morning?" It felt thrilling, to have the right to ask this question.

"I did." He stopped my hand and pressed it to his cheek, then kissed the base of my thumb. I wondered where he had learned to do all this. This Georgie was a stranger to me.

I drew my thumb across his lips; he bit it, gently, and my breath caught. I turned my head because this all, suddenly, seemed too much, too good, and I felt dizzy with the pleasure of it. The large bed of ivy in front of my house was blurry, but then a clear spot at the very edge, which gradually came into focus: my brother. I wiped my hand on my skirt and stood; Georgie jumped up next to me, and I waved at Sam, who had walked around the side of the house without me noticing. He nodded in our direction, his hands in his pockets. Take one out, I thought, take a hand out and let me know you saw nothing.

I put my hand over my mouth and turned to Georgie.

"Don't worry," Georgie said, "he didn't see anything." But it was all a guess, whether or not Sam had seen.

On Christmas Eve I sat between Georgie and Sam at the dining-room table.

I wore a gold silk dress that Mother said brought out the red in my hair. It was the last time I would wear it — the bodice had become uncomfortably tight, and by the time I had another occasion to wear a dress so clearly meant for a party, glimmering and unserious, I would be too broad and tall. But I wanted to wear it once more, and ignored Mother's suggestion to choose another dress.

I wore Mother's mink stole also. She lent it to me as if I were playing dress-up, which I was, but now the stole felt more mine than hers. Last Christmas I had been fourteen and all the same people had been here.

Father said grace. Georgie caught my hand under the table and held it, briefly. In my quick inventory of the table, everyone's head was still bowed. The last part of Father's prayer was for the orange groves. This was not unusual. Mother exhaled audibly.

"Amen," Uncle George added, "let us all praise citrus."

My father looked at his wineglass. I knew he was considering how to respond, that the glass simply bought him time. It seemed my father was always buying himself time, had a thousand little tricks he used to think before he spoke.

"Do you jest?" he asked. The word was so formal, like we were reading Shakespeare, and I felt so intensely uncomfortable.

Georgie watched the adults, carefully; I wanted him to pay attention to me, not them. I touched his hand, underneath the table.

"A man can pray for whatever he wants, can't he, Felix?" Uncle George asked.

My uncle was tense tonight, as everyone was. You could cut it with a knife — the phrase lingered in my head.

Then Georgie's hand was in my lap, on my knee. It was hot, even through my dress.

"Please," Mother said.

"It's true," Father said. "I suppose."

Then Georgie was moving his fingers up

and down my knee so gently, so rhythmically, that I wanted to moan. He did it for so long — three minutes, four — that I lost track of where he was. He was higher on my thigh, no, he was lower; he was too high, he was not high enough.

I put my hand on his and stopped him. It was madness, to touch each other in front of everyone, especially my brother. My thighs were trembling. The adults were talking about the Gainesville Christmas pageant, which my mother had read an article about in the newspaper; something lighthearted, chosen to counter the doom that had settled on the table, and though it wasn't working, though Aunt Carrie still looked like she might burst into tears, I thanked God that something had their attention. Thank God for Christmas pageants, I murmured, and Georgie laughed, quietly, but Sam looked at me strangely.

I'd never put much stock in dreams. Sam used to wake from nightmares, choked and panting, and all he could tell me as I held his hand was that he was falling from a great cliff, that a second before he met the ground he woke.

I never quite believed him, because I couldn't imagine such an insubstantial feeling, rootless, all in my brother's head. After the bonfire I fell asleep quickly and dreamed of Georgie, touching me. He felt through my underwear, gently, then harder, and then he put one finger inside of me. Then two. I woke not knowing where I was, the pleasure so intense I thought I must still be dreaming. I was on the cusp; I put my fingers where Georgie had, was surprised at how firm I felt against the pressure of my fingertips, the pressure that was felt more deeply here. Then I touched outside my panties, as Georgie had. I was wet, soaked through. Bright sparks flashed against my eyelashes. More, and more, then nothing but the tight, quick pulse in my groin. I rubbed my forehead with my wrist, my hands needed to be washed.

This sort of pleasure wasn't yet a secret, like it would become later. No, it was a thing that had never existed, so there was no attendant shame.

Sam woke me Christmas morning, tapped my shoulder gently. At first I thought it was Georgie.

"If you want to ride," he said, "you'd better do it now."

"All right," I mumbled.

"Merry Christmas," he added, as an afterthought.

"Merry Christmas," I said. He watched me as I sat up in bed, rubbed the sleep from my eyes. I smiled, and he smiled back, but his smile was off, somehow. For an instant Sam was inside my head, knew about Georgie.

Sam tilted his head and I felt a great surge of relief: he did not know.

I shook my head at him, and smiled again, to let him know everything was fine, and though Sam nodded, I knew he did not believe me.

I wanted to try a new jump that I'd built out back. In the ring commands were nearly invisible, it was supposed to seem as if you and your horse were in complete and silent agreement. But out here, the ring behind us, Sasi would only listen if I jerked and threw my weight, slammed my legs against his sides, shouted. It was ugly riding, but it felt truer.

I'd left my spurs in the barn. When I squeezed my legs against his sides, normally a command he half ignored, Sasi exploded into an elaborate trot, neck arched, ears forward, paying attention to everything but me.

I'd come out here for exactly that reason: I needed power, I needed him to clear the highest jump he ever had, not for me but because the jump was pointed into that great and mysterious beyond.

I realized as soon as I turned that I'd given us too much space — too long a straight line, too much time and reason for him to run away, for me to lose control. But I felt him gather his legs beneath him, in clear anticipation of the jump. "Yes, yes, yes," I murmured, in rhythm to his canter. My braid thumped on my back, my vision narrowed, and I was only aware of the particular way Sasi's hooves hit the ground — the hard sound that made — and the closing distance between us and the jump. It was all instinct now, there was nothing anyone could teach you about this instant before leaving the ground. "Now," I said, and we flew. I wished Georgie were here, watching. Then Sasi's left shoulder dropped and I was off, on the damp grass, but I still had the rein, I hadn't let go. "It's fine," I soothed, "it's fine." He half pulled, half dragged me away, rearing backward, scared, but also aware of the opportunity: if he could get rid of me, he could run away, listen to his brain, the deep part that told him to go, at any cost.

But I held on. I loved this pony; I would not let him go for anything. After he calmed down, I remounted. I pointed him toward the jump a second time, and we cleared it without incident, as I knew we would. This was how my mind worked, this was why I was brave in situations where others would not have remounted. The fates wouldn't align to throw Sasi off balance again, not twice in one day. You fell once in a while because that was your due, you rode a horse and expected him to do things he would not have done in nature. You fell once for every hundred clean jumps.

I sneaked upstairs after I had cooled out Sasi and fed him his morning oats. I stood at my brother's door and opened it a sliver.

Sam had returned to his bed, Georgie slept on a pallet on the floor. I was surprised that they slept apart — Sam's bed was large, there was room enough for two.

Sam's arms and legs stuck out at awkward angles, and his hair was matted down to his cheeks by sweat. His brown quilt had fallen to the floor, and his sheet was tangled between his legs.

I looked at him first, almost without seeing him. I looked because he was there. And then Georgie, Sam's comforter draped over his torso. He wasn't sweating. Perhaps it was cooler on the floor. He slept almost primly, his arms beside him in straight lines, his bare feet aligned, toes upward.

Georgie shifted, and I saw a brown flash as he threw off the comforter. He murmured, almost a groan, and then I saw his penis, erect through the opening in his pajamas. It was darker than the rest of his skin, had a purplish tint. I'd never seen a man naked, nor talked to anyone about male anatomy, but somehow I knew that my cousin's penis was erect.

I turned away and closed the door behind me. I felt ashamed, but complicatedly: he should not have shown me that, I should not have had to see, but he had been sleeping, he had not meant to.

Then I felt the opposite of ashamed: I felt a little powerful, like I knew a secret, a moment all my own.

11

"Boone is coming tonight," Sissy whispered. "Will you help?"

"Of course." The stakes were lower now that Mrs. Holmes was gone; everyone knew she was the one who disciplined us. She had left last Sunday, after worship, and would be gone for six weeks. When she returned it would be spring, which seemed impossible: everything was dead now, except the evergreens.

Through the window, night was black. We had just entered what Sissy called the doldrums: February. The sun set by five o'clock; we walked to dinner in total darkness now. Sissy said this was the most boring part of the year, when nothing happened. But I liked the calm.

I was riding again. I'd had to gain eight pounds before Mrs. Holmes would let me back in the saddle; I might have protested more if I hadn't been riding in secret already.

I still taught the Holmes girls, by my own request, at least for a little while, until they joined Mrs. Holmes at her mother's house in New Orleans. Mr. Holmes told us to write our mothers and encourage them to attend their Junior League or Garden Club meetings, where his wife would make appearances. It went without saying that all our mothers were members, yet my mother was not. She belonged to Emathla's Camellia Society, but for the flowers.

I watched Mr. Holmes and decided that he did not seem any worse for the wear, given his wife's absence.

Mr. Holmes came to our lessons once or twice a week, I never knew when he would appear, a specter perched on the side of the ring. Without realizing it, I began to anticipate his presence.

I lay awake that night until I heard Boone's rocks. He threw softly but precisely: from the sound it made, it seemed like Boone hit the same exact spot every time.

At the third rock, I rose.

"Sissy," I whispered. I shook her thin shoulder. "Sissy," I said again, and squeezed her forearm. She was sleeping in her clothes.

Her eyes opened slowly, and when she saw

me she started.

"It's only me," I put a finger over my lips. Her warm, vinegary night breath rose. You would think that such a delicate girl in such a delicate situation would be a light sleeper, or would not have fallen asleep at all. She rose and left.

We love each other, she had told me when explaining the gravity of the situation: we can't go too long without seeing each other. I smiled — she even kept the love of her life waiting. That girl was not on time for anyone.

"Sissy?"

I quickly slipped into Sissy's bed: there was no moonlight tonight.

"What are you doing?" Mary Abbott's voice was sleepy. I listened until I was sure she was asleep again. Out of all the girls, she would tell. Not out of spite, but because she was odd, had an odd conception of men, boys, the other sex. Whatever one wanted to call them.

They were no mystery to me. I fell asleep thinking, half dreaming, I was Sissy. They'd only kissed so far. But they would do more, they wouldn't be able to help themselves. Of course Boone would want it, and this was understood: he was a boy, he had urges, he could not be helped.

When I woke, Sissy stood over me, her hair wet. Rain beat against our roof. We exchanged beds, but I had trouble falling back asleep, could not stop imagining Sissy and Boone's embrace.

That charged, restless night, the threat not realized: Mary Abbott made no mention of hearing anything.

On our way to the barn the next morning, the Holmes girls' necks wrapped with scarves, Sarabeth spoke. "Our father's coming," she said happily, "to see me."

I squeezed Decca's hand, which I'd been holding, and she looked up at me curiously. I felt light-headed from lack of sleep, and now, happy. I should be more careful. But careful of what? I wasn't sweet on him; half of camp was sweet on him, the only man for miles and miles, except for the grooms, and they didn't count. But I liked that he spoke to me as if I were an adult.

"Us," Sarabeth quickly corrected, but Rachel had already taken offense, was staring at her sister with narrowed eyes.

Sarabeth could afford to be nice now, having already revealed her father's true intention. There were moments when Rachel seemed mean, but I could never tell with Sarabeth. They were children, sisters who fought over petty things. Sam and I had never fought; further evidence, according to Mother, of how charmed our life was. She had fought with her brothers, and Father with Uncle George. But we were twins, two sides of a coin.

I was sliding the bit into Luther's mouth when Mr. Albrecht told us that a tree had fallen in our ring last night, crashed into a rail during the storm. I paused and the bit clicked against Luther's teeth; he shook his head.

"It's fine," Mr. Albrecht assured me, stroking Luther's muzzle, "the tree is small. Most of the ring is still usable."

Sarabeth led Luther, Decca led Bright past the tree.

"Pat his neck," I told Decca, as she walked Bright by the tree, "talk to him."

Bright flung his head up suddenly, the rein snapping.

"There's a bird." Rachel pointed. I noticed a faint red scratch on her wrist. "I think it's hurt."

I knelt down in the sand. An owl, with its oddly shaped head, was nestled between the branches, so brown it blended into the leaves. It was clearly terrified, had resorted to keeping still because it couldn't fly. If Sam were here he would have known what to do, whether or not the injury to its wing was reparable. I guessed it wasn't.

"What do we do?" Rachel asked, her voice whiny.

"Leave it alone," I said, perhaps too harshly. My mood was spoiled. Mr. Holmes was coming to watch the lesson, and now this. If the owl tried to leave the tree, the horses would spook.

I made a fast decision. Sarabeth was already mounting Luther. Decca was pulling down her stirrups.

"Girls," I said, "do not come near this tree. The bird is hurt. It might scare the horses. So stay away." They all nodded obediently, even Rachel.

I stood at the center of the ring while the girls warmed up. I could see Sarabeth out of the corner of my eye. I focused on Decca, who was mastering posting.

Rachel sat on the fence, her slim legs twined through the slats. At first she sat there quietly as usual, her pale face calm. Her hair was braided in pigtails today, which made her look young. All of the Holmes girls had their father's hair: dark and glossy.

Then, again out of the corner of my eye, I saw Rachel come down from the fence to walk around the ring, timidly, as was her style, but also quickly.

"Rachel?"

"I'm going to look at the tree." Her voice again whiny.

"Don't you remember what I said? You'll scare the horses." I shook my head in disbelief.

"I just want to see."

I signaled Decca to slow Bright to a walk. "Rachel," I said, trying to make my voice a warning.

She acted as if she hadn't heard, her thin frame tilted forward. Sarabeth had halted Luther and sat straight in the saddle, watching her sister.

"I'm just looking," Rachel said. "I'm bored to death."

"It's almost your turn."

Rachel continued to walk.

"Rachel." My voice was high. She looked at me, her head cocked, and I saw she was daring me. My vision was blurry from the cold. "Rachel, sit down. Now."

She smiled, and for an instant I was relieved — she was going to pretend she had been joking — but then she took another step.

"Father's coming," Sarabeth murmured, and Rachel hopped onto the fence, resumed her waiting stance. Mr. Holmes smiled; he was thinking of something else, holding out his hand as if to ward off conversation.

I turned to Decca, my mood ruined. I wanted Mr. Holmes to be happy.

"Ask him to trot," I said.

Decca flapped her legs.

"Softly," I reminded her. "Gently. What you ask him should be a secret. No one else should be able to tell."

"I'm bored," Rachel muttered, but quietly so that her father would not hear. Decca ran through her exercises, and I turned my attention to Sarabeth. I almost forgot Rachel was there.

"Pinch your knees harder," I called. "Relax your elbows."

"Decca's just sitting there," Rachel called back.

"Rachel," Mr. Holmes said, "that's enough." Rachel looked as if she might cry. I was pleased by his anger. Rachel deserved it.

"Come, Decca." And I led Bright to the side of the ring, next to Mr. Holmes, so that Sarabeth could practice on the diagonal.

"Rachel," I said as we passed, "one moment. And you'll have an extra ten minutes. I want your father to see this."

Rachel ignored me. I took mean pleasure in making her wait.

"She's learning how to change leads. See how she moves her legs? Right one back, left one forward?" Changing leads was an advanced technique, and Sarabeth wasn't really ready for it, but Luther was so well trained, such an old schoolmaster, that a monkey could have gotten him to do it.

"And he switches."

"Yes," I said.

"Like he's skipping." Mr. Holmes drummed his fingers on the fence in rhythm to Luther's canter. Changing leads was something even someone completely unversed in horses could appreciate: it did, indeed, look like skipping. He bit his nails, I noticed. Men didn't wear wedding bands back then, so there was nothing that I could tell from his hands except that his skin wasn't rough from riding or another sport or hard work.

"She's good," I said. Mr. Holmes nodded. I wanted him to take more pleasure in his daughter's trick, in the things she could make Luther do already, but he seemed distracted.

I unclipped the lunge line from Bright's bit.

"Get down?" I asked Decca.

Everything happened at once then. Get down, I asked, but it was more of an order than a suggestion. I had taught Decca to slide both her feet out of her stirrups before swinging one leg over the saddle; this was lucky.

"Rachel," Mr. Holmes said, almost yelled, his deep voice cleaving the cold air. "I've had enough. Enough!" Now I knew for certain that Mr. Holmes was referring to some past wrong of Rachel's. She had been difficult today or for several days.

When I looked over, I saw that Rachel was gone from her spot on the fence, and Mr. Holmes was striding toward her. My impulse was to laugh: I had never seen Mr. Holmes angry, and it scared me. Rachel backed into the branches of the tree, watching her father, and then she started to speak.

"No!" she said, quietly at first, then louder and louder until her voice had reached a shrill pitch. "No, no, no, no, no, no!" She looked possessed. She was much too old for a tantrum.

"The bird," Decca cried as the owl flew straight up, out of the tree, and then faltered, diving unsteadily toward Luther. Luther backed up, quickly, his neck arched, his ears pointed forward.

"Thea," Sarabeth called, her voice trembling. I could barely hear her over Rachel. "What do I do?" I dropped Bright's rein and hurried toward Luther, speaking quietly and calmly. Out of the corner of my eye I saw Mr. Holmes kneeling in front of Rachel, his hands on her shoulders.

"It's fine," I murmured, "it's fine."

But as I approached the owl leveled out, flying past me so close I might have touched him. His wing was crooked.

"Thea." I turned and Sarabeth was pointing in the opposite direction, toward the gate I had left open. Bright had backed out of it, and I could see the liquid red of his flared nostrils, the whites of his eyes. His ears were flattened against his head. He reared back quickly, and Decca fell forward onto his neck.

"Slide off," I yelled. "Slide off!" Rachel was still yelling, and I had to scream as loud as I could to be heard, and still it wasn't loud enough.

Bright took off then, as I knew he would, and raced toward the barn. It was the worst kind of mistake, a novice's error, to have left the gate unlatched. And I remembered so clearly not having closed it: an instant of carelessness, in the same category as leaving a girth too loose.

"Thea," Mr. Holmes said, and he sounded almost calm. "Stop him." I broke into a run as Bright disappeared. When I rounded the corner, I saw that he was running at full speed now, flat out, as horses only do when they are terrified. Decca clung to the saddle. She wouldn't fall off now unless she made herself. But she was frozen.

The riding groups had all halted in their tracks, a dozen still horses, ears forward, waiting to discern the cause of the alarm. Alice Hunt watched me, not Bright, her face a mask of horror. That I had elicited a reaction from even Alice Hunt, who never seemed to react to anything, terrified me. Leona stared directly at me, her face wide and blank: she shook her head, once, as if she'd known my teaching the girls would end in disaster.

Mr. Albrecht climbed over the fence, yelling, "Turn him, turn him, turn him, turn him," until the words acquired a particular rhythm, until it seemed as if Mr. Albrecht was saying, "Tune him, tune him, tune him," his vowels arched in panic.

"Stop him," I heard behind me, "stop him now." The instruction was useless. Decca screamed, a sound so horrible, so close to a moan, I put my hands to my ears. Just then Bright veered left at the head of the trail; Decca fell the other way, to the right. Her head was not kicked: this was also lucky. It could have been kicked so easily. She fell cleanly, slid out of the saddle almost gracefully.

Mr. Holmes caught my shoulder as he sprinted past me, and I fell to the ground.

"Get the doctor," Mr. Holmes shouted as he passed. "Now."

Decca's eyes were closed, as if she were sleeping.

I rose and began to run, in a single motion. I looked back, once, at the girls on their horses, still standing as if statues. Sarabeth had dismounted, was crying quietly next to Luther, did not turn her head when Mr. Albrecht ran in front of her in pursuit of Bright, who might be lost in the mountains forever if he was not found quickly.

I emerged from the cover of the forest into the Square and screamed, "Henny!" — again and again until she emerged angrily from the house mistresses' cabin.

"Decca's hurt," I managed, and Henny yelled to Docey, who had followed her outside, to call the doctor immediately. We ran back through the woods, Henny so far ahead of me I lost sight of her brown skirt. Her speed surprised me. My chest felt like it was boiling, I could hear watery sounds when I inhaled. I slowed to a walk, tried to pace myself. I wanted rain, or snow, or wind. Something to make me feel not so alone. I wrapped my arms around myself.

No one noticed me when I materialized from the woods. The girls and their horses had disappeared. Mr. Holmes was kneeling next to Decca, had made himself small next to his daughter; Mr. Albrecht had his hand on her forehead. The first-aid kit was open next to him, the iodine overturned and running into rivulets. Sarabeth squatted nearby, rocking back and forth on her heels.

I focused on the pattern the iodine made in the dirty-beige sand. A complicated design, improbable and random. But I hadn't seen any blood.

I went to Sarabeth and smoothed her dark hair, removed a leaf that had gotten caught in her braid. Someone had taken Luther back to the barn. Her upper lip was covered with mucus, and she was crying, silently. I'd never comforted anyone besides Sam. And that was second nature to me; or it used to be, when we were young and so much a part of each other. Now I went to Sarabeth with Sam heavy in my mind and embraced her, and I was surprised at how eager she was to be comforted: she rested her cheek on my shoulder, and clutched my waist.

"It'll be all right," I murmured. I don't think Sarabeth heard me, but maybe later the memory of the words would resonate.

She would believe me. She was a child. Father had told me things would be all right, and I had believed him.

Rachel was nowhere to be seen. I would have hidden, too. She had hurt the wrong sister. Rachel was the sister who needed to be told it would be all right, that her world and her family had not collapsed. But whoever told her this would be lying. And it would not be me — I did not have the heart for it.

12

Word spread quickly through the camp about the youngest Holmes girl. There was an unfamiliar car parked behind Masters, where a girl would not notice it unless she looked. The doctor's car, I knew. Decca was hurt, it was just a matter of how badly. She had lost consciousness; I knew this was a bad sign.

On my way back from the bathhouse — for I was filthy, covered in dirt and sand — I saw a gaggle of young girls, Molly among them, whispering dramatically. She waved at me, brightly, and when I half-heartedly waved back she galloped over to me. She was still all arms and legs, like a filly. Her cheeks were bright red from the cold, her hair tied into some sort of knot. If Mrs. Holmes had been here to see it, she'd have sent Molly back to her cabin to repair her grooming.

"Thea! They're saying Rachel lost her

mind! That she tried to kill Decca!" Her voice was practically a squeal.

I wasn't taller than many people, but I was taller than Molly. I bent down and encircled her wrist with my hand. I could feel her bones like a bird's beneath her skin.

"Molly," I said, "that is nonsense. Do you understand me?"

Molly nodded, slowly, and I saw a gleam in her eye that had not been there before. I had handled this all wrong — I should have laughed off the rumor, brushed it away as if it were no more than a speck of dust.

I released Molly's wrist. She stared at me, her eyes wide in anticipation. What would I tell her next? What could she bring back to her clutch of friends, who were all waiting just ahead? Molly wasn't part of a group of girls that mattered, but still — gossip multiplied so quickly here, spreading through our ranks. Katherine Hayes walked by, coolly, but she was listening to every word. She'd rush back to her cabin and disseminate the information thoroughly and coldly. I glared at Katherine, who hid behind her screen of curls. She, who had so recently been the subject of the camp's scrutiny, should have sympathy for Rachel. But now her uncle was two months dead, and talk of him and the Hayeses' errant ways had disappeared. I saw Miss Brooks across the Square, her nose in a book. The adults at Yonahlossee were useless.

And there was always truth to the rumors, sometimes just a morsel of it, but still. Everyone must have heard Rachel screaming. And what of me, who had put the girl I loved most in harm's way because I wanted her father to watch me? I turned back to Molly.

"It was an accident," I said, loudly and uselessly.

The last time something terrible had happened, I had tried to explain myself, also loudly and uselessly. But I was smarter now, or at least not as foolish. I retreated to Augusta House and pretended to sleep, ignored even Sissy, whom I could feel behind me once or twice, waiting for me to turn around, to give a sign. Finally she left, all the girls did, for dinner. Life went on, it always went on, and Decca could be near death but still Yonahlossee would feed its girls three square meals a day. It had seemed so cruel, at home, that Mother still neatened my bed in the mornings, that Father still left after breakfast to call on his patients.

I could not force the image of my cousin from my mind, and I was usually so good at precisely that, at living a life at Yonahlossee that had nothing to do with Georgie, or Sam, any of them. I saw Georgie when I opened my eyes, when I closed them: not as he was when I left him, but as he had been when I'd known him best. Mother would be so disappointed in me. I realized that part of Yonahlossee's comfort was that it was a world completely separate from home, and now the two worlds felt like they were eerily merging, and why? Because of me, Thea Atwell, a wrong girl if there ever was one.

"Thea," Sam had said, over and over and over. "Thea, Thea, Thea."

I sat up in bed and pressed my fingernails into my forehead. I wished I could dig through my skin and skull into my brain, remove my memories of Georgie, of that day, entirely. But what of my soul? I knew from Father that though our brains stored our memories, our souls were the reason we remembered in the first place. And there was no way to get at the soul. The pain from my fingernails, though small, distracted, brought relief.

I was still in bed when Mary Abbott brought me a roll from dinner, knelt beside my bed, and unwrapped it from an embroidered handkerchief.

"Here," she whispered. The other girls

filed in: Eva, Gates, and then Sissy, who raised her eyebrows behind Mary Abbott's back.

"Thank you." The roll was cold and doughy in my palm. When warm, these rolls melted in your mouth. The air ruined them.

"You're welcome."

Mary Abbott stayed beside me, twirled a piece of hair around her finger, avoided my eyes. There was a faint rash across her forehead, where her wool hat chafed. The sight of her, so peculiar, suddenly enraged me.

"Do you need something?"

She looked at me, unsurprised. "Aren't you going to eat that?"

I shook my head.

"That's fine," Mary Abbott murmured. The other girls were preparing for bed; Eva's creamy shoulders, her back dotted with black moles; Sissy's fine, knotty hair, freshly brushed, a pretty gold bracelet on her wrist, which meant Boone would be coming again, two nights in a row. I felt like something awful was going to happen. I could smell it.

"Mr. Holmes came out and gave us a speech. I thought you'd want to know. Was I right?" she asked, suddenly bold, her cold, sticky hand upon mine.

I slid my hand from under hers, nodded.

"I knew you would." She smiled, but to herself, she'd made a bet and won. "He came out for prayer. He asked us to pray for Decca and his family. And then he asked us to pray for you, Thea." She paused. "For you and Decca."

Sissy watched us, from her bed. But I was all Mary Abbott's now.

"Are you glad he asked us to pray for you?"

"I'm flattered," I said, and closed my eyes, "and tired." Though it was not unusual to be mentioned in Mr. Holmes's prayers, right now his request felt like a betrayal. He hated me. Why had he ever agreed to put me in charge of his children? He knew something of my life in Florida. He knew enough to know I shouldn't be trusted. But now he hated me, he had to — since I had hurt one of his girls, what choice did he have?

"I thought you'd be glad, when I was walking over here I thought you'd be happy." Mary Abbot leaned in, conspiratorially. Her breath was dry and hot. "Because he's not mad."

I made my voice as cold as ice. "Leave me alone."

Mary Abbott backed away, but not before

leaning forward, so quickly I could not shield myself. I turned, and she caught my lips with hers.

I slept dreamlessly, hot and itchy, woke up dozens of times, unreasonably frightened, the tall bunk beds and the white-clad girls in them unfamiliar, terrifying. Then I calmed myself, it was a trick sometimes, remaining lucid, convincing yourself that the world had not arranged its enormity in opposition — to you, against you. I say I calmed myself but truly my mind was merciful in deciding not to unhinge itself as it had in the days before I was sent away, when I wept until my eyes were ugly pouches in my skull.

"Thea."

I sat up, startled.

"It's fine, it's fine," Sissy soothed, "you're fine."

"I'm hot."

"Are you feverish?" She felt my forehead with the back of her hand. "No. You were talking in your sleep."

"What did I say?"

"Nothing, babble. Are you all right?"

I nodded. "Have you heard anything about Decca?"

She shook her head. "I prayed tonight. I

haven't prayed in so long . . ." She trailed off. "What happened? Everyone's saying Rachel tried to kill Decca, that she lost her mind."

"An owl," I whispered.

"An owl?" she repeated. When I said nothing, she continued, "The doctor is here. Mr. Holmes must be worried sick."

"Mr. Holmes is alone," I muttered. Eva stirred above us. "I'd forgotten," I said, lowering my voice. I brought my hand to my mouth. My fingers smelled of leather.

"Thea, I have to go. Boone's here."

"Don't go," I said, "please."

"Oh, Thea," she whispered, and kissed my forehead. "I have to. But I'll be back."

She stood. Her hair was tucked into the back of her coat, her gloves stuck out of her pocket like hands. I felt the unpleasant bite of jealousy: I wanted so badly to be Sissy, going to meet a boy who loved me.

Sissy waited for a second, and then pointed to her bed impatiently.

"Oh!" I whispered, and went to her bed, a little wounded — all of these things had happened to me today, and still a boy was more important.

After she left, I rose, put my coat on, and stepped outside. Then, nervous I might have woken Mary Abbott, peered back into the cabin through the window. Mary Abbott slept almost peacefully. Eva's arm and head were flung over the side of the bed, hanging inertly. I couldn't see Gates, but I knew she slept in a tight ball, like she always did.

None of my sleeping cabinmates needed to concern themselves with the danger outside — as far as I knew, there had never been so much as a Peeping Tom at Yonahlossee. Danger presented itself, every girl knew, from within the family — your father's mistress; mother's thorny relationship with her mother-in-law, your grandmother; the first cousin who had tried to kill himself. But we were no one, nothing, without our families.

If anything happened to Decca, the youngest, the best and favorite of the family, Rachel would have ruined her own life as well as her sister's.

With a brief and distant shock I noticed a light beyond the Square where Masters was, not a part of the Square but not completely away, either; within eyesight, in case something happened, in case a girl needed something.

My boots stuck in the mud as I walked, their soles made a quick, sucking sound each time I lifted a foot; the noise was disgusting, and that was all I could hear, the night was so quiet, so utterly dead: Florida nights were never like this. There was always a chirping, a scuttling, a howl.

It was cold, the air was still, the sky was dark, but it's necessary to understand how dark. The stars were barely there, the twin gas lamps that bordered the Castle burned steadily, always, even during daylight, but they meant almost nothing in the face of so much black. So the small light, illuminating a Holmeses' window — it felt to me like it *meant* something: the light surged, ignited the reptilian part of my brain, and I wanted to move toward it, I wanted to be inside that house, that home, so badly I could feel the desire rise in my throat.

I began to run, clumsily, through the mud, stopping twenty feet from Masters. I confronted it. I was frantic, I knew that I could not trust myself but I also knew that I needed to speak to him.

I turned and retched into the mud. I felt dizzy, suddenly, unmoored. Beyond Masters was the forest, which led to the mountains; I could disappear into those woods. And who would miss me, if I left? And for how long, before my absence brought relief? I was already mostly gone from my family's life. Because I had done this once before, I had been careless. I had let desire dictate everything. I closed my eyes, tried to stop the world from spinning. If Decca was hurt beyond repair, then I would disappear into the woods. If Mr. Holmes hated me, if I had ruined another family, I would leave this place.

"I thought we knew each other," Mother had said, in my parents' room, where I had gone to find her on that other horrible day; she lay on their made bed, the yellow light of the late afternoon illuminating her delicate features, her head propped up at an odd angle. "You're not the girl I thought you were."

Who was I, then? When Georgie was pressed against me, I lost all reason. I acted dangerously with him and I would not have cared if both my dead grandmothers were listening at the door. All the various pressures of a boy against my body, the kneading, insistent pressure of his hands; the light, live pressure of his tongue; the almost unfelt pressure of his penis pushing through the fabric of his pants.

"Enough." I spoke now, startling myself, one of my tricks.

And because I was acting dangerously, I bridged the distance between myself and the Holmeses' front door, noticing how Mrs. Holmes or one of the girls had taken care to cover the pots of rosemary that flanked their door with old sheets, then fasten them with a neatly tied ribbon. The door was unlocked, as I had expected; I opened it slowly and slipped through; it was all darkness inside, a warm, dense darkness.

The Holmeses' stairs were spotless, the walls hung with family photos, silver frames dusted, gleaming. The portraits surprised me: to me, the Holmeses were a family without a place or past, even though I knew everyone had a past, and even though I knew specific details of their past: my mother, Boston.

The light came from upstairs.

It had been months, I realized, since I'd climbed stairs in a home — I'd forgotten how noisy they were, and my boots were still on. I half hoped the groaning stairs would announce me. I shrugged my coat off when I reached the top.

I could see the light at the end of the hall, pooling out on the pine floor so clearly.

I passed closed doors. I wondered where Decca and her sisters lay.

I noticed all his books, first, so many books the room reminded me of a library, a place I had been only once, in Gainesville, with Georgie and Sam. Those boys were on the tip of my brain tonight; everything I saw reminded me of them.

Mr. Holmes stood at a desk in front of the window, reading a newspaper. He turned a page, and I saw a grainy photograph, but I could not tell of what. It was an impractical place for a desk, where he could not see anyone enter, where the sun would bleach his things, his books, his letters, his photographs. But I understood why the desk was there: he could see everything below, all us girls coming and going through the Square; and beyond us, the mountains. Always the mountains. I touched the door frame.

"Who's —" He turned and glanced at me, startled. He was fully clothed, in a white dress shirt and herringbone trousers. He wore monogrammed slippers.

"You shouldn't be here, Thea," he said. He set the newspaper onto his desk, and I thought how different this man was from my father, or Uncle George. Or Sam or Georgie, for that matter. He didn't know me — that was why, and how, he was different.

"How is Decca?" I asked.

Mr. Holmes tilted his head, as if he were trying to discern me. I lowered my head; I hadn't been looked at so closely in such a long time.

"Are you worried, Thea? I'm sorry. I would have sent word sooner. Decca has broken her collarbone. The other injury is superficial — a cut on her hand. Her head wasn't hit; the doctor was very grateful for that."

The iodine had been for her hand. My eyes blurred.

"Thea?"

But I could not look up. Her head.

"Thea? Please look at me."

His voice was firm; he was still my headmaster. And so I lifted my head and saw Mr. Holmes now held a glass in his hand. Whiskey.

"Her personality is intact," I whispered.

He nodded, slowly.

"I left the gate open," I said. "I was distracted."

He set his glass down and directed me to sit, on an overstuffed armchair next to his desk. He pulled his desk chair opposite me — it looked so small in his hand, so light — and sat down.

"Thea," he said, "Decca will be fine. Just a bit of a scare, but nothing that can't be mended."

"She could have been badly hurt," I said. I thought of Rachel.

"That is true. But she was not."

I started to speak again, but he held up his hand.

"She was not," he repeated. "It was a series of events, Thea. Thank God they ended well, and leave it at that."

A door closed in my brain, then, unexpectedly. My understanding of our world shifted: it was a series of events, I thought, all of it.

"And I can't reach Beth. She's somewhere in Alabama, but I don't know exactly where. This day was already bad, to begin with. Our sponsors are not sponsoring. Our donors are not donating." He smiled, and took another sip of his drink. He was less guarded than I had ever seen him; this must be how he always was with his wife. But perhaps not. Perhaps Henry Holmes was rarely so undisguised.

"And the worst of it is that I don't blame them." He shook his head. There was a bitter note in his voice. "Forgive me, Thea. You always strike me as older than your years."

"Rachel?" I asked.

"Rachel," he said, and paused. "Rachel is beside herself."

"Are you angry with her?"

"Yes," he said, "of course I am."

"Don't be."

"But how will she learn, Thea, if I'm not?"

"She made a mistake," I said. I leaned forward in my chair. I could feel a flush creep up my chest, across my cheeks. "A mistake!" I thought of my brother and cousin as I had last seen them. It was all a mistake. "If it is a series of events, then let her be. She's learned her lesson."

Mr. Holmes seemed surprised. He finished his drink and set the glass on the floor, next to his feet.

"Has she?" he asked. His speech was looser. The alcohol, combined with his wife's absence. "I'd like to think so. But as a parent you never quite know what your child is learning."

Mr. Holmes turned his head at the sound of a door closing. He started to stand, and I caught the edge of his sleeve. He looked at me.

"Don't hate her."

"You never hate your child, Thea." He gazed down at me. I made myself meet his gaze.

He did not look away, so I did. I stood, then, and put on my coat. I realized all of a sudden how improper it was, me in front of a man I was not related to without even a robe to cover my nightgown. And yet I did not want to leave. I wanted to stay, to be with him, to go wherever he went, to be enveloped by Mr. Holmes and his books.

"I should leave," I said, "I'm sorry to come here like this."

He nodded and took a step forward, and he was so close I could smell him, the pomade in his hair, and it made me think about the time he had visited me in the infirmary, and told me I would grow to love Yonahlossee. He had been kind. It was only now, months later, that I was able to see how kind he had been.

"Rachel isn't bad. She made a mistake. There is" — here he looked at the ceiling, as if deciding how to phrase it — "a difference."

He departed then, mumbled something about checking on Decca, leaving me to quietly observe his office and all its books: neatly ordered, in bookshelves; stacked on his desk, with little slips of paper sticking out of their pages; one open, on the sofa.

I went to this book, and picked it up. I touched the pages he touched, the spine. I could see how Mr. Holmes lost himself in other worlds in here.

13

Dear Thea,

Did you like the coat? How was Christmas at school? Your father says we need to go away somewhere for a while but where? Here is where I want to be. I'm not lonely. Your father is working more than ever, even if everything else is changed there are always the sick and dying. And there seem to be more of them here now, the sick and dying.

I wish I could see you, Thea. I wish things were not how they are. You should have been my child longer. All three of you should have been children longer. I'll stop with that. Does it surprise you to read a letter like this, your mother so maudlin?

I cut back all the roses, mulched all the beds, hacked away everything dead. I worked for days, perhaps did too much. Sam helped. Your brother is still your brother. There is more to say, surely, but I can't think of it. I know you wrote to him. I know he has not written back. He is still reeling, Thea; I hope I am right in telling you this. I mean not to hurt your feelings, only to explain his.

Georgie is fine. Sam said you asked.

Bundle up in those mountains. Don't ride too long or hard. Remember your health.

Love,
Mother

I sat in the Hall with Sissy, in our usual spot, on a threadbare red velvet sofa, and read Mother's letter. I was exhausted. I'd been sleeping poorly since my nighttime visit to Masters, three days ago.

We weren't supposed to have roses in Emathla, in that humid, hot climate, but Mother loved them. She worried over them, and when they bloomed in the spring they were beautiful; you would not have known they did not belong.

My feelings were hurt. She had known they would be; I felt stung, crumpled. It was one thing to think of my family separately, going about their lives; another entirely to think that an alliance had been formed against me.

Katherine Hayes started playing something cheerful on the piano. Decca's accident had hushed Yonahlossee — girls had cried into each other's shoulders, and sported grave expressions, and looked sadly at Masters — but only for a day. Jettie stood at an easel, painting a watercolor of the view of the mountains from the window. I could see from here that Martha Ladue, who sat next to her, was idly flipping the pages of a magazine, and that Jettie's painting was very bad. Martha Ladue seemed to be interested in only two things: speaking French and being beautiful.

The day after I had gone to Masters, Mr. Holmes had told everyone during morning prayer that Decca had broken her collarbone, that she was recovering nicely. He seemed exhausted as he spoke to us. His eyes were tired. Since then he had appeared at most, but not all, meals. In his absence, Miss Metcalfe, the French teacher, presided. This was the first time I'd paid any attention to Miss Metcalfe. She fell into the boring category that most teachers and girls here did: plain but not ugly, nice but uninteresting. I knew she must go to Masters and speak to Mr. Holmes. I knew she must lend him her sympathetic ear. *I* wanted to do that. I wanted to bring him comfort. I felt a little like he belonged to me, now. He had let me into his office in the dead of night; he had comforted me, and I wanted more of that: more letting in, more comfort.

Henny had left with Sarabeth and Rachel yesterday, to chaperone them on the train to New Orleans to their grandmother's house, where they would be reunited with their mother. Decca stayed behind, because of her injury. Before they left, though, both girls had eaten their meals at the head table when their father did, and though I watched carefully for signs of distress, Rachel seemed unchanged. She seemed happy, even, and I understood that her happiness was an accident: it could so easily have turned out worse. I tried to be glad for the happy Holmeses. I tried to swallow the envy that rose in my throat like tar.

I was glad Sarabeth and Rachel were gone. I knew the feeling was base, petty, but I wanted to be closer to Mr. Holmes, and their absence would make this easier. He thought that I was good. Or at the very least he did not think I was bad. And that he thought so made me wonder: perhaps I was not as bad as I had thought.

It was so easy to be here among these girls, who knew nothing of my visit to

Masters, who knew nothing of the intensity of my thinking, which I could feel hurtling toward obsession.

"I'm bored," Sissy said, and drew a stack of Boone's letters from her schoolbag, which was what she did when she was bored.

There were a few girls who studied at the Hall — Gates, from our cabin — but most of us didn't; our classes didn't require it. We knew boys at boarding school received grades, which meant something in their lives, though *what* grades meant remained vague. We learned in class, were lectured to about wars and famines, ancient kings and queens, the habits of the presidents. But the lectures were cursory. We needed to know what had happened, because we were the well-bred daughters of men who could afford to educate us — but not why, or how. Not any of the stories that made the facts interesting.

We were ranked according to our equestrienne skills, but none of us would compete professionally, or do anything besides ride as a diversion once we left Yonahlossee. And many of us would go back to places where we couldn't sit astride a horse.

The few girls here who did truly care about learning — Gates, in our cabin —

were not popular. It meant you were too hungry, that you sought something unappealing and vague. It was better by ten to be charming and witty, like Sissy, than to care about books.

I watched Sissy hold the letter to her face, then draw it back again as if she were trying to trick her mind into seeing it for the first time. I wondered what she would be as an adult, whether or not she would still seem so young. Sissy's charm, her thin wrists, her easily tangled hair, her long, awkward neck, seemed so clearly and profoundly childish to me. She was lovely, Sissy, anyone could see that. But she was lovely because she seemed harmless.

What would it feel like to be Sissy? I thought of Boone gently and urgently kneading her breasts. Sissy smiled to herself, serenely, and I saw Boone's hands and felt a familiar sensation in my stomach. I turned my head and watched Jettie paint a disfigured mountain peak until the feeling went away.

Sissy would never have gone to see Mr. Holmes in the dead of night. The idea wouldn't even have occurred to her. She had chosen a normal beau. Boone came from a good family; the *good* implied that his family was wealthy. Their biggest hurdle would be that they were too young, that Boone was not Southern enough, not Alabama royalty. He was from Asheville, which Sissy had told me was fine, but not wonderful. But I gathered he had enough money to smooth that particular wrinkle. All of this seemed so ridiculous, the nuances of hierarchy, the subtleties of position, and though Sissy sometimes made fun of all this fuss, with me, I could see she took it seriously.

Outside, I hugged myself against the cold, my old coat too small. I squinted my eyes against the sun until I entered the woods, and then it was dark, the light dappled onto the forest floor and the effect was eerily beautiful, a pricked pattern engineered by randomness.

There was no trace that Decca had fallen. The iodine had been absorbed by the earth long ago; Bright was back in his stall, chomping hay; the felled tree had been cleared away. I lingered at Bright's stall and he whuffed into my hand, curious. He had no memory of what had happened, no idea at all. I envied a horse's dumbness, not for the first time in my life.

We took turns jumping the combination Mr. Albrecht had devised. I went next to last, and I watched girl after girl fail, go either too fast or too slow between the second and third jumps, then nick a rail.

"Well done, Thea," Mr. Albrecht murmured as I passed him.

Just then I saw Mr. Holmes walking alongside the ring, toward me, and I was hot and panicked but also terribly eager.

"Hello, Thea," he said, and smiled.

"Mr. Holmes."

"Well," he said, after a pause, and rested his arms on the railing in the posture that was so familiar to me, "Decca is feeling better." He looked beyond me, at the other ring, and I knew he was in front of me only briefly, before he continued his tour of the riding rings, before he would stop and chat with other girls. Jealousy was still such an odd feeling. At home, there had been nothing to envy, nothing to want that I didn't already have, or could get.

"Is Decca lonely?" I blurted, and then tried to speak more slowly. "I mean, does she miss her sisters?"

"I think she must. She's the youngest. She's never been alone before."

"I know that feeling," I said.

"You're the youngest?" he asked.

"No." I shook my head. I was relieved that he did not know as much about me as I had thought; and then also disappointed for precisely the same reason. He looked at me expectantly, waiting for an answer.

"I'm a twin," I said. "Fraternal."

"Ah," he said. He seemed neither interested nor surprised. He must hear so many things about us girls, all the time. He took his hands from the rail, preparing to leave.

"May I visit Decca?" I said, before I lost my chance. "Sit with her?"

He paused. I could tell I had pleased him. Parents liked when you were interested in their children. I wondered if Mother and Father had felt the same pleasure when people complimented me and Sam. But no one had, except occasionally, in town.

"She would like that, Thea. Thank you." He began to turn around, but then he stopped. "I almost forgot — I wanted to tell you that Rachel is fine. That everyone is grateful Decca was not seriously injured."

I wondered what his memory of that night was. I had been so bold, and he did not seem to mind.

I watched him walk away, his slim, busy hands swinging by his sides, then folded behind him, then in his pockets. I knew what the feeling was, now, that had embroidered itself in my brain. Knowing made me feel less horrible. I had what so many girls had: a crush. It was as simple and harmless as that. I had never had one before. With Georgie, things had simply happened, one after the next; I'd never had any control. But this time, I had control. This was just a crush.

I turned Naari around and saw that Leona stood at the gate, watching, and I got rid of the stupid smile that had been on my face.

The Holmeses' housekeeper met me at their door that afternoon, when everyone else was at the Hall studying, or feigning studying. I stepped into their house and unlaced my boots.

"There's no need," the housekeeper said. She was young, with golden-blond hair coiled into a braid. A smattering of freckles dotted her cheeks. When she spoke, I could see that her teeth were horribly crooked. Still, she was pretty. She had that Appalachian look, wan, thin. The mountain families were large, I knew, and inbred. Sissy told me that they thought nothing of marrying their cousins. But who else were they supposed to marry, I wanted to point out, isolated in hollers and valleys unreachable by automobiles and trains, places that never saw outsiders. When the only boy there for you happened to also be your cousin.

"I'll make a mess." I pried off my boots and handed them to her; she returned a moment later and led me up the stairs.

Decca's room was chilly. I was glad I'd kept my scarf and jacket. I felt Sissy's gloves in my pocket, lent to me for the winter, but to put them on would be impolite, even if I was only in the presence of a housekeeper and a child.

"Is she warm enough?" I whispered, because Decca was asleep.

The housekeeper paused a moment, as if considering whether or not to answer me.

"Hot-water bottles," she said, finally. She left, then.

I sat by a bed in a chair clearly meant for this purpose: Mr. Holmes must sit here, too, I knew, for hours, days if the hours were added together.

Decca was swathed in pink blankets. Her long lashes rested dramatically on her pale skin. Her hair — so dark it was almost black — was shiny with oil. I wondered if Mr. Holmes knew anything about washing girls' hair, about tending to a child of Decca's age. I touched her soft forehead and though she stirred she did not wake.

If he came into this room while I sat here with his daughter it would be happenstance. I could not be accused of being bad. I could not be accused of being forward. It would simply be a meeting engineered by chance. I wanted to be close to him again, I wanted him to speak to me, to ask me questions, to answer mine.

I would come again tomorrow, and the next day. I drew my gloves on and rested my head on the back of the leather chair. It was big and comfortable, meant for someone larger, a man's easy chair. The furniture in this room was the same as ours: washstand, desk, and vanity.

A homely embroidered mat hung between the beds, the Lord's Prayer stitched in green. Mother would have hated this room. It was clean, spotless, but looked mean. I took off a glove and fingered Decca's bedspread — made of some rough linen, with a thick border of dark red. There was a timeless quality about this room, perhaps due to its sparseness; except for the lamp, I could have been sitting in a bedroom from a hundred years ago. Was this house an accurate representation of Mrs. Holmes's taste, or had it always stayed the same, Mrs. Holmes only changing small things, grace notes? Pictures, maybe dishes. That would undo Mother, to live somewhere that was not her own.

At the end of the hour I was taken to the

front door and shown outside by the housekeeper, who managed to lead me through the house and hand me my boots while ignoring me. Decca had spent the whole visit asleep.

I looked up at the house, for some sign of Mr. Holmes. The drapes were drawn against the cold, and even if they hadn't been, it was impossible to see through a window lit by daylight.

Mr. Holmes had still not appeared. I asked the housekeeper where he might be — I had come three days in a row and seen neither hide nor hair of him. She shrugged. "You'd have to ask Mr. Holmes." I thought there was a note of challenge in her voice. Insolence. Or a note of satisfaction — of course I could not ask him, because he was gone when I came to the house. Because he was distant when we met in the dining hall — or did not meet, he made sure of that. He stayed away, it was not my imagination. And so I began to imagine that he also wanted to see me, that there was something that existed between us. I could not yet say what — I did not know. If I were a better girl according to Mother, I would stop all this, reinsert myself into Yonahlossee life, go to the Hall with Sissy instead of coming here every day. But I no longer knew what kind of girl I was.

I played with Decca, or read to her, or sang her songs. She had not slept after that first visit. I lay awake at night and rose when Boone threw his rock and shook Sissy awake, hard. Boone, so handsome and nice; he waited outside like a trap, waited for Sissy to fall. I lay in Sissy's bed and listened to her tiptoe out — she was so loud! — and hated her, hated Boone for making her furtive.

I hated the girls in Augusta House, who thought my visitation arrangement strange. "You only sit there?" Mary Abbott asked that night, sidling up beside me on the way to the bathhouse. "Why do you?" Wasn't that very apparent? Achingly clear? But no, it was not. Only to me, only I knew.

Now I was awake and knew I would not get back to sleep, and felt so hot, so ready.

"Do you love me?" I imagined Sissy asking. "Do you love me? Me?"

"Do you love me?" He would ask me that.

"Why did you stay away for all that time?"

"Because I loved you," he would say. He would put his hand on my breast, underneath my dress. Those slim, long fingers inside me, touching me, feeling parts of me, the odd pressures, the closeness.

Oh. I bit my pillow and there were sparks against my eyelids. If only this could last — longer, longer. If only, but it never did.

My breaths were quick but deep. My limbs were heavy against the sheets. I wiped between my legs with my handkerchief and left it there.

I could fall asleep now. I closed my eyes and was not ashamed. Mr. Holmes, Mr. Holmes, Mr. Holmes. When I closed my eyes, he was all I saw.

Dear Mother,

I do like my coat — thank you. It's so nice I don't know when I'll wear it. It's cold here, but beautiful. I think I prefer the cold to the heat. You can ride forever in the cold. I'm riding again, did you know? I don't know what else to report. There's nothing to report, I suppose. It's cold and I'm riding and camp life is the same. We do the same thing every day, exactly, except for Sunday but then our Sundays are exactly alike so everything has its order.

You wouldn't like it here, I don't think. There isn't any green in the winter except for the evergreens and they don't really count, do they? Everything dies and the world is all one color — white

— until spring. I never knew anything but colorful, humid Florida and I thought that was what I preferred, but truly it was simply what I knew. I wonder what the desert is like, or up north. Who knows what I prefer?

Mrs. Holmes was your friend? I didn't know. I didn't know you had friends. I would write more but we're kept so busy. Don't worry about me. Don't even think about me.

"My father spoke on the telephone," Decca said. "To my mother." I was reading to her from a book she loved, called *Winnie-the-Pooh;* she should keep still, the housekeeper told me. But Decca was back to her old self, a sling she had to wear to keep her right arm immobile so that her collarbone could heal the only evidence she had fallen. There was no need for me to come like this, I knew that, and though I told myself, and everyone else, that I came for Decca's sake, really I came for my own. I wanted to see him.

"Oh?" I asked.

"Yes. Father sounded angry."

I tried to hide my surprise. Mr. Holmes should speak more carefully. But clearly Decca did not know what this all meant.

"Why was he angry, Decca?"

"When will my sisters be here?" Her voice was plaintive. She missed them, I realized. She didn't understand their absence. I understood. Boone had told Sissy that a boy at Harris Academy had been sent back to school with a suitcase full of money, and told to hide it. He'd stored it in his mattress. It was such a dumb hiding place I didn't know if the story could be true, but the banks *were* failing, we all knew that; a girl's uncle was president of First National, Charlotte's bank that had closed in December. Yet the Harris boy's family had money — he was at Harris, after all, not beneath the earth working in some mine. His father didn't know what to do with their money, though, how to keep it safe, how to ensure that it would protect them.

There was enough money in the world for all of us to be here, to ride our horses, to wear our white clothes. I wondered if Mother's citrus fortune was in a bank. Surely it was. I couldn't imagine Mother hiding money among her furniture, her things. But I didn't know, I realized, I didn't know anything at all about how my family was handling their financial affairs. I had never known. The citrus income had shadowed us, all my life; it was impossible to imagine the Atwells without it: I saw now that it gave us an edge, a little way to feel better than people who did not have wealth from a distant, exotic source.

Mother would never have used the word *better*. We were simply different. Unique.

"Thea?"

I gazed at Decca, who looked at me curiously.

"They'll be back soon," I answered. I hated how vague I sounded, but I didn't know how else to sound.

Mr. Holmes seemed angry on the telephone. I would have given my left arm to know why. But Decca was just a child — she might have misheard. Perhaps Mr. Holmes had sounded upset, not angry.

I wondered how much she remembered about the accident. It seemed a mercy, that she was too young to understand Rachel's part in it.

Decca picked up her doll — its hair was patchy, its clothes smudged. It must have belonged to Sarabeth, then Rachel; finally, Decca. I had never had to share anything with Sam. I'd never liked dolls, but still I'd had at least half a dozen.

Decca whispered to her doll. I tried to listen to what she said but then drew back, embarrassed, a sixteen-year-old girl straining to hear the mutterings of a child. I should let Decca have her secrets.

If our lives had not been so blessed, if we had not had Mother's money — if, if, if. But this particular line of possibilities had never occurred to me. Then Father would have had to live in a city, where there were more paying patients. Then Mother could not have kept herself, and us, so apart from everyone else. We might have lived hours from Gainesville. We might have only seen each other once a year, for Christmas.

We would not have had money to give them. We would not have been able to help. We would not have been better. We would not have been lucky.

Did my parents hope I'd been taught a lesson? They thought they'd sent me somewhere safe. Away from men, away from cousins. Georgie, Georgie must be — I tried not to think of Georgie here. I stood — Decca was still playing with her doll, the room was still ugly and stiff, I was still alone in this house with his child.

I thought we knew each other, my mother had said, and then, later: This will all be fine, do as you're told, do as we say and this will all be for the best.

If my parents had kept me at home, I might have learned their lesson, I might have wanted to please them more than I wanted to please myself. In my head, I thought, if I can make Mr. Holmes love me, it will all be all right.

14

It was bitterly cold the next time we went to Gainesville. Aunt Carrie's mother had taken a turn for the worse and died very suddenly, and we were going to offer our condolences. I'd wrapped a scarf around my neck and head and face, left room for only my eyes. I watched the landscape speed by, punctuated occasionally by houses: they all looked the same to me, splintering wood, windows that were glassless black squares.

Since Christmas I'd seen Georgie only three times, which was, I thought, less often than we usually saw the Gainesville Atwells. But how often we saw each other was never something I'd tallied before. But now — now I wanted to see my cousin more than I could ever remember wanting anything.

Mother was concentrating on driving, which was new to her. There weren't many things that Mother wasn't good at, but driving was one of them. This new car had a backseat, which I thought was the height of luxury; right now Sam sat in front with Mother, and I was sprawled across the mohair seat in back. Sam sat tensely. He was a little afraid of how fast we went in cars.

That morning I'd gone through Mother's handbag, looking for the little pot of perfume she kept there. I'd found a blank envelope, unsealed, and inside a check made out to George Atwell for the largest sum of money I'd ever seen. Father's nearly illegible signature bit into the thin paper.

I dabbed perfume behind my ears, as Mother always did. Georgie would be George Atwell one day, lose his nickname, and what would he do then? Would I be his wife? I steadied myself on the counter. I didn't think I wanted to be his wife. But I knew from books that that's what you did, when you kissed.

There were no houses on the final stretch of our drive, as they would have been sucked down by the bog. It seemed so near on either side: if we stopped, the animals would emerge from the groves of cabbage palm and the thick stands of maiden cane. The bobcats hid — we almost never saw them — but the alligators often sunned themselves on the edge of the road when it was warm, their gnarly, muddy skin, almost black, their improbably white teeth that were visible when they lazily snapped their jaws, as — what else could it mean — a warning.

It was perhaps my imagination that Mother sped through this stretch, that the automobile shook violently, that she did not slow down as she normally did for dips in the road. Father loved this leg of the drive; he thought central Florida possessed the most beautiful landscape in the world: a little bit of swamp, a little bit of forest.

At Georgie's, we stepped out and waited while Mother gathered her things — a book for Aunt Carrie, a big crate of food: beans, Idella's bread, preserves. Surely Georgie's family did not need our food? I touched the sack of beans, and looked at Mother curiously.

"Just some extra things we had," she said. I walked toward the house: Was it my imagination, that it looked grim, in need of sprucing up? It was a matter of fact that paint flaked from the windowsills, that a gutter was hanging by a thread. But things could not fall apart so quickly.

"Georgie's at a neighbor's," Aunt Carrie told us after she had shown us into the living room. "He'll be back soon," she said, when she saw my face, which I tried to make look happy again. But I felt devastated. I'd waited for weeks!

"I'm sorry for your loss," I said — Mother had coached me — and Aunt Carrie put her arm around my shoulders and pressed me to her. She felt sturdy, next to Mother, who was all angles.

"Both my parents are gone," she said, her voice pitched as if she was asking me a question, and I realized she was close to tears.

"Carrie," Mother said, and led my aunt to a chair, "it will be fine."

"Will it, Elizabeth?" She offered my mother a thin smile. "You sound like our president." This had all turned Aunt Carrie mean, I realized.

Mother laughed nervously, and Sam and I slipped away.

"Want to go out back?" he asked, but I did not. I did not want to observe the natural world today; I did not want to follow Sam around.

"I'm tired," I said, even though I wasn't. Sam looked at me for a second — I always went with him — and I didn't meet his eye.

"All right," he said, hurt. "I'll go by myself."

I was sorry, but not sorry enough to go with him. I went to my aunt and uncle's bedroom, where I could think. Their bed was unmade. Beds were so rarely unmade in my world.

I pressed my forehead against the window and watched until Sam disappeared into the woods. Last night we'd stayed up far past our bedtimes and took turns reading to each other an Agatha Christie mystery we'd read a thousand times already. I spent nearly all my time with Sam — he should not be hurt now. I looked at my hands, my nails that I had carefully trimmed last night, painted with oil. They were not a child's hands. I stood and gathered my hair into a knot. I'd worn it down, brushed it ten different ways, decided on a side part.

I fell asleep in Aunt Carrie and Uncle George's bed; I opened my eyes and Georgie was there, and I felt as if I'd summoned my cousin through a dream.

I held out my hand. Sleep had calmed me. My fingers gleamed in the soft lamplight.

"Where is Sam?"

"Outside. Mother is showing Sam and your mother her first azaleas." He paused. "We'll hear when they come back in."

He rubbed my hand, I watched him, he rubbed my hand gently with his thumb and I wanted to moan.

He traced my eyebrow with his finger,

lightly. “So pretty.”

“Do you think Sam knows?”

He shook his head. “I’m almost certain he doesn’t.”

That was enough, in that moment. I looked out the window and was surprised to see that it had turned dark while I slept.

“You look so old,” I said, and he did, standing there with one hand in his trouser pocket, the other over mine, kneading slowly but insistently. I sat up and kissed him, he leaned down and opened his mouth, put his tongue into mine.

“Open your mouth, Thea, like this.”

I did what he said. He turned his head away and I didn’t know what he was doing, but then I saw he was taking his jacket off. The idea thrilled me: he was taking his clothes off, he was going to stay. He faced me again. I watched him for a moment. He was breathing heavily, his face was flushed. I knew that I was calm — calmer, certainly, than Georgie.

“Come here,” I said.

“Yes,” he said, “yes, yes,” and he climbed on top of me, propped himself up with his elbows. I wanted him closer, I pressed my hands hard against his back and at first he resisted but then he relented and he was pushing into me, and I wanted it, he was pushing into me and I reached down between us and felt for the hard pressure of his penis. I knew it would be there. It felt not like I expected it would, it felt swollen and very soft. I reached —

"No, no," he whispered, "not yet. Just feel me from the outside." So I touched him like he wanted, gingerly at first, but he kept pushing himself into my hand, harder and harder, and so I touched him harder, ran my fingers firmly along the length of it, and Georgie moaned while he was kissing me, moaned and moaned.

I ached. I pressed him to where I ached, shifted so that it touched more, harder, and I pressed and pressed and when it happened it was different, it was quicker, and when I was finished Georgie was still moving on top of me, kissing me, kissing my neck, my chest.

"Oh."

"What?" he asked.

I shook my head. He didn't know what I had just done. Georgie stood up suddenly. His pants were tented at his crotch. I'd done that, too.

"We should go down," he whispered, "they'll wonder."

I sat up and unknotted my hair.

"You're so pretty," he said, and knelt in

front of me, put his head in my lap. I combed his hair with my fingers. We heard the screen door slam, and then footsteps. "What if they catch us?"

"I thought you weren't worried?" I asked.

"I'm not," he said, "not really."

"I'm not either." In that moment I was so certain that they wouldn't. This was nothing they could conceive of, I felt. That we were in his parents' bedroom seemed to prove the strength of our secret.

And it was true, neither of our mothers had seemed to notice anything when we went downstairs, Georgie first, me ten or so minutes later, counting the seconds aloud because Uncle George and Aunt Carrie's clock wasn't wound.

By the time I came down Mother was gathering her things. Sam looked bored. But I caught his eye and smiled, and he smiled back.

On the way home I pretended to sleep in the backseat, so that I could think freely about my cousin.

"Are you all right, Sam?" my mother asked. So she could feel it also: Sam seemed too quiet.

"Sam?" Mother asked again. She turned to look at him, and the car swerved. "I hate this contraption," Mother muttered, shaken. "Sam, why so quiet? If you don't tell me I'll have to look at you again."

I smiled. When Sam spoke, I knew he was smiling, too, from his voice. "Georgie —"

I bit my lip, hard. He could tell Mother right now, and this would all be over. And in that instant, Mother and I both waiting, poised for Sam to speak again, I almost wanted him to tell her. "He ignored me, today." His voice was plaintive. I felt relieved that his malaise had nothing to do with me; then guilty. Georgie and I had both ignored Sam today.

"Things are a little tense right now, in your cousin's family," Mother said, finally. I could tell she was thinking of how to frame it so that Sam would best understand.

"Why?"

"They might lose their house, Sam."

My eyes flew open. I wanted so badly to speak, but I did not want to enter this conversation. To do so would feel like a betrayal, of Georgie.

"They won't," my mother continued, "because this family is generous, and we're glad to help. It's what family does. But it's hard for your uncle to accept charity. And it's hard for Georgie to know all of this. He shouldn't ignore you, but put yourself in his shoes. It must be hard for him, to see you." It made sense, suddenly, why we hadn't seen them in almost a month.

For as long as I could remember, we'd had more than my cousin's family. We were two children; one child, in those days, was noticeable. My father was brighter. And my mother won, in every contest, when put next to my aunt. My mother was from a wealthy family, with connections. And she was beautiful; my aunt was plain. I felt all this, but I didn't think much of it. And I did not have a girl cousin to compete with. I did not have to be prettier, or more graceful, or brighter.

But of course I knew my mother was wrong: Georgie had ignored Sam not because he was embarrassed or petty but because he only wanted me.

"Yeah, well," Sam said. "He didn't ignore Thea."

And I smiled: Sam was right. But then Mother spoke.

"Thea's a girl," Mother said.

For an instant I thought she meant that I was too pretty for a boy like Georgie to ignore. But then she spoke again.

"She doesn't matter like you do."

I felt as if the wind had been knocked out of me. My heart beat so loudly I was sure

Mother would hear it. But I calmed myself: I knew how to do that, because of Sasi. Horses could smell fear.

The shacks we had passed on the way up were lit by firelight, now. I tried to find some sign of poverty, but I didn't know what to look for. I was angry, suddenly, that my parents had kept me away from everything real.

Mother was wrong. I mattered, I thought, and tried to let the sound of the wind against the car lull me to sleep. I mattered. My name was Theodora Atwell, and I mattered to Georgie Atwell.

15

The news came through an old house mistress, who lived in Dallas and was friends with Henny. Leona's family had lost everything. Her father's oil was sour, we kept hearing, though no one knew what it meant. It was now worth less than drinking water. We knew what this meant. *Everything,* Henny said, but even she seemed to take no pleasure in this gossip.

"Where will they live?" I asked Sissy, on our way to the bathhouse, both of us swaddled in our winter robes.

She looked sideways at me. "They'll still have their house, Thea. Just not their lives."

When we arrived at the bathhouse, I scanned the room for Leona, whom I sometimes saw around this time, but saw only a gaggle of first-years, Molly among them. We were required to bathe every other day during the summer, but only every third day during the winter. Mrs. Holmes's standard of hygiene was high.

As I waited for Docey to draw my bath, I wondered what sort of life Leona was left with. Leona had done nothing wrong, nothing unforgivable. She would leave this place. She would give up horses, or at least horses like King, who had cost a small fortune. She would not go to a ladies' college, perhaps.

Docey motioned that the bath was ready and took my robe as I stepped in. I'd completely discarded any remnants of modesty after the first few weeks here. Docey's hand was red, from testing the water so many times. Leona's life might be limited, now, in a way that it hadn't been before, but she would not be a maid, like Docey. She would never go hungry. There was surely a rich relative who would help.

Victoria, Leona, all the girls who had been sent home — their lives would change in subtler ways. Rich suitors would not abound. They would have to choose more carefully. All the *Ladies' Home Journal*s mothers sent us were now full of articles about little jobs women could take in to support the household: laundry, sewing. I'd almost laughed. As if Leona's mother could save the family fortune. As if Aunt Carrie could have doubled the size of her garden and paid back the bank. That wives could earn even a fraction of what their husbands had lost was a fantasy.

I understood that our teachers, whom we had previously pitied, for they had none of our advantages, were lucky. Miss Brooks had a salary, and room and board; she talked about books all day instead of worrying about keeping her family afloat. It must feel like a relief, not to be saddled with a family right now.

In the days that followed, everyone watched Leona, for signs that she had faltered, would falter. But she acted no differently. And, gradually, the girls, as girls are wont to do, lost interest. If anything, she acted more imperiously. Watching her guide King over jumps as if they were playthings, clear the course beautifully, perfectly, then pass us on her way out of the ring without so much as a nod — well, it made us wonder if it was really true at all. But still she reminded us of our own precarious balance in the net of fate. If Leona's father could lose everything, what of our own fathers? What of us? The question floated above us, now, a cloud.

In Augusta House one night Eva switched off the lights and lit candles, brought out a

Ouija board, which she had borrowed from a first-year cabin. The first-year girls were consumed by them. We had been trapped indoors almost all day, unable to ride because of the rain. It almost felt like hurricane weather.

"Those," Gates said, as soon as she saw it, "are forbidden. And foolish, besides." But even so, she joined our circle, placed the tips of her fingers very lightly on the heart-shaped piece of wood. We sat on the faded Oriental rug that lay in the center of the cabin. I absently combed its fringed edges. They covered the floors of all our cabins; I knew how expensive they were. Mr. Holmes should sell all these, I thought, and pay a girl's tuition.

"My father says those are demonic," Mary Abbott said, from her bed. "You shouldn't."

"Oh, Mary Abbott," Eva said. "Don't be so grim. It's just fun."

"Who are we contacting?" Sissy asked.

"My grandmother," Eva suggested, "but she was so boring in real life. I can't imagine death has made her more interesting."

"Eva!" Gates said. Eva raised her eyebrows, lazily, and smiled. I stifled a laugh.

"How about you, Thea?" Sissy asked. "Is there anyone you'd like to contact? Do you know anyone dead?"

The question rang out like a bell, sounding clearly in my mind. Was Georgie dead? Tears came to my eyes, that old, familiar wetness. But no: Mother had said in her last letter he was fine.

"No," I said, and smiled, weakly, "no one I can think of."

Sissy tried to meet my eye. "How about an old Yonahlossee girl?" I asked, to interrupt the stillness.

"Which one?" Gates asked. She sat primly, her legs folded beneath her, the way we had been taught to sit in etiquette class if we ever found ourselves without a chair.

"Lettie Sims," Eva said. "She's why we can't swim in the lake anymore. Drowned," she added.

"When?" I asked.

"In the 1800s," Sissy said. "A long time ago." She smiled reassuringly. "A very long time ago."

I smiled back, to show her I was fine. But Sissy did look a little otherworldly in the candlelight; all of us did. I was not so fragile that a drowned girl from the previous century could alarm me.

We all touched the wooden heart, lightly. Mary Abbott turned off the electric lights, so all we had were candles. "Spirit of the occult," Eva began, and Sissy giggled.

"Spirit of the occult," she began again, "please let us speak to Miss Lettie Sims, who we know the girls called Simsy. We want to ask her a question. Respectfully."

The heart moved, of course it did, one of us pushed it. I watched the faces of these softly glowing girls and wondered what I would ask if I could ask anything at all and know the answer would be true.

"A-S-K-O-N-E-Q-U-E-S-T-I-O-N-I-F-Y-O-U-M-U-S-T-B-U-T-O-N-L-Y-O-N-E."

Gates's freckled fingers, I thought; she wanted to get this done with.

Mary Abbott whimpered, from her bed, "I'm scared."

"Shh," Eva whispered. "She doesn't want to hurt us."

Sissy's hands were shaking. Did the girls really believe this? We had read an essay about the occult with Father, how it was simply a way not to believe all the soldiers from the Great War were dead. I tried to meet Gates's eye, but she was watching the board.

"This is foolish," I said. "It's one of us moving it." I started to take my hands away, but Sissy shook her head.

"Please, Thea," she whispered. "Wait."

"Hurry, then. Ask a question."

The wind whipped against our cabin,

which felt unsturdy, suddenly, like a house made of paper. A branch hit the window and Eva gasped. Sam had briefly been afraid of Kate the Bell Witch, when we were seven; he said she could disguise herself as anyone or thing, recognizable only by her green eyes. A snake, a bird, a little girl. Georgie had told him the legend, scared Sam silly. Mother blamed him, he had let the outside world in. For years Sam looked carefully at the faces of people we encountered. But we didn't encounter many, and none of their eyes, to his relief, were green.

"A question?" I asked.

"I have a question," Gates said, which surprised us all. She closed her eyes and took a deep breath.

"Will we be all right?" Her voice wavered, ever so slightly, which it never had before and never would again, at least not in my presence.

That winter I got better and better on a horse. The cold seemed to agree with me. At the very least, you could ride longer without fear of overheating your horse. Faster and stronger, I jumped perfectly any course Mr. Albrecht arranged, usually on the first try. My legs no longer ached after I finished a ride. My arms were stringed with muscle. Eva had cut my hair off; now it fell to my shoulders, and I looked less like a child. When I examined myself in the mirror over my washstand, I liked what I saw, I liked what I'd become again: perhaps it was my imagination, but I looked in the mirror and saw that I was superior to the old Thea, I was more powerful than she'd ever been.

I cleared my plate most mealtimes. Henny watched and sipped glass after glass of cold water. Not fat, not yet — she was plump, very round, but anyone could see that she would be fat soon. It was her fate.

Sometimes I asked about her wedding. She was pleased with me then — oh, it was so easy to put myself into Henny's good graces. She talked less about her fiancé than about her flowers, the rolling cart of desserts, her dress from New York. Martha and Jettie were going to be bridesmaids. I wondered if it pained Henny to think of beautiful Martha standing next to her. Miss Metcalfe was silent when Henny spoke of her impending matrimonial bliss, and I realized with a shock that she was jealous.

I asked a question about their new house, the one they would move into after they were married, and Henny turned to me, excluding all the other girls at our table.

"You'll know what it's like, Thea, you'll

know how much joy there is." Her hot breath smelled faintly of chocolate. What an odd way to phrase it, the joy floating somewhere, an infinite quantity of it, as if you only had to stand in the right place to catch it.

When Mr. Holmes did appear, a week into my visits with Decca, it was nothing extraordinary. So many things were like that: you waited and waited and waited, and then it happened, and you were still you. I wasn't yet sure if this was a disappointment or a relief. It seemed to be a little bit of both.

We were downstairs, playing dominoes on the coffee table. I was drinking tea and watching Decca's milk — her glass rested very close to the edge of the table and I was afraid she'd knock it over with her elbow. I'd already told her to be careful, twice, and there was a limit, I'd learned from spending so many hours with Decca, to how many times you could warn a child.

There were expensive pieces in this room: a collection of tiny Limoges boxes in a glass case, six silver calling-card cases on an end table, all engraved with various initials. An oil painting of a girl sitting in a field, a sheep in the distance, that reminded me of *Tess of the D'Urbervilles.* There was nothing personal except for the initialed card cases; again I wondered if any of these things belonged to the Holmeses. Was there a discretionary fund that each headmistress was allowed to draw from? But that fund surely would have been stopped now, with the trouble. Even if the money in the fund hadn't been affected, it would be in poor taste to use it.

"Go."

"Sorry," I said, "sorry, let's see . . ." But I didn't see. I'd never played dominoes before and apparently the Holmes girls had played since birth. It was a dull, endless game.

Decca wore a summer dress, evidence of a father's hand. Decca could be obstinate, and she was picky about her clothes. I imagined she'd insisted on this, and Mr. Holmes had given in to his daughter's seasonally inappropriate whims.

I was wearing the Yonahlossee uniform but I didn't mind it. I had gotten used to the sight of us, all alike at first glance. I wore no jewelry.

Decca stood; I interrupted the caressing of my hair.

I was vain, I was sixteen years old and would never again feel so watched.

"Father's home," she announced, and twirled in a tight circle.

"Decca," I scolded, "behave."

There was always some tragedy that accompanied his arrival: the milk, this time.

"Decca!" I was furious. All this waiting, all my calibrations, and now the milk was spilled and Emmy unavailable — how to call her without sounding coarse?

Decca ran to her father and I busied myself with soaking up the milk with my skirt.

"An accident?" Mr. Holmes asked, and lifted Decca on his hip. He offered his free hand to me and I accepted it and stood.

"Emmy," he called, and she appeared so quickly I knew she must have been waiting.

"We were just . . ."

"Playing?"

I nodded, looked to the right and out the window. Everything was blank, still and cold. "Playing." I felt defeated. Decca sat curled and small on her father's hip, Emmy scurried on the rug, patting and feeling.

"That's fine, Emmy." And although he sounded distracted, he spoke gently to Emmy, who stood and curtsied and backed out of the room without ever meeting his eye.

I wasn't going to say a thing, I wanted him to speak next, after I'd waited and waited.

But it was Decca who spoke: "I'm winning at dominoes."

"Don't boast."

"She's not. It's true." I smiled at Decca, who grinned back.

Mr. Holmes put Decca down but she clung to his leg. He rested a hand on the top of her scalp, carefully extricated his leg from her grip.

"Is that right?" He smiled.

Decca nodded, unsure; there were adults laughing and sometimes that was fine and sometimes it was not.

"Go upstairs, now," he told Decca. "Please," he asked, anticipating her refusal. "I'll be up in a second." And we were to be alone, now! I wondered if he thought I was pretty. I willed him to look at me, to notice me, but he seemed distracted.

Decca kissed me on the cheek and my cheek flamed scarlet, she was so close to me, her scalpy smell and her thin shoulders.

Mr. Holmes patted Decca's head as she passed and smiled after her, and I knew that if she had not been his favorite before she would be now.

There was one thing in this room that did not belong, I thought, and it was me: I was intruding; surely Mr. Holmes thought I was a bother. Sometimes the house mistresses met here with Mrs. Holmes, but mainly the Holmes house was private, theirs, not a place for girls. As Mr. Holmes arranged himself in a chair, I knew that he did not want me here.

"Well," I said, ready to make my excuses. What had I thought? That Mr. Holmes would fall in love with me? This was how crushes made fools of girls. I resolved to never have one again, to never love someone until they loved me first: to control my heart.

"Sit, sit," he said, "please," and gestured toward a chair, and I had been wrong. He wanted me here. He seemed genuine. I had not imagined everything.

Just then Emmy reentered the room, carrying a tray, which she set on the coffee table. She refilled my teacup in careful, measured steps: first pick up the teapot, support it under its belly as well as by its handle. Angle your wrist, do not allow your arm to tremble. Pour. Straighten your wrist now, quickly, so that you interrupt the stream of tea decisively, so that no drops of boiling water leap from the weakening stream and land on the porcelain tray — or, God forbid, silver, which shows everything and more — or even worse, on the lady for whom you are pouring.

Emmy did not once raise her head or glance at me. Her hand was perfectly still. She was here in Masters for a reason.

She handed Mr. Holmes a tall, clear glass and left. My mouth felt chalky. More tea was exactly what I wanted least.

Mr. Holmes took a long swallow from his narrow glass, halfway done already. He was pale, but that could have been the quickly dimming light, orbiting us into darkness.

A bell rang. Everyone would still be at the Hall; I thought of Sissy, who was probably expecting me. I was going nowhere.

"Class time," Mr. Holmes said, but so informally, as if I needn't worry myself. He swallowed the rest of his drink.

I heard water run upstairs, Emmy drawing Decca a bath.

"Excuse me for a moment, Thea," he said quietly, and left the room.

Mr. Holmes returned with a glass decanter. We kept similar ones in our formal room.

I've gotten into a bad habit since Mrs. Holmes left, I imagined him saying.

He seemed very far away, at the other end of the room, mixing a drink on top of the piano, his sweaty glass on the bare wood — it would leave a ring, he was a man and did not think about rings — but no, he picked the glass up and smoothed away the dampness with his coat sleeve.

He sat down and examined his drink. We heard a noise from upstairs and both looked up. I caught his eye and smiled, he smiled back, this was how to be easy and natural with a man. I looked up again but Mr. Holmes was looking down, stirring his drink with his finger.

"Thea," Mr. Holmes began, then paused. He flicked his spirit-sopped finger and then smelled it, and I was suddenly and unbearably embarrassed — these were private gestures, I was not meant to see them. He took a long swallow of his drink.

And because I was nervous, the first thing that came into my head popped out, like one of Sam's tree frogs.

"Mrs. Holmes is still gone?" And it was precisely the wrong thing to say. It sounded like I sat in judgment of Mrs. Holmes's absence, when truly I was grateful: if she was here I would not be, that was certain.

He nodded slowly. "I'm of half a mind to send Decca there, brace and all, but I think I would be too lonely."

I smiled — it did not seem possible that an adult's loneliness could be relieved by a child. But I supposed we had relieved Mother's loneliness.

"Only a month until her return," he continued. "Hopefully I can hold the camp together for another month." He took a sip of his drink and grimaced the way adults did when they drank hard liquor. The grimace meant the taste was pleasurable. I knew from watching Uncle George.

"Are there more donations?"

He looked up at me, surprised. "You mentioned before," I explained, "that people were not donating as much as you'd hoped."

"Yes, yes. You have a very excellent memory, Thea."

"Not really," I said. "My brother is the one with the excellent memory. He knows all the names of all the plants and animals, hundreds and hundreds of them."

"Your twin," he said. "I remember some things."

I could feel my face flush with pleasure. He could remember one detail about my life and make me so, so happy, more happy than I could remember being in ages.

He finished off his drink and cradled the glass in his lap.

"Beth is having better luck, yes. Better her than me. I'm no good at separating people from their money. Do you know what has made everyone more willing to contribute?"

I shook my head.

"Horses." He laughed in disbelief. "For the women, at least, this seems to be their soft spot. There are girls here, girls on scholarship, girls who will be sent home if their scholarships are not funded. The women are unmoved by the plight of such girls. But mention the plight of horses and" — he snapped his fingers — "the check is signed."

"The plight of horses?" I did not want to align myself with the women he so obviously held in contempt, but I wanted to know what he meant. If I couldn't ride, I didn't know what I'd do.

"Oh, I didn't mean to alarm you, Thea. The horses aren't in any danger of being taken away." He sighed. "No one would buy them now, anyway. It's their expense that's daunting. Grain prices have shot sky-high, thanks to the drought. I never thought I'd be so familiar with the agricultural economy. Horses eat a great deal, as I'm sure you know well."

"Yes. They're big creatures." I understood the impulse to protect the animal that had no voice, no parents to look out for it. I would certainly be more willing to donate to a horse fund than a girl fund.

"I shouldn't bore you with all this," he said.

"I'm not bored." And I wasn't. I've never been less bored, I wanted to say, because this adult world, where I was not someone's daughter, or niece — well, this was entirely new to me.

"Thea Atwell, from Florida. So serious. Were you a solemn child?"

"I don't know." Usually Mr. Holmes held something in reserve; his current sociability seemed an act, bought with a drink.

He laughed. "I don't know what's gotten into me. Look here," he said, leaning forward, twisting his glass around and around, "thank you for all your help. You've been a blessing."

"In disguise," I said, and Mr. Holmes didn't laugh, as I had intended, but nodded, as if he agreed.

Walking to my cabin, I savored the quiet campus. I savored his hand that had glanced off my shoulder as I left, lingered — was that my imagination? — no, it had lingered, it had not wanted to leave. He leaned forward and thanked me and it was such a thrill, such a feeling of grace.

After dinner that night — a thick, dull stew, surprising for something so bland to emerge from the Yonahlossee kitchen, but I ate it anyway — Mr. Albrecht stood as we were eating our dessert of standard shortbread (rich but also a little dull) and told us to find our riding groups. Mr. Holmes sat next to him.

"But why?" I asked.

"The Spring Show," Molly answered, "it's soon."

"It's still February."

"There's a lot of planning. And then there's the Spring Fling, right afterward."

"You haven't heard of it?" Henny asked. "Everyone competes, everyone watches. It's splendid. If you're a house mistress you sip champagne with the adults and watch the rides."

"It is splendid!" Molly said. "There's a picnic lunch and then you get all pretty afterward for the dance."

The dining hall was a swarm of Yonahlossee girls as each of us tried to locate our group. I saw Leona from across the room, walking in a straight line. Girls moved out of her way in a neat sort of folding when they saw her coming, as if she were a thresher and they were the wheat. Her family's troubles only made us more careful of her. I remembered Leona's picture, on the wall outside Mr. Holmes's office. Most people were not themselves in a photograph: the camera rendered them too solemn, too straight-lipped, too unknowable. Sam used to say that the way people stared at the camera made it seem as if they were watching something awful. But Leona was not any more discernible in the flesh. She passed by me without acknowledging my presence and I fell in line behind her.

We found a table and sat down. My group, advanced, was responsible for designing a course for the intermediate girls. Gates sketched a triple, and we all leaned forward to watch, her pale hand flashing against the white paper. Jettie watched closely, murmured approval.

This was perfect: Mr. Albrecht still sat with Mr. Holmes at the head table; Mr. Holmes was close enough that I could see the details of his person — his crisp collar, his watch, the blunt edge of his hair — but we were arranged at such an angle that he could not see me.

Mr. Albrecht drew something in the air, Mr. Holmes nodded, his elbows rested on the table but that was fine, everything was cleared and men sometimes did that. Mr. Albrecht crossed his arms against his chest and listened to Mr. Holmes; then they were done speaking, for Mr. Albrecht was not the type of man who was good at speaking about nothing. Both their chairs had arms and ours didn't, because we were girls, not headmasters, not men. I watched their faces but they were like masks, neither looking at anything, staring past each other into the deep space marked by Yonahlossee girls.

It didn't occur to me then that it might be difficult to be a grown man surrounded by hundreds of girls, so certainly out of their reach that we could flirt, we could playfully take Mr. Albrecht's elbow in the tack room, let our hand linger in his when he helped us dismount, and he could do nothing in return. Mr. Albrecht wasn't a man, not to any of us, I don't think, because he wasn't handsome or rich or young. But we flirted with him because he was there and so were we. He probably touched himself at night, when we were ensconced in our cabins, he at home in town. He would hold himself and think of Leona's white hair against her naked back, the curve of Eva's breasts, contained by her white blouse — he cupped his hand against one, then the other, she wanted to unbutton her shirt but he wouldn't let her, liked to feel how her nipples stiffened against the cotton. She wouldn't be wearing her thick undergarments, there would be nothing except the thin, stiff cotton between his hand and her breast.

“Thea?” Leona asked.

“Yes,” I said, hopefully authoritatively, though I had no idea what they wanted.

“Does a triple meet with your approval?”

I shrugged, then tried to still my shoulders, nodded instead. Last week I’d had trouble with a triple. “It does,” I said, and wondered at her composure. Her world had altered dramatically, her family no longer what it was, and she acknowledged nothing.

Then Martha passed by our table, holding her group’s sketch (she was in Sissy’s class, and though she was a better rider than Sissy, Martha’s tranquility did nothing for her on horseback). She had little diamonds in her ears tonight, and I watched her and she was a sparkle, a glimmer, a flash — something not of this world.

Mr. Holmes seemed to be studying Martha, too. His face was very calm. I did not want to admit to myself that Martha was more beautiful than I was, though of course I knew she was, I knew almost everyone at the camp, if asked, would point to Martha as the most beautiful girl. But I also knew there wasn’t any real way to measure beauty, and perhaps something specific about my face was something Mr. Holmes might love.

Mr. Holmes turned his head, and it was a second before I realized he had caught me staring. I looked away, quickly, flustered.

"How does this all sound to you, Thea?" Leona asked again.

"I think," I said, and glanced at the sketches laid upon the table, "I think this all sounds perfect."

Leona smiled. "Are we distracting you?"

My cheeks flamed. Everyone watched me. Leona turned in her seat and looked pointedly at the table where Mr. Holmes and Mr. Albrecht sat. I shook my head. I didn't want to submit so easily to Leona, but it seemed like the quickest way to stop her.

"Well, good," she said. "We wouldn't want to do that."

Gates trailed beside me as we gathered our things and left, her sketchbook tucked neatly beneath her arm.

"Thea." Her voice low. Her cheeks red underneath her heavy freckles. "Leona won last year. She was the youngest girl to ever win."

"I know," I said. Didn't everybody know?

Gates nodded slowly. "Then you must also know how badly she wants to win again." She touched my arm. "Just be careful," she whispered.

I was surprised that Gates cared. She didn't usually involve herself in camp pettiness.

We watched Leona, who sat alone at the table, reviewing Gates's sketch. She seemed to be giving the piece of paper all her attention, which is how Leona moved through the world: whatever she did received her full attention.

"Who knows if she'll even be here by the show," Gates said, and what I felt was disappointment, not relief. Leona was my only true competitor.

That night I opened a letter from Mother. Sissy was gone, with Boone. I had been impudent in my last letter, I knew; addressing Mother as if she were my equal, when of course she was not.

Dear Thea,

You sounded angry in your last letter. I understand, of course. Yes, I was friends with Beth Holmes. She was Beth Babineaux, then. Her family was a great New Orleans family. Rich as the day was long. I don't suppose they're rich like that now, but who knows. I lost touch with her; I lost touch with everyone, and would you like to know why? I had all I needed with you and Sam and your father. I could have had twenty friends; I could have had thirty. But your family is your greatest friend, Thea. I didn't tell you I knew Beth before you left because there were so many other things on my mind. It wasn't a plot, Thea. I honestly wouldn't have imagined you'd cared.

We sold the house. Astonishingly, someone wanted to buy it; I hadn't thought there would be any takers but your father was right: there are still people with money. We are among them, luckily. I am packing up all our things now. We are moving to Orlando, where your father will work. We might eventually move farther south, to Miami. It's all up in the air. We needed to get Sam away. We needed a fresh start, as you have there, at Yonahlossee.

Love,
Mother

I tore the letter into tiny bits as soon as I was finished. I was not astonished that someone else wanted my house; it was beautiful, perfect. What shocked me was that my parents would do this. That it was gone. I truly hadn't thought that Mother would ever leave.

I knew even as I was ripping the letter that it was foolish, a gesture no one but myself would see. I'd have to get on my hands and knees tomorrow to gather any stray pieces from beneath the bed. And the other girls might notice, they might wonder what in the world I was doing, and then I'd have to come up with a lie, yet another one, to make my family seem like a different one.

My next thought was Sasi. I had known he was going to be sold, since I was getting too big for him anyway, but I had pushed the thought from my mind. Would we live on a farm in Orlando? Or a place where you could see your neighbor's house, or both neighbors' houses, from your own? Would they sell Sasi to a girl or a boy? Would Sam go to school in Orlando? And did she think I was dumb? That Yonahlossee was anything but a place to get rid of me? If it was a fresh start, I was a monkey's uncle.

A year ago and I would not have believed any of it: Father leaving his patients, Mother leaving her house. But I believed it now. The worst thing I could do, I knew, the thing to hurt her most, would be to not write a letter in return.

I was afraid he wouldn't come back, but he did, the very next day, sent Decca upstairs just like the last time, and I felt both grateful and fearful.

"Decca's doing well?"

I nodded. He was looking around for

another drink, had already polished off the first. I waited for his voice to waver a little, for his gestures to become less precise. Alcohol turned Mr. Holmes into a boy.

What I noticed about him in the flesh — that his pinky joint was swollen, rubbed raw by something, that there was a dry patch of skin on his forearm — was not what I noticed when I imagined him. It was the same with Georgie. I would dream about how blissful it would feel when he touched me, but then when he did I would notice strange things: how bony his elbow was, how he smelled faintly of stale hay.

"Have you heard about Leona's family?" he asked.

I was surprised. He'd never mentioned another Yonahlossee girl to me; he was breaking a rule.

"Yes," I said, "everyone has."

"Have they?" He smiled, and fiddled with a cuff link. It looked old. His father's, his grandfather's. "And what has everyone heard?"

His tone unsettled me. "It's none of my business," I said. I didn't want him to think I was nosy.

"Has that ever stopped anyone before? It would be unnatural, in a place like this, not to care about other people's concerns." It was all happening so quickly, this shift from fine to horrible.

"I don't know what you mean," I said, but I did. I tried to keep my voice light, so that we could talk about something else, but the sound of my light voice irritated him, and he shook his head.

"Oh, of course you do. You're always watching, aren't you? All these silly girls, you watch them, don't you? They come to you with all their worries and you listen and tell them nothing in return."

"They don't come to me that often."

"You watch, I know, because I watch *you,* sometimes, I see how you slink, how you creep around all the other girls and *notice* things —" He stopped. "Your face doesn't move, Thea. You hold yourself apart. What must the other girls think of you?"

I willed myself not to cry. "I don't think they do, much." I felt fragile, Mother's letter a week old but still every word fresh and stark; if I ever saw my home again I would see it as a stranger. It was lost to me. Would Sasi's next boy or girl love him as I had? It did not seem possible. I'd spent more time with Sasi than I had with Sam. I knew from the way he cocked his ears if he was frightened or simply excited; I knew from the way he nipped my shoulder if he was angry or playful.

"And I don't think you really believe that."

If he had been my friend, I would have asked him: Why are you being so mean? So cruel? But he was not my friend.

I stood. "I have to be going now." I had been so, so stupid. I wasn't Mr. Holmes's confidante. I wasn't his friend. I was no more, no less than a gossipy Yonahlossee girl. But I was even worse than that: Mr. Holmes believed I thought I was better than everyone else. Nothing could have been further from the truth — that was my first thought. And my second, which came so quickly I wondered if it was the truer thought, was that I *was* better. I didn't let myself get too involved with the camp because I felt, somewhere deep down, that I was better than all of those girls. That I knew more, had understood more, was destined for a different sort of life.

I walked past him to the coat closet, fiddled with the knob, I didn't know how to open it, I had never opened it before. Where was Emmy, she should be here, she should have interrupted us, stopped him. I wanted to tell him that the different sort of life I was destined for was not a better sort of life. That in some dark moments I would give anything to take back everything I had done.

My ears roared and I didn't hear him until he was right behind me. I stayed where I was; for the world, I wouldn't have turned and faced him. He drew a finger along my spine.

"Always hold yourself so straight, even when you're slinking. Did I ever tell you that was the first thing I noticed about you, when your father came here? That your posture was perfect." His finger traveled down my back, stopped at my tailbone. "I suppose I wouldn't have told you that, would I? Wouldn't have had the occasion. Leona will have to leave, Thea. It has all fallen apart, it is all falling apart. I can't get my tenses straight." His voice had turned soft.

I turned to face him, and he touched my cheek. "I'm sorry, Thea. I have a mean streak, it seems. It is all wrong," he said, and then he was gone.

I didn't open the coat closet until I heard him upstairs, above me, in Decca's room. I tried to button my coat but my hands shook, both of them, terribly. And my hands never shook.

I left and went to my cabin. I was alone, and even though I knew everyone else would be at the Hall, I was still grateful. Everything was in order, our nightgowns folded and tucked into drawers, our lotions and perfumes carefully capped and lined on our washstands, our beds made in the morning and then straightened by Docey after rest hour. There were personal effects: framed photographs, pictures from magazines, purple velvet jewelry boxes. Ghosts lived here, we haunted this cabin, we hadn't ever truly claimed it.

I felt tricked. I had liked his kindness, and now his kindness had disappeared, but I still wanted him. I wanted him more, if that was possible.

I didn't bother to pull the covers up. No one was here, no one would see that I hiked my skirt up over my waist, put my dirty shoes on the quilt, moved my hand so roughly that I was raw afterward. No one heard me. No one saw the smear of blood, no one asked why I stared so long out the window, what could I possibly be watching for that long? Nothing, nothing.

When I sat at my dressing table I straddled my chair like I was riding. I was riding, even when I wasn't, a horse was always in my head. I spent at most two hours a day on a horse, the rest on the ground like a girl, but even so, when I walked on my own two feet my gait was vaguely, constantly unsettling, as if I were always stepping onto dry ground from a ship.

I was on a streak, I cleared every jump with an inch to spare. With two inches. Mr. Albrecht had me lead demonstrations for the other classes. This is what it looks like. You are not a pretty rider, he told me once, you are not graceful but you are technically flawless.

I wanted to win. Leona was making it easy, to want to beat her. I saw now that her friendliness toward me coincided with my convalescence. And now that I was a threat, her only real threat, she ignored me when she saw me in the Castle. At the Hall last week I'd seen her giggling with Jettie. I'd smiled at Jettie but she'd turned her back, and Leona had looked over Jettie's shoulder for a long second, assessing me, until she'd whispered something else into Jettie's ear and Jettie's sturdy back was shaking from laughter. I'd looked down quickly and checked myself, but nothing seemed amiss; my cheeks burned and I'd turned to Eva, asked her a dumb question, and tried to look like I didn't care.

I realized that other girls probably wondered what was said about them all the time. But I had never before known the peculiar sensation of both wanting to know and then never wanting to know what someone else thought of you.

Being so close to Sissy had served me well; I was liked because she was liked, I absorbed some of her radiance and passed it off as my own. Mostly, though, I was not well known.

At dinner, Molly had once teased me about being too solemn. When I had said something funny in the Hall, the group of girls Sissy and I were sitting with had laughed and looked a little stunned that I had a sense of humor. Now Mr. Holmes told me that I slinked. What else slinked? Animals, criminals.

Did Leona and Jettie make fun of how solemn I was? Did they think I was proud?

During practice Leona cut me off, twice. And then I did a strange thing: I trotted Naari directly in front of King, passing them so closely King left a trail of spit on my boot. I polished it off later, still surprised.

It was unusual for two third-years to be the best. And it must have been doubly unusual that Leona had been the best last year, as a second-year. Besides me, Gates, and Leona, the rest of our class were seniors. And though Gates was a very elegant rider, she was too fussy, too appraising on the back of a horse, to ever be excellent.

But now I wanted to be inserted into Yonahlossee history. I wanted to be admired, I wanted my photograph to hang on the wall outside Mr. Holmes's office. I wanted him to pass by me a dozen times a day, every time he came or went. I wanted people to see me and think I was pretty, yes, but that I was more than pretty: that I was good at something the way few people are good at anything in their entire lives.

Was it too much to want that? Was it too much to want him? Yes and yes. In the back of my mind, the nasty thought always lingered that I would be happier if I did not want so much.

16

"When are we going to Gainesville?" I asked Mother, as we were stripping my bed.

"I don't know — let's move a little faster, hmm?"

I tugged the sheets from Mother and threw them on the floor, adding them to the pile of dirty linens. "All right," I said, "can we go soon, do you think?"

Mother glanced at me, but seemed distracted.

"Maybe Georgie could come here?"

She unfurled a sheet, tucked it beneath her chin, and smoothed out wrinkles with her palm. All in one motion — she was so deft at these chores, she could fold a complicated blouse in a second, iron my father's shirt in under a minute. We hadn't seen Georgie's family in three weeks, nearly a month. I understood that there was a reason we had not seen each other in so long; Mother had made this reason clear to Sam.

But I wanted to see my cousin. I wanted to see him badly.

"Why isn't Idella doing this?" I resented my mother's quick, able hands, scurrying over my bed, my private bed, tucking in corners and picking up invisible specks of lint, dust, something.

She ignored me. "There, all done."

"Is Father eating with us tonight?"

She turned from the curtains, which she had been shaking — particles of gleaming dust were suspended in the air.

"I don't know that, either."

"I guess nobody wants to see us."

She turned from the curtains. "What do you mean?"

"I'm lonely."

She sat down next to me; her breath smelled like coffee and the lavender toothpaste she used. She looked around my room, then finally spoke. "This house charms people. I've always thought that. It's so beautiful. It's so . . . lovely. You'll never live in a place like this again, Thea. You should love it."

"I do love it," I said.

"Someday you'll meet a man and fall in love and want to go where he goes," she said, as if she were reading aloud from a fairy tale, as if she were hardly listening to me, "and you'll have to make a new home for yourself."

"Mother!" I tugged at my hair. I hated when she did this, changed what you had said you wanted. I thought about my cousin's thick, sturdy hands. *That* was all I wanted. Not a husband. But she continued, trancelike.

"You will meet a husband, Thea." Mother stood, and I saw the crow's-feet that framed her eyes, the worry lines that creased her forehead. I said nothing. I gave her nothing.

"And you'll have to be careful to choose the right one. It will seem like fun and games, but it's not. Not at all."

"It was like that for you?" I asked. "Unfun?"

She smiled, and shook her head. "*Unfun* isn't a word, Thea. It was fine for me — look at the result."

She gestured around the room, grandly, and stopped at me, as if to say — You, you are what I got. Which I suppose I was.

But then Georgie's family did come, the very next week. Mother told us over breakfast, as if it was nothing unusual. And perhaps it wasn't. The money Uncle George had borrowed had fixed whatever needed to be fixed, like a paste, like the hay I stuffed into a crack in the barn's wall.

Greetings were exchanged on the front porch — I was kissed, exclaimed over.

"Perfect weather," Mother pronounced. It was perfect weather, the brief stretch of spring we would have before descending into the maddening heat of summer. But Mother thought it boring to talk about the weather. She was trying to be cheerful, I saw, trying to distract.

I kept my eyes trained away from Georgie as I spoke to my aunt and uncle.

The adults left us and then it was only the three of us, as it usually was. I smoothed my hands across my bottom to make sure I hadn't bled through, a movement so practiced it was unconscious. I wasn't menstruating right now, but I wasn't regular, as Mother put it, and so I could start any time, really. I wondered if other mothers kept such close track of their daughters' bodies.

"Let's go out back," Sam began, "I'll bring my tent, and Idella will pack us lunch, and . . ." While Sam was explaining his plan, I met Georgie's eyes for the first time. He met mine, I should say. I watched for a glimmer of something.

I felt almost insane with desire. Should I call it that? Lust. A specific yearning. I didn't know how this would be.

"Sam," Georgie said, taking his eyes away, "no. None of that for me today. I'm going to stay inside and work on homework."

Georgie's voice was cruelly casual. In an instant, I regretted everything; I wanted Georgie to be nice, I wanted Sam not to be hurt, I wanted it all the way it had been.

"Why?" Sam asked, crestfallen. He looked to me, then Georgie, like he was trying to put the pieces together. But I did not want to be a piece of this puzzle. I was furious at Georgie, suddenly. He should not goad Sam. He should not try to make him wonder.

We both waited for Georgie to speak. I did not want to say anything; speaking would mean choosing a side, and which side would I choose? I looked at Sam, his auburn hair cut just yesterday, by Mother. Then Georgie, who watched Sam calmly.

"Why?" Georgie said, mimicking Sam. My stomach turned, it truly did — a flip beneath my skin. "Because I don't want to pretend to camp. I don't want to pretend anything, today."

"Georgie!" I said, and they both looked at me, my brother and cousin. I shook my head. "Nothing. I'll go with you, Sam." I stood.

Sam shook his head. It was too late. "No,"

he said, "I'll go by myself."

"Thea," Georgie said, after Sam had gone inside, but I was so mad I felt sick with it.

"Why did you do that?" I asked. "Why?"

He began to answer, but I didn't want to hear. I slipped inside the house, quietly, in case the adults were near; I meant to follow Sam, but he had already disappeared. I could have found him if I'd wanted to, I knew all the likely places he had gone. But if he didn't want to be found, there was no point in looking.

I sipped Mother's champagne while the adults visited. Uncle George had said it was four o'clock in the afternoon, cocktail hour somewhere. Aunt Carrie's one sister was doing poorly; her other sister had responded to the death better than anyone had predicted. Wasn't it always a surprise, my mother said, how a person acted after he had lost someone.

"Where are the boys?" Uncle George asked.

"Out back, I think," I said, though I didn't know. They had both disappeared after this morning's squabble.

"Hunting," Father said. He looked at his glass, which he held with two hands, a child's grip.

“Maiming the defenseless and innocent,” Uncle George said, and then dropped the glass decanter stopper he had been holding on the mahogany coffee table, the one that was particularly hard to keep unblemished. Its surface had been buffed and varnished until you could see a blurry reflection of yourself in the reddish wood. That hadn’t been what Father had meant. He meant they were hunting animals for Sam’s terrariums, not hunting animals to kill. But they were doing neither.

“Oops,” Uncle George murmured, and spilled a little whiskey onto the rug. Mother moved to help but he waved her away. He was quick with his napkin, blotted the spilled alcohol instead of rubbing it, which would smear the dyes.

“You do that well,” I said.

“Thea,” my father said sharply. I turned my face. I was not myself right now, and it was difficult to be kind to Uncle George, who looked so much like his son. I didn’t think this was possible, but somewhere on the edge of my mind an idea lurked: Georgie would find Sam, tell him about us, and it would all end.

Uncle George laughed. “It’s fine. I might as well help myself to another while I’m here,” he said, and poured a neat glass.

We were all silent for a moment. My father stared into his drink. Mother watched the carpet; I knew she wanted nothing more in the world than to be able to properly clean it. I knew well the idea of self-preservation, from Sam and his animals. Georgie would not tell, because telling would mean something bad for him, too.

"Thea," Uncle George said, and my father's glass trembled when his brother spoke. "Thea, you're getting awfully pretty."

"Thank you."

"She looks exactly like her mother did at that age. She's the spitting image. Wouldn't you agree?"

My father glanced at me briefly, and shrugged. "No, I wouldn't know. I didn't know Elizabeth at that age, remember? Neither did you."

"She does," my mother said, and touched the end of my braid. I knew she was trying to distract my father, but I didn't want her to touch me. And besides, I didn't look like her. I wasn't ever going to be as pretty as she was. Which was fine — what had it gotten her? A house in the middle of nowhere. "My hair, mainly. She has Felix's forehead, more and more."

Father smiled, as if at a private joke.

"It's interesting," she continued, "to look

at photographs and see how you change year to year."

"Is it?" Aunt Carrie asked. "I've always thought looking at pictures of myself was an exercise in vanity. And boring, besides." I looked at Aunt Carrie, shocked. I'd never heard her speak to my mother like this.

Mother furrowed her brow and pretended the rim of her champagne flute was the most interesting thing in the world. She was close to tears. Aunt Carrie stared intently at the fireplace, empty, swept clean, and the men did nothing.

My father broke the silence. "You are quite pretty, Thea," he said. "A smart, pretty girl."

"The whole world's at her feet," Uncle George said, his voice picking up again, eager to help his brother relieve the pall that had settled over the room.

"I'll bet you have twenty suitors by this time next year," Uncle George said. "Thirty."

"I don't think so," my father said humorously. "Not in my house."

"I don't want any suitors," I said.

"That will change," Aunt Carrie said. Her voice was strange. I wondered how much she'd had to drink.

"It will!" Uncle George said. "Of course."

I heard the distant slam of the screen door.

Sam came in first. He walked to the coffee table and took a handful of cheese biscuits, then flipped the tail of my braid, and the relief I felt — it felt like another chance.

"One at a time," Mother said, and Sam nodded but continued to stuff himself.

Georgie came in and met my eye and smiled, then sat next to Sam — at his feet, because there wasn't another chair — and they continued a conversation they'd begun elsewhere, chattering about a swimming hole in Gainesville. And then the adults began their own chatter, about nothing, about everything, and I was so grateful Georgie hadn't told, I wanted to weep.

But the quality of the adults' chatter was off; they sounded tense, distracted. I noticed that while Georgie was pretending to listen to my brother, his attention was elsewhere. He was watching the adults, very carefully. He caught me staring, and grinned in a way that chilled me. Something about the way he had turned his attention from them to me, as if we were connected.

I understood then that my family could never know my secret. Money, money where money did not belong, had almost ruined us. I understood that loving, where loving did not belong, would be much worse. No, they simply could not know. But that did not mean that I would stop.

After I had lain on top of the covers for an hour, the rest of the house asleep, after I stopped feeling impatient and entered into desperation, my door opened, and Georgie motioned for me to follow. He was wearing his regular clothes, thoughtless, my brother would have noticed. The stairs were mercifully quiet. The remnants of a key lime tart had been moved from the dining room onto the kitchen table, a tacky, grotesque mess now.

He almost let the screen door slam, and I felt a flash of anger. I caught it and eased it shut.

A fog had come and made the outside world impenetrable. I slowed, walked more carefully; Georgie plowed ahead, almost disappeared into the white.

We were both barefoot, and as we walked blindly to the barn I was half afraid I'd step on something sharp. But not afraid enough to turn around and get my shoes, or to have paused as we left the house and slipped them on. Not afraid enough to make Georgie wait.

He dipped in and out of the fog, in flashes;

I saw a hand, an elbow, then nothing at all. He was a stranger to me, that's how I could do this, behave like a girl who would shame her family so easily.

When I reached the barn, I went first to Sasi. Before my brain caught up with my heart, I thought he was missing. But then I saw that he was lying down, asleep, his knobby, thin legs tucked carefully beneath him.

"Thea?"

I turned and put my finger to my lips, but Sasi was already hoisting himself up, illustrating in a second how improbable a horse's body was, how dainty and inadequate his legs were.

"Why did you do that?" I asked.

"Do what?"

"Don't play dumb," I said. I put my hand flat against his chest, and I could feel his heart thumping against bone, through blood.

"Oh, that." He touched my finger. I wondered if he could also feel his heart, through my hand. "He's such a child sometimes." I started to speak and he touched my lips, then put his finger inside my mouth. It tasted like dirt, and I liked it. "I'll be nice to him, don't worry."

And I didn't worry. I had other things to

think about, now. Sasi pricked his ears toward us, curious, and then Georgie was kissing my neck, then licking it, and there was a roar in my ears, and he roamed over my breasts with his thick hands, and the roar subsided, turned into a distant buzz. Georgie combed his fingers through my hair, tenderly, and I thought of my mother, who was the only other person who did that.

"You are certainly," he said, and then paused, and undid the top button of my nightgown and put his hand down the front, "very beautiful."

He led me to a stall, and slid the lock open and pushed me inside. There was a blanket from the house already draped over the packed-dirt floor; a good blanket, from Mother's stacks.

I pointed to the blanket. "Don't leave that here. Mother will notice."

He shook his head and relocked the stall door, the familiar sound of metal against metal. He turned back to me, his erection pushing against his pants, like a tumor, a growth. He backed me into a corner and thrust his groin into me. His pants were thick, wool — winter pants. My nightgown was thin cotton. I felt everything, his sensation was dulled. I closed my eyes and unbuttoned Georgie's pants on the second try, I reached inside and was surprised again by how soft and tender his penis felt.

There were little flashes where my brain should have been, as if it had receded for this. We were on the blanket, Georgie was on top of me, my nightgown was hiked to my waist, and Georgie's penis was touching me, was slippery because I was wet and he had parted me and put his penis against the slickness. Then it felt very big between my legs, almost painful, and I didn't want this to happen, not yet, not in this way, so I flipped him over, in one smooth motion, and he was surprised. *I* was surprised, too, but I wrapped my legs around his thigh and moved while I also moved my hand fast over his penis. The same rhythm in my legs and my hands, and I couldn't get it quite right, the rhythm, I was doing two things at once and neither was right. So I moved faster, and the intense ache between my legs subsided briefly before it exploded, and then I stopped touching Georgie altogether for a second. I could see more clearly now, could see that Georgie was watching me, his hands folded beneath his head as if he were looking at the sky on a clear day. I smiled at him. I began again where I had left off.

I remember feeling very adult, for the first

time in my life.

I came in from hitting golf balls with Georgie and Sam around lunchtime and saw Mother, who had been upstairs all morning. Uncle George was off with Father, but Aunt Carrie had made herself scarce on this visit.

Mother smiled at me and returned to her paper, the glasses she used when reading small print slipping down her nose. I took three sandwiches from the platter Idella had left on the table.

"Aren't you going to ride today?"

"We're playing golf." Mother nodded slowly. I didn't want to tell her I had started menstruating this morning. It was private. "We're not very good," I added.

She reached underneath the table; I didn't know what she was doing until I noticed that her arm was now weighed down by the blanket.

"This was out," she said. She pushed her glasses up. She hated to wear them, but Father said she would wear out her eyes if she didn't.

"Oh?"

"In the barn. Maybe Sam and Georgie were using it, for their hunting? Not you? Sam should know not to use the good blankets. This is an old carriage blanket, it's older than you, you and Sam together."

I nodded, and after I gave Sam and Georgie their sandwiches I went to the front, muttered something about the mail, and sat on the steps. I looked at the road that was only traveled twice a day: my father going, my father returning. I had been stupid. Stupid, stupid girl. I felt very desperate. This is what it feels like to be desperate, I whispered to myself. Stop it.

If Sam suspected, if he could no longer keep the secret and had confided in Mother, if, leaving Sam out of it, Mother had seen something on her own, peered through one of the hundreds, thousands of windows this house boasted — we did not shirk when it came to glass, Father said, your mother loves the light — if she had looked into my world with Georgie, and if in that moment in that world he had touched my cheek, kissed me, bitten my thumb . . . if, if, if.

17

The next time I saw him it was the same thing: he sent Decca away and accepted a drink from Emmy. We sat for a moment before he spoke.

"The girls are starting to apply for next year."

"Is it a rigorous application process?"

He smiled. "It can be."

"Are we handpicked from thousands?"

"You weren't," he said, "but yes, there is some handpicking involved."

From upstairs we heard Emmy's sharp warning, Decca's hysterical giggle. She often acted this way in the afternoons, like a horse who had been pent up in his stall for days. A few moments later I heard the front door open and close. Through the window I saw a glimpse of Emmy leading Decca across the Square.

Mr. Holmes sat in his leather chair, I sat on a couch, two, three feet away from him.

"How do you pick?" I put my hand on the couch, as if to make smaller the distance between us.

"Family connections. If your sister went here, or your cousin. What kind of family you come from. We try to have some parity among the states. Though St. Louis is as far north as we ever get. And then after all that I suppose we look at the girl herself. What her parents want her to achieve while she's here."

"What her parents want," I echoed.

"Yes. They write the letter, they answer the questions on the application. Her father, usually. Did you think it would be otherwise?"

I was silent.

"To have all your decisions made for you is a curse. But it's one you know well, I assume." He had known exactly what I had meant; he had articulated what I meant better than I could have. But he seemed distant, today.

"It wasn't always like that for me." I smiled at what I had said — why was I defending my father? But Mr. Holmes looked at me expectantly, so I continued. "I never felt like that, like everything was decided for me, until they sent me here."

"Here," he said, and seemed lost in

thought.

"Do you like it?" I asked. I was losing his attention.

"Yes," he finally said. "In the end I do. What I tell myself is that this world is changing quickly, that female education is becoming vital. But truly I fell into this position, and it's a nice enough life, a nice enough place for the girls. Though most of the time I think I'd rather be reading a book." He closed his eyes and rubbed his temples. "You don't think, when you are young, that you will simply fall into your life. But that," he said, and raised his head and looked at me, "is exactly what happens."

I stood and went to him, quickly, so that I wouldn't convince myself not to. I sat down beside him, in the small space the chair allowed. And what compelled me to do what I did next? If I had moved away, or simply done nothing — well, I feel certain Mr. Holmes would not have touched me. He had touched me last time, yes, but today it felt as if he would not; today felt as if we were going to erase the sins of yesterday. And I did not want them to be erased; if he erased how he had touched me — well, then he erased me, Thea, what small stake I had eked out in his life. And so I put my hand on his knee, and turned my face into his coat.

He did not move away. The pleasure of that moment was so extraordinary it felt almost unbearable, a gift too large. At first he was tense, but then I felt him relax. If a Yonahlossee girl walked in and saw us, she would be shocked, briefly, but then she would think that Mr. Holmes was comforting me; that I had been upset, that our headmaster offered solace.

Or perhaps I was fooling myself. Perhaps she would know exactly what she saw.

"It's a beautiful place."

"Yes, Thea." He put his palm on my cheek. His voice trembled. "We can't," he said.

"It's all right," I murmured into his shirt. I had been right in divining his feelings.

He stood, and looked down at me. "You have brought me comfort. I don't know why. It shouldn't be this way. Do you know how bad it is out there?" He wore a pained expression, now. "This place might close, Thea. Let's hope Mrs. Holmes works magic out there, but we are asking people for money they do not have, or money they want to hold on to." He shook his head. "But let's hope that's not true, let's hope that this is simply the worst year in everyone's life. And lucky you, to have the worst year come so early. You have nothing except hopeful years ahead."

I laughed, and then I stood so that we faced each other, Mr. Holmes and I. He raised a hand and I thought he might touch me, but then he brushed his hair from his forehead, and I saw that his hand shook, and I was thrilled, I was unnerved, I was exhilarated: his hand shook because of me.

"Why are you laughing, Thea?" he asked softly. "Everybody's life is falling apart. What do you want? I know what I want, right now. If things weren't so bad outside here maybe I'd want it less. But desperation leads men to do desperate things. Isn't that right? Tell me it's right."

Instead of answering I kissed him. Even in that moment I was shocked at my boldness, but grateful for it, too. He was so much better than Georgie, so firm and gentle. Georgie was sometimes rough. Mr. Holmes stood, and looked down at me, and took a step backward, and I couldn't tell if he was stepping away from me or asking me to follow him.

"Take me somewhere," I whispered. He looked at me for a moment, then turned his head and looked out the window, and I knew he was deciding.

"Where would you like to go?" His voice was so solemn.

If I did not answer, it was because his question didn't seem to require an answer. Because I knew precisely where I wanted to go. With him, anywhere.

In the end, after one hundred seconds, two hundred, he led me upstairs into his library. He moved quickly, almost clumsily, as if he was surprised by the course of this afternoon. He closed the door behind us and I glimpsed all the books that lined the walls before he laid me on the couch. He drew me to him and the way his hand rested on my back almost undid me; I moaned, and he kissed me. By the end, he lay on top of me. He kissed my mouth, my face, my neck. I'd never been kissed like this. I felt helpless, my arms pinned to my sides by his weight, but helpless in a very lovely way.

Mr. Holmes offered solace. But so did I. We took comfort in each other.

Leona caught me as I was leaving Masters, en route to Augusta House. I tried to ignore her, but she did not want to be ignored, today.

"Weather's turning," she said, and sidled up next to me. I said nothing. "I'm going to visit King," she said, when we were almost at my cabin. "Do you want to come?"

All the other girls disappeared into their cabins. I only had on a light sweater, and now I buttoned it against the chill. A storm had threatened all day but never come; one of those days that felt like a menace.

I could still feel the full weight of Mr. Holmes on top of me, even as I walked through the Square, even as I stood here, deciding what to say to Leona; as if some trace of what we had just done was mine to carry with me, now. I felt changed.

"Why?" I asked.

"Why? I just thought you might enjoy it. I just thought —"

"Stop. I thought that at least you, of all people, would have no tolerance for artifice. So stop, please."

Something shifted in Leona's stance. "All right," she said coolly.

She eyed a group of passing girls. That she could be so casual while we were having this discussion infuriated me. Again I felt the impulse to touch her, to hurt her.

She tilted her head. "I guess you're kept busy," she said, "by other things, now. You're such a busy girl, Thea." She paused, and I knew she was going to say the worst thing to me now, the reason she had sidled up beside me in the first place. "Why was it you were sent away again?"

I stood there speechless, foolish, aware of how helpless I must seem.

I spotted Sissy coming down the steps of the Castle, and walked, half ran past Leona to join her. She had undone me. Leona called out: "But I forgot. You're not a girl anymore. You're very adult now, aren't you? You spend so much time with adults lately."

Aren't you leaving soon? It was on the tip of my tongue to call out. But I couldn't. It seemed too bad, even for me.

We watched Leona walk away, disappear into the woods.

"Off to see King," I muttered.

"Did you hear?" Sissy asked.

"Hear what?" I thought she was going to tell me that Mrs. Holmes was returning.

"About Leona."

"No." I felt light with relief. I still had more time.

"She'll be gone by the beginning of summer. And when she goes, King stays here."

"Oh, no," I said. I was horrified. To have to leave her horse when she had done nothing wrong. I had had to leave Sasi, but I had nearly outgrown him anyway. And still, it had been miserable. But there was some small part of me that took pleasure in Leona's misery. She was so awful; perhaps that's why awful things happened to her. "That's awful," I said, because Sissy seemed to expect more of a response.

"Not as awful as everything else that's happened to her family," Sissy said, and looked at me curiously, and though I did not agree I said nothing. *This* was the most awful thing to happen to Leona, of course it was.

The next time I saw Mr. Holmes he led me to his library again, and closed the door, and I reached for him, but he stopped my hand in midair. Even that, his hand on mine, was thrilling.

I could feel what he was doing, the way he held my hand, as if stopping a child. He was asking if I wanted to stop. But I did not want to stop.

"Emmy's gone?" I asked.

"Gone," he echoed. "With Decca."

I kissed him, then, and the idea that we were going to stop, that we would not touch each other again, disappeared, a puff of smoke.

He kissed my neck, and unbuttoned the first button of my blouse. His hand shook, and I touched it.

"You're so lovely, Thea," he said. His voice was sonorous, trembling.

He brought my hand to his cheek, and held it there for a moment while he watched my face, and I had never before felt so observed, so carefully accounted.

Then I took my hand back and began to unbutton my blouse, began the process by which I would reveal myself to him, and the moment felt so tender, so utterly unlike anything I had felt before. Mr. Holmes touched my breasts, and then pressed me to him and slid down to the floor, so that he was kneeling in front of me.

The world today was dark, wintery, the kind of day we never had in Florida. I could only see the mountains from his window, the rest of camp below my line of sight.

"Thea," he said, and took my hands in his, "you want this?" And his voice was so kind, gentle. I wanted to please him; I wanted to be pleased by him.

I nodded. "Yes," I said, and I almost didn't trust my voice. "Yes."

He put his hand under my skirt and slid it up my thigh until he reached the line of my panties.

"Take these off," he murmured, and I let him peel down first my stockings, then my panties. I felt very relaxed, sleepy but not tired. He stroked the inside of my thigh.

I put my hands on his shoulders to steady

myself, and he looked up at me, and I saw this was going very quickly for both of us, now.

"Open your legs." I did. He put one finger inside me, and I tensed.

"Does it hurt?"

I shook my head.

"Here," he said, and pulled me down next to him, on the rug. He lay at my side and undid his trousers. He put his finger back inside me, then another, and pushed up my skirt.

"There," he said, "I can see you. You're so . . ." He stroked my forehead. His voice was so soft, so loose.

"Beautiful."

He smiled. "Are you supposed to give yourself compliments? I was going to say something else. You're so . . ."

I waited. He pushed his fingers farther into me, and it was such an odd pressure that I loved.

"Exceptional," he said. "Beautiful, too, but there are so many beautiful girls. Be something besides that, Thea."

"All right," I said. "I'll try."

He took himself out and I touched him, but he shook his head. "No, just lie there. Just lie there."

"And be exceptional."

"Yes." He kept his fingers inside me as he touched himself and looked at me until he came, and then he seemed like he was in great pain for an instant, closed his eyes and cursed.

We lay there on the rug together afterward.

"Can I ask you something?"

"Nothing too complicated, please," Mr. Holmes said. He patted my hand. I smiled. Everything was so easy, now. If I could lie right here forever, shut the door on my life and everything it held, I would. In that moment, I would have.

"Thea?" His voice was gentle.

"Mr. Holmes —"

"Jesus. Please call me Henry. I'm begging you."

I turned and faced him. He placed his palm on my torso. "So strong."

"You know Mrs. Holmes knew my mother?"

"Yes."

I waited for him to tense — he rarely spoke of Mrs. Holmes — but he didn't.

"Do you think you'll ever leave?"

He was quiet for a long time. "I'm sorry," I finally said. "Never —"

"No, it's all right. In a way. Will I ever leave Yonahlossee? It's a question I ask myself, of course. In a way I like it here.

When I was young all I wanted to do was leave Boston. I hated it there. And then I left." He seemed lost in thought.

"Where did you go?" I asked.

"New Orleans. And then we ended up here. I thought the South would be different. And it was. But not different enough." He turned to me. "But you can never really leave your home, can you?"

"I didn't want to leave," I said. "I loved my home."

He lifted a handful of my hair and inspected it. "You had such long hair when you came here. And then you cut it off, like everyone else." He smiled. "You should remember that the sins of youth seem very far away when you're no longer young."

I said nothing. I thought of my mother, my father, my brother. Sasi. My first pony, before Sasi, dead for years now.

"Do you see your family at all now?" I asked.

He shook his head. "After my father died, Beth and I met my mother in Philadelphia, when Sarabeth was a baby. But since then, no."

"What did you do?"

I must have sounded stricken, because he propped himself up on his elbow and touched my cheek. "Thea, Thea. I didn't do anything. My parents wanted me to be a certain person, and I wasn't that person. I was a great disappointment. But — and this took me years to realize — they were a great disappointment to me as well." He watched me. "Thea, I don't know what you did, but you came here so that your family could forget. So that you could forget, so that when you leave here what happened will have disappeared."

"I ruined my family."

"I doubt that," he said quietly. "If your family was ruined, it wasn't because of you."

"They trusted me."

"Who?"

"My parents, my brother."

"Your brother may have trusted you, but your parents never did. Parents never trust their children. I don't know what happened exactly, and you don't need to tell me. I believed for a long time that I had shamed my family. But it's in a family's best interest to make a child believe that." He spoke quietly, but also firmly. He taught a single class at Yonahlossee, an advanced literature seminar that the senior girls took. I wondered if this was how he explained the characters in books to his class. It seemed so important to him that I understand what he meant.

I nodded, but said nothing.

"Do you really see? You're sixteen years old. What your family thinks of you seems like everything. But it's not. They have their own interests to protect. I wish I'd known that, how much a family has to protect, how sometimes a child interferes with that."

"You know it now."

"Was that a question? I do. Yes, I do." He paused. "You have a brother, correct? Did they send him away, too?" But they weren't really questions, none of them.

"I have a cousin, too," I said.

"And where is he?"

I shook my head. "I don't know," I said finally.

The light was becoming dim behind the curtains. Mr. Holmes kissed my forehead and held me very close. "So your brother is home. Your cousin is some place unnamed. And you are here. With me." He drew his finger across my lips. "They traded you, Thea. They sent you here and kept your brother." I started to speak, but he shook his head. "Don't believe them," he said very softly. "Don't ever believe what is said about you."

I took his hand and put it in between my legs, and he looked at me uncertainly, and then he understood, and his fingers were cold at first. He knew better than Georgie what to do. He knew how to prop himself up on his elbow, so that he could watch me. He moved his fingers slowly, and I was not embarrassed, or shy to look at him, as I usually was.

"You're very wet, Thea. And exceptional."

There was something in his tone that I couldn't quite place. "Faster, please."

"Certainly."

I touched my breasts, and closed my eyes. He knew how to lead me very carefully up this path; he would not go too quickly, or slowly. I moaned, which I could do because the house was empty. I bucked against his hand, and he pushed me down, gently. My eyes were closed but I saw anyway — in quick flashes I saw my mother, my brother, Sasi, and then Georgie, Georgie, Georgie — and his hand disappeared, everything disappeared, and there were only bright flashes and my cousin's face.

I opened my eyes and stopped his hand. He was watching me very carefully. I pulled his head onto my chest, and we lay there like that for a while, until I heard the bell ring, and I tried to hold Georgie's face in my mind. It was the first time in a long time I had thought of him and not felt pain.

■ ■ ■ ■

So: I knew this would end, I knew Mrs. Holmes would return. It was the end of February. She would be back by mid-March. But I had always been expert at ignoring the unalterable. Sometimes it was as if God was watching, had narrowed His vision until Yonahlossee appeared, nestled in the mountains. I had wanted something very badly, and then I had gotten it, and the getting kept getting better.

Winter began to disappear. Lifted, like a second skin. Docey took away our comforters from the ends of our beds. Our yellow-and-blue scarves disappeared from our closets, along with our sweaters. We thawed, too; everyone seemed prettier, nicer, fresher in the spring air.

I spent every afternoon at Masters, and our days began to feel like years. It began to feel like we had known each other for a very long time. Mr. Holmes peeled away the layers of Yonahlossee in a way Sissy couldn't. She was one of the girls, she didn't have the vantage point he did. He told me Jettie's drinking was a known problem, that Mrs. Holmes would have sent her away years ago but for Henny, who convinced her that keeping Jettie on was their Christian duty. He told me Yonahlossee was keeping King in exchange for Leona's tuition, which hadn't been paid in over a year. He told me Katherine Hayes's father wasn't doing as well as Katherine thought, that her grandfather had stepped in and paid her tuition; that her uncle had shot himself because he was about to be arrested. He liked the Kentucky girls best because they were the least mannered. And the Florida girls, he'd said, and grinned. I like them, too.

I came back early from French class because I didn't feel well. My stomach was troubling me — cramps, it was that time of the month.

Docey was mopping the floors, her back turned. She was humming some tuneless melody, but I was certain she'd heard me. I waited for her to turn around, acknowledge me, but she drew the mop around and around, over the same spot. From the back she almost looked like one of us.

"Docey?"

She turned then, but said nothing.

"I'm going to lie down for a bit." I stopped short of asking her if this was fine.

She nodded, and watched me while I stepped out of my boots, tiptoed across the damp floor. She didn't offer to help. My stockings were wet, now. I lay back on my bed and peeled them off, surprised by the feel of my bare legs against the quilt. I closed my eyes and pretended to drift off.

Yesterday Mr. Holmes was melancholy, told me I'd forget this place. But I couldn't imagine.

Mr. Holmes's breath tasted like gin. Juniper berries, he'd told me, the perfume of the evergreens. If we had been married and a wedding portrait taken, we would not have seemed an unusual couple. Mr. Holmes was thirty-one. Women married men twice their age all the time. His hair was thick and glossy — Eva had joked she'd die for his hair — his carriage boyish, his lips very red. I carried my youth in the way I moved, in my speech and furtive gestures. But I didn't look young when I stood still.

A sharp sound. I sat up, disoriented. My mouth was dry.

"You were saying things," Docey said. She was cleaning under Mary Abbott's desk.

"Was I?" I got up and poured myself a drink of water. "What?"

"Nonsense. Nonsense words."

For a second I was frightened I'd revealed something. It had been a week since I'd seen Leona in the Square. Now we avoided each other, as if we had come to some mutual decision. I'd gone over and over my comings and goings from Masters. There was no possible way she knew anything. I'd thought of Emmy, too, but Leona wasn't the kind of girl to ever talk to a servant. I liked to think that there was some sort of mutual understanding between the two of us, that she knew I knew about King, that I felt sorry for her, a pure form of pity. But Leona wouldn't want to be pitied.

"Do you know Emmy, Docey? From Masters?"

She smiled, almost smirked. I was about to ask again when she answered: "She's my sister." She turned to face me, then looked me in the eye for the first time that day. Her lazy eye darted crazily.

"I didn't know."

Docey went back to her work. "I didn't know," I repeated. I should have known. I watched Docey drag her rag over the desk, carefully, paying attention to the finials and knobs — carefully, but quickly — and knew suddenly that they spoke of us.

"But your hair is brown." I paused. "You don't look alike." And this was true: Emmy was pretty, and Docey wasn't.

"Do you look like your sister?" Her tone was pointed.

"I don't have a sister."

"None?" She seemed surprised.

I shook my head. "I have a brother. And we do look alike, we're twins."

"A twin?" she asked. It was the first time I had ever heard her sound pleased. "What's that like?"

I smiled. "It's all I've ever known," I said. "It's like there's another you, out there."

"I don't know if I'd like that."

"You wouldn't like it or not like it, if you had it. It would just be . . . how things are."

Docey said nothing. I watched her lazy eye. I wondered if it could be fixed, if there was some corrective method available, or if people with lazy eyes simply had to live with them. I wondered what she saw, right now — did my face stay still? Did it move, wildly? But of course Docey would never be able to fix her eye.

I realized I'd been staring. "How many siblings do you have?" I asked, and then thought she might not know what that meant. I flushed. "Brothers —"

"Twelve," she said. "Twelve," she repeated.

I was astonished. I couldn't even name twelve relations. Between Georgie's family and mine, there were only seven.

Docey smiled at the shock on my face.

"What do they do?" I asked.

"What do they do?" she repeated. She

shrugged, and I understood how vile Yonahlossee must appear to Emmy and Docey. Mary Abbott's father, the preacher, had written of two little boys who lived not far from here, up in the mountains. They had died from eating poisonous berries. All the other girls thought they simply hadn't known they were poisonous, but of course they had; in Florida I had known exactly which berries I could eat, which would send me straight to death. And surely these boys had spent as much time outside as I had, or more. They'd eaten them because they were starving. I wanted to apologize to Docey, but for what? Luck, fortune, fate.

She'd turned away from me anyway, bent down, and wound up the woven rug beneath the desk into a tight roll. She seemed to linger. I helped Mother clean, I was familiar with the desperation it entailed, born of futility. It was a fixed system of entropy, like Father had explained by tossing a coin.

"Do you like to clean?"

Docey laughed. It was a stupid question. Mother liked to clean, enjoyed ordering her world like that. But this wasn't Docey's world; it was ours. I turned to slip my shoes on and then leave, but then she spoke.

"I don't mind it." But she was lying, we both knew that.

■ ■ ■ ■

He was quiet today, sat almost mournfully with his gin. His shirt was buttoned crookedly, and though Mr. Holmes was somber, his shirt made him seem playful.

"Let's go out back." I rose and Mr. Holmes followed. I knew he would, he was in his passive mood.

It was a little bit thrilling to walk through the parts of the house I'd never seen — the dining room, to a formal sitting room whose French doors opened onto the porch. There was a table next to the window, heavy with glass bottles, their necks slender. I went to it. The sight, up close, was a marvel — various exotic plants that I'd never seen before, growing in bottles like model ships.

"Beth's." Mr. Holmes had come up behind me. I remembered that Mrs. Holmes loved to garden. He picked one up. "She sends away for the seeds."

I imagined all the attention they must require, the special tools, the careful nurturing. I had not thought Mrs. Holmes capable of magic like this.

The back porch was clearly built for entertaining — there was a bar in the corner, and clusters of small tables surrounded by chairs. I imagined fathers of alumna who came out here with Mr. Holmes to admire the view and talk — about what? The purpose of a place like this. The goal of women's education. Things that none of us girls ever spoke about.

I didn't want to be here anymore, where fathers came and spoke of their daughters with Mr. Holmes. "Let's go outside," I said.

"I have such a headache."

"The fresh air will help," I said.

He opened the screen door to the woods that lay beyond the porch. Outside, the footing was rocky, but it was fine because Mr. Holmes had to offer me his hand, and he seemed reluctant to touch me, today.

"I come up here sometimes on Naari," I said. Mr. Holmes said nothing. I was still careful about mentioning horses around him. "It's easier when she does the climbing."

He laughed.

"Are you feeling better?" I asked hopefully.

"It's not a horrible one. When I was a boy I had to lie in a dark room on the floor. Always the floor, for some reason it felt better, and wait until it went away. There was no logic to it. Sometimes it went away immediately, and other times it took days."

"And you had to lie on the floor for days?"

"Mostly, yes." He stopped, and leaned against a tree. "My governess would sit outside the door and forbid anyone to come close. I couldn't stand any noise."

I closed my eyes and pictured a small Mr. Holmes, laid flat by pain, his English governess barring the door.

"You had a governess?"

"Yes. You sound surprised. My family was very wealthy. Is very wealthy. Well, less wealthy than they used to be, I imagine, but I'm sure they've survived." He gave a hard little laugh.

I hadn't been surprised. I knew he came from money.

"My family was very wealthy, my mother and father lived in Europe for most of the year, I had a governess. I failed out of Harvard, twice. Then I met Beth." I opened my eyes. "And the rest, they say, is history." His voice had changed, was stiff and distant.

"And the rest, they say . . ." I trailed off.

"Is history," Mr. Holmes finished. "I was very disappointing to my parents."

"So was I," I said.

"Yes. But there are worse things."

I was silent.

"Thea, when you're young, disappointing your parents seems like the worst thing in the world. But it's not. Believe me, it's not."

I nodded. We walked in silence for a moment. The air was warm, felt like spring. Sometimes I resented always having to wear a skirt — I could never play as wildly as Georgie and Sam — but right now a skirt was convenient, allowed me to take giant steps to keep up with Mr. Holmes. I thought pants — especially wool pants, like Mr. Holmes was wearing — would have constricted me, been too hot and smothering.

"What is the worst thing, then?" I asked tentatively. "If not disappointing your family?"

"Disappointing yourself," he said quickly. "Disappointing yourself," he repeated. "And it's such an easy thing to do."

I turned this phrase over and over — the thought had never occurred to me. Why should my disappointment matter? My parents were disappointed in me. And my brother, and my aunt and uncle. The word seemed to come unhinged, the way that words always did when you lingered on them too long — *disappoint.* What did it really mean? How was it even possible to disappoint myself? I was just myself. I was Thea, I was a girl, I was a daughter and a cousin and a sister and now a friend.

"Did you disappoint yourself?" I asked.

He laughed. "In too many ways to count."

I watched the back of his head, he was silent for a second. He was so strong, Mr. Holmes; we were climbing a steep incline and his breath remained even, his footing sure.

I thought he was done with the subject, but he continued. "If I could do it all over again, relive my youth, as they say, I would do things differently. But so would everyone, I think. The trick is not to get mired in the muck." It was an expression Father used. He turned, and I watched his profile as he spoke. "The past is the past, Thea. I hope somebody's already told you that. But if they haven't, well — it's something to remember."

Mr. Holmes stopped at a stand of trees and went through an opening I hadn't seen. A secret opening, I thought as I followed, for our secret affair. The idea thrilled me. The trees opened and I could see straight through to the sky. I think half the transgressions here were committed because of weather like this. And the other half — in the memory of the weather. I touched his jacket, soft against my fingertips.

"Where does Emmy think we are?" I asked.

"I don't know, Thea." He shook his head.

"You should be at the Hall, with all the other girls. You should not be here with me."

"But I want to be here."

We were quiet for a moment, and I knew that when he spoke again he might very well end this, send me back to be with all the other girls.

But instead he bent down and delicately picked up a transparent snake skin. "Snakes are coming out again."

I reached for the skin, a long tube, dirty and translucent. "This is old."

He looked at me, surprised.

"There are snakes all over in Florida."

"You're not scared of them?"

"Not particularly. Leave them alone, they leave you alone."

I turned my face up and kissed him. I kissed him hard, directed his tongue; drew him closer to me.

"We can pretend we're all alone out here," I said.

"Because we are."

Mr. Holmes kissed my neck, and suddenly we were on the ground, he was on top of me. My skirt was unbuttoned, and his jacket was off. I reached for his pants. Mr. Holmes above me, framed by the bluest sky I thought I'd ever seen, and I felt so lucky, that he was here with me, that I was getting again what I knew I shouldn't have.

"No," he whispered, and instead he licked my breasts, then my stomach, and continued down. His mouth was over my panties, and I started to sit up. He raised his head and pressed his hand into my shoulder and pushed, hard, until I relaxed. What are you doing, I thought of asking, but I felt if I spoke I might end this. My thighs quivered, and his tongue felt like it was inside me. Which was impossible, wasn't it, but it felt so large and it moved and I put my hands on his head as if in a blessing.

18

Sissy caught up with me on the way back from the barn. I usually waited for her, but lately I had been scurrying out of the cabin after rest hour before the bell had even rung; and then, when I was done with riding, rushing through cooling out Naari. It was easy to evade Sissy, who was always late. I had started to do whatever I wanted to. Sometimes I didn't even bow my head during prayer, but watched Mr. Holmes. He made small motions with his hands, even though he kept his eyes closed while he was speaking. I tried it once in the woods, closed my eyes and spoke to the trees. But it felt as strange as walking blindfolded.

"You're always hurrying," Sissy said. "I can never catch you." She sounded irritated, her raspy voice high.

I shrugged. There were girls all around us. I opened my mouth to speak but closed it again; I didn't really have anything to say.

Sissy shrugged, and I realized with a shock that she was imitating me. I stared at her.

"What?" She shrugged again. "I never see you, and you don't seem to care. You haven't asked about Boone in weeks."

So this was what this was about. I was relieved, and, strangely, disappointed.

"I know he still comes," I reminded her. "I'm the one who helps you. Takes your place in bed."

She drew me to the side of the path, into the woods. "Stop, Thea." Her voice cracked. "You've been walking around with your head in the clouds. You never come to the Hall anymore."

"Nobody studies, anyway."

"That's not what I mean." I started to defend myself, but Sissy continued. "You're in Masters too much. Girls are talking."

I waited for her to go on. But she didn't. "What are they saying?" I asked.

"They're saying you're obsessed with Mr. Holmes, that you're lovesick."

I laughed, but the sound was strange in my throat. "Sissy," I said, trying to sound incredulous, "I go there for Decca. She asked for me, you know." I offered this as if it were proof of something. And then there was also a feeling of relief, that what Leona had said in the Square was gossip, nothing more.

"Thea, don't!" Her voice was high. "I'm your best friend. Don't."

I was touched, even in that moment, that she considered herself my best friend. Sissy stood so rigidly; I took her hand, drew it from her side. "I just like being there. With Decca. With Mr. Holmes, too. We talk. He understands me."

"What does he understand about you?" She gripped my hand tightly, now, and looked at me plaintively. "You were sent away because of a boy."

I nodded. I had told her this, so long ago it seemed like another life, when I was settling in at Yonahlossee and wanted so badly to have a friend.

"Mr. Holmes isn't a boy."

I took my hand away. "I know that." I paused for a moment. If I had been brave enough to trust Sissy I might have asked her what she meant, exactly, what she had guessed.

"What about David?" Sissy asked.

"David," I repeated, confused. I'd nearly forgotten about him.

Sissy watched me. Eva walked by, with Gates, and I smiled at them over Sissy's shoulder. "He's not . . . I'm sorry."

"Oh, don't apologize. It's just, it would be so easy, to like him. So fun. Just come around more," she said, and her voice had returned to normal. "Please?" I'd seen Sissy do this before, decide that a quarrel was over and end it just like this, snuffing a candle. It was one of her gifts, never deigning to fight with anyone. But she had never acted like that with me. She had never needed to.

I thought about David the rest of the day, as I walked from place to place and nodded at various girls and knew that I was not like them, did not want the same things, had made my life unnecessarily hard, and would continue to do so. And why? Why, Thea, why, Mother's voice ringing, ringing.

I knew why, though. I was a smart girl. David was a boy, and he reminded me of Georgie, as any boy would. I was done with boys.

Suddenly Yonahlossee was a haze of color: candytuft carpeted the fields beyond the riding rings in all manner of pink; grape hyacinth lined the Square; and finally daffodils, my favorite, circled our riding rings in carefully planted beds. Mrs. Holmes had supervised their planting before she left. She has a genius for flowers, Henny said one night, and I had to agree.

There's no future in this. I kept waiting for Mr. Holmes to speak these words, but he never did. I knew this would end. I knew the date. I knew how. Mrs. Holmes would come back, and we would simply stop.

There's no future in this, Mr. Holmes might have said, might have prepared me for the inevitable. But I wasn't naive. I could have been called many things — shameful, cowardly, cunning — but not naive. Why did I act this way, first at home, then at Yonahlossee? I risked everything when I was old enough to know better. But there was always this: the hard kernel of want in my throat. I could not push it away. I did not want to.

Mother would be so disappointed in me. She would hate me, if she learned what I was doing. Yet if my family could cast me out so easily — out of their home, out of their hearts — shouldn't I be able to act in the same way? I wasn't weak. There was so much want inside me, there was so much desire. I felt it exploding when Mr. Holmes touched me, I felt it multiplying.

With Georgie I had felt desire, yes, but a fraction of what I felt with Mr. Holmes. He taught me that desire is divisible, that it changes in relation to its object. I wondered if Mother knew that. I wondered if Father did. Because you couldn't know, if you had only ever desired a single person, if you had been kept away from everyone else.

I thought about what Mr. Holmes had told me, that my parents had made an exchange. He didn't know them, he didn't know my father's tenderness, my mother's lovely home. He didn't know how we had loved each other.

19

Georgie was in Missouri, with his mother and father. Mother had said that we might see him next week, but I couldn't confirm the date without calling attention to myself.

I'd woken and gasped for breath, the air was so thick and soupy. The clock on my bedside table read three thirty; in another hour or so it would be light enough to ride.

In the summers you had a second skin, a layer of moisture and sweat that was always with you. And this was only the beginning of it.

Outside, the world looked dead and disinterested; there was no breeze to rustle the grass, no crickets rubbing their legs together to interrupt the stillness. I sat on the steps and unbuttoned the first button of my nightgown, which made no difference. I closed my eyes and thought of my cousin, the way he had touched me last time, the way I had touched him, how we were learning.

"Thea," Sam called, from behind me. I knew without looking that he was sitting in a rocking chair.

"Sam."

"You weren't scared?" he asked. He sounded like he had been up for a while. He had always liked to startle others, to jump out from behind doors, to wait in a bush and spring up, suddenly, a surprise.

"Who else would it be?" The question hung in the air for a moment, two. I spoke again. "Can't sleep?"

"Who can? It must be a record, this heat. It feels like it."

"It never is. A record."

"No," he agreed, "it never is."

We were silent for a few moments. Sam sighed.

"You'll be tired tomorrow," I said.

"I'll just sleep tomorrow. I won't miss anything."

"I guess not."

"I want to go away, Thea. I want to travel." His voice was strange. I turned and looked at him. He was barefoot, sprawled in the rocking chair in his normal day clothes. His head was turned, in profile, and I saw how handsome my brother was becoming. He was going to be more handsome than I was beautiful, our features more suited to a man's face; but I pushed the thought from my mind. I was fifteen years old; I wanted to be beautiful. I did not want anyone else to be more beautiful, even my twin — or especially my twin. "Don't you?" he asked again, and turned to me. Mother said some twins looked less and less alike as they grew older, but that didn't seem to be the case for me and Sam.

"Where would you go?" I asked. My brother had never spoken to me of leaving before. Not ever.

"I think I'd like to go somewhere on a ship," he said, and I couldn't help it, I laughed.

Sam wouldn't look at me.

"I'm sorry," I said, "it's just the picture of you on a ship. Would you be a sailor?"

He said nothing.

"Sam," I began, "I'm sorry —"

"No you're not. Anyway, wouldn't you be glad if I left?" His voice was high, and I understood that Sam did not really want to go anywhere, that he wanted nothing about our lives to change.

"Why would I be glad, Sam?" I spoke quietly. "I need you."

"Need me?" It was his turn to laugh.

"Need me for what? You spend all day on Sasi. You don't need anyone."

"That isn't true," I said. But, strangely, my feelings weren't hurt. I felt they should be, I expected them to be, but they weren't.

"No," Sam said, "I suppose it isn't true. You need our cousin."

I lay back against the hard brick, suddenly exhausted. I could feel Sam stand behind me; I thought he would go inside now, but instead he sat down next to me. I watched his back: he was growing broader as I was growing narrower.

"No moon tonight." His voice was dull.

I shook my head, even though he wasn't looking at me.

"Do you remember when you thought an Indian lived out there?" I asked.

"You believed it, too."

He lay down next to me, and I knew the coolness of the brick was a relief to him also.

"Thea?"

"Yes."

"Do you ever wonder what it feels like to be dead?"

I considered the question. Sam passed his hand lightly over my eyes. "Close them." I did. "It feels like this," he said.

"No it doesn't."

"Try and fall asleep. You might as well be

dead, when you're sleeping."

I tried to push all my thoughts away and make my mind go blank. I tried not to think about Georgie, I tried to lull my mind into stillness. I wanted to please my brother.

"I don't think this is working." Sam didn't respond, but I could tell he wasn't sleeping, only trying. "I wonder which one of us will die first."

"Me," he said, "it will be me."

I said nothing. To be alive without Sam — would that be any life at all, I wondered. I knew Mother and Father would die first, though I didn't know in which order; this made sense. They had lives before me, and I would have a life after them. But Sam and I had never existed alone, and now this existence seemed as much a burden as a pleasure. Or perhaps it was neither. It was merely a fact.

"Thea. Try again."

I listened to Sam. I closed my eyes. And what did I see? Mother's old carriage blanket, weighing down her arm like a stone. I tried to think of other things, put them on top of the blanket: Sasi, Georgie, the usual things. But they all led back to the blanket. Usually I was so good at plucking from my brain what I did not want to consider.

I almost fell asleep. The sun rose very slowly, by increments, and I kept my eyes shut against it, tried to make myself drift into oblivion. Then suddenly I could taste what it would be like to become nothing. And it was an absence so large I couldn't quite conceive of it, except to be terrified.

I opened my eyes and sat up, turned to Sam, who slept peacefully. My hand hovered above his shoulder. I needed to wake him, I needed to tell him I was scared. He would help me understand it. But then I let my hand drop, onto the brick. I wanted to be separate from Sam. I wanted to experience something he did not. And so I stayed on the porch for another hour, the sun turning us hotter and hotter as it rose.

I should have woken Sam to prevent the burn that we would sport for the next week, our forearms and faces bright red, then pink, then peeling. But I did not. My face was redder on my left cheek, almost like I had painted it with rouge; it had been turned to the sun while I had watched my brother. He had wanted me to follow him there, to wherever he was, and I hadn't. I could not. I watched him and saw very clearly that there were places I would not follow Sam, where he would not follow me.

■ ■ ■ ■

What Sam said rang over and over — You need our cousin. We love him differently. Georgie, his thick waist, his broad chest — what Sam could see. What Sam couldn't see: the trail of hair that split his navel, the taut surface of his stomach.

We love him differently, but what was the difference? My mother and father loved each other, shared a bed; I loved my mother, my father loved me, they both loved Sam. Marriage meant you included someone, permanently, in your family. That kind of marriage made sense. In the Bible, Jacob married two first cousins, Rachel and Leah, and it was a joyful occasion. Occasions. I didn't want as much as that — I only wanted a single person, a solitary being.

But that was so long ago. At the beginning of time, everyone must have been a cousin. Cousin-marriage, then, was a modern term, applied to pairs like Charles Darwin and Emma Wedgwood, their marriage an anecdote, woven into Father's lecture in order to entertain, trick us into caring. I'd wondered if Emma was related to the porcelain manufacturer. Neither Father nor Mother had known, and there was no way for me to find out at that time in my life, no matter how badly I wanted to.

And so the story of Emma and Charles lodged itself somewhere in my young brain. Mr. Darwin had carefully considered both the benefits and detriments of marriage, committing himself to Miss Wedgwood for as long as they both would live. Marriage meant less money for his work, less time to catalogue all the unknown species of flora and fauna in the great beyond. Miss Emma Wedgwood was already catalogued, already *known,* and Mr. Darwin couldn't have been less interested in what he already understood. In his huge, unrelenting brain, Mr. Darwin's capacity for love had already been filled by the vast inhabitants of God's earth.

If Mother found out what I was doing, she might want me to marry Georgie. And I did not want to marry my cousin. I did not want to live in Gainesville. I did not — and this thought shamed me — want to be poor. But still I wanted my cousin. I wanted him very badly. I tried to separate the two things in my mind. I could not make sense of it all, how I could want one part but not the other.

It was the longest Georgie and I had been apart. I didn't think of it this way then, but that night in the stall must have worked on my conscience, because suddenly I saw what I was doing clearly, and I was terrified that someone would know. I was still hungry for my cousin — I wanted him to touch me, I craved his touch — but my hunger was tempered by caution. Perhaps it was as simple as this: I was older. I saw my mother unfurling her precious carriage blanket, pulling it from beneath the table, and it unlocked the possibilities in my brain. If I had allowed things to go further I would no longer be a virgin. That was the first thing, and then the second was that if anyone knew, I wouldn't be marriageable. I could have conceived a child, *we* could have conceived a child. It was a possibility. I shudder to think of my life had that happened.

My mother held up the blanket, and in Georgie's absence it had revealed itself to me like a flare in the night sky that had come into view suddenly and terrifyingly.

Then Georgie was back, and we went to Gainesville for tea, just me and Mother, Sam was busy with something. His absence would have seemed like a blessing a month ago. But now I wished he was here. Georgie had tea with us, stared at me in a way that was obvious, but Mother and Aunt Carrie didn't seem to notice. I ate a scone and it was dust in my mouth.

I followed him upstairs later. He patted the space next to him on his unmade bed; I went reluctantly. I'd never liked his room.

"Did you miss me?"

"Yes."

"My cousins there aren't like the ones here," he said, and I looked at him. Georgie leaned in to kiss me, his eyes already closed, and I turned my cheek.

"You left the blanket in the stall last time."

"I did?"

"Mother found it. We could have been caught."

He smoothed the sheet between us, and though he came close to touching me, he didn't. I could hear my own heart. He kept drawing his hand in a pattern that brought it close and then away again.

"Georgie," I said, my voice nearly a whisper.

"My cousins in Kansas City aren't doing very well. Everyone's moved into my grandmother's house." He gave me a sidelong glance. "It was good that she died."

"Don't say that."

"What? It's the truth. They're all farmers, they don't have professions they can depend on, like our fathers. Well, like your father. People are always sick, aren't they? But it hasn't rained in months there. They're desperate."

I stilled his hand and held it between both of mine. This was the Georgie who was mine, who no one else saw.

"I'm sorry."

"Do you know how poor everyone is now? Father says it's just starting, that it'll be worse before it's better. The cows in the pastures are starving. You can see their spines."

I shivered. "They should shoot them, put them out of their misery."

"They can't. Then that would be the end of things. Think, Thea — they need their cows."

"It will rain again. It always does."

"Only God can say that."

"Or the ocean. The ocean decides when it rains."

"Tell my uncles. Tell them to ask the ocean."

I hadn't meant to be flip. "I'm sure it's awful."

"It is." He rested his head on my shoulder, which he'd never done before. It was usually I who leaned against him. I stroked his forearm, watched how the fine hairs stood at my touch.

"All I thought about was you, when I was

gone. How much I wanted you to be with me."

"Well, here I am."

"I mean be with you differently." He drew his finger across my lap. "Do you want to be with me like that?"

I looked around the room — the ratty bedspread, flung on the floor; the uneven floorboards; the secondhand desk; the framed photograph of a man I did not recognize, someone from Aunt Carrie's family. There was a small lockbox beneath the bed, which held his treasures: a silver dollar, a smooth stone from Ormond Beach, a postcard from Toronto.

These were all his things in the world. And now me, he had me, too.

"You don't need to answer," he said, into my neck. "Just stay here with me."

I came to Yonahlossee in late July, the summer nearly over. In Florida this was always the worst month, the heat so vicious it claimed lives, a dozen every July. The bugs were unbearable, biting, buzzing, trying to get at you any way they could. When I undressed, I found mosquitoes in my undergarments, nestled between my thighs.

Georgie was visiting, for the Fourth. I looked forward to seeing my cousin with a distinct combination of dread and exhilaration.

My uncle bought fireworks from a stand in Gainesville, a boxful of them, on a whim. We'd never lit fireworks before. I saw my father's expression as Uncle George revealed his surprise, and he was not pleased, anyone could see that.

"A gift," Uncle George said, "a gift," and my father said nothing, and I pitied Uncle George, and I was so angry at Father for his meanness.

"A fine one," my mother said, splitting the silence, "a fine one." But it was too late.

Sometimes when I think of that weekend — and I have thought of it often, wound and rewound the scenes — I am not impressed. What happened seems, if not normal, inevitable, unsurprising. My family emerged a different family, but that would have happened anyway. Sam and I would have gone to college, Georgie would have married. The children would have left.

And other times I think of that weekend and I am a young stranger, that weekend is impossible.

I did have the sense that someone was watching us. I was very careful, I diligently ignored Georgie when we were in front of anyone else, including Sam. Sam looked at me as if we had an understanding when I didn't laugh at a joke Georgie made, when I refused to even smile; it was so simple to please him.

We watched the fireworks late at night, when it was darkest. My uncle kept praying to the moon, in jest, to go away. Sam and Georgie carried the box to the end of the field, past the barn. Georgie did a little jump and clicked his heels in the air, gave a holler, and Sam smiled and so did I, in spite of myself, but then I went cold. The fireworks had not excited Georgie. *I* had, and what he imagined we were going to do later. I looked at my mother, who watched my brother and uncle and cousin disappear into darkness.

"I hope he'll be careful," my mother said, and I wasn't sure whom she was referring to. If only she knew; then she could tell me to be careful, she could stop things before they went any further. We couldn't see them anymore but I heard Georgie yell something to Sam, probably some instruction, and his voice ricocheting off my brain thrilled me, amplified some desire I hadn't known I'd had.

"I haven't seen fireworks in years," Father said quietly. I put my hand on top of his. He turned it over and held mine. He was very easy to love.

"Did you have them when you were little?"

"I don't remember."

I thought that odd — whether or not you'd seen fireworks in your childhood seemed like a thing you'd remember — but I sat quietly because I sensed that Father wanted to sit quietly. I would remember this night, I thought, but perhaps one day all of this would have faded into a vague, barely recalled memory; that seemed unbearable, that all of it could simply disappear.

We heard a whoop and Mother stood, terrified, and then we heard the bang of a firework, and the rays of color spread across the sky.

"It's fine, Elizabeth," my father said, and my mother sat back down.

"Do you like them, Thea?" my mother asked.

I looked at the sky. "Yes."

Aunt Carrie was quiet. I looked at her and wanted to scream. You should know, you should have stopped your son from falling into all of this.

I left before the men came back, went to check on Sasi, who was, as I'd anticipated, frantic. I stayed with him for a while, but he wouldn't be soothed. I walked him around the ring, let him graze, but he wasn't interested in grass. The air smelled scorched, and there was no way to explain to him that it had all been for fun, that there was no real threat.

Back inside, Mother told me she was putting the house to bed — a phrase I'd never heard her use before. She must have read it in a book. I found her in the living room, drawing the curtains, and told her I would be outside for a while, tending to Sasi. She told me not to stay up too late, and I promised I wouldn't, though I planned to sleep outside if Sasi wouldn't calm down. Perhaps Georgie was in the next room — in the kitchen or the hallway — and heard, or he went to find me in my bed and guessed, correctly, that I was in the barn. That was where we had met before. It was not inconceivable that I would wait there again.

I was dozing — not fully asleep, but nowhere near awake, either — when I heard him. I watched my cousin while he looked for me. Sasi was exhausted from working himself up, stood very still, his head in the corner over me. I loved him. The feeling rose in my throat.

Georgie walked by the stall. His face was sweaty. A moment later he walked by again and stopped at the stall, propped his elbows on the door, and smiled.

"Found you."

Sasi started, jerked his head up and walked over to the door; Georgie backed away.

"I wasn't hiding." I stood by Sasi and stroked his neck, ran my fingers through his knotted mane. I hadn't been taking good care of him lately.

"Thea?"

I turned my head and looked at my cousin, and he was so eager. He motioned for me to come, and I went, it was what was expected of me, after all we had done together. I followed willingly, and as soon as I was outside the stall he pushed me against the cold brick wall, which felt good through my dress. He smelled of sweat, and he bit my lip. I turned my face and he began to gather my dress around my hips. He pressed his erection against my bare leg, and I turned back and saw that he was watching himself, that he was aroused by the sight of his erection pressing into my leg.

"Georgie," I said, "wait."

"Why?" He took my hand and led me into our empty stall. His voice sounded deeper than it had a moment before. I smoothed the hair away from his forehead and smiled at him.

"All right."

"You," he said, "you are so good."

I would have done anything, then. I turned away from him and unbuttoned the front of my dress, and he was behind me, sliding the dress from my shoulders. He kissed my neck, and felt my breasts, and then he turned me around.

He put his finger beneath my chin and lifted it. "Are you all right?"

"No."

"I'll make you better." But I wanted him to ask *why* I wasn't all right; I wanted him to feel this risk half as much as I seemed to. He appeared so careless, Georgie, so careless about all of this. He didn't take his eyes away. Ask, I screamed, inside my head; ask, ask, ask. Instead he put his hand between my legs while he watched me, and he was gentle. He stopped, a little half smile on his face, and I knew he was goading me. It worked.

"Don't stop," I said, and he unbuckled his belt, and it all felt so good, and then I wanted him, I *needed* him, because what I felt in this instant was not pleasure, exactly: it was the promise of pleasure, an itch that needed fingernails raked across it. And maybe, I thought, as I felt him next to me, as he guided my thighs apart while he traced my nipples with his fingertip. Maybe, I thought, as he pushed himself into me, it was enough, that Georgie would try to understand me later, that right now there was a need and when we were done the need would not exist anymore.

"Loosen," he said, and I tried. It hurt, now, but the pain, I saw, was a part of the pleasure. I should not have done this, I had been very bad, and now I was being punished. It was all so clear, now. I looked out of the stall window into a black, black night. I felt the cloth of Georgie's shirt, I put my hands on his shoulders and brought him closer to me. If a door had slammed, if Mother had stepped onto the back porch and called my name.

Sam's face flashed in my head, not as he was now — angry, hurt — but as he used to be, a little boy who felt the world too deeply. "We should switch you!" Mother used to say, as if little girls were better suited to feel the weight of things than little boys. Georgie bent down and licked my breast like an eager dog and I shuddered, pulled him up — I felt excluded from what he was doing right now, he was inside me but he was enacting a private fantasy, one that required my presence but not my love.

Mother had been right. I was too much like a boy, too dumb to the consequences. I remembered the tent Mother let us make between our beds when we were little. Sam clasped my face between his fat hands: "Thea," he said, "Thea!"

Georgie heaved against me, once, twice, and he seemed so large inside me, impossibly large. Then he put his head on my chest and breathed deeply. It was over very quickly.

What had Sam wanted? I couldn't for the life of me remember.

I slid down the cold wall until I was sitting. Georgie stood over me, tucked his shirt into his pants, fastened his belt. It was something about seeing him do all those things, those normal, everyday gestures, that made me feel very alone. I put my head in my hands.

"Thea?"

"What have we done?"

"Don't you know?" There was, outrageously, impossibly, laughter in his voice.

"I don't mean that."

He sat down next to me. "It's all very natural," he said.

"It doesn't feel like it." I shook my head.

"Doesn't it?"

"We should have waited." I looked away.

He laughed. "Why?" he asked. "There was no reason to wait, for us."

I was naked and my cousin was completely clothed. He traced a pattern in the sawdust and seemed to consider what to say next, which was unlike my cousin, to think before he spoke.

"We were wrong," I said.

"I didn't make you do anything."

I shook my head. He understood nothing.

"I want my dress," I said, and pointed to it.

He retrieved my dress from the middle of the stall, and it seemed to me that he moved like a stranger. Then he stood over me, watched me.

"Didn't you think that would happen?" He sounded genuinely curious. I wanted very badly to be alone.

I felt very keenly that I had given up too much for ninety, one hundred seconds. And that minute, those two minutes, had been painful for me, it had all been for Georgie's pleasure. I saw very clearly our future: we would do this a dozen more times, two dozen more times, and then Georgie would be finished with me, with our arrangement. Boys could do this, I understood now, watching my cousin, how he stood over me, so carelessly, so confidently. Boys were meant for this world. "We're not the marrying kind," he said. "Thea? Did you think we were the marrying kind?"

"I don't know what I thought," I said. "Not this." I gestured at the stall, the walls brown with mildew; they needed to be scrubbed, one of my summer chores. Georgie followed my hand, followed it to where it stopped: him, in clothes my parents had bought him, the only nice things he had. My cheeks burned. "It's dirty."

He knelt next to me and touched my cheek. "It's not like that."

"It is," I said, and removed his hand. "It's exactly like that. It's what you do, in your family."

"In my family?" I felt all the words forming in my heart, ready to tumble out; I clutched my dress to my chest and saw how I would end this. I pitied him, now. He stood so dumbly; he was so confused. I didn't want to pity him. I didn't want any part of him. I wanted to wash my hands of him, and in this moment that felt possible: I could be done with him forever.

"You're like your father." I was speaking quickly; I pictured my kind, mild uncle and felt like a nasty, nasty girl but I had no choice. "Your father came to my father like you came to me, begging. You're just like him, shameful."

I held my dress to my chest and wished

for nothing more in the world than to be clothed. My cousin looked out the stall window, into the night, black as pitch, here where the lights of town did not reach. I felt sick. I wanted this to be over. But I watched my cousin's profile and knew it would never be over; we were family, we could not be rid of each other.

I looked down. When I looked up again, Georgie's face was mean. And what choice did he have? I ask that question now, years later, too late, everything a ruin. "Look at yourself," he said, and his eyes roamed over my body, the dress that covered me so inadequately.

"If you don't leave," I said, "I'll scream."

"You'll scream?" What if I had waited a beat before I'd threatened to scream? Or, better, if I had stepped back in time and said nothing at all and kissed him good night and acted as if everything was the same, and let our arrangement end slowly, as Georgie said, naturally. He could be thick and clumsy and cruel; he was also kind and funny and sincere. And anyway, none of that mattered. He was mine. He was my cousin. I wanted to take everything back. I wanted *him* to take everything back. For the first time in my life, I understood that certain words were brands, etched onto the brain.

"Who will hear you?"

"Everyone."

"I don't think you want everyone to hear you."

We watched each other. God knows what you were thinking, Thea. Only God knows. I could hear Mother's voice. Georgie watched me, but I wouldn't meet his eye. Finally, he left.

I slept in the barn. I felt unclean, but not unclean enough to wash. It seemed natural to fall asleep in this empty stall, to stay in the barn until it was light.

I slipped upstairs at dawn and bathed, thought of Georgie, who slept in the next room. I might as well not have bothered with closing the door. He had seen me naked. But there was Sam, who hadn't. I pressed my fingernails into my forearm. I had been used by my own cousin. I was a young woman when young women were powerless. You would think I could have predicted what would happen. But I never felt powerless in my home. I hadn't known to be careful in that regard.

When I went downstairs to breakfast, Georgie wasn't at the table, and neither was Sam. I assumed they were still sleeping — it was early, not yet seven.

"Has your pony calmed down?" Mother asked.

"Yes."

"Are you all right, Thea?"

I wanted so badly to tell her. I wanted so badly to be comforted. I'm so ashamed, Mother, I've done something so awful you won't believe me.

She tapped my wrist. "Thea?"

Her voice was so soft, so lovely.

"Yes," I said. "Only tired." She looked at me, her head tilted, and I knew I could never tell, not in this life.

After breakfast I saddled Sasi, headed out into the orange groves. I rode all morning, turned around and let Sasi canter back in the direction of the barn. I felt careless today. There would be consequences — Sasi would fight for his head the next time we went toward the barn — but they felt small, and I felt large and bad. And I felt scared, though I tried to ignore the feeling of fear as it rose, tried to dampen it, send it back; I had always been so good at being fearless. I'd felt near tears all morning; now the cantering lulled me into some sort of trance and I flopped around in the saddle like a rag doll. I began to cry, like a girl, like a child.

Then Sasi swerved to avoid something —

I couldn't see what — and I gasped and grabbed Sasi's short mane and righted myself in the saddle, just barely, while I tried to murmur soothingly, while I tried to pick up the slack in my reins. It was always like this when you rode, doing a million things at once, all by instinct.

"Sorry," Sam called behind me, and I wished I had fallen, so that I would have an excuse for my tears.

"Thea?" Sam asked. "Are you all right?"

No, I wanted to say, no, I am not, and then I started to sob. I had let Georgie do things to me that had turned unimaginable in my mind; I had done things to him that I could never speak of, not to anyone. Not to Mother, not to Father, not to Sam, not to — and this occurred to me only now, on the back of the pony I loved, in the middle of an orange grove I had ridden through thousands of times, no, millions — my husband. I felt sick and dizzy.

"Thea?" And this voice belonged to Georgie. Of course. Georgie was being nice to Sam, perhaps because I was no longer his favorite. "Thea?" he said again, and then Sam was beside me, holding Sasi's rein, speaking quietly to him. Sasi nipped Sam's shirt, nervously, but then calmed down. I remembered what Mother always said, that it was in our blood to love horses. And what else was it in our blood to do?

"Why are you crying?" Sam asked, but I could only sob harder. The beauty of the day amplified my misery; if it had been raining, I would have not felt so alone, so wretched.

Sasi panted heavily, and for a moment or two that was the only sound — his grave, rhythmic breaths.

"Thea?" Sam asked again. Stop saying my name, I wanted to scream. Stop. I turned my face so I wouldn't have to look at him and saw Georgie, sitting on a rock. He had not come near me. I noticed then that both he and Sam had guns slung over their shoulders. I wondered if Sam had shot anything. Surely not. You did not raise orphaned squirrels only to hunt them as adults.

"I'm sorry," I said, "I'm sorry, I'm sorry, I'm sorry." I wiped my face, thick with sweat and snot and tears. I felt slimy, like a monster.

Georgie rose and walked toward me, and before I knew it he had put his hand on my thigh, braving his fear of Sasi, and I screamed at him, "Don't touch me!" I had never felt like this before. I saw sparks against the clear blue sky. I felt hot, so hot.

"Don't touch me!" I screamed it over and over, until my voice was hoarse. I could feel both boys watching me, in wonder.

Sam turned to Georgie. "What did you do?"

"What did we do," Georgie said, and his voice had turned mean. "What did we do together." And then he began to walk away, and Sam lunged after him, and pushed him to the ground. It took Georgie a second to get up he was so surprised.

Sasi, wound up, trembling beneath the saddle, started to trot, but I was still looking back, so I saw Sam — the back of his head, which I knew so well, his thin shoulders, his graceful pose — raise his hand and slap Georgie across the face, his palm open, and then Georgie responded with a punch to Sam's face, and Sam began to bleed from his nose, heavily.

"Stop," I cried. I leaned forward; Sasi gave a small rear and I slammed down onto the pommel of the saddle because I wasn't paying attention. Now there was a sharp pain in between my legs, and I was almost glad for it, because it made things real again, Sam and Georgie were no longer surreal figures backdropped by a giant orange grove, hitting each other sloppily.

"Stop," I yelled once more, and waved my

hand, as if that would help. When I turned back again, I saw Sam raise the butt of his rifle and strike my cousin — his cousin, our cousin — on the shoulder, and Georgie, stunned, fall backward, regain his balance, and lunge at Sam. He looked like a child trying to throw an adult off balance. Georgie was scared of horses; I flailed my legs against Sasi's side and directed him to gallop straight toward my brother and cousin. I wanted to stop their fighting. And as I was galloping, I was most aware not of what might happen — that any one of us might be terribly injured, that I was putting into effect a course of action that would almost certainly leave one of us damaged — no, I was thinking of how sloppily I was riding, how ugly I must look on top of my frantic, overheated pony, and I was ashamed for Georgie to see me this way.

Georgie looked up at us, his mouth bloody, an expression of terror on his face; I shifted my weight in the saddle so that we would gallop right in between my brother and cousin. Sasi flew, I'd never gone so fast with him, the orange grove was a blur. There was a bitter taste in my mouth. I wondered if it was fear.

I did not divide them, as I'd hoped. Instead, Georgie panicked and ran in front of us to Sam. He thought that I meant to run him over, he thought he would be safe with Sam. He didn't know that a horse would never do that; a horse would rather stay in a burning building than trample a human. Sasi stumbled; his hoof hit something hard — the rock, I realized, that Georgie had been sitting on — and in that instant I saw Sam raise the butt of his gun and hit Georgie on the side of his head, but Sasi regained his balance and he was going so fast, he would not slow down. I put all my weight against the bit, but Sasi was an electric wire beneath me, so I slid off while he was still cantering and hit the ground hard.

I picked myself up and turned and there was Georgie, Sam shaking him by the shoulders as if he were a doll. I could see how Georgie's head flopped, I could see that he was not well.

"Sam," I yelled, "you'll kill him." Sam looked at me, aghast, and I saw that he was in shock. I was not in shock. There was blood all over his face, smeared across his cheeks and neck like paint; Georgie was bloody, too, and so was the ground. There was so much blood. I had never seen so much of it, but it occurred to me that surely

Father had, that surely he would know what to do.

I motioned for Sam to come to me, and he ran wildly, his limbs unrestrained, like a child. "Go get Father," I said. Saliva glistened around his mouth. "Go get Father," I repeated.

I was alone with Georgie while Sam ran to the house. I smoothed his hair from his forehead. His skin was hot. His hair was matted with blood; Sam had hurt our cousin with his gun, his gun that he had never before used against a living creature.

I knelt beside him and arranged him so that he did not look so disheveled. I straightened his vest and used my handkerchief to dab the blood from his lips, but his mouth was still too red, so I tilted his head back and ran the handkerchief along his teeth. He looked better when I was done. I smoothed his forehead again. He was breathing and I half expected him to open his eyes and smile at me, as if last night had never happened. But he would open his eyes and smile at me and I would not be able to smile back. I would not have forgotten.

I heard a shout from the house — Mother, or Aunt Carrie, I couldn't tell — and I noticed Sam's gun, which lay next to me. There was a little blood on it, and so, without thinking, I wiped it on my breeches, which were bloody already, and threw it away from me, as far as I could, which was not very far at all.

He was still lying like this when my father appeared, with the rest of the adults. I held his hand, and my father looked at me strangely for a second before I was pushed to the edge of the circle that surrounded Georgie — my mother and father, my aunt and uncle.

Sam looked at me. I took his hand, impulsively, and he shook it off. His eyes were glassy. He looked like he did not know me.

"Sam?" I said softly. I tried to ignore the circle of adults on the periphery, tried only to focus on my brother's bloody face.

He looked at me briefly and then squatted on the ground, wrapped his arms around his legs, and began to rock gently, back and forth. I squatted next to him, and put my hands on his shoulders, and he looked at me again, and again he did not seem to recognize me. Then I wanted to die, I wanted Sam to smash *me* in the head with his gun.

Mother peeled herself away from the circle and came to us. She looked to Sam, then to me, then back at Sam. She leaned down and grabbed each of our upper arms, like she used to do when we were children, my right and Sam's left, like we were a single person, and leaned down to see us at eye level. This was also reminiscent of childhood.

"Go to your rooms," she whispered, and her breath fanned across our faces. She squeezed our arms too tight, dug her nails through fabric, but we said nothing, Sam did not even seem to notice her, and Mother did not seem to notice how odd Sam looked. "Go," she whispered again, and released us with a nod toward the house.

Sam stood, and I watched him from the ground. I rubbed the place where Mother had gripped my arm. He wandered away, his gait unsteady, but then he turned around and stared at me. I looked away.

"Thea," he said, "Thea, Thea, Thea." He kept repeating my name. He sounded possessed; he was not himself.

"Stop!" I cried, "stop! Now!" I put my hands over my ears. This was what he did when we were little, when he wanted to bother me. I'd hated it, hated how my name turned into nothing more than a sound when it was strung together. I'd almost forgotten. He hadn't done it in years.

He stopped then, his lips parted. I wanted very badly to say something else, but knew there was nothing to say. Sam pointed behind me; I turned and saw Sasi, who stood at the entrance to the barn, his sides heaving. I'd forgotten about him. I went to him, took the reins and smoothed his neck, and watched the graceful figure of my brother disappear. I couldn't return Sasi to his stall like this, he would colic and die, and so I was hand-walking him around the ring when I saw Uncle George in the distance, trailed by the other adults, holding his son in his arms, his inert, damaged son.

"Is he dead," I shrieked, "is he dead?" and Mother hurried to me, stopped when she reached the railing.

"No," she whispered, but in a shout, "no, he's not, but he's hurt, and what happened, Thea?"

I said nothing.

"Thea," she said again, and her voice was so sympathetic. I didn't deserve that voice, and I knew it was the last time she would ever offer it to me. When she spoke to me again, her voice would have turned ugly.

She couldn't stand there forever, and as the other adults passed she reentered their assembly. I turned my face into Sasi's slick neck, I felt his dusty sweat on my forehead and tried not to look at my cousin.

20

I sat on my bed with a letter in my hand. Mr. Holmes was expecting me; if I waited any longer he would start to wonder.

I touched the handwriting on the envelope. *Theodora Atwell,* it read. *Care of the Yonahlossee Riding Camp for Girls.* The letters my mother sent were perfunctory, and she never addressed me as Theodora. She told me that she was packing all our things, that she and Sam and Father would live in a hotel while they looked for a house, that Father would go early to set up his new practice. I suppose I was glad for the letters, that she was preparing me for my new life, that I was able to imagine their life while I lived my own, here. She implied, but never stated, that I'd live in this Orlando house with them.

But this letter, which I held in my hands, bore Sam's handwriting. It seemed sometimes that God was toying with me. The day before the show, and a letter from my brother, who hadn't sent a single word since I'd been here.

Dear Thea,

I know you want a letter from me but why? By the time you read this it will already be old. You know we're moving. Everything is the same here but without you. But it won't be the same soon, because we'll be gone. The family that is going to live in our house has five children. Five. Think of it. You would like some brothers and sisters and like others less. That would just be the way of it. Father has given me more work to do. I think he thinks the busier I am the better. I don't know what to write, Thea. You said you wanted a letter but what do you want it to say?

There is something wrong with Georgie. Mother and Father won't tell me but I hear them talking. It's not hard, they think I'm a fool who doesn't know how to listen at a door but they're the fools. Father has said the same thing about him for months — "that he is not quite right." What do you think that means? Do you know that the police interviewed me? I wasn't scared, but

Mother and Father were. We haven't seen Aunt Carrie or Uncle George since you left. I think Father has seen Uncle George, but I don't know for sure. We're paying for everything. I know that. The Orlando house will be smaller. That's what Mother says. But we haven't bought one yet. They're still looking. They wouldn't tell me this but I think we can't afford to buy a new house just yet. I think they have to wait.

I am bored here. I wish I had a friend.

Your Brother,
Sam

I folded the letter into a hundred squares, until it wouldn't fold anymore, and then I unfolded it and looked at all the words, read it and reread it until I had it memorized. By accident; I would have preferred my brother's voice not be stuck in my head, a record playing the same song over and over and over until I wanted to scream. But I did not want to scream. I wanted to cry. To weep, like heroines did in novels. Mother had lied. Georgie was not fine. But I had wanted to believe her, and so I had.

I didn't know what it meant, his letter, except that he was lonely and angry. He hadn't been an angry person; all of this had made him angry, changed him into a different boy. I felt selfish, small, mean: I'd been sent away to a place where it was impossible to feel lonely. And Sam, well, he'd been made to stay, to be the only child in that world. And Georgie — how long had Sam known? How long had he borne that burden alone?

His letter, I decided, was a way to ask me to return. And at first I had wanted to go back. But now I did not. There was no future for me at home.

I rose and took Mother's earrings out of their red velvet box. They hurt to put in, but I had expected that. I hadn't worn earrings in months, not since I'd tried on Sissy's rubies. And then I hurried across the Square to Masters, where I knew Mr. Holmes would be waiting.

At Masters, Mr. Holmes led me to his library, but I did not follow.

"I want to go out back," I said, "like we did last time."

"All right," he said, "whatever you wish."

I led him through the house, and out the back porch. It was sunny, like it had been that other day, and I hoped the sunlight wouldn't be ruined for me forever. I hoped I would someday be able to not remember that day so clearly.

We walked up a steep trail, and I felt Mr. Holmes touch the back of my thigh. I turned and smiled at him but kept walking. I knew he was wondering about my silence. But he needn't have. I knew where I wanted to go. I knew what I wanted to do.

With Georgie it had felt like a violation, a thing we should not have done. A violation of what, I did not know. I knew that Georgie would never be the same again. I had known all along; Sam's letter had simply confirmed what I had suspected. A series of events. At first I thought I might have changed things, prevented the Atwell tragedy: there were so many ways it could have all been stopped. If I had not ridden, that day. If I had simply taken another route. If Sam had refused to go hunting with Georgie. If I had not cried like a little girl.

But I saw now that it had all started before I was even born. With two brothers, and their sons. A daughter, the odd girl out. And then we were all pressed on by circumstances that, at first, had nothing to do with us. Circumstances we responded to, badly, but did not create. The Miami land boom, which preyed upon my uncle's hopefulness; the Depression, which amplified my family's sense of being better than the rest of the world.

So to say it could have all turned out differently: only God could say that. It was like saying I should never have been born, which was the only way, I saw now, that all of this could not have happened. One of us would have had to go: me, Georgie, Sam.

I stopped at the clearing and turned to face Mr. Holmes. "Thea," he said, "Thea." He touched my earrings, the earrings that had been a gift from my mother. That Mother and Mr. Holmes had touched the same thing without knowing seemed outrageous, sad, but also comforting.

Nearly a year ago, what had he seen when he approached the car? He had been waiting for us, for me. Watched my father, who seemed hesitant; watched him hesitantly wind his way behind his automobile, filthy from the journey; then me, I sprang out of the car before Father could open my door. Did he think that I was bold? That I was impertinent? Theodora Atwell, from Florida, who behaved indiscriminately — worse than that, very badly, and so was sent away. First my legs emerged from the car, a girl's legs. Then me, smaller than he thought, and pretty, with perfect posture. Or if not pretty, interesting-looking. Saw all this through the gloom of dusk. And then realized he had watched too long and hurried outside to greet us.

"Thea," he said again. That was all he would say. Everything came to me by some sort of instinct I hadn't known I'd possessed. I had done things, of course, but never this confidently, this easily. There was an ease between us, now, that felt so correct, and it seemed impossible that anyone other than he and I had ever felt like this before. I had never wanted Georgie like this.

I kissed him, hard, held his cheeks between my hands.

Then I pointed to the ground, and he understood, he understood exactly what I wanted and he lay down on the ground, on the dirt, and I unbuckled his belt and helped him slide out of his trousers.

I lowered myself onto him, and he was so large and solid inside me, and I didn't want the feeling of that to end. The feeling that seemed to give me a reason for everything that I had done, starting with Georgie: for this, for this feeling that I was not alone. And even while the feeling burned bright in my brain I was sad, for I knew that this would be the first and last time we ever did this. And it did not seem possible, in this moment — I gripped his shoulders, and he pushed up my blouse and sucked my breasts, and pressed me to him — it did not seem possible that I would ever feel this way again. I stilled my hips for a moment, leaned down, and kissed him. Both our bodies were slick with sweat.

"Don't stop," he murmured, and I promised I wouldn't.

I watched his face, his half-lidded eyes; what had he loved when he was a child? Had he held his mother's hand as they navigated an icy street and been comforted by her touch? Had he loved his father's voice as he recited the blessing? He must miss these things now, the touch and sound that slipped so quickly from memory.

I moved faster, and he put his hands on my hips and pushed me down, down, down, into him; and then I was angled differently on top of him and closed my eyes against the pleasure of it, that feeling of hopefulness.

I didn't want to remove Georgie from my mind. I wanted to remove that night, the following day. And that, I saw now, was impossible. The pain was part of the pleasure, and both were my memory of my cousin.

It was a beautiful morning the day of the show, the kind of morning that anticipates a beautiful day. If I often call the days here beautiful it's because they were, because I can think of no other way to describe them accurately except to simply call them beautiful, like a postcard, a painting, a thing not real.

I walked into the forest path with Sissy on one side, Mary Abbott on the other, her breeches sagging at her knees. Sissy had wound her limp hair into a tight knot. My show coat felt tight across my back when I lifted my arms. In two months I would have outgrown it. But I wasn't thinking of that, I wasn't thinking about a year from now, or even a day: I was thinking about the next hour, when I would jump in front of all these girls, and Mr. Albrecht, and Mr. Holmes.

Mr. Holmes was standing at the gate with Decca. My body responded to him, now; it felt like there was a magnet embedded in my skin, telling me to go to him. But of course I would not, could not. I held my hand up in a wave, and looked away. I saw Leona's blond hair, woven into her tight braid; she counted the steps between a double.

I fell into place behind Leona, who was walking the course a second time. This irritated me; etiquette dictated it was someone else's turn. I counted the strides between each jump and tried to see the course from Naari's perspective, tried to anticipate what might frighten her — the potted plants that bookended each jump, the tents at the far end of the ring that shaded our lunch tables, the mere presence of all the people — so many things.

I was sore between my legs, but I knew from last time that the soreness would disappear quickly. And then all I would be left with was a memory, which would fade and fade and fade until I only had a memory of that memory. But Mr. Holmes had changed me. I was a different girl, because of him.

I tried to focus on the jumps. I was impressed by the course, which Sissy's group had designed. The trickiest jumps in the advanced course were a water jump, which led into a wide oxer, two jumps next to each other; and a triple combination that ended with a wall of bricks. The wall was the tallest and last jump of the course, designed as a final test. The bricks were fake, made out of lightweight wood, but the horses didn't know that: to them it was a solid obstacle.

Mr. Albrecht blew his whistle, and Leona passed by and her cheeks looked pinker than usual, and I was actually shocked — she didn't seem the type to wear rouge.

I knew I should let her win. Sissy had even hinted as much. And I had laughed, told her that Leona would probably beat me fair and square. But I hoped that wasn't true.

Qualifying rounds went quickly. I warmed up in the adjoining ring and watched as the water jump claimed three girls before it was my turn: two third-years from Louisville and Martha Ladue. I'd drawn the third-to-last slot. Mr. Holmes still held Decca; I couldn't see them very well, only their profiles, Mr. Holmes's blocked by Decca's. There had already been one fall, a girl I didn't know well tossed after her horse refused the oxer.

There was a break halfway through the qualifying rounds. I tried to make my breathing even, tried to relax Naari with consistency. This was not a speed round — I needed to focus on accuracy. I closed my eyes and pictured each jump, counted the strides in between them.

When it was my turn, I timed my start perfectly; when Mr. Albrecht's whistle blew, I was lined up with the first jump. Naari rolled her eye at one of the pots, but I pushed her through my legs and she cleared it. I jumped like I always did: everything, everyone else disappeared. All the people watching were a blur. I focused on the sharp smell of Naari's sweat, her trembling movement between my legs.

I *knew* we had the last jump, I knew it for a fact, but then the bricks tumbled beneath us and I cursed Naari under my breath. She hadn't picked her legs up high enough. But we'd been fast.

Leona flew by us in a trot, so close she created her own private breeze as she passed. Naari wanted to trot, too, was nervous and wound up. I wanted to ask Mr. Albrecht what my time was and I spotted him, his back turned, gesturing. He was talking to someone but I couldn't see who until I walked past, and when I did I saw that it was Mrs. Holmes.

I watched Leona from a safe distance. My head throbbed, and my mouth was bone-dry. It's over, I whispered to Naari as we watched, but even then I did not quite believe it. Perhaps my eyes had deceived me. Perhaps my mind was playing tricks. But I knew the truth, which was simple: Mrs. Holmes had come home a day early. People came home early all the time.

King cleared every jump, including the last combination, as if they were tiny playthings. His legs were miles long; he barely had to exert himself.

Sissy found me in Naari's stall, where she

stood with her head hung low, exhausted. Sissy slipped in and swung the gate shut behind her. I patted Naari's rump. She would have a few hours to rest. The advanced class went first, and then last, so that their horses would have the most time to recover.

"Why are you down here?" Sissy asked. Her cheeks were red, and her hair had fallen out of its bun. She was dressed completely in white, like we all were. I wasn't competing against Sissy, but she wasn't a threat to anyone. She wasn't good enough. She didn't care enough.

"I'm tired."

"But there's lunch. Aren't you hungry?"

I followed Sissy's finger and saw girls in white, milling around. "What kind of lunch?" I hated how plaintive my voice sounded.

"Sandwiches. But they're good."

"Mrs. Holmes is back."

"I know."

I held my throbbing forehead in my hand and would not look at her.

"I'm sad," I said, finally.

"But you knew she would come back." Her voice was soft.

"Yes," I said. "Yes. But isn't that always how it is? You can see it coming, but you can't stop it."

She drew me to her in a hug, and I noticed how fiercely she did this, as if she was afraid I would refuse her. But I didn't. Nobody had hugged me last year, after Georgie. Nobody had touched me.

The three top finishers — me, Jettie, Leona — were in the jump-off. I was first, not an enviable position, but I was glad to go. We had to be fast. I knew it would be between me and Leona; I had always known that. King was bigger, a more gifted athlete, but Naari was faster, as she'd proved that night long ago; and more than that, she was smarter. King was dull, unflappable. But if I could make Naari nervous enough, she would go as fast as she had that night, and we would win.

In the warm-up ring, I kept my eyes on the tips of Naari's ears and walked her in circles, smaller and smaller until she was practically pirouetting. I wouldn't let her trot — I wanted to reserve every bit of her energy. I hadn't looked at Mr. Holmes but, oh, how he watched me. I could feel it. Mr. Albrecht looked at me curiously as I passed him. I should have been warming her up slowly, gradually working into the course, but in the end, rules were rules, and we both understood that. I could handle my horse however I pleased.

I wrapped the reins around my hands, something I had only heard about. It was stupid; if Naari refused a jump at the last instant, I would be pitched over her anyway, still attached to her by the reins; at the very least, I'd break both my arms. But I felt my old fearlessness rising up, as I always did before a difficult course. As I always did, when people were watching. And now this crowd included him and I felt so reckless; reckless, as I wrapped the reins so tightly around my hands the leather bit into my skin; reckless, as I heard Mr. Albrecht's whistle and pressed Naari into a gallop.

I liked the fierce leverage wrapped reins brought; I bent my elbows and Naari slowed, quickly, and then I turned my toes out and dug my spurs into her sides, and I had her trapped, I had all her power harnessed between my legs and hands, beneath me. I'd never felt such energy, roiling beneath me like a violent wave.

We were going much too quickly; in a lesson Mr. Albrecht would have shouted at me to reduce our speed by half. All the white-clad girls were a blurry crowd, interrupted every few feet by a house mistress's hat. If I'd wanted to find Mr. Holmes in the crowd

I couldn't have.

I cleared the water jump, felt Naari change her footing, and knew, as she collected herself in preparation for the oxer ahead of us — and then as she soared over it, her ears flat against her head in concentration — that we understood each other: I wanted to win, and she wanted to be rid of me, this confusing girl on her back, goading her forward with sharp pains on her flank, then holding her back with a terrible yank on the corner of her mouth; she tasted blood from the pressure of the seesawing bit, which flattened her tongue against her teeth, made it difficult to breathe.

Naari snorted in frustration. "Good," I whispered to her, in beat to her canter, "good, good, good," and as we approached the last combination — it was a dirty trick, to put the tallest jump last — flapped my legs against her sides and moved my hands up her neck, and she felt the relief in her mouth, in her brain, and leapt forward.

This was a speed round, so knocking down jumps didn't count against us, but I *needed* to clear this wall of bricks; I needed Mr. Holmes to see me do it. As we were suspended above the last jump — for a second, two seconds — I closed my eyes and for an instant imagined I was at home again, on top of Sasi, jumping out back, jumping into the great and unknown beyond.

I had to circle her five times before she finally walked. The crowd was utterly silent. I had cleared everything.

Leona trotted in on King, ignored me completely. But Mr. Albrecht caught my eye, and I noticed that all the girls around the ring were also watching: me, not Leona. I slapped Naari's neck and she flinched.

"Cool her down well," Mr. Albrecht murmured as we passed.

I nodded. I tried not to notice that everyone was staring. Mary Abbott stood by the entrance, and as I passed she grabbed my rein.

"No," I said, furious, "let go."

"What a ride," she said, in a singsong voice, "what a ride. Good girl," she said to Naari.

"Don't touch her."

Mary Abbott looked up at me, unsurprised, blew her bangs out of her face as she considered me. "If there's a jump-off I bet you'll win that, too. You'll win everything today, if I had to guess."

"Leave me alone," I whispered, and nudged Naari into a trot, pulling her back into a walk when I had passed the crowd. I slid off her back and began to walk her in a circle, again watching Leona from a safe distance.

"You're fine," I murmured to Naari, but she didn't respond, hung her head low, almost to the ground. I tried to dry the sweat from the raw places I'd spurred into her sides, each the size of a dime, but she flinched at my touch. I felt so horribly sorry, suddenly. For all of this.

A first-year I didn't know by name — Holly? — scurried past, stared at Naari with wide eyes. When I tried to catch her eye, she looked away. Naari shuddered as a breeze swept past us, the air cool on her hot skin. The gentle, rushing sound of branches was all around us, and I felt suddenly calm, empty, free of whatever violent force had possessed me. I stroked Naari's neck and wanted nothing more than to be magically transported back to my bed, a soft quilt pulled up to my neck.

It was hard to tell how fast Leona and King were going — he was so lanky he always seemed to be moving slowly, as if through water. They were a beautiful pair, Leona and King; I couldn't help but admire them, the sheen of Leona's navy boots a glossy contrast to King's burnished coat. They were like royalty, I thought. Yonahlossee royalty. And soon they would mean nothing to this place, a barely remembered girl and her horse.

Again King cleared the final combination as if it were nothing.

The top three finishers — me, Jettie, Leona — filed into the ring. No one knew our times. I spoke softly to Naari, who pranced and arched her neck; Leona glared at me as Naari tried to overtake King.

"Check her!" she commanded. Leona would be fine, I knew; it seemed as if she could weather any of life's storms.

"I'm tired of you always being first," I said. This was easily becoming the second worst day of my life, but the flash of shock on Leona's chiseled face was satisfying. I pushed Naari ahead of King.

I saw Henny next to the gate, chatting excitedly with someone I didn't recognize until she turned her head and looked at me. Mrs. Holmes. Everything about her was shorter: her hair, which hung in a loose, small bun; her skirt, which no longer brushed the ground; her shirt, which was no longer fastened shut at the neck with a cameo but revealed a little bit of her pale skin. I felt dizzy, leaned forward in my saddle too quickly, as if I might faint.

"Are you well, Thea?" Mrs. Holmes asked. I looked at her, my mouth open. I could not hide my surprise. She looked fresher, as if she had returned from a spa. I could see how she had been pretty in her youth. Not beautiful, but pretty in a pert, compact way. I felt sick to my stomach.

"Yes, Thea," Henny said, and her voice was cold. "Are you well?"

I nodded and walked past, avoided meeting Mrs. Holmes's gaze, ignored Henny's admonishment.

"Thea," she called, "have you forgotten your manners entirely?" But I couldn't face Mrs. Holmes; I couldn't, not for anything, pretend to like her.

I had forgotten, of course, I'd forgotten everything. I'd forgotten she would return, lay claim to her husband, her life here. And yet, as I moved on into the ring, I still wanted to win.

We all turned our horses to face Mr. Albrecht and Rachel, who was awarding the garlands to our class. She smiled at me, her face freckled by the sun. She'd been gone for a month, but I guessed being the headmaster's daughter afforded you certain privileges. Mr. Albrecht had his arm around Rachel; protectively, I thought. She was still loved, here. Her cheeks were rosy and she looked hopeful. Of course she was hopeful. Her parents reunited, her family all of one piece again. I saw Molly in the front row, chattering excitedly with another first-year. All the first-years still seemed like fillies, their wispy hair and long limbs. They didn't seem to know where to put their hands and feet when they walked, how to control their legs that had grown so long so quickly.

"In a moment," Mr. Albrecht announced, and the crowd fell silent, "we will have our results."

Jettie was muttering to herself, furiously, and I turned and looked at her.

"Always staring," she said, when she caught me looking, which was something Henny had said to me once. I was silent, closed my eyes against all the people.

When I opened them again I saw a mass of faces, all staring solemnly. This meant so much to all of us. I saw Martha conferring with Henny, and quiet Alice Hunt watching attentively. Molly, chewing on a fingernail. I knew so little about any of them, except Sissy. I knew enough about Eva to call her a friend.

Rachel caught my eye and then looked away, quickly, and I knew that I had won.

"And this has never happened before," Mr. Albrecht began, standing in front of us, addressing the crowd. He could have been any man, from the back, his heavy English the only clue that he was not like the rest of us. "We have never before given the prize to a new girl." He paused. I saw Henny whisper something to Mrs. Holmes, who shook her head. Everyone knew it was me now, of course; Mary Abbott beamed, and Katherine Hayes eyed me with interest. I watched Mrs. Holmes so I would not look at her husband, who I knew was standing near the back of the crowd, Decca on his hip. Mrs. Holmes watched me as well, a calm expression on her face.

"Horseback riding," Mr. Albrecht continued, "is, if I may say so, a true partnership between human and beast, between the power of a person's mind and the sheer force of a horse's strength."

"Get on with it," Leona muttered quietly.

"And all is fair in the jumping ring, where there cannot be favorites, where what matters is skill and speed, in that order. Girls, it is a lesson that is well suited to life: in all your endeavors strive hard, and honestly, and great rewards will be yours."

He took the simplest garland from Rachel, where the others hung on her arm in a neat row. He pinned the garland of greenery around the neck of Jettie's horse, who flattened his ears and bared his teeth. Then a garland around King's neck, while he stood patiently as Mr. Albrecht fiddled with the clasp.

"And our winner today, Theodora Atwell from Emathla, Florida, who has impressed us all with her daring and skill." Mr. Holmes entered the ring, passed by his wife and Henny with a nod of his head.

He pinched Rachel's cheek after he took the garland from her arm, and she turned her face in embarrassment. Panic swelled in my throat. I didn't want him so close, but then there he was, so near I could see the part in his dark hair. Another Yonahlossee tradition.

"Thea," he murmured, "well done." He patted Naari's neck, gingerly, as only a person unacquainted with a horse would do. Then he fastened the garland around Naari's neck. Forsythia dotted with purple creeping phlox, the first bloom of each. And who would have thought that such an unlikely combination — the former so startling, almost electric; the latter so delicate — would have been beautiful? Mrs. Holmes would have thought of it. Mrs. Holmes was back in time to tend to her garden.

She was tending to Decca now, in the

crowd, dark and lovely Decca. Mrs. Holmes did not deserve what I had done.

King backed up, suddenly wary of the garland, and Leona dug her spurs into his sides. Mr. Holmes hurried Rachel over to the side of the ring. My mouth was very dry; to deny myself water was a punishment, the best one I could think of right now.

"It is fine, King," Mr. Albrecht said, and King's ears darted in his direction, and I felt so sorry for him, his master turned cruel over a loss he could not comprehend. I clucked, and King turned his head in my direction, eager for comfort, and Leona's face, for the first time, was easy to decipher: I should not have won. I knew in my bones that this was all over.

In books it was more of a gradual dawning, a slow and painful recognition. But I knew in an instant that Leona wanted to do me harm any way she could. I had gotten in the way of the one thing in the world she cared about: her last chance.

And I would not take it back. I would die before I'd lose. I was so good on a horse because I was fearless. I had always impressed people with my willingness to try jumps that were too high and wide for such a small girl. And now I licked my chapped lips and sought out Mr. Holmes. He held

Rachel's hand at the edge of the ring. Everyone was watching Leona, who was making a spectacle of herself, spurring King into a frenzy. But Mr. Holmes watched me, as I knew he would. When I met his eyes he shook his head, sadly, and if I could have turned a knife in my heart, I would have.

Instead I waited, like a good girl, waited for Jettie, then Leona, to complete her victory lap, then took my own, the applause thunderous, like a warning; waited for the photographer to take my picture, waited for Mr. Holmes to disappear with his family into the woods. Waited while a hundred girls congratulated me, my ugly riding forgiven.

"Oh, how pretty," they said, and touched Naari's neck, one by one.

Then I guided Naari out of the ring, walked past the barn and up the mountain on a trail that wound its way through the forest for a few miles before you came to a clearing. It was the only trail that didn't take you back, eventually, to the barn — it went all the way to Asheville via an old mining road. Or so I'd heard.

I gave Naari her head and untied my garland, the forsythia already bent, the phlox bruised, and dropped it somewhere in the woods. I'd ridden my horse too hard, with everyone watching. I didn't regret that.

I'd ridden too hard for this particular competition, but I'd won.

I came to the first clearing and dismounted. The air was so sharp and clear it pinched my throat to breathe deeply. Naari rested her muzzle in my palm, an unusually affectionate gesture for her. I knew it was an affection born of exhaustion, of uncertainty — we weren't anywhere she recognized — but I was grateful. I put my palm on her wide forehead, traced a circle around her liquid eye.

I was fearless. It was a trait that served me well in the ring, and badly in life.

I chose one of Sissy's dresses from her closet, which was bursting with this season's fine silks and satins. Her mother had just sent them. Sissy was embarrassed by the riches, but she shouldn't have been. A new dress would make her an object of envy, not scorn; it meant she was safe. She would not be plucked from this place, like Leona. The dress I chose was formal, hit my ankles.

"Do you want a necklace?" Eva asked.

"I don't think so." I watched myself in the mirror, which was too small to see my entire reflection at once. My hair was dirty, I hadn't washed it in almost a week, but it looked very heavy, dully auburn. I took a step back and addressed my body, the green satin clung to my hips in a way Mother would have considered immodest. The dress was tight across the chest, flattened my breasts. I wasn't sure if the effect was strange or attractive. The straps were off the shoulder, and I couldn't get rid of the feeling that they were falling.

I wore Mother's earrings again. For the first time I wore jewelry that competed.

I left the cabin before everyone else. They were still applying the bits of makeup they hoped Mrs. Holmes wouldn't notice: swipes of rouge and powder, light lipstick. I hadn't wanted any, and I was avoiding Sissy; that I was able to slip out of the cabin unnoticed seemed like an extraordinary bit of luck. I was buoyed by this feeling as I walked through the Square, lost myself in the crowd of girls headed to the Castle. It was seven o'clock in the evening, twilight, and the light softened us. The Holmeses stood at the entrance, which was festooned with navy and yellow ribbons, but I was calm. The girls were with them, clustered around their father.

I ached with a sadness that had nothing to do with him: they were a family presenting a unified front, even with their secret divisions and sorrows. Suddenly I wanted my twin very badly, was moved almost to tears by jealousy. I straightened myself, felt to make sure my hair was in place, those straps. What would our reunion be like, when it came? Would he be happy to see me? It didn't seem possible.

"Our champion," Mrs. Holmes said at the door. And because Mr. Holmes stood behind his wife, she could not tell how he avoided my eyes.

"Thank you," I said, even though she hadn't exactly congratulated me. I looked at the girls. They all watched me, Rachel especially.

"Are you glad to be back?" My voice was surprisingly steady. "To see your father?"

They all nodded. "We had fun with my grandparents," Sarabeth said.

"So much fun," Rachel echoed.

"They all had a grand time," Mrs. Holmes said. "And I met with so many old Yonahlossee girls." She smiled. "There are so many of you, scattered across the South."

It took me a minute to identify the you to whom Mrs. Holmes referred — but of course. I was a Yonahlossee girl now.

Seeing them was not as hard as I had thought it would be. In fact, the sight of them brought relief: I had not ruined the Holmeses.

"Well," I said, and turned my head to see if another girl was coming, to look away so that I would not see Mr. Holmes so calmly ignoring me. Molly and Henny were at the bottom of the stairs, Molly chattering, Henny half paying attention. I turned back to the Holmeses, curtsied, and slipped through the doors held open by Docey and Emmy, the first time I'd seen them together. And there was a resemblance, in the way they each held themselves, in the way their heads sat on their necks, the way their hands darted quickly about. I smiled at them. Docey smiled back, but Emmy pretended she hadn't seen me.

The dining hall was beautifully decorated, the flowers from the show transported here. Mrs. Holmes had only been back a day, and already she had organized things, put everything back into its proper place.

The boys all stood at the other end of the dining hall in suits, colorful bow ties at their necks, and I felt very conscious of the length and formality of my dress. Everyone else wore shorter, more formless dresses — Sissy had raised her eyebrows at my choice but I had chosen it anyway, and why? Why had I wanted everyone to look at me? I felt their eyes, a hundred eyes, track me across the dance floor. Yet it was not an entirely unpleasant feeling. I imagined Sam in their midst, waiting to dance with a girl. They should have sent him away, too; didn't they know how unfair it would seem, to let me go someplace but not him? They were fools, like Sam had said.

Sissy came through the doors with Eva. She glanced over at the crowd of boys, quickly, and I wished she wasn't so obvious, I wished her heart had been a little less on her sleeve that night.

"Is everything all right?" Sissy asked when she reached me. I noted her earrings, the ruby studs that I had found while I sneaked around our Augusta House, almost a year ago. How time flew.

I nodded, and bit into a tiny berry tartlet, hot from the oven, and the butter melted on my tongue. The music started, and boys began to approach. We stood there awkwardly, Sissy watching me closely, me pretending she wasn't. Why did she think I could so easily transfer my affections to someone else? Then, as if summoned, David appeared, as tall and handsome as the last time.

"Thea? We meet again."

"David." He was the kind of boy who refused to be refused. "You're here." An idiotic thing to say. Surely I could have come up with something better than that.

"I am."

I let him lead me into the throng of dancers, fold my hand into his, place his other hand on the small of my back. Mr. Holmes was taller than he was. Katherine Hayes was wearing a bright red dress, had painted her lips bright red to match. That was bold, to so flagrantly wear lipstick. But Katherine was nothing if not bold.

David was silent, led me fairly gracefully around the dance floor.

"Do you like this song?" he asked when the band finished the first song and started another.

"I like it well enough," I answered. He looked away, and I thought my tone was too harsh, but then I felt his fingers fan across my back.

"How has this year treated you?" he asked.

"Let's just dance," I said, and smiled to soften my request.

He pulled me closer, and I wanted to rest my head on his shoulder, close the little distance left between us. So I did. I rested my head on this strange boy's shoulder and let him pull me, guide me around the Castle, that place where I'd eaten hundreds of meals, said a hundred prayers. I wasn't afraid of being caught this time. The lights were dim, we were surrounded by dozens of other dancing couples, it wasn't a risk. He smelled faintly of cologne.

The song ended and he stopped and held me by the hand, seemed reluctant to let me go. I smiled apologetically, turned toward the last place I had seen Mr. Holmes, and instead I saw Mrs. Holmes, who stared at me without the slightest trace of kindness. I had to look away, finally, because she would not. I caught David's jacket sleeve.

"Another one?" I asked, and he seemed surprised. I threw myself into the rest of the night, took only one break from dancing, followed David and Boone and Sissy into the far corner and sipped from a flask of whiskey. Sissy took one swallow; I took as much as I could handle. After the whiskey I felt lovely, I felt like a lovely girl with a smooth neck and bright lips. I could feel David watching me as I tilted the flask to my lips, and I was glad I'd worn this dress.

Leona wasn't there. I'd looked, and she wasn't easy to miss. And maybe it was the whiskey, but I felt bold enough to forget about her, to put her out of my mind. Perhaps I had imagined the threat: she didn't know anything, not for certain, and could she really bring a rumor about me and Mr. Holmes to his wife? She would have to have proof.

"What are you doing?" Sissy whispered, when we switched partners, but she grinned as she said it.

"Nothing," I mouthed back. I fell into Boone's grip, then; he swung me away from Sissy. Boone and I were both a little drunk. Up close, Boone looked a little startling, with his shock of red hair. But more than his hair it was his skin, translucent in that redhead way. Thin green veins framed each eye.

"Are you having fun?"

"Yes," he said, and turned me out for a twirl. He was a good dancer.

"Sissy's made quite the catch."

He smiled. "Has she? Funny, I was thinking the same thing about my own catch."

It was a strange thing, to be held like this, close enough to smell the pomade Boone used in his hair, but with the implicit understanding that this was all quite platonic. Boone had on his face a bland smile he must reserve for girls who weren't Sissy. I looked at his beige trousers, light enough that I could see clearly where they wrinkled, and I wondered who clothed this boy. His mother, when he visited home? Did she bring him to a seamstress, wait while measurements were taken, then carefully flip through swatches of fabric? Did she think that by clothing him well she sent him out into the world prepared?

"Do you love her?"

He smiled and the folds of skin around his eyes multiplied. "Yes," he said, and paused. "Are you all right, Thea?" He looked concerned. "It's only — that's such an odd question."

My cheeks burned. He was so nice, Boone. My heart ached against his niceness. He looked across the dance floor at something, and when I followed his gaze I saw he was looking at Mr. Holmes, who was helping Mrs. Holmes cut an enormous sheet cake, decorated with sugared rose petals; she slid a piece off her serving knife onto the plate he held, and then he had another plate ready in an instant. Boone looked from him to me, and I bowed my head.

"It'll be all right," Boone said quietly, and I said nothing, just let Boone hold me in his kind, chaste embrace.

He gave me back to David, and I danced with him until it was time to leave. The band played a slow song, something with a melancholy tune, and David was telling me how much he liked me and I looked beyond his shoulder and watched the other couples.

Sissy was pressed into a corner by Boone,

and I was surprised they were being so bold; Sissy must have been drunker than I thought to throw her decorum to the wind like that. Or maybe it was a Yonahlossee effect, throwing one's decorum to the wind.

I felt Mr. Holmes staring before I turned around to acknowledge him. There was only one corner of the room where I hadn't looked, and that was where he would be, and then I turned so I could see if his expression matched the one I had imagined for him, if he stood casually, also like I'd imagined, and just as our eyes met he turned his cheek and left the room. I was stung. It was still mid-song but I muttered something to David about collecting my things.

He held on to my hand by the fingertips again and I yanked it from him, more forcefully than I'd intended, and his face hardened.

You're a tease," he said loudly, and I realized that he was both drunk and angry. It was on my lips to apologize, but then I spoke.

"You're just a silly boy," I said, and David's face crumpled, and he did look like a silly boy, but I couldn't worry about him now. I hurried away and realized I had no things to collect, nothing to keep me here so I wouldn't have to go outside, where Mr. Holmes would be waiting. Or worse, wouldn't be. The room looked dismal, the refreshment table littered with dirty glasses and plates, a wedge of cake disfigured on a stand. Docey was cleaning up, swaying to the tune of the sad song.

"Good-bye, Docey," I said, because there was nothing else to say, because I felt horribly out of sorts and embarrassed.

She smiled at me and held up her hand in a wave, a wistful expression on her face.

I hurried down the stairs and I would have left, but Mr. Holmes called my name. I knew then that Mrs. Holmes was gone. He drew me into a shadow, outside the light that the gas lamp projected.

"What do you want?"

He looked taken aback but then he gathered himself, visibly, a slow rolling of his body, as if he were preparing to give a speech. "Did you have fun tonight?" This was the public Henry Holmes, not the one I loved. His tie was neatly tied, his hair combed flat. I noticed that his hair had been trimmed, and of everything that had happened this day, this was the worst, by far, to see his hair resting in such straight lines against his skin, to know exactly who had trimmed it, that it would be months before his bangs fell into his eyes again.

"What do you think?"

He shook his head. "No." He stopped, rested a palm on the wooden shingle behind him so that he stood in a contorted position. I wanted him, but I could never have him again.

He started to speak, but I stopped him.

"There is nothing to say," I said. "Not really."

He smiled. "There are so many things to say, Thea. Too many."

"Then let's not say any of them." I looked at my hands, still red from my ride today. I should wear gloves, but they dulled my connection to the bit. "I am leaving," I said. "I have to, now."

"You don't —"

"No," I said, and just then Miss Brooks emerged from the Castle, and saw us immediately. Mr. Holmes waved, and Miss Brooks looked at us curiously, and I wondered if everyone knew, or if the idea of it was too unimaginable for someone as nice as Miss Brooks.

Once she had disappeared into the Square, I turned back to Mr. Holmes.

"You were right," I said. "I grew to love this place. I do love it. It's so beautiful."

"Then stay, Thea. Let it continue to be

beautiful. Don't punish yourself by leaving."

"I'm not. I've been punished enough, I think. It was a punishment, to be sent here, but that's not the way it ended up, is it? I came here under such bad circumstances, and now I'm leaving under such good ones."

"Are you?"

"Yes," I said, and I wanted so badly to touch him, but knew I could not, so instead I repeated my answer, and tried to make my voice emphatic, so that he would remember that he had helped me: "Yes."

"Where will you go?"

"Home," I said. "Home."

21

When I returned from the party, the rest of the girls in Augusta House were up, in various stages of preparing for bed. Sissy was gone, was fearless, at least for tonight. I slipped under the covers with my borrowed dress still on. Mary Abbott watched me, but no one else noticed.

"Did you have fun?"

I nodded. My eyes were closed, but it sounded like Eva was hanging her head over her bunk. "Did you?"

"Yes . . ." She trailed off. I thought she was finished when she spoke again: "I'll be so sad when we go away from here, no more dances."

"I see many more dances in your life."

"But they won't be like these," she said.

For better or worse, I thought. "No. You're so dreamy, Eva. Always dreaming about someplace else." That wasn't quite what I had meant to say, but I couldn't articulate what I felt. "You'll always be like this."

"Like what?" Mary Abbott asked.

"Young and beautiful," I said, and Eva laughed. I had pleased her. "Young and perfect."

After everyone's breathing had reached a steady pitch, I went to Sissy's bed and lay there for an hour or so — of course I was fooling no one. I must have fallen asleep, because I opened my eyes and was startled, then relieved by the darkness. I walked heavily across the room and poured myself a full glass of water, drank it, and poured another.

Before the lights had been turned off, Mary Abbott had asked where Sissy was, if we ought to tell a house mistress. Eva had laughed, and told Mary Abbott not to worry. After all our precautions, I felt a flash of anger; even I was being more careful than Sissy. She was taking foolish risks.

The next morning I came to the Castle just as prayer was ending, and picked my way through the throng traveling to classes. Girls seemed to part in my presence, as if they were a herd of horses and I was a snake. Katherine Hayes and an Atlanta girl whispered to each other; Katherine raised her eyebrows as only she could as I passed. But

Leona, who stood alone at the edge of the crowd, watched me impassively, and something about how she stood gave me hope: perhaps this was all my imagination.

I felt a hand in mine. Rachel.

"Hello," she whispered, and squeezed my hand. "Are you going to teach us again?"

I gathered her in a hug and kissed the top of her forehead. "I missed you."

Rachel smiled up at me, abashed, and I told her that we'd see about the lessons. She left and I saw that Mr. Holmes was watching me from his place at the lectern.

He looked at me sadly, and all the girls and their eyes disappeared. I would never be alone with him again.

I felt someone at my side: Sissy. She looked to where I was looking, then back at me again.

"Come," she said. "Let's go to class."

Later that afternoon, on our way to the barn, Sissy seemed giddy, and it was not hard to guess why.

"Boone and I are engaged," she told me as we walked, me with my hand shading my eyes, "secretly."

I squeezed her hand. "That's wonderful. I wish you all the happiness in the world." And I did, that was true — Sissy's shining eyes seemed proof of something.

There were only a few girls outside but it was not my imagination, now: Sissy did not seem to notice — the soothing effects of love, I supposed — but they all stared. I tried not to look but that was impossible. When I waved at Molly, she hurried away like a worried mouse. I almost laughed; as if I were in a position to frighten anyone.

"People are looking," I said to Sissy.

"Are they?" She surveyed the Square. "I don't think so. Maybe they're just glad to see you." But there her tone was off; she was lying, clearly.

When we were almost at the barn we saw Gates, leading her pretty chestnut to the ring.

"Gates," Sissy called, and Gates turned. When she saw us, her face tautened; she looked stricken, as if she had seen a ghost. Her horse looked at us attentively, his ears flipped forward.

"Hello," she called out, her voice tremulous. Her horse whuffed into her shoulder, and Gates gave a small smile before she walked on. But Sissy spoke again.

"Wait," she cried, "wait!"

"Sissy," I whispered furiously. Other girls were looking, now. I saw Henny eyeing the situation curiously, her head cocked, Jettie at her side, always at her side. I watched them for a second. It dawned on me that Jettie loved Henny. But then I hurried after Sissy, who was marching toward Gates.

"Is there something I should know, Gates?" she asked, her voice steely. "Some reason you're ignoring me?"

Gates shook her head, and I felt sorry for her. She wasn't ignoring Sissy; she was ignoring me. She was kind, Gates — right now she kicked at the dirt and looked like she might cry. I smoothed her horse's red forelock down between his eyes, and he looked at me warily. "It's okay," I murmured.

And to Sissy: "It's not you. Leave her alone," I said. "It's me," I added, in a whisper.

"But we walk together!" Sissy cried furiously, and she made me glad I had come, still, willing to be confined in this place if it meant finding Sissy. I looked at Gates and saw what Sissy did: a spineless girl.

"I've known you since you were twelve, Gates Weeks! You should be ashamed." I saw Mr. Albrecht coming toward us and pulled Sissy away. We almost ran into Alice Hunt, who led her giant bay; she managed not to acknowledge our presence.

"Sissy," I said, after I had pulled her into Naari's stall, and she had brooded silently for a few minutes. I was untangling the knots in Naari's tail to give me something to do — whatever else happened in the world, there were always knots in a horse's tail. "I'm going to leave, but you'll stay. Don't make an enemy out of everyone."

"You can't leave," she said. "And why would you want to?"

"It's time.

Sissy looked like she might cry. But when she spoke she was angry.

"It's not that simple. You can't just pick up and leave."

"I'll think of something," I said.

"I wish you'd never met Mr. Holmes," Sissy continued. "I wish Mrs. Holmes hadn't left. I hate him," she said, and looked up at me, her cheeks burning. "I know you don't hate him, so I hate him twice as much."

"He's —" I started, but Sissy shook her head.

"Please don't," she said. "I'll always hate him. It's wrong," she said. "All wrong. You could have loved someone else." I watched her for a moment, my good and true friend, her brown hair tucked behind her ears, her cheeks still scarlet, her forehead creased in anger. She meant I could have loved David; she meant I could have been more like her.

"I loved another boy before I came here."

"I know that," she said impatiently. But she didn't know. I had never even told her I had a cousin.

"You don't know the boy was my cousin. And not a cousin I never knew, a cousin twice removed who lived in another state." I spoke quickly — I had to say it all at once, or not at all. "He was like a brother to me."

Sissy said nothing, only watched me, so I continued, half out of fear, half out of relief, because the telling felt so good, and as I spoke I remembered that telling had this power, this sweet release I had not experienced in such a long time. When I was little, my eardrum had burst from an infection, and though the pus and blood that streamed down my neck horrified Sam, who had run for Mother, I had felt nothing but relief from a pain that had come upon me so gradually I hadn't even known my ear was hurt. And this was the same, but with the heart.

"My brother found out."

"Sam," Sissy said softly.

"Sam. My cousin told him. There was a fight, between my cousin and Sam. A horrible one." My voice broke. "That's why I was sent away."

"Was Sam sent away, too?" When I didn't

answer she lifted my chin up with her finger, like Mother would have.

I shook my head. "I'm not a right girl."

"A right girl," she said. Her husky voice was soft. "I wonder what that is, or where we would find her."

"You don't understand," I said, finally.

"No?" she asked. "I understand enough, I think. We don't choose who we love, do we?" She smiled, and I knew she was thinking of Boone. "We don't choose our families, either. But you can choose to be angry at least." She took my hand and squeezed it, hard.

"Ow," I said, but she would not let go.

"Don't let your family decide the rest of your life."

"That's what Mr. Holmes said."

"Then we agree on something, he and I. What do you think you're going to do?" she asked. "You're just a girl."

"I know," I said quietly. "I'm just a girl. But I'm his sister, too. I need to see my brother. He did nothing wrong."

"Neither did you."

She dropped my hand, and drew me to her. She smelled unusual, of sweat and dirt. "You've been unlucky so far," she whispered into my ear, "but luck changes, all the time. God grants happiness only to those who seek it."

Mary Abbott came back to the cabin while everyone else was at the Hall. This was when I would be with Mr. Holmes, at Masters. It wouldn't be long until Mrs. Holmes noticed my absence, observed that I wasn't studying enough. I needed to leave before that happened.

Mary Abbott looked at me for a long time, her head at an angle. "What's the matter with you?"

"Why do you care?" I snapped.

She looked away and said nothing.

"I'm sorry. I'm tired. I need to sleep."

"But that's all you do now. Sleep. We are friends, aren't we?"

"Yes, Mary Abbott." Why had Mary Abbott chosen me? Why not Eva, or Gates? Or Sissy? Sissy surely would have been nicer, would have known how to handle her. "What do you need?" I felt like I was daring her to tell me that everyone knew about me and Mr. Holmes, that all of camp was talking.

She lowered herself onto the edge of my bed. "Someone saw Sissy in the woods last night," she whispered, even though we were alone. "Did you know she was there? With a boy. Everyone's talking. The rumor's that

Mrs. Holmes knows."

I sat up, so that my face was only an inch from hers. "Who, Mary Abbott? Who saw Sissy?" Today played quickly through my mind: all the girls turning away, but not from me; all the girls staring, but not at me.

But Mary Abbott didn't know, or wouldn't tell me. She looked worried, and I wondered if she was afraid of Leona. Because I knew who had told. Leona, who hadn't been at the dance, who had probably been at the barn; walking back, she could have so easily seen Sissy and Boone. She was the only girl I knew here who would tell on Sissy. Who would hurt another girl so terribly in order to hurt me.

But anyone could have seen Sissy last night — she had been so careless. I felt a flash of anger, again. How could she have been so careless? I looked at Mary Abbott, who picked at my bedspread. Could it have been her? I didn't think so — I had always been her focus, her eyes burning so consistently into my back it felt like a strange sort of plague. Me, not Sissy.

I took Naari into the mountains that night while everyone else was at dinner. The light lasted until eight o'clock these days, and so I stayed out until I could see the faint outline of the stars.

It was so easy to close my eyes and see Sissy's fine brown hair, her wide-set eyes; I could see her face more vividly than I could my mother's, my brother's, my father's. When I left I would ask for a photograph. Mary Abbott said Sissy would be sent home in the next day or so, now that word was starting to spread, and though I didn't particularly trust Mary Abbott, I knew she was right. Mrs. Holmes would find out; she always did. And if Sissy was sent home because of a boy, she would never be allowed to marry that boy, the one who had shamed her, marked her otherwise pristine reputation. All her plans, all her life, in shambles. She who had been so sure just yesterday of how my family should have acted. Who could say what her family would do, would think of her, regardless of how she might defend herself? Certainly not Sissy herself. Not having permission to marry Boone might be the least of Sissy's troubles.

I saw Mr. Albrecht's silhouette in the barn as I dismounted. It was too late to remount and ride around until he disappeared.

"Thea," he said, and nodded.

"Hello."

"No more classes for you. Just the nightly trail rides."

I shrugged. His accent lent such a strange rhythm to his speech.

"I don't think I've had a chance to congratulate you on your success," he said, and extended his hand. "Well done."

I let him shake my hand, his coarse palm around my small, relatively soft one. "Thank you." And I felt near tears again, inexplicably. I placed my other palm on Naari's broad forehead. It would be as if I had died, once my scent disappeared, once she learned to stop expecting the sound of my boots against the floor in the afternoons, once she became used to the noises and smells of another girl. But I would always remember my first horse. I would never forget.

Mr. Albrecht looked at me for what seemed like a long moment. "You're a talented horsewoman. You could stay with it." He stressed the word *stay,* because of his accent.

"And do what?"

"You could do things that have not been done before," he said, still holding my hand.

I looked away. "Perhaps."

There was still kindness in the world, at Yonahlossee. It almost seemed irrelevant.

22

I rose early the next morning and dressed carefully, tucked my shirt neatly into my skirt, polished a scuff mark from my boot. I looked over at Sissy, who was sleeping on her back, her arms flung out beside her. I smiled. Last night she had told me that the girls knew about her and Boone; she didn't seem worried, though. She'd seemed a little bit proud. I'd acted surprised. She clearly had no idea of how far the rumor had traveled, how it had snaked its way through camp to Mrs. Holmes's ears.

As I examined myself in the mirror I was nearly certain I could feel Mary Abbott watching me, but when I turned around and looked her eyes were shut, her mouth closed in a thin line.

I got to the Castle early, to catch Mrs. Holmes before breakfast. The dining hall was nearly empty, except for a few second-years sitting at a table. I took the long way around them, and as I was passing the kitchen, the door swung open.

"Hello," Emmy said, and looked away, down to a spot on the floor. She carried a trayful of glasses, a dish towel slung over her shoulder. The door swung shut behind her.

I said nothing, and began to walk by when she spoke again.

"Aren't you going to say hello to me?"

"Hello," I said. "Hello, hello, hello. I'm on my way to see Mrs. Holmes."

Emmy gave a short laugh. We had never really spoken before. She held herself more elegantly than her sister, didn't have the wandering eye, but their voices were the same, high, so thickly accented I had to pay attention to understand them.

"Docey feels poorly for you." She shifted the tray in her hands.

"Pardon?"

"My sister. She feels poorly for you." She spoke quickly, almost impatiently.

"Oh," I said, at a loss.

"But we have a different feeling about this," she continued. "I was there. You can say what you will about Mrs. Holmes, and girls always do, but she's a good soul. A good soul," she repeated firmly, almost primly.

I thought about all those afternoons in the library, Emmy lurking behind closed doors. I leaned against the wall, a cold sweat on my brow.

"Does she know?" I asked quietly. I turned and stared at the table of second-years watching us; nobody conversed with the servants here. But this table I could handle — these girls were from Kentucky, and they looked away quickly.

"Isn't that something you should have thought on before?" She shifted the tray again. Her arms trembled, and I almost reached out to take it from her.

She waited, as if for an answer. I looked from the tray, crowded with glasses, to her face, watching me imperiously.

"Thought on?" I asked, and Emmy lowered her eyes. I had shamed her, and it had been so easy. "This isn't any of your business."

As I began to walk away for the second time, Emmy shrugged. "Not from me she doesn't. Know," she added.

I was glad no one had heard me mock Emmy, a servant, born with none of the advantages I had known since birth. I'd never once thought of her as someone who could be cutting. But just now I could have been sparring with Leona, or Katherine Hayes.

I turned around before I entered the stairwell and saw Emmy setting out the glasses on the table where the second-years sat, her eyes downcast, her face expressionless. Then I saw Henny, sitting at our table, a book in front of her. She saw me and I instinctively held my hand up in a wave, before I could think better of it. Henny only raised her eyebrows.

Even though I had more serious problems than Henny's cold shoulder, I still cared. If Yonahlossee had taught me anything, it had taught me that it was impossible not to care, not to marvel at the mysteries of girls' affections, which were hard won and easily lost. If no one knew about me and Mr. Holmes, then why was Henny acting so coldly?

It was a question that occupied my mind as I climbed the stairs, slowly, half hoping she wouldn't be there. But then I'd just have to come back.

"Thea," Mrs. Holmes said, and looked up from her desk as I passed through her door. She pointed to the chair as if she had been expecting me. Mr. Holmes stood behind his wife, looking out her window, but when he heard my name he turned around, his hands in his pockets, always in his pockets, a confused expression disfiguring his handsome face. I stood in the doorway for a moment, noticed that my own hands were trembling. I clasped them behind my back and went to the chair.

"You wanted to see us?" Mrs. Holmes asked, absentmindedly pruning the potted ivy that sat on her desk, snapping the dead leaves away with a flick of her fingers.

You, I might have said, I wanted to see you. I lifted my head. "Yes."

"About what?"

"Sissy."

She gave a little gasp. It was satisfying to shock her. He watched me impassively. Did he know me so well that he had predicted what was coming? Had he felt it this morning, had he insisted on accompanying Mrs. Holmes to her office? That would have meant that he knew me better than I knew myself, because I hadn't even known I would go this far. And no one knew me that well.

"I know someone says she saw Sissy in the woods. With Boone Roberts from Harris Academy?" I couldn't keep my voice from lilting into a question. Mrs. Holmes had stopped her pruning, now held a leaf in midair, her mouth parted. "But it wasn't her. It was me."

Now she looked confused, an expression I had never seen cross her face before. She looked mystified, for an instant, before she composed herself. She should have been headmaster, not her husband. And for all practical purposes, she was.

"Yes?" she asked. "And? Tell us."

I hadn't been sure I'd be able to do what I had to do next. But the way Mrs. Holmes used "us," the way she gestured at me like I was harmless, nothing more than a girl — Mr. Holmes caught my eye, and I suddenly felt so exhausted. So reckless.

I looked Mrs. Holmes in the eye. "Ask Eva," I said. "My bed was empty." I paused. My voice wavered, and I took a deep breath. When I spoke again my voice was clear. "Sissy is loved. Her family is loved. No one will want to see her go, least of all her father, her grandfather." I didn't need to spell out what I meant; if nothing else, Mrs. Holmes was a shrewd woman. "Especially if they think it might be a mistake. And I'll see to it that they think it's a mistake. People won't care as much when I am sent home." I shook my head. "Do you see? It won't get you anywhere, punishing Sissy."

"I see," Mrs. Holmes said. "I see perfectly well. How interesting all of this is. But let me ask you this: Have you thought about what got *you* here? Have you thought that perhaps it is best for Sissy to be sent to a place where she will not be tempted?"

I looked at her in wonder. "Where would that be? We're already on the top of a mountain."

Mrs. Holmes turned briefly to her husband, as if to say, Do you see this girl in front of me, so impudent, so presumptuous? She shook her head, gave a hard little laugh. Mr. Holmes looked outside the window again, and I knew he wanted nothing more than to be absent from this. He would never help me; he was not capable of it. Mrs. Holmes had always handled the disciplining of the girls, the unpleasant parts of keeping order.

"You're so lovely, Thea, just like your mother was. So lovely. Do you think you own the world? Do you think you have any say in what the world does with you? So lovely, so naive."

"Beth," Mr. Holmes said, a warning, but she acted as if she hadn't heard him.

She crumpled the dead leaf in her fist and flung it into the wastebasket.

"Your mind works in ways I do not understand, Thea. Usually I understand all my girls. You will pretend to have gone behind

Sissy's back with her fiancé?"

I must have looked surprised — and I was — because she continued.

"Yes, I knew they were engaged. I know everything, Thea." She smiled, and pressed a finger to her lips. "I don't think you really want to go home."

I thought of how regal my house looked on a gray day, its stately lines illuminated by the sky like ash behind it. I wanted to go to *that* home, the home of my childhood, the home that included Georgie, the home where my family loved me without reservation. But that home was gone now, sold to strangers.

"How could you want to go home?" she asked, her voice softer. "Do you know why they sent you here?"

Mr. Holmes's hand encircled his wife's upper arm, gently, as if she were a child. "Enough, Beth."

But of course I knew why they had sent me here. I almost laughed.

Mrs. Holmes ignored her husband. "They thought you might be carrying a child," she said. She stared at me, but it was she who looked stricken, not I. "They would have known soon enough, but your mother always was a worrier," she said, and turned her head sharply. "Henry. You're hurting me."

I could see how tightly Mr. Holmes gripped his wife's arm. "That's enough," he said quietly. "There's no use in all this."

"She'd rather I deal with the poor child, I suppose. I was always the problem-solver, between the two of us. I used to think that pretty girls didn't have to worry so much about the mechanics of life, the simple procedures. But your father, what of him? He's a doctor, he would have known soon enough whether or not you carried your cousin's child." She gave a little gasp, and put her hand over her mouth. Mr. Holmes let go, then, and Mrs. Holmes massaged her arm where his hand had been, a faraway look in her eyes. Her face had softened. I thought of all her plants in their slender bottles. It seemed incredible that she felt any sympathy for me. It was so easy to deceive people.

"She needed to know," Mrs. Holmes said, breaking the silence. Then she turned to me. "She should know what awaits her at home."

I shook my head, though no response was required of me. I remembered Mother checking my sheets every day before I left. I remembered what Mrs. Holmes had said when I first met her, to see her if I noticed anything about my body. Of course.

"It's not a surprise," I said quietly. It would have been a surprise if Mrs. Holmes had told me that Georgie was well again, that Mother had forgiven me. That my parents had considered and acted upon the worst possible scenario was really no surprise at all.

"I'll have to make an announcement, you know. I'll have to make an example of you."

"I know," I said quietly.

Mrs. Holmes spoke again, softly now; I had to strain to hear her. "Do you know why your mother was friends with someone like me? We didn't travel in the same circles, no. You'd never even heard of me when you came here. . . ." She trailed off, then shook her head, quickly, and continued. "Your mother was something of a fast girl at Miss Petit's. Not unlike you, Thea. I was Miss Petit's favorite. Your mother was given a choice: leave in disgrace, or align herself with me. She wasn't stupid, your mother. She fell into line. But I like to think that we were friends. I like to think that eventually she loved me as I loved her." She did not know about me and Mr. Holmes; of that I felt certain. A small mercy.

"My mother was fast?" I asked.

"Oh," Mrs. Holmes said. "The fastest." Her faraway voice had returned.

In the dining hall the tables were still being set. Docey looked at me curiously, and I smiled at her, eager to be kind to someone. Emmy was nowhere to be seen. I sat on a bench out of everyone's way. The smell of frying bacon was so pungent I felt sick to my stomach. More girls streamed in, their eyes small from sleep. They barely glanced in my direction as they passed by; strangely, I felt a vague sense of disappointment. I didn't matter anymore. I glanced at the clock; I had spent only ten minutes in Mrs. Holmes's office, which seemed impossible.

What were Mr. and Mrs. Holmes doing right now in her office? Perhaps assigning blame, deciding whose fault it was that a girl — two girls, if Sissy was counted — had slipped from their grasp. Or perhaps Mr. Holmes was soothing his wife, had drawn her near, was telling her that this strange thing that had just happened, with Thea Atwell from Florida, was fine, would be fine.

I closed my eyes against the movement in the dining hall and put my head in my hands. There was a dull ache at the nape of my neck.

I had destroyed one family, and then come

close to destroying another. The pain in my head deepened, I didn't know how I would be able to rouse myself when Sissy came in.

Sissy was late, of course. I would wait. I saw Katherine Hayes walk in, chatting with Leona, which was odd. Alice Hunt gaped at them. I almost smiled — I'd never seen a person look so astonished.

Mrs. Holmes burst through the stairwell, her face red. Mr. Holmes followed close behind, speaking urgently under his breath. Girls turned in their chairs, startled. Leona and Katherine stopped in their tracks. We'd never seen Mr. and Mrs. Holmes exchange a harsh word. To see them fight, openly — this was unheard of. Everyone started whispering, all at once, the hum of all those voices torture. I shut my eyes, put my hands over my ears.

"Thea?" A tap on my shoulder. I opened my eyes. Docey, with her darting eye. "Are you all right?" she whispered.

Beyond Docey I saw Sissy enter the Castle with Eva. Everyone turned in her direction, the whispering died down, and I watched Sissy notice — scan the room, slowly, put her hand to her throat. I put my own hand to my throat. I'd never seen Sissy frightened before. I saw Henny whisper something to Jettie. She was so typical, Henny — I understood then that's what I'd always hated about her. Of course she would look smug. She was too dull to seem any other way.

Mrs. Holmes raised her voice at the other end of the room, and everyone looked away from Sissy.

"Thea," Docey said, more urgently, "you should go. Go!" she said again, and tried to pull me up.

Time was operating according to a different clock. Everything was moving too slowly. Mrs. Holmes watched Mr. Holmes wind his way through the tables, now set with platters of thick fried bacon, tureens of oatmeal; he was searching for something, as he walked, quickly checking each table, girl after girl averting her eyes. He stopped at my table, and Mary Abbott pointed behind him, and Mr. Holmes followed her finger to me.

Everyone was deadly silent, the hum evaporated. He tilted his head to the door, as if we were alone, back in his library, surrounded by all of his books. Have you read all of them? I'd asked. Most, he'd said, and laughed. I'm old. I've had plenty of time to read. I'd smiled, because he was so young, we both knew that. Then I'd accepted his hand, let him pull me from the couch.

Now, in this dining hall where I'd eaten hundreds of meals, Mr. Holmes still seemed young, if being young meant you seemed untouched by the world. He *wasn't* untouched, I knew that better than anyone, but he didn't seem haunted, there was no eerie look in his eyes. He looked like an immortal.

He pointed a thumb to the door, and Martha Ladue, who was sitting a table away from me, gasped, a flush spreading over her white skin.

Follow me, he'd said that afternoon, but that was just a formality, a thing he said. I would have followed him anywhere. He took me upstairs, to a room I'd never entered. All done up in pink, with a narrow white bed. Sarabeth's room. I didn't understand why he had brought me here. He retrieved something from her dresser, a pretty marble-topped piece, while I was hungrily taking in the room, and put it in my hands. Look, he'd said, and he'd seemed suddenly shy, his hair falling over his eyes.

But now, in the dining room, I knew it was no longer true. I would not follow him anywhere. I would have, for a moment, and that's how it had been with Georgie, too. I would have followed him anywhere for a moment, and then the moment ended.

I shook my head, and Mr. Holmes watched me in that fierce way of his, as if he were inventorying my soul, and then he left. I looked to the head table; his children weren't here. He would have taken them away had they been. He would go to them now. This was where he would always be. I would leave, but he never could.

"Girls," Mrs. Holmes said, and stepped up to Mr. Holmes's lectern, where he usually led morning prayer, "your attention for a moment. An announcement." She was flustered, her voice unsteady, her hands fluttering in front of her. That I had undone her brought me no pleasure.

But the view, always the view: she stood in front of the window, the same window I had touched nearly a year ago, when Father had dismissed me from Mr. Holmes's office. She was framed by the mountains; despite everything, I could still sight a marvel. Both then and now.

"Theodora Atwell is leaving us. Tomorrow morning. It is all very sudden, of course." Girls started to whisper again, as I'd known they would, as I'd known what Mrs. Holmes would do as soon as I'd seen her enter the dining hall. It was an odd sort of comfort, to know all this and not be frightened.

"For an infraction. Involving a young

man." The din grew louder, and Mrs. Holmes raised her voice. "I expect that there will be no more talk concerning this matter. You are ladies, and ladies do not gossip." She looked at me then, across the room.

In Sarabeth's room, I'd looked at what he'd handed me. A photograph of a much younger Henry Holmes in a silver frame that needed to be polished, Mrs. Holmes's absence wrought in little ways like this. Me, he'd said. Me when I was your age. He stood in front of a lake, holding a paddle. He looked directly at the camera, as men always did. He looked the same, except his face was fuller, not chiseled into handsomeness by time. I touched the glass. So handsome, I'd said. But what I'd meant was this: So new.

"And let this be a lesson, girls, to act your age. To obey the rules."

Sissy looked at me from across the room, along with everyone else, a slow dawning illuminating her delicate features. She knew. She looked away, out the window, touching the diamond horseshoe that rested in the hollow of her neck, and for an instant I thought that what Mrs. Holmes had predicted might be the case: Sissy would believe I had betrayed her. She backed out of the door, everyone watching.

Mrs. Holmes watched me. Then I felt Docey's hand on my shoulder. I took it, and held it, and though Docey's hand was tense at first, she didn't take it away. I could tell by feel that we had matching calluses — mine from riding, hers from the constant work of putting things in order. Our hands felt the same.

I found Sissy in the woods, where she and Boone went. She sat on a fallen log, crying into her hands.

I told her what I had done, and gradually, her crying stopped. I sat so close to her I could smell her. That's what sleeping in her bed a dozen times had earned me — recognizing the scent, surprisingly pungent, she left on her pillow.

"You'll sleep in the infirmary tonight. That's where they'll put you, before they send you away for good." Still she wouldn't look at me. I tapped her shoulder, and she turned to me, her wide-set eyes swollen.

"Thank you," she said, her voice even more jagged, from the crying. "It was a brave thing to do."

"There's proof. Eva noticed that I was gone that night. I told Mrs. Holmes to ask her."

"Eva wouldn't tell."

Of course Eva would tell, if it was me versus Sissy. "It doesn't matter. She won't ask."

"No," Sissy said, "she believes you, along with everyone else." Her voice broke.

"Mrs. Holmes doesn't believe me. She saw right through it. Through me." I took Sissy's hand. "I'm sorry."

"I know." She flung her hand in the air, as if to say, We're done with all that. That gesture never left me. In my darkest hours I would recall it, extract it from the recesses of my mind. "But who will I talk to, now that you're leaving?"

I thought then that it was always a matter of exchanging one thing for another, losing one kind of love for a new kind.

"And why do you want to go home, Thea? I don't understand."

I smiled. She was right to ask that question: Why did I want to go home? My family didn't want me. "I want to help you. And my brother. I need to see my brother."

She nodded. "But your reputation. What will your parents think?"

I looked away. That was what I feared most, but I couldn't tell Sissy. I would be leaving this place in shame, which was exactly the opposite of how I wanted to leave it. I wanted my parents to love me;

no, they had always loved me, I was their child — I wanted them to like me again. And leaving this way, in the midst of a scandal — I had made sure they would not. But better me than Sissy, who still had a chance; in my heart, I knew I was ruined in Mother's eyes; one scandal or twenty, it didn't truly matter. The Thea I had been had disappeared, a puff of smoke.

"I think I am a lost cause, to my parents."

Sissy looked like she might start to cry again. She grabbed my hand. "That is awful, Thea. The most awful thing I've ever heard."

"It's not the most awful thing I've ever heard," I said. "There's worse. I need to do what's good, Sissy. I need to help my brother. I need to be a right girl."

I wandered the Castle the afternoon before I left Yonahlossee, sneaking out of the infirmary, which wasn't at all hard to do. No one watched me. I knew by the bells that it was rest hour. Sam would know I was coming home, by now. Mother would have told him. Surely he would be glad to see me, in his heart if not in his head.

I'd left a book in one of my classrooms. But the book didn't matter so much. I had become attached to this place, and I wanted to see where I'd gone first when I'd arrived almost a year ago, once more before I returned to Florida.

I knew what to expect, now, the rapid process by which Yonahlossee would turn alien.

The dining room was clear of the chaos of this morning. I tried to memorize each detail as it lay: the table where I had eaten hundreds of meals; the space where Mr. Holmes had stood and talked to us of God.

I climbed the stairs to the third floor, to see it for the last time, but perhaps I knew, somehow, that Mrs. Holmes would be in her classroom.

She leaned against the window in an odd posture, her forehead on glass, her open hand pressed against the wall, as if she were trying to push her way through. I knew the view very well: she was in the mountains, only a window between her and them. I thought she might be crying.

And then she turned and I drew back, certain she had seen me. But she went to a desk, where Decca sat, drawing. Mrs. Holmes smiled, and pointed to something on the paper. Decca nodded. I watched them for too long, Decca engrossed in her drawing — she kept looking at the window, and I realized she was drawing the mountains — and Mrs. Holmes watching, her face constantly moving — her lips, her forehead — in response to Decca's work. She looked pleased. They both did.

When I left, I wound my way behind the cabins — I was meeting Sissy — so that in case Mrs. Holmes returned to the window she would not see me.

A kitchen girl I didn't know by name brought my dinner to the infirmary. I tossed and turned against the hard mattress all night. I was going to see my parents soon. My brother. What had they been told? I was doubly bad, returned to them for the same sin for which I had been cast out.

The door opened. There was no lock, and for an instant I thought Mr. Holmes had come to see me, and I was so happy.

But the silhouette belonged to a girl. I sat up and turned on the lamp. Mary Abbott.

"Why are you leaving?" she asked in a normal tone of voice.

"Shh. Because I was bad." I sighed. "You shouldn't be here."

"But you weren't bad!" She knelt down next to my bed. "I know who was bad."

My stomach dropped. I remembered the night I'd lain in Sissy's bed and Mary Abbott had called out.

"She shouldn't have done that. She shouldn't have sneaked away all the time." She paused. "But don't be mad at me."

"I won't," I said, "I promise. Just tell me everything."

"I didn't tell Mrs. Holmes."

"Who did you tell?" I whispered slowly, as if I were coaxing a small child.

"Henny," she whispered, her eyes wide. "Henny."

"Oh," I said, and lay back against the iron headboard. "Oh."

"She asked!" Mary Abbott said defensively. "She heard rumors, it was something all the girls have been talking about for such a long time, and then I saw Sissy."

"The night of the dance," I said.

She shrugged. "Lots of nights. I know where they go. I've known for a long time. Sometimes I follow them." She seemed proud.

"You watch them?" I asked incredulously.

She shook her head quickly. "Just for a second, two seconds. Just to see Sissy's safe. I love her, too," she said. "Like you."

I nodded, assembling all this new information, which was, after all, unsurprising. Unsurprising that Mary Abbott should have followed Sissy and Boone into the woods, unsurprising that she had been an instrument of Sissy's demise without the malice that such action usually called for. She was lonely. That was all.

"You were bad at home, weren't you?"

"Yes," I said, without thinking. "Very bad." I felt my eyes warm.

"Oh, Thea," Mary Abbott said, and then she hugged me, fiercely, and whispered into my ear, "it's all right," and whatever spell she had cast was broken. I pushed her away, hard.

"Ow," she cried, and rubbed her shoulder, drew her arms to her chest as if to protect herself — she did need to protect herself. I recognized something in her, a certain deviancy, a certain need. A yearning she knew she needed to hide without knowing how. She hadn't the slimmest idea. She was too much like me; I could not be kind to her. The only difference between us was that I did not seem as strange, on the surface of things.

"It's better," I said, "not to be strange. Not to be noticed."

Mary Abbott looked pained, but she nodded. She reached for my hand, and this time I let her take it. She was always reaching for my hand, but this time would be the last time.

"Take care," I said, "take care of yourself."

■ ■ ■ ■

I found Sam that night after I had confessed everything to my mother, almost everything: I would never tell her that my cousin and I had slept together. I thought I was being merciful; I never imagined that she did not believe me, that she had her own ideas about what had happened. But she was right, in the end; she was correct not to trust me.

I believed, as I searched the house for her, finally finding her out back pruning roses, that telling might relieve me. I believed foolishly.

Sam was in our old nursery, reading a magazine, sitting Indian-style on the bare floor. He shook his head when I walked in; his eyes were glassy, and the room was very dim.

"Do you want more light?" I asked, my hand on the switch.

"Leave it."

Sam turned a page, and I saw an advertisement for roller skates, which neither of us had ever used.

"What are you reading?" I asked.

"I'm reading an article about people with unnatural desires."

"I'm sorry." My face was swollen from crying, it felt as if there was sand trapped underneath my eyelids.

"I should have stopped you." He looked miserable, his eyes swollen and red, veins I'd never seen before at their surface. His left eye was black from a bruise.

"You couldn't have," I said quietly. "It wasn't yours to stop."

"They're going to send you away."

I was stunned. "Who?"

"Who do you think? Mother and Father."

"Where?" I thought of my mother's brother, in south Florida; that was the only place they had to send me.

"To a place I've never heard of. It has an Indian name."

"I won't go, Sam," I said, my voice rising. I didn't stop to think how he knew this. He must have overheard something. "Don't let them take me."

"Why, Thea?" he asked. "Why did you do it?" He began to sob. "They'll send you away, and I'll be alone. Did you think of that? Did you? Did you think that you would go away and I would be all alone?"

I threw myself on him. I felt my twin relent, and this relenting made the next two weeks, before I was sent away to Yonahlossee — the utter awkwardness, the turned heads of my family, the acknowledgment of my deep betrayal — my brother yielding against me in that moment made all of this bearable.

"I should have known," he murmured into my hair. I could barely understand him.

I held his face in my hands. His cheeks were hot and sweaty.

"You did know," I said.

My father had been in his study. I knocked and his voice sounded the same as always, giving me permission to enter: quiet, firm.

"Thea."

"Father." He was in the middle of writing a letter. Now he tapped his chin with his pen and waited. "How is Georgie?" I blurted, because either I said it now, and quickly, or not at all.

"Georgie is in the hospital. Did you know that?"

I shook my head. "He was breathing when I saw him last."

"Yes. Unfortunately one can breathe and still be badly damaged. It seems his brain is injured." He paused. "When your mother told me what you had confessed I was sure she was wrong." His voice was even. "Was she wrong?"

I shook my head.

"I wish with all my heart that she was." It was strange, for my father to use a sentimental phrase like that. *All my heart.* "But your brother is involved in this, too. Georgie's wound" — and here he laid his pen down and put his hands before him as if he were cradling a melon — "is consistent with violent injury. Do you understand, Thea?"

I nodded, not understanding.

"Georgie was either hit, by your brother, or he fell. Either way the result is the same. But there is a great distinction between the two, as you must know."

I said nothing.

"It is plausible that Georgie fell on a large, blunt object. I told the hospital the rock. They relayed this information to the police. That your cousin had fallen and hit his head on the rock."

"All right," I said, because he seemed to require a response. "All right."

"Your brother did not know who I was when I found him later. He had been sitting under a tree for hours. He had wet himself. His recounting of what happened is faulty, at best." Father looked at me like he was surprised to find me there.

"I just wanted to find out about Georgie," I whispered. His name was dirty in my mouth.

"Well, now you know. He is not well."

"But he will be well again?"

I should not have asked, clearly.

My father shrugged faintly. "God willing." I made to leave, but my father spoke again. "Did you see, Thea? Can you tell me what happened? Can you be honest?" He looked so pained, my father, so lost. The top button on his shirt was undone; it was never undone.

"It was the rock," I said. "The rock, not Sam."

It seemed an easy thing, to let my father believe what he wanted so badly to believe. The least I could do.

My mother found me in the barn later, untangling the knots in Sasi's tail. It was something to do.

"Thea."

"Mother." I held the tail loosely; I did not want to let go of it completely.

"I was out for a walk." She gestured toward the wide expanse. My mother never took walks. She was either in the garden or in the house. She had spoken to me three times in the past week. Once she had asked me to sweep the front porch, which I had done, twice, even though it hadn't needed it.

She rested her forehead against the stall door; she looked tired, vulnerable. Perhaps she would have news of my cousin.

"We've decided to send you away from all this."

"I won't go." I looked my mother in the eye, and though she was surprised, all the rules of how we behaved with each other had disintegrated, as if into thin air.

She closed her eyes. "You have no choice. It will be better for you, to go."

"No. I'm fine here. I'll stay out of everyone's way. You'll see. I'll sleep out here. I won't be a bother. Please, it won't be better for me."

She laughed. "You'll sleep in a stall? You're not an animal, Thea. Are you?" She shook her head. "You will go."

"Oh." I wound Sasi's tail around my wrist. "I see."

My mother watched me for a moment. "Why, Thea? Why did you do it?" Her mouth was screwed into a small, ugly knot. She did not look so beautiful, in this moment. She looked betrayed.

"Why was it so bad?" I asked. My voice cracked. "You loved Georgie."

It seemed like she was ready for the question, like she had already asked it of herself.

"I wanted more for you!" she cried.

"Don't you see, that Georgie is not enough? And even if he was, it's all a horrible mess now, Georgie in the hospital, your brother the one who put him there. Uncle George and Aunt Carrie cannot forgive. And I'm so angry at Georgie . . . and at you." She gestured outside the barn, at our thousand acres. "We had everything, Thea. Everything. This place is ruined."

"Please," I cried, "where are you sending me? Don't. Please don't." I touched her arm. "Please keep me here. I'll be good."

She looked at her forearm where I had touched it, then up at me again.

"I'm afraid it's too late for all that," she said, calm now.

We settled into a semblance of routine in my final week at home. I woke up early in the morning and rode until Sasi was exhausted. I made jumps that were higher and higher, and Sasi cleared them because he could feel how reckless I was. Mother busied herself with chores, and I helped her by making myself scarce. I knew I was the last person she wanted to see. Sam disappeared for hours at a time out back. Hunting, I presumed. Father left before I rose and returned after I was in bed. When I passed him in the hall, he made some mention of a sickly infant who would not nurse. I did not ask again about my cousin. I assumed that Father would tell me if his condition changed for the worse. I was naive, I thought my parents' silence meant that Georgie was getting better.

I was supposed to be packing my clothes. Mother had been vague about what I'd need. I had gotten as far as emptying my drawers onto the floor. Now I combed through these piles of all my fine things: shimmering dresses, stiff cotton skirts, smooth silk scarves. I didn't deserve them. I couldn't imagine a future in which I'd wear them again.

A knock. I'd been keeping my door closed to spare my family the sight of me.

"Come in."

Idella's brown hand, first. I went back to my things. The disappointment was nearly unbearable.

"Your mother sent me to help pack."

I gestured at the piles. "I've made such a mess."

"Let me."

I watched as she made better piles, put skirts with skirts, breeches with riding shirts; deftly folded all the things I'd unfolded.

"Your mother says to pack lightly." Idella

glanced at me. "She says there will be a uniform."

"A uniform," I repeated. "Do you know why I'm going away?"

Idella smoothed the collar of a blouse. I knew so little about her. She wasn't married. She lived with her mother and two sisters; they were all deeply religious.

"I'm sure it's all fine."

I nodded, close to tears. "It's not," I said.

"God willing," Idella said. "God willing."

23

The train from Asheville to Orlando was half empty. There was another girl my age who sat in first class. We ate together in the dining car, at separate tables. I studied her. She did not look at the waiter when she ordered, and when her food came she ate in a hurry, shyly, as if she were in danger of offending someone by dining. She wore beautiful, teardrop-shaped emerald earrings, which she touched constantly, in the same way that Sissy touched her horseshoe pendant. The horseshoe pendant hung around my neck now, and I found myself tapping it constantly, as Sissy had, but not for the same reasons: I touched it because Sissy had, because I missed her.

I could not eat the tomato soup the waiter brought. It wasn't very good, but I should have been hungry; I hadn't eaten very much in days. I forced myself to eat the roll. As I sat here, on this train, this bland food before me made everything real again. I could feel my resolve scattering like dandelion fluff. It was so green outside the train window, so green and alive. The beauty of North Carolina lay in its austerity, the mountains so far away, so cold, so distant. Once we crossed into Florida, everything was alive, at you. I knew as soon as I stepped off the train the heat would greet me like an old friend, even though it was only spring.

I was jealous of the girl, whose name I didn't even know, who I would never see again. I had never wanted to be someone else so badly. I wanted to begin again: at birth, without a twin, without a cousin so close he was a brother.

"Do you know the next stop?" the girl asked. She stood before me. I hadn't even noticed that she'd left her table. For a moment the name would not come to me. But finally it did.

"Church Street," I said. "Orlando." The girl seemed nervous, and I wanted to take her by the shoulders, say, Look, please, you have nothing to be nervous about. But I didn't know that. I didn't know what or who she would meet when she stepped off the train, which was beginning the slow process of stopping. I could see the station, where I would soon be, and it seemed impossible that I could be here on this train but that in five minutes, ten, I would not be. And that I would not be by my own volition. Why, Thea, why. Why had I wanted to return to all this? To my brother who hadn't written me a single word for months, to my mother and father who had sent me away so quickly it was as if they'd known all along how they would handle a crisis, a tragedy, a thing Mother hadn't planned: Send the girl away, keep the boy?

And then I saw them, my parents, waiting on the platform, my father in a suit, my mother in a wide-brimmed hat. And I knew why I had wanted to come back. Yet I was not ready to see them. I faltered. I put my head in my hands.

I looked up again and saw the girl was watching me. At Yonahlossee she would not have been popular; she was too nervous, too needy.

"Who are you meeting?" she asked.

"My parents." I looked outside the window. My mother stood in front of my father; my father's hands were clasped behind his back, his head bowed. My mother looked agitated. My fast mother, who had once been beautiful and shameless. She looked thinner. Sam was not there.

I watched my parents as the train pulled

in, stayed in my seat as the other passengers disembarked and my mother peered anxiously into their faces.

I stood. I could already feel my legs weakening, atrophying ever so slightly from disuse. I hadn't been on a horse in days.

When I finally emerged from the train, the last passenger, my mother was visibly relieved.

"Thea," she said, her voice high. Her eyes roamed over my body, and lingered on the necklace; then her eyes hardened. But she couldn't help this; I saw that she was trying to be kind.

My father raised his head and I saw with surprise that he had aged. He had gone completely gray in my absence. Even his eyebrows were gray. We waited while a porter gathered my luggage, while my father tipped him and my mother wrapped a scarf around her hair for the drive. Passengers for the next train milled around, and I was glad. They were someone else. The women wore pinks and purples and greens, a surprise to my eyes after so many days of white. And nobody watched them. Nobody made sure they got to classes on time, or turned off their lights at nine, or rose at seven. Nobody cared.

My mother and father turned to go, and

they expected that I would follow. My mother turned first, then my father, and I waited for them to say something.

"It's time to go," my father said. "Come."

My father held out his hand; my mother's eyes were desperate.

"Yes," I said, "let's go home."

But still I stood where I was. I had misspoken. We wouldn't be going home. I looked behind me and saw my train leaving, another giant machine poised to take its place. There would be other trains. I smiled at my father and allowed him to take my hand. I had not wanted to let go of his hand so many months ago, and now I had to make myself touch it. We were all being very brave.

My father opened my door, and waited until I was settled to shut it. We were silent while my father navigated our car onto the road. Orlando looked so busy — I had not seen cars, or roads, or any other tall building besides the Castle for so long. Then my mother turned so that I could see her pretty profile and I knew that I didn't have to try at all to love my mother and father; I hadn't known how easy it would be. They had my heart on a string, and I saw that they always would, until they died. Then I would truly be free, except for Sam. One string, instead of three.

I watched Mother's profile, that old familiar view. It was sharper, now; I had done that. I waited for her to speak.

"Thea," she began, and I could smell her, even from here; I could smell her old familiar smell. I leaned forward in my seat.

"Yes?"

Then she turned and faced me, closed her eyes, and lightly touched her forehead with two fingers, a new gesture. "This headache," she said. "It won't leave me."

I wanted to say something before she spoke. I wanted to tell her about the strangeness of all this, the utter strangeness. So much had happened in this last year, the busiest year of my young life; I felt so old, now. I wanted to tell her, and Father, too, about the strangeness of all those girls at first; then how all those girls had not seemed strange any longer. How now *they* seemed strange, my own parents, even though I loved them, even though I wanted to please them. I wanted to say: You can't ever imagine a moment, it seems like it will never come, but then it does, and there you are, Thea Atwell from Emathla, Florida, the same girl you thought you were.

"Thea," my mother said. "We've been living in a hotel for the past month, but we'll be leaving next week. We've bought a house.

There are so many here, abandoned."

"Sasi?" I asked. I couldn't make complete sentences; all I could manage were words.

"He's sold, Thea. You were going to outgrow him anyway." Her voice was soft. She was again trying to be kind.

"Who has him?"

"A little girl," my father answered. "She loves him. The truth is, Thea" — my mother made a small noise of protest, but my father shushed her, which was shocking; more shocking was that Mother did as directed, and fell silent — "the truth is that we can't quite afford a horse for you right now."

"He was a pony," I said quietly.

"Pardon, Thea?"

"Nothing," I said, "never mind."

I looked at my hands, these hands that Mr. Holmes had held. My mother turned around and leaned her head against the window. "This headache," she said, "is murder."

It wasn't hard, not crying. My mother, after all, was a liar, a liar whom I loved, but still a liar. She had promised me that Georgie would be fine, that she would write if he was not. I had been foolish to believe her, but I had wanted to believe her. I watched the street, and saw a dirty little girl and I wondered if she was poor, if her parents had abandoned their house; or perhaps she was only a little girl dirty from her backyard. Her dress looked nice enough. I would never know.

The hotel we stayed in seemed grand to me, with red plush carpet and an elevator. A bellhop accompanied me and Mother to my room. It was going to be mine alone, I saw as soon as he opened the door, my brother not anywhere in sight. The room smelled moldy, but rooms often did in Florida.

The bellhop was young, and handsome, with thick brown hair and long, lean limbs. Of course, I thought, of course I would get the young and handsome bellhop, not the old, wizened one. I told him where to put my things, and when he was done he waited.

"That will be all," Mother said.

"Mother." I looked at her purse.

"Oh, yes," she said, "I'm sorry, so sorry." She seemed nervous, and I knew why. She was about to be alone with me. And that I had just spoken to a man, and told her what to do in regard to this man, could not have helped. She would rather I hid in the corner until he left, even after he left. Well, I was not going to do that.

He closed the door behind him, and I turned to Mother and looked her in the eye;

I waited for her to speak.

"Well," she said, "camp worked wonders for you, Thea. You look well."

"It was not a camp, Mother." She stiffened. But I wasn't going to get into all that. "No, it's all right. I'm glad I was there for so long."

She watched me for a long time, the electric fan the only noise in the room. She wore a dress I had seen a hundred times before. She was still beautiful; the bellhop had paid more attention to her than to me. I felt my nerve weaken. She was my mother, I was her child, and this was a fact, and this was unchangeable. I waited for her to scold me, to express her displeasure, to tell me she knew all about how bad I had been, for a second time.

"Well," she said finally, and took my hand, "what are we going to do with you now, Thea?"

I began to speak, but she hushed me.

"No, please. We'll talk about all that later. I'm tired."

"Sam?"

"Sam is in the room next door. I suggest you let him come to you. But you will do what you wish, I'm sure."

I nodded. I would. She was correct.

■ ■ ■ ■

I had meant to stay in the infirmary my final night. But I couldn't. I rose after what seemed like hours of tossing and turning, which had followed Mary Abbott's visit. I *wanted* to fall asleep, to take advantage of the brief respite slumber provided. But sleep would not come and I began to feel panicked, hot; my scalp burned on top of my brain. That's what it felt like, anyway, that my brain was thinking too many agitating thoughts, that it was on fire. I hoped I would not regret leaving. I hoped Sam would be glad to see me. I hoped Sissy's life would turn out exactly as she wished it to.

The Square was deserted. There was a full moon, which was so, so pretty. There wasn't a single light on at Masters. Augusta House was quiet, all my friends fast asleep. Boone would not come anymore, now that Sissy had almost been caught. It didn't seem that Boone's identity had been revealed, a bit of luck. I'd made Sissy promise to write him a letter, to be more careful.

I thought of Kate the Bell Witch as I walked to the barn, the woods deep and black on either side of me. It would be so easy, to disappear.

Most of the horses didn't bother to swing their heads over their stall doors. It was late, not near feeding time. But Naari did. She recognized my footsteps. And she would forget them, and not ever know what she had forgotten.

I held her muzzle to my face, breathed in her softly pungent smell and let her breathe in mine. Who knows what I smelled like. Like a girl. Like Thea.

I heard the sound of metal on metal behind me, and jumped; I thought I'd been caught. But what else could they do to me? I had nothing to lose, nothing left to give them.

It was Leona, emerging from King's stall, closing the gate behind her. She wore her nightgown, which fell only to her knees while mine hit midcalf. Though I had changed into my day clothes before I'd come down here. I noticed her feet were bare. It was the height of foolishness, to walk in bare feet around a horse. Her hair was wild. Or nearly wild, as wild as Leona's hair ever got. King put his giant head over the gate and looked at me. Leona reached behind herself and patted his muzzle, absentmindedly. I'd thought her capable of such treachery. But really my first instinct about her had been right: she only cared about horses.

"Thea Atwell," she said. "You beat me. Nobody has ever beaten me before."

"Sorry," I said, and in that moment I was: I should have been kinder, I should have let her win.

"Don't be. I would have done the same thing, in your shoes. In your boots." She smiled, and I did, too.

"I'm sorry about King," I said, and gestured behind her, at his big, handsome face. Leona turned and buried her face in his neck, and King relaxed into her embrace, like a child. In the ring he was fierce, but on the ground he was gentle. I thought she was crying, I knew *I* would be crying, but when she looked at me again her face was dry as a bone.

"There will be other horses," she said, "but not like this one. And not for a long time."

I nodded. I believed her. If anyone could find her way back onto a horse it would be Leona.

"You'll have to leave her, too," she said. There was no malice in her voice.

"Yes." I looked at Naari's small, dainty face. "But she was never mine in the first place."

■ ■ ■ ■

Sam did not come to my door. I lay in my bed for hours and hours. I fell asleep; when I woke, the window was lit by streetlights, though I could tell by the way the darkness hit the windows that it was nearly dusk. My mouth was dry. There was no Docey here to pour me water, no other girl to tell me what time it was.

I poured myself a glass of water from the sink and drank it, quickly, then poured another and drank that, too. My eye caught a slip of white; a note, placed under the door. My heart caught; Sam. But no, Mother, telling me they didn't want to wake me for dinner. They. Had Sam been with them? I saw how sad it all was; my family living in different rooms in a hotel. I heard something outside, in the hall, but I wasn't familiar enough with this place to know what it was that I heard.

I opened the door slowly, and there he was, my brother. The back of him, but I knew, the same way I would recognize my hand if someone brought it to me.

He turned and in the bright light of the hallway I saw that he had indeed become more handsome than I was pretty, as I'd predicted. He was a man, now, his shoulders broad, a head taller than I was, at least. It was so amazing, this life: it took a person I knew completely and utterly and made him into a stranger.

"Sam."

"Thea." His voice was deep. I'd never hear it again as I'd left it, soft and pretty. He had a voice that asserted itself, now, that directed other people, that made itself heard in a crowded room. A man's voice.

I put my hand to my throat. "What time is it?"

"Late," he said.

"You couldn't sleep?"

He said nothing, would not meet my eye.

"Come in," I said, and opened my door, "please."

He hesitated. "Please," I said again, "don't make me beg." And then he came inside without a word, and sat down on the bed; I sat down next to him. The bed was unmade, and I was embarrassed, suddenly, that a boy was in my room and the bed was unmade, which was vulgar. But then I remembered that Sam was not a boy but my brother.

We sat in silence for a long time. It was familiar, though; I preferred it to our conversation, which had been stiff, awkward. Sitting down, he did not seem so tall; he was my brother again.

"So much has changed —" I began, but Sam interrupted me.

"For you," he said. "For you more than me. I didn't leave."

"I came back," I said. "For you."

He looked at me then, and he was astonished, utterly. When I left him his face was bruised and beaten; now it was perfect. He laughed.

"For me?" he asked. "For me?"

"For you," I said, but my voice wavered.

"Let's not pretend that any of this was for me. Can we not pretend, Thea?" His voice had turned plaintive.

I shook my head. "I thought you wanted me to come back. I've said sorry so very many times." I touched my necklace, and Sam's eyes went to it, and I saw he was hungry for me, as I was for him; he wanted to see all the ways change had wrought itself in his twin, as I did.

"You left."

And I understood he was referring to both times: I had left him for Georgie, and then a second time, for Yonahlossee.

He smiled at me sadly, and I wanted so badly to touch him. Just his hand, his shoulder.

"Oh, Sam." I knew I would remember this

moment for as long as I lived. I could live to be a hundred and this moment would never leave me. "I'm sorry," I said, "I'm so sorry," and I meant I was sorry for all of it; for all of us, forever apart now. A sob caught in my throat, and that was all it took: Sam turned and hugged me, fiercely, and I knew then how impossible our lives had gotten. And Georgie, whom we had not spoken of, had not been mentioned by name. There was no need. He was between us, as real in his absence as he had been in his presence.

After a while Sam released me, then stood, and walked to the window. Because he was not facing me I felt bold.

"Where are they?"

He continued to stare out into the night. "They moved to Missouri."

"And the Gainesville house?"

"The bank owns it. Uncle George let them take it. They wanted to leave." He tapped his fingers on the glass. "I haven't seen them since. . . ." He trailed off. "Only Father talks to Uncle George. That's all. Father sends them a check every month. 'It is our Christian duty,' " he intoned, using the voice he always used when he imitated Father: deep, slow. But now he sounded just like Father.

"They said that?" It was unlike my parents, to be so frank.

"They had to say something, Thea. We had to sell the house. And besides, I think they want me to know that our life is not exactly the same, now. They want to prepare me."

He turned his head to look at me, to read my face, and then he turned back to the window. "There's enough money, don't worry."

"I wasn't worried."

"Just not as much as there used to be. And no one knows how long this will go on."

He meant the Depression, of which he had known nothing when I left. My brother knew so many things now. He was no longer a child.

"Do you remember what happened, Sam?"

He stared out the window; night in the city was so bright, so different from my Yonahlossee nights. He stared outside so long I thought he must not know what I meant, but then he spoke.

"Yes," he said, "like I remember a dream. Mother and Father blame the rock." I watched his back. He placed a palm on the window. "Do you remember how Mother used to say that our lives were blessed, that we had our own private patch of paradise?"

I nodded, and met his eyes in my reflection on the window.

"Well, she doesn't say that anymore." He gave a short laugh. "I thought God was watching us." He was quiet for a moment, and it was all I could do not to interrupt. I had never heard this before. I didn't quite believe it. "I know it's silly. But I thought that God knew we were special." He smiled. "I didn't mean to hurt him, Thea. It would be better if he were dead."

"Hush," I said. "Who can say that?"

"I can say that!" he said, almost shouted. "I can!" He shook his head. "I can," he said more quietly, "because I have been here and I have seen all of it. All of it, Thea."

"All of it," I repeated, surprised by the sound of my own voice. "You should leave, Sam. It's not your mess."

"Whose is it, then?"

"No one's. Just a series of events. A series of events," I repeated.

"No, Thea. It's ours."

"It's not mine." I rose, and walked over to the window, peered over his shoulder. The sun was rising, and street sweepers were making a neat job of clearing the sidewalks. "There's all these people in the world, and we are only two of them. Mother and Father thought they were punishing me, by sending me away. It was a reward, to stay here.

But they were wrong. It was not a punishment."

"You learned so much, at camp." I could smell his breath, the particular tang it had whenever he hadn't slept long enough.

"I learned enough," I said. I took his hand, and squeezed it. "You should leave, too. Our lives are elsewhere."

He laughed. "Where?"

I shrugged. "Who knows? But God grants happiness only to those who seek it."

The next day there was a knock on my door at noon. I was awake — I'd fallen asleep as the sun rose — but not dressed. I opened the door and found Mother, Sam behind her. He looked fresh, alert, and I wondered when or if he had slept after leaving my room. He caught my eye and looked away, and then Mother did, too, and I realized neither she nor my brother wanted to see me in my nightclothes. Of course.

"Shall we dine?" Mother asked, eyes averted, and I told them I'd be dressed in fifteen minutes, though it only took five. I waited on the edge of the bed, in a dress that was too small for me, covered my knees just barely and pinched my arms. It was pretty, though, white polka dots against brown fabric. I had picked it out from a catalogue last spring; it had arrived after I'd left. I had forgotten the dress existed. But there it was, hung in my closet by Mother, the plain fact of it greeting me after nearly a year. It had been expensive, and I'd wanted it so badly because of Georgie, because I wanted him to see me in it. Georgie's face came to me so quickly, then. It was all another life, I told myself while I waited on the edge of the bed, because I sensed Mother wanted me to wait for her, did not want me to come find her. All of it another life.

"Your hair," she said, in the elevator, held her hand flat and brushed the bottom, blunt edge of it, where Eva had cut it straight across. "It's pretty, Thea. Very pretty." I felt my cheeks flame; I couldn't help it. I turned my head, but Mother had already seen.

She and Sam and I ate a mainly silent meal in the hotel restaurant, which felt cavernous because it was so empty. Sam seemed distracted, watching the one other patron — an older man, dressed in a suit — reading and rereading the menu. Mother was subdued. She had not seemed subdued in her letters.

She barely touched her food, but made Sam finish what she could not, for fear the restaurant staff would think her greedy, wasteful. I had never before seen her want so badly to place herself in the good graces of strangers, and I realized that this was one of the rewards of hiding herself away from the world: she did not have to care. And it was exhausting, caring. I had gotten used to it, at Yonahlossee, but all the wondering of what other people thought of you — it could weigh on your mind. But sometimes it weighed pleasantly, when someone admired or wanted you. Mother had starved us, in that way.

I sipped my iced tea, which was not as good as Yonahlossee's, which Mother and Sam had never tasted, would never taste. Mother watched Sam closely as he gobbled down her sandwich — his appetite seemed to have doubled in my absence — and her eyes darted back and forth from the waiter to her son. I almost could not believe it, except that I did. Our lives were unimaginable to us; if a year ago a fortune teller had read our future to Mother, she would have laughed, uproariously. She would have closed the door, then, and sealed us off again. But here we sat, our home dismantled, and Mother cared, deeply, about the opinions of a waiter, a waiter whose name she would never know.

"That was filling," she said, when our

table had been cleared, "I think I'll go rest my eyes," and I realized that she worried about small things now because the big things had turned her sick. Which might be, I saw, to my advantage: no one had mentioned my disgraceful exit from camp.

I knocked softly on Sam's door after lunch, but he didn't answer. I thought perhaps he was sleeping. I hoped so, hoped that he wasn't avoiding me. He had been nice enough at lunch, but distant. I spent my afternoon writing letters: to Sissy and Eva and even a brief one to Mary Abbott. I was trying to be kind to her, as so many girls had been kind to me at Yonahlossee.

Father knocked on my door at six o'clock, promptly, the same time as the church bells down the street rang out, reminding me of Yonahlossee. We ate at six o'clock there, too, though Father of course would not know that.

Sam stood behind him, just like before.

"Your mother is not feeling well," Father said, and stepped aside so I could walk by, as if I were a lady. I met Sam's eye and understood that they were taking turns with us.

After we had ordered, Father asked me what I had learned at camp.

"Learned?"

"What did you read? Who did you study?"

I laughed, and Father looked at me strangely. "I learned to be around other girls," I said. Father nodded. This is what they had wanted, after all; he had told me so in his first letter. *You will learn how to behave around other children there, Thea. I hope that is not too much to ask.* I would never forget it. But Father did not remember what he had written; he looked vaguely disturbed, as if I were mocking him. Which I suppose I was, but not in the way he thought.

"Did you like it?" he asked. "After you settled in?" Sam looked at me, too; they wanted to know. They wanted me to tell them a story. But I would not. Yonahlossee was mine.

"I grew to love it," I said.

The next morning, both Mother and Father appeared at my door, Sam behind them in his normal place.

"We thought we'd go for a drive," Father said. He smiled faintly, in his way. "And see our house."

Mother clung to Father as we made our way through the hotel, and shielded her eyes against the sun when we stepped outside. Sam looked out the window, at the shops we passed, at Church Street Station, where I had arrived just the day before yesterday, at the groves of oranges the city eventually gave way to. The country, I thought; we'll live in the country again, because Mother couldn't bear to live in town. No one spoke in the car, not a single word, no one even tried, including myself. Now I was used to chatter, to noise, to the constant hum of girls' voices; I felt ready to burst, to explode this silence.

After a little while Father turned down a narrow road, and then turned again, after a minute or so, and I saw where my family would be living. It was pretty, Spanish-style white stucco topped by a red tile roof. Thick palm trees surrounded the house in a neat square. It was half the size, I estimated, of our home, but that house had been so big, too big, really, for the four of us.

"Is there a barn?" I asked, though it didn't matter.

"No," Father said, and led us inside, up the front steps. The door was locked. We had never, in all my life, locked our doors. But now it would be done, from this point on. We stepped inside the empty house, into an empty room, the walls stark white. I could see how it would be pretty, though, with Mother's touch. The ceilings were high, the staircase wrought iron, the wood floors even and richly brown.

"It's pretty," I said, turning to Father, and I could see that he still wanted to please me, us, that he hoped the house would be some sort of salve.

"Yes," he said, "isn't it?" And my mother did not seem to realize he'd asked that question of her.

"Yes," she said, finally. "Quite."

Sam and my father went to look at the garage, and my mother went back outside, to the car, I thought, to rest. I waited for a moment, tried to gather myself. It would not be easy; it would never be easy, and waiting would not change a thing. I went to the window and saw that Mother had not gone back to the car. She sat on the front steps, her legs folded neatly to the side of her.

She looked pitiful, and I was so angry with her, because I did not want to feel pity, which is the worst kind of feeling, for my mother. She should be beyond pity. Father seemed the same, quiet and kind. Sam was distant, but the elemental way he moved through the world, easily, naturally, was unchanged. But Mother was ruined. She had been taken away from her home. She had belonged to a place, not people.

I remembered a woman, a friend of Uncle George and Aunt Carrie's, coming to Emathla to see our house. She and her husband were going to build their own house, soon, and had heard ours was magnificent. And it was. But so easily destroyed: a fire, a hurricane, an old oak felled on its roof. A daughter behaving inappropriately.

I remembered Mother showing them all our rooms, even mine and Sam's, and the woman, who was very tall and thin, like a bird, saying, over and over, "Exquisite." I remembered her so clearly because we did not often have visitors. Aunt Carrie trailed behind; I closed my eyes against the image of her, trailing. I put my head in my hands; all these memories, of home before the mess, of Yonahlossee, swirling from my head like so much vapor.

"Exquisite," the woman kept saying, "exquisite," and I realized that our home was exquisite; I had never thought of it in any way before except to call it our home. By the end of the visit Mother seemed bored. And this woman *was* boring; she kept saying the same thing over and over, at each room. But Mother was bored because the woman was stating something so plain it did not need to be spoken. Like calling Mother beautiful. Like calling us lucky.

We stood on the front porch until their car had disappeared in a puff of dust and Mother took my hand.

"Well," she said, "let's get back to our exquisiteness, shall we?"

Now I watched her sit on the front steps, pretending to look at a yard that she would never love, in front of a house that would never be hers. Her house was her child, I realized; but no, that was wrong. Her house was her mother, her father; she took comfort in it, expected it to shelter her from life's slings and arrows.

I slipped through the front door quietly. The heat was at me immediately. There was no color in the yard, only the palm trees, and shrubbery. Surely my mother would add color.

"A nice yard," I said, from behind her, and she nodded but didn't speak. I sat down next to her, and she patted my knee, lightly.

"Mother," I said, "I want to leave again."

She turned to face me, languidly; she seemed to be moving underwater, and it occurred to me that Father might have given her medicine, for her headaches.

"Why not, I suppose," she said. "Why not?"

Her answer felt like a punch, a blow. I expected reluctance; no, I had *wanted* reluctance, some sign from her that she needed me. But I would have gone anyway, so wasn't I being a foolish girl? I was getting what I wanted, more easily than expected.

Tears came to my eyes. But then she spoke again, and her voice was firmer, like I remembered it. "I thought you might want to go away again. Once you had a taste of what it was like."

"You were right," I said, and began to cry, and hated myself for crying.

"Oh, Thea," my mother murmured, and pulled me close, and if I could have stopped time, stilled all the clocks, I would have. But I could not. I was just a girl. My mother was just a woman. "Beth mentioned something about a boy you were meeting." She laughed. "I thought there were no boys there, but of course, there are boys everywhere. You'll go somewhere else, and my advice to you, for whatever it's worth, is to find a kind boy." She stroked my hair. She sounded like her old self. "Find a kind boy, like Father. I was once in trouble with a boy." I tried to lift my head, to look at her, but she pressed it back to her chest. "Long before your father. It is such a wonderful kind of trouble to be in. As long as you can get out of it. And you couldn't quite." She paused. "Get out of it, I mean. Could you?"

She let go of my head, and I sat up, tried to look at the blurry world through my tears.

"I didn't leave because of a boy. You might not believe me, but I wanted to come back. I wanted to come back and see my brother."

"So that you could leave again?"

"What is there for me here?" I asked. "There is not even a horse, here."

Mother gazed at me for a moment. "It's true," she said, "it's true. There is nothing for you here, not anymore. I wanted something else for you and Sam," she said, her soft voice returned. "But that was my mistake, wasn't it? To think I could fiddle with your natures."

The week leading up to the Fourth of July had been our last together, mine and Sam's, before what I had done was laid bare. There was something between us now, we both knew that, though of course neither of us had any idea, really.

It was pouring outside, in buckets. I flung myself from chair to chair, bored to death. I wandered into my brother's room, opened the door without knocking. He looked afraid, but he turned back to what he was doing when he saw it was me, not Mother.

"A nest," he explained, as I stood over

him, "of baby squirrels."

"Only two?" Sam had raised squirrels before, but usually there were more of them. They were so ugly, the size of mice, hairless and pink, their eyes sealed shut. Sam had nestled them in an old blanket. It seemed impossible they would grow to be squirrels.

"A raccoon got the rest."

One of them shifted, and I reached my hand down to touch one —

"Thea!"

"Sorry," I said. "I forgot."

"Mother would kill you," I said, after a moment. She didn't allow Sam's animals in the house.

Sam smiled. "No." He shook his head. "If she saw, her eyes wouldn't believe it."

But chances were Mother wouldn't come to Sam's room again; she'd already made the beds and straightened the upstairs.

I watched Sam try to feed one of the squirrels with one of Father's syringes, absent the needle.

"Is it milk?" I asked.

Sam shook his head. "Cow's milk would kill them. It's sugar water, warmed. They're doing better now, I think." The squirrel opened its mouth and began to suck, and even I was excited, in spite of myself. "There," Sam said, "there."

I watched him for a few moments. "There, there," he said, over and over, a refrain for the nursing squirrel.

"Why do you love squirrels so much?" I asked.

He shrugged. "Why do you like horses so much?"

There were so many reasons, but when I tried to name one good one, I couldn't.

"See?" Sam asked. "And besides, I don't love squirrels. I just . . . I like being outside. I like the natural world."

"The natural world," I repeated.

"Yes," Sam said. "The natural world."

He began to murmur to the squirrel again, and I fell back onto the bed, and closed my eyes against the sound of his voice.

I lay there, close to sleep, hearing my brother's pretty voice, still pretty even as it turned deeper and deeper, as it had over the past few months, changing to match his increasing height. My brother was a flower, unfolding, shooting toward the heavens.

That night I went to his hotel room. It looked lived in, unlike mine. There was a jam jar filled with flowers on the bureau, and three snake skins, almost completely intact, with tiny holes where eyes used to reside. I touched one of them, very lightly.

"What happened to your terrariums?" I asked.

Sam perched on the edge of his bed, watching me.

"They're gone."

I nodded. "I'm leaving," I said.

"I know."

"You could leave, too. They would let you."

My voice sounded too urgent. But he should leave, too. He should not let this swallow him whole.

When he finally spoke, his voice was a challenge.

"But I don't want to leave, Thea. I don't want —" And he paused, but no, it was more than a pause. He stopped himself from saying whatever terrible thing he was going to say. But I knew.

"To be like me?" I asked.

He looked away. I knew I was right. It was not fair, of course. I had been made to go away. I had not abandoned him on purpose. But in the end I got the better deal. There were so many accidents in the world, some happy, some not. I would take what I had gotten.

I went to my brother and sat down next to him on the bed. My twin would not leave because he was a better son than I was daughter; he could not leave because he could not imagine life without them. Sam wasn't brave. He never had been. He was loyal and true and still belonged to my parents in a way I never would again. He wasn't brave, but one person could only be so many things. He was still my parents' child, and perhaps he always would be. Only time would tell.

"You're a Florida boy," I said. I reached into my pocket and pulled out the handkerchief I had taken with me to Yonahlossee. It looked no worse for the wear. I put it in his hand and closed his fingers around it.

He looked at it, and then at me. "Yes," he said softly, with his new voice. "Yes, I am."

That night I lay in bed and tried to summon Sissy's eyes, Mr. Holmes's elegant hands, Naari's dainty face. But I could not remember. Everything was slipping from my mind. I rose and dressed in my Yonahlossee uniform; it was the only thing that fit. The clothes still smelled of Augusta House, and I tried not to cry, I tried not to want something I could never again have.

Outside, the air was thick with moisture, the moon hung over us like a fat face. There were a few people, scattered on the sidewalks. A door swung open and I glimpsed a crowded, smoky room, a man in front of a piano.

"Excuse me, miss," someone said, and I realized I was in someone's way. I stepped to the side and a man walked in front of me, and I recognized him as the bellhop my mother had almost forgotten to tip. A woman was on his arm, but I could only see the back of her, her sheer dress, her black hair. He gave no sign that he recognized me. I watched him slip away into the night, off to another place, or perhaps his home, where he would touch his girl, she would touch him, and the night would open like a flower.

I walked and walked. An hour, two. I lost track of time. I thought, foolishly, that I might see Sam. I knew he wandered at night. I knew he roamed. But there was no sign of him. I walked away from the streetlights, in the darkness. Mother had not taught us to fear the world; she had taught us to scorn it.

I finally arrived at Church Street, visible from a block away. I knew it would be busy here, or if not busy, alive in some way. There were people going places, people returning, always, always.

The sky zippered open, as it did in Florida, suddenly and violently, and the lightning lit the sky in a way that was beautiful and fierce. I was unafraid. Nothing in the natural world scared me. This lightning was far away, and I was surrounded by things taller than me, where the lightning would strike first.

I sat down on a covered bench, next to an old woman who was clearly waiting for a train. She asked me for the time and I looked at the giant clock above us and told her. She did not thank me; she was agitated, and I understood why.

"I'm going to Miami," she said. "And my train is so very, very late."

I almost laughed. Miami. Sam had told me there were thousands of acres of land there, abandoned by their owners, our uncle just one piece of it.

I understood the woman's agitation. She was waiting to be taken away from this place. She was dressed like someone from another century, long, long skirts, a blouse that hid even her wrists. And she was from another century, I realized. She had been born long before me, and I knew someday some impetuous girl would think the same of me: that I was old and foolish, dated, born too long ago to matter anymore.

I sat there and waited for the train with this woman. I tried not to fear the future. I hoped it would be kinder than the past.

On my way to Yonahlossee, all those months ago, I had watched my father's profile as he drove, and felt ashamed. I hoped I would not always feel this intensely. But then I knew I always would. It was my nature.

I sat on the bench and felt the strong wind whip my ankles and tried to keep ahold of all my memories. I touched Sissy's necklace. I saw myself in future trains and wondered who I would travel with. I wondered where we would go.

I would travel nowhere with Georgie, who died six days short of his twenty-fifth birthday. I never saw him again, I never saw Aunt Carrie or Uncle George or their former home in Gainesville. Georgie would never be himself again, a curse worse than death. If he had died right away, the circumstances surrounding his death would surely have been examined more closely; mercifully for us, Georgie lived. However briefly.

Mercy eluded my aunt and uncle, who tended to Georgie for the rest of his life. At Yonahlossee I only remembered Georgie and his family in the past tense, I tried never to think about what my family, especially my cousin, was doing in the present. It was perhaps a flaw in my character that I could forget so easily about my wounded cousin. That's what I thought then. Now I'm glad I was able to put it out of my head, to survive. We did not speak of him often, but my father revealed to me, one night when he was very drunk and old, long after my mother had died, that Georgie often succumbed to terrible rages, that the part of his brain that controlled anger was damaged in the accident. The accident.

My mother became an invalid, locked herself in her room most days and tended to her migraines. I was sent to a proper boarding school, in the Northeast, a place of my choosing. There was a stable nearby, where I continued to ride. I exercised the horses of the rich, which was a good way, I learned, to put myself on a horse when I couldn't own one. I thought of Leona in those days, wondered how exactly she had found her own way onto the back of a horse again. I was certain she had; how was the only question.

I left the South. My brother stayed put. He lived his life with my parents, who stayed in Florida but did indeed move to a foreign and strange south Florida, to a busy, bustling Miami, where my father continued to practice medicine.

My father never saw his brother again, but

he continued to send him money. I saw the letter once, folded around a check: to George Atwell in Centralia, Missouri. Citrus continued to be good to my family; it kept us afloat in the thirties, and in the forties it made us wealthy again. It saved us, allowed me to go away to school, allowed us to live some semblance of the lives we had imagined for ourselves.

After Georgie died, Aunt Carrie sent us his obituary, cut from a newspaper. There was a note folded over the clipping, in Aunt Carrie's hand: "He has left us." She and Uncle George thought that there had been a fight between the male cousins; I'm fairly certain they never knew my part. I would have cut my tongue out of my mouth before telling them, and Georgie — well, if he even remembered what had happened, he was not quite right, they would not have, I am almost certain, believed him. I have lived my life and Georgie is a shadow, Georgie is a person who I once loved, whose death I had a hand in. He is a ghost. My ghost.

I am certain Sam did not mean to kill Georgie. He was a boy, turning into a man. He did not know his own strength. It was a series of events, Sam. A series of events.

I never told a soul about what I had seen, my brother raise his rifle and strike Georgie in the head. Did my father know? He was a doctor, surely he could have told the difference between a wound from falling and a wound from force. But only God knows this.

I came home twice a year, two weeks for Christmas and two weeks in the middle of the summer. One twelfth of the year. In a way our relationships remained the same — my father was still distant, my mother difficult. But the qualities of those feelings were complicated now by what I had done, by what my family had done to me. It's difficult to say what Sam thought about everything — we were twins, we never had to articulate our feelings to each other, we just knew. But not anymore, Sam and I didn't know each other, it was safe to say, any longer. He was distant and pleasant when I was home, which was the worst punishment I could think of, to treat me like a stranger. I never cried again in his presence, nor he in mine.

I came back and was able to eat meals with my family, discuss matters of no consequence, sleep in the same house as they only because of Henry Holmes. Only because he made me understand the exchange my parents had made. Me for Sam. But I had made the first trade: my brother for my cousin.

I experienced true love, joy, when my children were born, grief again when I lost a child in my fifth month. I had a life, separate from my family and what had happened when I was a child. And horses were always a part of my life, a blessing; taking comfort in them had always been something I'd done by instinct, and it was an instinct I never outgrew. I took pleasure in how good I was in the saddle, how well I knew my way around a horse. I was good at something in a way most people are never good at anything in their lives. Horses were a gift; how many people have such a constant in their life, separate from the rough and often beautiful mess that is their family?

At Yonahlossee I learned the lesson that I had started to teach myself at home: my life was mine. And I had to lay claim to it.

When I returned from the Northeast, I was always surprised by the palm trees, the blunt heat, the moisture in the air so heavy it was almost sickening. My parents lived in a neighborhood where they could see other houses from theirs; they lived in a house that was beautiful and cold.

Sam decided to be a doctor, like Father. He stopped exploring the natural world. He spent all his time inside, now, and when I was home I would study his cheek, made pale by his preference for the indoors; when he turned toward me, there was a flash of skin, a succinct feeling of desperation. We were lost to each other. At Yonahlossee I learned to live a life without my brother; I learned that what once seemed impossible was not. And my life all to myself was easier, in many ways. Lonelier, but a twin is as much a burden as a pleasure. I did not know life without him, we had a language all to ourselves in infancy, we shared a womb. When everyone else expected one — my mother, my father, my grandparents — we were two. And it is not easy to be two people where there should have been one. If there had only been one person, then Georgie would still be alive. Because no one else besides Sam would have cared so deeply, so irrevocably, about what his other half had done.

My parents had sent me away because they saw I was a girl who wanted too much, wanted badly, inappropriately. And back then all that want was a dangerous thing.

Woe be to you, Thea, Mr. Holmes said. We were in his library, surrounded by his books. My blouse was unbuttoned. He took my hand and kissed my thumb. Woe be to you for wanting too much. He kissed my wrist. For wanting so much. He lowered me down onto the couch, my uniform hiked over my hips.

I wanted everything. I wanted my cousin. I wanted Mr. Holmes. I was a girl, I learned, who got what she wanted, but not without sadness, not without cutting a swath of destruction so wide it consumed my family. And almost me. I almost fell into it, with them. I almost lost myself.

But I was too selfish. I wanted, as Mr. Holmes put it, too much. And none of it was a decision, a list written out, a plan articulated. We have no say in who we love. And woe be to all of us, for that.

Woe be to Sam, who never left Florida, who never lived in the world beyond its shores. He had a wife, he had a family. He did not have his twin. Woe be to Mr. Holmes, who I never saw again, who surely felt me as a loss, as I felt him. Woe be to Mother and Father, who allowed what I had done to unravel their lives. Woe be to Georgie most of all, whose first love was his last, who has turned to dust now, a stone in a Missouri cemetery the only evidence that he existed, proof that he lived and left some mark. Evidence that he existed, but not that he loved. I am proof that he loved. And perhaps that was my most important task, in this life: living a life for both me and him.

Seeing things that he never did. Doing what he could not.

But woe be to Thea — no. Take it back, Henry. And surely he would have, if he had continued to know me. Surely he would have seen that my life was full, and rich, and my own.

A photograph would hang on the wall outside Mr. Holmes's office, though I would never see it. I would never return to Yonahlossee, or my home in Florida. The photograph would serve as a reminder to him. A reminder to everyone that Theodora Atwell and Naari had won the Spring Show in 1931. I had left in disgrace, but still my picture would go up. It was tradition.

I heard a train in the distance, the familiar whining. The woman next to me stood, my presence forgotten. Woe be to us. The memory sprang up, unbidden. One of the countless afternoons we spent with each other, all flooding out now, flooding out of my head and turning into so much vapor. I faltered. I put my head in my hands.

But no. I looked up again. The train made its slow ascent into the station, and the woman marched into the rain, though it would be minutes and minutes until she was allowed to board. But she didn't care. She simply wanted to leave.

I thought of my picture in the Castle, which neither my parents nor Sam would ever see.

But what would future girls see when they looked at the photograph during their daily comings and goings, peered closely? Not the shade of my hair, rendered colorless by the photograph. Not Mr. Holmes, who stood beyond the frame. Not anything, really. Just a girl on a horse, like so many other girls.

ACKNOWLEDGMENTS

A deep debt of gratitude to my agent, Dorian Karchmar, who took on *Yonahlossee* when it was barely a manuscript, and guided me through many revisions. It would not be a book without her.

Thank you next to my editor, Sarah McGrath, whose care and insight made the book so much better. At Riverhead Books, thank you to the entire amazing team and especially Geoff Kloske, Sarah Stein, and Jynne Dilling Martin. At Headline, my UK publisher, thank you to Claire Baldwin.

At William Morris Endeavor, thank you to Simone Blaser, Tracy Fisher, Catherine Summerhayes, and Eugenie Furniss.

I owe many thanks to the creative writing departments of Emory University and Washington University, respectively — the former, where I took my first creative writing class; the latter, where I received my MFA and then taught while I wrote *Yo-*

nahlossee. At both schools, I studied under many fine professors. A special thank-you to Kathryn Davis, who has always been my most enthusiastic cheerleader, and Marshall Klimasewiski and Saher Alam.

Thank you to Tim Mullaney, David Schuman, and Curtis Sittenfeld, for support while I wrote.

Thank you to my mother, for teaching me to love a home. Thank you to my father, for driving me thousands of miles to and from the barn. And for not letting me go to law school. Thank you to my sister, Xandra, who has always been my biggest champion. As I grow older, I feel increasingly lucky for the love and support my parents and sister have always offered.

Finally, thank you to Mat, my husband. This book is for him; it couldn't be for anyone else.

ABOUT THE AUTHOR

Anton DiSclafani grew up in northern Florida, where she rode horses, competing nationally. She graduated from Emory University, and received her MFA from Washington University. She currently lives in Saint Louis, where she teaches creative writing at Washington University.

The employees of Thorndike Press hope you have enjoyed this Large Print book. All our Thorndike, Wheeler, and Kennebec Large Print titles are designed for easy reading, and all our books are made to last. Other Thorndike Press Large Print books are available at your library, through selected bookstores, or directly from us.

For information about titles, please call:
(800) 223-1244

or visit our Web site at:
http://gale.cengage.com/thorndike

To share your comments, please write:
Publisher
Thorndike Press
10 Water St., Suite 310
Waterville, ME 04901